Contemporary Authors
Autobiography Series

ISSN 0748-0636

Contemporary Authors

Autobiography Series

Mark Zadrozny

Editor

volume **11**

Gale Research Inc. · *DETROIT · NEW YORK · LONDON*

Copyright © 1990
Gale Research Inc.
835 Penobscot Bldg.
Detroit, MI 48226-4094

Library of Congress Catalog Card Number 84-647879
ISBN 0-8103-4510-2
ISSN-0748-0636

Contents

Preface

Each volume in the *Contemporary Authors Autobiography Series (CAAS)* presents an original collection of autobiographical essays written especially for the series by noted writers. *CAAS* has grown out of the aggregate of Gale's long-standing interest in author biography, bibliography, and criticism, as well as its successful publications in those areas, like the *Dictionary of Literary Biography, Contemporary Literary Criticism, Something about the Author, Author Biographies Master Index,* and particularly the bio-bibliographical series *Contemporary Authors (CA),* to which this *Autobiography Series* is a companion.

As a result of their ongoing communication with authors in compiling *CA* and other books, Gale editors recognized that these wordsmiths frequently had more to say—willingly, even eagerly—than the format of existing Gale publications could accommodate. Personal comments from authors in the "Sidelights" section of *CA* entries, for example, often indicated the intriguing tip of an iceberg. Inviting authors to write about themselves at essay-length was the almost-inexorable next step. Added to that was the fact that the collected autobiographies of current writers were virtually nonexistent. Like metal to magnet, Gale customarily responds to an information gap—and met this one with *CAAS.*

Purpose

This series is designed to be a congenial meeting place for writers and readers—a place where writers can present themselves, on their own terms, to their audience; and a place where general readers, students of contemporary literature, teachers and librarians, even aspiring writers can become better acquainted with familiar authors and make the first acquaintance of others. Here is an opportunity for writers who may never write a full-length autobiography (and some shudder at the thought) to let their readers know how they see themselves and their work, what carefully laid plans or turns of luck brought them to this time and place, what objects of their passion and pity arouse them enough to tell us. Even for those authors who have already published full-length autobiographies there is the opportunity in *CAAS* to bring their readers "up to date" or perhaps to take a different approach in the essay format. At the very least, these essays can help quench a reader's inevitable curiosity about the people who speak to their imagination and seem themselves to inhabit a plane somewhere between reality and fiction. But the essays in this series have a further potential: singly, they can illuminate the reader's understanding of a writer's work; collectively, they are lessons in the creative process and in the discovery of its roots.

CAAS makes no attempt to give an observer's-eye view of authors and their works. That outlook is already well represented in biographies, reviews, and critiques published in a wide variety of sources, including *Contemporary Authors, Contemporary Literary Criticism,* and the *Dictionary of Literary Biography.* Instead, *CAAS* complements that perspective and presents what no other source does: the view of contemporary writers that is reflected in their own mirrors, shaped by their own choice of materials and their own manner of storytelling.

CAAS is still in its youth, but its major accomplishments may already be projected. The series fills a significant information gap—in itself a sufficient test of a worthy reference work. And thanks to the exceptional talents of its contributors, each volume in this series is a unique anthology of some of the best and most varied contemporary writing.

Scope

Like its parent series, *Contemporary Authors,* the *CA Autobiography Series* aims to be broad-based. It sets out to meet the needs and interests of the full spectrum of readers by providing in each volume twenty to thirty essays by writers in all genres whose work is being read today. We deem it a minor publishing event that more than twenty busy authors from throughout the world are able to interrupt their existing writing, teaching, speaking, traveling, and other schedules to converge on a given deadline for any one volume. So it is not always possible that all genres can be equally and uniformly represented from volume to volume. Of the twenty-one authors from five countries in Volume 11, about half are poets, with the other half made up of novelists and essayists. Like most categories, these oversimplify. Only a few writers specialize in a single area. The range of writings by authors in this volume also includes drama, translation, and criticism as well as work for movies, television, radio, newspapers, and journals.

Format

Authors who contribute to *CAAS* are invited to write a "mini-autobiography" of approximately 10,000 words. In order to give the writer's imagination free rein, we suggest no guidelines or pattern for the essay. The only injunction is that each writer tell his or her own story in the manner and to the extent that each finds most natural and appropriate. In addition, writers are asked to supply a selection of personal photographs, showing themselves at various ages, as well as important people and special moments in their lives. Barring unfortunate circumstances like the loss or destruction of early photographs, our contributors have responded graciously and generously, sharing with us some of their most treasured mementoes, as this volume readily attests. This special wedding of text and photographs makes *CAAS* the kind of reference book that even browsers will find seductive.

A bibliography appears at the end of each essay, listing the author's book-length works in chronological order of publication. If more than one book has been published in a given year, the titles are listed in alphabetic order. Each entry in the bibliography includes the publication information for the book's first and most recent printings in the United States. Generally, the bibliography does not include later reprintings, new editions, or foreign translations. Also omitted from this bibliography are articles, reviews, and other contributions to magazines and journals. The bibliographies in this volume were compiled by members of the *CAAS* editorial staff from their research and the lists of writings provided by many of the authors. Each of the bibliographies has been submitted to the author for review. When the list of primary works is extensive, the author may prefer to present a "Selected Bibliography." Readers may consult the author's entry in *CA* for a more complete list of writings in these cases.

Each volume of *CAAS* includes a cumulative index that cites all the essayists in the series as well as the subjects presented in the essays: personal names, titles of works, geographical names, schools of writing, etc. The index format is designed to make these cumulating references as helpful and easy to use as possible. For every reference that appears *in more than one essay,* the name of the essayist is given before the volume and page number(s). For example, W.H. Auden is mentioned by a number of essayists in the series. The index format allows the user to identify the essay writers by name:

Auden, W.H.
    Allen **6**:18, 24
    Ashby **6**:36, 39
    Bowles **1**:86
    Burroway **6**:90

For references that appear *in only one essay,* the volume and page number(s) are given but the name of the essayist is omitted. For example:

CAAS is something more than the sum of its individual essays. At many points the essays touch common ground, and from these intersections emerge new mosaics of information and impressions. *CAAS* therefore becomes an expanding chronicle of the last half-century—an already useful research tool that can only increase in usefulness as the series grows. And the index, despite its pedestrian appearance, is an increasingly important guide to the interconnections of this chronicle.

Looking Ahead

All of the writers in this volume begin with a common goal—telling the tale of their lives. Yet each of these essays has a special character and point of view that set it apart from its companions. Perhaps a small sampler of anecdotes and musings from the essays ahead can hint at the unique flavor of these life stories.

Angelo Pellegrini, reminiscing about childhood chores in Italy: "Among less arduous tasks, I remember particularly stripping leaves from the mulberry tree to feed the silkworms, and cutting grass, especially clover, to sell in small neat bundles to draymen along the highway. I went frequently to the main thoroughfare early in the morning with two or three dozen bundles of grass, to await the prospective buyers. During the autumn months I gathered fuel for the winter—any combustible remnants that could be found on a landscape where everyone was a gleaner and a scavenger. I also helped with the spading, the hoeing, the weeding, and—most pleasant of occupations—the harvest. On market days I followed the cattle and horses along the highway. For amusement? For diversion? Of course! A child must have his fun—even in Casabianca. But I pulled behind me a two-wheeled cart on which was strapped a huge basket—in case! Why? Because we needed the manure to fertilize our small plot of land. And I kept my eyes fixed expectantly on the animals. When one of them hesitated in his jaunty strides, then humped his back and arched his tail, quick as a flash I was right there, shovel in hand. When the basket was full I retraced my steps to the stone cottage, as rugged and as proud and as confident as the president of the National Association of Manufacturers—though much less certain about the future."

Emily Hahn, making an impression as an author: "I stepped off the ship in Bombay and encountered a bookseller. Booksellers in Bombay, it is worth saying, have a very peculiar way of selling their wares. Do you remember when everybody smoked? and girls in nightclubs carried cigarettes around on portable shelves? They, the girls, I mean, wore seductive little costumes of long tights and very short skirts. Well, except that he wasn't wearing tights or a short skirt, this bookseller looked very much the same. At any rate, he carried his books on a little portable holder slung around his neck and he paused for me to make my selection. I was interested to see that the books were all in English. At least that is what attracted my attention at first, but then I saw something else, far more important to me personally: one of the books I had written and had not yet seen on the shelves of any bookstore at home. I beamed at the bookseller. 'I wrote this!' I said, pointing to it. Not unnaturally, he looked alarmed. 'No,' I insisted, 'I mean it. That's my book. I wrote it.' The bookseller grabbed his carrier tighter and hurried away. He was scared to death."

Anthony Kerrigan, appraising the music in his life: "I listen to music, or live it, outside a designated and confined space, the music of composers from Monteverdi to Bartók—and not much beyond....Except, of course, for the unison medieval—who could help it?—the plainness of plainsong and the like: and how now can then anyone find a moment for the noise of 'Rock,' when there are endless hours of plainsong chant, so much more deeply tense than the latest racket? The Beatles? I never understood how this soft exudation, this loose fungus, this ooze, could have spread beyond the pools of suds in Liverpool saloons, beyond the pubs of the Mersey. What a pop counterpart to Nazi hysteria were the squirming masses of pubescent and pimply adolescents, mostly not-yet-ripe girls, who squealed the hours away while the Beatles and their ilk opened their mouths and—were not even heard above the savage beat!...Jazz? Nothing in contra (though I have no trouble turning off Thelonius Monk, say...whenever such sounds as his take over the airwaves in my car, while I find it impossible to interrupt a Beethoven quartet). There is only so much time and space. I'd rather fill them with the most substantial fare, the best food for the brain, the richest music, what sticks to the imagination's bones with the longest-lasting effect."

D. M. Thomas, lamenting the fleeting glimpse of family afforded by old photographs: "I own a fine Zeiss camera, but it's wasted on me. I've used it about half-a-dozen times in twenty years. Whereas my father, with a clumsy Kodak bought in California almost seventy years ago (I still have it), took thousands of snapshots, filled album after album. And how I envy those smiling groups, those happy couples and brothers and sisters, cousins and close friends. I curse them, in the most affectionate way, for having been so barren, those six brothers and four sisters; for having stayed abroad, died in plane-crashes, married wives who died young, lost lovers in a war, lived in damp cottages that produced fatal illnesses...In a word, left so few of us in their wake. Is there some especially fine Zeiss, I wonder—product of Germanic brilliance—that could make them burst out of the photograph, laughing, singing, joking, and with potent loins?"

These brief examples can only suggest what lies ahead in this volume. The essays will speak differently to different readers; but they are certain to speak best, and most eloquently, for themselves.

Acknowledgments

A special word of thanks to all the writers whose essays appear in this volume. They have given as generously of their enthusiasm and good humor as of their talent. We are indebted.

Authors Forthcoming in *CAAS*

Ai
American poet

Mulk Raj Anand
Indian novelist, nonfiction writer,
and critic

Russell Banks
American novelist

Hal Bennett
American novelist

James Broughton
American poet and filmmaker

Algis Budrys
American science-fiction writer
and editor

Ed Bullins
American playwright

Cyprian Ekwensi
Nigerian novelist and short-story
writer

Philip José Farmer
American science-fiction writer

Isaac Goldemberg
Argentinian novelist

Charles Gordone
American playwright, actor, and
director

Daniel Halpern
American poet and editor

Ihab Habib Hassan
American critic and editor

John Hollander
American poet

Elizabeth Jolley
Australian novelist

Nettie Jones
American novelist

Etheridge Knight
American poet

Aharon Megged
Israeli novelist

Jessica Mitford
English essayist and journalist

Bharati Mukherjee
Canadian novelist and short-story
writer

Larry Niven
American science-fiction writer

Fernand Ouellette
Canadian novelist

Harry Mark Petrakis
American novelist and screenwriter

Alastair Reid
Scottish poet, essayist, and
translator

Carolyn M. Rodgers
American poet

Edouard Roditi
American poet

Sonia Sanchez
American poet

James Schevill
American poet

Vladimir Voinovich
Russian novelist

Ann Waldman
American poet

Paul Weiss
American philosopher

Acknowledgments

Grateful acknowledgment is made to those publishers and photographers whose works appear with these authors' essays:

Lawrence Block: p. 28, J.N. Adam & Co.; p. 39, Lightworker/Matthew Seaman.

Malcolm Boyd: p. 43, Robert E. Clark; p. 53, © Kathy Weiss.

Nawal El Saadawi: p. 68, Schwang.

Frederick Feirstein: p. 85, Wade Newman.

Kay Green: p. 101, Robert Chacksfield.

Emily Hahn: p. 112, © Mondiale.

Marianne Hauser: pp. 135, 137, Aina Balgalvis.

Samuel Hazo: p. 139, Jonas.

Anthony Kerrigan: p. 208, Camilo José Kerrigan; p. 220, Judith Barnes.

Samuel Menashe: p. 223, Andre de Dienes; p. 234, Doug Cornell; p. 238, © 1990 Adam Hume.

Toby Olson: p. 251, U.S. Navy.

Charles Plymell: p. 281, City Lights Books, Inc.

Tom Raworth: p. 297, Rob Rusk.

William Pitt Root: p. 319, poetry by William Pitt Root from *Striking the Dark Air for Music*. Copyright © 1969, 1973 by William Pitt Root. Reprinted with permission of Atheneum Publishers, an imprint of Macmillan Publishing Company; p. 323, Michigan State University.

Martin Jack Rosenblum: pp. 333, 346, 351, © John Mallow; p. 352, Ranger International Productions.

D.M. Thomas: p. 373, poetry by D.M. Thomas from *Personal and Possessive*. London: Outposts, 1964. Copyright © 1964 by D.M. Thomas; p. 378, poetry by D.M. Thomas from *Dreaming in Bronze*. London: Secker & Warburg, 1981. Copyright © 1981 by D.M. Thomas. Reprinted with permission of John Johnson (Authors' Agent) Ltd, London; p. 383, Sonia Ketchian.

Contemporary Authors
Autobiography Series

Dick Allen

1939-

Dick Allen, looking out his living-room window at Fern Circle, by Thrushwood Lake, 1984

I

I'm lost in the spring of 1946, separated from Miss Griffin's second-grade field trip to the forest above Round Lake. I'm walking a leafy tunnel through an incredible sun-dappled green of poplars and maples bordering a deeper shadowed green of fir, spruce, and pine. Robins, cardinals, English sparrows enter and leave the tunnel . . . a squirrel, a small deer, a partridge. I am not truly in my body, not seven years old. I am with the crow's voice in a meadow beyond the tunnel, its raw sound into blue sky. The wind shimmers the leaves. The wind, the sun, the leaves, and I are the same. If I knew the words then, if I had read William James and Evelyn

Underhill and Meister Eckhart, and looked into the eyes of Alan Watts, I would say *mystical, magical, miracle.*

The feeling does not last long. Soon, guided by their voices, I find my way back to the other second graders. Miss Griffin does not scold me. She is young and beautiful and forgiving. She will die of quickly progressing cancer three months later.

My life has always seemed a constant alternation of such mysticism and reality.

II

I don't know what particular body I inhabited before this one, but I'm almost certain I lived in the

Mother, Doris Bishop, 1932

Orient, probably China or Japan. There were bent trees, wind chimes, the crow cawing over the fields. There was mist and a mountain landscape. I wore robes and walked in a meditation garden. How else to explain the sense of calm that comes over me when a breeze chimes the Bells of Lun in my living room, or when I visit a Chinese or Japanese garden, or when I read a haiku by Bashō?

Yet my conscious mind tells me this is nonsense. Mr. and Mrs. Hirohara lived in Round Lake, New York. I was very young when my father first took me with him to visit them, and was overcome by their small Japanese garden, its tiny pool and scattered rocks and small stone path. It was my first sense of perfected beauty.

Do I vaguely remember a previous life or were my perceptions set by that garden?

III

What compels me to write poems? Sometimes I think I'm attempting repayment. "Rühmen, das ists!" Rilke wrote. Often, the poems are expressions of wonder, attempts to touch the beyond, to see through the veil. Always, they are searchings for calm. This

sudden rain on the stone fence and its bordering asters as I pause from my writing and look out the bedroom window between tossing maroon curtains. Thunder mountains in the sky. Now the rain gentling off, sounding like a small brook as it drifts through the leaves.

Views from open windows and open doors have always drawn me. I cannot remember a time when I was not looking out, myself not real, trying to be what I looked upon, contemplated, meditated upon. When there is a sense of calmness, of rightness . . . when a line or an image belongs to that sense, then I have the core of a poem. The outward events of my life are only the things my temporal body and mind have passed through. What is real are the poems, the capturings. Only when writing them am I real, in the time that disappears.

My father, Richard Sanders Allen, a service-station worker for the Shell Union Oil Company in Troy, New York; a dropout from Cornell University; former office boy in New York City for the Munson Steamship Line; a voracious collector of Americana; a man boyish in enthusiasms into his seventies; the postmaster of a fourth-class post office; possessor of a retentive memory for millions of scattered facts; obsessive reader; to become "the world's leading authority on covered bridges" as well as a leading scholar in the history of iron furnaces and commercial aviation; Guggenheim Fellowship winner; Director of the New York State Bicentennial Commission; lover of all things to do with travel; author of seven books and countless articles; son of my grandfather Charles Rollin Allen, a consulting civil engineer who worked on the Whiteface Mountain Highway and the Taconic Trail, and of my grandmother, Mabel Calef, once governess to the child who would become the mother of Vice President of the United States Nelson Rockefeller, as well as a member of the Daughters of the American Revolution and the Women's Christian Temperance Union.

Richard Sanders Allen married Doris Bishop, descendent of Egglestons, Greenes, and Angells of Corinth, New York—a small farming and logging town in the Adirondack Mountains. Some of the families scattered. Walk Angell Street in Providence, Rhode Island, sometime. Merton and Sadie Bishop, my maternal grandfather and grandmother, took teacher's training after high school and both taught public school for a time. My grandfather became a telegrapher and station master for the Delaware and Hudson Railroad. When he managed the Round Lake station, I would visit him for the dimes he gave me, and to put pennies on the railroad tracks so passing mail trains could flatten them to the diameter of silver dollars. He wore a green visor and would hush me now and then as he bent his head to the clacking telegraph. When I begged him, he would translate the messages into words of trains in the distance.

IV

My mother was the third of his four children, like my father a graduate of Saratoga High School but a year older than him; a graduate of the Albany Business College; dropout from Cobbleskill Agricultural and Technical College, where she was studying education; an elocutionist who loved to recite poetry; a former college cheerleader; a strong-willed woman who channeled her constant plans and ambitions into her husband and two sons; a reader, like my father; postmaster of Round Lake from 1944 to 1946, after my father had been drafted into the U.S. Army Air Force; postal clerk later when he returned from Biloxi and Westover Field to reclaim his job; a woman whose first priority was always knowledge.

I was born on August 8, 1939, in Troy, New York.

V

Mr. Gorsline's Town

Trying to write a poem simple as his town
is really, I
keep thinking how the streetlights all
shut off at dawn

and the paperboy, riding no hands
on his Schwinn
distinguishes between
who tips and who pays

by whether the big fat *News*
lands on doorstep or lawn;
and at noon
the firehouse whistles.

And at seven, an automatic switch
turns streetlights on;
a father throws his daughter
the last hard one

as Mr. Gorsline locks
his grocery store up,
walks seven blocks home,
meeting friends,

remarking the calm. And I know

the sentiment
must blur the horror out, but I say,
I say his town does exist.

(From *Regions with No Proper Names*)

I had lived in Troy; St. Johnsbury, Vermont; and Saratoga before my parents moved into the house in Round Lake Village on Janes Avenue which was to be my home from 1942 until college. My first memory is of being shown that house at night, by flashlight, when I was two and a half. There was an unmade bed placed diagonally in an otherwise empty room. A bare lightbulb dangled from a cord above the bed.

The village of Round Lake, until the 1960s, was an anachronism, a former Methodist church campground about twenty miles north of Albany on Route 9 whose residents did not own their homes but leased them for ninety-nine years. Almost all the houses were former summer cottages. The village was set among pine trees. The dirt roads that twisted through the village were oiled each spring to keep the

Father, Richard Sanders Allen, 1945

dust down. Cats were required to wear bells, so the squirrels could be warned. Dogs ran free. Pine needle-strewn paths rambled everywhere.

An underpass beneath Route 9 led to the edge of the lake itself, where Mr. Lavery ran a boat house and casino with rowboats and pontoon planes. There was a small beach, boat and plane docks. The edges of the lake were covered with lily pads. In a swampy area to one side, where the cattails grew, you could still make out the outline of a Holy Land living replica, including the Dead Sea and the Sea of Galilee. The lake adjoined Little Lake, site of a huge abandoned and fire-blackened icehouse.

When I was not at the lake, or in my parents' rowboat, I'd head off to the forests. To the left of the town, if you stood facing it from Route 9, was what we called "the pine woods," a large stand of evenly planted corridors of trees on each side of the road. On the hills directly above the village and the village's World War II victory gardens, the forest was "Mount Lookout." Paths led to a huge water tower, two ponds on which my friends and I played ice hockey with a stone for a puck and tree branches for hockey sticks; the paths rambled through marshland, snake-grass, then joined trails and half-abandoned logging roads. Mainly, Mount Lookout was extensive stands of old white pine, the needle carpet a foot thick beneath the trees. There were deep ravines and Tarzan vines to swing over them, stands of poplar and birch, a stream with banks of clay to dig out, mold into pots and snakes, bake on wood fires. We built hidden huts in fallen trees, elaborate lean-tos with woven pine-branch roofs smothered by needles, tree huts, and secret caves gouged into the sides of the ravines.

To the right of the forest, high above Round Lake, was Roerig's Farm: acres and acres of cornfields over which the crows floated . . . and our homemade kites. The dirt road past Roerig's farmhouse, cluttering windmill, and century-old barns led to Sheep's Hole, a swimming spot beside a shale bluff set at the bottom of a deep wintergreen-smelling gorge. We'd bicycle there on hot days when the lake "worked," the inflated inner tubes our parents insisted we take dangling from our handlebars. You could get back to Round Lake by walking along several miles of the D & H railroad tracks, or by following Tenendeharo Creek, or—even better—by hiking along an abandoned trolley-car bed that hugged the valley's side. A few miles from my house, by following a faint sound of falling water, I discovered a thin waterfall, its stream plummeting seventy feet into a hidden valley pool where water-skeeters raced.

VI

The village, the lake, the forests, dirt roads, white pines haunt my poetry. I remember always feeling nearly ecstatic in childhood. I chose isolation, liked my solitary woods wanderings and my nightly walks when I whistled my way through the village. I always seemed to know Round Lake village and the surrounding area were idyllic. "Once mountains were mountains and trees were trees," the famous Zen koan goes. It is only after we begin to intellectualize, taken over by what Blake called "Urizen," that "then mountains are no longer mountains and trees no longer trees." Many of my poems try to recapture the time before intellectualization, are based in, or set in contrast to, the Edenlike experience of my village. Yet they are not autobiographical, the "I" never a Confessional "I," although some are based on actual experiences and perceptions. Always, it is the meaning beneath the meaning I try to lead toward. Thus, poems about sledding at night or being lost in the cornfields of Roerig's farm are poems about ambition; a poem about walking across Round Lake's ice in winter is about religious apprehension; a poem about a boy who drowned in Round Lake is about how one encounters and tries to understand and accept death . . .

My juvenilia is about the woods and creeks, the village at night, trucks on Route 9, the lake, fields of stars seen through the pines. It's overly romantic, sentimental, but it sets the stage for the sense of mysticism, of a complete dissolving into wonder and beauty, that has been with me through my life. It is a miracle that birds have wings, that the sky is blue, that wind blows and the sun shines. Those last two sentences purposely are put baldly. I need the poems. One of my self-appointed tasks as a poet has been to find fresh language with which to tell small stories reawakening this sense of miracle. The task is terribly difficult. A lovely landscape attracts scores of painters whose art is not adequate for communicating the vision they set up their easels before, painters who have slopped on layer after layer of bad painting on top of the first true one. It took me a long time to learn enough technique to begin scraping off the paint.

VII

Janes Avenue

At the end of it, the school
that was once a museum: stairs from its second
    floor
led up to a huge locked door
and the reek, we imagined, of the missing
    mummy.

Get down from there,
our teachers—sad Depression things—
would shout. But we kept trying,
small shoulders pushing; hands on the pitted
    black knob.

They lied it wasn't there. We knew
as sure as we knew rowboats, wind and clouds,
in that cupola room, propped on a broken desk,
a mummy stood in brown-stained strips of cloth.

We hated them for lying. Oh, we knew, we
    knew
when the last bell sent us home, they gathered
by the door; the Principal unlocked it;

they entered and they gazed and they were
    shaken.

As we wished to be. The frogs that spewed
beneath our bicycles, the horseflies in the
    grass—
these were the small things they thought fit for
    us,
the happy children of Janes Avenue.

(From *Overnight in the Guest House of the Mystic*)

The realist in me—counter to the mystic—
comes from other elements of my childhood. The
Allens of Round Lake were poor, like almost everyone else in the village. We had no radio, no phonograph, no furnace. During the winter months when
my father was in the air force, my mother and
brother—Robert Bishop Allen, born in 1942, eventually to become Professor of Architectural Engineering at Washington State University—and I moved
into one room, sleeping around a space heater. There
we would listen to the blackout sirens that told
everyone in Round Lake to cover their windows—
war precautions because the top secret Hermes
nuclear project was located only a few miles away.

The Allen house on Janes Avenue, early 1940s

Dick Allen at Round Lake, about 1947

Our kitchen stove was ancient, converted to oil from the coal it originally burned. I can remember nearly a year of having only one pair of corduroy pants and one pair of shoes, and a Christmas during the war when my mother, crying, apologized to me because there were no more than token presents: a kazoo and a mail-order holster for the toy gun I didn't have. The poverty, in the context of a happy childhood, has contributed to my never valuing materialistic goods highly, though also to empathizing with those who have never escaped poverty.

I attended a small village school until the ninth grade, its classrooms in the former Round Lake museum. There were two grades in each room, one on each side of a center aisle, both grades taught by the same teacher. I had a perfect attendance record. By the end of first grade I was off in the corner with eighth-grade story and poem collections while my classmates were struggling with Dick and Jane. On the two or three nights a week the village's small public library opened, I loaded both arms with books—I had special permission to take some out from the adult section if the librarian consented— and staggered my way back home. By twelve, I was

reading and understanding a little of Plato and Montaigne, Hawthorne, Hemingway, Shakespeare.

I had known I would be a writer since the third grade. Words, images, the *sound* of the language always fascinated me. And the house held my father's and mother's books, as well as the Tennyson, Browning, and Shakespeare of my paternal grandfather, who had died before I was born. Too, there were always stacks of magazines: the *Saturday Evening Post, Life, Collier's, Reader's Digest, True, Bluebook, Field and Stream, Popular Mechanics* . . . My postal-worker father and mother could never bear to throw away magazines whose subscribers had moved and left no forwarding addresses.

Books, magazines, my father's home-editing of *Covered Bridge Topics* . . . And talk, constant talk, ceaseless talk from morning to night. Silence was not allowed, except when someone was reading. Everything was noted, discussed, planned, worried over, alternatives offered, dreams spelled out. My brother and I were always consulted, our opinions and observations having, we were made to feel, equal weight to those of our parents. If, in a discussion, I could present a more logical argument than anyone else, I could have my way. Emotions meant little. There was almost no touching. No anger or sorrow was allowed to stand for long. All was communicated through the best-put words. And often, to make or illustrate their points or express their suppressed feelings, my father would provide anecdotes from American history and my mother would quote from her large store of memorized poetry: Vachel Lindsay, Edna St. Vincent Millay, Longfellow, Dorothy Parker, Robert Frost, John Greenleaf Whittier.

The mind, then, must always be active, logical; there is a lesson to be learned from everything; nothing should be taken at face value; opportunities are everywhere, take advantage of them; plan the future carefully.

Little wonder I've been an overstressed, chain-smoking workaholic all my life.

*   *   *

So I talked and read and studied and took advantage of the "opportunities." I was a webelos cub scout, a Boy Scout, then patrol leader, then junior assistant scoutmaster. I delivered the *Schenectady Gazette* for four years and never missed a day, even when the mumps puffed out my cheeks, getting up at 6:00 A.M. to pedal my bike a mile to where the papers were dropped off at one edge of the village, and then to speed four or five miles throughout Round Lake throwing the papers on porches and doorsteps. In winter, I walked the entire route, once through a snowfall almost to my waist, when I was the only living thing moving in the buried village. Drawn to underdogs and outsiders and those who worked against the odds, I rooted for the Brooklyn Dodgers, particularly my childhood hero Jackie Robinson. Summer evenings, I relentlessly joined the sandlot slow-pitch baseball games, even though I could never hit, throw, or catch very well. But miracles happen. One evening, my side behind by three runs, I hit a grand slammer into the dusk.

Satisfied with their own company, my parents had no real social friends. Their main entertainment was taking car rides to neighboring Vermont or two hours away to the Adirondacks and Sacandaga Reservoir, where they would finally buy a cabin the year I entered college. We had occasional family gatherings, but basically my parents were "loners," as I tend to be.

VIII

At Shenendehowa Central High School, eight miles from Round Lake, I ran on the cross-country team, played center for my junior varsity and then my varsity basketball squad, was assistant manager and scorekeeper for the baseball team, played on the tennis team. I was vice president of the student council, columnist for the weekly newspaper, president of the classical-music club, main announcer for the public-address system, editor-in-chief of the yearbook, story writer of an original ballet put on by the art department, writer of the senior skit, harmonica player in the annual talent show, founder of the American Field Service program . . . the yearbook lists twenty-eight different activities and the saying someone chose for me: "He pleases all the world, but cannot please himself." I was also president of my hometown riflery club and vice president of the Round Lake Methodist Youth Fellowship. For the summers of 1956 and 1957, I was a lifeguard, swimming instructor, and riflery instructor at a YMCA camp, where I was also a cabin and section leader.

Knowing I wanted to be a writer, I had resolved to get every kind of experience possible for me.

But the activities were just things I *did*, a natural introvert, an "isolato" forcing himself to extroversion. As soon as I learned to drive, I caged my father's black and yellow Ford station wagon every chance I was given and, sometimes from dawn to midnight, drove by myself through upstate New York and

nearby Vermont. I continued to read avidly: Shakespeare, *Leaves of Grass*, Robert Frost's and Carl Sandburg's poetry, *The Divine Comedy, The Prince, A Shropshire Lad*, Will Durant's *The Story of Philosophy*, Kant, Hegel, Eugene O'Neill's plays, *Walden Pond* . . . But most importantly, science fiction and Emerson's essays, particularly "Self Reliance."

Science fiction—Robert Heinlein, Clifford D. Simak, Ray Bradbury, all the others—gave me a contrast with my historian father. More importantly, it contained the apprehension of wonder, awe, and religious mystery I continuously felt from life. It combined the epic adventures I loved with continual search. It provided perspective, ways to understand overall human motivations. From it, I learned a tolerance for different modes of life, a feeling of the unity of the planet and the human race, a sociological and religious way of considering human destiny. Science fiction was my *Iliad* and *Odyssey*. It also led me always to consider the role of technology in our century. By 1955, to the scorn of my classmates, I was predicting humans would be on the moon by 1970 and that computers would be a major part of our adult lives.

I've reread Emerson's "Self Reliance" every year of my life. It encourages me to be a nonconformist, to trust my intuitions, to not let "a foolish consistency" bind me. I'd had doubts about joining the Methodist church when I was eleven, argued into going ahead by a minister who said belief would come; then, in ninth grade, I'd read Thomas Paine's *Common Sense* and decided, like him, that I could not believe in traditional Christianity. Emerson's transcendentalism, so strongly influenced by Oriental religion, gave me a way to call myself a "religious agnostic" and I left the church finally, declaring myself a Zen Buddhist on my college religious preference form. I was directed toward the Unitarian Campus Club but later, when I briefly considered becoming a Unitarian minister, was told my mysticism disagreed too much with the rational and humanistic elements of Unitarianism.

I wrote poetry throughout high school, along with hundreds of letters in red ink to various girls I was too shy to attempt dating. Despite my high-school activities and a fair amount of casual friends, I continued to feel a separation from others. My favorite song—aside from Bill Haley's "Rock around the Clock"—was "Wayward Wind." I felt myself to be the observer, the future wanderer. I hoped someday I would find people as interested in literature, religion, philosophy as I was, but if I couldn't, I would continue to be the observer and recorder. In practical terms, I planned to earn my living as a journalist.

IX

It is August, 1957. Co-leading a canoe trip on the Fulton Chain lakes near Old Forge, New York, in the upper Adirondacks, I've settled the campers in my charge down for the evening and taken a canoe out on the river. Dip the paddle in, twist the wrist at the end of the stroke, lift and feather the blade, repeat. The J-stroke moves me easily. The banks hold pines and birch and deep shadows. Then night falls abruptly and I'm in total darkness.

Blind, terrified, I turn the canoe and make my way back up the river by instinct until I finally see our camp fire. That night, I wake in my sleeping bag trembling; chills shake my entire body. I make my way to the fire, but the cold continues. I am going to die. Finally, I relax to Death, to this mystery that has overcome me, let go, and sweat breaks from my pores. My co-counselor is already making plans to rush me to a hospital at first light. But I crawl back to the lean-to, sleep, and when I wake it is as though nothing has happened.

X

In 1957, I won a New York State Regents Scholarship and a full-tuition Citizenship Education Conference Scholarship to Syracuse University, chosen as one of the top four high-school student leaders of New York State. Syracuse University seemed what I had been waiting for all my life. I immediately found a home on the staff of the *Daily Orange* and was writing lead stories for it within a month, staying up to 2:00 or 3:00 A.M. each weekday night to do layout, make headlines on the Ludlow machine, lead the print columns. By the end of my freshman year, I was being groomed to be the paper's eventual editor-in-chief.

I met young men and women interested in books and music and art, including Reidar Bornholdt, a strange freshman who had read 150 important books I hadn't—all 150 of which I crammed into my head the first semester; and Peter Bennett, who taught me about jazz; and Robert Ira Karmon, who became my best friend and later introduced me to Hart Crane's poetry. I read Ayn Rand's *The Fountainhead*, which encouraged my feeling that fierce self-reliance could win over any obstacles, then balanced it with Erich Fromm's *The Art of Loving*. I joined the Unitarian

Campus Club, and Skeptics Corner—a Sunday-night group of agnostics and atheists who met in the living room of Dean Noble, liberal head chaplain of Hendrick's Chapel. I attended the Sunday-afternoon concerts in Crouse Hall, sitting while Pete Bennett stood in his seat to mock-conduct the orchestra.

One exciting night, a dorm-mate read a book of poetry aloud to me, Allen Ginsberg's *Howl*, as a group of us crowded into my room. I read Jack Kerouac's *On the Road* and decided I had to hitchhike around the nation, too. Classes were an afterthought. I failed Spanish and got a D in geology. At the start of the next semester, it took a threat of loss of scholarships to frighten me enough so I would keep at least a dean's-list average every semester from then on.

I had come to Syracuse wanting to achieve local fame. Through my often controversial essays in the paper and by helping to found the university's Fine Arts Festival, I was starting to receive it.

XI

I remain after Archibald Stadium empties, following another Syracuse football victory. I like the

High-school yearbook photograph, 1957

feel of having the huge stadium almost to myself. I haven't read a newspaper for weeks, or listened to the radio. I look down at the front page of the Syracuse *Post-Standard* someone has left. *Sputnik*. The human race has begun to leave the planet. I sit down, dazed, on the concrete steps, everything swirling. The adventure my science-fiction reading predicted has started. The world is completely changed for all time. I vow aloud that I will somehow be part of it, that I will devote much of my writing to space exploration, science, and the future.

XII

In the summer of 1958 I set out to see America, hitching rides on trailer trucks, going by train, bus, and car from Round Lake to Chicago, Denver, Salt Lake City, Seattle, San Francisco, Los Angeles, the Grand Canyon, New Orleans, and Washington, D.C. I went to Kerouac's places, the bars in Denver, Lawrence Ferlinghetti's City Lights Bookshop, and because the Kingston Trio's folk songs were all I knew then of satirical folk music, to The Hungry I. I stood in Indiana cornfields, crossed the Mississippi on a night bus, slept in cheap hotels with neon signs blinking outside my window, and bunk-bed rooms of YMCAs. In Chicago, fresh from having read Upton Sinclair, I wandered the stockyards. My first sight of the Rockies was exactly as Kerouac had said it would be. They *were* papier-mâché! I stalked Seattle at night, rode the San Francisco cable cars, hiked along the Grand Canyon's edge. In New Orleans, as I walked into an old chapel, I heard a choir burst into song from a balcony high above me and, as I have so often, felt the dissolving into mystery, wonder, and harmonies. I walked across the Potomac bridge to the Arlington National Cemetery, watched the changing of the guard, toured the White House, climbed the Washington Monument, stood before Lincoln's statue, read the Declaration of Independence in its glass case, listened to a speech in Congress. I weighed 156 pounds, was six feet, two inches tall: an eighteen-year-old boy carrying his father's World War II air-force duffle bag and sleeping bag, satiated with America.

XIII

University Students Strolling through Midnight

for Robert Ira Karmon

I think of the night we walked through
    Syracuse,

that park with yellow moths around its
    streetlights.
We were two young men, dreaming of being
    famous.
The last trains from Rochester and Utica
slowed into the station on Erie Boulevard—
lines of typewriters clicking in the distance.
Above the old city a gibbous moon hung tiredly,
casting shadows through the pines, along the
    paths.
The spring wind at our backs was the pressure
of jackets grown too tight across the shoulders.
We talked, as young men talk, of many books
we read as if we were wading a stream in a
    clearing:
in words to our knees, we balanced in the
    currents.
Such nights, I am convinced, occur but once
between two friends, before they part with a
    handshake.
Restaurants closed, we shared that special
    licorice
you always carried—as we paused in the
    moonlight
beside the tennis courts and you told your
    stories
of growing up in the Catskills, your twin
    brother
pulled out dead a few minutes before you were
    born.
I spoke of the Adirondacks, where my uncle
built a log road skirting a huge white lake.
Under the streetlights, the moths became our
    stories
corkscrewing up to the lamps and falling away.
Where we would live! Providence and Dayton,
Philadelphia, New York, Westport, Garden
    City.
We sought a fame that would never grow as
    large
as we vowed it would; we live still with our
    wives;
we raise our children: your daughters, my son
    and daughter.
You said the moths were dreams among the
    branches
under the streetlights, that they would vanish.
But you were wrong, for I see them now—
each bite of wings, each spiral, each mad
    dashing.
I see you raise your head to them, my eyes
following your gestures and I hear the
    typewriter trains:

their fading messages, the hands above them
    lifted.
I feel the night wind and the moon descending;
    the sky is a curious black and gray without
    ending.
Its surface is cracked but holding like the glaze
of a painting, or a bowl from the Corning kilns.
The flowers by the paths are wings of scattered
    moths.

(From *Overnight in the Guest House of the Mystic*)

Back at Syracuse for my sophomore year, I switched my major from journalism to creative writing and left the regular staff of the *Daily Orange.* After the breakup of my first serious romance, I spent two months living in a bare room, meditating for hours, trying to observe Zen Buddhist principles. The division between my meditative private consciousness and my public activities continued, however. Although I was writing poetry, short stories, and had finished about eighty pages of an abortive novel, I also managed to get myself elected as a student-senate representative and spearheaded a fight to have the Society Against Nuclear Explosives accepted as a campus organization, beating back charges that it was a "commie front." I was hanged in effigy by a Syracuse fraternity after I introduced a proposal to outlaw all racial and religious discrimination in the university's fraternities and sororities.

I learned techniques in poetry from Arthur Hoffman, a New Critic who used an anthology that omitted names of authors from its poems, dates of publication for the poems, any mention of historical relationships. Hoffman, his bewhiskered face holding a catlike grin, would perch cross-legged on a table in front of his class on "The Form and Art of Poetry" and throw out Socratic questions. He spent the first three weeks in an exhaustive analysis of "Stopping by Woods on a Snowy Evening," and gave as his term-paper assignment a twenty- to forty-page technical analysis and explication of a single poem. I wrote on Stephen Spender's "I Think Continually on Those Who Were Truly Great." From Hoffman, I learned of poetic fallacies, of the primacy of imagery, of meter and varieties of rhyme—almost everything. With Walter Sutton, who advised my Citizenship Education Honors Class project on the Beats and had introduced me to Malcolm Cowley's *Exile's Return,* I read William Carlos Williams, W. H. Auden, Wallace Stevens, and Ezra Pound. Dr. James Elson introduced me to John Donne, Ben Jonson, Alexander Pope, and John Milton. In Harlan Bro's class on "The Religious

Development of the Individual" I learned of the mystic Edgar Cayce, with whom Dr. Bro had worked.

XIV

I started the summer of 1959 working in the Saratoga County Highway Department, where I sorted sand, typed, and inked in maps . . . and read introductory books on Albert Einstein to try and keep my mind alive. The job was hopelessly dull, everyone in the office working at a lackadaisical pace, and it soured me for life on the nine-to-five routine. After I quit, I spent several weeks alone in my parents' Sacandaga camp, meditating and writing.

In my first week back at Syracuse, at a small "bohemian" party, I ran out of cigarettes and beer and was approached by a fiercely intelligent, waifish-looking but buxom young woman, a senior English major, who let me share her beer and smoke her Parliaments. We talked, exchanged names—hers was Lori Mary Negridge, originally from the Lower East Side of New York, where her Polish, Russian, and Ukrainian forebears had settled—and I walked her home to her sorority. The next day, remembering that she'd said she often passed my boarding house, I sat on the porch waiting for her to go by. She did, we went for coffee, exchanged double entendres and our hopes of becoming writers. We were almost inseparable after that, unofficially engaged within the month, officially engaged in February, and married August 13, 1960, five days after my twenty-first birthday and two and a half months before hers.

XV

Strangely, the same Sunday morning after I met Lori, I woke up with an overwhelming change of attitude toward my life and ambitions. I'd set out at Syracuse to achieve "fame" and had done so—I was a campus figure, pointed out as I walked across the quad. But I felt cheapened. It was too easy to be "known." Although I was deeply committed to the freedom they supported, I knew my journalistic writing, my satirical and occasional poems for the *Daily Orange,* my controversial political activities were too easily done. It seemed to me that I could continue such beyond college, entering journalism or politics, and earn the same type of recognition. But if there was so little effort involved, would I be doing something of true merit? I felt ashamed, guilty. That morning I decided to abandon my drive for early recognition and to concentrate on learning my art. I

*Allen camp at Sacandaga Reservoir in the
Adirondack Mountains, 1959*

still wanted "fame," but now I wanted it for my work, not my life. And the work could not be cheap or opportunistic. That morning the quality of my art became my goal, everything secondary to it.

XVI

My junior year, Lori and I worked constantly on our literature courses, played chess, sometimes double-dated with her roommate, Joyce Carol Oates, whose early short stories I admired, though I complained to her that they lacked sufficient violence. To earn money for Lori's engagement ring, I worked for the university's public-relations office. In the summer after Lori's graduation, we moved into a tiny apartment on Comstock Avenue. As a graduation present, Lori's parents sent her for a fifth year of college, to earn her secondary-school teacher's certification, and they also helped support us, since we had planned Lori's working would do that while I finished my senior year.

Like so many of the young, Lori and I admired John Fitzgerald Kennedy, and cast our two votes for him in the fall of 1960.

We worked hard. I'd had my first poems in the *Syracuse 10*, chosen by Joyce Carol Oates, who was one of the magazine editors, under its editor-in-chief, Robert Phillips. I'd also placed a poem in a national Methodist magazine. In my senior year, the *New York Times* took a short poem, "The Death of Adam," about the aftermath of nuclear war. My mother sent a

long poem I'd written about space exploration and nuclear-war fears to a subsidy press and paid for my first book. Its publication, when I was twenty-one, gained me some further admiration on campus and in the local newspapers. But it was poor, haiku-influenced free verse. I wish the book to be nameless.

I brought my grades up to nine A's in the ten courses I took that year—good enough to receive my university's nomination for a Danforth Fellowship, for which I was eventually turned down, and to convince Brown University to accept me into its graduate school. In 1961, it was usually graduate school or the draft and, although I planned to enlist eventually, I wanted to study more literature. The idea of becoming a college professor was seeming more and more attractive.

XVII

Syracuse brought many noted figures to campus. As a journalist on its summer *State Fair News*, I'd spent part of a day with Governor Nelson Rockefeller, and through my public-relations office work, had met Hubert Humphrey and had lunch with President Harry Truman. I'd listened to Ayn Rand; as chairman of the Footprints Intellectual Conference in my junior year, I'd spent separate days with the pollster Elmo Roper and philosopher Herbert Marcuse. Through the religion department, I'd met Alan Watts, and through the English department, Grace Paley, Robert Frost, Herbert Gold, and Richard Eberhart. But, by far, the most important visitors to campus for me were Robert Francis and W. D. Snodgrass.

As senior creative-writing majors, Bob Karmon and I were allowed to not only have individual conferences with Francis and Snodgrass—and to take them to lunch, since we were, by then, responsible young married men with cars—but to have them do manuscript evaluations of our work. Francis was kind, and praised my poems for their music and imagery. Snodgrass was devastating. He ripped through my verbiage, red-penciling almost every other line; he eliminated my abstractions, corrected my meter, scorned my bad rhymes. *Be concrete. Show, don't tell,* he wrote in huge letters. Stunned, I went to my creative-writing professor, Dr. Donald Dike. Finally, Dike—who, with me at least, had taken a basic approach of saying mildly encouraging words about everything—admitted Snodgrass was right. Dike told me to study Yeats, concentrating on "Sailing to Byzantium." I did, and found I'd been writing foolishly and badly, without compression. It took me over a year to recover. If Snodgrass had not been so harsh and truthful, I would likely have never written publishable poetry. I'm forever grateful to him.

XVIII

Variation on a Theme by Ernest Hemingway

In a city where I once lived, for many years
an old man sat on his doorstep, in his hand
a brown facecloth, which he turned
over and over, smoothed out
against his knee, crumpled up, smoothed again,
then held at arm's length. Sometimes he buried
his whole face in it, and since he was dressed in
      tweeds
I could never decide
if he was idiot or on his way to being wise,
or on his way back, the cloth
his rhodora. I never
asked; he never looked up
from his studies or madness, whichever
let him sit there every sunny day
thinking or not thinking. I never heard
anyone call him in; I never passed
his doorstep as he came out into the morning
or saw him sip from a glass, or even stand.

Like the streets and the marvelous pennies on
      sidewalks,
the iris that came out of nowhere,
he was a part of my days for a while and I
      trusted
him as only a question can be trusted,
never an answer
and I moved away from that city, never
      regretting
my silence or his
but missing the houses with the mansard roofs
and the tall brick chimneys, so red
against the snow falling, winters I lived there.

(From *Overnight in the Guest House of the Mystic*)

My first year at Brown was a combination of nightmare and pleasure. I wasn't prepared for the intense advanced-degree work, nor for the Brown University graduate English department's large expectations. The often-said rumor was that Brown, being about halfway between Yale and Harvard, expected its students to be better than both. I took a reading course in French and graduate seminars with such scholars as David Krauss, Hyatt Waggoner, and Israel Kapstein, as well as with the poet Charles Philbrick. Most Brown period and genre courses

required that the students read *everything* written by the main authors, all the major secondary sources concerning them, and every two weeks produce (that was the word) a twenty-page paper, using at least ten separate secondary sources. This meant writing about sixty pages a week. If the paper did not seem to the professor of publishable quality, it wouldn't receive an A. If the graduate student's average over the year wasn't at least an A–, he or she would be advised to leave the program. I recall that approximately thirty English- and American-literature graduate-school majors began studies in 1961. By 1964, only five of us remained.

Most of that first year is now a blur, but somehow I made it through. Unable to find a teaching job, Lori worked as a legal secretary until her boss had a coronary and died in his office. The firm released her and she could only find Kelly Girl temporary employment. We lived on handouts from parents, my tuition paid by a National Defense Student Education Act loan, and by our earning twelve dollars a week from teaching Sunday school in the Providence Universalist Church. I scarcely saw Lori. When I wasn't in class, I spent fourteen to sixteen hours a day at my typewriter or in the library, reading and researching books I couldn't afford to buy. Still, I found the Hall, Pack, and Simpson *New Poets of England and America* and carried it everywhere.

The pleasure came from the intense literary conversations the graduate students had during coffee breaks and from the one night a weekend a number of us would drink and party. But by our second year, we felt we couldn't take time even for the weekly escape. Our gatherings turned into playreading sessions, where we'd each take a part and give ourselves a reading performance of *Faust* or Ibsen or Arthur Miller.

Lori and I lived in an old haunted mansion on Benefit Street, where I swear one evening I saw a ghost floating outside the windows. The building had been a hospital during the Civil War. It had been broken up into thirteen furnished apartments. Our apartment had been the parlor: now a tiny kitchen and bathroom, separated by a plywood wall from a living room with a curtain across one part of it to make a bedroom. The apartment cost seventy-five dollars a month, furnished, with five dollars extra for space in a dilapidated garage.

Even so, we reached the point where we could no longer make it financially. I was almost about to quit graduate school and join the navy when I was given a teaching assistantship at the end of the second semester—perhaps as a result of my having won Brown's Academy of American Poets Prize, judged by Daniel Hughes, Charles Philbrick, and Edwin Honig, and of being encouraged by Leicester Bradner to expand a paper I'd written on the comedies of Ben Jonson into a master's thesis. I spent the summer working on the thesis, Lori continuing to work for Kelly Girl. Toward the summer's end, she was hired as a junior-high-school teacher in Pawtucket, Rhode Island.

*   *   *

Cuba has long-range missiles. The American military has been put on full alert. Round-the-clock meetings are being held at the Kennedy White House. Within a day or two, there may be nuclear war between Russia and the United States. Providence will be one of the major targets. I survey our apartment house and find a basement room with no windows, where I plan we will spend our last days. I buy cans of Sterno for cooking. Some of the international students at Brown are on planes back to their countries; some out-of-state American students have also left, hoping to reach their homes so they can die with their families. After Lori finishes teaching her classes, I take her with me to my late afternoon seminar. If the missiles come, we'll go together, listening to Hyatt Waggoner discuss T. S. Eliot's poetry.

XIX

At Brown

Mad John Berryman, who I walked home from
    class
To Edwin Honig's house
He'd rented for his raving on that year—
When was it? Sixty-four?
Told me, "Son, don't ever win an argument
Without you say a prayer
You not be humblepie." Oh, in his cups
He could take a single line by Yeats
And huff and puff it so it sang and sang
Like a bejesused thing. At the gate
He turned and wagged a finger. Providence
    stretched out
Before us, Christmas lights
Just coming on. And Kate came to the door
In a blue, blue dress. "When we go away,
The telephone won't ring." I saw him last
Gathering his children in his arms.

Poor mad John, poor goose, poor Tiny Tim;
Dear Poetry, the losses you sustain.

(Published in *Crosscurrents,* Winter, 1989)

In my second year at Brown I was advanced to a teaching associate and assisted Daniel Hughes for a course in modern poetry. When Hughes took sick for several weeks, I worked with John Berryman—then writing *77 Dream Songs.* At a faculty–graduate student party for Berryman and Oscar Williams, I argued with Berryman about the predominance of Self in modern poetry until he conceded a point to me and stalked off. Lori was pregnant with our first child. We began plans to delay my final Ph.D. studies and—jobs were plentiful then—I'd teach for a few years before returning to Brown to finish. Our son, Richard Negridge Allen, was born in Providence Lying-In Hospital in November, 1963.

*   *   *

At a faculty-student cocktail late afternoon party, I find myself telling S. Foster Damon, the great Blake scholar, that my wife has always been a fan of e. e. cummings, but she's never seen a copy of cummings's *CIOPW.* He says he has one—he was a friend of cummings at Harvard—and invites us to his house to see it. I ask Lori to come up to the campus and I run through the streets to meet her partway. Damon makes us dinner, serves us homemade wine, then leads us up to his cluttered bedroom, where, rummaging through books scattered on the floor, he finds the cummings volume. Later, he plays songs on his piano as he sings, then unlocks a glass bookcase and lets us hold an edition of Blake's poems, hand-colored by Blake, as he turns the pages and quotes the poems, points out the places where the watercolors ran. Lori says she envies him his collection of complete works of various authors, including Oscar Wilde. He says he needs more room in his bookcase and, after demanding a kiss on the cheek from Lori, presses the complete edition of Wilde on us. Late that night, half-drunk, Lori and I walk two miles through a snowstorm, carrying the many heavy volumes.

*   *   *

The door to my stuffy third-floor office opens and a fellow TA leans his head in to say that President Kennedy has just been shot. For a few minutes, I continue to go over my student's paper, then dismiss him and go downstairs to the teachers' lounge, where Professor Charles Anderson is bent over a radio.

Kennedy has died. Neither Anderson nor I wish to go to our homes yet, not wanting to tell our wives, me particularly since Lori is only a few days back from the hospital with our newborn son. We wait, talking in choked voices.

Since I am the "political expert" among the English-department graduate students, they gather in our living room, all of us blankly watching the thirteen-inch Zenith black and white. That night, I walk the streets of Providence for hours, nodding speechless to hundreds of other solitary walkers. All I can think of is that I must write poetry to somehow give tribute to Kennedy's dreams for America and his effect on all of us.

*   *   *

Those Hatless Nights . . .

Those hatless nights we walked through
    Providence,
Driven inward by the outward blow,
Skies gray, wind tossing hard, small blurs of
    snow
Appearing suddenly upon a wrought-iron
    fence,
Transforming, for a moment, what they pressed
    against
As lovers transform lovers in the portico
Of love or lose their balance in its vertigo
Of swirling into Death's indifference . . .
. . . those hatless nights, those nights we
    prayed for him
And for ourselves, it seemed the people came
From nowhere to our sides, and some of them
Embraced us, some kept crying out his name,
And some just wept, and some whirled off alone
Like snowflakes flying to a blank headstone.

(From *The Space Sonnets*)

XX

In December, I was hired by Wright State University, in Dayton, Ohio—to open the next September initially as a joint branch campus of Miami University and Ohio State University—as an instructor of English and creative writing, my position gained by the few poems and brief essays I'd published and the book reviews I'd started contributing to the *Providence Sunday Journal*. I finished out the year as Mark Spilka's teaching associate for his large class in modern British literature while also teaching another section of freshman English. I left Brown

three courses short of completing my Ph.D. course requirements, never to return.

Unable to obtain a loan from banks, broke, and in debt to a dentist who'd had to remove most of my teeth and give me false ones, we borrowed a little money from Lori's parents and, in August, 1964, moved to a jerry-built house we rented for $105 a month in Fairborn, Ohio, a few miles from Wright State. The new campus wasn't really even that. It was a single large building in a huge field of mud. The first semester, I taught four sections of freshman English and a beginning creative-writing course. Later, I would also teach courses in advanced exposition, a seminar in creative writing, as well as American-literature survey courses. Compared to the ordeal of Brown, I had an easy work load.

That summer, freed from graduate-school pressures and inspired by a new area of the country, I started to find my way to writing a social and political poetry, much of it to be set in the Midwest. I hoped the poetry would capture an America I sensed was starting to change drastically. For the first time since high school, I began reading science fiction again and

Lori Allen, 1987

became fascinated with its new relevance, how it was being turned toward speculative fiction by such authors as Samuel R. Delany, Judith Merril, Harlan Ellison, and Kurt Vonnegut. I'd stopped listening to popular music after high school, but now began turning on the radio again, first for the Beatles, then Bob Dylan and Simon and Garfunkel and later to the flood from Judy Collins, Jefferson Airplane, all the rest. My reading of science fiction also brought me to a renewed interest in science, to the connections I felt were being made between science and mysticism.

Bombers flew constantly from the Wright-Patterson Air Force Base, bombers we could hear and see taking off continuously from our front window. And all the revolutions were being enacted at once: the civil-rights revolution, the revolution of the young against the war in Vietnam, the revolution of Beat poetry. And I read Robert Bly's early books and essays, my own poems changed by his surrealism and political influence.

XXI

The Mad River

The one-eyed sachem, Laulewasika,
when he was young and hated all things white,
even the dogwoods white in the underforest,
saw rising off Mad River as it weaved and
    roared,
the slanted eyes of his twin brother dead.

And in his middleage, John Appleseed was wont
to thumb his Swedenborg, toes in the river,
under the marble-white arches of the sycamore,
singing, planning the day of his visit
to Mrs. Blemmerhasset on Isle le Beau.

Wilbur and Orville Wright landed boats
and rafts, and talked long hours here—
who knows of what? The river was calmed
and great Ohio fields spread out
on either side. The white sky sprawled over.

Sprawled over on my back beside the river,
I wonder am I next and what is vision.
Can it be tuned and ordered by a river?
Are there places in this universe more holy
than the river called Mad? Are there none?

(From *Regions with No Proper Names*)

I joined a charismatic young professor, Bernard Strempek, in founding a new national literary magazine at Wright State, the *Mad River Review*, designed to publish some of the new literature we felt vital, and to bring prestige to our school. Bernard was killed in a car crash just before Thanksgiving, 1964, on a rainy highway outside Dayton.

We went on with the magazine. As teacher, poetry editor, and by my third year at Wright State editor-in-chief, I found myself swamped by my usual practice of filling too few hours with too much work. Yet the experience of editing the *Mad River Review* had unexpected benefits. Because of its quickly achieved reputation as a quality publication, I began to receive hundreds of poems a month from all over the world . . . and found a great sameness to most of them, a lack of quality and craft and relevance to the transforming world of the middle 1960s. Most apparent was the obsession of the bulk of the poetry with the Self. The poems were lyric, mainly unrhymed, confessional—without the poet having anything very interesting to confess. Since my first years at Syracuse, studying Eliot and other moderns, I had come to feel strongly that the emphasis on the "I" was damaging to poetry, and longed for a poetry strong in narrative and dramatic elements, as well as one with a form flexible enough to contain elements of the revolutions at work in our nation. The poetry I received confirmed my feelings. I began to advocate and to attempt writing poetry of a different sort.

In the summer of 1965, propped against a poplar with a notebook before me, I sketched out the first few three-line stanzas that would evolve into my first nonsubsidy-press-published book, *Anon and Various Time Machine Poems*. The title, *Anon*, pronounced with a long *A* and an accent on the first syllable, came from a student's telling me he liked "Anon's poems" best of all in the paperback of Japanese poetry he was reading.

I was writing other poems, too, starting to publish them in such magazines as Loring Williams's *American Weave*, the Canadian *West Coast Review*, and the *Antioch Review*, but *Anon* was to occupy most of my writing time for the next five years. Briefly, what I wished to do was set an anonymous character wandering through the 1960s America, in a fantasy of brief canto adventures, often comic and surrealistic, which would capture, via surrealistic satire of the sort I'd found in Bob Dylan's "Talking World War III Blues" and the Beatles, the strange times we were having. I meant the book to be a psychic examination of the 1960s, able to be read easily, its rhythms for the reading-aloud rather than the reading-silently voice, its references and allusions usually to American history.

He'd find
his purpose as he rambled on
like Johnny Appleseed through time

and orchards. He would meet
Leif Ericson and ride
the great white stallion over Idaho.

He'd camp
with Navaho, and by
John Sutter's mill;

hunt well
with Natty Bumppo, slay
the passenger,

engage
himself to Miss America, and die
with Captain Ahab;

walk
through Disneyland, be where
the gantries rise,

zoom rockets
into atmosphere, and laugh
in topless luncheonettes;

eat hot dogs, hamburgs, golden brown
french fries,
then sleep

at Howard Johnson's in
a double bed
beside

a giant mirror
reflecting him and one
who wears

a bunny tail, long ears
of paper yes you can
forget the Viet Nam,

Cong, Nimn,
rice, Korea, bomb,
bing, bang

right through the head—
his head
of splattered brain

has dropped
on Jackie's lap.
God what's

the glory here?
His name
is ANON and I've let him go.

(From "Canto Zero: Anon Is Invented"
in *Anon and Various Time Machine Poems*)

         *   *   *

Martin Luther King has been killed in Memphis. Weeping, we stare at our television sets.

         *   *   *

During the four years I taught at Wright State, I also formed friendships with poets James Reiss, of Miami University, Judson Jerome, of Antioch College, and William Harris, then an undergraduate at Central State University, but a fixture in nearby Yellow Springs. Reiss and Harris published some of their first work in the *Mad River Review.* Jerome and I engaged in a friendly debate concerning the merits of folk-rock poetry (I guest-wrote a poetry column for *Writer's Digest* on it). I had some surprisingly talented students who did their first writing with me, including fiction writers David Chacko and Eve Shelnutt. Through running the Wright State Visiting Writers Program, teaching at the Indiana University Writers Conference, and visiting other area universities, I met a wide number of poets, including Donald Hall, Edward Field, Gwendolyn Brooks, Stephen Spender, Thomas Kinsella, John Woods, James Dickey, and Wendell Berry.

         *   *   *

Robert Kennedy is gunned down in Los Angeles.

XXII

After four years at Wright State, Lori and I agreed how terribly we missed the Northeast, she New York City and the ocean and I the pine forests, high mountains, and wide lakes. Although I was offered an assistant professorship and tenure at Wright State, we drew a map around New York City and I applied for every Assistant Professor of English and Creative Writing position advertised. The University of Bridgeport, in Bridgeport, Connecticut, made the most attractive offer. In 1968, I joined its faculty as an assistant professor, charged with teaching two creative-writing courses a year as well as freshman English and a few American-literature courses.

         *   *   *

Buzz Aldrin, Michael Collins, and Neil Armstrong are preparing to take the LM down to the moon's surface. We wake our son and he stares at the television set as Neil Armstrong says, "Houston, Tranquility Base here. The Eagle has landed."

*   *   *

I'm teaching an advanced freshman English class and hear yelling from outside the room. One of my students goes to the window and finds that four students have been shot at Kent State. I dismiss the class and go home. When the telephone rings, it is Bob Abel, a senior editor from Delacorte, telling me his company has just accepted *Anon* for publication. I thank him politely and tell him what he has not heard—about Kent State. An hour later, I'm back at a campus whose buildings are quickly being occupied by protesting students. The administration retreats. With other of the younger professors, I visit the students, helping to mediate between them and the administration. Within two days, classes are suspended.

*   *   *

Completely unable to celebrate Christmas, Lori and I go for a walk through the suburbs of Loudonville, New York, where we are staying with my parents, who have moved there from Round Lake. The United States has just bombed Hanoi and the war goes on. My students are being drafted, killed, or are fleeing to Canada.

*   *   *

Earth Day. Woodstock. The Vietnam War. The sexual revolution. Drugs. Space exploration. The population explosion. The increase in crime. The ecological crisis. Folk rock. Civil rights. Increasing technology. How can I record it all? How can I capture the sense of what is happening? Less than fifteen years ago, I was still in Round Lake, wandering the forests. The contrast, the abrupt transformation is almost past belief. We live in a time warp, all in flux, nothing ever to be the same again. I must devote my poetry to trying to reflect the times.

XXIII

A New Age

We walk into a new age
carrying knapsacks, twin sleeping bags.

The colors of the trees slightly turn.
We have stepped from one photograph
into a print almost but not quite perfect.

Your voice has a small new tone
to it; I feel
a slight new texture when I touch your hand.

I am not sure if this age
is darker or lighter.
The sun appears smaller,
shadows in the pines seem looser.

We do nothing to adjust. We walk a mile
and the difference goes forever.

I was thinking of having married another
  woman.
You were thinking of having married another
  man.

We lie down in the shade
of an oak with faded initials carved
ten feet up its trunk. Nothing, you say,
is wrong. It is just a new age.

(From *Regions with No Proper Names*)

Our second child, Tanya Angell Allen, was born in 1971. In 1973 we uprooted from a rented house in Westport to the Nichols section of Trumbull, Connecticut, where we'd found a small Cape Cod cottage bordering Thrushwood Lake. The location is perfect for us, with the willowed lake, forty-one acres of ponds, fields, and woodland behind our house which can't be built upon, for they've been willed in perpetuity to the Nichols Improvement Association.

Thrushwood Lake, fall 1989

The university is a ten-minute expressway trip away; New York City is about an hour and a half by train or car.

The house is small enough to remain relatively inexpensive to maintain, large enough to hold our collection of close to fifteen thousand books, with an old stone fence in back, a giant Japanese maple in front. It's towered over by tulip trees, with a wild apple tree to one side. Since the lake is owned by the twenty or so families whose houses border it, there is a private swimming beach for the summer, with a diving board and floating dock at one end of the lake, fishing, space for rowboats and canoes. In winter there are bonfires on the beach, and ice skaters. Our neighbors are lawyers and doctors, ex-cops and plumbers, businessmen, firemen and salesmen. In a sense, I've found my way back to the kind of small-town community where I was raised, and here are the spruce and pine woods, the crows all summer, crickets and cicadas. From the living room's twenty-four-pane windows, we can look out upon a small stone bridge across the stream that feeds Thrushwood Lake after the stream runs through a marsh, and at the three small ponds constructed by the grandfather of our neighbor across the way. As the stream eddies through the ponds, it creates a very quiet, Oriental feeling.

*   *   *

Exhausted, I send telegrams to five organizations which have asked me to conduct seminars or present poetry readings and lectures. I take long walks and sleep fitfully. One night I wake from a strange dream and—as I have never done before or since—immediately write a poem trying to capture the details of the dream. In the dream, I'd died and was whirled through a huge tunnel. I found myself in the After-life, comforted by two women. The last thing I remember from the dream was looking into an endless meadow of flowers, their beauty inexpressible. A brilliant light was speeding toward me from my right.

Over a year later, the first "Life after Life" descriptions receive national publicity. When one of my students shows them to me, I'm shaken. The experience related is the duplicate of the one I've had. Two years later, I meet a woman I recognize from the dream.

Did I die in my sleep, or have I been fantasizing? I can't explain this.

*   *   *

Blocked by the great argument of Stevens's "Sunday Morning," I find I can't continue writing *The Space Sonnets*, the book-length sonnet sequence I began in 1970, in which I hoped to tell the story of a sonneteer and his family who leave America after Robert Kennedy is assassinated and go to live in the hills outside America, at a Space Monastery built around a gigantic telescope and bordered by a broken time machine. I can't convincingly give my sonneteer possible answers to the religious and social questions he asks. I have struggled with Ted Hughes's *Crow* and think I've found a way to convincingly counter his baleful view, but "Sunday Morning" defeats me. I will return only sporadically to the sonnets during the next ten years.

XXIV

William Rimmer: Flight and Pursuit

I saw two men in flight and in pursuit,
Stone castle walls around them and their bodies
  bent
As if they were the same. They were not the
  same
But in the leaning shadows of my dream
First I wore a dagger and a sash—
I fled the Lord's white lash;
Then a curving sword, a hood across my face—
I sped through darkness on His headlong chase.

I could not gain; I could not lose. We stayed
Near, not closing nearer. I could hear the wind
Roaring through the turrets, fleshing out the
  flags;
Beggars' hands reached up from beggars' rags,
Doorways turned to rooms; we sped through
  rooms
To other doorways—eyes, hands, bare thighs
  numb
As gods in bas-relief. The rooms went on and
  on;
Neither of us stumbled as we ran.

My mind, like all minds, sought a single room
  without
Another doorway; or, another world beyond it.
In either place I could have turned and drawn
My dagger from my sash; I could have shown
The face beneath this hood. But as we passed
Each portal, sandals burning, thinking it the
  last,
One more, one more. His sandals raced before
And followed me across each stone slab floor.

(From *Flight and Pursuit*)

Soon after arriving at the University of Bridge-port, I had devised and then taught a special seminar in science fiction which became very popular with my students. After meeting with William A. Pullin, a vice president for Harcourt Brace Jovanovich, I was encouraged to edit a text anthology of science-fiction works, which would become *Science Fiction: The Future,* published in 1971. The book became a success, selling up to ten thousand copies a year in the 1970s. Its royalties were enough to help us afford the down payment for the house. Through Pullin and a fellow professor, Frederick Lapides, I had met Bob Abel at Delacorte. My publishing was going well, and *Poetry* had finally accepted poems from me, publishing four of them to lead off its first issue of the 1970s, then later awarding me its Union League Civic and Arts Foundation Prize for poetry. I met Daryl Hine, then *Poetry*'s editor, and became a regular poetry reviewer for the magazine through the first half of the 1970s.

In 1972, I received the Robert Frost Poetry Fellowship to attend the Bread Loaf Writers Conference, at which I shocked John Ciardi with my liberal ideas and political and explicitly sexual poetry, causing him to denounce me during his farewell address to the Bread Loaf Conference. What particularly seemed to outrage him was a poem I read concerning a fantasy about George McGovern being elected President and ending the Vietnam War.

In addition to my feeling that the pseudo-Confessional "I" was overdominating American poetry, the approach encouraged by thousands of poetry-work-shop poems, I started to become more and more wary of free verse. Like everyone else, I wrote it, but always with a strong iambic base. I found myself drawn back toward traditional form, most particular-ly rhyme, and began experimenting with a hybrid type of lyric-narrative, combining slant and exact rhyme, exact and varying metrical lines—a poetry influenced by jazz, a poetry in which I hoped to combine the use of American idiom and colloquial-isms with a loosened formal structure. Above all, however, the subject matter of American poetry, I felt, needed expansion. I wished to write a poetry that dealt with the same material novelists and nonfiction writers of the last three decades had been treating.

There is little way I can communicate the thousands of days and nights when the main "event" in my life has been reading, studying, experimenting, wadding into paper balls thousands of abortive at-tempts. The struggle to bring into balance sound and sense, form and subject, has been my obsession. But what can be said of interest about such a solitary

pursuit except that it has eaten years and years of my life away?

In 1974, buoyed by the success of *Science Fiction: The Future,* I coedited, with my former student David Chacko, another text-anthology for Harcourt, *Detective Fiction: Crime and Compromise.* It was also success-ful and, like the second edition of the former, became the leading teaching book in its genre and has stayed in print. I followed *Anon* with a collection of political and social and science-fiction poems, *Regions with No Proper Names,* the first book of poetry published by the American division of St. Martin's. In 1975, I coedited with my wife a second science-fiction-text anthology, *Looking Ahead: The Vision of Science Fiction,* designed to emphasize the ecological and religious elements of the genre. And Lori, too, had begun to publish her fiction in literary and science-fiction magazines, as well as winning the *Writer's Digest* Grand Prize in 1976, the same year I became a full professor.

Five books in five years . . . poems, essays, readings, lectures, teaching, reviews, increasing cor-respondence. Even as a workaholic, I was outdoing myself. I'd work and write and edit my usual fourteen to sixteen hours a day, seven days a week, eating no breakfast, often skipping lunch, sustaining energies on seven or eight cups of black coffee. I continued the habit I'd developed at Wright State, of drinking seven to fourteen shots of scotch a night in order to shut myself down. I was always a solitary drinker, never had a morning hangover, was a happy drunk—drink-ing each night until I'd start to see double.

One afternoon in late fall, 1977, I became extremely dizzy during a creative-writing seminar and felt myself close to fainting. I'd been worried prior to then, my anxiety increased by several bouts of phlebitis. I'd become obsessed with fear over the necessary upcoming operation to remove varicose veins in my left leg. I'd also been found to have extremely elevated blood pressure and had been prescribed heavy tranquilizers. Unfortunately, one doctor told me it was all right for me to drink and take tranquilizers simultaneously.

Somehow, I finished out the semester, but I'd created for myself a full-blown case of agoraphobia and severe depression. I became unable to stand in supermarket lines, sit in movie theaters, drive any-where but back and forth to my classes. These I canceled or cut as short as possible, teaching on Valium and antidepressive medication, sitting down with the classroom door wide open. I'd come home at all times when I wasn't teaching and curl into a fetal ball or read obituaries. The semester is almost lost

The ordination of Reverend Richard Negridge Allen at the University of Bridgeport, spring 1987:
Richard Sanders Allen, Doris Bishop Allen, Lori Allen, Richard Negridge Allen,
Tanya Angell Allen, and Dick Allen

from my mind. I sought out a psychiatrist and he helped some, however. After the semester ended and I had survived my leg operation, I felt somewhat better.

But although my depression had lifted slightly, it was still mainly gray within me. I couldn't write, turning down all requests to review, edit, or plan new books. My agoraphobia still kept me near home and I couldn't bring myself to enter most closed spaces without my wife present. Confessing all this to a neighbor, psychiatrist Dr. Bernard Raxlen, who had just begun getting interested in nutritional elements of his profession, I told him I was better but still in serious difficulty. I succumbed to his suggestion that his laboratory give me a glucose-tolerance test.

When he finished analyzing the test, Bernard returned to me laughing. I had, he'd found, a severe blood-sugar problem and was disinsulinemic (a condition that's somewhat of a cross between diabetes and hypoglycemia). The alcohol would have to go completely, as well as all sugar, most carbohydrates, caffeine . . . and I'd have to keep myself steadily fed with protein.

Within a few months, I began to feel the results. The dizzy feelings slightened and then almost disappeared. My blood pressure dropped to normal. I could begin standing on supermarket lines and attend movies and, eventually, I dared to give poetry read-ings and public lectures again. But the process of recovery, of regaining confidence, was a long one. Going through it removed me from active participation in the "poetry world" for five years, from 1977 to 1982.

XXV

In 1978, I was awarded the university's Charles A. Dana Endowed Chair of English. There have been other teaching honors, too: the Associated Departments of English–Modern Language Association award for distinguished undergraduate teaching, my being named by the school to Outstanding Educators of America, and the UB Alumni Association Distinguished Faculty Member of the Year Award in 1988. My working career at UB has typically been too full: four courses to teach each semester, directing the writing major, advising the student literary magazine, running the department's Visiting Writers Series. As at Wright State, I've had distinguished writers begin their studies with me, the most noted to date being poets Jeffrey Skinner and Jon Davis, now themselves both college professors of creative writing.

Some writers are adventurers, roaming their nation and the world. Others root themselves in one place and simplify their lives to get their work done. I have obviously tried to be the latter type. With a secure home base and a long-lasting marriage, I devote my life to teaching for eight months of the year, and writing from dawn to after midnight the other four. Most of the first drafts of my poems are begun in summers, one or two during the holiday break, and then these poems are left to simmer, to be drafted and redrafted, often twenty to a hundred times, for periods ranging from six months to as long as four years or more. During the academic year, in what spare time I have, I revise, write reviews and essays, do some editing and manuscript consultation, and continue a voluminous correspondence with other poets. Since 1981, I've primarily limited my writing to poetry and material connected with poetry.

XXVI

Veterans Day

You were the soldier shouting at the rain
Who walked the college campus with a puzzled
    look,
Brought back, without parade, from Vietnam.

Once I hated you, your uniform, your name,
The way you hunched with buddies in an open
    truck.
You were the soldier shouting at the rain.

I was the marcher with a cause to claim,
Jailed so many times I thought I'd crack.
We wanted no more deaths in Vietnam.

But the helicopter war went on . . . and on—
A country ravaged when green locusts struck;
You could hear them coming through the rain.

A child could kill you, or a crippled man.
You trusted nothing; you got high for luck
And stared through burning eyes at Vietnam.

I burned my draftcard with a lighter flame.
I marched on Washington. You marched the
    jungle muck.
Necessity? Or madness. *Who can stop the rain?*
We were young men in the days of Vietnam.

(From *Flight and Pursuit*)

At last, during the enforced calm of my slow recovery from depression and agoraphobia, and as I allowed myself to include in my poems a few more autobiographical elements than I'd allowed before, I slowly taught myself to incorporate into my poems the mysticism which I'd kept secondary to the social

and political concerns, a mysticism which did not mitigate Stevens's view but added, I felt, to it. The breakthrough finally came with "Overnight in the Guest House of the Mystic," part of which is a retelling of the "Life after Life" dream I'd had in 1972. After returning from a car trip to Florida, I began to write this poem, obsessively struggling with the first draft, barely doing anything but writing the poem for a month of fifteen-hour days. Then it all loosened and I knew that Stevens was right to celebrate earthly life so, but I also knew that there was something else, something that when felt makes life on the planet even more vivid. With this poem finally completed, I was freed to finish the main work of *The Space Sonnets*, to give its sonneteer some of the answers he sought. I have held the book back from submission to publishers for nineteen years of construction, still finding more I wish to do with it.

XXVII

But, in rough translation, David's masters say:

*Turn back the steed, replace the peach, attempt
to reach that place
where knowledge turns to wisdom, as a light green
    wash
of paint upon a pair of screens might turn
into a crane, a crescent moon, a morning glory
or Kōrin's bamboo forests by a lonely lake.*

*Live to praise
your being mystified, the accidental glimpse
of doors through doorways, flames inside the flames,
groundless triumphs and the wind
whistling through the halyards of Port Washington;
the touch of hands.*

*Make light of darkness; make of darkness light
as John Martin did, who cast upon
his canvas so much glory, even in
the drowning rush a hand reached out, a wrist
was grasped and all the angels sang
in unison to see the boundless Lord.*

. . . .

*Our task is to acknowledge how the moths
dance upon a hayfield, darkling speed
of bats in flight above the ocean's spume;
give thanks, his masters say, for all
that takes our breath away and makes us see
more clearly through Illusion's fading veils.*

*Our knowledge that we shall not pass this way
    again—*

almost unbearable—although it makes
each moment precious in itself,
strikes even deeper if we come to feel
the signs and patterns of the mystical
on every tree and bush and turning wheel.

(From the title poem in *Overnight*
in the Guest House of the Mystic)

Overnight was published in 1984, and chosen as one of the five National Book Critics Circle Award nominees of that year. Also in 1984, with a sabbatical semester, a National Endowment for the Arts Poetry Writing Fellowship, and selection to read on the Ohio Poetry Circuit, I felt at last truly back in the poetry world I'd had to leave in the mid-1970s. With the extra money the grant provided, I was able to maintain a decent car and travel some. An Ingram Merrill Poetry Writing Fellowship in 1986 further freed me to construct my fourth book, *Flight and Pursuit,* which combines the mystical with some of the political and social poems with which I began my writing career. I began reviewing for the *American Book Review* and later for the *Hudson Review.*

I had met Frederick Turner, editor of the new *Kenyon Review,* and Frederick Feirstein at the Minetta Tavern in 1981. During an extensive evening conversation over supper, the three of us—a philosopher with dual U.S.A./English citizenship, a psychoanalyst who'd grown up on New York's Lower East Side, and a mystic from the rural America—found we had much in common concerning our views of contemporary American poetry, the need for more form in poetry, expanded subject matter, and a strong narrative and dramatic element. We vowed, that evening, to do as much as we could to encourage such a poetry—later termed "Expansive Poetry" by Wade Newman.

Through Feirstein, I met the businessman-poet Dana Gioia and poets Charles Martin and Richard Moore; through Gioia, Timothy Steele, Robert McPhillips, Robert McDowell, Phillis Levin, Emily Grosholz, and others. The Connecticut Poetry Circuit brought Brad Leithauser and Mary Jo Salter to read at my university and with them, too, there was a strong encouragement of a more formal, less "I"-centered poetry. In 1987, I was selected by Richard Wilbur, Richard Eberhart, James Merrill, and others to read on the Connecticut Poetry Circuit. Throughout 1988, I solicited and then guest-edited work for a special issue of the California literary magazine *Crosscurrents,* bringing together New Formalism and

New Narrative poetry, essays on it, and a symposium concerning these new trends in American poetry.

XXVIII

Our elemental madness—that we know we live
  Today, this century, this year, this hour,
    minute
Everything is happening. Above,
  A flock of geese goes flying down towards
    Bridgeport.
Emerging in a high and cloudy cave,
  A Boeing's shadow is a crosslike print

To which you raise your head. The shore
  Is sand and willows—and our children
Floating near it, bobbing heads and figures
  Flattened on their plastic rafts. The wind
Blows them toward each other
  Or away, unless they link their hands

While we tread water. Look at them. Their
    moments
  Also disappear, yet last—the paradox
Of memory. Think of mullein weeds,
  Full and empty pods upon their stalks,
Dead flowers and the living seeds,
  The washcloth texture of their flannel leaves,

And turn around. Stay close to me. Leave froth
  Again behind us and to both our sides.
Nothing ever will be beautiful enough
  Unless we're satisfied with how we ride
Waves backward and can love,
  For what we fashion, though we cannot keep,
    we need—

As I, these living moments, need the lake
    against
  My back, those towers in the clouds, the cries
Of children linking hands, the houses fenced
  About the lake, their windows brimmed with
    sky
Blue and white—trapped in the way your
    glance
  Catches me, and holds me, and all meanings
    fly.

(From "Backstroking at Thrushwood
Lake" in *Flight and Pursuit*)

I have just turned fifty. Our son, after his years at Ohio Wesleyan University and Emory University, is a Methodist minister. Our daughter has graduated from high school and will begin college soon. Already, she is winning major writing competitions and beginning to publish her stories, poems, and essays. Over one hundred of my creative-writing students have published nationally. I have sat on scores of university committees, taught thousands of classes, run dozens of programs, published hundreds of poems and over fifty essays and reviews. I walk, swim in the summer, struggle with university and English-department problems, vote in elections, write letters to editors, watch television, read constantly—particularly in physics and cosmology, write letters, drive my black Honda too fast, sleep, shop for groceries, make insurance claims after my house is robbed, eat, make love, socialize, attend readings by other poets, listen to music, go to art galleries, vacation, chat with my neighbors . . . is this my adult life?

Much of autobiography is simply a record of dates and events. The real life is the daily life taken up by the hundreds of little tasks, and the overall ones of making a living, raising a family. Or is it? The things I do in the "real" life still do not seem real, or even very true. What is real, to me at least, is only the struggle to understand and praise. It is all, as it has always been, a flight and pursuit.

BIBLIOGRAPHY

Poetry:

Anon and Various Time Machine Poems, Delacorte and Delta, 1971.

Regions with No Proper Names, St. Martin's, 1975.

Overnight in the Guest House of the Mystic, Louisiana State University Press, 1984.

Flight and Pursuit, Louisiana State University Press, 1987.

Editor:

Science Fiction: The Future, Harcourt, 1971, second revised edition, 1983.

(With David Chacko) *Detective Fiction: Crime and Compromise,* Harcourt, 1974.

(With Lori Allen) *Looking Ahead: The Vision of Science Fiction,* Harcourt, 1975.

Expansive Poetry: The New Formalism and the New Narrative, Crosscurrents, 1989.

Other:

Contributor to numerous anthologies, including *SF-12* (Dell), *Contemporary American Poetry* (Random House), *The Modern Age* (Scribner), *Contemporary New England Poetry* (Texas Review), *Anthology of Magazine Verse/Yearbook of American Poetry* (Monitor), *American Humor* (Harcourt), *An Introduction to Poetry* (Little, Brown), *The Umbral Anthology of Science Fiction Poetry* (Umbral Press), *Expansive Poetry* (Story Line), *Light Year* (Bits Press), *Faster than Light* (Ace). Contributor of more than six hundred poems, articles, essays, and reviews to magazines and newspapers.

Editor-in-chief, *Mad River Review,* 1966–68. Contributing editor, *American Poetry Review,* 1972–. Regular reviewer, *Poetry,* 1970–76, *Hudson Review,* 1984–, *American Book Review,* 1983–. Over one hundred poetry readings, including Ohio Poetry Circuit (1985), Connecticut Poetry Circuit (1988). Member: PEN, Poets and Writers, Academy of American Poets, Modern Poetry Society, Poetry Society of America, Associated Writers Programs, MLA, AAUP.

Lawrence Block

1938-

When I was fifteen years old, I was in May Jepson's third-year English class at Bennett High School, in Buffalo, New York. We'd been assigned a composition, a couple of hundred words on our vocational choice. Having at this point no idea what I might want to do after college, I provided a presumably humorous examination of my various career choices over the years, beginning with my initial decision at age four to become a garbage collector. (I abandoned this choice when my mother advised me that garbagemen got chapped hands.)

I don't remember what else I wrote, or what other occupations I reviewed, but I do recall my ending. "On reading over this composition," I wrote, "one thing becomes clear. I can never become a writer."

Miss Jepson liked my composition and gave it a good grade. (This was not remarkable. I always got good grades.) And, in the margin alongside my last sentence, she wrote: "I'm not so sure about that!"

No scrap of marginalia ever had a more dramatic effect. Before, I'd never once had a conscious thought of becoming a writer. From that moment on, I never seriously entertained the idea of doing anything else.

This will be about my life as a writer. The quantity of words I've written notwithstanding, writing has not been my entire life. It is, however, the only part I feel reasonably comfortable telling you about. If you're looking for someone who will afford you all sorts of personal glimpses of himself and others, someone eager to write candidly about family and childhood and intimate relationships, don't pick out a fellow who's spent the past thirty years writing fiction. If I had any interest in letting you know who I really am, I'd have done so years ago. I wouldn't have sat up nights making up stories about imaginary people.

More to the point, my writing life is the only thing that's legitimately interesting about me. (The adverb is the operative word there. There are undoubtedly other aspects of my life you might find absorbing, in a *National Enquirer* sort of way, but they're really none of your business. An advantage the fiction writer has over the journalist, it has long

Lawrence Block with his sister, Betsy

seemed to me, is that he doesn't have to violate anyone else's privacy. As an autobiographer, I'd like to see if I can't manage to avoid violating my own.)

I was born in Buffalo on June 24, 1938 (sun in Cancer, moon in Taurus, Gemini rising), the elder of two children. My father was a native New Yorker. He met and married my mother, a Buffalonian, while both were attending Cornell University. He practiced law in Buffalo. My mother was (and is) an accomplished painter and pianist, but never pursued either direction professionally.

I had what I suppose was a conventional childhood, although I don't suppose I was a conventional child. The first creative writing I can specifically recall came when I was ten. Our Sunday-school class

*Parents, Arthur Jerome Block and
Lenore Nathan Block Rosenberg*

was assigned the chore of writing a Mother's Day poem. This was my poem, which I recall in its entirety:

*Mother so lovely, mother so fair,
You are as fresh as the fresh spring air.*

I can't say I see any hidden talent lurking in those lines, but what do I know? I do know that the teacher liked it, and asked if it was original. "No," I said. "I made it up."

I wasn't being cute. I'd heard things described as being an original Rembrandt, an original Picasso, and I guess I thought original meant by somebody famous, or something like that. All the same, I think my response was right on the money. I did make it up, and it wasn't particularly original.

A few years later, in the eighth grade, I wrote a 200-word essay on Americanism. So did every other kid in Erie County. The *Buffalo Evening News* and the American Legion cosponsored an essay contest, with winners chosen in twelve categories. I was the winning Buffalo public grammar school boy. Coincidentally, the winning girl was my classmate, Lorraine Huber, a set of circumstances which very likely led a lot of people to suspect that our teacher, Edna Johnson, rewrote our entries for us. No such thing. Mrs. Johnson left my essay strictly alone. She did rewrite my pen name, however. You had to submit the essay under a three-word pen name, and the one I selected was Rutherford Delano Quincy. (I figured something with a vaguely presidential sound would be American as all getout, so I took the Rutherford from Hayes, the Delano from Roosevelt, and the Quincy from J. Q. Adams.)

Mrs. Johnson persuaded me to change this to Ford Delaney Quincy. She felt Rutherford was long and effete-sounding, and Delano might alienate any Roosevelt-hating Republicans among the judges. Ford Delaney Quincy didn't sound very presidential to me, but I didn't argue.

The prize was publication in the *News* and a trip to Washington for the dozen winners. We were escorted by an editor from the *News* and an American Legion official and his wife. I read about the legionnaire a couple of times over the years. He led a batch of local anticommunist witch hunts in Buffalo during the fifties, and ultimately killed his wife and himself in what seems to have been some sort of suicide pact.

I don't have a copy of my essay, but that's all right. The opening sentence was *Americanism—what is it?* and the next 195 words were about what you'd expect. It strikes me now that it was very much in the tradition of my Mother's Day poem. It wasn't original, and I made it up.

Despite its handsome payoff, the essay contest did not launch a career. Miss Jepson's approval three years later did. I suppose it came at the right time, and that I was on the verge of discovering literary ambitions myself. It was around this time that I became a serious reader. I had always read a great deal as a child, but then there was a period of a year or two when I didn't read much, and then I began reading adult fiction and made my way through most of the more accessible writers of realistic American fiction. James T. Farrell was an early favorite, along with Thomas Wolfe and John Steinbeck. By the time Miss Jepson suggested that being a writer was not necessarily beyond my grasp, I already understood that it was something very much worth being.

Having made up my mind, I didn't immediately feel the need to sit down and write anything. I did write some poems, and I did give my creativity free rein in my English assignments, but I thought of writing as something I would do later on, when I knew how to do it, and when, presumably, I had something to write about.

In the meantime, though, I got my first writing income. My friend Mel Hurwitz wanted a love poem to impress his girlfriend, who was either Nancy or Natalie Shupe. (They were twins, and I don't remember which one he was going with.) I wrote him a poem that he could pass off as his own work, and he paid me a dollar. I remember nothing about the poem, or what I did with the dollar.

Years later I recalled this incident in a piece I wrote for *Writer's Digest*. Someone showed a copy to Mel and he wrote me a letter. He hadn't passed the poem off as his own, he assured me; Nancy (or Natalie) would never have bought it. But she was impressed enough by his role as patron of the arts, so he got his money's worth out of it all the same.

If Ford Delaney Quincy was my first pen name, I guess Melvin Hurwitz was my second. I don't remember my third and fourth, but they were whatever tags I stuck on my two entries in the contest for Senior Class Poet. The only nonelective class officer, the poet was chosen by a faculty committee, and pen names kept the teachers from knowing who was who.

I entered twice. One poem was eighty lines of stately iambic pentameter—*"Four years have passed since first we called you Home . . ."* The other was free verse, shorter, impressionistic. The first one won, and was printed in the yearbook, and it is no better than the first line would lead you to suspect. The second placed second, Miss Jepson confided. "I knew they were both yours," she added.

I never saw her again after graduation. I never went back to the school to visit. Twenty years later, when I acknowledged Miss Jepson in the dedication of a book on writing the novel, I tried to get in touch with her. She had long since retired and moved to California, and a letter I sent to her came back. For that matter, I never saw Mrs. Johnson after I graduated from PS 66. I had other teachers who did me good, at 66 and at Bennett, and I never went back to see any of them.

I wish I had. It doesn't keep me up nights, but it's something I wish I'd done.

I went to Antioch College, in Yellow Springs, Ohio. I majored in English, although I seemed to be more interested in taking history courses. I figured

At Elco Beach, Canada

you were supposed to major in English if you wanted to be a writer.

I wrote some stories for the college paper, because that also looked to be something you ought to do, but I knew I had no interest in journalism as a career. It was supposed to be good training, and I'm sure it is, but it wasn't what I wanted. I wanted to be a writer, and that meant fiction and poetry.

And I was busy trying to write both. I mostly wrote poems, probably because they were shorter and easier. The short stories I wrote were very short, little ironic vignettes for the most part. They weren't any good and they didn't amount to anything.

I sent them off to magazines. Of course they came back. I expected nothing less. I pinned the rejection slips to my bulletin board and sent off more submissions.

Let me stress that I did not find this process disheartening, nor do I see it now as having been a waste of time. What I wanted then, more than anything else, was to be a writer. By submitting my work and collecting a rejection slip for my troubles I was very definitely being a writer. I have heard it said that going fishing and not catching anything is the second best activity in the world, surpassed only by going fishing and catching something. For me, having my early efforts returned was second only to having them accepted.

Antioch had (and has) a co-op program; you spend half your time on campus studying and the other half away from Yellow Springs, working at some sort of job presumably linked to your interests or vocational aims. Like most freshmen, I spent my entire first year studying. The following summer I took a co-op job as a mail boy at Pines Publications, a magazine and paperback-book publisher in New York.

I had first visited New York in 1948. My father and I spent a long weekend there. We stayed at the Commodore Hotel and went all over the city. When I knew I was going to become a writer, I also knew this meant I would live in New York. I don't know how I knew this, but I took it as a given.

The three months I spent at Pines Publications were some of the best times I ever spent in my life. Two roommates and I found an apartment in Greenwich Village, on Barrow Street. We spent evenings in the coffeehouses on MacDougal Street and our Sundays singing folk songs around the fountain in Washington Square. At six, when the cops chased us off, the crowd came back to our place on Barrow Street and the singing went on until after midnight. I wrote some songs, then and during the next couple of years. Most of them were political parodies, and some were published. (Anonymously—we figured we were on enough lists already.) Dave Van Ronk recorded one of my songs, "Georgie and the IRT," an urban parody of an old Carter Family tearjerker. A few years later we heard that the Kingston Trio might cover the song, but then they came out with their *M.T.A.* song, "The Man Who Never Returned," and I guess they figured one subway ballad was enough.

There was nothing terribly interesting about the work I did at Pines, but it was interesting being there, and I could have stayed; the fellow who ran the promotion department was about to lose his assistant and offered me the job. I told him I was scheduled to go back to school in another month, and he immediately assured me I ought to do just that, that I'd be better off at college. I'm not sure he was right, but I never seriously considered dropping out and taking the job, although I would have liked to.

Earlier, the month before I came to New York, I read a paperback collection of short stories by Evan Hunter, who had not long before won some fame

with *The Blackboard Jungle.* These particular stories had been published in *Manhunt,* and they were all more or less concerned with juvenile delinquents. I identified enormously as I read the stories, not so much with the characters as with their author. These were stories that I very much admired, and at the same time they were stories I could imagine myself writing. I even tried one story about a young man and his girlfriend besieged by a pack of teenaged hoodlums. It didn't work and I didn't finish it, but the attempt was unquestionably prompted by what I'd read.

While I was working at Pines and living on Barrow Street, I did write one short story, a first-person piece with a narrator who lives by his wits. He pulls a couple of scams, and then the story ends inconclusively.

Back at Antioch, I dusted off the story and decided it was good enough to submit. I sent it to *Manhunt.* I had never seen the magazine, but I remembered that Hunter's stories had appeared there, so I got the address and sent the story out. It came back, but with a note from the editor saying it

High-school yearbook photo

had almost worked but that it needed some sort of a snapper for the ending. If I could think of a way to fix it, he'd be happy to look at it again.

I went out and bought a copy of *Manhunt,* read all the stories in it, and came up with an ending. My narrator, after all the little con games he pulled, knows he's going to be really rich because he's put all his money in some investment or other. Gold-mine stock, maybe. The reader knows that he's fallen for a scam himself. The ending owed a lot to O. Henry's *Man at the Top,* and the guy at *Manhunt* sent it back promptly with a note expressing regret that the new ending was pat and predictable and really didn't work.

Meanwhile, I was taking a short-story workshop and a poetry class and getting a lot of stuff written. I had two things going for me from the jump. I was fast and I was smooth. It was easy for me to get writing done, and I had a natural ability to write readable, inviting prose and dialogue. I didn't have anything much to say, and I had trouble getting my mind around the whole shape of a finished short story, but my writing itself was quite good and I could turn out a lot of copy. In the short-story workshop I found it curious that some students spent the whole semester struggling to get a short story written. I was submitting something every week without knocking myself out. At the same time, one older student was about two-thirds of the way through a novel, and I found the accomplishment awe-inspiring.

I don't remember sending out the short stories I wrote for that class, although I may well have done so. I did submit some of my poetry, and I actually had two poems published by *Poet Lore* magazine. They didn't pay anything, but they printed the poems and sent me copies. The poems themselves were quite cryptic, and I don't think they made any sense to me, although someone else may have made something out of them. I was getting notes on my rejection slips from a couple of other poetry magazines. No acceptances, but a sign that I was coming close.

Then I had my first sale. In January of 1957 I went to New York for a week and stayed with some friends who had a loft on the Bowery. (Four of them, and they paid sixty dollars a month.) The Salvation Army had a mission across the street, and one of the girls and I drifted in one night to catch the service the bums had to suffer through in order to get the bread and soup afterward. We found the whole thing terribly amusing, and afterward I wrote a smarmy little seven-hundred-word article for which I supplied an ending the episode lacked in real life. *We Found God on the Bowery,* I called it, and I told how my girl

and I had come to scoff but remained to pray. It was, now that I think about it, altogether unconscionable, but I wrote it up and sent it off to the *War Cry,* official magazine of the Salvation Army, and they ran it and paid me seven bucks.

The summer after my sophomore year I couldn't find an official Antioch co-op job that I liked, so I decided to find my own. I drove to Cape Cod, moved into an attic room upstairs of a barbershop on Hyannis, and worked for a day as a dishwasher at a place called Mildred's Chowderhouse. I worked from four to midnight, and when I finished the boss told me to come in the next day at eight in the morning. I never went back.

I spent the next two weeks writing. First thing I did was rewrite the story that *Manhunt* had liked. I'd thought of an ending that would work, and I sent it off and got a letter back by return mail. An assistant editor wrote that the boss was on vacation but that he was pretty sure the guy would like the new ending, and he was holding the story. (This, I subsequently learned, was nonsense. There was no assistant editor. The magazine was having what a later generation would learn to call cash-flow problems. The editor read my story, placed it in inventory, and wrote me a letter so that I wouldn't expect payment for a while. I wish I'd known right away that the sale was sure. I wouldn't have cared how long I had to wait to get paid. Months later I did learn that they were taking the story, and some months after that I got one hundred dollars.)

I wrote a story every day and lived on Maine sardines and peanut-butter sandwiches. When my money ran out I took a job at a resort. It was eleven hours a day, seven days a week, and you had two-and-a-half hours off in the middle of the day, so there was really no time to do anything, and no place to write anyway in the staff dormitory where I was housed. I quit after ten days, wrecked the car driving back to Buffalo, packed a bag, and took a train to New York.

Within two weeks I had a job as an editor at a literary agency. It was one of the best things that ever happened to me.

I got the job by taking a test. They gave you a story to read, one that had been written to order by Lester del Rey and that contained every structural flaw he could build into it. You had to read it and write a letter to the author, either telling him it was marketable, telling him how to revise it, or telling him why it was beyond redemption. I passed the test with flying colors and got the job and spent the next ten months doing what I'd done on the test—reading amateur efforts and returning them with detailed letters explaining what was wrong with them.

The manuscripts came from hopefuls who paid a fee for the privilege of having their work read by my boss. I wrote to them over his signature, and I invariably told them that they were talented, that they wrote well, but that various plot problems made this particular story unacceptable. Ninety percent of the time the stories were by people who couldn't have written their names in the dirt with a stick, and plotting was the least of their problems, but that was how we were supposed to keep them coming back for more. I got so I could write the letters in my sleep, and I barely had to read the crap to do it, and it was just as well.

It was the best possible learning experience for a writer. Reading inferior work is much more informative than reading good stuff. You get more from seeing what's wrong with something than from seeing what's right with it. I learned even more from being in the office and hearing all the trade talk and gossip.

I wrote a lot, and I started selling regularly, my scripts submitted by my employer. I sold another couple of stories to *Manhunt,* and a batch more to various *Manhunt* imitators, *Trapped* and *Guilty* and the like. A publisher of sensationalistic male-interest magazines would send over article assignments that got parceled out among us, and I wrote seventy-five-dollar articles with titles like *Reinhard Heydrich—Blond Beast of the SS.* An editor who'd bought crime stories from me was editing something called *True Medic Stories,* or something like that, and I enlisted the aid of a premed-student friend and plotted one that he bought. ("My name is Brad Havilland," it began. "I'm forty-two years old and I'm the best bowel surgeon in the state." It's hard to believe anybody read any further than that.)

I took the job in late July or early August, and plans called for me to return to Antioch in November. After I'd had the job for two weeks I knew I wasn't going back. I'd been an indifferent student anyway, and it was very clear to me that I was going to get a lot more out of this job than I could get at college. I dropped out, and a buddy and I took an apartment at the Hotel Alexandria, on 103d Street west of Broadway. Cornell Woolrich was living a few doors away at the Marseilles, but I never knew it at the time.

I stayed through May. Around the first of the year I started being bothered by the fact that dropping out of school meant giving up my draft deferment. The peacetime army was no worse than an inconvenience, but I didn't really want to devote two years of my life to it. I enrolled for the spring semester as a matriculated student at Columbia University's School of General Studies, and I took three writing courses, figuring I'd be doing writing anyway. I enrolled in a radio and TV course, a novel workshop, and a course called Advanced Nonfiction.

It was bizarre. Here I was spending eight hours a day reading amateur writing, and now I had to go listen to people read it to me three evenings a week. The radio and TV course taught a format they'd stopped using years ago, with the audio on one side of the page and the video on the other. I stopped going to it almost immediately, and I dropped the novel course after a couple of weeks. I stayed with the nonfiction class, but I never had to write anything for it. I would just hand in copies of the articles I'd been writing for the men's magazines.

The professor was a nice old fellow who wrote biographies of classical composers. He thought my articles were excellent but lamented that they weren't commercial. This left me wondering, because I knew they were commercial—I'd already been paid for them—and I also knew they were lousy. Eventually I stopped going to that class, too. He gave me a B, though.

Toward the end of the semester I began thinking I ought to go back to Antioch. The job at the literary agency, while not entirely valueless, had by now taught me most of what it had to teach me. Unless I wanted to go on to become an agent, I was approaching a point of diminishing returns. And I didn't think I was yet ready to try supporting myself as a freelance writer. The pulp market was mostly gone, and I was only getting thirty or forty dollars a pop for my short stories. If I was going to make even a marginal living, I would have to be able to write novels, and I didn't think I was ready to do that yet. I'd made a couple of starts at novels and they hadn't worked.

In addition, I had the opportunity to become editor of the college paper if I went back. It seemed a more inviting prospect than spending another year writing letters to the authors of unreadable manuscripts. ("Dear Mr. Vorpal, Thanks very much for sending your story, *The Awful Truth.* I can see that you are certainly no stranger to your typewriter. Your writing is strong and convincing, and you have a sure touch with dialogue. But I am afraid that there are a few basic plot problems in the present work that really cramp your style." At this point I'd read the damn thing to see what they were, and then I'd write the rest of the eight-hundred-word letter. No one should have to do that for more than a year.)

Shortly before I finished up at the literary agency, I woke up one morning with two things I couldn't shake. One was the worst, the absolute worst hangover I'd ever had in my life. The other was the plot of a novel.

I ate some aspirin and sat down and typed up a chapter-by-chapter outline. It was the story of a college girl who thinks she might be a lesbian and comes to New York to find out. In June I left the agency and went back to Buffalo. A buddy and I had made plans to go to Mexico in July. I had three weeks before we were going to leave, and I spent two of them writing the lesbian novel. It came out fine, as far as I could tell, and I mailed it off to my former employer and went to Mexico.

Back home a month later, I received an assignment: on the strength of the novel I'd written, which was making the rounds, my agent wanted me to try a book for a publisher who was about to introduce a line of paperback sex novels.

By the time I reported to Antioch that fall, I had written the book and been paid $600 for it. In the course of the next academic year, I turned out three more sex novels for that publisher. I also found time to do revisions on the original lesbian novel, which had sold to Crest Books, the second or third publisher to see it. (Crest was a Fawcett imprint, and paid $2000 for the book. This was in 1958–59, when the fee for tuition and room and board at Antioch was, as I recall, $1400. I had previously earned $40 a week at Pines Publications, $65 at the literary agency.)

It seemed to me that I'd made a mistake going back to college. I don't know that this was so, but in any event I found it impossible to take my academic responsibilities seriously. I held things together well enough during the semester when I edited the paper, but during the academic semesters I was less successful. I tended to stay up all night, either working on a book or pursuing a second career as a hard-drinking campus legend. I didn't get to many classes, and I didn't cover myself with glory when I did.

When school let out in June I went to New York, moved into a hotel room, and started writing. I got a letter from the school suggesting that I might be happier not returning in the fall. I think I might have talked my way back in, but it was the last thing I wanted to do. (I'd tried to drop out myself midway through the year, but had let my folks talk me out of it.) I stayed in New York a few weeks more, then moved back to Buffalo with an assignment to furnish yet another new publisher with a book a month. He would be paying me $750. Meanwhile, the other publisher would continue to take extra books at $600 if I had time to fit them in.

I didn't do many extra books because other activities took up my spare time. I became a partner in a jazz club and coffeehouse and began keeping company with a Buffalo girl, Loretta Kallett. (We'd gone to the same high school but hadn't known each other at the time.) In March of 1960 we were married. We moved to New York and I sold my interest in the Jazz Center to my partner, leaving him to go broke with it by himself.

For the next three years I wrote one of these soft-core sex novels each month. My total production probably averaged something like twenty books a year, because I was doing other things besides my assigned monthly book. In addition, I was fielding assignments that my agent steered to me, and I was writing other books on spec, trying to move up in class.

I did make some progress, but it always seemed to come more in spite of than because of my efforts. When I tried to write for a better market, I generally fell short. More often, I shied away from the task rather than risk failure. After having sold that first effort to Crest, for example, I never did manage to write a second lesbian novel for them. I never decided not to, but my mind simply failed to provide ideas, and I seemed to be much more comfortable going for smaller surer money and writing easier and less challenging books.

On the other hand, a few months after we were married I started my monthly sex novel and discovered a few chapters into it that it seemed to have possibilities as a straight suspense novel. I allowed myself to write it that way. My agent agreed with my appraisal and sent the manuscript over to Knox Burger, then editor at Gold Medal. It was published as *Mona,* the first book to come out under my own name. Berkley reprinted it a few years ago as *Sweet Slow Death,* which is an improvement on the original title, albeit a slight one. (Ralph Daigh, the boss at Fawcett, had bought a piece of cover art with a girl's face on it and wanted to use it for the book, so he chose the name of the book's femme fatale for the title. Berkley in turn lifted the phrase *Sweet Slow Death* off the blurb copy from the Fawcett edition. My original title was no good either, so I can't complain.)

Mona wasn't much good; it was immature work, which stands to reason, given that I was twenty-two at the time and no model of maturity myself. Instead of following it up by trying to write another suspense novel for Gold Medal, I resumed turning out sex novels as before. A while later, I got the assignment of writing a tie-in detective novel based on the TV show "Markham," which starred Ray Milland. I wrote the book, and by the time I'd finished it I'd decided it was too good to waste its fragrance on the desert air that greets TV tie-in novels. My agent agreed and sent it over to Knox, who bought it, whereupon I went through the manuscript and changed Roy Markham to Ed London. (Then, of course, I had to write a second book about Markham for Belmont.)

Gold Medal published the book as *Death Pulls a Doublecross,* a title that still triggers my gag reflex when I contemplate it. Foul Play Press has lately reissued it as *Coward's Kiss,* which was my original title. It's derivative, certainly, and fairly predictable, but it's not bad. You'd think that I would have written more books about Ed London, and the fact of the matter is that I tried, as I indeed tried other things more ambitious than the sex novels and other hackwork I was producing at the time. But the books either didn't get written or just plain didn't work out. If I was writing something I could take seriously, I invariably took it too seriously—and the creative mechanism went on strike.

I used to think that my problem had been a lack of courage, that I hadn't had the fortitude to give up the sure money and risk insecurity. But I don't really think that had much to do with it. The money was

Lawrence with his parents and sister, 1955

never really that important to me. The real problem, I think, was that I didn't have the self-esteem required to write books that were to be taken seriously.

And, all things considered, maybe I was guided by some inner wisdom. Because I don't think the world missed any great literature for my having spent a couple of years writing crap. I wasn't really capable of writing anything very good. I did have a remarkable level of technical proficiency for someone my age. I could write eminently readable first-draft copy that did not require any editing, and this is not that common at any age.

But I wasn't really ready to produce anything significant with that talent. All I could really do was exercise my skills and improve them, and what I was writing probably served me better toward those ends than anything else I might have done.

The books I was writing, it should be understood, were rather a far cry from what is to be met with nowadays on the shelves of adult bookstores. The current run is frankly pornographic, and what we were writing, while no more high-minded, was something different. The books were about sexual matters, certainly, and there was a sex scene in virtually every chapter, but one had to work within the restrictions of censorship. You couldn't use any of the seven words you can't say on TV, for instance. Precise sexual descriptions were similarly forbidden. The purpose of the books was the erotic arousal of the reader, but some subtlety was required.

As a result, the books had to be novels. They had to have characters and story lines and dialogue. They were never much good as books—the conventions of the form precluded that—but they were wonderful vehicles for growing as a writer because you could try anything with relative safety. The medium was a forgiving one. A plot could be preposterous, a subplot could remain forever unresolved, a secondary character could take over the book or disappear from it without an explanation, and nobody gave a rat's ass. If the book was written in acceptable English, if it was long enough, and if it was in on time—that was all anybody really cared about.

I think it was good training, an apprenticeship that paid a living wage. Two of my closest friends, Hal Dresner and Donald E. Westlake, came up the same way. Both began working as editors at the literary agency—although none of us were there at the same time—and both were subsequently represented by that agent and wrote for the same publishers as I did. I collaborated on two books with Hal and three with Don, operating without any advance discussion of story line.

Once half a dozen of us gathered at one fellow's house in Queens for a writing marathon—five of us would sit downstairs playing poker while a sixth was upstairs writing a chapter. We figured we ought to be able to turn out a book overnight. This didn't work— one of our company, afraid he wouldn't be able to stay awake, took a dose of amphetamine before going up to do his chapter. He was evidently addled by the drug and produced about forty pages of incomprehensible gibberish, and the fellow whose turn came next was relatively inexperienced and spent hours trying to write something that would follow logically upon what the speed freak had produced. If the evening failed to produce a book, at least it spawned a legend. I have since heard versions of the story told by several people, including one agent who claimed to have been there. (Imagine that—an agent telling a lie. Who'd have thought it?)

In March of 1961 my daughter Amy was born. A year later we decided we needed more room and moved back to Buffalo. I went on writing the same sort of books I'd been doing in New York. Jill was born in May of 1963. After we brought her home from the hospital I wrote an extra book to cover the birth expenses. I wrote it in three days, and I don't remember anything else about it. Every detail of it— the plot, the names of the characters—had vanished entirely from my memory a day or two after I finished it. I guess it was all right. I got paid for it, and it got published.

You have probably noticed that I have not supplied the titles of any of the books I wrote during this period, or mentioned the pen names under which they were written. This is not the result of oversight. For several years now I've declined to identify my pseudonymous early work.

There are a couple of reasons for this. First is the same reason I published them under pen names in the first place. They are inferior work, categorically inferior, and I'd rather not be specifically linked to any of them, although I'm not reluctant to discuss that apprentice period in general.

At least as important is that I am even less inclined to be linked to books I *didn't* write. And it's a fact that a majority of the books published under "my" pen names were written by other people. I became very much in demand as a writer of sex novels during those years. My regular publisher wanted not one but two books a month from me, which was more than I wanted to produce, and I

solved that problem by training a few other writers to produce the books. I oversaw some of this ghostwriting, but in the main my relationship to the books was purely financial; I received two hundred dollars for the use of my pen name and the ghost received the other thousand. (My price had edged up over the months.)

In addition, the publisher had a cavalier attitude toward pen names. Some of my books came out under other writers' names, and some of theirs came out under mine. One publisher was revision happy; for reasons nobody has ever doped out he kept a batch of editors on staff whose chore it was to rewrite virtually every sentence of every book he published. I guess he thought this was something publishers had to do, but Lord knows none of the books were helped by this treatment.

Finally, even more books came out under my name after I stopped doing them altogether. The publisher evidently regarded one of my pen names as his property rather than mine.

My sex-novel apprenticeship, and my relationship with the literary agent (whom, you will also note, I have failed to name), ended abruptly in the summer of 1963. He gave me an assignment which I elected not to accept, and he responded by dropping me as a client. This had the unforeseen effect of closing my major book-a-month market to me, and of simultaneously depriving me of the override I'd received on my ghostwriters' production.

Things looked bleak at first. I had a family to support and no credentials or marketable skills outside of writing. Nor did I know how to go about getting another agent or developing new markets for my work. Still, I found ways to write books and sell them, and I was able to make a living. I did sex novels for one house and a couple of sex-fact books for another. I sold mystery stories to magazines. I'd become interested in coin collecting a year or two previously, and I wrote articles on the subject which I sold to some numismatic publications.

This last activity led to a job offer. After I'd placed two or three articles with the *Whitman Numismatic Journal,* an editor came to Buffalo to meet with me. His company, a division of Western Printing, published a line of numismatic books, as well as producing the greater portion of coin holders and other supplies for collectors. He offered me a job as a writer/editor. I took it, and we sold our house and moved to Racine, Wisconsin.

I started work in July of 1964 and stayed there for a year and a half. I got up every morning at six, sat down at my desk at a quarter to eight, and stayed there until a quarter to five. After having taken it for granted that I could never make it in the corporate world, I was delighted to discover that I seemed capable of adjusting to the life and, furthermore, that I was very good at my work.

I wrote some of the magazine every month and did most of the editorial work, editing manuscripts, laying out and making up the pages, corresponding with authors, selecting photographs, etc. I also increasingly took on the advertising and sales-promotion activities within the coin-supplies division, and the result was that the job, which I'd taken originally as a way out of a rut, was beginning to look like a position with a real future. By the time I'd decided to leave, there were plans to move me out of the coin-supplies backwater and into general marketing at Whitman, with some sort of eventual vice-presidency no doubt looming on the horizon.

Once I saw that I had a future there, I realized it was time to get out.

Because I'd never had the intention of making a life's work of this. I still wanted to be a writer, and indeed I was still writing. I completed several books during my time in Racine, along with a handful of short stories. One of them, *The Girl with the Long Green Heart,* was a book I'd begun in Buffalo; a new agent sent chapters and an outline to Gold Medal, Knox Burger bought it, and I worked nights and weekends in Racine to finish it.

It was in Racine, too, that I wrote the first book that was uniquely my own. Earlier I'd had the idea of writing about a character who had lost the ability to sleep. I figured out a few things about his personality and life-style, but I never wrote anything because I couldn't think of a story to put him in. At Whitman I met a fellow who'd spent the past several years in Istanbul, earning a precarious living smuggling coins and antiquities out of the country and peddling them in Paris and Zurich. He told me how he and a pair of execs from ARAMCO had tried to salvage a hoard of gold coins stashed by Armenian refugees in Balakesir some fifty years previously. That gave me the plot component I needed, and I wrote the first of what were to be seven books about Evan Tanner.

Meanwhile, I had a new agent. Henry Morrison, who had worked for my original agent (and who indeed had been working there when I worked there myself), had gone into business for himself. I sent him *The Thief Who Couldn't Sleep,* he placed it with Gold Medal, and I quit my job and we moved to New Brunswick, New Jersey.

I think my time in Racine must have done me good. I evidently needed that relatively fallow period. While I did get several books written there, my writing was under very little pressure, and my production was nothing compared to the volume I had been previously producing.

Perhaps as a result, I was able to write on a new level when I returned to full-time free-lancing. The seven Tanner books, novels of foreign intrigue set all over the globe, were mine in a way none of my earlier books had been. Neither the character nor the plots were derivative, as my earlier work had been. The books were humorous, too, and before this I had never expressed humor in my work.

I'd hate to have to write a book about Tanner now. I've grown since then, and there was a carelessness about the books that I don't think I would allow myself nowadays. But I'm fond of them, and I can still reread them without shrinking in embarrassment. They were fun to write, and I was pleased a few years ago when they all came back into print.

The only disappointing thing about the Tanner books—aside from the fact that the reading public never did go absolutely nuts over them—was that a couple of my best titles got changed. The second book bore the title I gave it, *The Canceled Czech,* but the Latvian adventure, which I'd called alternately *Letts Do It* and *The Lettish Tomatoes,* was published as *Tanner's Twelve Swingers.* And the next book, a story about a Siamese youth who couldn't get anywhere with women, wound up with the uninspired title *Two for Tanner.* I had called it *The Scoreless Thai.*

The Tanner books were not the only novels I was writing over the next several years. *Deadly Honeymoon,* my first hardcover novel, came out from Macmillan in 1967. (While this may look like a great leap forward, I'd written the book four years earlier, and the only reason it wound up in hardcover was that I'd been unable to place it with a paperback house. Publishing has curious cycles, and around that time it was very difficult to publish a paperback original crime novel.) My second book with Macmillan, *After the First Death,* made use of some themes that I would return to later in my books about Matthew Scudder.

We lived in New Brunswick for three years, then moved to a farm near Lambertville, New Jersey, where my third daughter, Alison, was born. I loved living in the country, but there were too many distractions there, and I woke up one day and realized I hadn't written anything in the past five months. I went into New York, rented a room at the Royalton, and wrote a book in a week that I'd been stalled on for months. That set a pattern I stayed with for the next three or four years. I didn't try to get any writing done at the farm, but came into town to do my work. At first I used the Royalton. (I wouldn't advise this now. When I used to go there you could get a room for ten or twelve dollars a night. Since then they've glitzed the place up beyond recognition, and I think the price is closer to two hundred dollars now.) After I'd done a couple of books at the hotel I took an apartment.

During this period I did some pseudonymous writing in addition to the books under my own name. I wrote some sex-fact books, collections of sexual case histories; these began as complete fabrications, but they generated a great deal of correspondence and wound up over the years evolving into a sort of legitimacy.

I also wrote three books as Paul Kavanagh and four as Chip Harrison. The narrator and protagonist of the first Kavanagh book, *Such Men Are Dangerous*, is named Paul Kavanagh, and the book itself was written in white heat in about ten days, after a period of depression several months long during which I'd been unable to write anything at all. I chose to put the character's name on the title page with the thought that it could be effectively marketed that way, but it's not hard now to see a more significant unconscious motive. The book was deeply personal, emotionally if not circumstantially, and I'm sure I felt more comfortable going within myself with a name other than my own beneath the title.

No such considerations prompted me to do the same thing with the four Chip Harrison books. The lead character, also named Chip Harrison, is a sort of lustful Holden Caulfield trying to make his way in the world. I never expected to write more than one book about the character; after the second I still found the voice an enjoyable one to write in, put my lead character to work for a private detective, and wrote two more books that amount to a sort of homage to Rex Stout's Nero Wolfe series.

The Kavanagh books that followed *Such Men Are Dangerous* are third-person novels, one a political thriller called *The Triumph of Evil*, the other a fictionalization of the Charles Starkweather–Caryl Fugate murders called *Not Comin' Home to You*. There was no reason not to publish these under my own name, but I seem to have liked something about pen names.

Commercially, I think they were a great mistake. Looking back, you'd think I was doing my damnedest to avoid building a following. I could probably figure

out some of the reasons I found pen-name writing alluring, but the hell with it. In recent years all of the Kavanagh and Harrison titles have come back into print, and they're all under my own name now. I haven't written a book under a pen name since 1973, and I can't imagine ever wanting to do so again.

In the summer of 1973, my marriage ended. Loretta and I had separated briefly six-and-a-half years earlier, and this time the split was to be permanent. I moved into the apartment on West Fifty-eighth Street that I was already using for writing, and I lived there for the next two years, at which time I sold almost everything I owned, put my remaining possessions in storage in my mother's attic, and hit the road in a rusted-out 1968 Ford station wagon. I drove to Los Angeles and took nine or ten months getting there.

It was an interesting time. (The Chinese have a curse: *May your children live in interesting times.* That is the kind of interesting time it was.) I was by now an established professional writer with a fairly substantial body of work. I was also thirty-five years old, and clearly too young for a mid-life crisis, so that can't be what I was going through. But something was clearly wrong.

By the time I packed up and left New York, my career had hit a bad patch, and it's hard even now to say exactly what happened. It had looked as though I was doing fine since the marriage ended. I had done three books for Bill Grose at Dell, all about an alcoholic ex-cop named Matthew Scudder, and they were arguably the best work I'd ever done. But Dell was just sitting on them, and it was unclear when they would be published, and by no means certain that they would ever see print. The publishing industry seemed to be going through one of its periodic reappraisals, and I was by no means the only writer who was having a hard time. Whenever I called to complain, Henry would tell me about all his other clients who were doing just as poorly as I was. I'm sure this was supposed to be reassuring, but I found it cold comfort.

For my own part, I suppose what I was doing then was falling apart. I had trouble getting books started, and most of what I began ended abruptly fifty or sixty pages in when I found it impossible to think of a reason why any of the characters should go on, or anything for them to do if they did. I wrote a couple of ill-conceived nonfiction books that never did sell. I wrote a novel, *Ariel*, under contract to a publisher; when I finished he didn't like how it had turned out. (This book did eventually sell to Arbor House; I revised it along lines Don Fine suggested, and it did quite well.)

Mencken wrote somewhere that a divine hand must have seized the United States by the state of Maine and lifted it, with the result that everything loose wound up in southern California. I was, and I did. I moved into the Magic Hotel in Hollywood in February of 1976 and stayed there for six months.

In July my daughters flew out to spend the summer with me. We stayed at the hotel for that month, where I started work on what turned out to be *Burglars Can't Be Choosers*. We spent August driving slowly back across the country to New York. We stopped in Roswell, New Mexico, for what turned out to be my last visit with my sister, Betsy; she died suddenly two years later. We stopped to visit a friend in Denver, stopped for a few days in Newcastle, Wyoming, so that I could work some more on the new book. We visited my old office in Racine; I would have liked my old job back, if I could have thought of a way to ask for it. We stopped in Yellow Springs, Ohio, where I learned that my old freshman roommate, Steve Schwerner, had just returned to take the position of dean of students. I suppose it's possible to receive such information without suddenly feeling a good deal older, but I don't know how.

When we got back to New York I dropped the girls with their mother. (Loretta had moved to the city a year after the breakup, and we'd had the farm on the market ever since.) I had expected to turn the car around and go back out to L.A., but this never happened. I hung around the city and realized I wanted to stay. Meanwhile, Henry had sold *Burglars Can't Be Choosers* to Random House, and Dell had finally brought out the Scudder books. And, toward the end of 1976, we sold the farm. We had owned the place outright, and with my share of the proceeds I was able to pay off my debts and move into a small apartment on Bleecker Street in Greenwich Village.

It was at about this time that I began a professional relationship which continues strong thirteen years later. In the course of my *wanderjahre*, I wrote a variety of short pieces, propping my typewriter on various motel desks and trying to finish up before checkout time. Most of these were short stories, the bulk eventually published in *Ellery Queen* or *Alfred Hitchcock*, but one was a piece on the development of ideas in fiction which I submitted to *Writer's Digest*. They bought it, and when the girls and I stopped in Yellow Springs en route to New York, I made a side trip to Cincinnati where I had lunch with John Brady, then the editor of *WD*. I proposed a monthly column

on fiction writing and he agreed to take the column every other month on a trial basis.

I wrote my first column immediately upon my return to New York. Six months later, the *Digest* dropped the cartooning column with which my column had alternated, and I've been in the magazine monthly ever since.

This association has been wonderful for me. With both John Brady and his successor, William Brohaugh, I've had complete freedom to examine whatever aspect of writing I wanted, from nuts-and-bolts columns on technique to essays more concerned with the inner game of writing. Two collections of my columns have appeared in book form, *Telling Lies for Fun and Profit* and *Spider, Spin Me a Web*, the latter published by Writer's Digest Books, who are also the publishers of my book *Writing the Novel from Plot to Print*.

Every month, then, I've been called upon to think of some element of my profession upon which I can ruminate for some 2000 words. This has informed my own reading considerably; if I tended to read fiction analytically as a writer, I do so that much more as a writer about writing.

I certainly never expected the column to last this long. A year or so into it, I began to wonder when I would run out of ideas. A little further down the line I realized this might never happen; by the time each column was due, there was always something to write about, some problem in my own work or something I'd read that had struck a chord. And I haven't seemed to lose heart for the business, either. The magazine or its readers may tire of me sooner or later, but I don't seem to tire of my role in it all.

Not too long ago, someone pointed out to me that I may have written and published more sheer wordage on the subject of writing than anyone else around—or, indeed, than anyone else in history. In the column itself, I've probably written something like 300,000 words. When you add in *Writing the Novel from Plot to Print* and a fourth book, *Write for Your Life* (of which more later), plus occasional lead articles for *WD* and features for *Writer's Yearbook*, the grand total begins to edge alarmingly close to the half-million-word mark. I've no idea if that's a world record, and I'm not sure I want to know, or what I would prefer the answer to be.

It strikes me, though, that all of this writing about writing makes the autobiographical writing I'm doing right now both easier and more difficult. It's easier because I've already written about much of this material before, albeit in a different form and with a different end in mind. It's difficult because I'm more

Lawrence Block with his wife Lynne, Jamestown, North Dakota, 1989:
"The World's Largest Buffalo is in the background."

concerned in the present instance with the overall shape of a life and a career than with individual matters and the lessons to be drawn from them.

It was December of 1976 when I took the apartment on Bleecker Street. This was the first time I had actually lived in the Village since that job in Pines Publications' mailroom twenty years earlier, but in a sense the neighborhood had been home to me through all those years. Whenever I was in New York, no matter where I actually resided, I always gravitated there. It felt good to be back.

I settled in there, wrote my column every other month, wrote some short stories for *Ellery Queen* (including the first in what would be an extended series about a devious lawyer named Ehrengraf), and wrote two hundred pages of a crime novel which I

ultimately abandoned. I outlined and sold a World War II thriller about the defection of Rudolf Hess.

Then, in April of 1977, something monumental happened. I stopped drinking.

In the past twelve years, most of my fiction has consisted of novels about two series characters. Bernie Rhodenbarr, who first appeared in *Burglars Can't Be Choosers,* is an urbane and literate fellow, a nice guy who happens to be a burglar. (He knows it's a character defect but he's not able to do anything about it.) In each of five books to date, his criminal activities put him into a situation he can only resolve by turning detective and solving a murder. By the third book, *The Burglar Who Liked to Quote Kipling,* he had established himself as the proprietor of a used-book store and was best friends with Carolyn Kaiser, a lesbian poodle groomer. (That last phrase may be ambiguous. Carolyn is a lesbian who grooms poodles, not a groomer of lesbian poodles.) The Burglar books are lighthearted and great fun to write, and I wish I could write more of them, but it looks increasingly less likely that I ever shall. It's been seven years since I wrote *The Burglar Who Painted Like Mondrian,* and I have a feeling I'm done with the character.

But I could be wrong. I've several times thought I was done writing about Matthew Scudder, and he seems to have more lives than a cat. Scudder, the hard-drinking and angst-ridden ex-cop about whom I'd written three books for Dell, is a character through whose eyes I particularly enjoyed seeing the world. When Dell first delayed and then buried the books, it looked as though the series was a done thing; it's hard to get a publisher excited about a series with which another publisher has already failed. I did make a couple of attempts at a fourth Scudder novel during my wanderings, and on my return to New York I wrote two novelettes about him which *Alfred Hitchcock's Mystery Magazine* published.

In 1980 I had an idea for a Scudder novel and wrote it. By this time Don Fine at Arbor House had published a revised *Ariel,* and he liked the new book, *A Stab in the Dark,* and published it as well. The next book, the fifth in the series, was called *Eight Million Ways to Die,* and it was almost twice the length of the standard detective novel. In it, Scudder attempts to solve the murder of a call girl while struggling with his own alcoholism. Both themes are central to the book, as is the looming presence of New York City itself, in which, as the title suggests, there are as many doors to death as there are inhabitants.

The book was a great stretch for me, more ambitious and more effectively executed than anything I'd written previously. It was well-received by the public and the critics, was nominated for a Mystery Writers of America Edgar award, won the Private Eye Writers of America's Shamus award, and was eventually filmed. (So were *Deadly Honeymoon* and one of the Burglar books; none of the films were very good, or did very well.)

I had every reason to write further about Scudder, but I didn't know if I could. In a sense, all five books constituted one big novel which was resolved in *Eight Million Ways to Die* when Scudder came to terms with his drinking problem. With that ghost laid, what would drive him? His catharsis behind him, the man's fictional *d'être* had no *raison.*

Several attempts at a sixth book fell flat. Then I wrote a flashback novel, what Hollywood people call a prequel; Scudder, sober, recalls and narrates events which took place a decade earlier. I used the material first in a short story which *Playboy* published. It won several awards and was widely anthologized, and I subsequently expanded it into a novel, *When the Sacred Ginmill Closes.* I felt the book represented a further advance for me as a writer, that it was more novelistic, more a story of human relationships than I'd managed in the past. But it still looked like a dead end as far as the future life of the series was concerned. I couldn't see myself writing more flashback novels, and felt no more sanguine than ever about the prospect of chronicling Scudder's sober life.

In 1981 I met Lynne Wood, a model-turned-antique-dealer-turned-accountant. A year later we began keeping company, and in 1983 we were married. We lived in New York until 1985, when, for reasons neither of us can any longer recall, we moved to the Florida gulf coast.

During the first three years of our marriage, I got relatively little writing done—not, I hasten to add, for the dirty-minded reasons you're thinking, but because most of my time and energy (and Lynne's as well) went into a series of writing seminars we presented all around the country.

I had by this time led a writing seminar one summer at Antioch, and had taught a course in mystery writing at Hofstra University. (And, of course, my monthly column was instructional in nature.) All writing classes, my own included, seemed somehow beside the point.

Exposure to several New Age seminars, most notably one called the Loving Relationships Training, convinced me that the interactional seminar could serve as an excellent vehicle for increasing an individual's capacity to achieve his full potential as a writer. Accordingly I developed such a seminar, called it "Write for Your Life," and went into the seminar business. Over the next three years Lynne and I flew back and forth across the country, putting on several dozen of these intensive all-day seminars.

The whole thing rapidly became a business. I recorded a tape of affirmations for writers, designed for repeated listening. I wanted to make the seminar available in book form to the great majority of people who would never take it in person; in order to get the book out in a hurry, I published it myself. (Like most writers I'd had fantasies of self-publishing for years, and this seemed a low-risk way to do it.) In no time at all we were in the mail-order book and tape business, filling orders in the middle of the week, then flying off to hold a seminar.

All of this was exhausting, and although the seminars were successful in every other respect, they were never financially profitable. After three years, too, leading the seminars began to feel more like performance, and it was time for the play to end its run. Even more to the point, I was ready to focus more of myself on my writing.

In Florida I spent about a year and a half getting ready to write something without knowing what it was. I meanwhile dealt with a batch of projects I was happy to do once but wouldn't want to make a career of. I completed a Cornell Woolrich novel which the *noir* master had left unfinished at his death. I did a novelization of a film script; because of contractual problems with the screenwriter, the book remains unpublished. I spent months working with a friend on his memoir of his life as a mercenary, a criminal, and finally an undercover DEA bounty hunter. (This, too, was never published.)

I knew I had a novel to write and I knew it was going to be something completely different, but I didn't have a clue what it was. I had booked myself to spend a month at a writers' colony in June of 1987, and I just hoped I'd have something to work on when I got there.

In mid-May, I suddenly got an idea for a book about people walking across the country. Over the next several days the idea kept filling my mind. I drove to the colony and just started writing when I got there. Each day, everything I needed to know about the story was somehow available to me. It was an uncanny experience, as if an unconscious part of my mind was able to perceive the novel whole and complete. The book itself was a sort of New Age epic, the story of these people walking east from Oregon, and it was also the story of a serial killer who was driving around the Great Plains murdering women and enjoying it immensely. The two story lines didn't appear to belong in the same book, but I just kept on writing, taking it on faith that it would all make sense in the end.

The book, *Random Walk,* was exciting to write and gratifying to have written. It was a complete departure for me, and I had no idea what I would do for an encore. When it came out in the fall of 1988, it had all the impact of a rose petal dropped into the Grand Canyon. The few reviews to appear were negative, the publisher failed to advertise or promote the book, and sales were weak. My mail shows that people who like the book tend to like it a lot, but a good many readers don't know what to make of it.

"With Lynne at Mohonk (New York) Mystery Weekend,"
1989

Perhaps it will find its audience when it comes out in paperback.

I don't know that *Random Walk* will change the lives of its readers; there may be too few of them to tell. It does seem, however, to have changed the life of its writer. Having written it, I knew I didn't want to live in Florida any longer, and neither Lynne nor I was at all sure where we'd like to live next. Accordingly we decided to try a couple of years of living nowhere in particular. It is June of 1989 as I write these lines in the Irma Hotel in Cody, Wyoming. We have been living without a fixed address for about a year and a half, driving back and forth across America in an aging Buick and learning to rely upon the kindness of strangers.

And, much to my surprise, I've resumed writing about Scudder. After having told anyone who asked that I was finished with the character, I got an idea last spring and wrote a book last fall. It is called *Out on the Cutting Edge,* and Morrow will publish it in October. A sequel, *A Ticket to the Boneyard,* is already written and scheduled for publication a year later. And I have a new book in mind, and a space reserved this fall at a writers' colony. I find I'm eager to get to work.

It's a curious business, writing one's autobiography. I've nattered on autobiographically in my columns for years, and of course I've used aspects of my inner and outer selves in my fiction for as long as I've been writing, but this is a very different matter.

For one thing, I'm not sure how true it is. The facts are genuine enough, and my memory's reliable on dates and such, but I've been writing fiction for over thirty years, and that's bad training for this sort of work. I wouldn't have to come right out and lie in order to sell you a bill of goods, and I wouldn't necessarily know that's what I was doing.

Our narrator here, the "I" in this saga, is almost certainly a slightly different person from the fellow sitting at the typewriter. The narrator's a character created by the man at the typewriter, same as all the other narrators of my first-person fiction who are and are not me. All things considered, I have to say that I much prefer writing fiction that comes right out and says it's fiction, a made-up story about made-up people that aims at a higher truth.

Another thing that bothers me is that all of this has the air of a summing-up, and that strikes me as uncalled for. The same superstition that makes a man reluctant to draw a will would argue against the preparation of this sort of document. It would seem to presage the end of a life, or of a career, and either prospect appalls me.

I'm not done writing. Perhaps I should be; for all the years I've put in and pages I've turned out, in any other line of work I'd be pensioned off by now. You'd think I'd have long since said whatever I had to say and could be expected to maintain a decent silence for whatever time remains to me.

On the other hand, I'm doing my best work now. I've been able to continue growing as a writer, perhaps because I had the wit to start out at such a low level. But everyone who's read *A Ticket to the Boneyard* thinks it's my best book to date, and I'm of an age to have my richest hours ahead of me.

Of an age indeed. I'll be fifty-one in a couple of weeks. My children are grown—Alison is halfway through college, Jill was just admitted to the New York State Bar, and Amy has a daughter of her own. But I still wear jeans, and I still drift around the country and hang around the Village, and God knows I haven't managed to save a dime. I don't know that any of this adolescent behavior makes me young at heart. One can only hope.

I find myself profoundly grateful for the life I lead. It is, I suppose, an eccentric life, and its external circumstances can change radically from one year to the next. ("If you don't like Larry," Don Westlake has been known to say, "just wait a while. Next time you meet him he'll be somebody else.") Still, for all my wanderings and life-style changes, mine has been a rather stable life at heart, replete with lifelong friendships. My marriage is idyllic. I've been with the same agents (Knox Burger and Kitty Sprague) for over a decade, and the same primary publisher (Arbor House was absorbed into Morrow) for about as long. And I've been able to make a sort of living for all these years doing the only thing I ever really wanted to do.

And, when I have a book to write, there's only the typewriter and the paper and the words, the wonderful words. Everything else disappears.

BIBLIOGRAPHY

Fiction:

Death Pulls a Doublecross, Fawcett, 1961, published as *Coward's Kiss*, Countryman, 1987.

Markham (tie-in to a television play), Belmont Books, 1961, published as *You Could Call It Murder*, Countryman, 1987.

Mona, Fawcett, 1961, published as *Sweet Slow Death*, Berkley, 1986.

The Girl with the Long Green Heart, Fawcett, 1965.

Deadly Honeymoon, Macmillan, 1967.

After the First Death, Macmillan, 1968.

The Specialists, Fawcett, 1969.

(Under pseudonym Paul Kavanagh) *Such Men Are Dangerous: A Novel of Violence*, Macmillan, 1969, published under name Lawrence Block, Jove, 1985.

Ronald Rabbit Is a Dirty Old Man, Geis, 1971.

(Under pseudonym Paul Kavanagh) *The Triumph of Evil*, World, 1971, published under name Lawrence Block, Countryman, 1986.

(Under pseudonym Paul Kavanagh) *Not Comin' Home to You*, Putnam, 1974, published under name Lawrence Block, Countryman, 1986.

Ariel, Arbor House, 1980.

(With Harold King) *Code of Arms*, R. Marek, 1981.

Sometimes They Bite (short stories), Arbor House, 1983.

Like a Lamb to Slaughter (short stories), Arbor House, 1984.

(By Cornell Woolrich; completed by Lawrence Block) *Into the Night,* Mysterious Press, 1987.

Random Walk, Tor, 1988.

"Evan Tanner" series:

The Thief Who Couldn't Sleep, Fawcett, 1966.

The Canceled Czech, Fawcett, 1967.

Tanner's Twelve Swingers, Fawcett, 1967.

Two for Tanner, Fawcett, 1967.

Tanner's Tiger, Fawcett, 1968.

Here Comes a Hero, Fawcett, 1968.

Me Tanner, You Jane, Macmillan, 1970.

"Matthew Scudder" series:

The Sins of the Fathers, Dell, 1976.

In the Midst of Death, Dell, 1976.

Time to Murder and Create, Dell, 1977.

A Stab in the Dark, Arbor House, 1981.

Eight Million Ways to Die, Arbor House, 1982.

When the Sacred Ginmill Closes, Arbor House, 1986.

Out on the Cutting Edge, Morrow, 1989.

A Ticket to the Boneyard, Morrow, 1990.

"Bernie Rhodenbarr" series:

Burglars Can't Be Choosers, Random House, 1977.

The Burglar in the Closet, Random House, 1979.

The Burglar Who Liked to Quote Kipling, Random House, 1979.

The Burglar Who Studied Spinoza, Random House, 1981.

The Burglar Who Painted Like Mondrian, Arbor House, 1983.

"Chip Harrison" series:

(Under pseudonym Chip Harrison) *No Score,* Fawcett, 1970.

(Under pseudonym Chip Harrison) *Chip Harrison Scores Again,* Fawcett, 1971.

(Under pseudonym Chip Harrison) *Make Out with Murder,* Fawcett, 1974, published in England as *Five Little Rich Girls,* Allison & Busby, 1984.

(Under pseudonym Chip Harrison) *The Topless Tulip Caper,* Fawcett, 1975, published in England under name Lawrence Block, Allison & Busby, 1984.

A.k.a. Chip Harrison, (includes *Make Out with Murder* and *The Topless Tulip Caper*), Countryman, 1983.

Introducing Chip Harrison (includes *No Score* and *Chip Harrison Scores Again*), Countryman, 1984.

Nonfiction:

(With Delbert Ray Krause) *Swiss Shooting Talers and Medals,* Whitman Publishing, 1965.

Writing the Novel from Plot to Print, Writer's Digest Books, 1979.

(With Cheryl Morrison) *Real Food Places: A Guide to Restaurants That Serve Fresh, Wholesome Food,* Rodale Press, 1981.

Telling Lies for Fun and Profit: A Manual for Fiction Writers (collected *Writer's Digest* columns), Arbor House, 1981.

Write for Your Life, Write for Your Life Seminars, 1986.

Spider, Spin Me a Web: Lawrence Block on Writing Fiction (collected *Writer's Digest* columns), Writer's Digest Books, 1988.

Malcolm Boyd

1923-

*Malcolm Boyd, outside Saint Augustine by-the-Sea Episcopal Church,
Santa Monica, California, 1987*

Three parts of my life have defined me as far back as I can remember. I am a writer. I am religious. I am gay.

My childhood was very much out of the ordinary. Growing up in Manhattan as the only child of rich parents, I was terribly alone and lonely. Servants were the only people close to me. A chauffeur taught me how to tie shoelaces and read the face of a clock. Instead of playing with other children, I had a succession of governesses. One, English to the core, was tweedy, affectionate, but firm. My family resided near Central Park, and every day my governess and I made our way around the reservoir, she on foot, I riding my tricycle.

Inside Central Park was an old stone observatory which became a castle for me. My governess had given me a book about British kings, queens, princes, princesses, palaces, gardens, and wars. I lived inside my own fantasy world, and my fantasies came to life when I climbed around the observatory, its stairways and turrets. Of course, I knew the story of *The Prince and the Pauper*, and alternately played both roles in my daydreams.

Later, I had a German governess. Her name was Angela. She had an affair with the doorman of our apartment building. She knew that *I* knew, so discipline was out of the question. When I was supposed to be in bed and asleep, I insisted that she allow me to listen to "Chandu the Magician" on the radio. It was scary, all shadows and serpents, and I was blissfully terrified.

When my parents separated, I was nine years old. My mother was given custody of me. We left New York and visited my maternal grandmother in Oklahoma. Then we settled down to live in Colorado Springs, Colorado, and later, Denver. My father, Melville Boyd, a financier, remained in New York. I hated everything outside New York, and was an utter snob about it. The Sunday edition of the *New York Times* didn't reach Colorado Springs until the following Thursday (or Saturday, maybe even the next Monday in case of a blizzard). I devoured the "Arts and Leisure" section. Theatre, dance, opera, books: these were my real world.

I listened to opera broadcasts from the Met each Saturday. The first time I ever heard the "Liebestod" sung by Flagstad and Melchior was one of the most exciting moments of my early life. On Saturdays I also visited the public library. Always I returned a stack of eight or ten books, and brought home a new batch. I read avidly the most sophisticated novels and nonfiction.

These were odd years because I was, in the classic sense of the word, a sissy. I knew nothing of sports. My friends comprised one or two adult women. Lonely and isolated, I could not identify with anyone of my own age. The junior high school newspaper became a salvific force in my life when I began to write for it.

In that pretelevision era, major artists braved snow and ice to appear in Colorado Springs. I saw Paderewski, Flagstad, Lotte Lehmann, Marion Anderson, John Charles Thomas, Lawrence Tibbett, Lily Pons, and many others. More to the point, I got in the habit of interviewing them whenever they were available. God knows why they spent their valuable time with a kid in short pants from the local junior high school paper.

When violinist Mischa Elman sat for my first interview, my questions were awful, stilted, unimaginative, and obvious. He said angrily that I needed to do more research. Lotte Lehmann was a lovely and gracious subject. And, she treated me as an adult.

With father, Melville Boyd, New York City, 1925

Could it be she was simply lonely out on the road in the hinterlands? Did she see me as a sophisticated and sensitive boy providing a pleasant interlude? Carl Van Doren, urbane and kind (he gave me three hours for our interview), was joined by Harold Laski, H. V. Kaltenborn, and a small legion of authors and social critics as my subjects. After Josephine Antoine, a Metropolitan Opera soprano, gave a concert in the Ute Theatre, I interviewed her. Learning from our conversation that I sang, too, she asked me to perform "O Sole Mio" for her onstage. My mother, arriving to drive me home, was startled to hear my voice thundering through the empty hall.

My mother had gone to work as a teacher, for my family's money was wiped out in the Depression. Beatrice, who is ninety-one as I write this, has always possessed strong inner resources. In her youth she taught and cared for Navajo children in the Arizona desert during an influenza epidemic. Then, after working for forty years, she retired at the age of seventy and commenced another twenty years of volunteer teaching at the Children's Hospital of Los Angeles.

After my mother and I moved to Denver, I continued interviewing celebrated men and women in the arts and letters. Wanda Landowska entered my life unforgettably when she insisted on my staying to lunch after our chat. She prepared a salad and served it with fresh bread and tea.

During this period I won first prize in the Sons of the American Revolution essay contest, received an honorable mention in a *Scholastic* magazine competition, placed third in my high school's poetry contest, wrote editorials for my school newspaper, the *Spotlight*, and was the *Denver Post* correspondent from my high school. Chosen by the National Honor Society in my junior year, I was studious and deeply concerned about world events and politics. A regular reader of the *Nation* and the *New Republic*, I became sharply aware of racism at home and the emerging Holocaust in Europe. I wrote long letters expressing my views about these matters to the *Rocky Mountain News* and the *Denver Post*.

I still remember my first opera, *Rigoletto*, performed by a traveling troupe, and Noel Coward's *Private Lives*. Despite such icing on the cake, this period of my life was utter hell. I felt an alien in a strange place. No one, I was sure, understood me at all. Any serious attempt to communicate with another human being seemed hopeless. I was "different." How could I cope with forever being The Outsider? I looked at easygoing, popular, handsome athletes and knew I was totally shut out of their world of acceptance, glamour, achievement (in my eyes), and fun. Girls either ignored me or found me a eunuchlike jester, someone to laugh with and confide in. I quickly learned how to provide laughs and counseling for such people. Although I was convinced no one gave a tinker's damn about what I wrote, I continued turning out page after page of poems, essays, and reviews for any publication willing to print it.

Religion was at the center of my life, although I was not conventionally "pious." There was a lot of rage inside me. God was not distant, I knew, but close by and caring. Although God siphoned off some of my rage, a lot of it remained. The church, I understood, was a vastly amusing, very political, highly eccentric organization close to God, but also capable of the devil's subversion. I saw strong, dynamic church leaders locked in conflict with one another over careerism, absurdly minute territorial rights, and foppish matters of protocol. Egos were dominant. While the sheer drama of the church was compelling, both in its liturgy and behind-the-scenes soap operas, instinctively I knew Jesus the Galilean stood in stark contrast to such polished posturing and burnished gold. I could scarcely, and seldom, find Jesus in the church that seemed to go out of its way to condemn the world in his name. I perceived that the church, at its worst, was an imperial and self-serving empire whose own machinery took precedence over human needs.

Mother, Beatrice Boyd, at age forty-five, 1943

My paternal grandfather, who died before I was born, was an Episcopal priest in New York. I still have a photograph of him. Garbed in vestments, he appears a gentle and kind man with soft, compassionate eyes. While I was a youth living in Denver, Paul Roberts, an Episcopal priest, became a role model for me that cut sharply against my negative image of clergy. Dean of Saint John's Cathedral, he was gutsy, honest, plain, an eloquent preacher, and possessed a sturdy sense of humor as well as a keen social conscience. I stayed in touch with him through succeeding years. He was a marvelous man, an exemplary Christian. But even his positive presence in my life was not enough to make the church as an institution appealing to me.

When I went away to college, I dropped the church like a hot potato. It bored me, droning on

"As an acolyte"

endlessly with those whining, irrelevant prayers. Clergy seemed a breed apart, mostly cold, clammy men with whom one felt ill at ease. Did they *ever* take their clerical collars off? What did they do in *bed*? Were there *any* simply natural moments when they weren't "on"? I didn't want to hear any more about "sin"; I yearned to experience and enjoy life.

During my four years of college, I never found out who I was, and no one was able to help me. Still The Outsider, I learned how to play a splendid masquerade. I drank beer every night at the Speedway, the "in" bar for the college set at the University of Arizona. (My lungs were poor, and this was the reason I attended Arizona instead of Dartmouth; I remained the easterner in my allegiances.) My writing became perfunctory; there was no sense of intellectual challenge or creative growth, and my former idealism seemed to ebb. I wrote for the yearbook and newspaper, and published a gossip sheet called the *Bar Nuthin.*

While I dated girls, I longed for boys. Boys surrounded me in the highly erotic setting of my fraternity, the most macho on campus. I had to learn

to wear a mask, hide my feelings, repress my strongest desires, and show a face that bore little resemblance to my real self.

After college I moved to Los Angeles in the mid-forties, studied how to write radio scripts, and was hired by the Hollywood office of one of the largest and most powerful American advertising agencies. Soon I produced a fifteen-minute soap opera five days a week at Foote, Cone and Belding, along with a Sunday evening news broadcast. And, I wrote a few scripts for dramatic programs.

Hollywood was in the last stages of its "golden age" when I left the agency to work for a movie studio. All doors were apparently open for me, a good-looking, well-educated, clean-cut, hard-working young guy starting out. Quite innocent, I met the stars, dined in legendary restaurants and clubs, spun dreams, and became a success.

Serious writing was out the window. So was religion. I didn't know what to do about being gay— it didn't seem *gay* at all, just an awful burden to be "a homosexual." So I put my pent-up sexual energy into my work, and soon had the workaholic force of a one-person Niagara Falls.

When I met Mary Pickford, I was in awe. She was the empress of the entertainment world, the first great woman star, the first modern media celebrity (with Charlie Chaplin), and a millionairess. We met when I worked on a movie she coproduced, *Sleep, My Love,* starring Claudette Colbert. Pickfair, Mary's home, was at that time nearly as well-known as the White House. She entertained U.S. presidents, European royalty, and international stars. Mary opened Pickfair to me. I learned to swim in its pool and stayed in the guest house which had hosted the Mountbattens and Queen Marie of Romania. I quickly grew accustomed to Hollywood stars whose foibles were amusing but their egos tedious.

Mary and I formed PRB, Incorporated, a production company, and moved to New York. Shortly I was having brunch with Mrs. William Randolph Hearst, cocktails with Adele Astaire, and was being called the "Golden Boy" by society columnist Cobina Wright. As a young gay man in search of his identity, I entered into a close friendship with Mary, who called herself my "spiritual mother."

Mary drank heavily in a sad *Long Day's Journey into Night* sort of way. This boozing was dead serious, self-destructive, obsessive, and rooted in extreme human anguish. Mary, "America's Sweetheart," was lost. I cared for her deeply, but was unable to help her.

I was lost, too. I had settled for glamour (which I found quite drab) instead of pursuing spiritual and intellectual truth. The parts of myself that responded to this, I repressed. I was locked in an "I-Thou" relationship with God that was intense, troubled, and unfulfilled. I needed desperately to enter into a human relationship that combined sexual and spiritual elements, but that possibility seemed remoter than going to the moon. I lacked the basic rudiments of self-definition, and also feared the sexual mystery of myself. I wasn't able to share it with anyone else, except in the most casual and shifting of brief encounters.

Glancing around me at the personages inhabiting Mary's heady milieu, I realized I didn't *want* this. I couldn't bear to look ahead to twenty or thirty years of such aggressive success-manufacturing and image-making, accompanied by spiritual despair. I yearned to open up windows in my claustrophobic life. Was there a vaster and infinitely more comprehensive life outside? Could I learn to exercise my intellect and provide oxygen for my soul? I wanted to try. I withdrew from Hollywood, went out to the desert, prayed and meditated. Gradually an inner life came into focus as a possibility for me. And, I knew a fire burned there. My life was undergoing a major turning point, an extraordinary change.

I decided I wished to be an Episcopal priest, and, after applying to the diocese of Los Angeles, was admitted as a postulant to holy orders. In 1951 I departed Hollywood for a seminary in Berkeley, California. My going-away lunch at Ciro's, when the entertainment industry formally told me good-by, was star-studded and tearful. Columnist Hedda Hopper reported that even the bartender bowed his head for the Lord's Prayer. My departure shared newspaper headlines with actor Robert Walker's youthful death and Mary Astor's suicide attempt.

The following three years at the Church Divinity School of the Pacific allowed little time or energy for either writing or pursuing my gay identity. I devoted all my time to the Bible, liturgics, homiletics, church history, Christian education and ethics. The next year I went to England and studied at Oxford. Also, I closely observed such church experiments in evangelism as the "industrial mission" and "house-church." That winter was spent at the Ecumenical Institute of the World Council of Churches at the Chateau de Bossey, near Geneva in Switzerland. Then I commenced two years of graduate theological studies at Union Theological Seminary in New York City.

"With Mary Pickford at the Hollywood Advertising Club," Hollywood, California, 1949

Here, I wrote a graduate paper which became my first book. Carefully grounded in scholarship (my teachers included Reinhold Niebuhr and Hendrik Kraemer), it attempted to relate Christian theology to the mass media. In other words, I was constructing a bridge between two quite different worlds I'd inhabited. Doubleday published *Crisis in Communication* in 1957. When the book was completed, I had to be hospitalized briefly. I was as close to a nervous breakdown as I would ever be. The stress had been relentless.

During the next year at Union Theological Seminary I completed my second book, *Christ and Celebrity Gods* (Seabury Press). It should have been Part II of the first book, as it explored the same themes. Now I went to work in my first parish, a tiny church in an impoverished inner-city area of Indianapolis. The sophisticated young mandarin of academia was, at least on the surface, turning into a kind of worker-priest. The dean of the nearby cathedral was Paul Moore, Jr., who would later become bishop of

New York and remain one of my close friends for a lifetime.

In 1959 I was asked to become the Episcopal chaplain at Colorado State University in Fort Collins, Colorado. In that small-town environment I staged a series of "Espresso Nights," with readings and dance, and directed a reader's theatre-style presentation of T. S. Eliot's *Cocktail Party*. The diocesan bishop strongly opposed such outreach and the implicit meaning of my work. I was forced to resign.

Four books emerged from this period, all published by Morehouse-Barlow of New York. They are *Focus: Rethinking the Meaning of Our Evangelism* (1960); *If I Go Down to Hell* (1962); *The Hunger, The Thirst* (1964); and *On the Battle Lines: A Manifesto for Our Times* (1964), which I edited. I had gone to France in 1957 to spend three months living and working in the Taizé Community, an ecumenical Christian brotherhood. It engaged in farming, medicine, and art, as well as theological work. Taizé combined the contemplative with the active life, believing each necessarily complements the other. My

*Malcolm Boyd at Taizé Community
in France, 1957*

experience at Taizé, which deeply affected my life, I wrote about at length in *If I Go Down to Hell*. However, the book proved to be a disappointment because I was unsuccessful in communicating my ideas and feelings in a clear way that embodied their urgency, and in relating these to my own inner struggle and a more universal, existential one.

Compelled to leave my chaplain's post in Colorado, I was invited to become Episcopal chaplain at Wayne State University in Detroit, which occupies a sprawling, urban campus in the heart of the city. I lived in a ramshackle apartment house across from the university. At this time I became involved in the civil rights movement, participating in a 1961 "Prayer Pilgrimage" Freedom Ride and dozens of other demonstrations, frequently being arrested for my beliefs and actions to combat racism. Nothing else I ever did meant so much to me. I was ready to lay down my life for what I perceived as justice. I was with Martin Luther King, Jr., on numerous occasions and had great admiration for him. In Detroit, I held discussion meetings about civil rights in my apartment, which were often impassioned and attracted large and diverse groups of people, including the brother of Malcolm X and Viola Liuzzo, whose murder would shortly make her a nationally known activist martyr.

I wrote four dramatic sketches, all related to the civil rights struggle. *Boy* was about a middle-age African-American shoeshine man; *A Study in Color* featured a white man dressed in black, wearing a black mask, and a black man dressed in white, wearing a white mask. I appeared in both short plays when we presented them in Detroit coffeehouse theatres. Neither Detroit paper would review them, but the *New York Times* did. They were later performed nationally on college campuses, off-Broadway, in cathedrals, and on NBC-TV. The two other dramatic sketches were *They Aren't Real to Me*, a comedy about a reverse racial situation, and *The Job*, a humorous but bitterly ironic monologue.

During 1963 and 1964, I wrote *Are You Running with Me, Jesus?* At the outset I rented a small house in a Detroit suburb to provide a space where I could work completely alone without interruption. A friend, Richard A. English, who later became the dean of the School of Social Work at Howard University, drove me there, and planned to come back once a week during a two-month period to bring me a supply of food. I settled down to write.

However, the civil rights struggle would not conveniently leave me alone. These were the days when the youthful civil rights martyrs Goodman,

Schwerner, and Chaney were missing in Mississippi. Every night I watched the Huntley-Brinkley news on TV for an update on the search for them until their bodies were found.

Not long before, I had visited Jackson, Mississippi, to attend the funeral of Medgar Evers, the black civil rights leader who was killed there. Going to the Evers home, I saw a field of tall grass nearby in which the killer had hid, holding his gun. Now, in my rented house in an all-white Detroit suburb, I noticed there was a vacant lot alongside it that was also filled with tall grass.

Soon telephone calls started. When I answered, I heard heavy breathing, but no word was ever uttered. The calls came intermittently throughout the day and night. I had given the number of the house to no one. I realized these calls must be placed by someone trying to terrify me. Then it dawned on me that they must be coming from someone *who could see me* from a nearby house. The caller had apparently watched Richard and me arrive. His black face in that determinedly all-white neighborhood had triggered fear and hatred.

Seated at my typewriter, with my back to a window that opened on the field of tall grass, I nervously waited for the phone to ring again, and again, bringing its message of hate. When I answered, I pleaded in vain for the caller to talk, or listen to me; to permit some kind of an honest, open dialogue between us. A sullen silence prevailed, which clearly carried a genuine threat to my safety. When Richard arrived the next time, bringing my food, I asked him to get me out of there as fast as he could.

During the coming months I worked on *Are You Running with Me, Jesus?* in my inner-city apartment overlooking the Wayne State University campus. As I structured these poems/prayers, I found my voice. I was able to communicate my thoughts and feelings effectively, it seemed, for the first time. I felt battered and tired; I had just been fired from the chaplaincy in Detroit because rich, powerful people in the church opposed what I was doing. Why was I so controversial? I didn't know where to go from here. I felt down, drained, unaccepted, and perhaps even unacceptable. It is no wonder that my prayers have been compared to psalms in their swings of up and down, their primitive cries from the heart and unvarnished look at life.

William Robert Miller became my editor when he accepted the book for Holt, Rinehart and Winston. Bill offered invaluable advice in helping me complete the book for publication. But he was shortly fired, gone in a bureaucratic shuffle. Joseph Cunneen

replaced him as editor, leaving his own strong mark on the book. Holt expected *Are You Running with Me, Jesus?* to sell around four thousand copies, and ignored the book.

It changed my life when it became a sensation and a best-seller. Arthur Cohen, editor in chief at Holt, suddenly took me seriously as a writer. So did other people. Sales mushroomed. Soon I read the prayers during a month's engagement at San Francisco's *hungry i* and on campuses in every part of the U.S. Visiting Newport, Rhode Island, to read them at the Jazz Festival, I was invited by Hugh D. Auchincloss, the financier, to use his family's cabana at Bailey's Beach. When Auchincloss unexpectedly showed up, he didn't greet me or shake hands, but blurted out, "Why don't you write any prayers for stockbrokers?" The book's title quickly became part of contemporary folklore, appearing on banners in parades and demonstrations, and seen as an integral part of pop culture.

Are You Running with Me, Jesus? had fourteen editions in hardcover, fourteen in paperback (Avon).

"A coffeehouse theatre performance of my play Study in Color," *1963: the author, left, wears a black mask; actor Woodie King, Jr., right, wears a white mask.*

Malcolm Boyd, second from right, "at the ruins of a bombed black church
in McComb, Mississippi, with four other Episcopal priests in the civil rights movement," 1964

The *New York Times* wrote, in a review published months after publication: "Terse, sometimes slangy, always eloquent prayers . . . Their eloquence comes from the personal struggle they contain—a struggle to believe, to keep going, a spiritual contest that is agonized, courageous, and not always won . . . A very moving book." The *San Francisco Chronicle* observed: "These prayers are vital, extremely contemporary, and have caught on in the ferment of the new cultural revolution." Senator Eugene J. McCarthy wrote a poem titled *Are You Running with Me, Jesus?* that was published in the *New Republic*:

> Are you running with me, Jesus
> asks the Reverend Malcolm Boyd
>
> May I ask the same?
>
> I'm an existential runner
> Indifferent to space.
> I'm running here in place.

I didn't wait long enough for my next book to appear. The pressure from Holt was unyielding. I was caught in a very heady experience of success. So I let *Free to Live, Free to Die* come out perhaps a year earlier than it should have. In retrospect, I wish that *Are You Running with Me, Jesus?* had been followed by *As I Live and Breathe: Stages of an Autobiography,* which I wrote a bit later. I find *Free to Live, Free to Die* an uneven work, containing both some of my best writing and some of my worst. The *Christian Century* wrote: "I give thanks for it. Boyd is a prophet for our times. His words speak with disturbing power to believer and unbeliever alike." The *Chicago Tribune* called it a "drama of redemption." The book's first printing was eighty thousand copies. It moved into two paperback editions (New American Library). The seemingly stark secularity of this book was a shock to many readers who expected a sequel to *Are You Running with Me, Jesus?* I believe these people had never understood how deeply radical that work is. Did its subject matter of "prayers" mask its offense? *Free to Live, Free to Die* possessed no such layer of protection. Yet it is a profoundly spiritual work, albeit without stereotyped trappings. To a number of people it appears even antireligious. It is largely misunderstood.

James Silberman was my editor for my next two books at Random House. The first was *Malcolm Boyd's Book of Days* (1968), with a subsequent paperback edition from Fawcett. A number of people fell in love with this book, but it was distinctly a minor work. I find it curiously detached from myself, having a format that is more packaged than personal. Bennett Cerf thought it should be titled *Half Laughing/Half Crying*, a title that I used nearly twenty years later for another book. *Book Week* wrote: "Malcolm Boyd wants to break down ghetto walls, tear off masks, remove barriers." *Look* exclaimed amusingly: "A smashing iconoclast!"

Within seven months I was arrested twice for participating in Peace Masses inside the Pentagon. It seemed the epitome of theatre of the absurd, enacted in real life. In one mass I delivered the sermon. A police officer with a bullhorn engaged in an unrehearsed dialogue with me. He tumbled out the words "You are under arrest." I responded antiphonally, "If the salt has lost its taste, how shall its saltness be restored?" My image at this time was defined by Robert Frank's photograph on the cover of *Are You Running with Me, Jesus?*: sophisticated but sincere, tense-eyed but with soul, a swinger but certainly on the saintly side.

When *As I Live and Breathe: Stages of an Autobiography* appeared, R. W. B. Lewis wrote in its foreword: "Malcolm Boyd's mission is altogether in the American grain. It harks back to the days of Emerson and Theodore Parker and Orestes Brownson, to those restive ministers who found their church had gone dry . . . and who in their attempt to restore vitality to the religious life expanded their ministerial activities into the whole range of human experience . . . Malcolm Boyd is the irregular man, the informal man, but (anything but an alienated man) he always prefers to do his work and have his say *within* the peripheries of whatever establishment he is inhabiting . . . How Malcolm arrived at his so-to-say regularized irregularity is the subject of this book, and an utterly absorbing account it is."

I attempted to tell my story chronologically in the book, but spent almost no time on my youth, and an inordinate amount of it on civil rights. The *New York Times* called the book "a story of our times" and noted: "The vibrations of church and society and race and war are so tightly interwoven that you can never separate them." I felt this book was my proudest, most elegantly written, most beautifully produced book. The *New Yorker* wrote: "His experiences are moving and his concern is affecting." The only problem with *As I Live and Breathe*—and it's a major one—is that I remained closeted at the time. So did an indispensable part of my life in the book.

Washington, D.C., became my home for a couple of years after I left Detroit. I found it a cold and impersonal city. Also I had a back problem, felt terribly lonely in a harsh spotlight of celebrity, and withdrew into myself. My personal life was spartan and devoted to writing. I made appearances on national television as "the rebel priest" and read my celebrated and now-familiar prayers and meditations. At this point I could not walk through an airport without causing at least a slight stir, being asked for autographs, or even running into a vociferous, demanding, youthful group of fans. All this only served to heighten my isolation.

From the church I heard conflicting messages. A fundamentalist minister in the Midwest, obviously critical of me, asked almost accusingly (as if expecting a negative response) if I had ever experienced an act of conversion. I told him offhandedly that I sometimes had three in a good day, but could go five weeks without one. The minister seemed an enemy. However, I perceived the essential church as passionately alive in the midst of sensitive, crazy, changing, and growing people. Here, I found a quiet celebration of Jesus, the antihero, who died on the cross in God's identification with human injustice, suffering, failure, and hope.

I went to Yale in 1968 in response to R. W. B. Lewis's invitation to reside in Calhoun College as a visiting fellow. (I returned there for a second year in the early seventies.) Now I was quite estranged from the institutional church. Indeed, I felt that it and I were in a *Who's Afraid of Virginia Woolf?* marriage. Love and hate ran deep. At Yale, William Sloane Coffin, Jr., who was the chaplain there, kindly asked me to preach. But aside from an occasional visit to the Yale chapel, I seldom attended a service.

Norman Mailer was also a fellow of Calhoun College. I remember when he visited the college and held court. Everybody sat on the floor around the chair where he sat. He pontificated, issuing opinions as from a throne. Norman apparently viewed himself as Hemingway's literary heir. He seemed to enjoy his role as an avant-garde filmmaker, drank a lot, and cultivated a persona of an aging social and political enfant terrible.

Years later, when I lived in Los Angeles and was president of PEN there, Norman visited from New York as president of PEN American Center in the

East. We were at a literary cocktail party in Venice given by producer-restaurateur Tony Bill. The bartender was Mac McNeel, a young woman who worked at Bill's Venice restaurant, 72 Market Street, and was a faithful member of my parish church, Saint Augustine by-the-Sea. After handing Norman a fresh drink, she told him, "Mr. Mailer, it's a shame you missed Malcolm's sermon last Sunday. It was great. You would have loved it." Norman looked completely nonplused.

Twenty-five years earlier Norman had addressed a Vietnam Day protest in Berkeley when I preached at a jazz mass in San Francisco's Grace Cathedral. Columnist Ralph J. Gleason compared us under the heading "Two Moments in a Revolution" in the *San Francisco Chronicle*. He wrote: "Agnostic that I am, Rev. Boyd's sermon was the most impressive I have heard in years, and . . . [Mailer's] was the most impressive political speech in a generation."

While I was at Yale, I lived in the Master's house of Calhoun College with R. W. B. Lewis and his wife Nancy. They became close friends. Nancy and I particularly enjoyed cooking together. It became a hobby, and, with the assistance of students, we prepared ambitious and mouth-watering dinners for various celebrated visitors. Nancy and Dick's own home in nearby Bethany, Connecticut, became a familiar and welcome haven. Here, I enjoyed meeting friends of theirs, John and Barbara Hersey, Bill and Rose Styron, and the Red Warrens.

I'll always remember fondly my first dinner invitation to their Bethany farmhouse. I came out from Calhoun College for the evening. It was snowing, but seemingly no more than usual for a winter's night. We dined informally at their kitchen table, with a Helen Frankenthaler painting looking down at us from a vantage place on the wall near the stove. When it came time for me to go, we opened the front door and an icy blast of air hit us in the face. We beheld a maelstrom of swirling snow. I stayed there three days and nights as a blizzard raged.

Neither milk nor the *New York Times* reached the door. Of course, we could not get out in the car to shop. So Nancy and I found a lamb bone, placed it in an iron pot, added vegetables, herbs and spices, and prepared a stew. With the passing of days, we added whatever ingredients we could lay our hands on. It became miraculously like the feeding of the five thousand with loaves and fishes. Inside the house we had fire, food and drink, intermittent conversation, stretches of silence for reading or writing, and the slow, easy formation of an emerging friendship. I hated it when the sun came up on the morning of the

fourth day, the *Times* appeared at the door, and it was time for me to go. But Nancy invited me to dinner on Friday, two days away.

During this period of my life a publisher would inevitably expect me to go on a national book tour, visiting major cities for media appearances, when a new title of mine came out. A book tour is, I believe, as physically and emotionally demanding as Wimbledon or the U.S. Open. F. Scott Fitzgerald never rose at dawn for an author's appearance on "Good Morning America." Neither George Sand nor Elizabeth Barrett Browning ever raced in a cab on a rainy morning to be interviewed on "Today." One day in New York when I was on the move from dawn to 9:00 P.M., a Boston radio station asked me to do a telephone interview from my hotel room that night between 11:00 P.M. and midnight. I was exhausted, but my publisher asked me to accept the interview, saying it would be a snap. At ten o'clock I dozed off.

When the phone rang, I picked up the receiver and a voice asked, "Is Malcolm there?" I moved my head on the pillow. As I listened, the radio announcer told his audience that Pauline Kael would join us. Kael, the most articulate of film critics, was seated in the Boston studio. I pulled my body to a sitting position in the bed. I was plunged headlong into an erudite, sophisticated, fast-moving discussion, like a lobster pointed toward boiling water. I never caught up.

All interviews are arduous, but long ago I learned not to give a print interview over a meal. Without fail, a waiter barges in at a key moment of one's confession. My two best print interviews took place in taxis racing toward airports. One was for the *Toronto Globe and Mail*, the other for the *Chicago Tribune*: No frills, all existentialism.

My relationships with other writers have proved highly interesting. Naturally I have interacted with many of them as president of PEN. I have dined with Christopher Isherwood in Los Angeles, shared a microphone with Studs Terkel in Chicago, given a reading with Langston Hughes in Cleveland, and shared a speaker's platform with Ralph Ellison in New York. (Nancy Lewis shared with me his wife, Fanny's, recipe for a salad that's become a favorite of mine; its ingredients include marinated mushrooms, a sliced tart apple, a sweet onion, and watercress.)

One night in Madrid I missed going out on the town with James Baldwin because my back hurt, and I rested instead. I never met Graham Greene, but, in October 1954, Mrs. Greene asked me to dinner at her home near Oxford. She showed me her doll's house. It was immense, expensive, intricate; each

"At a Los Angeles literary party with Shelley Winters and Norman Mailer," 1985

little room was perfect with a carpet, chairs, tables, drapes, and she was inordinately proud of it.

I was visiting New York in 1989 when R. W. B. Lewis was asked to read from the work of Henry James at the Cathedral Church of Saint John the Divine. That night, James and Henry David Thoreau were formally inducted into the American Poets' Corner. Nancy and I sat together as James Merrill read two speeches from *The Ambassadors*. Then Dick read a Jamesian letter written in 1896 in Rome, the concluding pages of *The Wings of the Dove*, and a letter to H. G. Wells. He appeared remote and distant, robed in black, as he stood at the cathedral lectern. How different he looked in this public setting from the close friend with whom I have shared hour upon hour of conversation over food and drink. I felt such a somber, heavy image did not capture his great humor, vitality, irony, anger, and passion. Years before, his photograph in the *Times* accompanied the announcement that he had just been given the Pulitzer Prize for *Edith Wharton*. (Later, Dick and Nancy were co-editors of *The Letters of Edith Wharton*.) Following Dick's extremely formal and sedate appearance at Saint John the Divine, it was good to engage in the most ordinary of chats with him while holding a drink in Paul and Brenda Moore's home.

Authors and artists as celebrities are fascinating to me. In the mid-seventies when I lived in the creative center of Mishkenot Sha'ananim in Jerusalem, Friedrich Durrenmatt was there when I arrived. Virgil Thomson had just departed, and soon to arrive

were Simone de Beauvoir, Lukas Foss, Stephen Spender, Alexander Calder, and Arthur Rubinstein. Interaction was quite natural and left to the individuals involved. I lived there when the thirty-ninth International Congress of PEN met in Jerusalem in 1974, and guests of honor included Saul Bellow, Heinrich Boll, Eugene Ionesco, V. S. Pritchett, and Yehuda Amichai.

The "celebrity factor" of becoming a well-known writer touched my own life during this period. I was written about and interviewed. I found myself in situations with other well-known people. For example, Teddy Kollek, the mayor of Jerusalem, and I became friends. At first we kept seeing each other in the streets. I walked two or three miles daily. Teddy was never a mayor to sit in his office. He was constantly out, on the go, moving rapidly, interacting with a wide variety of people. When I was a member of Teddy's invited party for a Christmas Eve midnight mass in Bethlehem, I found a pleasant companion in a middle-aged woman in the party who dressed plainly, wore flat shoes, and had an engaging sense of humor. Afterward we became separated from the others in a great crush. Seemingly we missed our ride. We started to walk on foot the highway leading from Bethlehem to Rachel's Tomb. The night was bitter cold.

"We haven't formally met, have we?" she asked. "No. I'm Malcolm Boyd," I replied. "I'm the Baroness de Rothschild," she said. Hiking beneath the stars, we engaged in an animated conversation. Shortly a car appeared to whisk us back to Jerusalem. A couple of days later the Baroness asked me to tea at her Jerusalem home. "But you don't really want *tea*, do you?" she asked. "Let's have scotch." And she invited me to join friends at her home for New Year's Eve. Stephen Spender was among the other guests. It was a low-key, quiet evening. In a few days the Baroness returned to her castle in France.

While living in Jerusalem I ate many meals at a popular "French kosher" restaurant that was a bit like a private club. The staff became familiar and, in fact, once catered a party in my honor in another part of the city. Often I would just sit at the bar in the restaurant, order a drink, and dine on a salade Nicoise or a light plate of veal piccata. One evening, the owner asked me to sign a leather-bound guest book which he placed in my hands. I thumbed through its pages. Henry and Nancy Kissinger were on one page, Elizabeth Taylor and Richard Burton on another. It seemed everyone, from Frank Sinatra to Zubin Mehta, had written a few words. What should I say? Sipping another drink, I drew a picture.

Soon it covered two pages in the book. I had arrows pointing everywhere. A few days later the owner told me the president of Israel came in to dinner the next night. He had never signed the guest book and was asked to. But when he got to my mini-mural, he called the owner to his table. "What's *this*?" he asked. "Tell me, what's *this*?"

We authors have public lives and private ones. Some of us do not wish to have the former; or we try to place a fence around the latter. During the sixties my public life was under klieg lights, while my closeted sexuality kept my private life a hidden preserve. In 1968, when I edited *The Underground Church* (Sheed and Ward; Penguin paperback), I became publicly identified with the book almost as if I were "the bishop" of the underground church. *Time* said that I named it. The publisher's jacket copy, which I did not see until the book appeared, offered this commentary about me: "He is the unofficial national chaplain to the disaffected or alienated Christian of whatever age who has been 'turned off' by the official Church. At the same time, he serves the official Church as prophet-preacher, critic-gadfly, and quintessential priest."

My own picture of my life and role was not nearly so neat. I found myself plunged into seemingly endless controversy. I had a persona that aroused the strongest emotions, positive and negative. I hated that kind of polarization of attitudes. Was I a kind of battleground for other people's wars? People who didn't read me apparently had as many opinions about me as those who did.

I moved to fiction for *The Fantasy Worlds of Peter Stone and Other Fables*. The stories concerned (1) a Jewish candidate for the U.S. presidency, (2) a coffeehouse priest who comes close to secular canonization by the New Age, (3) a woman's visions that cause her to found a new worldwide religion, and (4) a young man selected by a celebrated Italian filmmaker to portray Jesus Christ in a spectacular biblical movie. I wrote an additional story about a cathedral that was bombed, but the piece never seemed to come together, and I dropped it. Harper and Row published the book; Avon did a paperback edition. *Publishers Weekly* wrote: "Boyd is lighter, brighter and fresher than he has ever appeared before in print. The fables are delightful and wise." It surprised me that the book was not a sales success, because a number of critics went out of their way to praise it. For example, the *New York Times* wrote: "Malcolm Boyd turns his considerable talents from off-beat apologetics to satire and shows himself to be provoca-

tive, witty, and highly entertaining." Too provocative? Too witty? Did "highly entertaining" cut against the image created by *Are You Running with Me, Jesus?* that called for a soberer, self-conscious moral tone?

I followed *Peter Stone* with an altogether different book. Looking at the traditional interview—and having been interviewed myself more than two thousand times in various media—I wished to open up the form, freshen it, try something new, find some offbeat life and energy. So when I decided to write a book of interviews, I set out to correlate my central subject with a group of related people surrounding him or her. I began with a Chicano leader in Colorado, and interviewed a dozen or so associates and followers. Next came members of a midwestern commune, intellectuals and idealists trying to forge a new life with a new set of rules or approaches. One chapter comprised a group of Vietnam veterans. Another I devoted to Hugh Hefner and his *Playboy* empire. He intrigued me as an American folk figure. I interviewed his mother, college roommate, girlfriend, valet, and A. C. Spectorsky, author of *The Exurbanites*, who had become a *Playboy* editor. The book was published by Holt, Rinehart and Winston. The *Rocky Mountain News* observed: "His service here is that of a medium . . . [He] transmits, with honesty, straightforwardness and no small measure of integrity, an inexorable heartbeat of America, in its steady pulse, in its worrisome murmur."

For several years I crisscrossed the U.S., speaking on countless campuses. Airports and motels seemed to frame my life. When I read my prayers with guitarist Charlie Byrd, Columbia Records taped us and produced two albums of our work. In my personal life I felt lonely and driven. While I was a fellow at Yale, the *Yale Daily News* invited me to write a weekly column. On September 24, 1968, I said in my first column: "As I feel strongly that we have come to a period of necessary and painful silences, I hope to share them in creative community instead of bearing them simply in isolation."

After *My Fellow Americans*, which was such a secular book, it seems strange that my next books narrowed to tighter religious themes. *Human Like Me, Jesus* was a new prayer book. I like parts of it very much. It epitomizes my belief that prayer is light years away from talking to God in Old English and occurs in everyday life, mostly in our actions. Prayer is found in a supermarket and on a highway, in bed and the kitchen, beneath a tree and clouds, on a picket line; in anger, frustration, joy, betrayal, fulfillment, ordinariness, and ecstasy. I wrote prayers while visiting an old cemetery, and about a black-student center on a university campus, a rollicking party, people in love, and reading letters and scrapbooks in an attic. Simon and Schuster published the book; Pyramid did the paperback. The *Boston Globe* wrote: "He has come of age. Concerned, caring people across the nation will be pleased with his latest book."

However, *Human Like Me, Jesus* clearly lacks the raw energy and spiritual power of *Are You Running with Me, Jesus?* By this time dozens of imitations of the latter book had appeared. A few were superb, others pedestrian and banal, imitating style while largely ignoring content. At this time I wrote my next three books for Word Books. *The Lover* is a tapestry interweaving stories that tell, again and again, of the immanence of God. Word Books was more a religious than a mainstream publisher; my readership had always been more mainstream than religious. Consequently, this book did not reach my readership. This frustrated me because critics loved it; it is a shame that a bridge between critics and readers could not be traveled. The *Atlanta Constitution* commented: "Modern life seen with poetic vision. He is the secular saint." *Publishers Weekly* said: "Malcolm Boyd is fast becoming an American institution."

In *The Runner*, which followed—and was designed to complement *The Lover*—I attempted to portray Jesus Christ in a new, and different, light *in relation to* his followers. "It is a kind of Pilgrim's Progress a la Bunuel, Ionesco or Arrabel," said the *Christian Century*. *Publishers Weekly* offered this highly interesting observation: "He may stand the best chance among a small group of his writing contemporaries of revealing the common meeting ground where young and old alike might put down roots in a Christianity seen freshly without cant or cliché."

My next book was an attempt to do this. A rather obvious idea on the surface, it turned out to offer fresh and innovative insights. I keep running into people who say *The Alleluia Affair* remains a favorite book of theirs. A favorite of mine too, it's about a Christ nailed to a cross in an Indianapolis church who climbs down and starts walking the streets. Other Christs come down from crosses all over the world from Rio to Johannesburg, Beirut to Paris. These Christs go to work, talk to people, enroll in school, and live ordinary lives. Soon the crosses are empty.

On the Mount of Olives, Jerusalem, 1974

But they start filling up again. People begin to notice other men and women whom *they* place on the crosses. My favorite scene in the book takes place inside a lavish new cathedral by an ocean. Jesus is the central figure in an immense stained-glass window. He leaps from it, shattering the glass.

I paid my visit to Mishkenot Sha'ananim in Jerusalem before I wrote *Christian.* It is a collection of essays. These concern such diverse topics as Jewish-Christian relations, Israel, mass evangelism, Billy Graham, religious films including *Godspell* and *Jesus Christ Superstar,* and the future of faith in America. I wanted to call the book *Bread and Butter Issues of Faith.* I never managed to pull the various pieces together into a unified work. To my surprise, *Publishers Weekly* called it "His most mature and searching book." I wasn't terribly angry in the book (perhaps I needed to be), and took a somewhat lofty, objective view of things. But I had fun writing about a restaurant that had previously been a church building. The bar was allegedly where the choir loft had stood. I saw lots of irony and "post-Christianity" in the situation.

Am I Running with You, God? is something of a mystery to *me.* I wonder why I wrote it, but the answer seems to be that the material within its pages existed mainly in the form of various published magazine pieces, and the publisher wished to collect these in a book. The form is largely meditations. *Publishers Weekly* said that I mingled "intense prayer-poems with confessional meditations and personal responses to the world of social and spiritual struggle," and added: "His insights into what is spiritually 'phony' and 'true' go deeper than most of the self-help psychotherapy books that flood today's market."

Inevitably one might ask why I have written so many books. In one sense, they are my children. Quite a family. I have learned that they have lives altogether separate from mine. They grow up, leave home, and embark on the damndest adventures. I can't help them from getting burned, entering into relationships I question, or cultivating wrong company. I have my favorite books, but should keep this information from the others.

Writing is my passion. Some people breathe; I write. "Keep breathing" one might say to others. "Keep writing" is invaluable advice for me. I know that I am not a "great" writer. Fine. That is not the point at all. I strive to be professional, to dig ever deeper into my own truth, and to communicate. Communication is very important to me, though paradoxically, I am not a gregarious person, and its practical requirements do not come easily to me in ordinary, daily living. I am, in fact, a classic loner who needs to integrate one's own life with others, yet sets up barricades and spins spiderwebs.

I collaborated on my next book with Paul Conrad—and loved the experience. I want to collaborate more often with interested, skilled, creative coworkers. Paul, who draws editorial cartoons for the *Los Angeles Times* and its syndicate, joined me in a book entitled *When in the Course of Human Events.* Paul has won three Pulitzer Prizes for his work, and is an enormously gifted man with a strong social conscience. His editorial cartoons, at their best, deal with such subjects as racism, the homeless, political corruption, and world peace. He has both a sense of humor and a sense of outrage. I wrote short texts to complement his cartoons. The *Chicago Daily News* wryly commented: "Should be right next to every Gideon Bible in every hotel room in the land."

These days my life was changing. I slowed down, allowing myself much space and time for reflection and introspection. Based in Ann Arbor, Michigan, I spoke on a number of U.S. university campuses and wrote reviews and articles for magazines and newspapers. Gradually I was building up to the moment of coming out as a gay man. I found it an extraordinarily sensitive thing to do.

The mystery of being gay puzzles and astonishes me. What, if any, unique mission or vocation is involved in this? Gay used to stand for pretense and patterned choreography, playing prescribed roles and wearing masks. "Make it gay" was the watchword. It meant "put on the ritz," "keep the act going," "don't let down your guard," "keep on smiling"—especially to conceal one's sadness. But there has been a change. Gay now means new honesty. Where it used to signify wearing a mask, now it is a call to take off the masks. Its definition has shifted from form to content, sheer style to reality.

So, gay has something (I believe) of universal meaning to say to everybody. Take off the masks of repressed anger, self-pity, sexual deceit, hypocrisy, social exploitation, and spiritual arrogance. Let communication be an event that involves people, not a charade of puppets. Be yourself. Relate to other selves without inhibition and pretense. Help others to be themselves too.

Taking the matter this seriously, it is only natural I should have needed time to burrow inside my consciousness and explore my faith. I have always done this when I approached great turning points of my life. Often I have stayed in monasteries. In 1957, for example, when I lived in the Taizé Community in

France, during the days I worked hard in the fields. At morning worship I liked to watch the subtle reflection of stained-glass on the stones in a restored twelfth-century Romanesque chapel. Sunlight streamed through small windows behind the altar, creating a pool of color on the floor. At first I perceived simply pure blue or yellow. Then, red ran slowly along the sharp edge, making a design, a movement.

One of the artistic ministries of the Taizé Community was filled by a lay brother who created sculpture, mosaics, canvases, frescoes, stained-glass windows, and etchings. When he visited Algiers for the first time (he told me), he had contacts with the nationalistic movement, saw police brutality, and discovered the racial problem. Afterwards he made a stained-glass window for a church in Strasbourg showing a black man playing a saxophone. And, he painted "Vierge Noire," a black Virgin and child. She wore a yellow gown, white hennin, a blue ring on her finger, and a single gold bracelet, this against a vivid red background. I remember that he used dehumanization as his theme in a painting, *David and Goliath*: "transposé dans un univers modern la victoire de l'Esprit sur la matière." Young David stood naked and quietly confident, holding a flower, in front of monolithic structures of steel in which people were cruel to each other, and helpless, and there was a sense of demonic power.

Always I have observed a sense of strongly contrapuntal values within monastic communities. Not that they're perfect. But, at their best, they struggle for an ideal, and reject any too easy, glib solution for either social or personal problems. There is an authentic intellectual vitality within any spiritually alive community. Always I love being literally astounded by a new idea, challenged by a thought that never occurred to me.

One day in the madly energized sixties I found myself near the Trappist Abbey of Gethsemani in Kentucky. I decided to drop in on Thomas Merton, who lived there. He greeted me as a long-lost friend, showing remarkable high energy and humor. He had read and liked *Are You Running with Me, Jesus?* Inside his hermitage we talked, laughed, shared, gossiped, and discussed a world of ideas and topics within a span of a few hours. He provided Kentucky bourbon, which we sipped as a form of communion.

Now a major turning point in my life beckoned once again. In 1976, grappling with the idea of coming out as a gay man and immersing myself in reflection, I sought the meaning of Marianne Moore's words, "The cure for loneliness is solitude." I identi-fied strongly with Sam Keen's description of his experience with solitude: "A drop of calm, a moment of silence, a thimbleful of the Void is enough to reverse the paranoid movement of the mind." I settled into the seasons, getting to know their moods and qualities. It required me to look into a mirror, see Malcolm Boyd without flinching, and decide that I must not run away any longer from God, other people, or my true self. As I wrote later in *Take Off the Masks*, I reduced the speedometer of my life toward zero. The arrival of the daily mail took on all the significance of a visit from a god. Wrapped in silences, I slowly became at ease with demons whom I had feared.

Vistas outside and inside myself merged in landscapes of stark whites, blacks, and browns. Sometimes flowers punctuated, or even splashed, these landscapes with marks of color. Snow on the ground provided the whiteness for nearly half the year. Trees were black sentinels then; later they became brown, surrounded by the greenness of their foliage. A few of the trees were among my beloved friends. I talked to them, touched them, more than once I placed my arms around a tree to hug it.

I fed, and watched, birds. For a time a lively cardinal visited me daily. I felt a closeness grow between us. Then on an ice-cold morning I found its small red body resting in death outside the door. What could I do as a final gesture of friendship? I carried it into a nearby area and buried its remains beneath frozen winter leaves.

After blocking earlier escape routes of my life, and working my way through a number of dilemmas and problems, the moment finally arrived for my coming out. Afterward, *People* magazine tried to describe how many people had apparently viewed me: "blunt, restless, eloquent and above all, open." Yet it noted the brooding presence of a mask in my public life: "He kept one aspect of his life deeply private: his homosexuality." In 1978 I wrote a book about my experience, *Take Off the Masks* (Doubleday). New Society Publishers published the paperback, still in print. I wrote in its introduction: "My life is in midcourse. I want to involve my life in the whole struggle for human liberation and understanding . . . I do not *ask* for my right to life, liberty and the pursuit of happiness in what will inevitably be the final years of my life. This right belongs to me. I claim it. For anyone who knows what it is to wear a heavy, stultifying, and imprisoning mask in life, I write this book. I offer my witness. Let's take off the masks."

The book proved to be an event. The *Washington Post* called it: "Boyd's honest, courageous account

"With my life-partner, author-editor Mark Thompson," Los Angeles, 1988

of his freedom march toward integrity and psychological health." *Library Journal* wrote: "A man reborn who learns to love himself, other people, and God, step by bloody step. He reveals the flesh and soul of a media-myth we thought we knew."

A few years later I wrote another book that is a recollection of my gay relationships over a life span, some lasting and significant, others fleeting and transitory, a few mixed with fantasy. *Look Back in Joy: Celebration of Gay Lovers* was published by Gay Sunshine Press in 1981. I consider it daring, original, and a work other people can identify with. A new edition is to be published by Alyson Publications of Boston in the fall of 1990, accompanied by photographs by Crawford Barton. Poet Will Inman said of the book: "He tries to lead us to see ourselves, not with guilt but compassion, with clear eyes and courage, reaching to the roots of the spirit within us toward healing. His book is one of the necessary ongoing gospels of our uncertain and struggling time." The *Los Angeles Times* said: "By sharing the unextraordinariness of love's long suffusion into his life, Malcolm Boyd has shared with us his neatest trick of all."

St. Martin's Press published *Half Laughing/Half Crying,* which is, in effect, a reader containing a goodly sampling of my written work. It may have been a bit premature; in any event, it moved out-of-print fairly briskly. *Publishers Weekly* commented: "Boyd has explored how people maintain their humanness in the face of forces that try to break them or reduce them to stereotypes . . . [His] relentlessly honest self-portrait inspires the reader to examine his or her own preconceptions."

Gay Priest: An Inner Journey followed from St. Martin's, with a subsequent paperback in Stonewall Inn Editions. Michael Denneny of St. Martin's Press became a friend in the process of our getting out the book. He had emerged, along with Sasha Alyson, as one of the key figures and best editors in gay publishing. In order to understand this book, one must take note of the subtitle. It is, truly, an *inner* journey. The *New York Times* called it "Part memoir, part meditation, part manifesto."

After I came out, my first telephone call was from author Frank Deford, then a senior writer for *Sports Illustrated* and an old friend. He had read the story in a New York newspaper on a plane en route to

Dallas. He said, "Gee, I don't know what to say. They don't make Hallmark cards for this." We laughed, but a human tidal wave of reaction struck me within a few hours. The story was carried on the wire services and featured in newspapers, TV flash announcements, and radio broadcasts throughout the country. I sensed instinctive human support rather than hostility or rejection, although I heard that someone burned all my books. Paul Moore, as bishop of New York, supported me courageously in the face of scattered demands that I be punished by the church. I had to adjust to a new life out of the closet. I found this moment a painful one because I felt stark naked in front of the world. Yet it brought me personal freedom and the most remarkable opportunity to start over with a new lease.

During the eighties I resumed an anchored place in the church as writer-priest-in-residence at Saint Augustine by-the-Sea Episcopal Church in Santa Monica, California. It meant that I returned to regular preaching in a church pulpit. I regard the sermon as an art form, albeit a neglected one, and love to preach. To my surprise and delight, I feel very relaxed and at home within the church as I prepare to celebrate my thirty-fourth anniversary as an Episcopal priest. I am impressed by the depth of faith shown by congregations like St. Augustine's that engage in serious social activism and remain open to the world as well as to God. I find staggered levels of incredible meaning in the eucharist, the church's central act of worship, and rejoice in a liturgical role as its celebrant.

In the past few years I have served three terms as president of the Los Angeles Center of PEN (1984–1987), and have been a member of the Los Angeles City/County AIDS Task Force and chaplain of the AIDS Commission of the Episcopal Diocese of Los Angeles. My life has come together in ways I would not earlier have believed possible. My gay personhood is integrated with the rest of my life. I live in a fulfilling relationship with my life-partner, Mark Thompson. Also a writer, he has been senior editor of the *Advocate*, the national gay newsmagazine, for fourteen years, and is author of *Gay Spirit: Myth and Meaning*. The twenty-fifth anniversary edition of *Are You Running with Me, Jesus?: An American Spiritual Classic Revisited* will be published by Beacon Press in the spring of 1990, and I am presently writing a new book.

At sixty-six, I look forward with a certain childlike innocence to the year 2000. A reviewer for the *New York Times* once called me "a balding Holden Caulfield." Perhaps I am. I realize that I have always been more like *The Glass Menagerie*'s Tom, who was "pursued by something," than like a knight consciously searching for the Holy Grail.

BIBLIOGRAPHY

Nonfiction:

Crisis in Communication, Doubleday, 1957.

Christ and Celebrity Gods, Seabury, 1958.

Focus: Rethinking the Meaning of Our Evangelism, Morehouse, 1960.

If I Go Down to Hell, Morehouse, 1962.

The Hunger, The Thirst, Morehouse, 1964.

Are You Running with Me, Jesus? (prayers), Holt, 1965, twenty-fifth anniversary edition published as *Are You Running with Me, Jesus?: An American Spiritual Classic Revisited*, Beacon Press, 1990.

Free to Live, Free to Die (secular meditations), Holt, 1967, revised and abridged edition, 1970.

Malcolm Boyd's Book of Days, Random House, 1968.

As I Live and Breathe: Stages of an Autobiography, Random House, 1969.

My Fellow Americans (interviews), Holt, 1970.

Human Like Me, Jesus (prayers), Simon & Schuster, 1971.

(With Paul Conrad) *When in the Course of Human Events*, Sheed & Ward, 1973.

Christian: Its Meanings in an Age of Future Shock (essays), Hawthorn, 1975.

Am I Running with You, God? (meditations), Doubleday, 1977.

Take Off the Masks, Doubleday, 1978, revised edition, New Society, 1984.

Look Back in Joy: Celebration of Gay Lovers, Gay Sunshine, 1981, revised edition (photographs by Crawford Barton), Alyson, 1990.

Half Laughing/Half Crying: Songs for Myself, St. Martin's, 1986.

Gay Priest: An Inner Journey, St. Martin's, 1987.

Fiction:

The Fantasy Worlds of Peter Stone and Other Fables, Harper & Row, 1969.

The Lover, Word Books, 1972.

The Runner, Word Books, 1974.

The Alleluia Affair, Word Books, 1975.

Plays; all produced in New York City:

The Job, 1962.

Study in Color, 1962.

They Aren't Real to Me, 1962.

Boy, 1964.

The Community, 1964.

Contributor:

Christianity and the Contemporary Arts, Abingdon, 1962.

Edward Fiske, *Witness to a Generation,* Bobbs-Merrill, 1967.

You Can't Kill the Dream, John Knox, 1968.

Mark Thompson, editor, *Gay Spirit: Myth and Meaning,* St. Martin's, 1987.

Editor:

On the Battle Lines (essays), Morehouse, 1964.

The Underground Church, Sheed & Ward, 1968.

Other:

Also coauthor of screenplays, including, with Ervin Zavada, "Are You Running with Me, Jesus?," based on Boyd's book of the same title; author of weekly column, *Pittsburgh Courier,* 1963–65; motion picture columnist for *Episcopalian, United Church Herald, Christian Century, Presbyterian Survey,* and *Canadian Churchman;* contributing editor, *Renewal* and *Integrity Forum;* reviewer of devotional books, *Christian Century,* 1974–81; contributor of reviews to *Los Angeles Times Book Review;* occasional contributor of articles to *Ms., New York Times, Washington Post, Los Angeles Times, Parade, Advocate,* and many other periodicals.

Boyd's books have also been published in England, Germany, Sweden, Finland, and Italy.

The Malcolm Boyd Archive is housed at Boston University Library, 771 Commonwealth Avenue, Boston, Mass., 02215.

Nawal El Saadawi

1931-

AN OVERVIEW OF MY LIFE
(Translated from the Arabic by Antoinette Tuma)

Dr. Nawal El Saadawi, president of the Arab Women Solidarity Association, 1983

My mother told me that I was a quiet child, that I spent hours alone humming musical tunes to myself before I could even speak.

Once I learned to speak, I started asking those questions that parents do not answer, such as "Where did I come from?" or "Where did my dead grandfather go?" and "Why does my older brother enjoy more freedom and privileges than I do?" . . . etc.

Once I learned how to read and write, I started writing stories to myself where the protagonists were my mother, my father, my brothers, and my sisters.

I used to take a pencil and draw the faces of the members of my family. I felt a strong desire to draw portraits of people around me. I also had a strong urge to express my moods through my writings, and to register the events I witnessed in a way that reflected my thinking and my view of them.

My mother was a woman of great intellectual ambition, which was "aborted" when her father took her out of school at the age of seventeen so she would marry my father. And though her married life was relatively happy, she yearned for her old dream of being a woman of importance, intellectually or scientifically.

I have probably inherited from my mother this ambition, since I used to hear her repeat, when I was a child, that she would have loved to visit the whole world by plane, or that she would have wanted to be a scientist like Madame Curie, or an accomplished pianist, or a poet, painter, or surgeon.

I never heard my mother praise marriage as an institution even though my father was, in her view, an ideal husband. She was very perceptive and considered my father a rarity among men. She witnessed the life of her mother and father, and she lived the sadness and misery of her mother, whose husband imprisoned her in the house.

My mother hated marriage because her own mother hated marriage, and she heard her curse marriage as a cemetery for women.

So as a child I hated marriage, and I never dreamed of myself in a wedding dress. But rather, I dreamed that I was a physician, a creative writer, an actress, a poet, a concert musician, or a dancer.

I grew up in a large family of nine brothers and sisters—six girls and three boys. I had a brother who was one year older than I who tried to dominate me, but my father did not permit it.

At the age of ten, while I was getting ready to go out, I heard my brother tell me, "You will not go out by yourself. I shall come with you to watch you." That greatly angered my father, who scolded my brother. He then gave me permission to go out by myself and told my brother, "She is capable of protecting herself, and you should mind your own business."

This was an important lesson for my brother. He never tried after that to impose his will on me. He might have tried to do so once or twice when my father was not there, but I was capable of standing up to him.

My father always encouraged me to read Arabic poetry, for he loved literature. For this reason I was a fortunate child compared to other Egyptian girls who grew up in the forties. I excelled in my studies because I loved reading and the sciences. I had many girlfriends at school, and the teachers usually liked me because I was an excellent student, but I was also a source of trouble and rebellion against the administration of the school.

Deep within me, I resented authority. This was due to my mother's resentment of her father's authority, and also to my father's resentment of the Egyptian government's authority and of the British

occupation. My father was, all through the forties, one of the revolutionaries who rebelled against foreign occupation and the king's cooperation with the British. As a child, I used to hear him curse the occupation and the Egyptian authority that cooperated with it.

The evolution of my personality was therefore based on two fundamental principles: (1) my love for the arts and creativity, (2) my love for Egypt, independence, and justice.

My father was a firm believer in the merits of education. His education helped him obtain a high position in the Ministry of Education, which allowed him to escape the lot of his poor provincial class and marry my mother, who came from a bourgeois family from Cairo.

Because he valued education, my father sent all nine of his children to college. He never made any distinction between boys and girls in this respect. On the contrary, he used to encourage me more than he did my brother because I was a better student.

I used to love school and prefer it to home. There was never anything exciting at home. At school, there were friends, and there was a big playground where we played ball. I used to love to play sports and to run. I also loved reading and books. I loved to understand. I always asked, why? I was liked by some teachers and hated by some others. I, for instance, used to dislike the history class as well as the history teacher. History was not a subject we were made to understand. Rather, it was a series of dates and events that we memorized for the purpose of reciting them at the end-of-year exam. The same applied to geography.

On the other hand, I loved Arabic literature and poetry, and I used to write my compositions with a sense of pleasure. Writing was for me something of beauty, and I enjoyed sitting by myself at night to write my thoughts and ideas.

One of the important people in my life was my paternal grandmother. She was a poor peasant with a strong personality and a superior intelligence even though she never went to school and had never learned to read and write. Life was her school. Her husband died very young of schistosomiasis, which was a common sickness among Egyptian peasants. My grandmother was widowed while in the prime of youth, having had seven daughters and one son (my father).

When I was a child, my grandmother would sit next to me on the couch and tell me about my father's childhood, how she sent him to school, then to the university in the capital, in spite of her poverty. She used to wake up at dawn and go to work in the fields and save one piastre after another, even deprive herself of food in order to save for his education. My father had decided he was not going to be a peasant like his father, who died in the prime of his life. He appreciated his mother's sacrifices and worked harder at school. He was always successful and ranked first or second in his class. When he was ranked second, my grandmother would ask him, "Why aren't you the first? Wasn't the first in the class conceived in a womb like mine?"

And my grandmother would pat her abdomen with her veiny rough hand and say laughingly, "That is why your father ranked first, always."

Despite her intelligence, my grandmother was not conscious of women's causes. She was the poorest of the family. She worked in the fields to support her children, but she was independent. She refused to remarry although she was still young, but she was unaware of women's liberation. Like all the other women in the village, she preferred boys to girls. She preferred my brother to me, and used to tell me that a boy was worth ten girls. She also was ignorant of the

possibility that a woman can have a future without having a husband and children.

It was therefore natural that, when I graduated from elementary school, my grandmother and my maternal and paternal aunts, conspiring together, started talking me into marrying a wealthy peasant from the village. This was not only because I was the oldest daughter, but because I had reached puberty at an early age (I was nine) and there was no secondary school for girls in the village. I still remember them telling me that this man would build me a beautiful palace and that I would not have to work in the field in the burning sun.

But I resisted and threatened to commit suicide if they insisted on marrying me off. My mother objected to my marriage at such an early age, and encouraged me to pursue my studies. My father was also proud of my accomplishments at school, and he agreed to let me travel to Cairo to enroll in a girls' secondary school.

I lived the first year with my aunts in my maternal grandmother's house in the suburb of Zaitoun. My maternal grandfather had died a few years earlier, and my grandmother had died shortly

At a medical meeting, Cairo, Egypt, 1964

Establishing the Women's Writers Association in Egypt, 1971

thereafter. I lived in the big house with my aunt Fahima, my aunt Na'amat, my uncle Yahya, and my uncle Zakaria, and I did not like them. They were in a different world than mine; they lived in the world of the decadent bourgeois class, a world of laziness devoid of activity; they lived in the past on the bygone laurels of the family. My aunt Fahima kept in the drawer of her desk an old worn-out piece of paper which certified that the khedive Ismail had borrowed large amounts of money from her grandfather, and that he had seized a piece of land. As for my aunt Na'amat, she used to drink black coffee in the morning, tie something around her head, and mourn the loss of her husband who divorced her for no reason known to her. My uncle Yahya had failed at the university and worked for the railroad administration, where there was no work for him except to make sure that the clocks at the railroad stations rang regularly. My uncle Zakaria was still a student at the university but he stopped studying, lost faith in education, and fell in love with horse racing and cigarettes.

The year ended after I had fights with all of them, and I told my father that I could not stand living in the likes of this miserable, decadent house.

My father moved me to the Halwan secondary school for girls, where I boarded. I lived in a dormitory with more than twenty students. I made many friends. I discovered in this environment many problems that girls face because of the strictness of their fathers. My father seemed to me a caring, loving man compared to other men.

Ever since I was a child, my father told me: use your mind in everything, even matters pertaining to the belief in God. My father told me that God is justice and not a veil on a woman's face. My mother never wore the veil.

I inherited from my parents a hatred for foreign occupation. I was proud of being Egyptian, and I had read since I was a child about the old Egyptian civilization, and about the goddess of the sky, Nut, and her daughter Isis, the goddess of knowledge, and about Ma'at, the goddess of justice.

I was proud because these goddesses were my first ancestors. They lived in the Nile valley, and they played a very important role in promoting knowledge, arts, justice, philosophy, astronomy, and everything.

For this reason, I often asked my parents why no mention of these Egyptian goddesses was made in the Koran, and why the goddesses have disappeared from history, and why God had become a male and was no longer a female.

My father convinced me when I was a child that God was neither a male nor a female, that He is a spirit without a body, that He is the origin of the world, the creator of mankind, of Adam and Eve.

My mother had a strong personality, and my father respected her. I never witnessed any disagreement between them, nor did I ever hear my father shout at my mother or reprimand her as other men in our village very commonly did with their wives.

My father prayed regularly and fasted during Ramadan, but my mother prayed only during Ramadan. I learned to pray as a child of seven. I memorized some verses from the Koran at school without understanding their meaning until my father explained them to me.

When I was in elementary school, I had a Coptic friend whose name was Angel. During religious classes, Angel used to go to the playground and read the Bible with other Christian students.

I always asked my parents why God created some people Muslims and others Coptics, and I always resented discrimination among people. I especially resented the discrimination between my brother and me on the simple basis that he was a boy and I a girl. Despite the relative freedom that I enjoyed, my brother had more privileges than I did. He used to go out to the street and play with his friends into the late hours of the night, while I stayed home most of the time and went out only to go to school. I had to help my mother with her chores at home while my brother was playing ball in the street.

In secondary school, I was an excellent student of Arabic literature and wanted to specialize in that field. I also liked chemistry and biology, and decided to enroll in the scientific section during the last year in high school. At the finals, I had the highest grade in the school. As a result, I entered the school of medicine.

In Egypt, the best students enter medical school. There was no discrimination against girls entering medical school. They had the same chances as the boys provided they had the same high grades.

At medical school, I was introduced to new sciences, the most important of which was anatomy, which involved dissection of the human body. But I still liked literary writing. I used to write down thoughts and stories, which I sometimes published in the university journal.

I never stopped thinking about writing. I used to see myself as a free writer who obeys only her mind. I did not dream of being a wife, nor of being a physician.

Actually, I hated practicing medicine, and I hated the smell of hospitals and diseases. There was in me this deep desire to create, whereas practicing medicine did not offer me the proper environment for scientific or literary creativity, just as my studies at the university did not encourage my creativity but rather my capability to memorize and copy other people's views.

Literature and the arts then became the only fields where I could satisfy my appetite for innovation and creativity.

In spite of all this I used to pass my exams at medical school with high grades, since I was brought up to be responsible and to perfect anything I did. I used to like science, anatomy, and medicine, since they offered much that satisfied my appetite for learning and discovery. That is why I received excellent grades in anatomy while I detested the smell of cadavers and of formalin. And during the two years we performed dissections on cadavers, I could not eat any meat because I became nauseated. I nevertheless did my dissections with precision, interest, and curiosity.

Two strong traits dominate me—my mind and my emotions. My emotions are always very strong, be it in love or hatred. I am also rational; therefore, sometimes my mind dominates my emotions; at other times, my emotions dominate my mind. There is in me a strange balance between mind and emotions which sometimes produces a sort of mental and emotional rebellion towards many things in life. That explains why my rebellion is based upon action and productivity, why it is not a mere intellectual rebellion.

I used to lead nationalistic demonstrations against the British and King Farouk while I was a secondary-school student, and at the time when I was a student at the University of Cairo (a few months prior to the revolution of 1952), Cairo was the scene of student protests. Encouraged by my mother and my father, I used to take part in these demonstrations as well. I was the only female medical-student demonstrator among thousands of male students at one of the rallies. The female medical students were mostly interested in passing exams and getting good grades. I had a friend at the university named El Menesi who was killed while fighting the British at the Suez canal in 1951. His death triggered demonstrations. I stood at one of the rallies at the school of medicine and delivered a stirring speech about El Menesi. That is how I found myself, as a student, entering the world of politics with a burning desire to liberate my country from foreign occupation and from the governing authority which collaborated with the British.

But I was not interested in any one of the political parties. I always felt that politics was a game and a kind of ruse played by different forces in order to attain authority and political power.

I never knew a political party that worked for me or for the people. Therefore, I never joined a party even though I participated in demonstrations and yearned to liberate my country.

I wanted to regenerate everything around me. But traditions and customs presented hurdles to men with such ambitions, let alone to women.

I felt surrounded by physical and moral restrictions. These restrictions bound me as a woman, as a member of a family, and as a patriot in a country occupied by foreigners.

When I was at the medical school, I pursued my readings outside the medical field—arts, philosophy, history, and religions. I loved reading very much. I had a great understanding of books.

My study of history and various religions helped me understand the roots and the hidden causes of many phenomena around me and of many inequities that I witnessed.

My studies in medicine, as well as those in psychology and psychiatry, helped me understand the human personality and its motives.

When I graduated from medical school in 1955 at the age of twenty-four, I was a very young woman, extremely idealistic, daydreaming that I would live in a poor, sick village where I would treat everybody without ever charging them, where I would never be afraid of contagion, where I would work day and night until I died of a contagious disease.

I was very influenced by these persistent dreams that were enriched by all the novels that I read. No

Nawal El Saadawi (right) in her village, Kafr Tahla, Egypt, 1978: "A journalist interviews my cousin Zenab, with her son on her lap, while her husband stands near. Zenab is an illiterate peasant woman who works in the field with her husband."

wonder then that I started practicing medicine in the country. But after a few years I realized that the diseases of the peasants could only be cured after their poverty and their ignorance were cured.

From this point on I realized that writing was a stronger weapon than medicine in the fight against poverty and ignorance. A book reaches thousands and influences large numbers of people.

I started off by writing poetry. Then I wrote short stories, novels, and plays. Writing was a release for my anger. What angered me most was oppression: oppression of women and oppression of the poor.

I used to write about love. Love that was inexistent in the relations between men and women. I used to praise freedom and justice, without which life would have no value.

Then I discovered the relation between love and politics. Between poverty and politics. Between sex and politics. I realized that the political regime imposed the will of men upon women and imposed poverty and slavery upon the poor and the destitute.

Later I discovered the relationship between the local rulers and the international ones. And I understood what constitutes global imperialism, class exploitation, and paternal oppression of the family.

I realized the connection between the liberation of women and that of the poor and that of the country from subordination or occupation or any form of new or old colonialism. I understood the connection between sex, politics, economics, history, religion, and morality. This might be the reason why my writings led me to prison and to the loss of my position in the government, to the confiscation of my books, and to my being blacklisted.

The boldest of my writings were hidden in the drawers of my desk, since no publisher would dare to publish them. They dealt with the taboos (sex-politics-religion).

Despite governmental authority, my writings spread among the Arab people, from Morocco and Algeria to Egypt, Sudan, Iraq, Syria, and Yemen. They even penetrated Saudi Arabia.

This triggered the enmity of the Arab government towards me, enmity that got stronger as the number of people (women, men, and the young) reading my writings increased.

The same authorities tried to alienate me from my readers. And I became the target of attack of the political forces that dominated the Arab countries, including Egypt.

Among the means of attack was what we call the propaganda war. The authorities claimed that I was instigating women toward absolute sexual freedom and immorality, even though in everything I wrote I tried to combat reducing women to being sex objects fit only for seduction and consumption. I was even opposed to women wearing makeup. I encouraged them to be intelligent human beings and not mere bodies to satisfy men, to produce children, or to be slaves.

They also claimed that I was a Communist because I wrote about the subjugation of the poor and the causes of poverty and hunger. They claimed that I was against religion because I discussed rationally matters pertaining to religion and because my faith was not like theirs, inherited blindly as one inherits land or camels.

During the eighties, when my books were being translated into English, French, German, and other languages, they claimed that I was writing for Western consumption, even though I always wrote in Arabic, and all first editions of my books were published in Cairo. Only when my books were confiscated did I move publication to Beirut, Lebanon.

If my books met the approval of readers in Europe, America, or Japan, they met a greater degree of approval in the Arab countries, including Egypt.

The authorities in Egypt and the Arab world tried to prevent my message from getting to the people; and they succeeded, since they dominated all media of information and propaganda.

The most dangerous medium of information in our country is television, which explains why I have been banned from speaking on television in Egypt and in most of the Arab countries to this day.

I still remember my last visit to Tunisia in 1983. I was invited by a television director to talk, on the screen, about the Tunisian woman. We talked for about half an hour, and the conversation was aired on television. As a result of the program, the television director was fired by a decree signed by Bourguiba. Why? Because in our conversation about the Tunisian woman, I failed to mention that Bourguiba had liberated her.

During my last visit to Baghdad in 1981, I was invited by young men and women to give a talk at the university. I talked about the Iraqi woman without mentioning the governor; it is not one of my habits to talk about governors. I would always rather talk about the governed and not the governors.

During my last visit to Morocco in 1984, the president of the university almost cancelled my speech simply because the students wanted to open the large hall, since the small hall had three hundred

Nawal El Saadawi (right) at an international conference on women, Vienna, Austria, 1982. Also pictured are Germaine Greer and Robin Morgan, among others.

seats and three thousand people had gathered in the courtyard.

I have numerous memories of my travels to the Arab countries; I was always met there with hospitality and love on the part of the people, but with hatred and enmity by the rulers.

That was natural since everything I wrote unveiled the close connection between antiquated forms of government and all sorts of poverty, repression, and discrimination based on sex, social class, religion, or race.

I am opposed to authority and against bonds of all sorts. I defend freedom and justice everywhere. For this reason I was moved by the Palestinian cause, as I was moved by the cause of the people of South Africa. I feel stronger about the Palestinian cause for the simple reason that it has closer ties to Arab political and economic causes, and because of the ties of the Israeli government to the world capitalist and colonial powers.

I have met Israeli women who side with the Palestinians against the Israeli government, which proves that a woman who praises justice transcends the artificial boundaries between countries, and sides with the truth even if that pits her against government.

The women's liberation movements have played a very important role in the last twenty years against new colonialism, multinational companies, against wars, the arms race, nuclear armament, against racism and discrimination based on race, color, religion, or social class.

I always felt that the "pen" was an effective weapon I could use against injustice and oppression. But writing is also a very private undertaking, which could lead to one's isolation and removal from the battles of life.

In order to avoid such isolation, I founded, in 1982, the Arab Women Solidarity Association. We have been working diligently since then toward the advancement of the Arab woman. Our motto is: "Power of Women—Solidarity—Unveiling of the Mind."

Power is necessary, for what is right is lost without power. Just as power without right is tyranny.

Awareness is also necessary, since knowledge generates power. It is impossible for a woman (or a man) to know her or his rights if she or he wears a veil on the mind.

What the media accomplish in the Arab world (as in the rest of the world) is that they delude the people by placing a "veil" on their minds through which they cannot see what is happening to them or around them.

This delusion takes different forms depending on the country. In the industrial capitalist countries, there are modern technological means to brainwash the people.

The governing bodies in our country imported this modern technology, and television, for example, became a most dangerous device for destroying the human mind.

What is the role of the book against this octopus? Millions watch television, but only thousands read books. Such is the tragedy which is compounded by the fact that the books promoted by the authorities are not among the best; rather they are the ones that could best be used to mislead and delude the mind of the people. "Mind" is not here limited to the conscious but also refers to the subconscious.

In spite of all that, I still believe in writing. I still believe in the power of the truthful "word" to reach the minds and souls of people in spite of barriers erected around them.

Writing was the most important thing in my life, more important than marriage and more important than medicine. It is no wonder that I walked away from marriage and from medicine in order to write. I did not completely quit medicine, but I never devoted much time to it. Similarly, I did not reject marriage completely, but I refused to be married to a man who would hinder my writing.

Even though my parents were relatively liberated, I sometimes clashed with them when I felt that they restricted my freedom.

For example, I married my first husband without the approval of my parents, and I assumed full responsibility for doing so. The marriage ended in divorce when I discovered that he was not the man I dreamed he was, that he was imposing restrictions on me, and that he was standing in the way of my creativity. I had a daughter with him. She was still a baby when she and I left the house. My daughter and I lived together alone for a few years. Then I married my second husband whom I left. I remember my second husband telling me one day: "You have to choose between me and your writings." I answered, without hesitation, "My writings." Because I was pregnant, I had an abortion to get rid of the fetus. I decided never to get married again. But several years later, I met a truly liberated man who became my third husband. We got married in 1964 and I had a son with him, so that I now have a daughter and a son.

I was unable to become a "mother" without becoming a "wife," and I have always liked to experience life to the fullest, including motherhood and love. I have experienced marriage three times, and I am still married to my third husband, who respects the freedom and dignity of women. He is also

a creative writer and artist in addition to being a physician. He knows the value of literature and creativity to human life. He encourages my rebellious and revolutionary spirit; he is also a revolutionary and a rebel. Literary writing, medicine, and the liberation of human beings—men or women—brought us together. His name is Sherif Hetata, and he has a long history of struggle against the British and against oppression and exploitation. He was among the best students at the medical school, but he spent thirteen years in prison because of his intellectual and political rebellion.

I also was imprisoned during the regime of Sadat, but I was luckier than my husband. After Sadat was assassinated, I was set free by Hosni Mubarak, the president who succeeded him, after having spent only three months in prison. Were it not for these circumstances, I would probably have spent thirteen years in prison as my husband did.

Imprisonment in my country is always possible for any person who thinks and writes freely. Most of

Third husband, Sherif Hetata, 1983: "Medical doctor, novelist, fighter for socialism, and founder of the Arab Women Solidarity Association"

the men and women I know have been in prison at one time in their life.

As for women in my country, their husbands are their permanent prisons. It is very difficult for a woman not to be married. Extramarital love and sex are forbidden to women, but men are free in this regard. I have fought this moral double standard in my writings.

The first nonfiction book I wrote about women was titled *Women and Sex*, published in 1971, and confiscated by the Egyptian censorship. It was because of this book that I lost my job as general director at the Ministry of Health, and that the publication of the health journal of which I was editor in chief ceased.

During the Sadat regime, publication of my books was forbidden in Egypt; therefore, I started publishing my books in Beirut. I was blacklisted under the Sadat regime. I wrote articles that criticized his policies and uncovered his ambivalence. He preached democracy but practiced dictatorship.

Nothing proves Sadat's dictatorship more than the fact that he threw me in prison because of what I

Daughter, Mona Helmi, and son, Atef Hetata, 1982

wrote even though I never belonged to any political party. It was well known that I was a writer, independent from political parties, who expressed her opinions freely.

That is why I write. I write everywhere and under any circumstances. Even in the prison cell, I wrote. Every morning the prison guards would enter and search my cell from floor to ceiling. Their chief would shout, "If we find a paper and a pen, that would be more dangerous for you than if we found a gun."

They never found the paper and the pen that I hid. This was my small triumph that filled me with hope in my prison cell.

But even outside of prison, life is filled every day with small triumphs over the oppression, aggression, and tyranny of the authorities.

Because of these small triumphs I live my life and never lose hope or optimism even in the gloomiest and darkest of circumstances.

We are going through times of decadence, not only in the Arab world but in the world in general, but such decadence shall be outweighed by a new awakening, and a new rising dawn.

Women pay dearly with their freedom and dignity to obey the laws of marriage and the patriarchal class system that dominates society. Women also pay dearly in order to become free and escape domination.

I have chosen to pay such a price and become free rather than pay the price and become a slave. In either case we pay a high price. Why pay it to attain slavery and not freedom?

My third husband and I have succeeded in forming a family that does not abide by the prevailing laws of marriage nor by the inherited traditions. We instituted our own law based on equality among us. We also succeeded in creating a new understanding of motherhood and fatherhood in relation to our daughter and our son. Our daughter, Mona Helmi, studied economics but favored literature and the arts, and she has become a young creative writer, publishing a number of short stories and poems. Our son, Atef Hetata, studied engineering but favored cinematography, and he is now training to become a movie director.

All four of us joined hands in founding the Arab Women Solidarity Association. We are all active in its various committees. The educational and the youth committees are among the most active in the organization. They are committees founded by my daughter

Dr. Nawal El Saadawi with Yasser Arafat, leader of the Palestine Liberation Organization, in Sanaa, North Yemen, Egypt, 1983

with the help of my son and other young men and women.

What distinguishes the activities of our organization is that men and women are involved, for we do not classify people according to their sex. There are some male members who are more zealous toward women's causes than some of the women.

We succeeded in abolishing the arbitrary distinction between science and art and between literature and medicine. I still read the sciences as I do the arts. My varied readings in varied fields made me understand the women's causes scientifically, and made me understand the relationship between the sciences and other unrelated specialties.

My work as a psychiatrist allowed me to meet many women (and men) who are victims of subjugation, oppression, and fear. But I always considered myself a writer rather than a physician. Today, I devote most of my time to writing, and in my spare time, after I am done writing, I tend to other work that awaits me at my office. Very often, I escape to my village where I spend a few days, weeks, or months tending a new literary work away from the congestion and noise of Cairo.

The last novel I wrote was *The Fall of the Imam,* which was published in Arabic in Cairo in 1987. A few months after its publication, my telephone rang, and a high official at the security department was at the other end of the line. He told me, "Doctor, we are putting you under supervision." Supervision, I wondered? That normally meant confiscation of one's property or freedom. But the official added that he was sending guards to protect me. I wondered if anyone was threatening my life. He simply said that he had information. Who is threatening my life? He did not want to tell me.

Armed guards were stationed in front of my house in Giza without my knowing why or who threatened me. Maybe they were religious extremists.

I lived with this suspicion about a year and a half. One day, I walked out of my house and did not find any guards. To this day I do not know why they left. But I was happy that they disappeared. Their presence meant that I was in danger. Their disappearance meant that the danger had vanished.

I must admit that I was worried the first couple of days after the guards were stationed in front of my house. But soon I became accustomed to the worry and stopped feeling it. Which reminds me that before I entered the prison I was afraid of it, but soon after I entered I shed my fear. We are frightened by the unknown. If we knew and understood death, we would not be frightened by it. We fear death because it is unknown to us.

Since then, every time I emerge safely from a bad experience I tell myself that an incident that does not kill me makes me stronger.

BIBLIOGRAPHY

Nonfiction:

El ma'ra wal ginse (title means "Women and Sex"), El Shaab (Cairo), 1971, El Mu'assasah El Arabeya Lil Tahrir Wal Nashr (Beirut), 1972.

El rajol wal ginse (title means "Man and Sex"), El Mu'assasah El Arabeya Lil Tahrir Wal Nashr, 1973.

El ma'ra heyal asl (title means "The Essentiality of the Woman"), El Mu'assasah El Arabeya Lil Tahrir Wal Nashr, 1975.

El ma'ra wal sira el nafsy (title means "Woman and Psychological Conflict"), El Mu'assasah El Arabeya Lil Tahrir Wal Nashr, 1976.

El wajh el ary lilma'ra arabeya, El Mu'assasah El Arabeya Lil Tahrir Wal Nashr, 1977, translation by husband Sherif Hetata published as *The Hidden Face of Eve: Women in the Arab World,* Zed Press, 1980, Beacon, 1981.

Mozakerati fi signel nissa (autobiography), Dar El Moustakbal El Arabi (Cairo), 1983, translation by Marilyn Booth published as *Memoirs from the Women's Prison,* Women's Press (London), 1986.

(With Georges Tarabishi) *Untha did al-untha*, Al Saqi (London), 1988, translation by Basil Hatim and Elisabeth Orsini published as *Woman against Her Sex: A Critique of Nawal El Saadawi, with a Reply by Nawal El Saadawi*, Al Saqi, 1988.

Fiction:

Mozakerat tabiba (novel), Dar El Ma'aref (Cairo), 1958, Dar El Adab, 1979, translation by Catherine Cobham published as *Memoirs of a Woman Doctor*, Al Saqi, 1988.

Talamt el houb (short stories; title means "I Learned to Love"), Maktabet El Nahda (Cairo), 1958, Dar El Adab (Beirut), 1980.

Hanam kalil (short stories; title means "Little Sympathy"), El Kitab El Zahabi (Cairo), 1959, Dar El Adab, 1980.

Lahzat sidk (short stories; title means "A Moment of Truth"), El Kitab El Zahabi, 1962, Dar El Adab, 1980.

El gha'aeb (novel; title means "The Absent"), El Kitab El Zahabi, 1965, Dar El Adab, 1976.

Emra'atan fi emra'ah (novel), Dar El Kitab, 1968, Dar El Adab, 1973, translation by Osman Nusairi and Jana Gough published as *Two Women in One*, Al Saqi, 1985, published as *El bahitha an el hub* (title means "The Searcher for Love"), El Haya El Misreya Elama Lilkitab, 1974.

El khait wa el gidar (short stories; title means "The Thread and the Wall"), El Shaab, 1972.

El khait wa ain' el hayat (contains stories from *El khait wa el gidar*), El Shaab, 1972, Dar El Adab, 1980, translation by Shirley Eber published as *She Has No Place in Paradise*, Methuen, 1987.

Kanat heya el ada'af (title means "She Was the Weaker"; contains stories from *El khait wa el gidar*), El Shaab, 1972, Dar El Adab, 1980.

Emra'a enda noktat el sifr (novel), Dar El Adab, 1975, translation by Hetata published as *A Woman at Point Zero*, Zed Books, 1983.

Mawt el rajoh el waheed ala el ard (novel; title means "The Death of the Only Man on Earth"), Dar El Adab, 1976, translation by Hetata published as *God Dies by the Nile*, Zed Books, 1985.

Oghniat el alfal el da'ereyah (novel), Dar El Adab, 1977, translation by Booth published as *The Children's Song*, Zed Books, 1989.

Mowt ma'ali el wazin (short stories), Dar El Adab, 1979, translation by Eber published as *Death of an Ex-Minister*, Methuen, 1987.

El ensan (play; title means "The Human Being"), Maktabet Madbouli (Cairo), 1983, published as *Ethna ashra emra'a fi zinzanah* (title means "Twelve Women in One Cell"), Maktabet Madbouli, 1983.

Isis (play), Dar El Moustakbal El Arabi, 1986.

Rihlati awl el aalam (title means "My Travel around the World"), Kitab El Hilal (Cairo), 1986, translation by Eber published by Methuen, 1990.

Sokout el imam (novel), Dar El Mostakbal El Arabi, 1987, translation by Hetata published as *The Fall of the Imam*, Methuen, 1988.

El Saadawi's books have also been translated into Danish, Dutch, Finnish, French, German, Italian, Japanese, Norwegian, Portuguese, Persian, Swedish, Urdū, and other languages.

Frederick Feirstein

1940-

My mother's favorite book was called *Life Is with People.* I suppose that's the way I can best describe my life and the central theme of my poetry.

I was born in Manhattan in 1940, hours after the New Year. My family was in mourning for my paternal grandmother, who had died four months earlier. My mother had promised her on her deathbed that she would take in her family. So I arrived in an extended family of seven people, including my grandfather—a Polish immigrant who signed his name with an *X*—his three daughters, his son Bernie, and my parents.

We lived in an elegant apartment building on the Lower East Side called the Aigiloff Towers. It's still there and wraps around half a city block from 3rd Street to 4th Street on Avenue A. It was built as a cooperative in the late twenties, but when the stock market crashed Aigiloff jumped off the roof and the building became a rental.

We lived on the 4th Street side, where my father paid one hundred dollars a month for a five-room apartment, a doorman under a canopy, an Art Deco lobby, and two elevators manned by uniformed elevator men.

I remember my early years by the different places I slept in. First my parents' bedroom, where I stayed too long waiting for a vacancy. I remember lying in bed, maybe trying to distract myself from forbidden noises, tapping out an intricate ten beats with different finger variations of my right hand. I've often wondered if my interest in the iambic line didn't start then.

When my younger sister Rosalee was born, I moved into the foyer. It was a way station for my grandfather's three brothers, my mother's five sisters and brothers, their wives, husbands, and children, and assorted family friends. It was my childhood's Tabard Inn, where I'd pretend to be asleep while gossip, snatches of arguments, secrets passed me by. But one night I was allowed to stay up well past midnight. My Uncle Bernie had been away in the army, the only white with an all-Apache troop scouting the Pacific islands for enemy soldiers. Now he was

Frederick Feirstein in Central Park, New York City, 1980

coming home to a celebration beginning around my bed and ending hours later in the living room.

Bernie was one of my childhood heroes. He was a double for John Garfield and would teach me over the next few years how to comb a pompadour, flirt with girls, box, play basketball. Just as he was in the middle of teaching me the give-and-go, he decided to get married. I took his place sleeping in my grandfather's room. At first it seemed a lousy trade-off. But soon I discovered a literary adventure awaiting me there. At night it became the place where I'd first learn the art of storytelling and what would become narrative poetry.

My grandfather Willie was a big street-fighting man. On Friday nights, instead of going to synagogue, he'd go down to the bars on Avenue A and pick fights with neighborhood anti-Semites. Then he'd come home with a sheepish look, down a schnapps, and spend the evening watching the wrestling matches with me on television.

My mother was very strict; in fact my home was a matriarchy. But at bedtime my grandfather would riskily keep me up, making barnyard sounds which I'd echo, or telling me stories such as how his mother first came to this country.

My great-grandmother had been the young wife of an old well-to-do farmer in Poland. When he died his five sons, Willie among them, immigrated to America. My great-grandmother regularly received news of America from the *Forward,* the Yiddish-American newspaper that was mailed to her town and shared by her neighbors. But one day no one seemed to have the paper. She became suspicious and sent her young daughter Mary to find out why. As my narrative poem *Family History* tells it, this was the shocking story my great-grandmother discovered:

HARRY FEIRSTEIN SLAIN. No! No! No! No!
WILLIE FEIRSTEIN JAILED. From
　　Brody . . . Jews . . .
Were brothers . . . Harry's stable . . .
　　blood . . . hook . . . Will . . .
The letters crumpled in her vertigo.

That very night my great-grandmother sold
Her farm, her livestock, bailing hooks and forks
And steered an ocean liner's rail to New York's
Lower East Side. Trying to stay self-controlled
She softly pressed the bell marked "Feirstein,"
Then climbed six flights, often pausing to lean

On Mary, then Hallucination: *Gut!*
Her angel Willie at the door! Or Cain?
Mary squeezed my hand when she told me this.
The paper got the melodrama, but
Mixed up the facts. A thug saw Harry kiss
His girl, his doll, his skinny scatterbrain

And lead her to the shadows of his stable.
They fought. Harry reeled against a table.
The thug lept on him. Harry reached for his nuts.
The thug reached back and pinned him with a
　　hook
And with another opened up his guts
And made his girlfriend, crazed already, look.

Shrieking she zigzagged down the street. She
　　reached
The barbershop where Willie was stretched out,

Listening to the barber smack his strop.
Harry is what? She's talking so damn fast!
Come on, Willie, sit down, sit down. I doubt
Your brother's . . . Someone hurry, get a cop!

My Grandpa Willie was over six feet tall.
He swept the thug against the stable wall.
He broke the wrists, the elbows, cheekbones,
　　nose.
He almost drowned him, turning up a hose
Inside the killer mouth before the cops arrived.
Mourning nearly wrecked him. Jail he survived.

Next door to my grandfather's room lived, at various times, my two aunts Sylvia and Annabelle and Renee, my father's baby sister but only eight years older than I and raised as my sister. I've described Renee, Annabelle, and Sylvia in *Family History.* Perhaps this excerpt about Sylvia will give a feeling of what growing up among them in that time was like:

Frederick, about two, with his grandfather
Willie Feirstein, in front of the Rivington Street Baths
on the Lower East Side, New York City

At five I thought Aunt Sylvia romantic
In fox fur, nylons, spiked heels, pillbox hat
—A working girl beneath a John Sloan El.
The others didn't think of her like that
But as a spinster, unlike Annabelle.
Though she was 27, she was frantic

And said despite my protests she was "plain"
And sat her rimless glasses on my nose:
"Boys don't make passes at girls who wear glasses
Or feminists who wear designer clothes."
She'd prink a mocking smile and bat her lashes
And say she should have been a scatterbrain

And I'd protest and tell her she was funny.
She'd laugh, "You'll have to play John Wayne
One day with fists, one day with money,"
And crack her gum like Ginger Rogers tapped.
I'd dance to it, my baseball bat my cane.
At every little thing I did, she clapped.

Though my grandfather was the nominal head of the extended family, his ice business was failing and my father's new coal business came to support the household.

My father was smart, ambitious, and in his younger days an athlete. I idealized his accomplishments, though he was self-effacing. My father had a different relationship with my grandfather than I did. My grandfather, who grew more and more financially dependent on my father, constantly put him down. My father wouldn't say a word back. At eleven I pasted photos of my dad in my sports scrapbooks: My father, quarterback of his high-school football team, set to pass in Yankee Stadium. (My father laughed, "We never won a game all season.") My father, the sprinter, setting track records that stood for a long while in New York City. My father the catcher and Spud Chandler the pitcher on the University of Georgia freshman baseball team. My father would drop out of college and work in my grandfather's business, lugging blocks of ice up tenement steps. Spud Chandler would go on to pitch for the New York Yankees. I'd go with my father to watch him. We'd go to all the sports events we could. We were Yankee fans and spent many afternoons from the time I was little watching Joe DiMaggio, Charlie Keller, and Tommy Heinrich. We'd go to the first games the Knicks ever played—against such teams as the Providence Steamrollers and the Tri-City Hawks. Often we'd go to Tompkins Square Library, then in a lovely setting among Eastern European barbershops and cafes, across the park that later became a drug market.

Mother, Nettie, with Aunt Sylvia, late 1930s

Through the late forties and early fifties, my father persistently developed better and better coal accounts till he had a flourishing business. Yet he was embarrassed by the work he did. He had two coal trucks and in the busy winters drove one of them. I remember coming home from junior high school and seeing my father's truck, Universal Coal Corporation, making a delivery. Excitedly I'd rush around to see him. He'd shyly try to hide himself. It took me a while to catch on that he was ashamed to have me see him covered with coal dust. When he wasn't driving the truck, he was meticulously clean and an elegant dresser.

My mother was an immigrant but you'd never guess it. Her English was flawless, and she too was an elegant dresser. I have a videotape made from old movie reels showing my mother decked out in chic dresses and flamboyant hats, gloves, scarves, and pocketbooks. She had incredible energy and patience, running a house of nine people. My mother was a survivor of a little-discussed type of event in Jewish history, the pogrom. But it's in-between the lines of Jewish fiction and, I think, has a lot to do with the anxiety behind much Jewish comedy.

My mother survived two pogroms as a little girl in Komenitz Podolsk, a town in the Russian Pale of Settlement. I don't have many details because like most survivors she tried to protect her children from knowledge of it. But I sensed something hidden in her overprotectiveness, her thwarting my fistfights as a little boy, her waiting up for me at the window as a teenager.

What I learned of her early terror was this: While my maternal grandfather worked as a tailor in America, trying to save money to bring his family over, my grandmother ran a tearoom in Russia, with my mother and her sister Belle as tiny waitresses. During one pogrom they hid from the Cossacks in a cemetery. Just before the next they got a warning from the young revolutionaries who came to the tea shop. That night they fled through the European underground and came in steerage to New York.

I didn't discover even these details till I was grown and began to sense a hidden story of survival in my poetry. My first book of poems was called *Survivors,* and the first poem in it was based on a dream of a friend of mine, with no direct reference to my background, or so I thought.

With father, Arnold Feirstein, in Tompkins Square Park, New York City, about 1943

Walking Away

There were no cans or prayerbooks or dead
    dogs
Along the road, no snapshots or headstones,
No broken dolls, butts, newspapers—nothing.
Only a few memories troubled him,
And these he could suppress, he could.
And he could name the trees and sun and sky
And name the names: green, yellow, and pale
    blue
For the first time. And the sick or the mass
    dead . . . ?
Pine needles and the wet sun, the bluejay
Splashing among the branches, the Oz-green
Lichen on rocks: he was so curious,
Out of himself for the first time, since when?
There at the end of the road . . . the smell
    first,
He closed his eyes, of honeysuckle, yes,
Of thyme and bier roses and the man there
At the road's end, a bent-over harlequin
Singing an old song, old sentiments, yes:
Half-red his back half-green, half-red his hat
Half-green. Could such a private thing exist?
Oh, he would talk to him, become a boy,
Sit cross-legged at his feet and lose control.
The cold sweats began. The planes dove again,
The big guns . . . buttercups, spiderwebs,
The peacock green and spotlight red: keep still.
Still. Envy the white moth its folded wings,
The slimy things that Coleridge praised, praise
    them.
He did. And thought of poems. Four three two
    one . . .
Color drained from everything at once,
Except the clown, except the clown, the clown
Turned like a ball-turret gun upon his rock:
Rock upon rock, his buttocks: rocks, back: rock,
Head: rock. There was no more. His arms and
    legs
Were gone, as were the woods, as was the sun.
Nothing except the rubble's mystery,
Its quizzical last smile that was itself
An answer: "Did you expect a comedy?"

The next poem in *Survivors* is "'Grandfather' in Winter." In 1968 I had been directing publicity for the American Committee to Keep Biafra Alive during the Nigerian Civil War. I didn't fully understand then why I wanted to help the children under siege or how it was connected to my mother, until I wrote this poem:

"Grandfather" in Winter

The overcoats are gone from Central Park
—In the sudden Spring.
A clump of leaves, that lay in a white crypt
Of roots for months, loosens, looking for life.
Bare feet of hippies on the sunny walk,
Rock-heaps of pigeons bursting like corn, food
From brown bags, from white hands, from
     black hands,
Black and white kids kissing in the high rocks,
In the Rodin laps, in the hands of God
Above. Below, an old man, in a rough coat,
Wearing my grandfather's frown, lifts his face
Up to the sun and smiles smacking his lips.
His sky-blue Buchenwald tattoo has healed.
Below him, in the skating-rink, a small
Girl, Jewish, repeats the rings of the park:
The ring of her father skating around her,
The guard around him, the border of the rink
Around him, the rings of the pigeon-walks,
The rings of clouds, of jets, of the young
Sun around it. Me on the parapet,
The blood of the false Spring ringing my heart.
My wife beside me aims her camera at
The girl. The girl falls. The rope jerks. Nine
Iraqi Jews are falling through the air,
The Arab horde around them cheers. *Shema.*
The feet clump like leaves. The eyes turn up:
     white
Rocks. Israel in winter prepares again
For war. Around the gas-house are the guards,
Around the guards, pogroms: Deserts of dead,
Miles wide and miles thick. The rings around
Her border are of time. Grandfather knows.
His dead eyes scrutinize my eyes. He knows
Tomorrow snow will fall like lead, the news
Will be obituaries, Kaddish will
Be sung. It is the eve of war again:
Shema.

Only after I wrote such poems as these did I press my mother for details about her background and begin to understand how much my mother's childhood experiences in the Russian Pale were a part of me and my poetry.

My poetry was not only shaped by the world I found in my extended family but also by the world in the streets, the carnival of Manhattan. Then New York was a safe playground for a child with games to play, people to meet, exotic places to visit. Next door to us was a storefront where an old Ukrainian woman painted Easter eggs and made patterned collections of butterflies. Across the street was a cabinetmaker who also carved puppets and told us stories out of the Bavarian woods. Down the block was Harry's Grocery, which functioned like a general store in a small town. New York then was a series of small towns, Europeans' towns with each block having a unique identity. The Aigiloff was a shtetl Jew's fantasy of America. At the end of the block were tenements packed with southern Italians. Down the avenue were Ukrainians, Czechs, and Poles.

In my early years we all played together. PS 63 in the middle of the block was a true "melting pot." We all played outside. Women sat in front of the buildings on folding chairs or orange crates, on fire escapes in the summers. There was very little traffic; few people owned cars. We'd play Off the Wall—flinging a Spaldinger (a pink rubber ball made by Spalding) against the brickface of the warehouse across the street and then the opposing team would have to catch it in the gutter or sidewalk or without a bounce off our building. We'd play Chinese Handball (slapping the ball first off the bottom of our wall), Grounders (skimming the Spaldinger at top speed on the surface of the sidewalk), Punchball, Stoopball, Stickball.

We'd travel the city on roller skates, metal skates we'd tighten with a key, or on bikes—to the UN or to the ferry slip where we'd boat ride to Staten Island and then bike it. We'd play basketball in Houston Street Park, where we'd learn by watching stars from Harlem like Cal Ramsey, and then eat our way from the pickle barrels of the Essex Street Market to the hard-salami sandwiches at Katz's Delicatessen.

We were the children of the last generation of European immigrants and friends of the new immigrants—the first wave of Puerto Ricans. I remember evenings strolling down 4th Street between Avenues A and B, listening to the Puerto Rican men playing guitars and singing in Spanish.

Music was a very important part of my childhood, and I think there's a correlation between the classical music education I got in street-slangy New York and my use of meter and rhyme with colloquial diction.

From the time I was seven I studied music at the Third Street Music School. I had extraordinary teachers. Jacob and his wife Elfrieda Mestechkin taught me the violin. Both had been pupils of Leopold Auer, the master teacher of all the great Russian violinists. Both played in chamber groups with Fritz Kreisler and Jascha Heifetz, and Elfrieda was the concertmistress of the Sadler Wells Ballet. The conductor of our children's orchestra was Julius

"In front of the Aigiloff Towers, Third Street side, with my sister, Rosalee, in the carriage, and my mother, Nettie," about 1944

Rudel, and my theory teacher Ralph Shapey. I'd love practicing, sometimes in front of an open window, entertaining my friends or spontaneously accompanied by gypsy musicians. By the time I was eleven I was picked with two other little violinists to play with the All-City Orchestra in Carnegie Hall. By fourteen I'd travel to Queens to play professionally with the Queens Symphony and to Brooklyn to play with the All-City Orchestra. It was easy then for a child to travel freely (with a violin) in New York. This carefree access to a city full of joyousness and music I tried to capture in my second book, *Manhattan Carnival*, my most written-about work. It's full of passages that celebrate the city:

> The world looks simple in these fancy blocks.
> There are no grandmothers in army socks
> With all their worldly goods in paper bags,
> No windows warped or cracked and stuffed
>   with rags.
> Instead old mansions, churches, private schools,

And rooftop gardens, rooftop swimming pools.
This market selling jumbo squab and goose,
That florist selling miniature spruce,
This dress shop with its leftist magazines
And racks (here poor is chic) of faded jeans.
We squatted here, pitched pennies at the wall
And through that ladder hooked a basketball.
We bicycled and rowed in Central Park.
We necked, defying muggers, after dark.
We sauntered nibbling sauerkraut like grapes.
When maids or doormen sneered we swayed
    like apes.
We ran like blind men once for seven blocks,
Both stricken by a midnight urge for lox
And settled for a closing pizza stand
And once . . . Your life now? Mine seems
    second-hand.

I need the windows of the Tourist Boards
On Fifth—their beaches, lower Alps, and
    fiords—
The students playing clarinet duets,
The mime in top silk hat and epaulettes,
The Hari Krishnas spreading incense, joy,
Their flowing peach robes, shoes of corduroy,
The blind man singing hymns, St. Thomas
    Church,
The scaffolding where whistling workmen
    perch,
The haughty English manager of Cook's,
St. Patrick's nave, Rizzoli's picture books,
Tiffany's clock, the pools of Steuben glass,
The pocket park with cobblestones for grass.
Remember how we'd stroll on your lunch hour?
My nickname for you then was "City Flower."

That was in 1974. Now when I celebrate Manhattan, as in my sixth book, *Manhattan Elegy & Other Goodbyes,* it's mostly its past in contrast to its present full of the homeless, drug dealers, teenagers going "wilding." But that Manhattan of my past gave hints of disappearing even as I came into my adolescence. It began losing its small-town feeling as "city planners" began demolishing neighborhoods. And it began losing the extended family to our American need for more independence.

By the time I was twelve Renee, Sylvia, Bernie, and Annabelle had married and moved out. My grandfather died, in an instant, of stroke. The house seemed shockingly empty. We became a nuclear family, characteristically one with troubles. With those troubles my childhood came to an end. About the time the extended family left, the American fuel economy began to change from coal to oil. My father's business began to suffer. My father, with several creative ideas and a lot of confidence, tried other ventures. But they didn't work out and he became cynical, telling me everything was contacts, that talent and creativity counted for little. More difficult for me then, he began to act like my grandfather, diminishing my accomplishments with ambiguous mockery which I couldn't bring myself to counter.

My mother also was deeply affected by the loss of the extended family. She was like a woman executive suddenly forced into retirement. She focused her managerial energy on my grades (though I was an "A" student) and on my sister's, nagging me to practice the violin more when I'd had enough, to study when I'd studied, to get up, not lie down, to do something when I was playing in three orchestras, chamber groups, and on a settlement-house basketball team at night.

By the time I was fifteen, I'd had enough. I stopped studying, dropped the violin, and picked up a raucous saxophone. I bought a brown leather jacket, white scarf, grew sideburns, and greased my hair like a fifties hood. For a while I felt free. But my sad masquerade provoked my mother to nag me more, to turn off the radio and study without rock and roll. I'd slam my books down and storm out. My father, who hadn't gone beyond his freshman year, was bewildered and let me slide. My mother, who had only finished junior high school, became more anxious and angry. I became more defiant.

After a while we couldn't talk. We'd have dinner at the table with my father watching television, my mother talking on the telephone with relatives, my younger sister Rosalee, who was having her own school difficulties, afraid.

I was in turmoil and couldn't express what I was feeling. My mother suggested I talk to Ben Hertz, the family doctor, an obstetrician who had delivered me as a baby and would help deliver me in adolescence.

Dr. Hertz wanted to be a psychiatrist but for some reason didn't fulfill his ambition and chose to remain with basically a general practice, mostly among the Lower East Side poor. I'd stop by once or twice a week after school. He'd listen empathetically and speak frankly to me. We'd talk about my relationship with my family, my awakening sexuality, and my curiosity about the larger world around me. I began to identify with him, feeling guilty all the while about betraying my father by confiding in Dr. Hertz. In part my becoming a psychoanalyst grew out of the two years I spent talking to him.

At sixteen and a half, I began my premedical studies at New York University, with the view of going into psychiatry. I was passionate about learning what made people do what they did, the same passion that later on would attract me to narrative and dramatic poetry and theater.

I did very poorly that first semester because I tried out for the freshman basketball team, going to constant practice sessions, surviving every cut but the last. Satch Sanders, who'd become the center with the Boston Celtics, was on the team with his high-school teammate Russ Cunningham, a guard about my height. Cunningham was the leading scorer in New York high-school basketball and I outscored him in a game. But I didn't make the team, and all the time away from my studies cost me. I wound up on probation and had to work around the clock to catch up. By the end of the year I made dean's list but began to feel that premedical studies with its learning by rote was a grind. I was ready to become distracted by poetry.

The poetry that first made an impact on me was French, particularly Rimbaud's and Villon's. They articulated, in ways I wished I could have, feelings of defiance and loss. The rough colloquial yet "formal" style of Villon later led to my fascination with Chaucer and eventually to my writing *Manhattan Carnival*, which is in New Yorkese and in couplets.

My interest in studying psychiatry faded. In a manner becoming typical for me, I followed my passion. After my sophomore year I transferred schools to the University of Buffalo, where I majored in French and tried to separate from my background. I hung around with a rowdy crowd at first but then they bored me. They wanted to go deer hunting and I wanted to read "Yates"— as I remember first writing his name.

The choice of French turned out to be lucky. At Buffalo I met Madame Burrell, a French professor who was amused by my combination of recklessness and naivete. She was black and married to a physician. She guided me into a more sophisticated way of thinking about myself, as Dr. Hertz had, and the Mestechkins had earlier. She pressed me to think about how I'd support myself as a poet. During Christmas vacation I had seen my first Broadway plays. I told her that they excited me, that I thought I could write them as well as poetry, and so support myself. She explained how risky that could be and asked me what other ways I could make a living. I said I sometimes still had thoughts of going to medical school and becoming a psychiatrist. She told me that if I wanted to be a therapist it would be less time-consuming to take a degree in clinical psychology ("There are such programs?"), which would leave me with energy to write. I didn't know what I wanted to do. All I knew was that I had a passion to write. I could write plays, I could become a therapist, I could teach. At her further suggestion I switched my major to English. I worked hard learning technique in my language. Madame Burrell liked my scribblings and discussed them with me at length. I finished college just as I turned twenty. Two weeks before graduation she died, suddenly. I didn't stay to pick up my diploma. My first real poem was an elegy for her.

I remember standing in the lobby of NYU after I'd come back from Buffalo and calling the clinical psychology department. But the department told me I couldn't begin in mid-year. So I enrolled in the English Department's Ph.D. program. It was another haphazard choice and a lucky one. Otherwise I wouldn't have met Linda.

One day, two years later, I went to the 42nd Street Library to work on a paper about Ezra Pound, assigned to me by M. L. Rosenthal. Of all my teachers, after Madame Burrell, Rosenthal influenced me the most. Interestingly Rosenthal was the critic who defined modern poetry as being the lyric and lyric sequence and brought the Confessional Poets to critical attention. But Rosenthal also taught me the crucial lesson of being open to all kinds of poetry. At the time I was writing free-verse lyric poetry but, given my lifelong interest in other people, I'd become intensely interested in the narrative and dramatic poem as well and started experimenting with a style that combined meter and rhyme with colloquial diction. Many years later this would lead to my helping to begin the Expansive Poetry movement, which is devoted to opening poetry up to other forms besides the free-verse lyric and lyric sequence.

Taking a break from Pound, whom I both admired for his devotion to poetry and detested for his anti-Semitism, I stepped outside the Main Reading Room and talked to a friend. I watched him wave to a beautiful young woman approaching from the other direction. He introduced us. Three months later we would be engaged.

Besides being beautiful, Linda Bergton was academically brilliant. She was a Phi Beta Kappa in economics and political science at the Heights campus where I was a graduate assistant. She was the only girl in those departments and, in those pre–Women's Lib days, she successfully competed with the boys and won the medal for being the top economics student.

She was also unlike the women I knew in my matriarchal family. She's kind and careful with peo-

Frederick and Linda Bergton Feirstein, 1987

ple, uncritical and loving. These qualities she combines in her work as a psychoanalyst and in mothering David, our son.

Like many people of our generation, believing that children can't have children, we waited, deliberately, for fifteen years to have him. We wanted to grow up first, indulge ourselves by finding the right careers, traveling, taking our difficulties to analysis instead of out on a child.

Lucky for us David is a warm, outspoken, funny, athletic, creative eleven-year-old. One of the central themes of my poetry is the importance of raising a family. Naturally David is at the center of our lives; and our work, structured at will, frees us to spend a great deal of time with him.

But now we're back in 1962, wanting to get married and about to contend with Bernard, Linda's father. Bernard was in his fifties, overly attached to his daughter, and planning for her to marry a businessman like himself. He laid down strict terms to Linda. He told her that unless we waited a year to get to know each other before we married, he'd have nothing to do with her again. He had a heart condition which frightened Linda. Reluctantly we waited.

All year Bernard and I would fight. He thought of me as a beatnik, a wild poet stealing his daughter.

He was in real estate. I was writing sexual poetry that I once read to his startled friends. We played a version of Archie Bunker and Meathead. But after Linda and I married, Bernard and I became good friends. Two years later he died, shocking us just before my first play was presented in New York.

It turned out I had a natural gift for drama. While I was in graduate school, I taught myself the craft of playwriting as I did the craft of poetry. Though I'm happy the proliferation of workshops has made life easier for the writer teaching in the university, I felt taking writing courses wouldn't be helpful to me. I had to find my own style and subject matter myself by practicing the craft and by painstakingly studying those writers who knew how to say the kind of things I wanted to. So, for instance, I learned how to write *Manhattan Carnival* by translating the "General Prologue" to *The Canterbury Tales* and studying William Carlos Williams's successes and failures in *Paterson*.

Right after we were married, Linda and I moved to Milwaukee, where I took a teaching job at the University of Wisconsin. We hadn't seen Milwaukee before and were expecting a sullen industrial city. Instead we were stunned by the beauty of the town, particularly Shorewood, the area we came to live in. We rented the top floor of a wooden two-family house on a street lined on either side with elms arching above the rooftops. We'd walk such streets for hours till we'd come to richly landscaped parks that rolled down to the shores of Lake Michigan. When we weren't out enjoying the city, I wrote like a released prisoner telephoning everyone. I'd spend hours on the porch (except in the Arctic winter) writing the free-verse poems of "The Comedy: Dream, Associations, and Waking," experimenting further with meter and rhyme, and struggling with twenty drafts of *Simon and the Shoeshine Boy*, my first play, a full-length expressionist drama.

In the summer of 1964, I met Kenneth Rexroth and Gene Frankel, who were artists-in-residence at the university. Rexroth, a great formalist whose work I loved, was very encouraging about my poetry, *Simon and the Shoeshine Boy*, and *Harold*, a one-act comedy. Kenneth gave the work to Gene Frankel, then New York's most interesting director. Frankel told me he wanted to do *Simon and the Shoeshine Boy* on Broadway as part of a season of four original dramas, with Morris Carnovsky playing Simon and Alvin Epstein the Shoeshine Boy. To a still somewhat naive twenty-four-year-old, building a theater career seemed easy as playing the violin in Carnegie Hall. But then the producer died and along with him my production,

and I was to soon learn that American theater would be a crapshoot I'd eventually stop playing.

One of the disadvantages of being self-taught as a playwright soon caught up with me. I didn't know how to gauge talent in the other theater crafts, particularly the director's. *Simon and the Shoeshine Boy* was done the next year in a series at the Chelsea Theater Center. But when I arrived backstage, Simon was stretched out like Christ on the floor doing "acting exercises" but really spacing out. The director was nowhere in sight. Finally I found him hiding in the light booth. I brought him down to try to wake up the actor. Simon was supposed to begin with an exuberant speech and wind up committing suicide at the end. But the actor committed suicide in the first line.

The next year *Harold* and a companion piece, *Sondra*, were scheduled for production at the Provincetown Playhouse in New York. I chose a director who turned out to be depressed, inadequate, and uncommunicative. The choice was partly masochistic for reasons I described in *Family History*, and partly from a lack of knowledge. *Harold* was a very good

The author with his son, David, 1979

absurdist comedy and would be published as *The Family Circle* in England in Davis-Poynter's Modern Classics series. But the director didn't know what to do with it, panicked, and totally obscured both plays with the kind of shtick that would come to dominate American theater in the sixties and drive many playwrights away from the stage and into film.

In the sixties, partly under the influence of pop-culture theorists like Marshall McLuhan and academic Marxists, American culture was becoming half-witted, all right brain, no left. A "revolution" in communications was taking place as it supposedly was in society. Form in art, particularly if it was linear, was considered not only outmoded but "reactionary." In theater, stage images and movement would no longer supplement but replace the text—as TV was supposed to be replacing books. "Serious" theater, under the influence of groups like the Living Theater and the Open Theater, was to become a director's medium, with visual gimmicks replacing dramatic structure. It was also to become a pop-therapy forum, where actors prodded by directors would throw off the constraints of mere words and talk about the real stuff: their lives, their boring thoughts and childlike feelings, to captive, mystified audiences.

This revolting development was paralleled in poetry, where the large forms of the dramatic and narrative poem were replaced by the narrow mono-dramas of the Confessional Poets and the short autobiographical free-verse lyrics anyone merely wanting to express his feelings could scribble. It was a maddening time for someone who wanted to write well-crafted plays and poems about people other than himself. I found myself feeling like a *samizdat* writer. I was living in a cultural world that talked about "liberating" art from form, which really meant devaluing the writer and his craft.

I found the same destructive attitude toward the text in academic life, which years later would become formalized as deconstructionism. In the seven years of teaching (the act of which I loved) I found the "scholars" who controlled English departments hostile or at best ambivalent to creativity. I felt, as did the other writers I taught with, that the "scholars" seemed to need to see creative work as mere raw material for the real stuff, their articles; and the writer as merely infantile, unaware of what he or she was doing until the critic, by explaining it, gave the work shape.

This attitude was epitomized in a conversation I had at Temple University, where I went to teach in order to be closer to New York. One day, near the

Linda and David, 1987

end of the sixties, I was telling a colleague I was upset that, though I was an assistant professor and had had plays produced and many poems published, I was stuck teaching freshman and sophomore English. "Don't you get it?" he told me with malicious pleasure. "We consider you the Department Nigger. We all envy your virility as a writer so we'll be damned if we let you get into our bag of teaching." Those were his exact words. Bigotry mixed with sixties slang, epitomizing the hypocritical times. A few months later I left teaching.

Linda was also affected by the anti-intellectualism and fashion-mongering of those days. She had taken an M.A. in history at NYU and planned to go for a Ph.D. and teach. But universities were eliminating history courses under pressure from Know-Nothing students who demanded only what was relevant. History was old news, like television reruns, boring. New jobs in the field were not to be found.

So, as the seventies began, Linda took a job with *Library Journal* as a book-review editor, in charge of history and social sciences. Her income gave me the opportunity to try to make a place in the theater with my kind of plays. I determined that if I couldn't make a go of it financially in a couple of years, then I'd find something else to do. I wrote feverishly. I wrote *Masquerade,* a play about Jonathan Swift. It won a prize in the first Audrey Wood playwriting competition and an alternative theater in Washington put it on. There was talk of a commercial production of *Masquerade,* and *Simon and the Shoeshine Boy,* which I'd rewritten, was optioned for Broadway. I wrote *The Children's Revolt,* a play with music about Marie Antoinette and Louis which would win a Rockefeller Foundation–sponsored Office for Advanced Drama Research fellowship and be produced by another alternative theater, in Milwaukee. But it was becoming clear to me that, in an age uncongenial to Aristotelian drama, I wouldn't be able to survive with plays based on plot and character development. In a last-gasp effort, I cofounded a playwright's theater at the Manhattan Theater Club. We wanted to develop work centered on the text rather than directorial shtick. But I found administrative work counterproductive, taking the time and energy I needed to write.

During those two years I finished my first book of poems, *Survivors,* which was made up of mostly short dramatic and narrative poems in meter (which of course was "reactionary" for being "linear"). No large press or university press would touch such an unfashionable book. But the New York bookseller Stanley Lewis (who ran an adventurous small press named after his son) brought it out, and, against all odds, it would be picked by the American Library Association's *Choice* as one of the two outstanding books of poetry for 1975–76. Encouraged in my defiance of what was now the Establishment, I started to structure a long historical poem about New York City. But I found myself walking around Manhattan taking notes on the dramatic vignettes I was seeing, laying the groundwork for what was to become *Manhattan Carnival.*

I found out what I wanted to do for a profession in the hours after I wrote. In my spare time I found myself returning to my interest in psychoanalysis and read one psychoanalytic book after another. I began to talk to Linda about going into psychoanalytic training. Linda was intrigued by the idea and, fascinated by the psychology books she dealt with at her job, began to think of doing it too.

We learned that the National Psychological Association for Psychoanalysis welcomed people from the arts and related academic disciplines. In 1972 we began analytic training that would take a dozen years.

Eventually we'd both develop successful practices. I'd also come to teach one of the final courses to analytic candidates, "Symbolization and Creativity," and out of my work in it begin to develop my own theoretical ideas. Linda would become an excellent, sought-after clinician. But getting there was a financial struggle. As we studied, we built small psychotherapy practices. But that wasn't enough for living in the expensive city New York had become. During the seventies we lived on the edge, with me writing film and television scripts and winning grants like the Guggenheim to keep us going.

By the late seventies I gave up writing plays and concentrated my literary talent on writing poetry. I had already completed *Manhattan Carnival* by 1974, after two drafts. The first was made up mostly of dramatic vignettes with a love story lightly sketched in. Feeling uneasy, I showed the draft to the now well-known Rilke translator Stephen Mitchell. He confirmed my feeling that I should strengthen the story of Mark and Marlene and develop it into a plot, which I did.

Though I felt I found a good dramatic style for myself in *Manhattan Carnival,* I wanted to keep my range of poetry truly open or "expansive," as it would later be called by critics. I wrote lyrics and lyric sequences as well as dramatic and narrative poems. In 1978, when David was born, I wrote the joyous lyrics that would form the first section of *Fathering.* But then, within four months, my extended family was decimated. Renee developed chronic leukemia, Sylvia died, my father died of Guillain-Barré syndrome after taking a flu shot I begged him not to take. The next day Bernie's son committed suicide. A week later, grief-stricken and exhausted, I was sitting in session. Rosalee called and I simply asked her, "Who is it this time?" "Nelson," she said, Belle's second husband.

The sense of loss I learned in childhood when the extended family left or died I was experiencing again. *Fathering* became tragic, a lyric sequence contrasting the joy of my son's birth with my father's death. In 1981 I began *Family History,* partly in an attempt to recapture my extended family and partly for the reasons I gave in the "Afterword" in the *Quarterly Review of Literature* (which awarded it the Colladay Award and published it):

Apart from the obviously intense personal reasons I had for writing *Family History,* I wanted to write an autobiographical poem that wasn't a monodrama—as much Confessional Poetry has been. I wanted to write a narrative poem that would develop the characters of others as fully as I could, given the form. I also wanted to explore further the style I'd begun working with in some of the poems in *Survivors* and in *Manhattan Carnival*. The style combines what is called "formal" in America with idiomatic speech —and hopes to illustrate that there's nothing intrinsically stuffy about form and that, in fact, it can be as natural as prose.

After finishing *Family History,* I wanted to return to the purely fictional poem, as were the shorter monologues in *Survivors* and the book-length dramatic monologue *Manhattan Carnival. Manhattan Carnival*'s vignettes were episodic. Now I wanted to push beyond the episodic and write a series of interlocking dramatic monologues that would develop a more complicated plot and subplot. So I wrote "The Psychiatrist at the Cocktail Party," a long comic poem that appears in *City Life.*

While I was writing *Family History* and *City Life,* I was helping to develop the literary movement later called Expansive Poetry, devoted to opening poetry up to the narrative and dramatic, to combining colloquial diction and form, and to introducing content that would be meaningful to an audience that was finding the short free-verse autobiographical lyric uninvolving.

The movement began in 1981 when Frederick Turner, Dick Allen, and I met. Turner and Allen were also trying to expand the resources of American poetry in their own work, and Turner was doing an important job of it as coeditor of the *Kenyon Review.* He had published most of *Manhattan Carnival* in an issue of the *Kenyon Review* and wanted to meet me. When he came to New York we found we had a lot of ideas in common. We knew others who shared our ideas and were working in compatible ways and should be ready to form a movement that would confront the Establishment.

That weekend we had dinner with Dick Allen at the Minetta Lane Tavern in Greenwich Village and laid plans to put everyone in touch with one another. At first we centered the movement around the *Kenyon Review,* which published several of the key essays that formed our aesthetic. Then, through Dana Gioia, who would become the fourth main driving force of the movement, we discovered that Robert McDowell and Mark Jarman were trying to do on the West Coast what we were trying to do on the East Coast and in the Midwest. Their platforms were their magazine the *Reaper* and their publishing company

Story Line Press, which Robert was developing with his wife Lysa. As the decade passed, each of us developed hard-won but solid reputations and the movement grew. In 1989 Dick Allen edited a special issue of *Crosscurrents* devoted to the movement. Shortly afterwards Story Line brought out a collection of our best essays, which I edited. It is called *Expansive Poetry: Essays on the New Narrative and the New Formalism.* Both the magazine and the essay anthology have begun to create the kind of excitement and controversy we hoped would be helpful to poetry.

As I was finishing the editing of *Expansive Poetry,* I realized my sixth book of poems, *Manhattan Elegy & Other Goodbyes,* was taking shape. It is an elegy for the city of my past, the New York of extended families and neighborhoods—my version of the America many of us mourn.

Manhattan Elegy

The past is like a library after dark
Where we sit on the steps trading stories
With characters we imagined ourselves to be.
Neighbors in clothing from our childhood stroll by
Unmolested, nodding at us benevolently.
One with your father's face tips his fedora.
You lower your eyes in shame. I look back.
Someone is sitting at a long table,
Reading in the moonlight. I must look startled.
He holds a forefinger to his lips
As if it is a candle for the dead.
You tap me on the shoulder and I turn back.
The street is dangerously empty
Except for the newsstand on the corner
Lit yellow where a woman in a nightgown
Showing beneath her blue coat buys the morning
    Times,
A pack of Kools and, eyeing us, lights one.
You race to her, turn a corner. Goodbye.
I'm frightened, as if I am a foreigner
In a city under siege. Yet I know
It is still mid-century. Underground
Are only the subways carrying boisterous
Party-goers or somber family men
Working the night-shift or harmless bookies
Respectful of the No Smoking signs.
I walk to the corner where the newsstand, shut,
Advertises brand names I'd forgotten.
I shove my hands in my pockets and whistle
A song my parents danced to when they were
    young.
I walk on hoping for a passerby,
Even to the burning borough of the Bronx.

Linda and Frederick Feirstein with Frederick Turner, 1988: "This photo was taken by Wade Newman, who named us the Expansive Poets in his Crosscurrents *article."*

Like most elegies, though, *Manhattan Elegy & Other Goodbyes* looks for hope. But as I show in poem after poem, hope doesn't come easily in the demoralizing, drug-ridden, greedy times we live in. Yet when I look at our age from a longer historical perspective and think of the family life and friendships many of us manage to nurture in the face of social chaos, then our present difficulties seem a part of human destiny, endurable with a bit of courage. These two poems from the sequence "A Day in Disney World" perhaps will illustrate that aspect of my present vision:

Spectacle

Out of the shtetl, out of pogrom
(My mother whimpering until America),
My son, nine, sits among macaws and hibiscus
At a white piano bar, handsome
As a movie star, smart as a physicist,
Chess champion, Judo player,
Ignorant (my doing) of his heritage.
We listen to a tinkling
Of T. S. Eliot's poems about cats

Until my son yawns. It is getting late,
Near the end of a millennium.
The sky over Disney World is turning black,
The stars breaking through report light
From a time more primitive than my mother's era.
We leave the gentle fascist to his audience
And rise, American angels, in a glass
Elevator over the posh lobby
Of the hotel with its three story palms,
Its narcotizing fountains.
I stretch out safe on the turned down bed
And nibble the Godiva chocolates the maid left.
My son flicks on the end of a t.v. show
About a war orphan foraging
For roots in the Russian countryside. We watch
Until an artillery of fireworks
Begins bursting over The Magic Kingdom:
Red orange yellow blue indigo violet.
We kneel to watch between the bars of our
    balcony
As my mother, nine, kneeled behind a tombstone
And peeked out at the spectacle of her burning
    town.

Parade

Wheeling down Main Street in technicolor light
Are Disney's heroes, our mythology,
A comfort in the middle of the night.

Mickey Mouse, Minnie, Uncle Donald, help.
The children of America are sick
Of AIDS, religious hypocrites, and greed.
Snow White, Bambi, Lady and The Tramp,
It's midnight now, Help us in our hour of need.

You helped us with the witches' ovens and
Her poisoned mushrooms. Goofy, Pluto, please.
Those childhood traumas were much worse than
   these.
Teach us to be courageous and naive.

BIBLIOGRAPHY

Poetry:

Survivors, David Lewis, 1974.

Walking Away, Advent, 1975.

Manhattan Carnival: A Dramatic Monologue, Countryman, 1981.

Fathering: A Sequence of Poems, Apple-wood, 1982.

Family History, Quarterly Review of Literature, 1986.

City Life, Story Line, 1990.

Plays, selected first productions:

Simon and the Shoeshine Boy, Chelsea Theater Center,
New York, 1966.

Harold [and] *Sondra,* Provincetown Playhouse, New
York, 1967.

The Exhumation and Installation of Robert E. Lee Haines,
Actors Studio, New York, 1971.

John Wayne Doesn't Hit Women (revision of *Sondra*), New
York Theater Ensemble, 1972.

Dr. Rush Pays a House Call, Berkshire Theater Festival,
Stockbridge, Mass., 1973.

The Family Circle (revision of *Harold;* published in
England by Davis-Poynter, 1973), Theater Rapport,
Los Angeles, 1974.

Masquerade, A.S.T.A. Theater, Washington, D.C.,
1974.

The Children's Revolt, Theater X, Milwaukee, 1976.

Manhattan Carnival, The Medicine Show, New York,
1985.

Other:

Also editor of *Expansive Poetry: Essays on the New
Narrative and the New Formalism,* Story Line, 1989.
Contributor to poetry anthologies, including *Contemporary Poetry: A Retrospective from the Quarterly Review
of Literature,* edited by T. Weiss and Renee Weiss,
Princeton University Press, 1976; *New York: Poems,*
edited by Howard Moss, Avon, 1980; and *Strong Measures: Contemporary American Poetry in Traditional Forms,*
edited by Philip Dacey and David Jauss, Harper & Row,
1986. Contributor to literary journals, including the
*Kenyon Review, Ontario Review, Quarterly Review of Litera-
ture,* and *Shenandoah.*

Kay Green

1927-

ROSES ALONG THE WAY

Kay Green at a resort on Mallorca, Spain

At five years old I was notorious. I'd had a brush with the law, lifted what wasn't mine, and dabbled in forgery.

I think it was all to do with the high-legged boots we were forced to wear which labelled us as from "the home." Miss Goslin, the matron at the orphanage, used to sit me on her knee and tell me stories, but she was a stickler for discipline and she and I had some colossal clashes of will. Below the rambling old house, the huge cellar had been converted into a kitchen. There was a stone sink under the only window and little else. Whenever my pans were insufficiently scoured, which was often for I hated

domestic chores even then, she would point to the cellar in a way that brooked no argument and I would stump back down the stairs and fling my pan in the sink. I had a wicked temper in those days.

Once I slammed a pan down and forgot to remove my thumb. It festered and had to be swathed in cotton wool and bandages. Miss Goslin nursed me close to her bosom, and sang me lullabies. She was my anchor in a lonely world.

It was in the subterranean kitchen that I came to know a boy much older than myself. He was very friendly and said he knew some good games. We would stand behind one of the big pillars and he would ask me to do things to him. They seemed odd games to me, especially when he tried to explain something of his anatomy.

Then one day I was summoned to that part of the house that was sacrosanct. In a room filled with solid furniture, I was given a chair against the wall and a policeman started asking me questions. I had no idea why he wanted to know so much about the boy in the cellar, but I felt there was something sinister behind his enquiries, and when he became insistent I burst into tears.

I would dearly have loved to wear shoes like the other children, but rules were rules, and the boots which laced up to the shin were apparently a uniform of "the home." I think the stigma of the boots had a lot to do with my painful reserve in later years.

The other children at school certainly ostracised us because of the boots. I longed to have a friend, and when one day a new girl was put in the desk beside me, to impress her I told her that I had some sweets (pure invention) and that at break time, if she liked, we could share them. Sweets, for those lucky enough to have them, always had to be put on top of a small cupboard during class. When the bell went I filed up to the cupboard and chose a bag of sticky, boiled black-currant sweets. The girl and I were sitting munching happily when my crime was discovered. There was an uproar and I was branded a thief.

One day I found a bankbook on the way to school. I saw it had several sixpences deposited and I felt extremely proud at owning a school bankbook. I scrawled my name inside and joined the queue for withdrawals that very day. Of course my felony was discovered and I sank a notch lower on the way to depravity.

But I think my most heinous act was one day in the school playground. I was standing on my hands when a girl came and dug me in the ribs. I collapsed on my head in a heap, and I was so furious I leapt up and bit her in the chest. Later in the day I was confronted by the mother of the child in the headmaster's study. I stared fascinated at the victim's chest. Now turning slightly brown was a perfect impression of my teeth.

I was told that any more savagery would be a case for the police—a dread word, for I remembered my grilling over the cellar "games." For my wickedness I was made to bite on a bar of soap. When I got back to the orphanage my infamy as a defacer of infant bosoms followed me, and I was made to bite on another bar of soap.

Every Saturday morning I went with an older child to the local butchers to buy the week's supply of meat. I never understood why there was always a tray of freshly baked buns on the counter, but I used to eye those buns with all the longing of a starving cur. The proprietor would smile, take his time in handing me one. Sometimes, oh bliss! he would give me two. He was another anchor in a bleak and hostile world.

I wasn't an orphan. It was the days of the institutions. There were institutions for the poor, for the sick, for the maimed, for the homeless. My father, brothers, and a sister were in an institution. I was in an institution. My mother was in an institution. But my mother was a fighter and as soon as she had recovered from a debilitating illness she was battling with the authorities to reclaim her brood.

Born in Doncaster, orphaned at sixteen, she went to live with a married brother in nearby Mexborough. A small Yorkshire town with neat red-bricked houses and wide avenues, there was employment for the men in the coal pits but little else. She eventually gravitated to Bradford, where work was plentiful.

My father's family hailed from Buckinghamshire. My mother would relate stories of his comfortable background. But somewhere along the way the family money had been lost and, like so many others, my father drifted northwards where industry was booming. The only reminder of his affluent days was a Buckinghamshire newspaper cutting and photograph of my paternal grandmother celebrating her ninetieth birthday, which my mother would get out and show us from time to time.

My mother's name was May Sydney. In Bradford she met and married my father, Wilfred Sutton. She would often recite to us the old proverb "Change your name but not the letter, you marry for worse and not the better."

I think she had a trying time with my father. She would tell us how she dreaded him asking for sausages for his dinner. If one burst during the frying, he would pick up the pan and throw the lot across the room.

I was born on the very last day of the year 1927 in Hall Street, one of a warren of alleys at that time, off the main Leeds road. I remember nothing of that period of my life, but from what I heard later, it seems that Mother and the rest of the family spent most of their time keeping clear of Father.

When I was seven years old Mother won her tussle with the authorities, and she and I and my three brothers were reunited. My sister, fifteen years older than me, had been born mentally retarded. She spent her short life in an institution. My father was considered a danger to his family and did not obtain his ticket of leave. Mother would tell us how he had been a model husband and father until he was thirty-six years old, when his identity changed. She reckoned it was all to do with his mother hitting him over the head with a water jug when he wouldn't get up for work. One wonders if, by this time, my paternal grandmother was feeling the strain of the dwindling family fortunes.

Mother had distant relatives across town and this is where she set up home. Bradford nestles in a valley in the Dales, with main roads climbing out on all sides to other parts of Yorkshire. Our street, Sterling Street, was only a stone's throw from the busy centre. It sloped down the hillside along with dozens of others lining Manchester road, a narrow thoroughfare teeming with horse-drawn carts, trams, double-decker buses, and lorries.

Across the main road from our street, down in the valley, were the woollen mills, huge buildings with great smokestacks which belched smoke all day long. But the employment the mills provided brought a certain prosperity to the community. The shops and businesses lining the busy road thrived, the pubs were full every Friday night, with many a fistfight in the later hours.

Those were the days when the milkman came round door to door, with his gill and pint measures and his churn of fresh cow's milk. There was the pea and pie man; freshly baked pies and hot peas. The staple diet was fried fish and chips, or most of the time a pennyworth of chips, the fish at the exorbitant price of tuppence ha'penny being only for the affluent, or as a Friday-night treat. Pay night was always the most exciting night of the week. If one couldn't rise to an actual fried fish, at least there was the fishcake—two slices of a large potato sandwiching a kind of mashed-up fish, and dipped in batter. Other Friday-night treats I remember were two ounces of dolly-mixtures (a kind of small scented sweet) with which to gamble recklessly on the family card game, and crunchy brandy-snap.

This was my world and I loved it. The rattle of the trams late at night. The early-morning sound of the thickset dray horses pulling the coal carts over the cobbles. The smoke, the dusty streets, the constant clamour of booming industry.

But plans were afoot where I was concerned. Everybody we knew worked at the woollen mill. Mother had had no difficulty in obtaining employment as a spinner. She, however, wanted something better for her family. She apprenticed Ralph, seventeen years old, to a cabinetmaker as a polisher, and

John, fourteen, as a joiner. My younger brother and I were at school but Wilfred, being eleven, was considered adult enough to watch out for himself, whereas I, the baby, posed something of an onus with everyone being out at work all day.

After a family conference it was decided to send me to a boarding school—or what was called an open-air school. The authorities were becoming aware, at this time, of the danger of the smoke-filled valley, and had opened a school on the hilltop at Odsal, a tramride out of town, where the classrooms were walled only on three sides and set in the heart of woodlands and rolling country.

Mother had no trouble in convincing the authorities that I would come to no good playing in the soot, and so I was torn from the family bosom and deposited in the clean air.

Needless to say I hated it. The classrooms looking out onto sombre woods and grey skies were freezing. The crows built their nests in the tall trees and caw-cawed bleakly in the chill air. I lived for the weekends when I was allowed home, but come Monday morning that dread place would loom again. I remember one such morning when I sobbed and pleaded with my brother Ralph not to put me on the tram, but he had his duty and he ushered me aboard, giving me a sheepish wave as I departed weeping bitterly.

I arrived at the school tearstained, smudged, and late. Miss Walker was a formidable type. She had short sandy hair, a matching hoary complexion, and a disposition of steel. She wore mannish shirt-blouses and a tie atop a tweed skirt, and would face the class confident of her power. When I crept into the classroom she paused until all attention was focussed on me, then addressed me with her usual sardonicism. Not only had I arrived late after the privilege of being allowed home for the weekend, I had also returned dirty.

I can still feel the hurt at these words. At the time I was utterly miserable. It wasn't enough that I had been abandoned by my family and banished to an alien place. On top of this I was being held up as an object of ridicule before my classmates. With time children live down these humiliations, but they sometimes leave a scar.

Looking back, the open-air school ought to have been paradise. Everyone had my interests at heart, but as far as I was concerned it was another institution. Oddly enough, I was just coming to terms with the strange environment and proudly displaying the turnips I had grown myself when I was brought home

"My father, Wilfred Sutton, at about thirty years old. Beside him is his concertina which he loved to play."

and installed in St. John's primary school, just a street away from where I lived.

I don't recall putting much effort into my schooling, but miraculously at the age of ten I won a scholarship to go to the then elite high school in an exclusive area of town. Everyone fussed and exclaimed. My three brothers looked upon me with awe and I was regarded as some strange form of intelligent life.

Mother took me to the store in town where the school uniforms were sold. I remember us eyeing the rich-looking blazers with gold braid and smart felt hats in the shop window before turning sadly away. What she made at the mill plus my brothers' apprenticeship wages was barely enough to keep us. There was nothing to spare for luxuries like school uniforms.

I went to the high school in mufti, as it were, but like all Capricornians I resented any kind of upheaval. True to my horoscope, I have fought change all my life, even though most of it has been for the better. I found the school strange and unwelcoming, and I missed my friends. When the question of the school uniform became a major issue, I gladly opted for my old school and mother, relieved to see the end of the dilemma, left it at that.

My old teacher was very unhappy at my return. She knew the value of the education I'd turned down and it greatly upset her that it had all pivoted on the question of a school uniform. Often after that she would call at my home and leave for me a new woollen garment for the winter or warm underclothing she had bought with her own money. There were gems in the teaching profession as well as ogres.

I think the first words that interested me from a literary point of view were those in our school songs: "Philomel with Melody" . . . "Ye Banks and Braes o' Bonny Doon". . . . Each song told a story—like "The Trout":

> As by a crystal brooklet
> I wandered on my way
> Among the gentle ripples
> I spied a trout at play
> And here and there he darted
> As swift as swift could be
> Was never fish so lively
> And frolicsome as he.

As the story goes on to describe the fate of the trout at the hands of a fisherman, we had to put all the nuances and action in our voices as we sang and I loved it. Some of the words to a particular song I sang with gusto were:

> Dirty British coaster with a salt-caked smokestack—
> Butting through the Channel in the mad March days . . .

This song fascinated me. If words conjured up pictures, nothing did it, to my mind, as vividly as these. And with them came a breath of the exotic; something beyond my own small world.

> With a cargo of ivory . . .
> Sandalwood, cedarwood, and sweet white wine.

I think I must have tried to capture the spirit of these songs in the compositions I wrote. They would often make the teacher smile.

Three months before my twelfth birthday the war came. Much of the confusion was over my head, but I remember feeling a childish sympathy for Mr.

Chamberlain, a man, it seemed, with good intentions, but poor political insight.

My two older brothers who were members of the army reserve were among the first to be recruited. Wilfred at sixteen was working alongside Mother in the mill. That left me, once again, a source of worry to the rest of the family. There was a lot of talk about evacuating the children out of the cities to safe zones. I paid no attention to it until I found myself on a train along with hundreds of other children, heading for the open country and rural homes.

It turned out to be one of the happiest periods of my youth. I was billeted outside Ripponden, a village near Halifax. Although only a few miles from Bradford, it could have been another planet. In the summer there were rolling cornfields and green valleys, and the snow in the winter was so deep it left only the tips of the lampposts showing along the road.

Mr. Smith was a fat farmer type. His wife ran the only shop on the route through from Ripponden to Littleborough, in deep country. Their own family were grown up, so I came in for a certain amount of spoiling. Before leaving for school each morning I was given a handful of chocolates, and there was sparkling Vimto and Tizer to be had whenever one developed a thirst.

The Smiths' house was one of three cottages which faced onto the dam of a derelict mill. Here nature abounded. From the forecourt of the cottages you could take the few steps down to a stream gushing through a hole under the road, where red-spotted trout plopped into the dam at the rate of about a dozen a minute. I would try to catch them with my hands, an impossible task, but one always hoped.

An unexplainable mystery to me was when the dam was frozen over in the winter. I would find several trout frozen stiff on top of the ice. Was it possible they had jumped, as trout do, and failed to make it back to the depths before the rime formed? I remember turning one over and over in my hands. I was now face to face with the character in the song. Either way his fate didn't look rosy.

In the summer I would wake at dawn and creep over to my bedroom window. In the early-morning hush I might see a heron stalking in the shallows, a water hen bustling among the weeds. I had never heard of hens swimming before. All this was new and wonderful to me. I would watch with suppressed excitement, sure that I was the only one who knew such things existed.

The dragonflies flitting over the water were another source of astonishment to me. I couldn't believe the fantastic metallic blues and pinks of their bodies. I wanted to capture that beauty for all time and once imprisoned three in an aerated jam jar. I was amazed the next day to find that they had all turned a dull mud colour. Years later I wrote a story using the simile of the lovely dragonflies and their drab other selves.

Henry was the youngest of the Smiths' grown-up children. He was twenty and I was twelve. He was in the army but stationed only a few miles away at Littleborough. He came home regularly and always brought me a present. I remember a smart red-leather purse with a zip along the top which he gave me with his shy smile. When I was twenty I cycled all the way to the Smiths' home to say hello. Henry was by then quite mature, and I had grown up. We went for a country walk and held hands. Henry was a quiet gentle type, but my fate didn't lie in that direction.

Ever since I'd persuaded Mother to buy me a decrepit machine, brightened with blue paint and going for a song in Bradford market, I'd been mad on cycling. Pedalling round the back streets of Bradford

"My mother, May Sutton, at about twenty-seven years old."

had been fun, but out here with mile upon mile of deserted country road the mind boggled. Then an opportunity to take advantage of the space came unexpectedly.

Mrs. Smith fell ill, and so I moved next door to stay with her daughter Elsie and husband, Ray. Uncle Ray had a bike. Unlike my miniature model back home it was a great big country bike with tall wheels and high frame, but I still eyed it longingly, and pestered daily. Finally Ray agreed to let me take it out for a run. The road alongside the cottage coursed downhill for about three miles. I remember doing that stretch proudly without holding the handlebars once all the way down. When I got back to the house, exhilarated after my feat, Ray was waiting for me grimly. He had been watching me from the bedroom window and flatly refused to let me use the bike again.

Not long afterwards my country days came to an end. Mother was not happy about me being shifted next door without being consulted. She saw Elsie, a woman slow of speech and manner, as an unlikely foster mother and promptly took me away.

I was plunged back into the roar and bustle of city life, and unlike Ripponden, where one only heard the sirens faintly across the fields, or the distant crump of guns, the war here was on our doorstep. Mother must have had a latent wanderlust in her which I eventually inherited, for I can remember at least five moves in and around Sterling Street during that period. Houses were cheap in those days. You could rent a "two up and two down" for two and sixpence a week, a mansion for five shillings. At that time we were living at the bottom of the street, and on top of the German targets, the woollen mills, just across the road. The wool was used to make uniforms, therefore strafing at source was considerable.

One evening the mills suffered a direct hit. Unfortunately, the air-raid shelters were situated in the same direction. As the three of us, Mother, Wilfred, and I, ran down the hill, the valley was a holocaust of flames. A piece of shrapnel as big as a soup plate fell at our feet as we hurried for shelter. I remember getting my first crush on the air-raid warden in the dugout where we ended up most nights. He had blond wavy hair and was about thirty-five years old. I would willingly have braved incendiaries and buzz-bombs just for the opportunity of worshipping him from afar.

During this harrowing period my sister, Annie, died. She was twenty-seven years old. I knew her as a strapping matronly woman when we had been to see her on visiting day. She weighed less than six stone when she died. They said it was pneumonia. Mother was sceptical of the findings, but she abided by them. Despite her tussles with officialdom, she had been brought up to fear authority and she instilled this fear in me. This was to prove a considerable handicap in later years when I was making my own way in the world. I would sweat and quake, and lose all ability to function properly when confronted by anyone higher than the tea-boy.

The waxen doll-like figure lay in a coffin under the window. Mother had to go out, so she got a school friend to come and stay with me. We ran up and down the stairs and chased all over the house. Such is the indifference of youth. But I remember being moved when we sang "Rock of Ages" at the funeral. I could never hear the hymn after that without getting a lump in my throat.

Here were words again which gave me food for thought. In a world where books were unheard of (I don't recall being inspired by anything I read at school) it was these occasional brushes with emotive expression which fed a flickering spark in me. And I hadn't settled down to city life as easily this time. Now I had a longing for the open spaces, and whenever the opportunity arose I would take a tram out to Bingley, or Shipley Glen, Thornton or Howarth—Brontë country, which I was only to discover later.

Mother mourned her firstborn more than I could understand. Looking back, I wish I could have been more of a comfort to her. But we are not given compassion until it is sometimes too late.

Apart from the bombs and the shortage of food, growing up in the war years proved no particular hazard for me. I left school at fourteen and was apprenticed to a dress-pattern firm. But after two weeks of being cooped up in a room lined with pigeonholes with only a list of figures for company, mother relented and took me with her to work in the mill. I had six glorious months in the spinning section running my own machine as long as a cricket pitch, but the novelty wore off and I was already developing itchy feet.

For want of something better I developed an affinity with a sewing machine, and suppose I must have helped the war effort sewing army holdalls for a firm on war work. It was here that I met Joan. She was small of build and extremely thin. A most unlikely candidate for the footlights, but it turned out she was taking tap-dancing lessons and expected to go on tour with a pantomime. I crammed a tap-dancing course at the same school and also won a place in the chorus. We toured with G. H. Elliot, "the chocolate coloured coon.'' He had known considerable fame in the music halls, blacking his face and singing minstrel songs. Now, getting on in years, and reduced to a third-rate show, he still had a quiet dignity and was greatly liked by all. I saw him take a ten-shilling note out of his wallet (a lot of money in those days) and give it to a stage-door Johnnie who spun him a hard-luck story.

The tour did not live up to my expectations. I was already romanticising the mundane. There were dreary train rides every Sunday, to even drearier cities like Sunderland, Middlesborough, Gateshead. The dressing rooms were tawdry, the digs cheerless. After six weeks smoky Bradford seemed a haven.

Wilfred had failed his medical for the army. A patch had been discovered on his lung. He was sent to Grassington, a country sanitarium bursting at the seams with tuberculosis patients. But the weekly bus rides on visiting days were a treat for me.

Mother and I had to manage alone. John, an army sergeant, was training recruits in Scotland. We had almost lost Ralph, now stationed in the Middle East. Unable to swim at Dunkirk he had been up to his chin in the sea before someone had hauled him into a boat. Instead of allaying Mother's fears for the family unit, I added to them.

The blackout was so complete at nighttime, you could barely see a hand before you. Ever since a school friend of mine had been found murdered on a lonely path on the way to school, I had been terrified of the dark. This didn't stop me popping over the main road one night, to the fish-and-chip shop. Package in hand, I was returning over the road when my imagination convinced me that someone was creeping up behind me. Glancing wildly over my shoulder, I ran for all I was worth and flew smack into an electricity box at the side of the road. Fortunately for me, a father and son were passing by in the dark. They heard groans in the roadway and pulled me clear from the path of an oncoming bus. Dead-set against the idea in the first place, Mother almost swooned when I was delivered home still clutching the blood-stained package of chips. We had to cross the main road again to a police box, where a pad was put over my eye and an ambulance called. I had stitches in the cut but nobody paid any attention to the egg-sized lump on the back of my head where I had hit the road. This lump plagued me for many months, then one evening when I sat in the cinema I felt it ease as a warmth trickled down my head. After that it never bothered me again.

These incidents are linked in my mind because it was at the cinema—or the "tuppeny rush," as it was

"With my mother at age two"

called—that I found fodder for my fertile imagination. I would spend every cent I could earn watching films that were making fortunes in those days. Stories like *Mrs. Miniver*—*Blossoms in the Dust*—*Love Affair,* where Irene Dunne is hurrying to meet the love of her life at the top of the Empire State Building, and looking up gets knocked down by a car. Because she is crippled she never lets the man know what has happened. And he assuming she has let him down marries someone else. They were real tearjerkers.

Charles Boyer was the big heartthrob at that time. I adored him in *Algiers* where Hedy Lamarr, as the woman who loved him deeply, was tricked into betraying him to the police. Marlene Dietrich and Boyer starred in an earlier film, *The Garden of Allah.* Though nothing like the book (which I was to discover later), the story had a haunting quality which affected me greatly.

There were the war films like *The Mortal Storm, Three Comrades,* and those typifying the American way of life which were immensely popular. Though they boasted some of the finest actors, they're considered syrupy and unreal today. But they were a tremendous source of inspiration at the time, and I truly believe, to our generation, they were the main motivator in many of us to improve our lot. Today the young have their pop idols, but little else to aspire to.

With the coming of video many of us can "wallow" again. There was a fantasy romance which fascinated me in the old days—*The Thief of Baghdad*. I went to see it six times. It was the first video I ever bought and to me it's still a wonderful story. Some years back I acquired a brand-new edition of Robert Hichens's *Garden of Allah*. I've read it several times. It has pride of place on my bookshelf. To my mind it is one of the most beautifully written works ever published.

There's probably some indication here which way I was heading, but the romances I fantasised had no relation to those budding in my own life.

The boys had an added fascination in uniform. I played fast and loose like most girls of my age. One summer evening I was chatting to Ernest, a strapping army sergeant, in his jeep outside the house, when I remembered I had promised to see Eric, an aircraftsman. I had to make some excuse and dash round the corner. I was only just in time, for Eric was halfway up the street (we had moved house again). I told some lame story that I couldn't go out. He went away sad and disappointed. Enjoying the popularity, at the time I didn't feel at all heartless.

But though I dated, they were fleeting affairs and did nothing to fulfil the need I had, for what I wasn't sure.

I'm not certain how I discovered the town library. I think a friend told me you could actually walk in there, choose any book you liked, and take it home free of charge. It sounded crazy to me, but I tried it and found it worked. I chose a book at random. I've never forgotten it. A mystery, it was about a corpse found in a locked room with a dog. The dog had got so hungry it had chewed the corpse's head off. I read boggle-eyed for a while but lost interest when the gory details gave way to supposition.

I had no yardstick for reading. I chose books with visible appeal rather than for their contents. I have always liked the look and feel of a handsome book. I don't ever recall seeing a book in our house. Reading was considered a waste of time. Whenever I retreated to a corner to lose myself in some saga, the cry would go up, "She's got her head in a book again."

Towards the end of the war my father died. I recall sitting on his knee when an aunt brought him to visit us once. He had a moustache and fierce eyes and I could feel the rough serge of his suit. That's the only memory I have of him.

I met a boy who played in a dance band. He was a keen cyclist. We cycled all the way to Liverpool, caught the ferry, and cycled round the Isle of Man. We had a difference of opinion over food. He was so mean with his money he bought himself barely enough to survive on. Cycling is a strenuous sport, and I was about to keel over, so I wandered off on my own to find a restaurant. Most of them were closed for the afternoon. In desperation I pounded on the door of a cafe of reasonable appearance. A pretty middle-aged woman came to open the door. She was most obliging and sat with me throughout my meal, chatting pleasantly and eyeing me thoughtfully. A tall Negro passed through the room towards the outdoors. She called him over and introduced us, repeating what I had told her, that I was drifting round the island on a bike. They exchanged glances and he left. While I was finishing my sweet, she offered me a job in the cafe with good pay. I declined simply because the idea didn't appeal to me. It wasn't until years later when I came to know the ways of the world that I realised I had walked straight into a brothel.

I said good-bye to my cycling sweetheart and took up roller-skating. There was a small rink adjoining the Hippodrome cinema which my friends and I haunted. To glide round at high speed between two boys in trios, to blaring music, was to us the thrill of a lifetime. Then much to our dismay, the rink closed to make way for a supermodern one on Manningham Lane. This didn't have the friendliness or the intimacy of our old rink, but we had nothing else, so we were obliged to patronise it.

One evening I was making an attempt to skate backwards when I collided with a young man. He said he would show me how it was done, and he's been doing just that for the past forty years. He was known as Fred to his friends, but I thought Gavin, his second name, had more dash, and he's been Gavin ever since.

A native of neighbouring Leeds, he had been reading since he was three years old, and in later years had developed a taste for American literature. He introduced me to Sinclair Lewis, O. Henry, Mark Twain. Soon I was as hooked as he was on the American way of life.

He was full of ideas. I was reserved in my thinking. To Gavin anything was possible. Whereas I shirked meeting anyone outside my own station, he thrived on striking up friendships with people from all walks of life. The social ladder meant nothing to him. He simply enjoyed getting to know people.

Twenty-five years old and ex-RAF, he had several schemes afoot to make money. He was excited about the potato-crisp business but lacked the funds to get launched. I was sewing tailored shirts for wealthy mill owners at the time. Gavin was working on a Hoffman press, but that was just a standby occupation, one that he was to turn to often over the lean years, just as I found a sewing machine handy.

A few weeks after our meeting he acquired the position of skating manager at a Butlin holiday camp, and invited me to accompany him. I got a job as a barmaid at the same camp, and we took the train together to Pwllheli in North Wales. It was while the train was negotiating a stretch of track between sombre mountains that I suddenly felt unsure in strange surroundings, and burst into tears. Gavin comforted me without really understanding my bout of nerves. To him life was just one big adventure and the future always looked rosy.

"Gavin and me on the Butlin's Roller Rink," 1949

As it turned out, it was one of the most wonderful summers of our lives. That year, 1949, the sun shone almost every day. After my stint at the Pig and Whistle serving Double Diamond to the campers, and flirting barmaid style with the male element, I would join Gavin on the rink. One of his patrons was Freddie, the son of Haile Selassie, Emperor of Abyssinia (now Ethiopia). We had the use of all the amenities at the camp, and were served the same meals as the campers. On days off we would visit the local beauty spots, discovering the ethereal shapes of transparent shrimps swimming in the clear water at Criccieth—a phenomenon to us city-bred types. We always thought shrimps were bright pink!

It was an idyllic existence, but one that left us totally unprepared for the coming winter. We had decided that we wanted to spend the rest of our lives together and, having tied the knot, drifted around Wales still under the influence of being cushioned by a big organisation.

We took a train to Aberystwyth because it sounded interesting, found nothing there but the university and a cluster of languid students. We visited Caernarvon Castle. In Swansea, the money we had saved during the summer ran out and we were forced to hitch a lift up north.

My three brothers were married. Mother had sold the home and gone to live with an aunt of hers in Manchester. We put up there for a week or two, then found a house and dry-cleaner's shop in Salford. We soon discovered why the rent was so low. The surroundings were grim, the clientele nonexistent. I did a brisk business a few weeks before Christmas dressing dolls for local customers.

Our daughter, Valerie, was born under the grey skies of Manchester, and our son not long afterwards. But when Philip was a month old, we decided we'd had enough of industrial cities and moved to the seaside at Blackpool. Gavin passed an audition for the Blackpool ice show, and I had a high old time taking the children on the beach every day.

Gavin was an avid reader. He could get through a book in an evening. He soaked up information like a sponge, whereas I tended to read deeply, to analyse. I read *Jane Eyre,* couldn't get on with Dickens, and was greatly attracted to Somerset Maugham after seeing the film *The Moon and Sixpence.* It seemed inconceivable to me that a man should want to leave his comfortable way of life, his wife, his family, for something as capricious as art. Today I can understand that.

I was attracted to Maugham's writing often after that. I loved his *Liza of Lambeth, Cakes and Ale*—and of course I had seen his *The Letter, The Razor's Edge, Of Human Bondage* on film. Much of what I saw at the cinema influenced my reading. The two were, and still are, my twin loves.

Both Gavin and I were interested in writing, but living was taking up all our time. We'd tried different ways of making money: selling jewellery by post from somewhere deep in the Welsh mountains, sewing garments for wholesalers. I'd made up a blouse and sent it off. We got an order back for ten thousand. Riches, but we had only one sewing machine! In Blackpool we made plastic neckties for the holiday trade.

Having put together a comedy act with a friend, Gavin signed a contract for a summer show in Bournemouth. Our stay there lasted fourteen years. Bournemouth is a gracious old town on the south coast. Many celebrities have made their homes in the exclusive residential districts like Canford Cliffs and Talbot Woods. We used to see John Creasey, the prolific author of crime novels, typing at his open window overlooking Horseshoe Common, a charming little park bordered by graceful houses. And Dennis Wheatley was a regular visitor to the locale from his home in the nearby New Forest. A well-known journalist typed out his pieces on the porch of his beach chalet.

I don't think it was this wealth of talent on the doorstep, so much as our own personal quest, that led us to buy a typewriter. We rented rooms in a lovely old Victorian house adjoining Horseshoe Common (both featured in *Across the Lagoon*). While Gavin skated in the evenings and the children were asleep, I would tap out little bits on the typewriter. When I read them back they didn't seem to make much sense. It was only later that I learned that writing is *feeling*, not just arranging words prettily on a page.

Gavin was such a success in the ice show, he was given the opportunity to tour with "Holiday-on-Ice." This presented us with a dilemma. The thought of world travel was mouth-watering, but the children were young, and they would need schooling. Neither of us cared for the idea of separation, so reluctantly we turned the offer down.

Soon after that the owner of the Victorian house died. We were made homeless. Bournemouth is a holiday town. The rents then were (and probably still are) exorbitant. Carting the children round, looking for something practical, I became the angry young woman and my writing career was born. I wrote a scathing letter to the *Bournemouth Echo* berating Bournemouth landladies, and the sedate owners of large houses, who looked upon small children as

"Our children, Valerie and Philip, on a trip to London," 1953

vermin. It caused a furore, as the editor knew it would, and missiles were fired back and forth through print for weeks after.

I was exhilarated at the fight but there was no money in it, and we needed money more than ever just to pay the rent. The ice show had come to an end. Gavin found a Hoffman press. I worked evenings when he was home with the children at a variety of occupations. I served tea to customers in a Lyons cafe and made such a hit over the counter I was ear-marked for manageress training. More to my taste, as an ice-cream girl in the Westover cinema, I got to see snippets of films showing at the time: *Rebel without a Cause, High Society, Bhowani Junction*—the latter starring Stewart Granger. His mother lived in Talbot Woods. When she came to see her son on the screen, the red carpet was laid out for her. She was a tall woman with angular features and blue-rinsed hair. I caught sight of her profile against the spotlight as I served ice creams. It was like looking at Stewart Granger in the dark.

We had decided that Bournemouth was a good place to raise our children, but sometimes it was a case of hanging on with our teeth. Employment was scarce, accommodation a disaster. We would just get settled when the season was upon us and we had to move out to make way for the holidaymakers. We shunted around, working long hours, crippled by high rents. But we did rear our children in beautiful surroundings; something they, and we, have always been thankful for.

I used my pen often in those days to let off steam, especially when our daughter, Valerie, passed all her exams to go to grammar school, but was denied the privilege because of shortage of places, those excelling in maths taking precedence. Many other mothers were up in arms and the *Bournemouth Echo* was once again the battleground for the fors and againsts. But apart from this and the odd guinea here and there for letters to magazines, I made little headway as a writer.

I didn't have Gavin's flair for stepping out of line. He sat down and wrote a screenplay—"Johnny Bull"—and was invited to London. Aptly, at the time we were living in an area close to the sea where everywhere was named after the poets. There was Shelley Avenue, Browning Avenue, Byron Close. We lived on Wollstonecraft Road, Mary being the second wife of Shelley and paradoxically the author of *Frankenstein.* Gavin met Patricia Green (now a Hollywood producer) in London and sold an option on his film for twenty-five pounds. Some time later he optioned it again for a hundred pounds, but though the second party were keen, they couldn't raise the production money.

I was cautiously trying my hand at writing picture strips for teenage romances and gathering a nice supply of rejection slips. I had always viewed life through a romantic haze. At thirty-five, with nothing but hard work and little reward to draw on, I suppose I was ripe for the kind of romantic fiction which transports you to exotic places, where a superhuman hero (nearly always wealthy) tenderly provides and shelters you from the storms of life.

I found my escapism here. I had discovered Mills and Boon, and would haunt the library for my favourite authors. It's curious that the only three (out of some sixty-odd in those days) I could read avidly turned out to be one and the same author. I learned this years later from Alan Boon. The woman behind Kathryn Blair, Rosalind Brett, Celine Conway, wrote with enviable restraint, while brilliantly portraying romance in all its subtleties. I tried to emulate her, as did many others, but hers was a unique talent. Typically she was not appreciated. Probably in rebellion, her last novel, left unfinished when she died tragically in a car crash, was laced with drugs, sex, abortion. Of course, after reading it, Alan Boon wouldn't touch it with a barge pole. It's sad that she was lauded after she died, and a great fuss made on each reissue of her books. One in particular was *The House at Tegwani,* considered to be among her best. But I was just a reader at the time, and though I experimented with other authors, they lacked something that I found in her writing.

Of the top musicians around in those days, Tony Osborne wrote "The Swinging Gypsies" and Acker Bilk "Stranger on the Shore." Both tunes appealed strongly to my imagination and I wrote lyrics and sent them off. I received a harsh reply from the Acker Bilk management instructing me not to tamper with people's music. Tony Osborne, on the other hand, wrote me a charming letter telling me that he liked my lyrics very much, but felt that the musical piece should stand as it was.

I retired into my shell and didn't emerge until an urge to put some kind of romantic thoughts on paper had me retiring to the bedroom each evening while the rest of the family watched television. I must have been what is called dedicated, to sit down with a pen after a day's work sewing overalls, plus household chores. But somehow I got a story together and tentatively sent it off to *Woman's Weekly.* They were doing digests then, of two or three authors in one volume, and that was as near to a real book as I felt equal to. But even this seemed a shot too high. I received a terse rejection note in which the editor explained that the story I had written was not very clear. I experienced the abysmal misery that only a writer knows when his/her work returns unwanted. Then I got mad. I had been accused of woolly writing. Well, I would make sure that the next story was crystal clear. It turned out to be useful criticism.

I was having a frustrating time on the reading front. I couldn't find one of my favourite authors in the bookshops, and I had read and reread those in the library. This was a publishing lack I experienced in my own writing career. Friends and acquaintances I met later in different countries would ask the same question, "We never see any Roumelia Lane books in the shops. Why is this?" I rarely saw any myself and hopefully assumed they had all been sold. But why no fresh supply?

Sir Bernard Chacksfield, the author, husband Gavin, and a friend, 1984

It was this lack of my favourite reading matter which drove me to produce something which might prove equally satisfying creative-wise. I suppose we write what we would like to read, and I needed the escapism of romance.

The *Sunday Times* had a colour supplement. I was browsing through it and came across photographs and an article all about the oil fields in Tripoli. (This was long before the oil crisis.) It gave me an idea for a novel. I set to work. I hadn't been writing long when I experienced a curious nervous distress. It was probably my subconscious battling with my inherent dislike for change, which had kept me hanging on to my sewing machine. One evening I came home from the daily stint, and knew I couldn't go back. It goes to show what a wonderful family I have when I state here that they were unanimous in their support. Though it would mean less in the weekly kitty, all agreed that I should stay home and write.

I called my novel *Rose of the Desert* after the pieces of sandstone blown into rose shapes by the desert winds and, of course, the heroine, Julie, an oil-field secretary who clashes with the hard-bitten field manager, Clay Whitman. I took my pen name from a

little back street I used to pass every day on the way to work. When I look back, I don't know how I managed to tap out sixty thousand words on a typewriter. I've never got on with machines. I was always happier with pen and exercise book; Gavin (never known to stop at anything) took the typing of all my books in his stride. All I can say about that first manuscript is, it must have been pretty rough.

I was uncertain where to send it. Gavin had read Dale Carnegie's *How to Win Friends and Influence People.* I think it was here that he had come across the advice "Always go to the fountainhead." And from this had evolved his own philosophy, "Always aim for the top." He thought I should send it to Mills and Boon. I was awestruck. Mills and Boon were not only the biggest (if not in size, in prestige) publishers of romantic fiction in Britain, they had also cornered the market.

I overcame my nerves and in June 1966 sent off *The Rose of the Desert.* I didn't hear anything for four months. In October I wrote a letter of inquiry and received a reply almost at once from Alan Boon saying that they liked the book and wanted to publish it. There was one condition. I had strayed from the house style at the end of the story by leaving the heroine in a tricky position and concentrating on the hero. This would have to be corrected, so that everything was seen from the heroine's point of view.

I was in such ecstasies at being accepted, I think I would have written the entire story backwards to conform. I wasn't aware at the time how restricting house style can be.

Rose of the Desert was published in the spring of 1967. By that time I had completed *Hideaway Heart.* We were living in a pleasant garden flat. Valerie at seventeen was doing prenursing training at the Victoria Home for Crippled Children. Philip, a mathematical wizard, had had no trouble getting into grammar school and was moving towards his A levels. I was more or less launched. Gavin felt it was now safe to try his own luck.

He had had several writing successes, supplying material for top TV comedians, and publishing short stories and articles, but he hadn't the staying power for long-term projects (I was always the plodder) and liked to experiment. It's typical of him that he applied on this occasion for a top position in the Central Office of Information in London. Out of the three hundred applicants, narrowed down to a shortlist of ten, he walked away with the job, and later proved he had the flair for it by producing the scripts for the *Concorde*'s maiden voyage to the USA, British Week at Macy's, New York, The Royal Tournament of 1968 at Earl's Court, London, plus public relations for the Investiture of Prince Charles, etc.

While I was extricating my heroine from the hands of the villain, Gavin was rubbing shoulders with Princess Margaret in the royal-box enclosure, meeting the Chiefs of Staff of the armed forces (among whom was the descendent of Captain Cook), visiting the Microbiological Establishment along with the Duke of Edinburgh. Working on the "World of Shakespeare" for the British Exhibition in Tokyo, a portrait of the Bard was required. Lord Montagu of Beaulieu was known to have one in his collection, so Gavin got in touch. It was while he was talking on the phone to Lord Montagu that an amusing incident came to mind. On a family outing to the Beaulieu stately home years before, Gavin spotted a sailing craft about to cast off on the river and, without thinking twice, dashed up, family in tow, and asked if it was the ferry to Buckler's Hard. About to enjoy a sail with a group of friends, Lord Montagu at the wheel wasn't sure whether he was having his leg pulled or not. Without letting his face slip, he replied that, no, it wasn't the ferry. It was only when we

turned away that we realised who it was we'd taken for the ferryman.

Christmas 1968 we had our first holiday abroad. With only a week to go before the festive season, booking was heavy. All Gavin could come up with after scurrying round the London travel agents was a week in Mallorca. I was disappointed. I had pictured somewhere traditionally snowy, maybe singing carols in some rollicking Swiss tavern. Also the stories we had heard about Mallorca suggested it was no more than a glorified appendage of English seaside resorts at their worst.

We bought the plane tickets simply because there was nothing else (strange how fate decides for us) and immediately fell in love with the island when we arrived. We went to see the usual tourist sights— Chopin's living quarters along with George Sand's in a monk's cell in Valldemosa, the Gardens of Alfabia, Lluch Monastery. But I think it was these trips into the hinterland of pine-clad hills, gnarled olive trees, lonely hermitages perched on mountain tops, which opened up another world for me; one to which I had a curious feeling I belonged. It was as though I'd come home. It may sound corny, like something straight out of one of my own books, but Mallorca had a magic for me. I felt it instantly. And in the twenty years I've been fortunate enough to reside here, that magic has not diminished.

In our usual nonchalant way, we decided before we left that we would be back. We gave ourselves a year to settle our affairs and sell the home we had got together. I had written six novels by then, the latest one being *Sea of Zanj.* This had been sparked off by pictures and an article in the *National Geographic* magazine. I had discovered some old *Geographic*s in a bookshop and considered them gold for writing. The information was invaluable, the pictures superb for description, and in those days I relied heavily on them, not having firsthand knowledge of exotic places, a must for Mills and Boon books. But we did manage a trip to Italy in that year, visiting Cortina and Venice, and the latter I was able to draw on for *Across the Lagoon.*

We had a little soul-searching before we burnt our boats. Or should I say I did? To Gavin it was just another adventure. He gave up the job he enjoyed at COI and promptly got himself a retainer with one of the biggest advertising agencies, Young and Rubicam, as Market Intelligence Adviser for Spain. I was forty-two, an odd age, I thought, to be scooting off to some Mediterranean island. Not a bit of it. Gavin put everything into perspective in his inimitable way.

Philip was installed in Canterbury University. Valerie was training to be a nurse at a London Mission hospital. We had reared them in the best possible surroundings often at a cost to ourselves. Now it was time to do a little living of our own.

So with just £825 in the bank we booked an hotel in Mallorca for two weeks. After that we were on our own. There are monstrosities on the coast which give the island its bad name, and inevitably our hotel was situated in one of these spots, but we knew of that other world far removed from the tourist belt, and we were not dismayed. Valerie and Philip were having a last fling before settling down to studies, and we all thoroughly enjoyed ourselves regardless of the infamous El Arenal surroundings.

Someone had heard of our determination to pioneer on the island. One evening while we were dining, the waiter brought a card to our table. It announced "Air Vice-Marshal Sir Bernard Chacksfield, KBE, CB, FRAeS, RAF (Retired), and Lady Chacksfield." I had a hard time trying to give the appearance of sangfroid. Gavin might take these kind of titles in his stride. I tended to want to scuttle away and hide. As it turned out, they were the most genuine couple one could wish to meet, and from that first encounter, when they voiced an interest themselves in buying a *pied-à-terre* on the island, blossomed a friendship which has lasted twenty years. It cured my inherent fear of authority. Bernard, a giant of a man, proved invaluable, delivering my typescripts to Alan Boon in London, and acting as a go-between in various negotiations. And this from a man who was a fighter pilot in the Royal Flying Corps and who has an inexhaustible supply of stories to tell on aspects of his career, including his close friendship with Lord Mountbatten, and his meetings with the royal family. Myrtle, his wife, had been born in India, and could talk at length on the colonial days. As a writer I couldn't have asked for more colourful companions.

When our two weeks were up, we said good-bye to the children, collected the family dogs, Mitch and Andy, from the kennels, and set up home in yet another flat, this one bought for all of ten pounds deposit. One has to smile now when one thinks of the easygoing Mallorcans in those days. They're a lot more businesslike now. The picture window of our studio-flat overlooked a blue bay. The view was fabulous, but we wanted a house of our own and eventually found the one of our dreams outside a village called Santa Eugenia. We had only thirty-six pounds in the bank at the time. This didn't stop us deciding that this was the house for us, and we signed all the legal papers. Nowadays one would go grey at

the thought, but once again, thanks to the trusting Mallorcans, who even waived the rule that we would lose our deposit if we didn't find all the cash in time (the cavalry arrived in the form of an advance from Alan Boon several days late), we got the house by the skin of our teeth.

While house-hunting my writing output had been poor. I eventually completed *The Scented Hills* and sent it off. After waiting several weeks, I received a terse letter from Alan lightly rapping me over the knuckles for not keeping in touch. It was the first sour note in our relationship. He had enthused over my books while I was in England and had wanted me to travel down to London so that we could have lunch together. In those days I was in horror of meeting anyone as exalted as a publisher and, convinced that I would choke over the meal, had declined the offer. Finding my feet in Mallorca, I was under the impression that, as I had nothing to offer, there was little point in getting in touch. He considered it my duty to let him know what I was up to, and perhaps he was right. *The Scented Hills* had a cool reception.

Once we were established in Casa Mimosa, I began to draw on local colour and produced *Cafe Mimosa* (we named the house after the book). This was received joyfully in London, and I felt secure once again. When we weren't working, we indulged ourselves in travel, doing the whole of the Costa del Sol by bus. We saw Spain in the raw, as well as the beautiful white villages of the south, touching on Granada, Seville, Jerez, and even stretching our resources by crossing the Guareña River and exploring the near reaches of Portugal. One never-to-be-repeated trip was a tortuous five-hour journey from Málaga to Almería atop steep cliffs, with the wheels of the bus only an inch from dizzying drops into the sea. It was the longest five hours of our lives.

During our stopover in Seville we had a peculiar experience which I later used in *The Tenant of San Mateo.* The hostel we had booked for the night was an ancient establishment still steeped in an atmosphere of about a hundred years before. Our room was a small L-shaped affair with two single beds in the narrow section. Beside the beds was a low window which gave a view of a well courtyard where the rain pattered persistently on the huge potted palms. I had been lying awake for some time thinking idly when Gavin suddenly sat up and put on the light. When I asked what was wrong he couldn't explain. He said all the hairs were standing up on his arms and he sensed an invisible presence in the room. This coming from Gavin was laughable. His was the logical mind. I was the one with the overactive imagination, who saw shadows round every corner, and I hadn't felt a thing. But I had to admit there was something eerie about the darkened courtyard outside, where the palms glistened in the light from the room, and something equally eerie about the bleak interior, with its bare table at the far end and a shuttered window on the opposite wall. We agreed to leave the light on while we tried to get some rest, but when the shutter on the wall suddenly creaked open of its own volition, all thoughts of sleep vanished and we sat wide-eyed until the first sounds of the hostel staff brought some small reassurance. We examined the shutter in the morning. The closed window behind adjoined an unused room. There were no open doors or draughts, no explanation as to why the shutter should suddenly unlatch itself and creak open in the middle of the night.

We saw the Louvre in Paris, the Tivoli Gardens of Copenhagen, crossed the split on a hydrofoil and saw a little of Sweden in Malmö. Once when we went to Tangier we became political pawns in a row between Spain and Morocco. Because we had journeyed from Spain and had for our occupation "Writer" on our passports, we were given the cold-war treatment and held up for half an hour while the rest of the ferry passengers gaped as though we were some prize terrorist catch. To make matters worse, when we were finally freed and a figure in djellabah and fez came rushing up gesticulating excitedly, I told him, in a few choice words, where he could go. Unfortunately it turned out Ahmed was our guide for the day. His pride wounded, it was some time before he would forgive my faux pas. But eventually we became bosom friends. During working hours as he was taking us through the Casbah, which wafted strongly of urine, he met his wife (or one of them), a black-shrouded shape in yashmak. While they were discussing some domestic matter, and he handed over something to help with the housekeeping, I had time to admire his pointed yellow slippers.

My writing career was going through a series of ups and downs. I was feeling the restrictions of formula romance and would keep adding a dash of adventure, even danger, for my heroine to cope with. This kind of straying from house style was severely frowned upon by the editors and I was pulled into line by readers' adverse criticism. It's a curious thing that the books which received the thumbs-down sign from the readers made the most money. Alan Boon, who had faith in my work, had the last word in those days. Harlequin, the giant Canadian publishers, were Mills and Boon's lifeline. They were considered

tough to deal with and only the cream of Mills and Boon writers were accepted for publication. I'm proud to say that almost all my books were sold through Harlequin.

Casa Mimosa looks out onto an almond orchard above which, in the near distance, rises the village of Santa Eugenia, with its windmills, on the lower slopes of a mountain. The house is situated at the side of a disused railway track. On the other side of the track is an old Mallorcan cottage. I got the idea that both houses would compete for ownership of the track to convert it into a much-needed driveway, and put the hero in one house and the heroine in the other. I added Twiggy, our cat at the time, and Mitch, our cairn poodle, disguised under the name of Dale. The result, *Stormy Encounter,* left the readers cold, but it was one of my top money earners. I read a charming little write-up of the book in a magazine in which the reviewer fell in love with the antics of the dog and the cat!

In actual fact we did later have a tussle over the track with a sea captain who eventually bought the Mallorcan cottage. He was so angry when we acquired the track, he tried to run Gavin down with his

"My good friend Merle Chacksfield, author of Armada *and* The Glorious Revolution.*"*

"Son, Philip, boating on the Norfolk Broads in the 1970s"

car. But those days are long gone and now he tolerates us.

Once again, I used the old *finca* on another hill, looking east from Casa Mimosa, and placed in it a golf-course designer (hero) living there without the permission of the owner (heroine), who has come all the way from England to take up residence there herself, but who, because of some clause in the rent contract, can't get rid of her tenant, and is compelled to dig in on the lower decrepit floors—haunted of course—while he lives in comparative luxury and old-world splendour on the upper floors. The publishers loved this one, *The Tenant of San Mateo.* And that's how it was. A minor triumph every once in a while.

In that same year, 1976, my brother Ralph died. From his army days he had developed a liking for drink and it had finally lowered his resistance to living at the early age of fifty-seven. I must have used up all my tears, for when, two years later, my youngest brother Wilfred collapsed and died, I didn't shed one. But the grief went much deeper. Closest in age, we had grown up together, and I can still remember those nights in Woodroyd Road Home when he would sing from his bed in the boys' dormitory, to me in the girls' dormitory below. We would all lie and listen as his clear contralto drifted down:

> Roses whisper goodnight
> 'Neath silvery light
> Asleep in the dew
> They hide from our view
> When the dawn peepeth through
> God will wake them and you

When the dawn peepeth through
God will wake them and you.

Living on an island away from it all, we had lots of time for reading. We bought all the classics to fill the bookshelves. I read Kafka, Chekhov, gave up with Plato. The complete works of Shakespeare I haven't attempted yet. Conversely those of Somerset Maugham I read avidly, one after the other, a rare feat for me. Perhaps because he has a very easy style. I remember his advice to budding scribes was to write as though you are writing a letter to a friend. I think this is good advice, and it was probably paramount in getting me started. The *Hola* magazine gave me an insight into the Spanish way of life. Together with its colour photographs of celebrities around the world, I learned to read Spanish out of a burning curiosity to know what was going on.

The first Spanish novel I attempted was *Valz Mefisto,* actually a translation of an American author's *The Mephisto Waltz.* The plot was so gripping and the translation so superb, I read it from cover to cover with little difficulty. Later, perhaps because of writing so much fiction myself, I developed a liking for biographies. I've always been passionately interested in people, and this is now my mainstay in reading. I keep abreast of the current best-sellers by reading them in Spanish.

We improved Casa Mimosa whenever resources would allow. The writing of romantic novels provided certain comforts, but not riches. They were never that. On our shopping visits to the city of Palma, for fruit trees, etc., I would often see a tall figure in black suit and Cordoba hat striding down the Borné—a tree-lined avenue where the Mallorcans stroll in the evening. This striking personality, I discovered later, was none other than the poet Robert Graves. Once when we passed close by on the pavement, his glance caught and held mine, and for a second I felt something like—not exactly the meeting of kindred spirits, considering the tremendous gulf between his work and mine, but an empathy. Later when our daughter, Valerie, nursed him in the Clinica Miramar, she described him as cheerful and absentminded. His books, pens, and papers were scattered over the room, and each time she went in, he was in a different bed. Valerie and his wife, Beryl, whom she nursed six weeks later, became good friends, and Helen Graves, their daughter-in-law, is one of Valerie's walking companions.

Valerie fell under the spell of the island in 1973. As a Nursing Sister in those early days at the Clinica Miramar, she often knew more than the doctors about the intensive-care apparatus. Later she married a Santa Eugenian and became the local resident nurse. The villagers are very proud to have an English nurse to look after them, and the resident tourists find it a relief not to have to explain their problems in stuttering Spanish. Our grandson, now ten years old, has grown up bilingual. He speaks Mallorcan with his father, English with us and his mother, and Spanish at school. Valerie walks for relaxation. She hired a guide and did all the mountain routes on the island, plus others, later producing a book, *Landscapes of Mallorca,* which, now published in several languages, has become invaluable to hikers visiting the island. When we see groups of walkers in the cooler months, they invariably have *Landscapes* tucked in their rucksacks.

Philip, who published a book on statistics in his position with Maidstone County Council, would probably have gravitated to the island, but he married an Anglophile and he and Deirdre and their two boys, Robin and Tristan, live happily in West Malling, Kent. On the other side of the coin, I knew quite a few writers who wanted to come and live on the island, but were not sufficiently self-supporting in their work, especially when property began to soar in value. Ann Hoffman, a researcher of mine (and for many of the top writers, like Morris West, which puts me in good company), wrote about Mallorca for the David and Charles "Island" series, but always wanted to write that "special book" in some hideaway among the olive trees and the blue lagoons. This is a dream she is on the point of achieving, after thirty years as a visitor, having invested in an apartment on the more remote east side of the island.

Someone who turned out to be a dark horse, where writing achievements are concerned, was Merle Chacksfield, Sir Bernard's sister-in-law. We had met Merle and Bob Chacksfield when the two brothers and their wives paid us a visit while on holiday, and Merle and I became good friends. She was formerly a headmistress of a large infant school in Chandler's Ford, very close to Bournemouth, while Bob was headmaster at a Christchurch school, also a stone's throw away from Bournemouth, which proves it's a small world. As I discovered much later, Merle has written pioneering books on the teaching of music and language, and history books (her first love) about Dorset smugglers, a famous rebellion in that county, and others. But I think her *pièce de résistance* is her *Armada,* written to commemorate the defeat of the Spanish Armada in 1588, and it's like Merle that the proceeds from *The Glorious Revolution,* her other anniversary book, about the rebellion of 1688, she

has donated to charity. As a contemporary writer myself with modern-day life there for the picking, I can appreciate the hard work that goes into these history compilations. I might add that Bob has contributed some very fine photography for the books.

Midway in my own writing career I entered into a bumpy period. I wanted to do a good job and I was a great believer in research, but here again I was going beyond the barriers of the given formula and much of what I produced in the seventies raised barely a murmur in the publisher's office. There were one or two exceptions—the aforementioned *Cafe Mimosa* and *The Tenant of San Mateo.* My first book as an expatriate, *The Scented Hills,* was chosen by Avon Cosmetics for a USA coast-to-coast gift promotion, as was another book of mine for a Coca-Cola promotion. But on the whole I felt I was posting my typescripts to somewhere on the moon and getting no feedback. This would leave me dispirited at the end of a day's work as opposed to that feeling of exhilaration one has after a good creative session.

I seldom reread my books, but sometimes when glancing through a new edition I would see that certain names had been changed. Often my fair-haired blue-eyed heroine would turn up red-haired and green-eyed. I was never consulted on these points nor did I make any comment, believing that the publishers knew the business better than I. But it was hard to pin down exactly what they wanted relying on intuition alone. In the late seventies I was so fed up with all the hard work and little reward, I didn't send my publishers anything for a year. What drew me back? Funnily enough the healthy royalty statements for past "mediocrity."

During that year Gavin had advised me to cut loose from formula writing once and for all. But the publishing scene had changed vastly since the sixties. Now earthy sagas were in. The best-seller was the god in publishing. Everything else of literary value fell by the wayside in the stampede for the blockbuster. Also it was my nature to fight changes, so I clung to the niche I had. But after I submitted *Second Spring,* my maverick tendencies could no longer be ignored and I was invited to London to take lunch with Alan Boon and his editor. I took Gavin with me for moral support, and in the Mills and Boon offices I met Alan Boon for the first time, and his twenty-eight-year-old editor. Their argument, why wasn't I repeating my successes of the past? Mine, no one expects an architect to design the same building every time, or a painter to paint the same picture, so why was a writer expected to write the same book? The editor came back with, Ah but there was a Japanese artist who painted the same picture every time and he was selling very well. What could I say to that? Eyeing me sternly her words of wisdom were, "You can't write what you like, you know." And I who have always been under the impression that that was what made every writer unique. I can't imagine Shakespeare writing what someone else liked, or Colette, or to come nearer home, Barbara Cartland, who, I hear, will not have a comma altered in her final typescript.

We lunched at Claridges without the editor, who wasn't feeling well. Ex-king Constantine of Greece sat at a table across from us chatting earnestly with his companions. I'd like to say that I enjoyed the experience but if my morale was low before the meeting, it was about ankle-level when I departed. I did, however, get an inkling of the reason for their steely attitude. Harlequin was breathing down their neck for good stories and few among their stable of writers seemed able to come up with that magic formula. Romantic fiction has always been a joke to other writers and the layman, but it's not generally known that it's the hardest thing in the world to capture that magic which makes a romance unique. The writer behind Rosalind Brett, etc., did it every time and I believe she enjoyed a certain prestige. Unlike us of today, as I was to learn on a visit to Canada in October 1984.

Sir Bernard, president of the Burma Star association, had organised a reunion of the Four hundred thirty-fifth and Four hundred thirty-sixth Squadrons First Canadian Branch at the Holiday Inn in Toronto, and Gavin and I went along. Sadly, Myrtle had passed away the previous February after a long battle with multiple sclerosis. We had a wonderful time, found the Canadians warm and friendly. In the banqueting hall I met a retired schoolteacher from Ohio. We got on like a house on fire, jigged together round the hall to country and western music, but he took me to task for writing for Mills and Boon, saying that his girl pupils filled their heads with this piffle instead of reading Keats and Browning. I explained that I had always tried to write intelligently, and that one of my books had been chosen by a Canadian teacher to demonstrate the good English therein. (I know this because the publisher passed on a request from the teacher for more information regarding me.) But this cut no ice with my friend from Ohio, and I suppose he had a point. Nowadays, I would say, he has more than a valid grumble.

Harlequin eventually took over Mills and Boon, and for a while many of their writers, including myself, experienced a bonanza with our books selling in Canada and North America. But this, alas, was short-lived and, in a way, the beginning of the end for the romantic novel as we knew it. Simon and Schuster tried to make a deal. Harlequin refused, so Simon and Schuster set up their own romantic department, wooing away many Mills and Boon writers with their exciting adverts in the British press. They flooded the market with light porn disguised as romance, and Harlequin lost millions in sales. They have never recovered. Harlequin eventually bought the Simon and Schuster "Silhouette" series, and it gives one food for thought wondering what happened to the Mills and Boon writers who turned traitor and went over to "Silhouette." I myself wrote them a letter of enquiry (which was no doubt in the files), but I didn't fancy writing to their guidelines, so I didn't take up the offer.

During the panic stations in London while sales plummeted, a German expert was brought in. I never personally met Horst Borch, but I received his circular letters from time to time. One presumes he was responsible for the sweeping changes in which many of the writers were also swept away. I myself was back in favour, having produced the hits *Lupin Valley, Summer of Conflict* (I wince at some of these titles, not my own), *Night of the Beguine*. I wrote *Master of Marraxt*—later changed to *Master of Her Fate*—and received these golden words from the editor: *Thank you for sending* Master of Marraxt *which I have read and enjoyed.* But you're only as good as your last book, and I had been clinging on for ten years.

I shall always be grateful to Alan Boon. Without him my writing might never have seen the light of day. But we were growing apart. He was dogged by young editors crying out for Silhouette-type romance, and I did tend to stick to the old-fashioned formula. I had won out with these only as long as he held the reins, but when he was "retired" my position became increasingly shaky. Still I hung on. Then the decision was made for me.

After twenty years of producing romantic fiction, my thirtieth book was turned down. The rejection was like a kick in the stomach. I took stock of the situation, asked for guidelines, received them, and produced *Tempest in the Tropics* (not my title), the nearest I could get to light porn. This was received with open arms in London. I tried it again with *Turn of the Tide*. Much to my amazement it was returned. The typewritten criticism accompanying it was so hilariously contrived, I knew there was no going on.

"At Casa Mimosa with brother John and wife, daughter Valerie, grandson Julian, and family dogs including a very old Mitch of Stormy Encounter *fame."*

A fellow Mills and Boon writer of the same long standing living in Australia tells me that nowadays the trend is to write two or three books on the off chance that one will get accepted. She is still battling on with this, but I can't think of anything more time-consuming or hit-and-miss. Besides, my final break with formula romance had opened up a new and exciting field of writing.

I've always written visually, that is, seen vivid pictures of the action in my mind; and nothing thrills me more than to see a really first-rate film. Spanish television has always had a spot for NBC's "Movie of the Week," and though the dubbing leaves a lot to be desired, it still rates as some of the best entertainment around. Often, after that glow of seeing a fine performance, I would think what it must feel like to have written a script like that. But these were heady thoughts for a lowly pulp writer and true to form I shied away from them.

As a free-lance writer, I produced two books, both of them gathering dust with an agent. The second of these, a tight suspense involving soap-opera stars spirited away to the Swiss Alps, was crying out to

be written visually. I was very tempted to try my hand at a script, but though I resisted I've always felt that *Icebound* was something of a hybrid. From my old love of films I had many books on the subject. I was browsing through one of these, Mason Wiley and Damien Bonas's *Inside Oscar,* when I came upon an interesting snippet of information. It seemed that in the early days of the Oscar awards, when a recipient had been unable to attend, a mystery figure had walked up to claim her Oscar, and neither were seen again. This gave me an idea for a story, and I felt it had to be a script. I had grown up on a diet of motion pictures. Maybe I'd always had a latent affinity with this mode of expression. It was a bit late to discover this now. But perhaps not too late.

I leaned heavily on Alfred Brenner's *TV Script-writer's Handbook* for technical know-how. When the script was finished we gave it the working title of "Phantom of the Oscar" and posted it off. I was surprised and delighted when a letter came back from a top Los Angeles agent saying that my script was too long, and needed tightening up, but it was good enough that he would try and sell it for me. I was sufficiently seasoned in the business by then to know that this was only the very beginning, but it proved one thing. I was on the right track.

As it turned out, the agent didn't sell the film. (Does that only happen in fiction?) While I was producing my second and third scripts, Gavin set to work. Ever since the *Johnny Bull* days he had maintained a keen interest in films, and while on the island had been involved with the financing of *Journey to Judgement Rock, The White Schooner, All the Queen's Men.* We had met Guy de Montfort, author of the latter, when he had come over to Mallorca for a meeting. It's significant to mention here that Guy was disenchanted with book writing and eager to make a name for himself in the film world. Gavin had many contacts, and though it has taken time we're beginning to feel that we're edging nearer to that possible success. In May a British producer and an American casting agent from Rome came to see us. The producer was excited when he read "Phantom," the casting agent equally keen about "Death from the Past," another script of mine.

The names of big stars were tossed back and forth—James Stewart, Brenda Vaccaro, Michael Douglas. "Phantom" is scheduled to be shot in Arizona later this year, "Death from the Past" in the hometown of the casting agent in Ohio. But it's a long road between acquiring two producers and seeing your work on celluloid. Oddly enough I'm in no hurry. For the first time in my writing life I'm a free spirit. I've discovered the real me and this, I think, is worth all the success in the world.

Santa Eugenia, Mallorca
14 August 1989

Copyright © Roumelia Lane, 1989

BIBLIOGRAPHY

Fiction under pseudonym Roumelia Lane:
Rose of the Desert, Mills & Boon, 1967.

Hideaway Heart, Mills & Boon, 1967.

House of the Winds, Mills & Boon, 1968.

A Summer to Love, Mills & Boon, 1968.

Sea of Zanj, Mills & Boon, 1969.

Terminus Teheran, Mills & Boon, 1969.

The Scented Hills, Mills & Boon, 1970.

Cafe Mimosa, Mills & Boon, 1971, Harlequin, 1972.

In the Shade of the Palms, Mills & Boon, 1972, Harlequin, 1983.

Nurse at Noongwalla, Mills & Boon, 1973.

Across the Lagoon, Mills & Boon, 1974, Harlequin, 1984.

Stormy Encounter, Mills & Boon, 1974, Harlequin, 1980.

Where the Moonflower Weaves, Mills & Boon, 1974, Harlequin, 1984

Harbour of Deceit, Mills & Boon, 1975, Harlequin, 1983.

The Tenant of San Mateo, Mills & Boon, 1976, Harlequin, 1983.

Himalayan Moonlight, Mills & Boon, 1977.

The Brightest Star, Mills & Boon, 1978, Harlequin, 1979.

Hidden Rapture, Mills & Boon, 1978, Harlequin, 1982.

Second Spring, Mills & Boon, 1980, John Curley & Associates, 1985.

Desert Haven, Mills & Boon, 1981, Harlequin, 1982.

Dream Island, Mills & Boon, 1981, Harlequin, 1982.

Lupin Valley, Mills & Boon, 1982, Harlequin, 1983.

Bamboo Wedding, Mills & Boon, 1977, Harlequin, 1982.

The Fire of Heaven, Mills & Boon, 1983, Harlequin, 1984.

Dear Brute, Mills & Boon, 1984.

Master of Her Fate, Mills & Boon, 1984, Harlequin, 1987.

Night of the Beguine, Mills & Boon, 1984, Harlequin, 1986.

Summer of Conflict, Mills & Boon, 1984, Harlequin, 1984.

Tempest in the Tropics, Mills & Boon, 1985, Harlequin, 1988.

Emily Hahn
1905-

The Hahn children in St. Louis, about 1918: (back row) Mannel, Rose, Dorothy, (front row) Helen, Emily, and Dauphine

O h, sure, I do believe there's something," I used to say during those long, somewhat stupid conversations we had in college about God and all that. I was studying the various branches of science in the engineering course, first year. It was the time of Rupert Brooke. I fooled around with these muzzy ideas because my fellow students did, but my heart wasn't really in it. Concepts of God did no more than ruffle the surface of my mind, because my father had vaccinated me against religion: he was the first really dedicated atheist I ever knew. I wonder which of us in the family were similarly affected, and how strongly. My sister Helen, with whom I share a flat, took it really hard. Even today any mention of church gets a hostile reception from her, whereas I

can take it or leave it. My only brother—but I can't really speak for him, he was so much older that I relegated him to the adult world and in my mind still do. Anyway, it is said that as an adolescent he and his good friend Charless made a round of all the available churches in St. Louis, attended their services, and made up their minds which made sense and which didn't. I am not sure if any met with their approval. I only remember their indignant repudiation of Christian Science, but then Mark Twain probably had a hand in that. At any rate, Mother sent us for a while to the Sunday school offered by the Ethical Culture Society. There my class studied the "Lives of Famous Men and Woman," which I recall lacked savor somehow. It all was singularly juiceless.

"We might as well be in everyday school," I complained, and stopped going. No, there seems to have been no hunger for spiritual nourishment in my house. Later, it was a different story, at least for my eldest sister, Rose, who with her children tied up with—Unitarian? Congregational? Is there any difference? Something, anyway, and it was rumoured that for a time her elder daughter wore a silver cross at her throat.

But what is all this? "Were we Jews?" one of my daughters asked hopefully. "Sort of," said Helen.

Sort of. But my father grew up determined, for some reason, to be a Methodist minister. This was in his birthplace, Memphis, where Methodism was probably very big. He changed his mind at the age kids do change, because he read a book by the then notorious Robert Ingersoll which, as he put it, opened his eyes to the futility of—oh, the Bible mainly, but religion generally. It certainly put a stop to his Methodism and when, years later, his daughter Helen married Herbert Asbury, he was happy with Herbert's book *Up from Methodism.* Now, as for writing—for this is to be an autobiography of a writer, isn't it?

Emily Hahn "in the tam-o'-shanter" with sisters Helen and Dauphine (front), about 1913

To me, the remarkable thing is not so much that I finally became a writer, as that we all did not. There were six children who grew up—there were two more; the first one, Carrie, or Taddy, died very young and has been execrated by all her siblings ever since, though we did not know her, because Mother talked so much of her genius. I think she was eighteen months old when she died, but Mother was convinced she was a genius and we got tired of hearing about it. The other, a boy, died practically at birth, also long before we realized it, and we bore him no rancour.

As for writing—well, Daddy wrote a lot, mostly poems in the style of the South and the eighties, when he had time. We all read, practically all the time as I recall, but perhaps I read more than the others: I don't know. I do know that Mother read to us a good deal at bedtime. I was four years old when, in the annals of the family, I "taught myself" to read. I am not sure how it happened, though I have a vivid memory of it. Let me explain. One of the books Mother read to us was *Sunbonnet Babies,* a large, flat book that was mostly pictures, with a line or two, in big letters, across the bottom of each page. These lines I soon memorised, not on purpose but because my mind works that way, and at some glorious moment the memory of each word melted, as it were, into its actual shape on the page and . . . Presto! I was reading. After that there was no holding me, though Mother tried to, because she was firmly convinced that too much reading was bad for the eyes. She laid down a law that applied to all of us: half an hour of reading a day was enough for us until we reached the age of twelve and after that we could have a whole hour. (I don't know how she counted the minutes spent on homework.) As a result I took to smuggling books out of the house and hiding them here and there—under the back porch was a good place. It was not much hardship in St. Louis, where we were all born, because the weather was mostly clement.

I read everything I could lay my hands on after graduating from *Sunbonnet Babies* and its cousin, *Overall Boys.* I read not only *Little Women* and its sequels, but a whole row of Victor Hugo's works that I found higher up in the living-room bookcase, and *Webster's Dictionary,* which lived on its own lectern, and the choice books collected by my elder sister Dorothy, who went in for illustrations by Rackham and Dulac, and, as soon as I was old enough for a library card, everything I could get hold of. But it was the school library that gave me my first taste of Shaw, when I was twelve. Why, then, you might ask, didn't I start writing seriously before I did? Because it never occurred to me, that's why. I did write, copiously, when it was called for. I wrote long letters and loved doing it. I wrote poetry when I reached the right gloomy age, but didn't everybody? What fascinated me was science: the lives of the ants and bees, the formation of rocks, and, first and foremost, nonhuman primates. (The St. Louis Zoo was an excellent one as zoos went in those days and it was not too far from our house.) Fascinated by the fact of the opposable thumb and the difference it made to the evolution of humankind, I wrote an essay about it which Rose took along to Smith and showed to her psychology professor.

"I like the way her mind works," he said kindly as he handed it back. I was twelve at the time. Earlier, a teacher at school gave me a book on frogs—I think it was frogs—with the inscription "To a dear little scientist, from one who loves her." They don't make teachers like that any more, or do they?

Sitting here thinking about it, I realize that my childhood was not the stuff from which novels can be made. There was no great stress in it, no tragedy—although the loss of my brother's great friend Charless, in a plane accident during his training in the First World War, could count as such. Even had there been tragedy, however, I doubt if it would have impinged on me. I moved about in a cocoon of dreams, that is how I remember it, a kind of daytime sleep in which I lived not my own life but anything I was reading about. I took hard whatever I was reading, but real life did not affect me. At least, I don't recall much of what went on in the true world, but if you ask me questions about the books of Dickens or Thackeray—oh, that's quite another matter. We took *St. Nicholas* and the *Youth's Companion:* I memorized a long poem in *St. Nicholas* which I still remember, though not every word, and there was a science section in *Youth's Companion* that showed me how to make a mineral garden: you take a fairly large goldfish bowl—oh, never mind. Whatever happened to *Youth's Companion?*

It was easier to find a place to read in than to read right out in public where any member of the family could come along and interrupt me. So I found places. We each had a shelf in the playroom, for example, to keep our toys in, and for housewifely reasons the shelves were hidden from the world by curtains. My shelf, it turned out, was a splendid place to hide in and read. Then there was the Folding Bed, which did just that: it folded into a sort of bundle on wheels. If you were young enough you could burrow into the thing and remain hidden. I did that quite often. Really, though, school turned out to be the

most private place of all if you gauged your lessons right and came out of the fog in time for arithmetic or whatever.

These bad habits seem to have persisted until I was halfway through high school and Life broke in. We had moved to Chicago. One day I came into the literature class a little late and found the teacher chalking a poem on the blackboard with furious energy—and I mean furious: she was fit to be tied, Miss Peterson was. The poem was something by e. e. cummings. "Look at this," she said, in a voice half strangled. "He left out all the punctuation *on purpose.* Why? Why did he do that?" She stared at us, waiting for an answer that never came. I should have liked to reply but I couldn't. Still, I sort of liked the poem—and I liked Miss Peterson too, for caring that much. I began to listen to Miss Peterson in class. You might say that I woke up that day.

But I still didn't think of writing with a capital *W*, even though in English class—not Miss Peterson's, it must have been the next year—I got a commendation from another teacher: "The distinction between Shelley and Keats is good." I mean, of course it was good. It was easy to write. It was always easy to write. Now if I'd had a commendation on a maths paper . . .

I have written elsewhere and often, or anyway talked often, about why I took mining engineering for my major in college. I liked geology and wanted to take a course in inorganic chemistry in the engineering college at the University of Wisconsin because I preferred the professor there to the one who would have been my fate in the College of Letters and Science. They said I couldn't do that, because it would upset the way things were. At the age of seventeen I was spoiling for a fight anyway. Any fight, anywhere. I think most people of that age are, aren't they? So I transferred to the College of Engineering. They didn't want me, so I persisted. They went on not wanting me, so I went on persisting: it still seems to me obvious why I did. In due course, a bit battle-scarred but triumphant, I got my degree. English? Writing? Don't be silly. All students at Wisconsin, no matter what the course, did have to undergo one English course in the freshman year, so I did that one. I remember that the professor was a very nice little man who had, as one might suppose, an enormous class, and he made the best of it by following his own tastes, never mind whether or not we followed. Naturally, most of us didn't. One day, talking along happily, he leaned over his desk to ask

"Mitchell Dawson, my brother-in-law and mentor"

of the front row of pudding faces, "Have you ever *peered* into Confucius?"

So that was my only training for writing.

In our sophomore year my great friend Dot Raper, who had started out with me in geology but later dropped out, went into a very adventurous project with me. We bought a car. It was not a ruinous proposition—just a Model T Ford—but it was new and that was certainly a change. I had owned a fifty-dollar racing Ford before that but it broke down the first time I took it out for a long trip and this was different: new, glossy black, and dependable. We had plans for that car and we carried them out, driving all the way to the Pacific coast, then back again to Dot's hometown of Cleveland, and from there to Winnetka, where my family was now living. The reason the trip should be mentioned here was that I started writing elaborate letters, turn and turn about with Dot. We wanted to keep a record and we did. The letter-writing habit was well ingrained by the time I got back to school and it carried on. I think that is a sign that the letter writer is a genuine writer: find someone who enjoys it and you have found a writer. At least that is what my brother-in-law Mitchell thought. He was a writer himself but not all the time. He shared a law office with his father and, once in a while, he wrote poems. Oftener than that he read other people's poetry. After he married my sister

Rose he took her family seriously. One day he found me reading Nietzsche. Instead of laughing it off—I was going on fourteen at the time—he said, "But of course you are acquainted with the works of Schopenhauer?" "No," I said, "Who's he?" Mitchell said, "A philosopher. I think you'd find Nietzsche easier if you worked up to him through Schopenhauer."

So I read Schopenhauer. I have no idea if it was a good thing or not. Probably it didn't matter. What did matter was that when I wrote a poem making fun of "People who can say things," Mitchell read it and said, with a little sigh, "Well, you're one of them."

That was why I paid attention to my letters home that summer and later when I had jobs. My first job was that coveted thing, work as a mining engineer—coveted because everyone at school had said I would never get one because I was a female. I was overwhelmed with my luck. Why, a lot of the men in my graduating class hadn't even got themselves fixed up when I set out on my career. I was so eager I didn't bother about the graduating exercises but let them send my diploma after me.

It was a few weeks before my jubilation died down and I realised that it wasn't really what I had hoped for: it was a desk job and part of my duty was to help send men out on field trips that I could not share. I gave it a year to the day—Mother was not to accuse me of being a restless type—then I quit and went out to New Mexico to be a guide, or a courier as we were called. This was more like it, I felt. I wrote enormous letters home, really aimed at Mitchell.

It took Mother and a determined effort—she actually came out to Taos—to extricate me from what she considered an idle life and a terrible waste. Instead, I went to New York to take up a job at Hunter College as assistant to the professor of geology. Hunter was then for women only, but the professor was a man, an amiable gentleman of what I thought were advanced years. He was probably not quite fifty. I liked teaching all right and New York was full of new scents and sounds and sights, but what brought a change into my private existence was that a friend who worked now and then for the *World* asked me to fill in for him on a feature story and cover a cabaret presentation of Helen Morgan. I can't recall if this first step into the genuine, professional world of journalism had any effect on me or not. Was I timid when I went into that nightclub? I should have been, but I simply cannot remember. What I do remember is that Miss Morgan made a tremendous impression on me when she came out, sang, and for the second number sat on the piano. So I wrote about that and the *World* printed it and paid me TWENTY-FIVE

DOLLARS. Twenty-five! Why, that was what I earned for a week's work at Hunter. Not that I didn't enjoy Hunter but this was even better; more enjoyable.

Even so, I still thought of myself as a mining engineer. A somewhat frustrated engineer, it is true, but only for the time being, and I did an extra class at night, not teaching, but learning about gemology. I would probably have gone on like that but for Mitchell. Back in Winnetka he had a sort of idea. There was a new magazine that for a few years he had been paying attention to: it was called the *New Yorker*. Mitchell took two of my letters and doctored them a little. In other words, he took off the salutation and the signature. Then he had them copied at his office and sent them to Harold Ross—and Mr. Ross bought them.

This did have some effect on me. I still felt like an engineer, but I was doing more and more writing in my spare time. Coming in one evening to my sister's apartment in New York—another sister this time—I said, "What a silly man I just went out with." "How, silly?" asked Helen's husband idly. (He was a *genuine* writer. He had had books printed and published and all that: his name was Herbert Asbury.)

I said, "Oh, his line. It was so obvious. Really I could write a book about all the different seduction lines one hears. There aren't as many as all that." Herbert said, "Well, go ahead, write a book about it."

His agent handled it and Brewer and Warren bought the idea. They paid me an advance of—I am pretty sure—five hundred dollars, but how did it happen that they gave it to me in cash? That is how I remember it, because I said, "Yippee!" when we came out of the office—I was with a man—and started throwing the money around in the street. The man ran around collecting it, saying crossly, "Idiot!" as he handed it back to me. Yes, they must have given me the cash.

But still my fragile connection with geology remained until, toward the end of the semester, I had an offer from an American writer to go to Italy and help him read in the English Library in Florence: he was doing a book on Lorenzo de' Medici. No, I had no Italian but it didn't matter, he thought. There was all that stuff in the English Library, wasn't there? So I handed in my notice and the professor at Hunter said, very kindly, "Be careful."

A lot of one's life in those days, if one travelled very far, was spent in ocean liners. This liner took its time crossing the Atlantic. We paused for a bit at the Azores, for one thing, and later at Lisbon, where the passengers were taken around in carriages to look at the arena—but no bullfight. Only the other evening I told someone, at dinner, that we had disembarked at a place called Split. "Split," said my husband knowledgeably. "That used to be in Yugoslavia." I said in amazement, "Have I been in Yugoslavia?" Yes, I have. But after Florence—several months of it, very cold and wet—we started home by way of England, which I loved even then.

"I'm coming back," I vowed to myself.

In New York it was hard to pick up the ribbons of my old life. I went on living there because there didn't seem much point, now, in going home to the Midwest. I picked up little jobs here and there; one as a telephone operator plus copywriter in an advertising company, at which I was a miserable failure. The copy I wrote did not meet the boss's standards, and as for the telephone exchange, something went wrong very soon. The boss, who spent a lot of time yelling at business associates on that telephone, was just getting into his stride when I, listening raptly to it—though it was none of my affair—inadvertently cut him off. He stormed out to the entryway and fired me.

Oh well, I still had the advance on the book. I was saving up to go to the Congo, the Belgian Congo that is, which is now named Zaire. I got another job: was it the one that involved pasting clippings into an album? No matter. I had several jobs, and then I decided I had enough money to go to Africa by way of London. It was firmly in my mind to aim for the Belgian Congo for two reasons: the first, because Dot Raper and I had long ago decided to go there, for the good reason that Lake Kivu, on the east, was evidently a nice place and its waters were three degrees too cold for crocodiles, and the second, because I knew somebody in the Ituri Forest. Dot had dropped out of my calculations by getting married and calling off the Congo but Pat was still there and, as I happened to know, had with him a chimpanzee he had brought to New York the year before. I was nuts about that chimpanzee. So, with the advance on *Seductio ad Absurdum* and the *World*'s twenty-five dollars, plus what I had saved from Hunter College—an acquaintance of mine had once said aggrievedly that I never spent *anything*—I set out. About spending he was almost right. One didn't have to use much money in those days. My bed-sitting room in New York was eight dollars a week. Breakfast was—well, let's see: a quarter for coffee and a nickel for a doughnut. That sort of thing. I cannot recall what the *New Yorker* paid but they used only short pieces, a column or so. Whatever they paid, I saved it.

"Embarking from a medical station on the Ituri River, the porters carrying my little tin boxes,"
Belgian Congo, 1932

But I still thought of myself as an engineer. "Mining Engineer" was written in my passport.

My bed-sitting room in London cost about the same as the New York one. It was near the British Museum, of course: all Americans visiting London lived near the Museum, unless they went to the posh hotels in the West End.

I plunged heavily when it came to preparing for the Congo. I stood out firmly against buying a tent or a bathtub or all that fancy stuff, but I had a pair of boots made especially to walk in African forests or—and I love this—to ski. You can make ski boots out of any kind of sturdy shoe merely by hammering in two brass nails at the right place on either heel. I must admit that I never had occasion to use those boots for skiing, but it is as well to be prepared for every eventuality, and the brass nails never interfered with walking.

A more important purchase even than the boots was the twelve tin boxes, painted a bright brown, just big enough to hold about twenty pounds of assorted stuff, be it clothes or such supplies as groceries, canned food, medical supplies, even paper for writing on, though now I think about it I did not take a geological hammer. Twenty pounds, Pat had told me, was the approved weight for a porter to carry on his head all day. Any more would constitute hardship. Those were good boxes: I wish I had a few of them now, dented though they were to become in the

months that followed. I went third class in a French ship, along with a number of noncom officers from Corsica. Their accents lent a certain original flavour to my French which, I am assured, I have never lost. Added to the African accent I later acquired, it has given such French as I have a tang that is, at least, individual.

That time in Africa I have written about, as I have written about practically everything that happens to me. I kept a diary in the Congo—something I haven't needed since—out of which came *Congo Solo* and, a little later, the novel *With Naked Foot,* which I suppose was boiling within me for a long time because the situation of African women made me so indignant. I stayed in the Congo almost two years because, chiefly, I couldn't get out: I went broke when my careful hoard of money, going through England, got devalued along with the pound. But I got out at last through the east coast, landing at Genoa, from where I sent two of those battered tin boxes full of black wood carvings and such straight to New York via American Express. Sixty dollars it came to, I remember. I was scandalised, not to say worried—but then I was always worried about money. I had time in London, anyway, to see my friends and go through whatever it is that divers go through when they have the bends. Debriefing? You might call it that. Anyway I was afraid to go back to America in the middle of the Depression, but in the end I had to, of course.

Slowly New York, and I, crept out of the Depression. I find it impossible to remember how many piddling little jobs I held and lost in the following year or so but, like all Americans, I was resilient. The *New Yorker* bought one or two pieces. And when it was time to get a new passport, at last, at last, I put on the right line, instead of "Mining Engineer," "Writer."

It was through a relationship, to use modern language (I would prefer the word *liaison* or even *affair,* but custom is custom), that I got a job in Hollywood. My lover was a Hollywood writer, so that is what I became although I never earned the enormous sums he did. The relationship took me back to England to work on a rather awful film there, and I opted for a term in Oxford, where I took the degree known as a Diploma in Anthropology. Looking at Africa from the ivy-smothered walls of Oxford is not at all the same as living in the Congo. It was a valuable truth to learn.

Back in America, the relationship fell apart and I decided to go abroad again. I had written the novel about Africa and another one, *Steps of the Sun,* about New Mexico, as well as the diary, *Congo Solo.* The African novel was about to come out and the New Mexico one not long after, so I had some advance money. Why not go away and forget all about relationships in the Congo? I started out, this time by way of the West Coast—might as well see Asia while I was at it. With sister Helen I embarked on a Japanese ship which was to stop in Japan on the way. But, on the way also, we were told that the ship went no further than Japan. What now?

Never mind: we would see Japan while we were at it, and we did. Then, because Helen couldn't stay away much longer, we went on to Shanghai for a weekend—at least, I stipulated a weekend: no longer, I said firmly. The upshot was that Helen went home after a few weeks, but I stayed nine years. How did it happen, you ask—at least you ask if you haven't read my book *China to Me,* which came out after the Second World War, when I was back in the States. Well, I liked China—loved it, in fact, and I had plenty of work to keep me busy. I had a job on the local newspaper, an English-owned one. I taught school at various colleges. I wrote a lot for the *New Yorker* because, luckily for me, Harold Ross, although he had never been to China, loved the idea of it. For some intoxicating years I could not put a foot wrong in my *New Yorker* stories and, of course, after Pearl Harbor whatever I wrote was that much more attractive to people at home who couldn't get enough news from the Far East.

Besides, about 1939 I signed, at long distance, a contract with Doubleday to write a book about the Soong sisters, the three ladies who all married influential Chinese. The reason I got that job was that John Gunther didn't want it, or didn't think he knew enough about China. He had visited China long enough to have lunch at my house, but even for John, a wonderful on-the-spot reporter, that wasn't quite enough experience for a book. At least he thought so, and he suggested my name as a substitute. I did have contacts with the Soong family, at least enough to get clearance from them for the enterprise. So I began trotting after them whenever it was possible. Keeping track of three ladies, each of whom had her career to follow, was strenuous and time consuming, but fun. Madame Sun Yat-sen, the middle sister, was the most difficult, as she wasn't really happy about the projected book, but Madame Kung Hsiang-hsi, the eldest and most influential in the family, kept her in line, and Madame Chiang Kai-shek, the youngest, did not mind. I interviewed them when I could and went to Hong Kong when I was tipped off that they were

"With my first monkey, the Punk, a Javanese macaque,"
New York, about 1932

In Nanking, at the Sun Yat-sen memorial, with poet Zau Sinmay and another friend, 1937

meeting there and at last, in 1941, followed the trio to Chungking to where the government of China had withdrawn after the Japanese began flooding into the country.

I sent the finished manuscript of *The Soong Sisters* from Chungking. I even saw the book, one of the first printing, before the shades of Pearl Harbor came down, but I was sorry I had done so because Doubleday had made a bad mistake. The red cover of the book had been embellished with the Soong character embossed on it: nice idea, but it was upside down.

"Bad omen," said Madame Kung, shaking her head. Of course I telegraphed Doubleday right away and the error was rectified, but it *was* a bad omen. Fortunately, superstition apart, the book didn't suffer. I had no idea if it was doing well or not until I got out of China several years later, but it did very well. All of this, of course, did not seem to mean much when one was cut off from one's normal world by a war. I was stuck in Hong Kong for two years without anything to do in the way of writing—indeed, without a typewriter. But I had other things on my mind. Just before Pearl Harbor I had had a baby, Carola, a

sort of *cause célèbre* in Hong Kong, or anyway a big scandal which the war wiped out of the public consciousness: she was illegitimate, though she isn't any longer. So I had my baby to feed and the task of getting food to send in once a week to the baby's father in prison camp. Otherwise, like everybody else, I was preoccupied with staying alive and all that. It is astonishing how quickly, though, you can get used to anything at all. I got used to living in a war-isolated city. When I was exchanged towards the end of 1943, my mind was not fixed on that missing typewriter. It was—well, I don't know what it was fixed on. Seeing people, I suppose, and finding out what had happened to my world in America. We had been fed a lot of strange Japanese news, very strange when I come to think of it. The news was supposed to break our illusions of the West and destroy all hope of getting back to prewar conditions but it was rather badly judged, I think. For example, every week or so the newspaper—there was a newspaper in English, for us—printed the item that Carmen Miranda had been badly hurt in a car accident and had had to have her legs amputated. That was supposed to break our morale. Strange . . . and I didn't even think of checking up on Ms. Miranda when I got out: is that bad? What I did check up on was the Japanese story that tanks had levelled New York, skyscrapers and all. I half believed that, but of course I shouldn't have.

The first news that really percolated into my fogged brain was that *The Soong Sisters* had been a best-seller long enough to rack up considerable sums in the bank. To be sure, it took a little while to get the money out—the government had sequestered it, suspicious of me because I hadn't grabbed my first chance to get out—but in due course I got hold of the cash and then, naturally, I bought clothes. Secondly, naturally, I grabbed a typewriter. I might even have begun on that before getting the clothes. The *New Yorker* was very nice to me, taking a hotel room before I landed and supplying the typewriter.

I wrote a lot after that. First I got *China to Me* off my chest, but there were many more pieces to write about the war experience—*New Yorker* pieces and even children's books. People were all writing books for children; they still are and it was a natural thing to do when you had a child. Then after Carola's father, Charles Boxer, got out of prison camp, I started on a biography of Stamford Raffles—the man who founded Singapore. There was *Beginner's Luck*, the novel that had come out while I was living my first days in China. There were, in time, collections of my magazine pieces. I was very busy. One of the children's books (it was for adolescents really) was of the life of Mary, Queen of Scots, and after that came out, the editor, who was Bennett Cerf, had another suggestion: why not the story of the Borgias? This gave me pause. I repeated it: "The Borgias? Are you sure?" I felt that he might be right but, if so, things had certainly changed since the days of the *Sunbonnet Babies* and the *Overall Boys*. "I'm sure," said Bennett enthusiastically. "Think of all the local colour! The Florentine background and so on!"

Well, all right. Back in England I read what I could find at the London Library and got to work, but my heart wasn't in it. I wrote three chapters. I left out the murders, the incest, and the buggery, but, with the best will in the world, I could not leave out the Church, or the fact that one of the Borgias was a Pope complete with children. I sent those three chapters to Bennett with a note: "This is the best I could do. Should I go on?"

Quick as a flash came back the reply, by cable: "Hold everything." I sighed in relief and started work on something else until Bennett's letter came. Yes, he admitted, he had been wrong.

With Carola in Hong King, 1941

But all that lovely local colour was not wasted. I wrote another book for Random House, about Leonardo da Vinci. Still, it all seemed rather strange and I went on wondering. It came to me in a flash, a couple of years later. I sat up in bed one morning, having just woken up, and said aloud, "Bennett meant the Medici!"

Yes, that is what he meant. How do I know? Because not long afterwards Random House brought out a book for teenagers about the Medici.

I did a number of articles for an English daily, the *Evening Standard*. The editor wanted to use my nationality as a selling point, an aim that he pursued in a roundabout way by cashing in on my unpopularity as an American. We would chat for a while about what I thought of this or that British aspect and when it was really juicy he would cry, "Splendid! Write about that!" So I did. I was really horrid about the way English girls did their hair, or called their mothers "Mummy" long after they had grown up. I didn't really have such uncharitable feelings, but if the editor wanted me to express them, why not? For a time the technique had unfailing results. People

Emily Hahn, with Amanda on her lap, surrounded by (clockwise) niece Zoe, sister-in-law Anne, brother-in-law Myles, Nanny, and Carola. "Zoe gained everlasting fame that summer because she slapped Nanny, something everybody had long wanted to do." England, 1949

telephoned him to say unflattering things about me and I got so much vituperative mail that they had to set aside a desk just to accommodate it. He was delighted. Fortunately for me, I left the country for a while just before being shot down, and the public had a chance to forget or, anyway, forgive.

Harold Ross died and William Shawn took his place. I went on writing for the *New Yorker* with hardly a break. Sometimes I wrote a book instead and the magazine used parts of it as, for instance, when George Weidenfeld suggested that I do something about the diamond trade. This was a pleasant assignment as it meant going back to Africa, though not of course the same place on that continent, to look at the diamond mines. I felt relieved to be back in the world of mining—almost shriven, one might say. It was all the better when my plane, on the way back to London, had to land in the Belgian Congo and stay there for several hours. We passengers were told to get out and to go around the countryside a little to

get out of the pilot's hair. I wandered through a village near the airport and was assailed by memory. The sights were the same, so were the smells and, tied to a post, was a baby baboon. I used to keep baboons when I was there. No other visit to Africa, and I made several, was to be as nostalgic.

Then there was India. Not long after the end of the war I had gone there with friends and I wanted to go back. When Shawn suggested that I do, to see what was happening after the independence had settled down a little, I was very glad.

"I understand they have done away with the Maharajahs and all those," he said. "They're still around, of course, but without their old powers. I thought you might go and have a look at how they're managing. What's happened to them? It would be a good idea to go and stay with a Maharajah if you could manage it."

I could manage it, quite easily as it happened. I was staying with an Englishwoman who used to be my neighbour in England and who was now living in Bombay, when we got an invitation from a British photographer to come and celebrate the birthday celebrations of a Maharajah in Rajasthan. It was his habit, the photographer explained, to make a big thing of it—a birthday banquet complete with other Maharajahs and the photographer.

"But we need ladies to dress up the table," explained our friend. "The princes all have wives, of course, but they're in purdah and won't come to the party. That leaves the table very plain and bare. They need ladies to dress it up. It should be fun. They're celebrating the feast of Holi at the same time and His Highness is putting on a tiger shoot for his guests." Of course we accepted, bringing with us our prettiest party dresses. Not all Indian ladies were in purdah; there were a few who accompanied us. The palace was beautiful, His Highness was beautiful, and the table made for a lot of good photography. So, even more so, did the feast of Holi when it came around. Drums beat, coloured water was thrown all over everybody and we danced and danced. The tiger shooting couldn't have turned out better because nobody got a tiger. After the weekend I didn't go away, because His Highness discovered that my brother-in-law had been his general in Burma: he was quite happy for me to write about him. I stayed two or three more weeks.

Was that the most pleasurable book to write, I wonder? Or was it the one about zoos? That one meant going all around the world to look at the zoos in most countries (not Norway though—Norway has a law against keeping exotic animals in zoos, as pets, or whatever). Yes, I guess that was the best. It's been a busy, happy time on the whole.

Not everything I've done has been successful. For a time, of course (I say "of course" because I think we writers are all in the same boat on that count), I thought maybe I ought to write a play, and I did try, but I couldn't do it. I couldn't get people on and off the stage. That might not have been the whole trouble, but that is the way it seemed to me. A friend asked me, tentatively, if I really *had* to get my people off-stage or on-stage: "Why not let them just come and go without explanation?" he asked. I was staggered: I had never thought of that. Anyway, I never wrote more than one play; I was helped on that one and we sold an option but no more than that, so I forgot about plays. I've always been busy enough without.

Going back and forth between England and the States, as I have to do because of the complicated tax laws of both countries, has taken up rather a slice of my time—not that the trip itself is so long nowadays, but one is subject to jet lag, sometimes as much as two weeks of it, during which the brain is not very active. Writing is really very much mixed up with what is sometimes called "private life," which makes it difficult at times. I can understand some of the writers I have known who make a valiant effort to keep the two things—life and work—separate. They rent special rooms a long way from home and go there to do their work and put all thought of work out of their minds when they go home. At least that is the theory. I have never gone so far. I do keep a room where I live supposedly dedicated to work, but life has a way of slopping over these boundaries and, anyway, why shouldn't it? There is no hard and fast line between the two. Oh yes, when the children were small and thus, by their very nature, little nuisances, I did try to keep my room out of bounds, although I never went as far as poor Mitchell, who was driven to hanging a sign outside his door, "KEEP OUT." My daughter would stand outside the door and say in tones of ever-increasing volume, "I mustn't bother Mummy because she's working . . . I MUSTN'T BOTHER MUMMY . . ."

Naturally, getting old as I am, I tend to sit back and wonder a little what it was all about. Perhaps I always did wonder. But I have never really come up with an answer. The nearest apology I can make for all this is that, well, I do love to read. What would all the people like me do if we didn't keep turning out our writing? Still, one can't help having misgivings now and again. Once, in Oxford, I found myself, for some reason, upstairs in a bookshop. Perhaps one of the clerks had suggested that I go up there to find a book I was looking for—anyway, there I was, staring around in the attic gloom at heaps, piles, thousands of books, stacked up each according to subject. Dusty books. Miles of paper printed with words: leather or paper or celluloid bindings—and what for? It was a gloomy, miserable thought. For just a few minutes, there in that Oxford attic, I seemed to see my life reduced to emptiness. Then I found the book I wanted and went downstairs again, into light and air. But I remember.

Fortunately there are other more cheerful moments: like the time I stepped off the ship in Bombay and encountered a bookseller. Booksellers in Bombay, it is worth saying, have a very peculiar way of selling their wares. Do you remember when everybody smoked? and girls in nightclubs carried cigarettes around on portable shelves? They, the girls, I mean, wore seductive little costumes of long tights and very short skirts. Well, except that he wasn't wearing tights or a short skirt, this bookseller looked very much the same. At any rate, he carried his books on a little portable holder slung around his neck and he paused for me to make my selection. I was interested to see that the books were all in English. At least that is what attracted my attention at first, but then I saw something else, far more important to me personally: one of the books I had written and had not yet seen on the shelves of any bookstore at home. I beamed at the bookseller. "I wrote this!" I said, pointing to it. Not unnaturally, he looked alarmed. "No," I insisted, "I mean it. That's my book. I wrote it." The bookseller grabbed his carrier tighter and hurried away. He was scared to death.

It was quite a bit later that I had another Indian adventure. I was on my way back from Bombay to England. They had an arrangement in those far more difficult days of travel; you went partway to the airport and spent the night in a hotel before getting your plane. It was near Juhu Beach, I think. Anyway, I was just putting the finishing touches next morning to my luggage at the hotel, in my room, when there was a gentle knock on the door, and I opened it to reveal a shy-looking youth, student age, in white clothes. He grinned nervously and said, "Miss Hahn?" "Yes?" "Miss Hahn, the American novelist?" Well, it was near enough, so I said again, "Yes?" "Miss Hahn, I represent the school near here, and we would very much like it if you could come and take a class in English for us."

I said, "It's very nice of you but you see I am catching a plane in just about an hour, to go to

England. I can't possibly take a class at your school." He writhed a little and said, "Oh, please, Miss Hahn, do us this favor." "You don't understand. I have to catch a plane, I can't . . ." He begged again, just as if I had never spoken. He all but lay down on the threshold. "Do us this favor, please, Miss Hahn. Dear, kind Miss Hahn . . ." It was getting ridiculous. It was even beyond flattery. The minutes were ticking by. Finally I said, "What is this anyway? Who mentioned my name? Who told you to come and get me?" "The school, the English department," he said. "They told me to go and find a novelist, any novelist who writes English . . ."

"Ah!" I thought fast and remembered some people with whom I had had a drink the night before. "Listen," I said. "On the second floor of this hotel is an American couple, very nice people, and they are *both* novelists." His eyes lit up with hope. "They are here for a week," I resumed, "and I suppose they have plenty of time. I am sure they'd love to take your class. Here is their name." I wrote it out on a piece of paper. "Now you go and ask them nicely," I said. He thanked me and writhed away and I went and caught my plane.

What incident among all these comings and goings has stayed in my mind the most vividly? It is not easy to answer this question or, rather, it is too

"Helen, Rose, and me in St. Louis, where I got an honorary degree," about 1977

easy. It all depends on when I start to think. Different memories are strong in different ways, on different days. Let's see—how about South America?

The only South American country I know is Brazil. Oddly enough I did not go there in pursuit of zoos but only because I was with my husband and he was collecting material for a book later entitled *The Golden Age of Brazil*. We met an attractive if somewhat mad woman in Rio—no, it was São Paulo—who decided we should see the Matto Grosso and came with us part of the way, across Minas Gerais and up to the banks of the Amazon, which was flowing with an unusual amount of water after a very wet spring. There she left us and we flew in a taxi-plane (plane-taxi?) to a *fazenda* run by friends of hers. In the ordinary way it was on the banks of the river but now it was on an island in the middle of the water. The family, alerted by our somewhat mad friend, by telephone I guess, were gathered at their private airfield to meet us: man, wife, and two young daughters. Naturally, I noticed the daughters first because each one was wearing a monkey, a South American–type monkey with tail curled around the girl's neck. As we entered the farmhouse a small deer jumped nervously. It was standing at the empty fireplace, trembling all over. "We pretend not to notice it," our hostess explained. "It came yesterday, swimming in the river. We get all sorts of animals in flood times like this. Just ignore it: when the time comes, it will go away."

Our host took us in his little motorboat to see various other estates along the river, each as isolated as his. The girls came along. Once the outboard motor got choked with leaves and he told one of the girls to get out and unchoke it but she hung back and refused, for fear of piranha I think. Finally he unwrapped the weeds himself. That night, getting ready for bed (in a hammock), I went into the shower room and found three large frogs sitting on the water outlet. It was a memorable visit altogether. Now, what else stands out in my mind today? I know, the leopard. Probably because our hosts there on the Amazon had mentioned that they would not have welcomed a puma guest quite as calmly as they had the deer, I am thinking of that time along the Ituri River when I strolled out after a hard rain to see how things were going. It was evening and I sniffed the fresh air. For a reason that puzzled me, I thought suddenly of circuses. What was this? Circuses in the Belgian Congo? I shrugged and went back to the house. Next morning, however, it was explained: we found the traces of a leopard in the bush near where I had been standing. Which naturally brings me to the night I was going to bed in that same house.

The house was constructed of branches and leaves, stuck onto the walls of the hospital where I was working. My bed was a hospital cot, over which, at night, a mosquito net was draped. Well, I was just getting undressed when I had this strange sensation that someone was looking at me. Who on earth . . .? Nudity was not exactly in short supply in the Congo, where the girls used to strip down, take a saucepan of water, and go into the bush to bathe, quite undeterred by any public that might be around. And nobody could be peeking through the window anyway because I didn't have a window. I took off my last garment, a singlet, and looked up to meet the eyes of a snake that was lying comfortably across the top of the mosquito net.

I have no explanation or excuse for what I did next. I got dressed again, all the way, even my shoes—though I won't swear I tied the laces—and *then* I opened my mouth and screamed. Enter a mixed group of servants complete with weapons: exit snake. I went to bed.

Strange how most of these memories entail some brush with the animal kingdom. There was my first day in Dar-es-Salaam in Tanzania, when I encountered a camel, a genuine real-life camel, and was so fascinated I followed him or her and his or her driver all over town. It was a good thing I did too, or I would have missed the dance going on over on the other side of town, among Moslems celebrating Ramadan. They flourished curved knives and threatened one another but never stopped dancing in a ring and they didn't seem to mind that I watched: in fact, I don't think they noticed. By the time it was over the camel had disappeared.

Well, perhaps it isn't so strange. If you are born with a taste for investigating animals, you are born with it, and I am not the only one by far. In fact, I think people without this curiosity are stranger. At any rate, I don't understand them. But at least I think, as I look over my list of books written, to a certain extent I have been consistent, a lot more consistent than I used to think. "You have covered the field pretty widely," an interviewer once said, a shade of disapproval in his voice. "Most people specialise. Why haven't you?" "Because I don't want to, I suppose," I replied. "I don't want to get stuck in a groove. I've always been sorry for actors who are called on to interpret the same part in play after play. I have tried to avoid the same fate."

And so I have avoided it, I tell myself, but then I look at the list and realize that animals keep coming

forward. Oh well, I tried. We all have certain cut-and-dried notions about ourselves, some correct, some mistaken. I *think* I am correct in saying that I don't write good novels. After all, if I did, wouldn't I have written more of them? Some writers go ahead and write nothing but novels, whereas I write biography, history, even poetry. I don't even read very many novels, come to think of it. Some, of course—not to mention masses and masses of mysteries. Apart from these, I read poetry, old and new, and scientific papers.

Nobody, even Emily Hahn, reads absolutely all the time. When I do break off I have one enthusiasm which disturbs my nearest and dearest, who suspect me of insanity—I'm crazy about miniature things. I don't mean the fine paintings that artists used to do, but genuinely miniature things like the furnishings of dollhouses—but they must be of a certain scale, one inch to the foot. A friend studying psychology once told me a scientific word for it and I misunderstood and called it "pygmophilia," which satisfies me better than the original word: I am a pygmophiliac. It comforts me to think that I am not the only one. There are lots of us, thank God, otherwise there would be no shops and catalogues to pander to this strange taste. We aren't all alike. There is a Swedish company, Lundby, I think, that makes

Emily Hahn and Charles Boxer in England, 1980

and sells dollhouses and dollhouse furniture, but it's the wrong scale: one foot to three-quarters of an inch, which will not do. Crazy? Well, I warned you. By the way, I am not nuts about dolls. Dollhouses yes, dolls no. The houses I drool over either have no occupants at all or, if I have had a hand in creating them, they are tenanted by teddy bears about three and a half inches tall.

I once made a house for my elder daughter's Christmas, when she was four years old. I got a wooden packing case of the right proportions, divided it up, and planned the rooms very carefully and lovingly. There were pieces of furniture made from kits when necessary and everything else I could adapt to my sense of proportion. I even managed somehow to get a mouse-skin rug for the bedroom, right by the bed, ready for cold feet. I may have outraged my sensibilities by procuring the right size of doll; I don't remember, probably I did, because I knew that Carola, unlike me, loved dolls. There was a man in the neighbourhood who arranged to electrify the place, so we had ceiling lights, bedside lamps, the lot. It was a beautiful dollhouse. Only one thing marred its triumph. I gave it to Carola and SHE PLAYED WITH IT. Her first action was to take handfuls of the furniture, carry it—I mean, bundle it—upstairs to the second storey and push it out the window. Her second, before I could interfere, was to try to get in the tub. I mean that: a human child of four tried to put her great hulking foot into a six-inch-long bathtub. Well, naturally, I took the whole thing away from her and never let her go near it again. I am not sure when, if ever, the child developed a normal sense of proportion. I think she must have, because she now draws and paints and—oh yes—takes baths without any trouble, as do her children, but it was a near thing.

Teddy-bear houses are all very well and I've had a wonderful time outfitting rooms for them. At present mine have a study full of what I assume are their favourite pursuits, chess sets and butterfly collections and tiny pianos and violins, all those things for very intellectual teddy bears. It is the unexpected things, the *little* things, that cause trouble. There was the matter of Daddy's spectacles, for instance. I call that particular bear "Daddy" because he—well, he looks a bit like my father. He is sitting on the porch in a rocking chair, reading the *New York Times* through a pair of spectacles, and, at his elbow, not that bears have elbows, but you get my meaning, is a tray on which sits a can of beer, a glass, and a can opener, very nearly the size of a thumbnail cutting. Unfortunately, the child of our cleaning lady came to look at

the whole thing and—I think it was that child, but one cannot be sure—swiped Daddy's spectacles. I couldn't find them anywhere. How to find another pair? Originally the lost pair had been found on some souvenir card, now forgotten. I thought and thought. I went to several shops that had carried those souvenir cards but they told me the line had been discontinued. What to do?

(Instead of all this foolishness I should have been finishing a book, but I couldn't concentrate.)

The Barbie dolls one saw everywhere were about the right size. Did Barbie ever wear specs? If she did, I couldn't find the proper costume, but there was one chance. An imitation Barbie was sold at Woolworth's: did this interloper ever go to the beach and use sun spectacles? It seemed possible. Early one morning when I should have been at my office, I went to the Woolworth's nearest the building and found it still closed, and small wonder, it being only 9:00 A.M. I went to work but at the lunch hour Woolworth's found me hovering at the door. Inside, quickly, I looked around for the Barbie substitute. Not there? Where, then? Oh, the basement. Down in the basement I wandered around for a long time before I found the toy department, but I did at last locate it. I found the Barbie substitute. I shuffled through all her wardrobe and there, at last, oh joy! oh success! I saw a pair of spectacles. Of such are life's better triumphs made. Daddy wears them now.

We have come a long way from writing, but it's not as far as you might think. My pygmophilia goes far enough to encompass books. I collect miniature books. I have lots and lots of them—not those nasty blocks of painted wood that they use to dress up dollhouse interiors, but the real thing. Of one fact you can be sure; they don't take up a lot of space like the books that line the walls of my working room. It is hardly necessary to say that I have a miniature Bible, but I am saving part of my choicest shelf for a copy, if I ever find it, of *Sunbonnet Babies.*

BIBLIOGRAPHY

Nonfiction:

Seductio ad Absurdum: The Principles and Practices of Seduction—A Beginner's Handbook, Brewer & Warren, 1930.

Congo Solo: Misadventures Two Degrees North, Bobbs-Merrill, 1933.

The Soong Sisters, Doubleday, 1941, reprinted, Greenwood Press, 1970.

China to Me: A Partial Autobiography, Doubleday, 1944, reprinted with new foreword, Virago Press, 1987.

Hong Kong Holiday (memoir), Doubleday, 1946.

Raffles of Singapore (biography), Doubleday, 1946, reprinted, University of Malaya Press, 1968.

China, A to Z (for children), F. Watts, 1946.

The Picture Story of China (for children), Reynal & Hitchcock, 1946.

England to Me (memoir), Doubleday, 1949.

A Degree of Prudery: A Biography of Fanny Burney, Doubleday, 1950.

Aphra Behn, J. Cape, 1951.

Love Conquers Nothing: A Glandular History of Civilization, Doubleday, 1952, reprinted, Books for Libraries Press, 1971, published in England as *Love Conquers Nothing: A New Look at Old Romances,* Dobson, 1959.

James Brooke of Sarawak (biography), Arthur Barker [London], 1953.

(With Charles Roetter and Harford Thomas) *Meet the British,* Newman Neame [London], 1953.

Mary, Queen of Scots (for children), Random House, 1953.

Chiang Kai-shek: An Unauthorized Biography, Doubleday, 1955.

The First Book of India (for children), F. Watts, 1955.

(With Eric Hatch) *Spousery: His Edition,* F. Watts, 1956.

Diamond: The Spectacular Story of Earth's Rarest Treasure and Man's Greatest Greed, Doubleday, 1956.

Leonardo da Vinci (for children), Random House, 1956.

Kissing Cousins (memoir), Doubleday, 1958.

The Tiger House Party: The Last Days of the Maharajas, Doubleday, 1959.

Aboab: First Rabbi of the Americas (for children), Farrar, Straus, 1959.

Around the World with Nellie Bly (for children), Houghton, 1959.

China Only Yesterday, 1850–1950: A Century of Change, Doubleday, 1963.

Indo, Doubleday, 1963.

Africa to Me: Person to Person (memoir), Doubleday, 1964.

Romantic Rebels: An Informal History of Bohemianism in America, Houghton, 1967.

Animal Gardens, Doubleday, 1967, published in England as *Zoos,* Secker & Warburg, 1968.

The Cooking of China, Time-Life, 1968.

Recipes: The Cooking of China, Time-Life, 1968, revised, 1974.

Times and Places (memoir), Crowell, 1970.

(With Barton Lidice Beneš) *Breath of God: A Book about Angels, Demons, Familiars, Elementals, and Spirits,* Doubleday, 1971.

Fractured Emerald: Ireland, Doubleday, 1971.

On the Side of the Apes, Crowell, 1971.

Once upon a Pedestal: An Informal History of Women's Lib, Crowell, 1974.

Lorenzo: D. H. Lawrence and the Women Who Loved Him (biography), Lippincott, 1975.

Mabel: A Biography of Mabel Dodge Luhan, Houghton, 1977.

Look Who's Talking! New Discoveries in Animal Communication, Crowell, 1978.

Love of Gold, Lippincott, 1980.

The Islands, America's Imperial Adventure in the Philippines, Coward, McCann & Geoghegan, 1981.

Eve and the Apes, Weidenfeld & Nicolson, 1988.

Fiction:

Beginner's Luck, Brewer & Warren, 1931.

With Naked Foot, Bobbs-Merrill, 1934, reprinted, Transworld, 1952.

Affair, Bobbs-Merrill, 1935.

Steps of the Sun, Dial, 1940.

Mr. Pan (short stories), Doubleday, 1942.

Miss Jill, Doubleday, 1947, published as *House in Shanghai,* Fawcett, 1958.

Purple Passage: A Novel about a Lady Both Famous and Fantastic, Doubleday, 1950.

Francie (for children), F. Watts, 1951.

Francie Again (for children), F. Watts, 1953.

Francie Comes Home (for children), F. Watts, 1956.

June Finds a Way (for children), F. Watts, 1960.

Other:

Contributor to *New Yorker* and other magazines.

Marianne Hauser

1910-

ABOUT MY LIFE SO FAR

For centuries my birthplace Strasbourg and its province Alsace-Lorraine provided a stage for historic lunacy and political spite. Coveted by Germany and France, now ruled by Prussia's "Iron Fist," now liberated in the spirit of "la Gloire," we never could be sure whose flag to wave next. Wars have maimed and decimated our population, have colored our folklore, and sustained our cynical contrariness. A popular song may illustrate our disposition:

> Hans in his mosquito hole
> Has everything he wants
> And what he has he doesn't want
> And what he wants he doesn't have . . .

I've translated from the Alsatian patois, a curious mixture of Swiss-Alemannic gutturality and French idioms. The mosquito hole refers to the swampy basin left of the Rhine which breeds an oversize species. But some regional scholars believe that here too we may be dealing with an allegory of war.

Memory contracts the start of World War I into an image. I am stroking a toy pig the size of my hand as I peer through the window guard, down at a crowd. I hear a voice (Mother's?): That man (the Kaiser?) has dragged us into it (la guerre?). The scene, the sounds are afterthoughts. The soft toy pig in my hand remains a constant.

Other images evolve as the war gains momentum. Posters, printed underground, provoke my curiosity. Why is Alsace shown as a half-naked bride? Her wedding scarf is torn. Why is she screaming? That spike-helmeted Prussian, leering from behind a bush, he stole her from France, he's chained her to a cliff, he'll plunge his bayonet into her bosom. That's why.

Across her breasts, the slogan REVANCHE coils like a crimson rope. Mediocre art work. But effective propaganda, says Mother. She, like Alsace, is a paradox: of French blood, yet born and raised in Berlin. The name of her Huguenot ancestors, Fou-

Marianne Hauser, age seven

quère, had been simplified to Fiquert or Fickert. However, her millionaire father, an oddball, to put it charitably, adopted any spelling at will. In France, he played the Prussian gentleman. In Berlin, he was the Frenchman déplacé. When Mother arrived in Strasbourg as a young bride, the patriarchal seesaw must have hit her like a déjà vu.

My grandfather's type—poseur, acteur manqué—pops up throughout my writings in endless disguise, maybe because of Mother's endless anecdotes: how he threw a fortune out the window, literally, tossing gold coins to the poor kids in the street; celebrated his wife's birthday by hiring the royal ballet to perform at his house. A munificent megalomaniac, obviously. Still, his contempt for mon-

123

"My maternal grandmother, Claire Fiquert"

ey had a touch of the heroic, with his sudden, total bankruptcy fitting the mold. The financial collapse took his family by utter surprise—proof what a thorough actor he was to the end. When his inherited fortune had vanished, his estate gone under the hammer, he switched roles from Midas to tramp, gadding about in ragged old togs, and left his family destitute, with my mother, then barely fifteen, the chief victim.

His wife attempted suicide. It was up to his underage daughter to provide for her and for two baby brothers. She had to take whatever job was available—in sweatshops, eateries; in the exploitive factories of the Industrial Age. Worst, she would have to stand up against the nineteenth-century male ethics which treated a teenage working girl, like any adult female worker, as a potential whore. Small wonder that the child feared every male as a potential rapist.

I see her narrow lips tense as one of us girls would coax the conversation toward sex, already sure how she'd reply: "The sole purpose of intercourse is reproduction." We'd giggle behind her back. Who does she think she's kidding?

But she is dead serious. Throughout her youth, men have symbolized aggression. For her it isn't a matter of morals, but of survival.

She may have seen her former, menaced self in her three daughters. For on the whole, her views on sex and women's rights are far ahead of her time. Self-educated, she studies nights: Rousseau, Havelock Ellis, Marx, Shaw, Heine. In her twenties, she joins the protests against Oscar Wilde's conviction. She comes to Zola via the Dreyfus affair. She moves in Bohemian circles. By then she has become a successful dress designer, one of the first women to enter that field.

Many of her friends are painters. Father, studying at the University of Berlin, meets her at a vernissage where her portrait is on exhibition. A life-size canvas, technically perfect, and incredibly idealized. Her work-scarred hands are smoothed out to a feathery white. The artist has transformed her into a languid, swan-necked lady in chiaroscuro.

Father bought the picture and I remember it well. It was the most intrusive presence in our home, the pretended realism of her likeness perhaps the one fixed element of my childhood and youth.

The portrait, hung and rehung by her from room to room, appears in my short story "The Sheep" and, more prominently, in *Green Apples for Hermes,* a yet to be produced play. Father enjoyed the canvas for its meticulous craftsmanship. He couldn't abide shoddy work. He himself was a "Sunday painter," and his crayons of landscapes, flowers, and faces have authenticity and tenderness. I own one of his many sketchbooks, perhaps the only one which has survived two wars and related horrors. From a fogged Strasbourg harbor I turn the pages to forgotten toys. I search for my face. At twelve I sat for him in a red dress. But I can't find myself. I must be in one of the other sketchbooks, those that are lost.

In contrast to Mother's, his background seems unspectacular. The Hausers were sober, middle-class shopkeepers and, at least officially, they were Jews. The fact that they were a mixture of Jewish and Arab blood, the family preferred to hush up or deny, God or Allah knows why. By the turn of the century, they had crossed the Rhine from a townlet in Baden to Strasbourg, where their tool store would ultimately develop into a modest manufacturing plant.

My paternal grandfather died around the time of my birth. But Grandmother was much alive, sharp-witted, matriarchal, and a tireless storyteller. I could count on her for company while my older sisters, Dorette and Eva, attended school. The help was glad to get me out from under foot. They said I was a little monster and needed a father's firm hand. But Father had been "enslaved by the war machine," as Mother put it. A patent attorney by profession, he had also a degree in engineering and a doctorate in chemistry which may be the reason why he was whisked off to serve at an ammunition factory somewhere along the mutant, bloodied frontier.

And Mother? But she too wasn't there. During his absence, she had taken full charge of his office and I saw her even less than before. From the start of their marriage, she had been working for and with her husband. She had the business expertise he sorely lacked. Both by necessity and inclination she was always a working mother.

A patent lawyer's world is a crazy combine of practicalities, dreams, gadgets and science fiction. (To Father, Jules Verne and H. G. Wells are prophets.) Downtrodden inventors, on the verge, perhaps, of momentous discoveries, are pitted against an industry hungry to buy them out. I've used the setting in my novel *Dark Dominion* where the office of a patent lawyer, the heroine's lover, merges with the phantasmagoria of her dream life.

Mother deals with the practical side of the show, a growing office staff, an international clientele. She has a knack for what we now call PR; a gift for balancing efficiency with patience. But at home, that balance might break down and she would burst into irrational anger.

However, I rarely see her when she makes it home from work, bone tired. I only hear her. I've been put to bed before she arrives.

Autumn 1917: the third, most frightening year of the war. The nightly air attacks increase. So do Mother's fits of despair. Is she raging against the Kaiser? More likely, she's upset over my oldest sister, Dorette. Her bed next to mine is still empty. I hear shrapnel splash into the river Ill below the house. So far the air-raid siren hasn't howled. I hate to be driven out of bed and into the cold cellar.

Yes, Mother is scolding Dorette for staying out late. I don't catch every word. But I instantly side with my sister. She is my best friend, fourteen and beautiful, not another dull blonde like me or Eva. Her hair and eyes shine dark, her skin is like a summer tan all year around. I won't sleep until she's told me where she was, with whom. We have no secrets.

But when she creeps into the room, she says nothing. She only moans. Through the dimness I hear her drop onto the bed in her white party dress.

That night she went into a coma, already dying of meningitis, one of the epidemics brought on by the war. For over forty years I could not write about her death, or of the war and Strasbourg—components both of that one death and of a grief I was too young to concede. I didn't cry when I was told that she had "left" us. Instead I broke into moronic laughter. Only when I was finally able to write about her, did I burst into tears, my crying spell as uncontrollable as had been my laughter.

I happened to be in Texas when I found the key to the long deferred story. My husband, Fred Kirchberger, and I were on our way to Mexico when the old car broke down and we had to stop in San Antonio for repairs. And as we waited at an outdoor café in the sun above the Arenson River, my memory tape reeled backwards to childhood and war. Whatever the catalyst—the algaeous green water, the dank

"My paternal grandmother, Rosalie Hauser, with her husband ensconced in her locket"

*"My parents, Anne and Fritz, newly 'betrothed'
in the Vosges Mountains"*

smell or the lazy slap of a wavelet against the embankment—I was back in Strasbourg among the canals that zigzag, dark green and narrow, through the thousand-year-old inner city.

In no time, the timeless trip had stopped. Fred was folding the Texas road map, ready to leave, when I divulged the news: I had the clue to my story. The clue was water.

Water music? Fred, the musician, responded.

I named the story "Allons Enfants." And, of course, I wrote it in English. I only mention this because I've been asked (as was Nabokov): do I translate from my native tongue? I don't. Besides, I have two native tongues, though (unlike Nabokov) I lost my fluency in both.

"Allons Enfants" comes perhaps closest to autobiographical writing. However, beneath superficial data, facts merge with fiction for a more complex, unsettled truth.

To highlight the essential drama, the milieu had to be simplified. "Allons Enfants" called for an average middle-class home. Ours was too consciously

aesthetic: handcrafted ceramics, hand-bound books; art behind glass and on the walls, and carved art nouveau furniture designed by father. Such a stage set would have overshadowed the players. The extraordinary drama needed ordinary living quarters—like Grandmother's.

Nothing "strange" about her cozy rooms. I rock in her old rocking chair until the myriad family photos on walls and étagères spin through my head and the waxen apples seem to tumble off the credenza. She lives like what I call "real people."

I loathe the ethnic clothes Mother makes us wear. When I'm alone, I play "real people" with my dolls. I crave conformity. I want to be like the bourgeois I soon learn to distrust.

Food, already strictly rationed, gets scarcer than ever toward the end of the war. I'm over-active, underweight, and often sick. I'm always hungry. When the maid manages to buy a slice of beef on the black market, it turns out to be crawling with maggots. Still, she serves it up as boeuf à la mode. No one at table will touch it. But I devour my portion. My favorite uncle, a cousin of Father's, approves, although he is a vegetarian. I'm starved for meat. Maggots too are meat, he says. Eva retches. I gloat. For once, my stomach isn't empty.

Father is home on a furlough. He has grown a beard and I don't recognize him. But on the following morning, Mother, too, looks like a stranger to me. Are these people my real parents? More likely than not I was left on their doorstep. I think I'm a foundling. I tell my uncle. But, to my disappointment, he shrugs. We all may be foundlings, he says—a statement which confuses me completely, up to my twelfth birthday when he arrives with a gift which will influence me for years to come: two volumes on Caspar Hauser, a collection of documents pertaining to that early nineteenth-century foundling known as "The Child of Europe."

The enigma of his origin and death absorbs me to the exclusion of homework and games. I make him the hero of a puppet play for which Eva creates the puppets. Even ages later, after I've come to live in America, he remains my ghostly double to remind me that he will yet be a novel.

I was close to forty when I started and discarded various tryouts before I found my voice, or rather Caspar's, in *Prince Ishmael.* The actual writing took well over ten years. The rejections, before the book was published, were astronomic. If it weren't for my agent Perry Knowlton, his strong faith in my work, Europe's Child may well have dissolved in the smog of America's literary horizon.

I was far from the final draft when I was introduced to Gore Vidal at a party. A cousin of Caspar Hauser? he asked to my shock, resulting in an eerie feeling that he may have second sight, as my uncle claimed to possess after he had consumed a quantity of Alsatian wine.

Uncle Ludwig, his eccentricities and wisdom, has had a lasting impact on my development. He is a professor of science and math—two courses I regularly flunk. But he is also an accomplished musician and, above all, a prodigious reader and bibliophile. The books he gives me for keeps (and not just on birthdays) range from fiction (Gogol!) to African folklore (Frobenius) and Central Asia (Sven Hedin). However, the one book I've read so often I know whole chapters by heart, I filched from a school chum: Hector Mallot's *Sans Famille,* the wonderfully sentimental tale of a waif and his travels through France with a small circus.

My parents' library, too, is at my disposal. There are no "forbidden" books, not even *A Thousand Nights and One* of which Father owns the unabridged Burton edition. There's only one caveat: I must first wash my hands.

So far it hadn't entered my head that I myself might write a book. To explore the world had become my supreme ambition. When "old" people would ask me the inane question what I'd like to be once I grew up, I'd promptly answer: ballet dancer or missionary. Always, my response made them chuckle. But to me, the choice was logical. Either career meant travel. To put my restlessness to some good use, Mother signed me up with a dancing class. And doing my exercises at the bar, I saw myself as a prima ballerina, on tour to the world capitals.

The missionary career was more fuzzy. Of course, it had the advantage of getting me even further away, maybe to Africa. But once I was there, I'd have to convert the heathen which seemed a senseless job to me. Having delved into Frobenius, I considered the native's rites and religions by far superior to our own. The more gods, the safer. In a sense, that still is my credo.

My belated puberty and the riddle of Caspar Hauser engender universal riddles. I ponder the reflection of the mirror in the mirror. (Infinity may

"Ludwig Hauser, my remarkable uncle"

be another mirror, Caspar will tell us in *Prince Ishmael.*) I ponder the rectangular Quaker Oats box with the Quaker man holding the box with the man in the box ad infinitum . . . The label poses questions within questions. . . .

A commercial trademark, symbolizing cosmic mystery: perhaps that's what pop art is all about. I had no idea that the image of limitless repetition on our kitchen shelf advertised a product from the New World. America was a concept to me, based on the stereotype l'Oncle d'Amérique with his pockets full of gold, and a fat belly.

But here I shall take an enormous leap, forward in time or backward in sanity: from Strasbourg Bas Rhin to Berlin an der Spree. Alsace—the Vosges Mountains with their Gustave Doré forests, the luxuriant vineyards and ancient cathedrals—all the wonders I took for granted have been traded for the sandy wastes of Brandenburg. I'll never know how Father came to make this drastic decision or why Mother failed to dissuade him.

She couldn't have approved. Indeed, she had an ominous nightmare: a giant monster in frock coat and

"Mother with my sisters, Dorette and Eva"

top hat was rolling his bulk across Europe, burning villages and farms with his cigar. The monster was the war machine of industry. That was how Mother read the dream, as though she foresaw the coming of another war.

But wasn't war supposed to be past history? The League of Nations, our stupendous progress in technology, had made all wars impossible, if not suicidal. At least that was my father's firm opinion.

Berlin in the late twenties: Eva is studying painting. Father's new practice is a success, with Mother working by his side as of old. I'm the one who gets the worst of the displacement. For I am trapped in a high school system so moronically Teutonic, chauvinistic and pedantic, it brings out the devil in me. The strict curriculum at the French lycée was tough. But it stayed within the boundaries of sanity.

The Weimar Republic, still in its infancy, is already being systematically murdered by its educators. I can't keep my mouth shut. At assembly, when the principal delivers a tirade against the republic (which pays his salary!), I shout back at him and am expelled from school. A public disgrace. A personal

triumph. No more demented teachers in stuffy classrooms. Or so I fantasize. Mother gets me into another school, one of the few peace-oriented institutions. But at that point, formal education has lost me. Whenever feasible, I play hooky. I forge sick notes, so I can swim or skate or just "hang around." That I ever wormed my way through the final exams and into the famed University of Berlin is nothing short of a miracle.

I'll skip the farcical chapter of academe, as indeed I skipped most courses in law school. I can't be sure why I enrolled in the first place. Maybe I tried to impress Father. He had in vain wished for a son, and sometimes would hint at partnership with one of his daughters. But if he ever did consider me, he must have quickly realized that I was unqualified beyond hope.

I audit lectures which attract me—on Provençal literature, Etruscan art, Oceanic masks. My urge to travel is undiminished. But it no longer involves a career. I may write stories, little fantasies for my amusement, never suspecting that writing would become my profession. I'd gladly spend my life dancing or skating; or lying with my feet in the lake

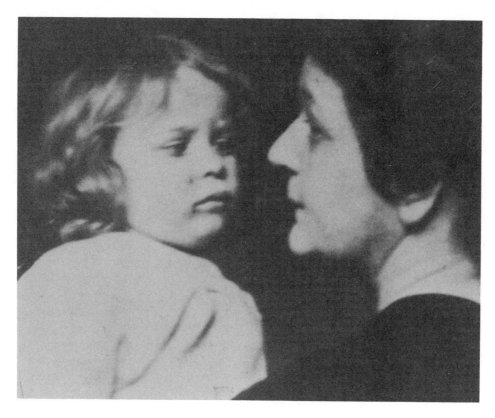

"Mother with me," 1911

and doing nothing, except to hope for a suntan so dark, people will take me for a Hindu or mulatto.

We are advancing toward the thirties. Nazi Brownshirts spill from the alleys and flood the streets and beer gardens like liquid manure. The bashing of homosexuals and Jews, the murder of socialist and communist workers, have ceased to make front page news. The German Republic is finished, Mother predicts. Hitler, with the unemployed for mercenaries and Big Industry a silent partner, will drag the world into another war.

But Father stands by his conviction that the Nazis are a passing phase. Is he deceiving himself on purpose? It occurs to me how little I do understand him—or Mother. She with her dire prophecies—why can't she make him see?

But few, except the organized, militant left, are willing to see. And we, the progressive young, are in a bind: conscious of the imminent threat to freedom, yet swept along with the avant garde in a carnival spirit. The iconoclasm in the arts, the innovative theatre of Piscator which places Berlin in Europe's

cultural center, are short interludes in the long dance of death.

And so, as the world turns (not as a soap . . . TV is in the laboratory stages), I get married to a gentleman who shall remain nameless. My choice of a husband with whom I have little in common defies reason, as did my choice to study law. And yet this absurd union gives me the break of my life: it gets me out of Germany in time. We are on Capri, playing husband and wife, while the Nazis perpetrate their first shrewd hoax, torching the Reichstag and blaming the communists.

Soon the marriage falls apart. I split. And we later divorce.

Paris. I'm twenty-two and looking for work. No more support from my parents. Hitler is in power, and the transfer of money abroad is punishable by death.

I've taken a room in a shabby hotel on the rive gauche. Days, I see Notre-Dame. Nights, I fight bedbugs. Plain food is cheap, and horse meat, sufficiently peppered, doesn't taste too bad.

During the first weeks of marriage, I had, out of sheer boredom, started a "novel." Now, out of sheer necessity, I finish the juvenile opus at top speed. The simplistic writing may explain why the instant novel finds an instant publisher, in Germany, and in Switzerland where it is serialized. I don't remember the plot, except for the ending: my teenage heroine's departure for Washington, D.C., which I believed to be the cultural hub of America.

Since I write in both French and German, Swiss periodicals offer the best outlet. I submit extra short pieces (minimalist fiction, in today's lingo). I interview "personalities." I deliver fashion reports. The snobbish rites of the haute couture, devised to keep the rich in tow, intrigue me as possible fiction material. However, eventually the scenario repels me and I lose interest.

But maybe it's my old restlessness that has revived the urge to get away, to travel. For months I've inquired about Asia, have studied books and maps and mapped out routes. But I haven't figured out how to finance the venture. Until one night,— I've just finished Céline's *Voyage au bout de la nuit* (fresh off the press)—I have a brainstorm. As long as I earn my living by writing, why don't I travel at the same time?

Tomorrow I shall take a train to Switzerland and try my luck at Basle's great newspaper, the *Basler National Zeitung*.

Amusingly, the paper, a first among the Swiss press to declare against the Nazis, was called by its acronym NAZI long before that self-styled Aryan tribe existed. The literary editor Otto Kleiber has published prominent anti-fascists and exiles, among them Tucholsky, Brecht, Thomas Mann, and his less famous, more modern and politically wiser brother, Heinrich Mann.

I've made an appointment with Kleiber. Of course we'll have to arrive at some kind of financial agreement, provided he goes for my plan. Else, the exhaustive trip I'm about to lay out for him must remain a dream. So, to look older—for, unlike today, youth is not yet a business asset—I've borrowed a matronly suit from my aunt, and plastered my face with make-up.

The masquerade doesn't fool him. He guesses my age during the interview. But he is willing to take a chance with me and back my project: a journey through India, Malaysia, Cambodia, Ceylon (Sri Lanka), Siam (Thailand), China, Manchuria, Formosa (Taiwan), Japan, and lastly the U.S.A., to me a country as exotic as the rest.

I am to contribute a weekly feuilleton (a column of approximately twelve hundred words). The feuilletons are to transmit spontaneous, personal impressions. Traditional travelogues or run-of-the-mill journalism are out. Kleiber emphasizes, with a smile, that the NAZI is noted for humanity, vision, and style.

The monthly sum the paper has agreed to pay is modest. But with added income from various periodicals, and free transportation provided by an Italian shipping line, I ought to manage.

In the early spring of '34, I sail from Brindisi on the *Conte Rosso*.

Transportation by air is still the exception. But the unhurried mode of travel, by boat, by ferry, on trains or busses, and often for miles on foot, has a tremendous advantage: it gets you in intimate touch with a cross section of the people.

The British Empire continues to rule over huge chunks of Asia, and segregation by race, oldest weapon and predictable doom of colonialism, extends to the farthest settlements. (In India, segregation by caste is an added curse.) Englishmen, from high officials down to minor clerks, throw me the same cliché: Never mix with them. "They" can't be trusted.

"They" are the millions of natives—a human ocean. The best I can hope for is that at least a few will trust *me*. I need to get the feel of their lives, their everyday rhythm. Without it, landscapes, dwellings, and temples will be mere props on a dead stage.

My travelling third class—a taboo for whites— helps. The lengthy train rides invite conversation. I don't find it hard to make friends. Sometimes, as we get off at the same stop, I'm asked to meet the family. We take our meals together. I'm even put up for the night—a special honor.

By compressing a mass of material into specific moments, I'm learning my craft. I write and rewrite. A weekly column of three or four typed pages now takes me a week to complete.

I'm in no hurry. I have all the time in the world—that grandest of all young illusions.

"Inscrutable Mother India, veiled in eternal mystery": the romantic concept, in vogue then (as again today) has a numbing effect. It masks the stink of poverty and urban horrors. The country is too large and multiform. The sacro-erotic statuary overpowers. I'll have to withdraw to one small corner to clear my mind.

The corner is in Kathiawar, a peninsula smaller than Ireland, yet composed of 189 princedoms. One of them, a busy harbor province, will be my residence. A former student of my uncle's, anti-British and my guide in Bombay, has given me a letter of introduction. So now I am the guest of a maharajah. His tiny realm, where ancient customs clash with ultramodern business, is to become the scene for a novel.

In real life, the maharajah is a highly visible prince. In the novel, my aborted efforts to meet him are self-deceiving, his whereabouts the mystery of my India.

I wrote most of the India book during a year's travel through China. Excerpts from the work-in-progress appeared in the NAZI. In '37, Vienna's Zinnen Verlag published the finished novel *Indisches Gaukelspiel* (Indian Phantom Play). My French version, *Fantômes des Indes*, came out with an Underground Press which was destroyed by the Germans during the occupation of World War II. As far as I know, all copies of *Fantômes* are lost. Also lost are the original manuscripts, clippings of my French writings,

and photos I had, for safety, stored outside of Paris. But what I had stored with my cousin Gisèle in Zurich, was safe—one of the blessings of Swiss neutrality.

An epitaph for the India book: when John Hall Wheelock read my German copy in New York, he suggested I translate the novel for Scribner's. However, I'm a poor translator, and wary of regurgitating past work. So I let a professional chance slip by. It wouldn't be the last time that I acted on impulse against myself—business-wise, of course.

I finish the novel during my stay on Hawaii which has yet to become the fiftieth state. But it does afford a mini-preview of American aloha hoopla, hot dogs, iced drinks, and young-bronzed-gorgeous Californian tourists.

From Honolulu, I sail on a Japanese freighter to San Francisco. Surprisingly, after the many strange countries I've seen, the U.S. seems to me the strangest. I'm back in Western civilization. Yet I feel more like an alien than I did in Manchuria.

The culture shock is memorable. As I amble through the typical drugstore, past the soda fountain

"Me at nineteen"

"Fred Kirchberger with our son, Michael," 1959

in a smell of fries, malts, deodorants and medications, with Pearl Buck's *Good Earth,* the Bible and other best sellers adjacent to cosmetics and prescriptions, I might be a latter day Alice caught in the Looking Glass House.

Little do I suspect that one day Paris will celebrate, with American hype, the grand opening of its own drugstore.

Nineteen thirty-seven: I've finished the last lap of my journey. I'm back in Basle, in Kleiber's office at the NAZI, and faced with a decision. He'd like for me to return to the States for a year. The press is allotting increasing space to American affairs, and my feuilletons might shed some light into the corridors of politics.

I'm caught unawares. I don't want to return. In fact, I have already thought up a very different trip—via the Oceanic Islands to Australia. Yet to my own surprise, I don't so much as hint at my new plan, but accept his proposal without hesitation. Something must be telling me that The Looking-Glass House is the right house for my work.

After a Swiss vacation, I sail for New York on the SS *America.*

While I was still in Switzerland, Father met me for a week of skiing. He was as athletic as ever, and—at least on the surface—in good spirits. Because of censorship, our letters had steered clear of politics, though I had taken it for granted that my parents would leave Germany. However, each time I asked, Father switched to other topics. It seemed he had made no preparations to pull out of the fascist morass.

A short while later, when I met Mother in Paris, she confirmed my worst fears. Although the Third Reich had not intervened in his daily life, it had killed his childlike utopian world view, and with it his will to act. No matter how relatives and clients abroad, as well as some Germans (in high position but secretly against the regime) had promised to assist in every possible way—he would not budge.

He was seventy-one when he died of prostate surgery in '43. By the end of the war, Mother died of cancer. She was seventy-three.

I've spent the larger part of my life in America—over half a century, to put it into perspective. And though I've never aimed to assimilate, or lose my Alsatian accent, my true voice as a writer emerges in the U.S.

I heard English spoken as a child, and loved to speak it myself. But now it's a matter of writing in English or, more important, of dreaming in it. No longer will I look at another language. I read indiscriminately—Joseph Conrad, the tabloids, Ezra Pound, Arnold Bennett's *Old Wives' Tale* from cover to cover. I read aloud to myself late into the night. I learn through sound or rhythm, not grammar rules.

On my walks through Manhattan, I listen wherever I stop—in cafeterias, automats, libraries, parks. I learn from shopgirls, mailmen, housewives, and bums. Preachers and prostitutes are among my most loquacious mentors.

Now, when I run into an acquaintance from the old country, my French or German is flawed. The feuilletons resemble awkward translations. Perhaps my total involvement with English has cut me off from the audible past. I wish I had the ease of a Raymond Federman who writes brilliantly in two idioms.

But back to my earliest New York weeks. I've rented a furnished room near Columbia University, advertised in the *Times* as "modestly priced and EXCLUSIVE." Exclusive of what? Pets? Kids? Obviously not roaches which crawl all over the so-called Residence Club. Had someone told me that "exclusive" stood for WASPS only, I would have laughed it off as a joke. I'm new in the land of the free and have yet to discover that racism is as prevalent here as in the colonies, though more cleverly disguised and often interlaced with the great American phobia of socialism.

I've cut my link with European publications, and must find work in New York. Amy Loveman, Malcolm Cowley, and notably Quincey Howe, help me make contacts. I review books for the (old!) *New Republic,* the *New York Times, Herald Tribune,* the *Saturday Review of Literature,* etc. But the pay is minimal and I need to supplement my income.

Simon and Schuster, Knopf, and several other "big houses" take me on as outside reader at ten bucks a manuscript. I also ghost write, and lecture to church-related groups on the link between racism and fascism. As to our noted publishers, most of them, like Hollywood in the thirties, are jittery about such issues, lest they should be identified with "Jewish interests" or—God forbid—be labeled "red."

Clearly, the melting pot mustn't be stirred. It dawns on me that bigotry in the U.S. is a way of life

rather than an isolated phenomenon. Not that I have gazed at the Statue of Liberty through the rose-colored glasses of the mythicized immigrant. I have no mind to stay past a year. Then I'll move on.

But the city and the landscape beyond, with its resonant space so uniquely American, conveys a sense of constant transmutation. Every day is a new trip. I am on the move in my head in the narrow room, with its window open to the Hudson—an everchanging stream whose grays and blues melted north into the clouds or hills of Bear Mountain.

I don't believe I ever longed for roots. Perhaps that's part of my Alsatian paradox. But air roots, yes. To me they are the essence of freedom.

Coby Gilman, editor of *Travel,* has asked me to write a piece on Alsace—an imaginary province, not to be found on any map he ever laid eyes on, he swears. His budget is small. But his humor and enthusiasm are boundless. He commissions further articles, modeled in approach on my old feuilletons.

He has the rare gift for spotting new talent. With his encouragement I start on a novel which is to become *Dark Dominion.* The theme evolves from a brief, intense relationship with a psychoanalyst I met prior to World War II, on Nantucket.

My knowledge of Freud is nil. Now I make up for past neglect. My paramour, himself a victim of interminable analysis, is a living textbook; so much so that I feel almost tempted to deliver myself to a dream surgeon's scalpel. (Anaïs Nin is in error when she states in her *Diary* that I was analyzed by Otto Rank. He knew me well, and was far too smart and ethical to mess with my peculiar psyche.)

Dark Dominion goes through many drafts and is finished on Monhegan Island. Told in the first person, in flashbacks by a Swiss hotelier, it centers around his sister in New York who has married her analyst. My role as male narrator is still judged weird by some in '47 when the novel is published. Literary cross dressing is perhaps safer for men. I don't think anyone censored Defoe for using Moll Flanders as his mouthpiece.

The early forties. I'm an occasional camp follower. Fred Kirchberger, my future husband, is in the army, his music studies interrupted, his pianistic career in the clouds.

By the start of World War II he is stationed in Georgia where I receive my basic history lesson in black and white: I'm returning from Atlanta to New York. The night train is crowded with soldiers and I am lucky to find a seat. Deeply tanned, with my hair tucked under a bandana, and my eyes behind shades, I'm ready for sleep when I hear the conductor order me off the seat and to the back of the train.

I rise, a befuddled alien, unfamiliar with Jim Crow's sacred law. I remove my shades for better vision. The conductor's face has turned purple and puffed as though he had choked on a bone. With a trembling hand he motions me to sit back down—please! He couldn't see in this poor light that I . . . He thought. . . .

At last I catch on. The poor fellow is in a mortal funk because he mistook me for black—an unforgivable insult to every white lady, if not the whole white race, and sufficient reason to cost him his job.

So much for Southern mores during our war to save democracy. Ironically, my adolescent dream to look so tanned I'd be taken for a mulatto has come true with a vengeance.

Fred and I were married on a three-day pass. He would be overseas with the Army's Counterintelligence Corps through '45, the year our son Michael Kirchberger was born at Sydenham Hospital, Harlem.

As usual, I worked at home, so taking care of the infant posed few problems. I went on with my regular book reviews, ghosted an autobiography for a mummified investment banker, and wrote short stories for *Harper's Bazaar*. Today, my young students are astonished that the *Bazaar* was once a highly regarded literary monthly whose authors comprised Ionesco, Colette, Flannery O'Connor, Terry Southern, Paul Bowles, and several other fine writers, with George Davis and Alice S. Morris the memorable fiction editors. Morris edited *The Uncommon Reader*, a selection of stories from *Harper's Bazaar*, which includes my story "The Abduction" (also anthologized in *The Human Commitment*).

"The Abduction" tells of a once famous and now forgotten musician on an American plane, in flight from his native Budapest, yet not sure whereto or what he is escaping, which one of the many revolutions or wars.

I wrote the story in '56, the year of the Hungarian uprising when we were living in Tallahassee. Fred, on leave from a teaching job in Missouri, was working on his doctorate at Florida State. And it was there that I met the celebrated Ernst von Dohnanyi who set off the spark for the tale. Hungarian-born, composer and conductor, and a gentleman of the old school, Dohnanyi rose to stardom before the finale of the Austro-Hungarian Empire.

But let's regress to '48. Fred, after years in the army, has applied for a teaching position at Bennett, in Greensboro, North Carolina—"a college for colored young ladies," in the parlance of the day. Allen Tate (with whom he enjoys making music) has offered to write him a letter of recommendation. A well-known poet and Son of the South, he has pull with the white board of trustees, though *pro forma,* the letter must be addressed to the black president. However, what about the salutation? Can't bring himself to call a Negro "Mister." Problem solved when advised that addressee is a Ph.D. "Dear Dr. Jones." That should be quite appropriate, says Mr. Tate.

The incident on the Georgia train has prepared me for worse. Michael and I have to stay behind in New York for close to a year, while Fred hunts for suitable living quarters. It isn't his employ at a black school that marks us as undesirable, perhaps dangerous tenants. It's the prospect of our entertaining nonwhites at home. After a tedious search, and resigned, though scarcely able, to pay twice the normal rent, we have an apartment.

I could cite other, more revolting incidents, still common enough today, and no longer confined to the South.

The mix of cruelty and human folly has brought Caspar's fate into the foreground again. I'm playing with different narrative approaches, reluctant to go by my instinct and use the first person as I had at the start (and would revert to in the end).

Caspar's short life unrolled in Nuremberg and came to an abrupt halt in Ansbach. Except for photos and early nineteenth-century gravures, I was unfamiliar with either Bavarian town. So, in the winter of '50, I knew I'd have to travel there, especially to Nuremberg which, after heavy allied bombing, was still partly in ruins.

I can't explain why caved-in buildings and heaps of rubble were quintessential for my perception of Caspar. Already on Monhegan Island where we spent summers, he seemed ubiquitous among the rocks and caves. I had even sketched out a chapter or two which placed Caspar into our age—a lost child of war, a *desperado.*

Nor can I justify the urgency of the trip when we had no money. Cheap tourist flights overseas didn't exist. Only first class was available, and I had to take five-year-old Michael with me on a full ticket. Expectedly—as happened many times before and would again—I had to borrow, enough to get us to Paris. I had already pawned whatever trinkets of value I owned.

We took off for Orly in a heavy storm. And once in Paris, I scared up more money for the train ride to the wintry haunts of "Europe's Child."

Accompanied by an alert five-year-old, I track Caspar's ghost amid the rubble of Nuremberg, and Ansbach's baroque tombs. I search for sights that have vanished or never were. "Just make it up," my son advises. "It's only a story."

Kirksville, Missouri, 1951. Fred has joined the music department at the Northeast Missouri State College. In New York we had been warned that the Bible Belt would strangle us. But we breathe freely enough. The skies look enormous, and the infinite horizons of the flat land invoke the childhood mystery of the old Quaker Oats box.

But I'm still a novice to the lore of the heartlands. A local farmer's remark that out there in that shack in the corn the James brothers used to hide out fills me with awe (such literacy!), though I do wonder just why Henry and William would be hiding in the Missouri corn—from whom or what.

Have lots to learn. But in a rural town of ten thousand "friendly people" (quote from welcome sign donated by Lions or Elks), information is easy to come by through gossip, that bottomless treasure trove or sinkhole for novelists.

I was seven when someone gave me a diary so I would keep an orderly record of what I was up to. But the first and last entry I made was one smug line: Today we had noodle soup. Since then I haven't tried to keep a consistent record, and so can only guess the date (1953?) when I drafted my novel about a small Midwestern town I dubbed Ophelia. The hero (a bank clerk, choir master, and operatic tenor manqué) has been diagnosed to die of leukemia within months. Inspired to live his allotted time to the fullest, he breaks family ties and conventions, though in the end he is back where he started, in his yard, with his wife and the kids.

The plot builds on dual tensions: the town's shifting view of their choir master, and his own duality, foreshadowed by the suicide of his father, a faith healer and bogus M.D. Though in subject matter the most American of my writings, the novel

"Autographing Ashley *at a book party with, from left, Robert Beers, Kathy Hirliman, and her husband"*

was first appreciated in England where Victor Gollancz published it under its original title *The Living Shall Praise Thee.* For the American edition, the title was, inexplicably, altered to *The Choir Invisible*—a worn-out quotation from a George Eliot poem, Edmund Wilson had cautioned me.

While *The Choir* was making the rounds of the publishing industry, Alice S. Morris excerpted three chapters for the *Bazaar.* She also bought some separate parts of the Caspar manuscript *Prince Ishmael,* and we had enthusiastic responses from a cross section of readers, including W. H. Auden, while the "big houses" continued their myopic rejections.

I didn't fit into their pigeonholes. I was a maverick. When the *Bazaar* went commercial, my short fiction too was tougher to place. *Botteghe Oscure* and *The Tiger's Eye* had folded. The latter, a quarterly designed with exquisite care, was founded by Ruth Stephan, dedicated writer and a woman of great personal courage who died in the early seventies under mysterious circumstances.

The paying market for good short writing had shrunk pathetically. One of my most provocative stories, "One Last Drop for Poor Abu," remained unpublished until it appeared in my short story collection published by the University of Texas. Abu, an Arab, metamorphosed into a born-again Christian Missourian, was too far out (even?) for *Partisan Review.*

March 1964: The start of Fred's sabbatical, and ahead of us lies an exciting year of travel; by boat from New York to Tangier; by car through Morocco, land of magic, and worlds removed from the tourist Mecca it has become. Spain, also, is still relatively untravelled, though foreign land investments along the Costa del Sol are being advertised on garish billboards along the highways. But we'll avoid the busy routes. We'll travel leisurely on country roads, on to northern Italy, and cautiously up the rocky paths into the mountains to Yugoslavia's monasteries. Then on to Greece.

(I was in Greece with Michael about ten years before, when "island hopping" through the Aegean wasn't yet the popular tourist attraction it will be in '64, not to mention the '80s.)

Michael, between semesters at Kenyon, will travel independently with his friends. By the end of the summer, we'll have a reunion in Orsay (near Paris) at the house of the Swiss artist Jean Weinbaum.

Instead of taking notes on the spot—for me an inadequate memory aid—I've promised to write a letter a day to my old friend Rae Hargrave. This method of keeping track of the road for a future rerun was suggested by the late Joe DeMartini, one of America's most shamefully neglected painters.

New York, 1966: Already the letters are proving invaluable for the Moroccan pieces Alice S. Morris has asked me to do for the *Bazaar.* A commissioned article on Yugoslav frescoes was to be finished in Kirksville. However, my attempt to arrange the letters into a book was interrupted by divorce proceedings. The divorce itself went smoothly, and Fred and I have remained friends. We've always travelled well together. During the past twenty-five years, we've met repeatedly for trips through Mexico, Central America, Peru, Turkey, etc. When Fred spent two years in Vienna, we took a boat down the Danube to the Black Sea.

I've rented an apartment on Christopher Street, in earshot of the waterfront of lower Manhattan. Nostalgic wailings of the foghorn. But also a nightly pandemonium of rock-rolling sadomasochist tenants above, and the interminable scream of police or ambulance sirens. The cacophony pervades "The Seersucker Suit," my first short story after the divorce.

The Talking Room is informed by the same waterfront life. The Sapphic theme, intrinsic to the milieu, came as easily to my androgynous nature as any other sexual variant.

The first draft of *The Talking Room* was written fast and in a boozy haze during a visit to Paris. Until a few years ago, I liked to drink, though since I was apparently born with a "high," I don't need or want to drink at work. But thanks to Lizette, my generous hostess, there always was a bottle on my desk. Amen.

I didn't read over the draft until I was back in New York. It seemed a careless piece of work, disorganized, and hardly worth a rewrite. Fortunately, I didn't destroy it (as I've done with other works I gave up on). In fact, it may have been by accident that I packed the untidy manuscript when I moved to a more peaceful Village apartment with lots of sunshine.

There, late in the fall, William Kienbusch, the painter, and a loyal friend of many years, said he was curious to read the draft because I had dismissed it with such rash certainty. I let him have his way, but I was scared—scared all at once he might agree with me? He had a sharp, critical mind and we were

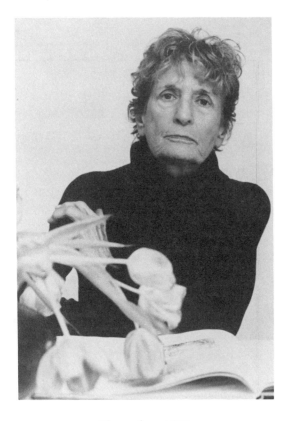

The author, 1988

committed to absolute honesty, at least in respect to each other's art.

I corrected papers while he read. His verdict: This could well be my best novel. It just needed work.

Suddenly all doubts were gone. He had given me the needed push, and saved a book from extinction.

Before it was published by the Fiction Collective (a promising new enterprise at the time), the manuscript went through the usual rejection mill. One wonders at the acumen of our trade houses, their editors' reluctance to read in depth; the fantasy of "cost effectiveness" on which too many decisions rest. (I've worked for publishers and I know their often self-defeating maneuvers.) My protagonists in *The Talking Room* couldn't be more timely: an ill-matched lesbian couple and their daughter, a pregnant teenager—most likely a test-tube baby.

Admittedly, structure or style are neither Krantzian nor Oatesian. Yet the novel, published in '76, continues to be bought and taught in '89.

In the spring of '66 I had become a writing teacher at Queens College of the City University of New York. The campus, fenced in by chicken wire, was once the site of a reformatory. Subway plus bus connections to my place of employ were a nightmare. I was a night teacher, paid per diem. Once I was given tenure, the pay improved.

I've had short-term employments at other institutions of higher learning or lower expectancy. At Queens, I endured until '79. Of course, an old discomfort with academe made me shun most faculty doings. I spent my time and energy with the students whom I advised right off that the term "Creative Writing," as listed in the catalogue, should be abolished. (Only God is creative, Balanchine is said to have said.) More to the point, I taught the class how to unlearn the rules pumped into them by grammarmanic pedagogues and style manuals.

Perhaps because of my unorthodox method, I had a surplus of promising talent to draw on. Gifted students—Hrutch Zadoian, Joanne Anderson, Arlene de Strulle, Iria d'Aquino, Aina Balgalvis, Dan Frueh, Kathy Hirliman, Scott Sheer, and the great Jamaican poet Lee Vassel—published distinguished work during my employ and after. (The motto for *The Talking Room* is taken from one of Vassel's poems.)

But Queens proved fruitful in other ways. A chance encounter with Carol Chu led me to her husband, C. K. Chu, acknowledged master of T'ai Chi Ch'uan, an ancient Chinese discipline and martial art. I enrolled at his T'ai Chi Center.

Now my mornings start with the form: thirteen movements, strictly defined thousands of years ago, and performed at the slowest possible tempo, a coordination of body and mind to relax and stimulate at one and the same time. I'm also learning the basics of Nei Kung from one of Chu's books.

The Vietnam War has blasted pacifism into action. Michael, graduate student at Columbia (poetics, film, anthropology), receives an additional education in live politics via the student uprising of '68. At Queens, we also rebel, though with less media attention. And though I'm not a joiner by habit, I take part in the demonstrations, the sit-ins, the March to the Pentagon. (Today I articulate my opposition to the lethal dogma of "pro lifers" and nuclear defense apologists.)

The social climate of the Vietnam years reflects in my novel *The Memoirs of the Late Mr. Ashley: An American Comedy.* Already dead and incinerated, another acteur manqué, Ashley tells his story through wild monologues and mea culpas, and through the tapes he makes to dupe his wife, though he is destined to be the fall guy of his own tricks.

Ashley resides in New York, married to a conventional heiress he leaves for a male lover, yet can't escape—a repetitive dilemma. Fugitive from the Bible Belt and the seedy boarding house of a pious mother, he keeps going back there in his imagination, powerless to shake off what he wants to lose.

While I was writing the Ashley novel, I saw to what extent my own imagination had intertwined with the Midwest—the source for such recent stories as "Heartlands Beat"; or "Conflicts of Legality," which centers around Ophelia, town of *The Choir Invisible,* and, by the way, Drew Ashley's place of birth, though in his *Memoirs,* local folks pronounce it "Off-the-Liar."

A new novel, still in the works, is also haunted by Missourian echoes. I sometimes wonder . . . if the Alsatian in me did hook up with America, it must have happened in the "Show Me" state. Our beginnings never know our ends. Or vice versa. . . .

BIBLIOGRAPHY

Fiction:

Monique, Ringier (Switzerland), 1935.

Indian Phantom Play, Zinnen (Austria), 1937.

Dark Dominion, Random House, 1947.

The Living Shall Praise Thee, Gollancz, 1957, published as *The Choir Invisible,* McDowell, Obolensky, 1958.

Prince Ishmael, Stein & Day, 1963.

A Lesson in Music (short stories), Texas University Press, 1964.

The Talking Room, Fiction Collective, 1976.

The Memoirs of the Late Mr. Ashley: An American Comedy, Sun & Moon Press, 1986.

Prince Ishmael, reprinted by Sun & Moon Press, 1989.

Samuel Hazo

1928-

Samuel Hazo

Except for my father and several uncles, the closest members of my family are buried in a single six-grave plot in Calvary Cemetery in Pittsburgh, Pennsylvania. The graves there are those of my grandfather John Abdou; his wife, Zarifa; his daughter and my mother, Lottie; his sister, Katherine; his son, George; and George's daughter, Frances Mae, who died before I was born and is known to me only as a name. Of this group my grandfather, my mother, and my aunt Katherine are the dominant figures, and I begin this profile with them because it is to them that I trace the strongest sinews of my life.

My grandfather immigrated to the United States from Lebanon around the turn of the century.

Within ten years he brought over his wife, his two children, his two brothers, his mother, and his sister. He settled for a time in Maine and then gravitated to Pittsburgh where he became a manufacturer of textiles. Although he died while I was still in elementary school, I remember him as convivial, hearty, and generous. Some say he never recovered from the death of his daughter (my mother); they sang Arabic songs together, and he was so proud of her that his friends often kidded him by saying that "Lottie is not only your daughter but your sweetheart."

My mother, who died of Bright's disease before I was six, was an exceptional woman. She sang in Arabic and English, accompanying herself on the lute (which I still have). She wrote witty letters and kept a diary in three languages. She mastered vernacular Greek in less than a year in order to deal with the patients of a Greek doctor for whom she worked for a time. She had a serene Mona Lisa beauty of face, and she was extraordinarily kind and generous. As a young girl she so excelled as a student that she was asked to teach the children of other immigrants, and to this day many of her students or members of their families approach me to tell me that so-and-so's daughter's or granddaughter's name is Lottie in memory of my mother. In one of life's inexplicable coincidences, I now work a few blocks from the school where my mother taught as a young girl (my office almost overlooks it), and, in another coincidence, I maintain an office as Director of the International Poetry Forum across the street and in full view of Saint Paul's Cathedral where my mother married my father in the mid-twenties.

I mentioned earlier that my mother kept a diary. It was in my aunt Katherine's possession for years after my mother's death, and she finally shared it with me in the late fifties. I read it from cover to cover in a single night and on the following day wrote this poem:

To My Mother

Had you survived that August afternoon
of sedatives, you would be sixty-three,
and I would not be rummaging for words
to plot or rhyme what I would speak to you.

Tonight I found a diary you kept
in 1928, and while I read
your script in English, Arabic and Greek,
I grudged those perished years and nearly
        wept

and cursed whatever god I often curse
because I scarcely knew one day with you
or heard you sing and call me by my name.
I know you were a teacher and a nurse

and sang at all the summer festivals.
You made one scratched recording of a song
I often play when no one else is home,
but that is all I have to keep you real.

The rest exists in fragile photographs,
a sudden memoir in my father's eyes
and all the anecdotes of thirty years
remembered like a portrait torn in half

and torn in half again until a word
deciphered in a diary rejoins
these tatters in my mind to form your face
as magically as music overheard

can summon and assemble everything
about a day we thought forever past.
For one recovered second you are near.
I almost hear you call to me and sing

before the world recoils and returns . . .
I have no monument, my beautiful,
to offer you except these patterned lines.
They cannot sound the silences that burn

and burn although I try to say at last
there lives beyond this treachery of words
your life in me anew and in that peace
where nothing is to come and nothing past.

Because my aunt Katherine was my grandfather's sister, she was actually my great-aunt. This made my mother her niece, but, since they were quite close in age, my mother and my aunt were almost like sisters. My aunt respected my mother in ways that went beyond love, and it was reciprocated. On her deathbed, my mother called my aunt to her and, as I was told, said to her, "I am entrusting my boys to you. Raise them for me."

My story actually begins right there. Living subsequently with relatives and then on our own, my aunt, my brother, and I proceeded to live a life that none of us ever expected but which, in retrospect, seemed destined to be what it was. My father, I should add, subsequently remarried, and we remained close over the years until his death from a stroke in the early seventies. A merchant of linens and rugs, my father traveled constantly and would never have been able to give us the stable upbringing that my aunt provided for us. Many of her friends and some of her relatives told her from time to time that what she was doing was a thankless task, but she never wavered. She worked, shopped, washed, ironed, disciplined, encouraged, scolded, and spartanly made us what we are. And she did this miraculously on the salary of a seamstress.

My aunt was determined, stubborn, outspoken, moody, courageous, often too proud for her own good and, in the language of her generation, a spinster. She admired people who had both brains and bravery, who somehow were or seemed underlined for emphasis in their respective destinies. Terence McSweeney, the martyred mayor of Cork, was one of her heroes, as were Franklin Delano Roosevelt, UN Ambassador Warren Austin and, late in her life, John F. Kennedy. I insert at this point an anecdote vis-à-vis President Kennedy and his family that occurred in 1962. My aunt at that time was in the hospital because of an attack of congestive heart failure. She had suffered a heart attack in 1957, and periodically thereafter had instances of heart failure

"Lottie Hazo, my mother"

that necessitated hospitalization. At that very time I was scheduled to give a poetry reading in Washington. I was hesitant about going, but the doctor assured me that my aunt was recovering nicely and that I did not have to cancel. While in Washington, I telephoned the White House, spoke to Mrs. Kennedy's press secretary, Trish Baldridge, and mentioned that my aunt was a great admirer of the Kennedys, was at that moment in the hospital, and would be helped immeasurably if she could receive an encouraging note from the first family. I expected to be dismissed politely but firmly, but Ms. Baldridge seemed to understand perfectly, asked me for my aunt's full name and the address of the hospital. When I returned to Pittsburgh, I discovered that my aunt was the talk of the hospital. It seemed that a special delivery package had arrived for her from the White House in which there was a letter from Mrs. Jacqueline Kennedy as well as an inscribed photograph of Mrs. Kennedy and her two children. Of course, my aunt eventually learned that I was the guilty party in this scheme, but until she did she told one and all that President and Mrs. Kennedy and the whole Democratic party were wonderful because they even kept track of sick people and made sure they were not forgotten.

To my aunt Katherine I owe not only my upbringing but the beginnings of my love of books and education, my belief that a selfless love is not only possible but invincible and, finally, my wife, Mary Anne. One night, after returning from a benefit, my aunt told me that she was introduced to a girl there who impressed her with her politeness, her conviviality, and her palpable goodheartedness. My aunt's final judgment was delivered in more telegrammic form: "Sam, she's not like the rest of them. Dumb." But more of Mary Anne later.

It was many years after my aunt's death in 1965 that I was able to write a poem that really satisfied me as being faithful to the person she actually was. I called the poem "Kak." We always had trouble as children saying, "Aunt Katherine." It eventually became "Aunt Kathy," then "Aunt Kakie," then "Kakie," then simply "Kak."

Her heroines were Pola Negri,
   Gloria Swanson and Mae West—
   one for glamour, one for style,
   one for nerve.
          First on her scale
of praise came courage of the heart,
   then brains, then something called
   in Arabic "lightbloodedness."
                        All
birds but owls she loved, all
   that was green and growable,
   including weeds, all operas
   in Italian, the schmaltzier the better . . .
Lightning she feared, then age
   since people thought the old
   "unnecessary," then living on
   without us, then absolutely nothing.
Each time I'd say some girl
   had perfect legs, she'd tell me
   with a smile, "Marry
   her legs."
          Or if I'd find
some project difficult, she'd say,
   "Your mother Lottie mastered
   Greek in seven months."
Or once when Maris bested Ruth's
   home runs by one, she said,
   "Compared to Ruth, who's Harris?"
Crying while she stitched my shirt,
   she said, "You don't know
   what to suffer is until
   someone you love is suffering
   to death, and what can you do?"
On principle she told one bishop
   what she thought of him.
On personality she called one
   global thinker temporarily
   insane.
         She dealt a serious
hand of poker, voted
   her last vote for Kennedy
   and wished me a son two years
   before he came.
         She hoped
that she would never die
   in bed.
         And never she did.
"When you and your brother were young,"
   she said, "and I was working,
   then was I happy."
         And she was.
The folderol of funerals disgusted
   her enough to say, "I'm
   telling no one when
   I die."
         And she didn't.
One night she jotted down
   in longhand on a filing card,
   "I pray to God that I'll be
   with you always."
         And she is.

Central Catholic High School in Pittsburgh is run by the Christian Brothers, and in retrospect I can say unequivocally that I am still indebted to the education I received there. Latin was a four-year requirement in the sequence I chose, and our instruction in mathematics went up to but did not include calculus. In addition to regular academic work, I edited the school newspaper and was on the debating team. Although I did well enough to be the valedictorian of my class, I did not receive a single scholarship offer until the eleventh hour. A week or two before graduation I learned that the Notre Dame Alumni Scholarship of Western Pennsylvania had not yet been awarded. I made an appointment for an interview with an alumnus named Dr. Leo D. O'Donnell, must have made a good impression on him, and, three weeks later, found myself on the campus of the University of Notre Dame in South Bend, Indiana.

Notre Dame in those years (1945–1949) was in transition from war to peace. When I enrolled, the school was still on a trimester program to accommodate the various naval programs that were still operating or just phasing out. My high-school education made the first-year programs in English, biology, but not history, largely a matter of review. I worked as a waiter to supplement my modest scholarship. Matriculating with me, I would later learn, were Thomas Dooley, subsequently known as Dr. Thomas Dooley for his work as a medical missionary, and José Napoleon Duarte, the recent President of El Salvador. These were also the halcyon days of Notre Dame football. After my first year at the university I never saw Notre Dame lose a football game until long after I was graduated. This was due to the fact that the returning veterans created at that time a dynasty of teams that probably will never be surpassed. The conventional wisdom in those days had it that the varsity's toughest games were on Wednesday when it scrimmaged with the second team.

My original intention was to be a lawyer. At the conclusion of my sophomore year I inquired into a program that would permit an undergraduate to combine his last two years with interspersed law studies and thus graduate in five rather than the usual seven years. To my chagrin I was turned down by the then dean, Clarence Manion (subsequently one of the cofounders of the John Birch Society), because I was too young. (I had matriculated at the age of sixteen and was eighteen when I met Manion.) I then decided to major in English, have never for a moment regretted it, and have given grudging thanks to Clarence Manion ever since for saving me, albeit inadvertently, from a false ambition.

Notre Dame had a number of inspiring English teachers in those days: Frank O'Malley, Reverend Leo L. Ward, Rufus Rauch, John Frederick, Richard Sullivan, and Ernest Sandeen. Through them I was introduced not only to the major writers of English and American Literature but to a number of Continental writers as well. I also learned at that time what I have continued to believe ever since, namely, that the final questions in literature are ethical or, if you will, theological. Mere semanticism stops short of this. Art for art's sake avoids the question entirely. In a course that spanned my junior and senior years (appropriately entitled "The Philosophy of Literature"), I became convinced of the fact that poems, novels, and plays all eventually create and reveal an image of man, and that the revealed image reflects the author's vision of man's nature, and that this has ethical or theological dimensions. In other words, literary creations confront us with man's nature as perceived by writers, and these perceptions are as complete or as limited as the author's view of man is. This imposes the burden of judgment upon the reader-critic to determine how complete or how limited such perceptions are and to explain why he thinks so. The same, I suppose, could be said of political philosophies and schools of psychology. In any event, the presence of a theological dimension to literary criticism and to writing itself has always struck me as being inseparable from both disciplines.

I continued my interest in debate while at Notre Dame, and in 1947 was a member of the team that won the Sigma Tau Delta National Championship. I also wrote a number of short stories, poems, and one play that received the James V. Mitchell Memorial Award for Playwriting in 1948. Academically, I did better than I expected, graduating *magna cum laude.*

In retrospect I am able to say that my years at Notre Dame were my intellectual and spiritual preparation for almost everything that followed, up to and including the present moment. My interest in literature both as a teacher and writer remains as fresh as it always was, and, although I've tended to be an eclectic Catholic in the profession of my belief, I still think that the Christian view of the nature of man is the most persuasive one I can name. I should add at this point that it was at Notre Dame that I heard my first poetry reading. It was given by Karl Shapiro, and it convinced me once and for all that the old maxim about poetry and prose was true: "Poetry is to be said, prose read." Although I did not know it at the time, the experience of that initial reading would arm me for what has since become a major aspect of my life, but that too will receive more elaboration later. Many years after graduating from Notre Dame I was invited back to give a poetry reading in my own right. The invitation came from the students so I had the double pleasure of returning to the university and of being asked to do so by members of another generation. That visit eventually transformed itself into a poem called "Breakfasting with Sophomores."

When I was what you are, the world
   was every place I'd yet to go.
Nothing near, now or here
   meant more than something anywhere
   tomorrow.
           Today, the ratio's reversed.
Back from anywhere, I watch
   the Indiana earth I walked,
   measure Indiana's level weathers
   and remember . . .
               Where did twenty-five
Decembers go?
          North of action,
east of indecision, south
of possibility and west of hope,
I stare into the now and then
of all those years at once.
A sophomore who has my name jogs
   by in ski boots and an army-surplus
   jacket.
         Netless tennis courts
turn populous with players only
I can recognize.
         Oblivious,
the campus pines still celebrate
their rooted anniversaries.
           A DC-7
seams the zenith with a chalkmark
wake, and clouds rush over
lake, dome and stadium
like bursts of smoke from field
artillery . . .
         No different in its bones,
no greener, not a foot more hilly,
Indiana's real for the acknowledging.
I sit back, listening, observing,
   memorizing everything.
           Two-decades-worth
of meals and months and mileage
consecrates this minute.
         Even
an eyelash swimming in my coffee
seems important.
         When I was half
my age, I never would have seen it.

"My mother and Aunt Katherine as nurses"

After returning to Pittsburgh from Notre Dame, I worked as a newspaper reporter until a newly appointed editor and I concluded that it was not the work I really wanted to do. (To that man, as to the aforementioned Clarence Manion, my thanks as well). After that, I worked on a farm for more than a year to sort things out, did a little graduate work, and, when the Korean War began, enlisted in the U.S. Marine Corps as a private. Like many other college graduates who were in the enlisted ranks, I was given an opportunity to become an officer and did, serving the rest of my tour as a disbursing and legal officer in Portsmouth, Virginia, at the Marine Corps Forwarding Depot. To this day I do not know what was forwarded to or from that Depot to wherever, a gap in my military memory that I'm quite content to leave as is. Because disbursing officers had a great deal of time on their hands between pay periods, I turned my attention to the writing of poetry again, wrote a few tolerable poems, and decided that I wanted to be a teacher as my work in life. The one poem that emerged from this experience is called "Toasts for the Lost Lieutenants." It grew out of my recollection of some of the officers with whom I served in the early fifties, and there is not a shred of poetic license in it.

> For Karl, the Cornell rower,
>   who wore the medals he deserved.
> For Grogan of Brooklyn, who left
>   no memory worth mentioning.
> For Foley, who married the commandant's
>   daughter, though nothing came of it.
> For Clasby, who wanted out,
>   and, when he could, got out.
> For Schoen, who married, stayed in,
>   thickened and retired a major.
> For Chalfant, who bought a sword
>   and dress blues but remained Chalfant.
> For Billy Adrian, the best
>   of punters, legless in Korea.
> For Nick Christopolos, who kept
>   a luger just in case.
> For Soderberg, who taught us
>   songs on the hot Sundays.
> For Dahlstrom, the tennis king,
>   who starched his dungarees erect.
> For Jacobson, who followed me
>   across the worst of all creeks.
> For Laffin and the gun he cracked
>   against a rock and left there.
> For Nathan Hale, who really was
>   descended but shrugged it off.
> For Elmore, buried in Yonkers
>   five presidents ago.
> For Lonnie MacMillan, who spoke
>   his Alabamian mind regardless.
> For Bremser of Yale, who had *it*
>   and would always have *it.*
> For lean Clyde Lee, who stole
>   from Uncle once too often.
> For Dewey Ehling and the clarinet
>   he kept but never played.
> For Lockett of the Sugar Bowl
>   Champs, and long may he run.
> For Lyle Beeler, may he rot
>   as an aide to the aide of an aide.
> For Joe Buergler, who never
>   would pitch in the majors.
> For Kerg, who called all women cows
>   but married one who wasn't.
> For me, who flunked each
>   test on weapons but the last.
> For Sheridan, who flunked them all,
>   then goofed the battle games
>   by leaving his position, hiding

> in a pine above the generals'
>   latrine until he potted
> every general in sight, thus
>   stopping single-handedly the war.

As a footnote to this poem, I learned recently that the officer referred to in the first line, Karl Ulrich, is currently the Director of Athletics at West Point, and that Philip Sheridan, referred to in the last section, retired as a general. *Semper fidelis et semper mirabile.*

Armed with the GI Bill, I returned again to Pittsburgh, found a job loading trucks, and enrolled in the Graduate School of Duquesne University while I looked for a teaching position. The result was that I taught for two years in a boys' prep school, finished work on my Master's, kept up my reservist's status with the marines, and was subsequently hired as an instructor in the English Department at Duquesne University where, because of devotion, interest, sloth,

"My brother, Robert G. Hazo, Aunt Katherine, and myself," about 1960

orneriness, or resistance to what is often called the broadening effects of relocation, I have been ever since.

In all seriousness, teaching at Duquesne, with which I have always had what Robert Frost identified as a "lover's quarrel," has always been an ongoing renaissance for me, and I can think of no other university where I would rather have been for the past three decades. The students are unpretentious and hardworking; the faculty, though sometimes too conservative, invariably manages in due course to stand for the right things; the alumni and alumnae have distinguished themselves in so many ways that I am convinced of the value of the education they received there. The students also have (I am generalizing) a basic good humor and an unexpected altruism toward the university. In the mid-sixties, for example, when students on other campuses in the country were barricading themselves in administrators' offices or vandalizing campus buildings, the students at Duquesne on their own initiative were engaged in a capital drive to save the university from an unforeseen indebtedness. And they did. Now that I am in my fourth decade at Duquesne and now that the children of former students are appearing in more and more of my classes, I am learning that having remained in one place for all my teaching life has given me the privilege of observing at first hand the turnover of generations at the genetic as well as at the intellectual level. This is fascinating.

Many writers have told me that the only reason they teach is to make a living. The implication is that they would not teach at all if they could make their livings by writing. My view tends to be more vocational. I have always seen education as one of the few professions where one can share one's ignorance as well as one's knowledge with others who voluntarily do the same. I have received insights as a teacher that I never would have received otherwise, and I regard them as some of the most valuable insights of my life. Randall Jarrell once said that teaching was one activity he would pay for the privilege of doing. I've never been tested to find out if I am capable of that kind of magnanimity and munificence, but I do understand what he meant. The contact with other minds over the course of semesters is a kind of marriage, and like marriage it requires and rewards continual rededication and rediscovery. In the long run it exposes the intellectual vices of sarcasm, cynicism, and dilettantism for the dissipations they

truly are. It teaches one that truth is a pursuit and that perseverance is as necessary as intelligence in its quest. Like poetry, it is done best by those who are irresistibly drawn to it (or called to it if you prefer vocational language) since it is finally its own reward. For those who are called to it, it does not spare them from asking themselves the question that all workers eventually must ask themselves vis-à-vis their work: "Even on my worst day, is what I am doing worth it?" Most true teachers would say, however reluctantly, that it is. I certainly would, and I do, often with no reluctance at all.

One thing I was not anxious to do as a teacher was to become involved in creative writing courses. My reasons were twofold. First, I did not believe that writing could be taught (*that* kind of writing). Second, I did not want to put myself in a position of feeling that I had to cough up a book at regular intervals to justify my teaching of such a course. Consequently, I taught mainstream undergraduate and graduate courses, became the Director of Freshman English, and, for a four-year period, the Associate Dean of the College of Liberal Arts and Sciences. But after being at the university for almost twenty years, I finally agreed to conduct a poetry workshop. By then I'd published five books of poems and did not feel that I had to "prove" myself in that way any longer. But I still had (and have) my doubts about whether writing of a creative nature was teachable. Confronted with the work of student-writers, one can tactfully suggest improvements, encourage workshop discussions about what has quality and what does not, try one's damnedest to tap whatever it is that brings the imagination of students to life, and then just hope for the best. At most, one tries to fail as nobly and fruitfully as one can. And at times there are rewards that are beyond expectation and almost beyond one's deserving, as, for example, this single line written by a young woman who was still hopelessly in love with her former husband and who realized the hopelessness of it while being unable to "un-love" him: "Love, for me, is like the bubble in the stem of a wine-glass—a defect." Lines like that are worth the wait. Recently I had the good fortune to have a particularly good class of writers, and during the course of the semester I wrote a poem in which I found myself imagining their future in contrast to the work of some contemporary poets whose work I did not respect at all. The poem is called "Whatever Makes It Happen Makes It Last."

This one's a good translator
   but a public fool.
           These clans
have such a consanguinity of views
that all their books seem interchangeable.
That one has let her cause
   corrupt whatever poetry
   was hers, and what was hers
was not dismissable.
           Those two
have never grown beyond awards
they won too soon.
           I could
go on, but what's the point?
Poets are not poetry.
           Who knows
what wakens fire in the blood
of saints and sycophants alike?
Who cares?
           The gift's in the awakening—
in words that flare and flame
across the white adventure
of a page.
           If you are one
so visited, imagine you are
speaking to an audience.
           Imagine
every listener is you
plus ten times fifty.
           Hearing you
by choice, they compliment you
just by being there.
           You share
each other as you'd share
the steady goodness of a book,
the sun in all its indiscriminate
democracy, the presence of the very
air.
           Because your listeners
are guests as you are theirs,
they keep returning you like mirrors
to yourself.
           You stay in touch
with them as lovers stay
in touch, withdrawing only
when the poem they alone have made
returns them to their separate
but undivided lives.
           But while
in touch, you hold back
nothing.
           You give beyond
the point where giving says enough.
The worst defect is stinginess.

Earlier in this writing I mentioned that my wife, Mary Anne, was brought to my attention by my aunt. Subsequent to that, I went out with Mary Anne on a blind date arranged by a mutual friend. I was still teaching at a prep school at the time, and my salary, in the language of the underpaid, was "modest." That first date spawned other dates, and we eventually became engaged, and were married in 1955. We have now been married for thirty-four years. At the conclusion of this paragraph I will quote one of several poems I have written about (and to) her, but as a preface to that I can say that she was and remains the most generous person I have ever known, not merely with things but much more importantly with her time, her attention, and her concern. A bit impatient at times, somewhat mercurial (and inexplicable by my perceptions), she nonetheless has that unique blend of foresight and consideration that remains the bedrock of her personality. Like many raised during the Depression she places perhaps too much stock in savings (funds as well as things), but her innate generosity converts them immediately into use or gifts when the needs present themselves. Children and flowers can bank on her love, absolutely. She is tall, beautiful in the classical sense, and willing to take on anybody, any institution, or anything when she perceives an injustice. In my brother's language, "she is hard to stop once she gets started," and that applies to everything from making a meal to helping somebody out. In short, she has those two qualities that are essential to human life: courage and generosity of spirit. She has no noticeable vices except the minor ones of not agreeing with me about the sterility of working out crossword puzzles, the fact that Miss America competitions are essentially cheap ways to select a model as well as being social comedies, the aesthetic dimension of smokers' pipes, the strategic importance of the bunt, and the hard truth that there is life after Cary Grant.

Expecting a family, Mary Anne and I worked to conserve and augment what little savings we had. I taught at Duquesne University, fulfilled my weekly reservist's commitment with the U.S. Marine Corps, and continued to work toward a doctorate under the much appreciated GI Bill of Rights at the University of Pittsburgh. (I eventually earned it in 1957.) Mary Anne worked as a legal secretary. In fact, she became so good at what she did that she eventually was named one of the top three legal secretaries in the United States from a field of more than ten thousand. What we thought of as a temporary division of labor actually became permanent for the next eleven years. Like many couples whom pregnancy somehow elud-

"As Marine Corps Captain," about 1958

ed, we consulted various doctors, underwent tests of numerous kinds, were told by the well-intentioned to pray to so-and-so or eat such-and-such until we both finally had enough and resigned ourselves to what would be, regardless. At that point, I was invited by the State Department to represent the United States during Literature Week on the island of Jamaica. Mary Anne went with me, and for reasons known only to God and the Fahrenheit of the tropics returned pregnant, although she did not become aware of it for a month or more thereafter. She was treated by two doctors for everything but pregnancy until a routine specimen test assured one and all that she was indeed pregnant. The results of the test were made known to me by a doctor we had consulted as a last resort, and I had the pleasure (unusual in any locale and at any time) of informing my wife of her condition on, of all dates, April Fool's Day. We celebrated by going out to dinner, looking at one another in total happiness and equally total disbelief, and thanking a generous God. When our son was born on November 15, 1966, Mary Anne insisted on naming him Samuel Robert after my brother and

myself. It turned out to be a foresightful decision since, despite our hopes, the lightning of pregnancy struck only once in our lives. If we ever had a daughter, Mary Anne was determined to name her Lottie in memory of my mother, but that, like the children in Charles Lamb's dream-essay, was not to be. Although I have written three or four poems to or about Mary Anne, my favorite is the following entitled "Anne's on Any Anniversary":

Remember Canada?
　　　　　　　We pooled
our dollars and we went,
relying only on each other
and a car that had its problems.
Since then our counterpoints
　persist.
　　　　　　I hate fast
and love slow while you're
the opposite.
　　　　　　　I'm Centigrade.
You're Fahrenheit.
　　　　　　　　I throw away.
You treasure.
　　　　　　　I hear the words
and trace the silhouettes.
　　　　　　　　　You learn
the rhythm and enjoy the colors.
If every day's the picnic
after Adam's dream, we're picknickers.
En route to anywhere, we bicker
as we go but come home
happy.
　　　　　What bonds us then?
A love of figure-skating,
manners, courage and the poetry
of being kind?
　　　　　　　Or just
that difference makes no
difference to the heart.
　　　　　　　　　Confirmed
by how we faced three deaths
together and a birth that answered
everything, we're sure of nothing
but the going on.
　　　　　　　We take
our chances like Freud's "group
of two" whose only books are stars
and waves and what the wind
is doing . . .
　　　　　　　Queen of the right
word and when it should be
said, I love you for the way

you keep surprising me by being
you.

    Who else could whisper
through the pentathol before
your surgery, "If anything goes
wrong, take care of Sam."
Then, to prove the woman in you
never sleeps, you added, "How
do I look?"

        Darling, no wonder
every child and flower opens up
to you.

    You can't be unreceiving
deceiving if you want to,
and you've yet to want to.
That's your mystery.

          If "love
plus desperation equals poetry,"
then love plus mystery is all
the desperation I deserve to learn.
On cold nights or warm
I'll turn and tell you this,
not loud enough to wake you,
but in secret, softly, like a kiss.

By the early 1960s I had had several books of poems published (two by Sheed and Ward under the then editorship of Philip Scharper and two by the University of Pittsburgh Press). At this point the god of the fortuitous intervened. As the Associate Dean of the College of Arts and Sciences, I was determined to bring in speakers of note to address the student body. On one such occasion I presented W. H. Auden after having previously presented Mark Van Doren, Mortimer Adler, Senator Eugene J. McCarthy, and George N. Shuster. In introducing Auden, I mentioned that it was regretful that there was not a forum in every major American city where poets could read their poems to the public at large and not only to students and faculty members. What I did not know at the time was that there was in the audience a lawyer named Theodore L. Hazlett, Jr. Later, Mr. Hazlett was named the President of the A. W. Mellon Educational and Charitable Trust. In that capacity he asked a mutual friend to tell me to give him a call at my leisure. I eventually did call and was invited to luncheon. During that luncheon he reminded me of my introductory remarks at the Auden lecture and then asked me if I was willing to create such a forum

"With students in a poetry class"

for poets in Pittsburgh. Seeing how dumbfounded I was, he proceeded to explain that he wanted to direct the A. W. Mellon Educational and Charitable Trust toward the arts and that poetry, being one of the most neglected arts, was in his plans, provided I would be willing to "run" the program. Apart from stating that poetry appealed to the generalist in him rather than the specialist, he claimed to know little else about poetry except that he thought it was important to Pittsburgh. For more than nine months thereafter we discussed various formats and schemes for making poetry part of the cultural fabric of the city. What finally emerged was the International Poetry Forum whose announced purpose was to present poetry readings (by poets and recitationists alike from any-where in the world) for the paying public. The Forum was under the sponsorship of the Carnegie Library, which was directed at the time by an exceptional librarian named Keith Doms, and the Forum's pro-grams were presented in the Carnegie Lecture Hall (capacity 635) or the Carnegie Music Hall (capacity 1,900). I might add that these venues are still used by the Forum to this day.

In the spring of 1966 I established an office in the library with a young coordinator named Karen Falkenhan, and in the fall we presented an inaugural reading by Archibald MacLeish. Much to Mr. Haz-lett's surprise, the Carnegie Lecture Hall was filled to capacity for Mr. MacLeish, and we even had to turn away two hundred people in the rain. The rest of the season was so well supported that I had to add matinee readings for Richard Eberhart and Richard Wilbur. In addition to all the inaugural hullaballoo, our son was born in November of that very year, three days before the arrival of Yevgeny Yevtushenko for a special reading. At the suggestion of Galen Williams of the Poetry Center in New York, I had extended the official invitation to Yevtushenko that made possible his being able to travel to the United States from Russia. His performance was superb. Despite reservations that many may have (and I am one) about his politics and some of his poetry, there is no question in my mind that he has outstanding dramatic presence on stage. Moreover, he recites almost all of his poems from memory—a practice that all poets, American and otherwise, should follow. Such recitations put the poet in direct touch with his audience and obviate the intervening prop of a book.

Since the mid-sixties the International Poetry Forum has been one of the central occupations of my life. Apart from enjoying the work in and of itself, I consider myself lucky to live in the city of my birth and of my choice at the level of my professional and

civic interest, and to have brought to Pittsburgh many of the leading poets and actors of this era. The poets have included representatives of more than twenty-five countries, not including the United States. Of these there have been Nobel Awardees, Pulitzer Awardees, National Book Awardees, as well as younger poets and those numerous others who, though without citation or prize, are among the most significant poets of our time. The actors and actresses who have appeared are by any standard among the most literate of stage and screen: Hume Cronyn, Jessica Tandy, Eli Wallach, Anne Jackson, John Houseman, Melvyn Douglas, Colleen Dewhurst, Maureen Stapleton, Brock Peters, James Earl Jones, Claire Bloom, Danny Glover, Zoe Caldwell, Richard Pasco, Pat Carroll, Jason Miller, Ellen Burstyn, Jill Balcon, Dame Judith Anderson, and, on two separate occasions, Princess Grace of Monaco.

The first visit of Princess Grace to Pittsburgh occurred in the midst of a threatened coal strike. Her arrival reminded many that the real source of our energy is not coal but the soul. She arrived without fanfare (she traveled on commercial air with a single companion), made no demands at all, and proceeded to ready herself for her first professional appearance in the United States since her marriage. She also received an honorary degree from Duquesne Univer-sity on that occasion. The ceremony, in the memory of those in attendance, was as close to a wedding as any such convocation has a right to be, and all of us at Duquesne remain extremely honored in knowing that this was the first and only degree that Princess Grace ever agreed to accept. She subsequently became a member of the International Poetry Forum's honor-ary board of directors and cosponsored with the Forum a poetry festival in Monte Carlo with Jean De Sailly, Simone Valere, William Jay Smith, and Andree Chedid. She later made a second appearance in Pittsburgh in 1981. The last time I saw her was in the summer of 1982, two months before her death. She and I were planning a benefit that she had agreed to have for the International Poetry Forum at Wolf Trap (we had just begun presenting our annual programs there as well as in Pittsburgh). As a matter of fact, on the day of her death I was returning from Washington to Pittsburgh, having completed ar-rangements for the benefit and being totally unaware of the severity of her injuries because of the mislead-ing reports that were then coming out of Monaco. In the brief time that I knew her, I found her a woman of outstanding good judgment, taste, and dramatic ability. She had a superb comic touch and possessed the kind of courage, goodheartedness, and generosity of spirit that made knowing her a privilege.

The visits of Princess Grace to Pittsburgh, though high in civic interest, constituted but a fraction of the varied sponsorships that were presented under Forum auspices in the two and a half decades of its existence. Here are a few postcard-memories: George Seferis giving a bilingual reading shortly before he received the Nobel Prize; Czeslaw Milosz in *his* pre-Nobel days reading to a sparse audience composed largely of Pittsburghers of Polish extraction; Archibald MacLeish returning for a special curtain call when we presented the world premier of his verse play "The Great American Fourth of July Parade" in 1978 to celebrate the American bicentennial; W. H. Auden, all crankiness and erudition, reading his cerebral poems in his bedroom slippers (a foot problem made it impossible for him to wear shoes); readings by William Stafford, Derek Walcott, Stanley Kunitz, Linda Pastan, Eugene J. McCarthy, and Richard Wilbur with Jerzy Kosinski serving as Master of Ceremonies on the occasion of the Forum's twentieth anniversary.

Supplementing these annual public readings was an ongoing poetry publishing program. Mr. Hazlett had agreed with me from the beginning about establishing a national award for poets, and I suggested an award of two thousand dollars plus publication for a first book of poems by a United States citizen. The United States Award thus came into being. One of the first of its kind when initiated, it spawned other first-book awards throughout the country during its ten-year existence. Rather than have the awardee's books published by subventing the series with a New York publisher, I insisted that the University of Pittsburgh Press be the publisher, and the Forum and the Press were associated for ten years in this cooperative arrangement. The current Pitt Poetry Series in effect grew out of this venture.

Meanwhile, I had published two more books with the University of Pittsburgh Press and would subsequently publish a third plus two translations (poems by Adonis and essays by Denis de Rougemont). A collection of my poems entitled *Once for the Last Bandit* was a National Book Award finalist in 1973.

During the early and mid-sixties I made several poetry reading junkets under State Department aus-

Samuel and Mary Anne Hazo on their wedding day, June 11, 1955

pices in Lebanon, Jordan, Egypt, Greece, and Jamaica. The Middle Eastern trips brought me face-to-face with the ongoing tragedy of the Palestinians, and I have steeped myself in the history of Palestine and Lebanon ever since. The biases and outright ignorance vis-à-vis American culpability for this interminable agony remains inexcusable to me, and I have felt compelled in a variety of public forums to speak or write out for what I consider to be a more accurate historical view of the situation there. My personal views are summed up in a poem I wrote after I returned from my first trip to Jerusalem, during which I met a young shoeshine boy, a refugee from one of the camps north of the city. The poem is called "For Fawzi in Jerusalem."

Leaving a world too old to name
and too undying to forsake,
I flew the cold, expensive sea
toward Columbus's mistake
where life could never be the same

for me. In Jerash on the sand
I saw the colonnades of Rome
bleach in the sun like skeletons.
Behind a convalescent home,
armed soldiers guarded no man's land

between Jordanians and Jews.
Opposing sentries frowned and spat.
Fawzi, you mocked in Arabic
this justice from Jehoshophat
before you shined my Pittsburgh shoes

for nothing. Why you never kept
the coins I offered you is still
your secret and your victory.
Saying you saw marauders kill
your father while Beershebans wept

for mercy in their holy war,
you told me how you stole to stay
alive. You must have thought I thought
your history would make me pay
a couple of piastres more

than any shine was worth—and I
was ready to—when you said, "No,
I never take. I never want
America to think I throw
myself on you. I never lie."

I watched your young but old man's stare
demand the sword to flash again
in blood and flame from Jericho
and leave the bones of these new men

of Judah bleaching in the air

like Roman stones upon the plain
of Jerash. Then you faced away.
Jerusalem, Jerusalem,
I asked myself if I could hope
for peace and not recall the pain

you spoke. But what could hoping do?
Today I live your loss in no
man's land but mine, and every time
I talk of fates not just but so,
Fawzi, my friend, I think of you.

I have already written that I consider myself lucky to be directing a poetry forum in the city of my birth, that I enjoy teaching at Duquesne University, and that the central interest of my life is my family, my close friends and, for lack of a better phrase, a life of letters. But I also confess to other interests and propensities. I love sports of all kinds as a participant and observer (exclusive of golf), think we are in a time of national decadence vis-à-vis films, national leaders, popular music and public speech, believe that jogging is all right for the young if they wish to expiate past vices but is a waste of time (and possibly of life) for those over forty, hate fluent liars more than flagrant crooks, think that laureled poets like Ashbery, Rich, Ginsberg, Sexton, and the like are secondary or tertiary figures in contemporary American literary history compared to Merwin, Pastan, Wilbur, Stafford, Nye, MacDonald, Kumin, and Kinnell, write all versions of my poems except the last with a fountain pen, find it difficult to understand why people find science fiction of any interest at all, ditto Tolkien, double ditto historical romances, cannot fathom the attraction of drugs of any kind to anyone in any age group, enjoy the comedy of Peter Sellers but not Bob Hope, Jerry Lewis, and most other stand-up comedians, with the exception of Robin Williams and Eddie Murphy who, when not shocking their yuppie audiences with mandatory vulgarity, show traces of real comic genius, treasure the cinematic performances of Brando, Olivier, Newman, Streep, and Loren, place the scenic beauty of Western Pennsylvania in the summer and autumn quite high on the scale of such, concluded from watching in person the last fight of Sugar Ray Robinson (against a young boxer named Joey Archer) that age is nothing more nor less than not being equal to what you think you can and want to do, regard Hemingway still as a master stylist of American prose, have yet to discover what in the hell is so great about Henry James (with the exception of *The Turn of the Screw* and his travel prose), deplore

With Archibald MacLeish, about 1966

teachers who try to turn their students into facsimiles of themselves, find the city of New York an unavoidable pain in the mind, find the city of New York overrated in the national consciousness, particularly among those who have never been there, ditto California, love to listen to late-night jazz while I'm driving, believe that all institutions in which people put their deepest faith will disappoint them eventually and usually totally, distrust people who speak in the passive voice, distrust true believers of any sort, think that Donne and Shakespeare are without equal in the English language, find T. S. Eliot a greater critic than he is a poet or playwright, never tire of spring, summer, or autumn, tire quickly of winter, think that silence is more eloquent than language, deeply and truly regret that President Kennedy was murdered more than I am curious about who actually did it, enjoy the cuisine, climate, and pace of the south of France, think that this paragraph is long enough.

Since poetry has been the dominant occupation of my waking hours, I have come to regard it not simply as another use of language. It *is* another language. Its purpose is not to command, explain, persuade, deceive, inform, diagnose, or demand. Its only purpose is to attempt to say what cannot be said or, in a seeming contradiction, to say what is best said in silence—a fertile silence which at times cannot prevent itself from springing into sound, into words, into a voice. Once shared, once said, poetry tells a different kind of time. It is not clock-time nor calendar-time nor any other kind of time created by man to chain us to history. It is akin to the time of love, of suffering, of play. Lovers know that time is measured only by their time together, and it is never

time enough. In suffering, there is only the time it takes to heal or else the time or duration of pain itself. In play there is only the time of the exhilaration of the body in action; we play until we are tired. Poetry never addresses itself to masses or the crowd. It speaks to each of us personally and with absolute sincerity (like a private letter), and we nod and assent to the truth of it as we would to the mention of our very names. It places us in a time when it is everlastingly now, a time when we go from present to present, a time when we live in that all-too-quick eternity where nothing is ahead and nothing behind but somehow totally within and between us. It makes us more ourselves and more profoundly everybody else at the same time. Understood in this way poetry is as indispensable to life as bread. Like bread it is daily and shareable. It roots us in the only permanence we have, which is the eternal human person we each bear within us in a way that is beyond change and beyond denial. Poets address themselves to that inner person. And they are among the few who do. We live in a time when numerous institutions and their representatives look at man in partial terms. To advertisers he is a consumer. To politicans he is a voter. To television producers he is a viewer. To corporations he is something called personnel. To some orthopedists he is bones. To the military he is a rank. These are all partial views, and they owe a great deal to the influence of technology since technology assumes that all reality—man included—is divisible into parts. This may be true of machines. It is certainly not true of life; divide anything living into its component parts, and it dies in the process. Only poetry regards man in his totality. It is what John Henry Newman calls his "autobiography." It bonds us in the common nationality of flesh and bone. We respond to and are attracted to it as to a source or shrine—a power that does not and cannot lie. In our time and perhaps in any time the explicit is for those who lack imagination. The totally explainable is for those who have no place in their lives for mystery, which is to say that they have no place in their lives for life. Poetry is for those who know that some things (and they are usually the most important things) are forever inexplicable while being forever undeniable.

Although poetry has been the main preoccupation of my life as a writer, I have written prose when the impulse was there to do so. By prose I mean literary criticism, personal essays, and fiction. I have published critical pieces on John Donne, Wilfred Owen, Gerard Manley Hopkins, Hart Crane, and recently T. S. Eliot. The study of Hart Crane was published in the Barnes and Noble American Writers and Critics series and was the first book-length study of Crane ever published. This book was subsequently republished by Holt, Rinehart and Winston and then re-republished with an updated bibliography by the University of Ohio Press under the title *Smithereened Apart.* My essays have usually been personal essays on subjects as varied as my dislike of travel as an end in itself to my failure to be impressed by the Wizard of Oz aura of the Reagan administration. I did strike an unexpectedly rich vein when I began writing a number of short essays on the myth of Icarus, which I interpreted as being concerned with the fascinating question of how much is enough and not simply how high is too high. This collection of essays was eventually published under the title of *The Feast of Icarus* and has recently been included in a general gathering of my essays and marginalia entitled *The Rest Is Prose.* My fiction consists of four books. The first was a trilogy entitled *Inscripts.* The second was *The Very Fall of the Sun,* a parable of sorts about justice. The next was a love story set in the south of France. Its title was *The Wanton Summer Air.* (Many who did not recognize the title as coming from a speech by Friar Lawrence in *Romeo and Juliet* —"A lover may bestride the gossamer / That idles in the wanton summer air / And yet not fall, so light is vanity"— thought of it as an oriental novel, presumably Chinese.) My most recent novel is called *Stills* and is a love story about a photojournalist who is permanently stigmatized by his experiences in embattled Beirut.

For me the difference between writing a poem and writing a novel is traceable to a difference in inspiration, which in turn necessitates a difference of utterance. A poem possesses you like an obsession, a matter of writing out what you are just now discovering so that in the process you find words for what it is that you are trying to understand or at least describe honestly. As a poem demands that you "die" into your subject so that it can reveal itself through you, a novel demands that you die into the characters and their stories so that they can express through you how they behave and talk and think and grow over a period of time. To me that is essentially the mission of fiction—to reveal man in action. And I understand action as Aristotle understood action—whatever reveals the nature of man.

As a rule, I do not move in circles where writers tend to meet with other writers. Even if I could, I'm not sure that I would. Literary consanguinity has hurt more writers than it helped. But there are a few men and women with whom I correspond periodically and whose work I regard highly. By *highly* I mean that they pass a simple personal test—I buy their books. There are other criteria that come into play after that, but purchase is primary. Poets of the present and past whose work I admire are John Donne, Shakespeare, Hopkins, Robert Frost, Randall Jarrell, Richard Wilbur, W. S. Merwin, Linda Pastan, and Naomi Shihab Nye. There is also a fine poet named Sue Ellen Thompson whose talent is self-evident in *This Body of Silk,* her first book but assuredly not her last. It is always a pleasure to like those writers whom one admires (I mean to like them personally), and in the case of Wilbur, Merwin, Pastan, Nye, and Thompson I am happy to say that such is the case.

What are my immediate plans? Hopefully to go on doing what I have been doing since 1966: directing the International Poetry Forum while continuing to teach at Duquesne University, being a family man, writing as well as I can and trying to be intelligent in public about one or two issues that I regard as important. When asked what I would do if I were suddenly to be given a million dollars, I usually answer that I would probably go on doing what I'm doing. Thus far it has not made me in any way unhappy. My concept of happiness, I might add, is not exalted. At one time I defined happiness as knowing that my son, because of the Salk and subsequent vaccines, would not contract polio. I still hue to a definition of happiness that is not far removed from that. It is linked to appreciation. Like mercy it is a quality that is never strained. In a poem addressed to my son and entitled "The Quiet Proofs of Love," I like to think that something of that appreciative spirit is present:

With Princess Grace of Monaco, 1980

"My family: my son, Samuel Robert, Mary Anne, and myself"

Don't wait for definitions.
                    I've had
my fill of aftertalk
and overtalk, of meanings that don't
mean, of words not true
enough to be invisible, of all
those Januaries of the mind when
everything that happens happens
from the eyebrows up.
                    If truth
is in the taste and not
the telling, give me whatever
is and cannot be again—
like sherbet on the tongue, like love . . .
Paris defined is Paris
   lost, but Paris loved
is always Orly in the rain,
broiled pork and chestnuts
near the Rue de Seine,
the motorcade that sped de Gaulle
himself through Montparnasse.
                    Viva
the fool who said, "Show me
a man who thinks, I'll show
you a man who frowns."

                    Which
reminds me of Andrew, learning
to count by two's and asking,
   "Where is the end of counting?"
Let's settle for the salt and pepper
of the facts.
                    Oranges don't parse,
and no philosopher can translate
shoulders in defeat or how
it feels when luck's slim arrow
stops at you or why lovemaking's
not itself until it's made.
Let's breathe like fishermen who sit
   alone together on a dock
   and let the wind do all
   the talking.
                    That way we'll see
that who we are is what
we'll be hereafter.
                    We'll learn
the bravery of trees that cannot
know "the dice of God
are always loaded."
                    We'll think

of life as one long kiss
since talk and kisses never mix.
We'll watch the architecture
of the clouds create themselves
like flames and disappear like laughter.

As for the rest I am pleased that my brother and I work in the same city and see one another quite often. (He is the founder and director of the American Experience program at the University of Pittsburgh and the author of a definitive work on the nature of love entitled *The Idea of Love*.) Other than that and what I have mentioned previously, I try to face each day with the faith it deserves. I am not a great devotee of excitement. I incline to a few bankable pleasures—a pipeful of a mild English mixture of cavendish, perique, and latakia, a breakfast of ham and eggs, a swim, a walk, a chance to converse with good friends, being able nightly to return to a book that I am in the midst of reading or writing, additional time to listen to my son's music and to watch him develop his talent as a composer and band director and music educator, the opportunity to do physical work, the pleasure of watching the expression in my wife's face when she is watching flowers she has grown. I know that the world offers much more to searchers and yearners, but they don't beguile me. Some would call that a shortsighted vision of the world, but I can only answer that there is a world more vast and more mysterious within us that is no less real. As long as we live we are citizens of both worlds, but the inner world has always had my first allegiance.

BIBLIOGRAPHY

Poetry:

Discovery, and Other Poems, Sheed and Ward, 1959.

The Quiet Wars, Sheed and Ward, 1962.

Listen with the Eye (photographs by James P. Blair), University of Pittsburgh Press, 1964.

My Sons in God: Selected and New Poems, University of Pittsburgh Press, 1965.

Blood Rights, University of Pittsburgh Press, 1968.

Twelve Poems (prints by George Nama), Byblos Press, 1970.

Once for the Last Bandit: New and Previous Poems, University of Pittsburgh Press, 1972.

Quartered, University of Pittsburgh Press, 1974.

Shuffle, Cut and Look: Poems, Book Press, 1977.

An America Made in Paris, Byblos Press, 1978.

To Paris: Poems, New Directions Publishing, 1981.

Thank a Bored Angel: Selected Poems, New Directions Publishing, 1983.

The Color of Reluctance, Dooryard Press, 1986.

Nightwords, Sheep Meadow Press, 1988.

Silence Spoken Here, Marlboro Press, 1988.

Prose:

Hart Crane: An Introduction and Interpretation (criticism), Barnes & Noble, 1963, revised and republished as *Smithereened Apart*, Ohio University Press, 1977.

Seascript: A Mediterranean Logbook, Byblos Press, 1971.

Inscripts (fiction trilogy), Ohio University Press, 1975.

The Very Fall of the Sun (parable), Popular Library, 1978.

The Wanton Summer Air (novel), North Point, 1982.

The Feast of Icarus (essays), Palaemon Press, 1984.

The Pittsburgh That Starts within You (essays), Byblos Press, 1986.

Stills (novel), Atheneum, 1989.

The Rest Is Prose (essays), Duquesne University Press, 1990.

Translator:

The Blood of Adonis, translation from Arabic of the poetry of Adonis, nee Ali Ahmed Said, University of Pittsburgh Press, 1971.

The Growl of Deeper Waters, translation from French of the essays of Denis de Rougemont, University of Pittsburgh Press, 1975.

Transformations of the Lover (additional poems of Adonis), Ohio University Press, 1983.

Shelby Hearon
1931-

Shelby Reed in Dahlonega, Georgia, 1935

The grandest thing about my childhood was the freedom. At six, in 1937, I travelled alone from Midland, Texas, to St. Louis, Missouri, on the train, a tag around my neck giving my name and destination. It seemed quite natural to deal by myself with the dining car, the porter about the ladder to my upper berth, the bathroom in the middle of the night, and to converse with the elderly gentleman on whose hat I sat. My mother's father, whom I adored, met me at the station and drove me to Marion, Kentucky, the town where both my parents (and I) were born. There I divided my time between the houses of my two grandfathers, who lived at opposite ends of Main Street and did not speak.

We spent the summer I was nine in the Davis Mountains of West Texas, at a family-style guest ranch called Mitre Peak. While my parents got reacquainted with old friends and tended my two-year-old sister, Frances, I was free between meals to go wherever I liked. I recall being on a huge horse when a six-foot rattler crossing our path caused her to bolt a fence and lope us back to the stable; watching a sheep drown in a flash flood as a sudden deluge roared down the dry gulleys of the mountainside; finding a swimming hole hidden below a ledge and taking a dip with a bunch of teenaged boys. I recall also, that fine summer, getting the itch, impetigo, and being sprayed by a skunk. But all that seemed a fair price to pay for being on my own.

Part of the liberty I enjoyed was certainly connected with being reared in a gender-general way. I remember a car trip I took at four with my father. I had a boy's barbershop haircut, boy's pants and jacket, my ambiguous name, and whenever we stopped for the night at a filling station, I was taken for his son—a confusion that went uncorrected.

Later, entering school in Midland, where Daddy, a geologist, was hunting oil for Shell, a group of kids crowded around me on the playground to ask, Are you a boy or a girl? I thought that pretty dumb, but there I was, named Shelby Reed, with my cropped hair, corduroy trousers, checked shirt, lace-up shoes. The year was 1938: the Age of Shirley Temple. Then, as if to prove their point, I spent most of my time hanging around with a boy named Kingsley, competing with him for smartest kid in the class, learning pig latin and how to use his father's jigsaw. Even finding it necessary to bloody his best friend's nose for trying to make something out of our friendship.

Closely associated in my mind with the mobility and androgyny of those early years is science, which was in the very air I breathed at home. My earliest memory is of being three, in a snowsuit, in the piney woods of north Georgia, where my father was prospecting for gold in the Smokies. When he called my name and I knew which direction to turn, that seemed a marvelous discovery: to be able to locate by sound. Shortly after that, when I proudly identified

Mother, Evelyn Roberts Reed, Midland, Texas, about 1939

an anthill, he responded, passing on his training, "Can you prove it?"

In Midland, at the age of eight, I remember Daddy and his friends—in the living room of our house with the windmill in the backyard and the fine shingled roof for sliding down—inventing math problems for me and waiting while I walked around the block in a sandstorm, solving them in my head.

Later, when my family moved back to Marion, Kentucky, so that my father could prospect for fluorspar, my mother could have my sister Susan, and I could enter fourth grade, I remember Daddy and Darrell Hughes (a physicist who later worked on atomic energy at Los Alamos) bringing in a block of ice, stacking *Encyclopaedia Britannica*s at an angle, and sliding it down them in a vain effort to explain glaciation to me. I argued, as I recall, that it melted from the top faster than from the bottom, which, to their chagrin, turned out to be the case on our hardwood floor.

At that time, too, I met King Hubbert (who later, married to Miriam Berry, my mother's closest

friend from boarding school and Vanderbilt days, won Columbia's Vetlesen Prize, the "Nobel Prize" of earth science) and Eddie Mayer (who did top-secret operations analysis at the Pentagon during and after the war.) Together and in pairs those men talked and talked and talked, argued and argued, so that I came to feel that truth in science was directly proportional to the volume of words marshalled in support.

The women, less voluble, took refuge in the text to make their points. I can picture my mother, Evelyn, waving some book in the air at my father, Charles; producing a passage that substantiated her claim, settling a dispute in which he did not intend to budge an inch, by citing, as they said, chapter and verse.

Back on their home ground, my parents, housed midway on Main Street between the remnants of their families, seemed romantic figures to me. My father, sent off alone at eight to a clinic in St. Louis with polio; his baby sister dying of the diphtheria he brought back. My father with blood poisoning, the doctor ready to take off his arm, his dad saying he'd rather have the boy dead than a cripple. My father born the very day his older brother, John, died of tetanus, leaving three sisters behind. Him going off at fifteen to the University of Virginia, the school for gentlemen, with one jacket to his name, and making all A's. (That these stories were not all true—my aunt claims brother John had had rheumatic fever all his life and died of it one winter—didn't matter; these were the legends I grew up on.) My mother losing her own beloved mother at fifteen; my grandmother, having lost a third daughter and been told that to get pregnant again would kill her, closing her bedroom door and dying young of hypertension; my mother and her sister raised under the cruel rule of a jealous young stepmother (a Wallis Simpson look-alike named Maude whom I was not allowed to call grandmother), who substituted fake pearls for the real pearls my mother's father gave her. Him dying of a heart attack in the same town with her, the two of them not speaking.

Evenings in the house on Main when the Red Seal shellacs of Galli-Curci, Caruso, and Schumann-Heink played on the turntable, I was a little bit in love with both my parents.

In those years Daddy sang. He had a beautiful high tenor voice, most like John McCormack's in its range and timber (and when I play his records now I can still see my father standing, hand on his heart, pouring out the lyrics to such songs as "Drink to Me Only with Thine Eyes" and "When Other Lips and Other Hearts"), and for seven years I took piano lessons so I could sit on that bench and accompany him.

My mother swam. Summers we went to Dawson Springs, a lake surrounded by pines that had echoes of Dahlonega, Georgia, for me. While Frances and Susan played on the raft and learned to dive, Mother and I sidestroked across the deep cold lake together, she on her right side, I on my left, facing. And I can see her yet, thin and tanned, pulling the still water away from her with long smooth strokes.

For my part, being back in Marion meant having a whole small town to explore. My great new friend Patty Jo Babb and I went everywhere and did everything that came into our heads: sneaking out for sunrise breakfasts at City Lake, where we scaled and fried up the perch we caught; hitching rides around town on horse-drawn wagons; swinging from the railroad trestles while the trains went by overhead; catching crawdads in the creek with empty cling-peach cans; swapping clothes with Joan and Louise in abandoned boxcars; smoking cigarettes under the bridge. (We bought them at Small's Grocery, pretending they were for Patty's mother, who the grocer knew had died when she was born.)

Even at eleven, after we got our periods and began to wait expectantly for the big breasts of Patty's sisters Betty Lou and Dottie Sue, nothing really changed—not even later when we wore flame red lipstick, read pornographic comics (bought at the newsstand, where we claimed imaginary older brothers), played Post Office and Spin the Bottle, exercised our legs until they matched Betty Grable's (7″, 12″, 19″), gave each other Toni Home Permanents, began to date. In the wartime forties, sex seemed just one more adventure awaiting us around the corner.

Then into this Eden came boarding school; and my formal education, in several senses, began.

Because the high school in Marion was no longer college preparatory, as it had been, teaching Latin and Greek, in my parents' day, I was sent off at fourteen to Sayre School in Lexington, a financially shaky girls' academy in the Kentucky bluegrass, run by a group of Presbyterians, formerly missionaries to Korea. It was a staggering adjustment. Or would have been, if I had made it.

It was not the religion, to my surprise, which was the problem. If not raised in a church, I had lately attended my Grandmother Reed's Methodist services and so had the general idea; more importantly, by training I was a textualist. So reading the whole Bible was fine; and reporting on it, as long as testimonials were not required, was fine as well.

Father, Charles Boogher Reed, about 1939

The trouble was the confinement. Everything was not all right: Leaving the freshman-sophomore floor after a certain hour. Leaving study hall. Leaving the campus ever, except with chaperones or Saturday morning in sign-out, sign-in groups of four. Staying too long in the bathroom. Taking more than one shower a day. Unauthorized use of the phone. Eating except at mealtimes. Going too far, or rather going anywhere at all, with boys.

The first time I got campused was for sitting with a date in the parlor at four in the afternoon, with the light out. "Abstain from all appearance of evil," the housemother reminded me. Not caring a fig, or drawing a distinction between, whether I had been necking up a storm or talking Einstein's theory of relativity with my boyfriend, a physicist's son.

The trouble also, implicit in the rules, was that I did not "know my place" as a middle-class female.

Rescuing me for occasional weekends, my aunts and uncles in the area were very generous—my mother's sister Ethel, a favorite of mine, in Cincinnati, my daddy's brother Avery and his family in Lexington, his older sister Katherine and her chil-

In Marion, Kentucky, 1943

dren in coal-mining Cumberland—but in their homes, also, I learned that certain manners and behavior were expected of a proper teenaged girl.

Then in 1947 we moved to Austin, Texas, where my father did seismic work for oil companies, my sisters went to better schools, my mother, who had a six-week-old baby named Linda, put a distance between her and her wicked stepmother, and I tried to break away. I wanted desperately to take early admission to Chicago, the school that had turned Darrell Hughes from a rural Kentucky boy into an atomic physicist and King Hubbert from a Texas redneck into an earth scientist. It seemed (and probably was) my last chance to escape the gender expectations of the postwar years.

When my parents vetoed the idea (I'd had my time away at Sayre; they had three other daughters to consider), I gave in as gracefully as I could. At Austin High I joined a social club, wrestled my smile to the floor for the upperclassmen, made girlfriends, stuffed Kleenex in the points of my conical bra, and, in my white two-piece Rose Marie Reid bathing suit, went out for the Beauty Revue. I gave Coke parties, went

to graduation teas, was a high-school debutante, dated the boy across the street and one around the corner.

And was the only girl in my physics class.

My salvation in those years before the university was a dark and hungry boy I met when I went out for debate. Painfully thin, troubled, brilliant, he spent most afternoons in detention hall for one violation of school rules or another. Clearly my type. We spent hours and hours a week together. He biked the three miles from his house to mine, then we walked or took a bus to the campus, where we both planned to go, sitting in a booth over iced tea, or rummaging in the open stacks at the University of Texas library where he worked.

We argued heredity and environment, compared all the books we'd read, read piles of those we hadn't, wrote long confiding letters. Yet even when we were wriggling out of whatever clothing was permitted to be removed in those days, on the dark hillside near my house, we were much like grade-school buddies. Being with him was in many ways like being back in second grade with Kingsley.

His name was Bob Hearon, and I married him six years later.

Before entering UT in the fall of 1949, I took all the tests offered by what was then the Testing and Guidance Center. When it came time for the conference, my guidance counselor said that, although all my scores were high, my highest by far was a category known as mechanical. It went off the top of the page. He didn't know what to do about that or what to suggest. Since I was a girl, perhaps the honors liberal-arts program . . . ? I said I'd already signed up.

The university was a very wonderful time for me. I loved each and every course, and, in Plan II, had all the best professors. Ettlinger for pure math, Riker for history, Ayres for economics, Engerrand for anthropology, Hughes for physics, Roach for government, Ransom for English, Bullard for geology. None of my outside activities (the Pi Phis, Orange Jackets, Mortar Board, the university Y) detracted in any way from the feeling that I was finally a fish in water.

In 1951 I got my first car, when a small annuity left me by my Grandfather Roberts matured. It was a 1949 Desoto Club Coupe, dark green, and the first week I drove it some old man stopped dead in the middle of traffic and I ran into the back of his car. "I'm J. Frank Dobie," he explained to the traffic cop, as if this were information enough about our wreck, and proceeded on his way. It was my introduction to

Texas letters, and my first taste of the freedom of wheels. I haven't been without a car since.

By the time of my graduation in 1953, my wedding two weeks away, the idea of a life of science had given way to the intention of someday being a writer.

I think there were two reasons for this, quite apart from the cultural pressure of the times.

The first was that my attempts to question, to argue matters of mathematics or science in school, had been met with less than enthusiasm. At Sayre I remember asking the plane-geometry teacher why a certain proof couldn't be worked in a quicker way, and being sent from the classroom for the remainder of the period. At Austin High, at the board, I suggested to my trig teacher that there was a simpler equation, and she threw a chalk eraser at my head. At UT I tried once, after biology class, to question Darwin as presented in the text and lecture. Surely, I argued, the varieties of species we had today could not have come about through random selection in the time given. Was it not possible that Lamarck had been right? That changes in the environment might alter individuals and be inherited? To which the professor responded with ridicule and by lowering my grade.

The other obstacle was that I simply was not good enough. In Darrell's introductory physics course for physics majors (in which I was the only girl), he graded on a curve that kept most of us with a test average between 35 percent and 45 percent, so that he could see whether there was anyone able to make a high score on that scale. There was. One student had a 98 percent; I was not that student. I wish I had been.

In sharp contrast, every time I turned in a written paper, I got an immediate and positive response. At Sayre my roommate and I, the only two students in Latin, were urged to read novels and plays set in early Roman times and invent scenes of our own; at Sayre, also, my first English theme ("The Fifty-Cent Cigar") was passed around to all the other teachers. At Austin High the composition teacher held up my first essay and asked, "Whose paper is this?" When I claimed it, she told me to stay in after class. "Who wrote this for you?" she demanded. Which I found to be an amazing concept: that there could be homes where people knew what you were taking; where people had the time to do your homework for you; where they could do it better than you. "Nobody," I told her. And, after satisfying herself it was mine, she put a list of words from the paper on the board the next day. My senior year, I

won the state interscholastic-league extemporaneous writing contest. I felt I'd come full circle when the local paper carried a banner headline: AUSTIN BOY WINS READY-WRITING.

English teachers seemed to welcome rather than resist dissent. I could say to Willis Pratt that *Hamlet* was not a tragedy as he himself had defined tragedy, if I gave chapter and verse; could argue with Harry Ransom that *Sons and Lovers* was not about a silver cord, or not mainly, provided I could substantiate my claims for what it was about. And in my seminar on Proust, under Stephenson, reading a volume a week to catch up with the graduate students who had already read them in French, I could argue my points and not have to go stand in the hall.

There was yet another consideration in my decision to try writing. Looking ahead to being wife and one day mother, I recalled my mother and grandmother in Marion. Women, I concluded, lived their lives by the word; texts were their dowries. My mother owned the large annotated library that had belonged to her great-aunt, May Shelby Wyatt, an educated woman who read Cervantes and Victor

Shelby "in high-school debutante dress," 1949

Hugo on a pig farm in Fredonia; she cherished the remaining books of her mother's, a suffragist who had been the first woman on a Kentucky board of education. For my grandmother Reed, who had grown up in the shadow of Washington and Lee University, which she could not attend, books meant education. Before and during the Depression, she put seven children through college, Daddy's brothers becoming mining and ceramic engineers; his sisters, all of whom had advanced degrees, teaching math, Latin, English, psychology.

Texts were also women's histories. My grandmother Lutie Boogher Reed could trace her neat, branching family tree in this country back to 1622; my mother, born Evelyn Shelby Roberts, to 1620. Both tended boxes of handed-down letters, wills, inventories, journals. Writers as well as readers, both kept records, my grandmother in a series of fat, locked five-year diaries, my mother in a tiny loose-leaf notebook that held character sketches from her teaching days at Shady Grove.

Between entering and leaving UT, I had also got my first taste of paid employment, instruction of a different sort. At nineteen, I applied for a job as playground director in East Austin, the Mexican sector of town, thinking that I knew nothing of this community which was a large part of the Texas culture. The director of Parks and Recreation, Beverly Sheffield (he had trouble with his name, also), tried to discourage me. They had run through a series of ten leaders on Palm Playground the year before; it could be rough. Try me, I said, and he did.

Having no concept of the assumption of failure, I looked at the chart of citywide events available to playgrounds and started getting up teams and programs so we could enter. At first I had trouble; a couple of the big guys got up on the clubhouse roof and threw Coke bottles down, so that I had to rely on my second-grade nose-bloodying stance to get them back in line. Other boys made rather different propositions, spelling out the words for me on the ground with sticks. When I told them thanks, no, that I was getting married in two years, they were insulted; nobody waited that long.

I found myself coaching the boys' softball team, teaching swimming to the little kids on the lifeguard's day off, and—perhaps my dumbest move and our biggest success—cutting Thurber's *Thirteen Clocks*

Sisters, Susan, Frances, and Linda, with their father at Barton Springs, 1949

into a one-act play. When our production was one of three citywide finalists, and we got to perform it (Hagga crying diamonds) for the hillside theater at Barton Springs Park, over a thousand people from East Austin sat on the grass to watch. Another milestone event for Palm was sandbox sculpture. Every playground hosed down its six-foot-square sandpile and got some high schooler to carve a picture in bas-relief. This had never worked for them; big boys always trashed it, stomped or peed it, sending the little kids home in tears. But this time, when we were serious contenders, and the whole community with its network of families was rooting for us, the big guys stood guard over our sculpted state of Texas (complete with mountains and rivers) all night long in shifts. We placed fourth overall in the city, beating out at least eighteen middle-class, achiever-oriented neighborhoods, and the Palm Mothers' Club gave me twelve place settings of pink dishes as a thank-you.

I was equally untrained and ill-prepared to be the secretary-bookkeeper at the university YM-YWCA, a job I took to help put Bob through law school. The head of staff, W. A. Smith, known as Block, a man well loved in the world's YMCA movement, became very much a father figure to me. I went to Nixon-Clay Business College to learn typing, and from him got the rudiments of double-entry bookkeeping. So dumb was I about the ways of government and payroll that I put the social-security number of my predecessor on my forms, thinking that was the number which went with the job. Block was patient, rewarding me with a milkshake whenever I got the debit and credit columns to balance on the first try; he took upon himself my general education. When he presented me with Tillich's *Shaking of the Foundations* and I said I didn't have any foundations to shake, he gave me *The Courage to Be,* inscribed "a good book for a good mind." That he could see me in that way—someone doing rather badly the ordinary clerical work of a meagerly paid job—was as confirming as my B.A. degree. I left that job and Austin feeling for the first time since the summer at Mitre Peak one whole person named Shelby.

The years in which I had my babies were a wonderful oasis in my adult life. We ended up Bob's military service during the Korean conflict on a hill in Alexandria, Virginia, living in a cottage that belonged to my father's old friend Eddie Mayer. His first wife, who had been a close friend of my mother's, had died of a cerebral hemorrhage; his second wife, Kay, became a wonderful friend and

Reed and Anne Hearon, Austin, 1960

surrogate mother to me. I went there with a new baby named Anne Shelby, and while I grew big with my second, I trotted along after Kay, watching as she milked goats, saddled horses, fed and talked to dogs and cats. I'm sure, in hindsight, this easy farmlike atmosphere both loosened my tongue and soothed my mind, assets at baby-making time.

I had worked at the Pentagon early in my first pregnancy, making travel arrangements for and writing to a group of scientists stationed around the world, and when one of them on leave said to me, "Don't you know there are too many children in the world?" retorted earnestly, "There aren't too many of *mine.*" That conviction remained with me, that there was something fine and amazing about replicating the species, something that, just as sex had been, was an expansion and not a limitation.

At Eddie and Kay's I had a wonderful freedom. Plagued with insomnia because I couldn't sleep on my stomach, I used to wander around Eddie's apple orchards in the middle of the night, check on Kay's goats, who would come silently to the fence for a nuzzle in the moonlight. Soon Anne, by then a year old, could push open the door of the cottage and run across the yard to Kay's house, open her screen, squeeze by the dogs and cats, and take out all the pots and pans to play with while we had our toast and coffee. Even my Siamese male, Satchmo, followed the goats to pasture every morning and came home with them at night, while my female, Delilah, spent her time chasing the laying hens around their pen.

Having my children so close together was my idea, although it happened rather sooner than I expected. Because I knew I'd not have such a wonderful breathing or breeding space again, it seemed a fine time to begin another child in that lovely Virginia landscape. So I read up on the biology of reproduction—which sperm lives longest, which travels fastest—and figured I would leave my diaphragm out one night a month, ensuring that if I did get pregnant (as I recall that required the male sperm to live five days before the egg came down) it would be a boy. When it happened on the first try and then I began to bleed all over the living-room rug, I figured I was right. Only a perceptive nurse ("Honey, you're not bleeding inside; your bladder's just full") kept the doctors at Fort Belvoir from doing a D and C, and by such a slim accident I kept the baby.

The arrival of my son Reed got a response I had in no way anticipated. "He's the first Hearon born in fourteen years," my father-in-law announced, explaining that Anne didn't count because "girls don't keep their names." My own father's joy, relayed from Houston where he was working, and his pride, were apparent. For the first time I looked head-on at the fact, long denied, that my family had without doubt been disappointed by the arrival of four girls, each of us in turn.

The first handful of years back in Austin felt like boarding school revisited, made worse by the suspicion that this time it was for life. Everything not required was restricted, especially my behavior, as a lawyer's wife, and my mobility, in a neighborhood that required a car to get anywhere, that didn't even have sidewalks to stroll along. Anne, who had had free rein at Kay's, now had to be spanked for stepping off the yard into the street. And even the planks and nail-kegs I got them, the sandpile and slide and tubs of water, lived in a fenced yard with a high gate.

Although raising small people—the whole exploration of cognitive learning, motor development, how the young of the species developed personality—was endlessly fascinating and grand, it seemed to bring with it a whole host of communal expectations I couldn't shake, boundaries and limitations that took my breath (and sometimes my spirit) away. Lawyers' wives did not work, so that my being a part-time bookkeeper for my father and his geophysical partner must be sub rosa. We did community service, so that I ended up places like the board of the Pan American Center with a bunch of politicians and no direct access to the people I had worked with on Palm Playground.

Central to the perception of being trapped was the fact that the three adults closest to me had altered beyond recognition, raising the terror that my fix had nothing to do with women's place or role-playing at all, but rather with growing up, with the inevitable passage of time. My slim, raven-haired mother was now a stout blond, no longer swimming laps at Barton Springs, the rock-ledged, spring-fed city pool, and, with her youngest in her teens, at loose ends. My father, the boyish athlete with the lilting tenor, was no longer singing, was drinking heavily, was gone for weeks at a time. Quite simply, my sisters had been raised by different people. Bob also was unrecognizable: the intense outsider, the hungry biker, had put on forty-five pounds, a suit and tie, and disappeared into the fortress of his profession.

The cumulative effect was one of substantial loss.

At that point, I decided that if I couldn't get out and wasn't to go nuts, I'd have to go *in*. And in I went.

I read Karen Horney, Erik Erikson, Karl Menninger, Erich Fromm. I kept a journal, recorded my dreams, studied my high-school diaries, listened to the words of my mouth, compared what Bob and my parents had said in letters and in my memory with what they said now. Looking for patterns. Had anyone truly changed? Was my mother again just the wide-cheeked girl she'd been before her stepmother entered her life? Was what had seemed a young man's wanderlust in Daddy now perceived as running away? Was what had appeared moody and troubled in Bob at seventeen now seen as depressed, unreachable? If determinism before had had to do with Darwin, with biological necessity, it now had to do with Freud, with psychological destiny.

I got reacquainted with my sisters; asked them about "their" parents. Linda, at six, had cried when I got married because we weren't going to be sisters any more; I tried to prove her wrong. When Susan, who had been to Poland with the Experiment for International Living, gave up graduate school in Russian Studies to marry her junior-high-school sweetheart, we were all in the wedding, wearing cherry red satin bridesmaid dresses, matching high heels, and bouffant hair. Frances, already bilingual, had married a South American engineer, had a daughter, and was teaching languages; Linda, dreaming of being a doctor, was already dating her future husband. Why did we all end up with those early boyfriends? Was it fear of not finding someone new? Or were our masks too fixed for anyone later to get past? I asked.

Frances, Shelby, Evelyn, Susan, and Linda at Susan's wedding, Austin, 1962

But those personal pryings went against the grain. If the temperament of the therapist is to intervene, the temperament of the writer is to let each scene play and replay itself. The therapist is the participant; the writer the observer.

When I was thirty, we built a house outside of town, in a hilly, woodsy area largely undeveloped, on a geologic fault not far from a lake and fossil outcroppings, where the children and I could climb rocks, hike old caliche trails, and feed visiting raccoons and possums.

And I began my first novel.

For three years I struggled with a draft of it. Every day I got up at five, did my yoga exercises and zen meditation, then wrote at the dining table with my yellow pad and pen until time to wake the children for school. I felt back on Palm Playground; back with the double-entry ledgers. Trying to learn by doing what I had no training for.

Winters, I still put in my time on Planned Parenthood, the Junior League, the PTA, serving my term as president of each. Summers, my good friend Valerie Sellers Dunnam and I took picnic lunches and our kids to Barton Springs to swim laps and visit. Val

led a similar divided life, having been both homecoming queen and a competitive diver at Southern Methodist University, and, in what we later referred to as the Age of Sylvia Plath, we compared notes on juggling it all.

Then, in 1964, mortality reared its head in the form of two cerebral hemorrhages a month apart, followed by a craniotomy. I recall thinking quite clearly the night before my chancy operation that, well, the main thing had got done: Anne and Reed at eight and seven were wonderful kids and could finish the job of raising themselves. But I never got that book finished. Once back on my feet, with the breath of that threat blowing down my neck, I got to work. The draft of the novel I had written was bad, really bad, every word. I threw it out and started over. In two more years I had another draft with ten good pages—on armadillos, biochemistry, and art. Working from those ten pages, while the children were at camp, I rewrote the whole and in July of 1967 sent it off to Knopf, unsolicited and unagented.

In a later novel, *Painted Dresses,* I have an artist who has taken six years to complete her first decent canvas. She conjectures that perhaps Matisse spent

Anne Hearon, about 1974

thermos and a piece of sourdough bread, making the forty-five-minute, two-thousand-foot climb at the edge of town, writing until midafternoon, taking off for a three-hour hike to one of the nearby glacial lakes at twelve thousand feet, having my steak, then writing until bedtime. When my family arrived for the last two weeks, we did longer, overnight hikes high in the Maroon Bells.

Those were wonderful lifesaving summers: Aspen in June with the sounds of the music festival floating on the air, the Physics Institute nearby, a door I could walk out at any time, was heaven to me. I can shut my eyes still and feel the rocky trail under me, and smell that rare, clear, fir-filled air.

In those years my children, also, were making choices. Anne, who'd worked for a summer as the only volunteer with a team of professionals (psychologist, psychiatrist, social worker) treating preschool autistic boys at the state mental hospital, was heading for Sarah Lawrence and psychology. Reed, who'd backpacked most of the Rockies and the length of the Cascades, got accepted at the University of Chicago after his junior year of high school, to study mathematics.

fifteen years arranging the fruit for his still life, then painted it in an afternoon. That was how the acceptance of my first novel, *Armadillo in the Grass,* the fall I was thirty-six, seemed to me.

As I began to make time for my writing, I also began to make a place for it, to create an alternate world into which I could move when the children went off to school.

Seven years before, when they were small, Bob had done a stint with the National Guard in Colorado. Leaving them with his mother, I took a twenty-six-hour train trip to join him. It was like water to someone on a desert, that time alone, a wonderful echo of the train trip I'd taken by myself at six. Forgoing sleep, I sat up reading Fred Hoyle, soaking up the different dimensions that astronomy provides. Once there, we took a burro pack trip to the top of Pikes Peak, reaching timberline at sunrise—and I fell in love with the Rockies.

Now I began an annual return to Colorado, in time taking a month in Aspen each summer, renting the place myself, setting the schedule, writing and climbing the mountains. For two weeks I was there alone, rising each morning at dawn, taking my

Reed Hearon in the Rockies outside Aspen, about 1974

By the time I officially left my marriage in 1976—moving with rented furniture into a rented apartment in the treetops near a hike and bike trail that led to Barton Springs—it seemed an outward and visible sign of a move already made.

In the fall of 1987, with *Owning Jolene,* my eleventh novel, I returned to Knopf and Judith Jones, the wonderful editor who had selected *Armadillo* from the unsolicited pile twenty years before. In the decades between those two books, writing has provided me with the ongoing opportunity to learn new things. First, the novels have permitted me the joy of pursuing my abiding interest in science in an amateur way. For example, in *Painted Dresses* I again tackled the matter of the inheritance of acquired characteristics, but this time in a vastly more receptive climate. My scientist is a biochemist at the Menninger Foundation who works on the way microevolutionary changes in the brain affect the genes. Currently, I am digging segments of trilobites out of samples of shale collected along Lake Cayuga in New York in order to explore the paleontological theory of punctuated equilibrium, which brings Darwin's random selection and gradual change into question. (Needless to say, these expositions are not always picked up by the reviewers: *Painted Dresses* was called "a lacy valentine" by the *New York Times* and a "junk food binge" by *Texas Monthly.*)

My novels have also allowed me to keep up with psychology, starting in each with a theoretical construct in order to see how it plays out when set in a particular place among particular people. Here I've been influenced by Harry Stack Sullivan, Frieda Fromm-Reichmann, Melanie Klein, Heinz Kohut, Alice Miller, and Jerome Kagan, to name a favorite few. In this regard, it was quite a high point a few years ago to be invited to give a reading at the Menninger Foundation. I felt as if I had taken coals to Newcastle—and they were recognized as coals.

Two asides about the books as a group may be of interest. For one thing, the novels seem to arrange themselves in pairs, the first of each being a special instance of a problem, the second more a class-action treatment. For another, I find I travel back and forth in a sort of rhythm between the classless small-town world of western Kentucky and the stratified professional society of Austin, Texas.

All of which is not to suggest that once I got myself and my books out there all my problems were solved. I still have ongoing trouble with being misperceived, as though somehow my concrete embodied self is not convincing.

Shelby, about 1974

For instance, the *tall* myth. This has happened to me half a dozen times or more, but one example will do. I arrived at the Rochester airport to give a reading at a nearby college. No other woman was in sight; in fact, no one else got off the tiny plane on that flight. I wandered around looking for my contact, wondering if there had been car trouble, and finally had him paged. He was standing right there by the phone, talking to the airline clerk. Looking, he confessed, surprised at my appearance, for someone 6'2" tall. And, as he loaded all 5'6" of me into the car, I felt he was secretly convinced he was escorting an imposter.

Or, take the phenomenon of being invisible. When I went for a job interview at a local college, Sarah Lawrence, and the door opened on time and a dean came out, I stood, held out my hand, and introduced myself. He walked right past me and spoke to a woman reading on a sofa against the wall: "Miss Hearon?"

Or being told I'm not me at all. Back when my second novel was condensed in *Redbook,* I went to the supermarket in Austin where I regularly bought my groceries. When I purchased five copies of the magazine, the checker asked me, "Why so many? Good recipe?" I told her, modestly, that I had a story in there, opening the page to my name. She said at once, "That's not you. I know the woman who wrote that. She comes in here all the time."

The gender confusion still plagues me, too. When I complained to Brown University about a letter addressed to "Mr. Hearon," the chair apologized by explaining that "it was a form letter"! At the New York Public Library, during a benefit that included fifty writers reading snippets of their works, I was introduced as Mr. Hearon by the man at my elbow, and, while waiting my turn at the mike, heard "his" oeuvre cited at length. The first time I applied for a Guggenheim Fellowship and didn't get it, the letter of regret informed me: "Mr. Hearon, your work was given every consideration." And more than once a student, wanting to get into a workshop, has written, "Dear Mr. Hearon, I've read and enjoyed all your books."

I still have problems also with losing my voice—still plagued with the notion that men talk it to death and women put it in writing. If as a teenager I could

Bill Lucas and Shelby Hearon at home in Westchester County, 1988

and did frequently retreat into a bout of laryngitis, as an adult I've found myself on a colloquy or panel more than once (painful to recall) tongue-tied—quite simply speechless. In later years, I've found a partial cure: I shake out my fingers, in an old reflex as if about to play the piano, recall the anticipation that went with waiting backstage at a recital in my yards of scratchy blue tulle, and then begin. This usually works despite whatever heavy intimidation is being handed out. (Readings on the other hand are a pleasure, but then that isn't my voice, it is my character's.)

Writing happy endings is hard, especially one's own. When I met Bill Lucas, a philosophy teacher, at a dinner party in Austin in 1978, I'd moved into a German stone farmhouse twenty miles west of town, where I meant to live out the rest of my life. I'd my three cats from my former life with me, and had acquired two battered dogs, a shepherd and a husky, that I'd nursed back into delinquency. It was a great life. I'd bought Adidas and jeans and baggy shirts, telling the kindly shrink who'd guided me through my divorce that this time I was hunting for a man who could tell the girls from the boys without a program.

Bill and I sat by one another at dinner and talked of job and work. "Hmmm," he said a lot. That in itself got my attention, accustomed as I was to the deluge of words on the part of important males in my past. "What does 'hmmm' mean?" I asked him. "What is philosophy?"

"Hmmmm," he said, "means you didn't say what I expected you to. Philosophy is figuring out how to decide what's true."

That first warm September night he stayed with me he said he couldn't get serious; he had a lot of irons in the fire. The first time I stayed with him he said he couldn't possibly move in with me until February.

From the start I liked his style and that of his family: direct. "What do you want from me?" he asked, walking the dogs with me through the lavender hill-country twilight. "I'm offering you sex," I told him. He thought that a howl; that I was the nearest thing to a Girl Scout he'd ever met. But I intended it on several levels, and he took me up on all of them. His mother, meeting me and suspicious of the motives of anyone interested in a logician still working on his dissertation, asked me why I'd picked him. "For his money," I answered, and Bill liked that, too. First because he was only making five hundred dollars a month at the time; second, because she believed me and was reassured.

I left my house and he left his garage apartment in East Austin, moving onto neutral ground together near the campus, both of us having a major amount of terror about giving up our private space, our own quarters. In the early months he padlocked his workroom door, and I packed up and left enough times to be sure I could.

It took us forever to believe, to trust, that you could be in the same vicinity with someone who didn't breathe your air or devour your thoughts. "Where are you?" we asked one another often, to signify permission for the other to be miles or worlds or chapters or proofs away. We have a blackboard in the living room, file drawers in the bedroom, reference books in the bath: reminders that no place is off limits to work.

Shortly after our wedding in 1981, Bill accepted a teaching job at Manhattanville College, a thirty-minute train ride from the publishing world in New York City, and I received fellowships from the Guggenheim Foundation and the National Endowment for the Arts. In Westchester County we found a Cape Cod house set in a 1940s time warp. Here we can safely walk out the door any hour of the day or night—to the grocery, the cleaners, the drugstore, the five and dime still called the Five and Dime, the train, or just around the shady neighborhood. Set squarely on an outcropping of blackened Precambrian rocks, our village is only minutes from the Cranberry Lake wilderness area, a bird migration route, and the Pound Ridge conserve, where stands of hemlock grow. Some days it feels as if I'd picked up Marion, Kentucky, and set it down in Colorado.

From the start, we worked to recover loss. We looked up my friend Patty; saw Marion's Main Street; made contact with Eddie and Kay. We hunted down Bill's father, whom he hadn't seen in fifteen years. We recovered all his books from the garages and storage rooms in Houston, so that his favorite ten thousand volumes can be at all times close at hand. We framed pictures of his grown daughters, and remember the birthdays of all his grandbabies. Most importantly, perhaps, we rekindled my old affection for my parents, who, trim and white-haired in their eighties, still talk and read and write with the same gusto. My mother graces us with the holographic histories that are her biweekly letters; my father sends us manuscript pages of his days as a seismologist in the twenties, prospecting and mapping in the North Woods, 385 miles north of Winnipeg.

I swim my laps at the college pool.

With the house, we inherited a wondrous garden: white dogwoods like those on the hill in Alexandria; iris, lilies, and tulips like my grandmother Reed grew in her long yard; peonies like those that bloom along the fences in Aspen; violets massed like those on the grounds of Sayre; lilacs that smell like the purple mountain laurel outside the house in Austin where I worked on *Armadillo.* The preacher next door shares her white tomcat with us, and we have a birdbath presided over by a resident jay, and a water tub on the ground for visiting possums and raccoons.

Here in my workroom that looks out on traffic accidents and the rising sun and moon, my stereo plays Pavarotti and John McCormack when I am starting work.

Bill gives good and perceptive true love. He spells it out. He says, speaking of himself generically, "Boys wouldn't mind a little popcorn." "Girls," I answer him in kind, "could eat a steak."

On days like today, when my son, a chef in California, reports he still reads mathematics, and my daughter, a family therapist in Florida, calls to say the baby is to be named *Shelby* whatever it turns out to be, I'm content.

I haven't made it look so bad.

BIBLIOGRAPHY

Fiction:

Armadillo in the Grass, Knopf, 1968, reprinted, Pressworks, 1983.

The Second Dune, Knopf, 1973.

Hannah's House, Doubleday, 1975.

Now and Another Time, Doubleday, 1976.

A Prince of a Fellow, Doubleday, 1978.

Painted Dresses, Atheneum, 1981.

Afternoon of a Faun, Atheneum, 1983.

Group Therapy, Atheneum, 1984.

A Small Town, Atheneum, 1985.

Five Hundred Scorpions, Atheneum, 1987.

Owning Jolene, Knopf, 1989.

Nonfiction:

(With Barbara Jordan) *Barbara Jordan: A Self-Portrait,* Doubleday, 1979.

Other:

Contributor of short fiction to *Mississippi Review, Shenandoah, Southwest Review, Cosmopolitan;* anthologies, including *Available Stories,* Ballantine, 1985, and *New Growth,* Corona, 1989; and various newspapers, with five PEN Syndication Project prize stories. Contributor of articles and features to periodicals, including *Cosmopolitan, Harper's Bazaar, GQ, The Writer, Texas Monthly, Reader's Digest, Poets & Writers, Publisher's Weekly.* Contributor of book reviews to *New York Times, Philadelphia Inquirer, Dallas Morning News, Houston Post.*

Madison Jones

1925-

"The house my father built at Sycamore Farm"

1

The great event of the year when I was fourteen was my father's buying a farm in the hill country twenty-five miles north of Nashville, Tennessee, my hometown. Sycamore Creek, then a clear virgin stream, wound through and partly bounded the farm, running for nearly a mile beneath towering sheer-rock bluff. The great sweep of the creek and bluff half-encircled bottom land that rose slowly to hills all in timber, from whose crests the farm dwellings in the valley looked like the houses of dwarfs. The hollows among the hills had names like Julie and Campbellite and Sodic, and in the central pasture was a graveyard with nameless markers of rude fieldstone. I think Sycamore Farm was one of the last places where, when people stopped talking, true silence would come down.

But my father's buying that farm was more than the great event of a single year. The place, with its people white and black, came to play a large part in my life, including my life as a writer. It created, or at least incarnated, a new world for me, fulfilling something I must have been yearning toward.

Outwardly, given the circumstances of my earlier years, it must not have appeared that I was possessed of any such yearning. I spent my first few years on a residential street in Nashville, a city boy. About the time of my sixth birthday we moved out of town to what was even then a swank suburb, Belle Meade, where my grandfather Webber, just retired, had built a house designed for his wife and himself and also for his daughter's family. This was my home, my literal home, until my grandfather died when I was nineteen.

My father was a very successful small-businessman, and I grew up among prosperous people and friends from rich or well-to-do families and had access to an elegant country club within easy walking distance. As a child I spent much time at that country club, swimming in the pool or wandering over the beautiful golf course. Later I attended private high schools, where I was a fairly good football player but not much of a student, and I was a member of a fraternity most of whose members were from rich families and more than a little snobbish. The dances that fraternity gave, always at the aforementioned country club, with big bands of national renown, often elicited howls of rage from the minority of not so wealthy fraternity members' fathers. "Exotic" is the word that describes my memory of those occasions.

Left alone, however, this account of my early experience would badly distort the picture. My parents, and especially my grandparents, were in no way social butterflies. They were all people of character. My father was a person of great authority and, if I am able to judge, as honorable a man as I have known. My brother and I grew up under rather stern discipline, with "Sir" and "Ma'm" for our elders and instant obedience to our father's voice. Failure in such matters was sure to call down what is here properly described as a "threshing." Our Presbyterian religious training had real teeth in it. No doubt was entertained in our home, and both of us grew up with moral consciences that today's vision could only see as overabundant. I remember three great virtues as being cardinal: honor, courage, and purity of heart. I overdid the first one and did moderately well with the second. With the last one I was a failure, though I suffered such pangs as consciences like mine were designed to inflict. I sometimes shudder to think of what Freudian sages would have to say about my growing up.

We were, I believe, a not untypical Southern family, traditional in our thinking. We were very conscious of family. Uncles and cousins and the rest were a part of everything. The past was persistently with us, and the War, the Great War, was not World War I, in which my father had fought as an infantry officer. My own feelings about the Civil War were the stronger for the presence in the house of my grandfather Pa Webber—or Fat Pa, to distinguish him from my paternal grandfather Skinny Pa.

"My father, Madison Jones, Sr.," 1951

Except for a Prussian paternal great-grandfather, all the recent generations of my family were of Welsh descent, and so with Pa Webber. He was a very old man when I knew him, born before the Civil War, in 1857, on a farm outside of Nashville. He remembered a great deal and also read Civil War history. The summers in particular were often lonesome times and I spent many an hour listening to him talk about the war—or the "waugh," as he called it—and about the life he remembered. The result was almost as though my own memory went back all those years and experienced the life and events he talked about: moments with the little black slave boy who was his early childhood companion; his actually seeing a kinsman, a Confederate soldier, captured by the Yankees; the time the Yankee soldiers came and confiscated the whole stock of food in his home. Such things are indelible in my memory—personal, you might say. I still look with pain on the defeat we suffered in that war.

Pa also read to me a great deal, mostly Bible stories from the Old Testament, stories I loved. There were Samson and Delilah, and Joseph in Egypt, and David and Goliath. This reinforced my religious training, of course, but it went further than that. To this day, when asked what writer has been the major influence on my work, I can truthfully say, "Moses"—because he is thought, or used to be thought, to be the author of the Pentateuch.

We had a number of black maids and part-time yard and house men when I was growing up. I was good friends with nearly all of them, but one in particular who worked for us from the time I was about six until I was twelve was very much a part of my life. Her name was Birdie (I am not sure now that it wasn't supposed to be "Burtie") Cannon Keith, though she had three or four additional middle names that she used to reel off when I asked her to. I guess that I spent, in the years she was with us, as much time in her company as I spent in my grandfather's. She was a mine of old tales and stories of her rural childhood, and she also sang to me. She sang songs like "Froggie Went A-courting" and the "Crawdad Song" and "Little Brown Jug." Many of her "true" tales were, as I later realized, at least partly untrue. She seemed to have had a wide experience of snakes and to have spent a considerable part of her childhood fleeing from them. There was the hoopsnake that would put its tail in its mouth and roll in pursuit of its victims. There was the fleet black racer and the jointed snake that, upon being struck, would break into pieces and later reunite.

As I recall, Birdie was barely literate, yet she knew tales which I later discovered were virtually identical with tales from the Brothers Grimm and Hans Christian Andersen. I have wondered about this, whether she had learned them from white people or whether these tales had somehow got to be part of the lore of the American black folk independently of Grimm and Andersen. Anyway Birdie created many a magic hour for me with these tales. "Fee, fie, fo, fum," she would say, transfixing me with the drama of Jack's peril in the castle of the giant. I owe her a great debt for such hours. She was like a member of our family and it was a blow when, shortly after my grandmother Webber's death, Birdie's husband was accidentally killed while driving his ice wagon and she had to leave us for good.

I was a fairly lonesome kind of boy, secretly timid in spite of some athletic prowess, and I did not make friends easily. I remember a later time when my

Sycamore Creek beside the house

Arthur Shearon and mules on Sycamore Farm

mother, concerned about my withdrawing nature, said to me, "Madison, I want you to be 'Hail, fellow, well met.'" But, as I told her, "Hail, fellow, well met-ness" simply never had had a place in my capabilities. I was not greatly dissatisfied with the fewness of the good and lasting friends I did have, with whom I played and wandered over the considerable extent of the Belle Meade area.

It was a beautiful area, with many handsome homes, including especially the splendid antebellum home after which the suburb of Belle Meade was named. It was one of our recreations to sneak, fearfully, into the big turreted horse barn that had used to house the finest of racing thoroughbreds, among them a winner of the English Derby. In my childhood there were many vacant lots and patches of woods scattered among the clusters and rows of houses in Belle Meade, and from almost anywhere in the area you could see the big hills around. A fairly short walk in most directions would put you in woods or pastureland or cornfields. In the woods, alone or with a friend or two, was where I spent a considerable part of my time—just wandering, or else, once I owned a gun, hunting squirrels or quail.

It may have been old talk and old tales that inspired my romantic feeling about the woods and wild things, a feeling that has lasted. A beautiful spot discovered beside a creek or on a hilltop would seize my imagination and accompany me home that day and draw me back again. I liked to imagine Indians still in those woods and to look for signs and relics of their vanished presence. There were spirits in the woods, a religious feeling. All this was what gave me, when I encountered it in college, an instant under-standing of Wordsworth's nature poetry. It was also one of the reasons for my elation when my father bought Sycamore Farm.

2

It was not only the natural beauty and mystery of that farm that inspired my love for it: there were the farm people. Before my father built a small house for his own family to summer in, there were three dwellings on the place, each occupied by a family. After several years there were only two families—the Hoopers, white, and the Shearons, black—and the men of these families were people I came to know about as deeply as I have known anyone. I also came to respect them. The country around there in the thirties was still not much more than a generation removed from the frontier, and these people were in many respects its children. They were honest simple people for whom a ten- or twelve-hour working day was merely the stuff of life. They had long memories and knowledge of every person and thing in that part of the country. They had due respect for us, my family, but they also had a proper and demanding pride in themselves. I came to know them through the summers and, in other seasons, the days and nights I spent there on the place. But I got to know them best in the eighteen months when I lived there exclusively, after I dropped out of college during my freshman year with the intention of becoming a farmer.

I learned what work was. Tobacco, both dark-fired and burley, was the principal money crop in that part of the state and a man earned what he made by growing it. In particular those interludes when each of thousands of plants had to be set in the ground and, when they were nearly grown, stripped of their suckers were an unprecedented test of my metal. I think I had never considered what it would be like to bend down hundreds of times in the blazing summer sun, while tobacco gum accumulated on my hands and arms and sometimes got into my eyes like fire. Of course we rested now and then, repairing to a shady place where we kept a common water jug and spent a few pleasant minutes in talk. But I could never see that Nell, the white man, and Arthur, the black one, were in dire need of rest. It is astonishing what a man can get accustomed to.

Besides tobacco we raised corn and hay and a good many hogs and cattle. We also kept walking horses, a few of which I broke and trained and sometimes took to horse shows, where I was successful on several occasions. And we had mules, inevitably. Until after World War II every smaller farm in the South had, and always had had, at least one team of mules. In my mind their demise is one of the saddest items in the long catalogue of things now all but vanished. They were among the most interesting of creatures, stubborn and cantankerous and perversely intelligent. A whole philosophy had developed around the mule, illustrated for me by what I heard Nell Hooper say more than once: "A mule'll be good all his life just waiting for one clear chance to kick you." Nell had a fiery temper and you could hear him for half a mile cussing one of our mules for some act of perversity. Arthur by contrast was even-tempered,

given to persuasion or resignation when a mule, with every appearance of deliberateness, stepped on one of his garden plants. The mule lived in song and story as well as on the farm. There is not an old-time farmer still surviving who is not able to recount at least a couple of mule-committed outrages.

Sycamore Farm had, in hollows and on hillsides, a great many acres of woods, and my father was interested in increasing our pastureland. So, at times when corn or tobacco required no work, we often went to the woods with ax and brush hook. It was not all sweat and strain. Usually there was running talk, only punctuated by those intervals when real muscle was needed. But there were interludes when we worked in silence, in sunlight filtered or slashing down through roofs of foliage overhead, dragging brush or saplings to a pile. At length I made a discovery. There are times in the woods when unexplained voices call to you. Once when I heard one I asked Arthur, who was close by, if he heard it. He turned a grave black face to me. He did not like to hear them; they frightened him.

Nell Hooper's father-in-law, Tom McCool, a man up in his seventies, came to live with him. Tom had, evidently, lived a good deal of a rogue's life, from place to place, with his whereabouts unknown to anybody. He still liked to go to town, to little Ashland City four miles away, and gamble and get drunk, but for all that he was first-class help on the farm. Even in the woods, where he used an ax slowly but with dead accuracy, he was as good as a young man. He had seen the world from its underside and as our friendship grew he told me about it—within, I suppose, discrete limits. But once, in the woods, evidently dropping discretion, he electrified us all. It was a story about his being in jail in Cairo, Illinois, in a cell with a black man, and how the two of them killed the jailer and escaped. He was a wanted man, I guess, but I think the event was years behind him and he felt himself in no danger. Unless it was danger from the devil: I sensed that he did not like even to think about his own death. When he was dying and the preacher came to see him about his soul, he turned his face to the wall.

High up on the ridge, on a small briar-choked piece of land adjacent to ours, lived a man named Red Ford. He had one son who left home for good as soon as he was nearly old enough, and after that Red lived entirely alone. Seated in his house you could see through the wall chickens walking around in the yard, and when the wind blew you could watch pieces of paper go fluttering across the floor. It never bothered Red, even in bitter weather. He seemed a pleasant, good-hearted, intelligent man; I never saw evidence of the truth of tales about him that might have put a person on his guard. It was a time when store-bought whiskey was expensive and sugar was cheap, and homemade whiskey was his business, his only business. His life had a regular rhythm to it. It consisted of something like four months making whiskey and three months in jail, repeated over and over down through the years. As soon as he got out of jail he would start up again, as everybody, including the revenue people, knew he would. But he was ingenious and hard to catch in the act. The stories of where and how he hid his stills were classics around that part of the county. But Red was an honest moonshiner. If the stuff was not good he would not sell it. After I was married and we spent summers at Sycamore, I used to buy from him. Once, because he did not think a run of whiskey was first-rate, he gave me a free gallon. My wife and I found it quite good enough to drink.

During the year and a half when I lived at Sycamore regularly, I had my meals at the Hoopers' and then retired to my own house well out of sight and hearing down on the creek bank. On winter nights I built fires that only occasionally got the place really warm. It was one of my recreations to stretch out on the hearth with my big half-shepherd dog on the cold side of me, and doze, and dream. I read some and went to bed early, with my dog on the bed for a source of warmth. With no local friends except the farm people and my old Nashville friends now in the armed forces (I was 4-F because of a blind eye, an accident suffered in early childhood), I was often extremely lonely. But it was a kind of loneliness whose memory I cherish. I think that loneliness had something to do with the development of my imagination, perhaps by nourishing my longtime habit of conversation with my alter ego. In any case I will never forget the ghostly night mist in the valley around that house, or the voices of hoot owls, a whole contending congress of owls, from the steep wooded hillside along the creek.

3

After an undistinguished high school career in which I had nevertheless imbibed a good deal of Latin and some French, I entered Vanderbilt University, at seventeen, with practically no academic ambition. Off and on I had toyed with the idea of becoming a newspaper writer but I was not serious even about this. The consequence was poor grades and, after two academic quarters, my decision to quit school and go to work at Sycamore. This interrup-

tion, lasting a year and a half, was the first of two in my college career. The second one came when, 4-F or not, I was unexpectedly drafted into the army in the spring of 1945. They sent me to Korea, where there was nothing doing at the time, put me in the Military Police Corps and set me to driving jeeps and guarding warehouses. In a little less than a year I was discharged because of eye trouble, and three months later I was back in college.

The first interruption particularly had made a considerable difference in my academic outlook. One of the reasons was a notion, inspired by praise from a freshman English teacher and brooded over during my long absence, that I had a gift for writing. Soon after my return to Vanderbilt, I enrolled in an advanced composition course taught by Donald Davidson. He also praised my writing and, though it was not yet apparent to me, my career was launched. So it is that people seek to do what they think they can do well. But in my case, as in most cases, there was more to it than this.

A part of what moved me was Donald Davidson himself, aside from the praise he gave me. He was a fine poet, critic, historian, and, by reason of his great character and learning, a powerfully inspiring teacher. He had been—along with John Crowe Ransom, Allen Tate, and Robert Penn Warren—an original member of that group of Vanderbilt-connected poets called the Fugitives. A few years later, along with these same and other prominent writers and scholars, he was also an important participant in the Vanderbilt Agrarian Movement, contributing one of the twelve essays that appeared in *I'll Take My Stand.* Of all the participants, Davidson was the one most serious about the South and its agrarian heritage and, as these men saw it in 1930, the imperative need to roll back the encroaching forces of an industrialism that was in the process of annihilating all traditional life. Although practically speaking the movement had already failed when I knew Davidson, the fact had not diminished his passion for the ideals involved. With my traditional background and agrarian experience, I was ripe for his teaching and became one of his many disciples. He articulated for me so great a part of what I had half-known and often felt.

If Davidson's thinking about social and philosophical issues played a part in sending me on my course (my creative life had acquired a center now), so did his subtle capacities as a critic of writing. He perceptively praised and criticized my fiction, knowing always just how far to go, and sent me on to do what every writer finally must—learn for himself. He remained my respected friend until the end of his life

"My father's home on Hillsboro Road near Nashville"

and did me many favors. It saddens me to recall that some of the earnest and forthright stands he took—like those against the Tennessee Valley Authority (he wrote a prize-winning history of the Tennessee River) and against racial integration—cost him so dearly in reputation. If his great passion pushed him sometimes to extremes, beyond the prudent and even the possible, his ideas in their essential nature continue to inform my most serious opinions.

There were other excellent professors at Vanderbilt, including especially Monroe Spears, who taught me virtually everything I was to learn about eighteenth-century literature and much of what I know about poetry. He went on from Vanderbilt to a distinguished career as critic and scholar, serving for some years as editor of the *Sewanee Review* and later occupying an honorary chair at Rice University. Monroe is another of my former professors who has remained a friend and with whom I have regularly and profitably asked for advice about my work.

Although I began writing while still in Vanderbilt, it was several years yet before I settled down to serious work. I became a conscientious and rather successful college student, though I also spent some time whooping it up. I learned to drink and was diligent in my pursuit of one fair broad after another (which resulted mainly in nothing except a more finely whetted appetite). For a while I was a fraternity boy but about the beginning of my junior year I seceded. I am able to look back with a good deal of nostalgia on my college years.

When I was nineteen, my grandfather Webber died and my father bought a new home, a large farm on Hillsboro Road a few miles out of Nashville. There was an impressive antebellum house with high hills rising behind it and a branch of the Harpeth River just south of the house. Until I graduated from Vanderbilt, I lived there with my parents. We brought the horses from Sycamore, and I continued to care for them when time allowed. But now one of our horses, a stud acquired not long after we moved to Hillsboro Road, was among the most magnificent I have ever seen.

The horse, Chief's Allen, had belonged to Lem Motlow, a man famous for his ownership and production of Jack Daniels whiskey and also, in Tennessee, for other (and morally mixed) reasons. But Mr. Motlow had got old and partly paralyzed and paranoia had come on him. Some years earlier the horse had been Reserve Grand-Champion at the prestigious Shelbyville Walking Horse Celebration and, considering his splendid qualities as a stud, he had become in Mr. Motlow's mind an object of lethal jealousy on the part of rival horse breeders. So, with the idea of moving the horse out of harm's way, Mr. Motlow sold it to my father for less than its worth.

He was an animal of rare beauty, extremely large and powerful, a red roan with blaze face and flaxen tail and a mane that, when the horse was at a canter, made you think of falling water. He was also gentle, except in one respect, which I discovered to my consternation on my first try at breeding him.

Instead of routinely leading the horse from his stall to the waiting mare, I found myself instantly airborne at the end of his leadrope. He would simply catapult himself at a mare, and Hercules could not have restrained him. It was dangerous, of course, to the mare especially. It took me a long time to think of the piece of trickery with which I solved the problem. This was to tie the mare to an outside wall of the barn with her rump just shy of the corner. This put her where she was invisible when I took Chief out of his stall, and though he was raring to go he could not discern the direction in which to charge. When I got him to the corner where he could see her, there was not space for him to do anything but act like a normal horse. Or almost like a normal horse. The mares usually had a glazed look in their eyes for the rest of the day.

The horse died in the fire when our barn burned. The news nearly killed Mr. Motlow; when he phoned us he was incoherent with grief. He was certain that his enemies were responsible.

"On a mare I showed several times," about 1943

I graduated from college at Christmastime of 1949 and lived and worked at Sycamore until the following September, when I went to graduate school at the University of Florida. I went because Andrew Lytle taught courses in creative writing there. Andrew is still another of the people who has been important in my career and in my life, perhaps more so than any. He was also a member of the Vanderbilt Agrarians, contributing to *I'll Take My Stand*. He is best known for his fine fiction but has also written volumes of literary and social criticism, historical biography, and a striking book of personal memoirs. Like Davidson, he was an inspiring teacher, though radically different in style and temper.

A surprising number of good and established writers came out of those small classes that Andrew taught at Florida. One story I wrote in his class was collected in Martha Foley's *Best American Short Stories* (1953). Another has since appeared in a couple of anthologies.

Andrew Lytle is, I believe, the most remarkable man I have known. His great courtesy, humor, imagination, and what I would call his gift of grace have made him literally hundreds of friends. He must

be, even now in very old age, one of the most visited men in America. And I should think that few leave his home without at least some consciousness of having been in the presence of a very special human being.

I went to Florida because of Andrew, but secondarily with the idea of getting an M.A. degree which would enable me to get a teaching job. I got the M.A. but was unable to get a job, so I stayed on and completed, except for the dissertation, classwork toward the Ph.D. I was married by then and had a baby (the first of five), having met my beautiful wife Shailah in my first year at Florida. I never did complete the dissertation. I got a job as instructor at Miami University of Ohio, not far from Shailah's hometown of Cincinnati, and there I began work on my first novel.

The novel was named *The Innocent*. Of all my novels this was the one that came nearest to being autobiographical. Not very near, however, except perhaps in some inner, psychic sense, as is the case with many novels. Duncan Welsh, the protagonist, and his story are related to me and my literal story only in tangential and accidental ways. I did give to Duncan certain of my own mental and psychological characteristics. The locale, pretty faithfully transcribed, was Sycamore and surrounding areas. Most other important characters were not so much based on as suggested by some of the farm people and people I knew around the countryside. I derived the horse from Mr. Motlow's stud and had him die prematurely, though not in the way his prototype had died. And further borrowings from actual circumstance could be extended to considerable length.

But certainly the story itself is a long way from any actual one. Duncan, after some years of absence out in the modern world, returns in disillusionment to the home place, the simple world of his childhood. His parents are dead and except for the black family on the farm he is alone, living in the old house. He sets out trying to restore for himself an order of life that has essentially passed away. He breeds a colt from an old and nearly extinct bloodline, the animal being for him the symbol of restoration and the immediate object of virtually all his love and hope. More and more Duncan finds himself shut off from the world outside. His enmity with that world leads to the destruction of his horse and to his falling, now completely, into the hands of a thoroughly isolated and vicious moonshiner who in a way represents the dark side of himself. Their alliance leads finally to the destruction of them both.

My idea for *The Innocent* began as one thing and ended as something else, changing shape as I proceeded. At the start of the novel I did not conceive of my hero as possessed of any specially marked human flaw. I thought of him mainly as social victim, a man whose temperament and rearing had made him intensely conscious of an emptiness in modern life, who very naturally sought to go home again but who would find in the end, to his own ruin, that the world would not let him be. So I proceeded, without much of anything in mind more than developing the circumstances which the original plot idea had offered, in the faith that new plot elements would grow out of the old ones.

But quite by surprise, the moonshiner got into the story. This was one of those lucky accidents that writers learn to count on, and indicated to me, in terms of plot and idea at the same time, the direction that my story must take. Of course the appearance of the moonshiner (Aron McCool was his name) was not really an accident. It seems clear now that he was the

"My wife, Shailah, and the children," about 1962

image which my idea supplied to the end of achieving full development and coherence. I soon perceived that the sinister McCool was more than just another important person in the novel: he was like a part of my hero's self, the full-blown development of a logic implicit in my hero's moral condition. So, then, in a manner of speaking, McCool was born of a moral flaw in my hero, and this was what gave McCool his power over him. After this I was no longer able to see Duncan as social victim. He was a victim all right, but in the most important way he was a victim of himself, of the flaw in his character.

I cannot remember at what point the novel's title, *The Innocent,* had come into my mind, but after the appearance of McCool this title began to take on a rather different meaning for me. It became increasingly clear that my hero was not an "innocent" in the way of a victim who is blameless for what he becomes. Instead the title now suggested what the nature of his flaw was—a determined rejection of the inescapable evil of life, with consequent deliberate return to the garden of innocence. Adam ate of the tree of the knowledge of good and evil and was cast out forever, and we all share his condition. Evil is a prime fact of our existence: we may be forgiven for it but we cannot escape it. The "innocent" who reenters the garden is destined to find that it is not God but the Prince of Darkness who walks there now. So with my hero. His flaw leads him into the hands of the Enemy, who destroys him.

I have devoted disproportionate space to this novel for two reasons. The first is that I want to illuminate a theme that, in one form or another, is close to the heart of all my first five novels and has at least some relationship to the three I have written since. The second reason is that my description of how the novel came to be what it is supports a theory about serious writing, and serious art in general, of which I and many other people are persuaded. This theory views the process of creation as the author's instinctive seeking after harmony or wholeness, but first of all as a seeking after an understanding of the self. It is a form of self-discovery, and therefore, in this sense, the author's subject is properly himself. To allow his efforts to be directed by his own true subject, then, is the author's calling and constitutes his integrity. Instead of the other way around, his theme, a reflection of his incompleteness, chooses him.

4

I taught for one year at Miami of Ohio as an instructor in English. What I taught was mostly freshman English, a chore that few teachers really enjoy and I was not one of the exceptions. But it was a chore that continued to fall on me for many years to come. More and more, as Shailah and I accumulated children, I came to realize that my dream of living by my pen alone was a dream whose fulfillment was far in the dark and indefinite future. But toward the end of that year at Miami I got a break. I was awarded, on the strength of the little I had so far written on *The Innocent,* a *Sewanee Review* Fellowship which granted money enough to support my family and me through the coming year. Though Miami was quite a pleasant place, I wanted to live permanently in the South, so I gave up my job for good.

We spent the summer at Sycamore and in the fall sought out a place near the beach on the Gulf Coast of Florida. It was a fairly miserable little cabin of a house, bitter cold in the dead of winter, and we had two babies now. Also Shailah had a miscarriage during those months. Yet both of us recall that time with considerable, if qualified, affection. We were between the Gulf and the Everglades, and in the river behind the house alligators bellowed at night, and close around there were fields and woods. *The Innocent* was going well (there is nothing like a first novel, because fictionally speaking all things are new) and when not at work I fished and hunted or, perched close to the tiny fireplace, read *War and Peace.* That place, that area, most of the Florida Gulf Coast in fact, is no longer recognizable to us.

At the end of that year I got a job at the University of Tennessee. I had by then finished *The Innocent* and my first month or two in Knoxville was a time of much nervous waiting to hear from a prospective publisher. That first rejection was almost as hard a lick as I can remember taking; Shailah said I turned pale when I read the letter. But there were two more rejections before that luminous day when Harcourt Brace accepted the novel with enthusiasm. I suppose the experience of being several times rejected was, if painful, salutary. At least it helped to educate me as to the bewildering diversity of judgment and taste that exists in the publishing world.

I was asked to stay on, with advancement, at UT but I was still full of my romance with the South, and UT with its big city location and its kind of ethos, was not South enough for me. So, in the spring when I received a surprise offer from Auburn University, in a small town way down in Alabama, I immediately accepted. I was still to do routine teaching but the creative writing course was mine alone. I took to the job at once, soon made friends who were to become lasting friends, and decided that Auburn would be my permanent home. So it became. I was a member of the faculty for thirty-one years and, though I retired in 1987, remain a resident of the town. It may well be that residence in a place more accessible to the literary world would have advanced my career as a writer, but I have never found persuasive reason to regret my long-ago decision. I think that, in spite of being a college professor, I have been able here to live my life closer to the heart of my fictional material than might have been possible in most places.

The Innocent was published a few months after I came to Auburn. If the reception was not all that I and my publishers had hoped for, it was, as I saw in retrospect, a quite respectable reception. Sales were hardly spectacular but the novel got reviewed, generally well reviewed, in most parts of the country and *Time* in particular gave it a satisfying and extended notice. It was also encouragement that I received praise from people whose literary judgment I greatly respected. In any case I was soon forgetfully deep in a second novel.

Forest of the Night would turn out to be, I believe, the least successful of my novels. Yet I sometimes feel

"The cabin at Sycamore Farm where I wrote part of The Innocent*," about 1955*

that it could have been my best. Impatience is often a scourge upon young novelists, and in the last one-third of the book impatience drove me on when I should have stopped and waited for things to mature in my mind. I should have waited, in other words, for the kind of discovery that the Muse, when patiently dealt with, can produce.

Though in no strict sense a historical novel, the action takes place at the beginning of the nineteenth century in the Tennessee wilderness. The story was suggested to me by accounts of outlaws along the old Natchez Trace, specifically the two Harpe brothers. The accounts, half-legendary, present them as a senselessly brutal and monstrous pair, and stipulate further that two women, one a preacher's daughter, accompanied them on their murderous sojourns. The question that seized my imagination was the question of what had set the Harpes on such a course, how they had become such monsters. The tentative answer in terms of which I conceived the novel was surely derived, learned, from my experience in writing *The Innocent.* It was the Garden of Eden idea, original innocence at last disillusioned and corrupted by intractable evil in the world. The Harpes came to the wilderness, the new world believed by them to be an untainted garden, only to find, like Duncan Welsh, that the Prince of Darkness ruled here as elsewhere. If Hawthorne's "Young Goodman Brown" comes to the reader's mind, it is, as I recall, because that story too contributed to my conception.

But as heroes of a work of fiction—in which probability instead of possibility must be a first consideration—the Harpes were too monstrous and also too well established as such in the popular imagination. For this reason, plus the further one that it would have been most difficult to credit them with any intellectual stature, I could see no way to make them dramatically and fully human. They were simply too much, they were freaks. Better, then, to keep them in the background, a sort of evil shadow, an ultimate potential of the human spirit. The more interesting dimension was the route to the desolate condition they had reached, and in order for me, as well as for readers, to follow this route in imagination it was necessary that there be a hero with whom I could at least partly identify myself. In effect he would have to be, with inessential differences, another "innocent," and so I made him.

My hero, Jonathan Cannon, is a young idealist smitten with Rousseauesque ideas (ideas that entered importantly into the thinking of makers of our constitution) about the goodness of man in the state of nature, and evil as mere negation created by the dead hand of the past. As such he is peculiarly ill-fitted to perceive the shape of the reality waiting for him in the wilderness. For him the Harpes can only be madmen, grotesque aberrations from the human norm. To even the possibility that they could embody a potential within himself and within all men, he is entirely blind, for his vision had prepared him only to see evil as the product of factors external to human nature. Largely through his involvement with one of the Harpes' discarded women, he sets his foot on the path, and finally comes dangerously close, to realization of that potentiality. In the late stages of the novel the woman, in her dementia, identifies Jonathan as one of the Harpes. Indeed it is a story about the making of a Harpe. With very modern ideological rigor, Jonathan rejects all the signs that would have pointed out to a different cast of mind the truth about what he confronts, for his whole stake is in his view of man as naturally good.

Insofar as it is successful, *Forest of the Night* is like a terrible ballad or legend—or like a controlled nightmare, perhaps. It is the darkest of my books, though none of them can be described as even approaching the playful. Rightfully, I suppose, I have been criticized for this. The reason is not that many terrible things have happened in my life; on the whole I have been fortunate. I attribute it mainly to an accident of temperament and let it go at that. I did once, in the 1960s, write a comic-satirical novel but it was never published (if partly because I stepped on too many egalitarian toes). In the years when the work of other writers was most important to me, my greatest enthusiasm was for such authors as Dostoyevski and Hawthorne and Thomas Hardy, those I think of as the tragic writers. At least in major fictional undertakings my imagination is most at home in semidarkness.

A Buried Land shares a great deal with my first two novels. Partly my idea of my hostility to the Tennessee Valley Authority which, in flooding so much of the best agricultural land, struck a blow to the traditional life of the region. But the novel's immediate inspiration was an anecdote told me by a friend, about a young man who, having made a girl pregnant, took her to an abortionist. As a result she died and the young man secretly buried her body. The rest was my invention.

I made the young man of the anecdote my hero, Percy Youngblood, from a firmly traditional farm family, and had him bury the girl in a valley already denuded in preparation for the rising of the water. Thus he makes sure of burying his guilt forever. This act, both literally and symbolically, is connected with his renunciation of his past and its traditions, in effect including his family. Henceforth he will be dedicated to the future, a strong advocate of the new enlightenment already oncoming in the form of an industrialized world. For him the past will be as dead as the girl lying buried under the lake. But Nemesis pursues him. It comes in the form of the girl's brother, a hill man to be reckoned with, who will not allow the memory to die. At the end of his long blind pursuit, though he dies as a consequence, he brings all to light. It is light for Percy also, whose repentance goes beyond the crimes of which he is legally guilty.

In spite of first appearances, as I later recognized, *A Buried Land* is essentially an extension of, rather than a departure from, the idea behind my previous novels. Here my hero, in flight from a world he finds intolerable, like Duncan and Jonathan before him, commits himself to a different world where imagined redemption lies. But what awaits him is not redemption. No worldly rejection can separate us from the evils that are ours.

Considering only the money that I have made through my writing career, the game has barely been worth the candle. But I have made money two times. The first time was when I wrote my short novel *An Exile*. Conditioned as I was, it was no small astonishment to me when Hollywood bought the book. They paid only a fair price for it but that price seemed like a fortune to Shailah and me. Gregory Peck, the star of the movie, did not like the title, so it was changed to *I Walk the Line*, the name of one of the songs that Johnny Cash sang in the background. I finally decided that, after all, they had made a pretty good movie of it, despite the fact that they twisted my characteristic theme in such a way as to make it more familiar to moviegoers. At least, however, they did present my hero, the sheriff, as yearning his way back into a world essentially extinct. Reviewers generally, with my full accord at the time, condemned the movie and praised the book.

This novel was published in 1967, about the time of the climax of the civil rights movement which had been visibly underway for a decade and more. Auburn, fifty miles from Montgomery and eighteen miles from Tuskegee, was close to the heart of it. I say "close," because such raw physical evidences of the conflict as marches and violence never touched us directly. Like most places in the South (and this is a fact not usually realized by people outside the South) and indeed like the rest of the country, we got our information not through on-the-scene experience but through the news media and through verbal report of friends and acquaintances. Television in particular

*Robert Penn Warren, Walton Patrick (head of English department), Taylor Littleton
(executive vice president of Auburn University), and Madison Jones, about 1977*

conveyed the notion that the South was one boiling cauldron of racial turmoil, with the Ku Klux Klan (which we never saw in Auburn) raging everywhere. This was by no means the case: statistically speaking, those who witnessed or were even very close to violent incidents were few, because in fact such incidents were few. There was widespread turmoil, all right, or at least distress, but most of it was in the minds and psyches of Southerners (and sometimes in the arguments that went on incessantly between those Southerners for and against the movement).

By this time, the late sixties, there had been a great many novels treating of the civil rights movement and racial injustice generally. As I saw it, these treatments on the whole amounted to a distortion of the reality, loaded with stereotypes, with lynch mobs and stupid red-faced sheriffs shooting or, usually from behind, knocking saintly black people in the head with nightsticks. I was not of a mind to contend that no injustice existed or that these things did not sometimes happen. But I was convinced that a true picture of conditions in the South as presented in fictional form required a treatment far more subtle

and more balanced than had been the case in all but the rarest instances. This included the requirement that credit be given where credit was due, even when it was due to white people who opposed the civil rights movement. So I decided, at a time when the movement had all but finally achieved its immediate goals, to make assay at such a fictional project.

Excepting *Forest of the Night*, this was the first of my novels for which I did not imagine the Sycamore area as locale. I chose instead, and played loosely with, a small town south of Nashville where the tradition of the Old South, the Cotton South, was stronger. The title, which I took from one of John Crowe Ransom's poems, is *A Cry of Absence*—an apt title, I believe, because it suggests the sense of loss that afflicts my heroine. Her name is Hester Cameron Glenn and her town of Cameron Springs has its name from her father's family. "Hester" in Roman mythology is a keeper of the hearth, and Hester in the novel, a proud, well-bred, aristocratic mother of two sons, is the self-appointed guardian of her family's and her community's heritage. When a young black activist is brutally murdered, Hester is outraged and determined that the guilty ones will be brought to justice. What she is finally compelled to accept, mainly by the agency of her elder son, is that her beloved younger son—in her mind the true scion—is one of the two perpetrators of the crime. Her agonizing moral dilemma and the resolution at which she finally arrives constitute the remaining action of the novel.

It is sometimes ironic how in the process of composition a work of fiction can compel radical and, from the writer's point of view, even unacceptable change in the original intention. But, willing or not, the writer must follow the developed logic of his creation or else in all likelihood produce a book that is at once dishonest and artistically unworkable. So it was in this case. I loved, and still love Hester; she is a part of me. I feel it almost as a betrayal that, by unearthing subterraneous aspects of her character, I put her seriously in the wrong.

I think that *A Cry of Absence* is, and probably will remain, my best novel. I had long wanted to write a book that could properly be termed tragic in the classical sense (there are so few of them in the twentieth century) and I was gratified that a number of capable reviewers so considered it. But the greatest satisfaction of all was seeing it described, by Allen Tate and several other distinguished critics, as a masterpiece. That I happened to make some money this second time was also not disappointing.

5

At some point after *A Cry of Absence* was published in 1971, I began to feel that I had come to the end of something and that hereafter I would need to find a rather different stance in respect to my fiction. It seemed to me then, in the seventies, that the South as a traditional entity within the nation as a whole had in the more important ways come to an end. Not that segregation of the races, now abolished, had constituted the South's essence. But this arrangement had been part and parcel of that essence and, having drawn virtually the whole network of Southern pieties into its defense, included the rest in its demise. The sense of an honored past, for one example, was now to be contemned. So, to speak somewhat too largely, the rout was at last complete. I felt that my novel, at least for me, had finally dramatized this debacle and that as a consequence my fundamental theme must be, if not abandoned, reshaped. For I had always thought of myself as, in a way probably obscure to readers, a sort of metaphysical apologist for the South.

My difficulties were, I suppose, manifested in the false starts and the length of time I took to write my next novel, *Passage through Gehenna*. Perhaps compounding my problems was the fact that I, along with most of my family, was abroad on a year-long Guggenheim Fellowship through most of the time when I was writing the earlier part of the book. We were in Ireland for some months and then, when the weather got too cold for us, in Majorca for some more months, in both of which I spent no little time ingesting new sights and experiences. But I had been away on fellowships before and the distractions had not disturbed my concentration. The real cause of my problems was surely the need to find a different light in which to view my fictional world.

The writing of *Passage* required more than three years. What I came up with, not by calculated intention, was a kind of novel that may be seen as manifesting my cousinship with Nathaniel Hawthorne. As before, I made use of rural and small-town characters and setting. The story centers upon a religious country boy's helpless infatuation with an evil older woman, designedly named Lily to suggest the lengendary Lilith, who uses him as agent for her own malign and destructive purposes. But the notable difference from my former novels, and what relates it to works of Hawthorne, is its quality of moral allegory. Much more than I had realized in the process of the writing, the characters are defined by the system of ideas they represent, creating in the manner of allegory a conflict of good and evil principles. A learned friend of mine, using a different basis of comparison, likened it to opera. He praised the book—with sincerity, I am sure—but predicted that, given the point of view of present-day readers, it would appeal only to a limited audience. In this he was on the mark, but I also like to think that his praise was justified. Aside from my friend's and my own opinion, there is perhaps reason to think so. The reviews, though not so many nor in the most helpful places, were quite satisfactory. And recently, after ten years or so, a fine essay in a prominent literary journal indicates that there is yet life in the novel.

I was not always writing, or teaching, of course. A dozen years ago I bought a small farm some miles out of Auburn, a purchase made possible by the inheritance my parents left me. (Their sad deaths, in less than a year of each other, were made the sadder by the fire that destroyed their beautiful home a few days after my mother's funeral.) The farm consists of both pastureland and woods, and wild turkey and deer are there in great abundance. I bought some Hereford cows and keep a small herd for pleasure and a little profit. Along with one of my sons and irregular help from others, I built a cabin of pine logs we cut and treated, and stones we took from the foundation of a vanished house on the place. The stillness there almost equals that which I knew at Sycamore Farm so many years behind me.

In the late seventies in Columbus, Georgia, not very far from Auburn, there was a series of stranglings. Women, all but one of them old, were the victims. The stranglings continued for a year and more, then suddenly stopped—but not because the strangler had been caught: his identity remained unknown for ten years. During his rampage I had had no thoughts of writing a book on the subject. But afterwards, one day when I was reading Sherwood Anderson's *Winesburg, Ohio,* the idea came to me. Why not a book in the style of *Winesburg,* a suite of narratives not about the strangler himself but about the considerable effect of his brutal and unsolved crimes on the community? In light of this idea, using the voice of a member of a community a good deal smaller than Columbus, I wrote *Season of the Strangler.* It consists of twelve loosely connected narratives in which emotions—fear, anger, inadequacy, even envy—generated or intensified by the strangler alter the lives of the various protagonists.

Unfortunately the result following publication of *Season* was much like the one that followed *Passage through Gehenna:* few reviews in prominent places and unsatisfactory sales. Assuming the book's merit (which I do assume, for I do not think my creative powers have diminished), one partial but important reason presents itself. The reading public has a short memory and unless a writer has produced one or two big and memorable sellers, he had better not allow too many years to pass between books. For whatever reasons, I have been slow with my later books, including the one I have forthcoming, named *Last Things.*

To start with, this novel was delayed for most of a year by my work on another novel which I finally abandoned. Then I began *Last Things,* changed in midstream to a different handling of the situation, finally returned to the original chapters and after important adjustments felt that at last I had it right. Not quite right, though. Some time after I had thought the book was completed, I saw that a good deal more was necessary in order to make it really

Shailah and Madison Jones

work. So I spent nearly four additional months on it. Such are the trials of fiction writing. In considerable measure I had experienced this kind of stumbling, of trial and error and feeling my way, in the writing of earlier novels, so I was not led to suppose that all my stumbling meant either bad or good in respect to the quality of the book. Books come both ways, hard and easy, and one way is as likely as the other to produce success. At least this has been my own experience.

Last Things in one way gives much more prominence to the South as subject than do my previous two books. But here it is the new South, with the old appearing mainly as contrast in the person of an aged lady who is murdered by her daughter-in-law at the instigation of the daughter-in-law's lover. He, the novel's protagonist, of redneck origin, is a graduate student who by blackmail though half assenting has become involved in the narcotics traffic. Now the Southern small-town locale is all but severed from the past, a victim of the kind of moral blight now common everywhere.

A new thing, for me, in the novel is the introduction of supernatural elements into the story. Employing an old Hawthorne device, I leave to the reader the final decision as to whether or not my villain is in fact the devil in person and whether or not certain events are real or hallucinatory. This may be called a sort of secular effort to achieve a sense of transcendence. I am now awaiting the result, which will be upon me shortly.

I have had little to say about my life as a teacher, mainly because the writing of fiction has always come first for me. Except for a few intervals when I was on fellowships, I taught for thirty-four years at universities. At first I taught mostly freshman English, though when I came to Auburn the creative writing course was included in my regular assignment. In time, as I came up through the ranks, I began to teach such courses as American Literature, Greek Literature (in translation), the Short Story, and a graduate course in Theory of the Novel. Creative writing remained my specialty, however, and after I became Writer-in-Residence, teaching creative writing became the greater part of my assignment. I took all my teaching seriously. In my writing courses, where I knew best what I was doing, I concentrated on the elements of fiction writing, without pressing my students to try for publication. Some of them did later publish, but not at my urging. I always assumed that those who were real writers would continue under their own power and that those who were not really writers were better left to find it out for themselves as soon as possible. As for the rest, the vast majority who did not even think they were writers, I believe that they learned a good deal by their effort—both about literature and about themselves.

For the sake of the success of his work, no writer can allow himself to preach through his fiction, but inevitably the import of what he most deeply believes is available in what he writes. Every serious writer, however clearly aware of the impossible odds, would like to persuade the world of something. In this I am no different—unless I am different in that what I would wish to get across is a viewpoint that seems increasingly, even radically alien to the modern mind. We are children of the Enlightenment, a movement promising among other things to replace with pure reason the darkness that had misguided traditional thinking. In this light, the old darkness dispelled, we would be able to discern the true features of justice and order and all the necessary virtues that tradition had so partially and imperfectly defined. In this light, step by step, we would advance into the millennium.

But what was promised did not happen. The commitment to Reason was of course enormously fruitful in its way, bestowing countless and unheard-of material benefits on the modern world. The kicker was that this commitment bore the seeds of our present increasing disorder. After two centuries of "enlightenment" it can now be seen, if not often admitted, that the claims of pure reason have been destructively overstated. In respect of the attempts to find acceptable definitions of justice and virtue and the rest, the burden of modern philosophy is a practical lesson in the futility of pure, unembodied reason: as the scholar Alasdair McIntyre points out, the review pages of the philosophical journals are simply the graveyards of all such efforts. In the world at large, outside of those diminishing circles still guided by tradition, it is for every man to furnish his own personal definitions. This is the world of Autonomous Man, of "lifestyles," and of doing one's own thing. It is right for a person to believe as he chooses, but woe to the person who insists that those who reject his truth are in error. In the end, the one shared absolute is the idea of equality, from which intellectual and moral relativism and finally cynicism derive. The consequences of this condition, notably the disintegration of community, grow more apparent daily in our society.

This is a text that I hope is reflected, though in unmitigated fictional form, in my books. It is also one of the reasons that I hope to produce still other books before I go.

BIBLIOGRAPHY

Fiction:

The Innocent, Harcourt, 1957.

Forest of the Night, Harcourt, 1960.

A Buried Land, Viking, 1963.

An Exile, Viking, 1967, published as *I Walk the Line,* Popular Library, 1970.

A Cry of Absence, Crown, 1971.

Passage through Gehenna, Louisiana State University Press, 1978.

Season of the Strangler, Doubleday, 1982.

Last Things, Louisiana State University Press, 1989.

Nonfiction:

(With Thomas Davidson Dow) *History of the Tennessee State Dental Association,* Tennessee State Dental Association, 1958.

Work is represented in anthologies *Best American Short Stories* (1953), edited by Martha Foley, and *Stories of the Modern South,* edited by Benjamin Forkner and Patrick Samway. Contributor of short stories to *Perspective, Sewanee Review, Arlington Quarterly, Delta Review,* and *Chattahoochee Review.*

Anthony Kerrigan

1918-

MOCK-UP OF A NOVELLA OF MYSELF

Picasso's "portrait of Tony Kerrigan," contributed as frontispiece for
At the Front Door of the Atlantic

After conception in the Panama Canal Zone, birth occurred to me by design in Winchester, Massachusetts, the birthplace and home base of many Yankee moguls (at the time) of the economico-"imperialist" (to use the fashionable Marxist term) United Fruit Company, a shipping and plantation company of shuddering renown to nationalist-"inter-nationalists." Years later I did not translate Neruda's ludicrously anathemizing stanzas against this company (following on his laudatory "Ode to Stalin," two of them), only because they were not good poems, merely agit-prop, agitation/propaganda, although I did translate the bulk of his *Canto General,* and saw it published in New York and London.

I was born in the USA "by design" because my "imperialist" father had put my mother on one of his banana boats so that she could be delivered of his firstborn at the center of empire—and the child, hopefully a son, would be eligible for high office. The decision may also have had to do with Yellow Fever and Yankee Hygiene. (Despite the latter, my father died at forty of a "tropical disease" and our world came asunder.) Once my birthplace was determined, my sister was allowed to be born in Cuba, where my father had installed us for good and all; the move was terminal.

Autobiography, even unwritten, said Unamuno, is simply the novel of oneself. Here then a mock-up of the novel of myself.

I had been conceived in the Panama Canal Zone, not in transit, for my Irish-American parents lived there, and I often mention this fact/feat because it strikes me as symbolic of the entirety of my life. That I could have been begun, so to say, on what I take to be the world's most dramatic and effective frontier, lying as it does between two mighty oceans and two mighty continents, was a mark of my destiny. I have lived a frontier life ever since, always at saltwater's edge, until my exile to Siberia USA. Most of my meaningful life has been lived outside the United States, and five of my six children have been born abroad, all but one on pivotal islands (Ireland and Mallorca), sea-frontiers in themselves and by nature. My own years have transpired in foreign (to Americans) parts: years in Cuba, years in Spain, years in Ireland, and even a year in France.

For his part, my father, Thomas Aloysius, left New England at nineteen to work in the Philippines. All his life he maintained that the world's most beautiful women were the Polynesians, Malays, and the *filipinas* with Spanish admixtures. My son Elie, working now as a journalist in Indonesia, repeats his grandfather's encomia; his brother Patrick, in college in Los Angeles, is skirting the pool of betrothal to a *filipina* at this writing. My son Camilo, the painter, married a young Spanish woman. The latest-model university-educated feministoid American woman is scarce fancied by the new generation of our clan. Notwithstanding his own proto-eulogies, my father, their grandfather, married the class beauty from his Massachusetts high school, Madeline Flood, who was of the same stock as he, so that my surname all the years in Cuba was, in the Hispanic fashion, Kerrigan y Flood.

My father never again resided in the States, where his parents lived only the short latter part of their lives after Ireland. His mother, Maria (mah-RYE-ah) MacDonagh, had taught school in County Mayo, *barefoot*, like her pupils. She spoke English with a heavy brogue. His father's surname in Irish was O Ciardhubhain ("son of Black," blackness, or black-visaged: *dhub* is black, but Blacks are *Blue* Men, *Fir Gorum*), a surname anglicized to O'Kerrigan. They were all, the lot of them, out of the black bogs, bogmen. So? History is cyclical: there are descendants of mine who, on pot and Rock, are better than bogmen only materially; spiritually they may be worse.

For all that the permissive-promiscuous, puritan-pornographic, now inverse-racist USA may be the best country in the world for exiles and refugees, three generations of my own family have lived here only cursorily. In *The Bellarosa Connection* Saul Bellow wrote that for a Jew "secular America is a diaspora within a diaspora." Similarly, for our imme-

"My ma as a lass: Madeline Flood on the eve of leaving Boston on the epoch's 'Grand Tour' of Europe—and Ireland—at age seventeen," 1907

diate clan, ousted from Ireland by famine and transported without duress to the USA in the nick of time (I, later "dropped"—for as soon as the deed was done I was whisked to Cuba, a recent foetus—rather than "Born in the USA!"), the exile seemed to put us out of kilter with a consumers' entrepôt nation: goods goods goods and no good sod left: little inscape and ever less landscape. Like so many of the Roman Imperialists, my father preferred the outposts of empire. I have always felt the inverse: I prefer Rome, that is, Europe as a whole, the center of American heritage so far, even as we assimilate more and more exiles like Joseph Brodsky, both Russian and Jewish, and parcels of even farther-East culture, along with Oriental intelligence and order, an evolution my Asian-beauty-bedazzled father would have hailed.

As regards language and my own children, four of my five sons speak only in Spanish to this day when they speak to each other, always in Spanish on the telephone and preferentially even in company. My daughter, however, answers them in English (and Catalan to anyone else who will understand her). Her English was fashioned in Celtic Ireland, and her Spanish in Catalan Spain. On Mallorca, the sons studied French, and equally-universal Castilian: a couple of them also learned un-universal Mallorquí, a Catalan dialect now nationalistically compulsory in the island's schools, a tongue suitable (like its cousin, Provençal) for poetry—or for the barnyard, according to Gertrude Stein—but not suitable for normal converse.

My daughter was born out of our place on the Boulevard Raspail, *chez nous,* in the fourteenth *arrondissement* in Paris, France; whenever I looked into my shaving mirror I saw—a crown on my head—the baroque serpentines of the monumental statuary over the tomb of Catulle Mendès, in the Cimitière Montparnasse, which we abutted; a few feet away lay the barely marked grave of Baudelaire. In the bidet by the mirror I washed my daughter's diapers.

Apart from the perfect dactyls of his forename and surname, Malachy Kerrigan, youngest son, boasts a miracle-laden set of given names (not all of them Christian, unlike the saints' names given at baptism to the eventual *soi-disant* Communist painter Pablo Picasso), and these names unite the three main language stocks of the family: Malachy Ciaran Diarmuid Lawless Antinomy Jordi Cayetano y Todos los Santos Kerrigan y Gurevich. (The latter collective prename appellation, Todos los Santos, French *Toussaint,* all Saints, to cover all other saints' names left out, was also Picasso's.) Malachy's names and their consequences appeared in 125 daily newspapers in the USA on 10–11 February 1972, as sole subject for an essay by Russell Kirk, who used them and their antecedents to make a traditionalist point in his then nationally syndicated column. For current purposes this son goes by Malachy Lawless Kerrigan-Gurevich, and thus signs his school essays.

Mostly, for most of the family, life has been lived in the tropics, or in the subtropics (in the USA, it was in related warm zones: California and Florida), while it has always been Irish weather I truly fancy, being a devotee of haze mist fog drizzle brume sleet frost hailstorms hoarfrost lowering cloud banks squalls cloudbursts thunderstorms lashing downpours sheets of rain snowstorms blizzards snowdrifts. And I doted, and dote ever more, on half-frozen waterfalls with dead trees lining the banks or caught in the ice-sundered rush.

My first sight of blood, of human blood in the world (of beast's blood it was to be shortly after in an open-field *matadero,* abattoir, in the Cuban province of Matanzas—"Massacres": by Siboney Indians of boatloads of shipwrecked Spaniards) was when our Spain-born maid walked the length of the corridor that ran alongside all the bedrooms, in the tropical fashion, leaving behind a trail of red drops. She glided silently, like a somnambulist, although that is not what I thought then as I ran to my mother with the news. It was in our first Havana house in the old Spanish-built section of *La Havana Vieja,* just off the inner docks, a block from the saltwater of the Caribbean.

First things, and Last: a recent story of mine (the first section published in *Fiction* magazine) has the protagonist drinking his girlfriend's (periodic) blood in Hungary, in the course of a largely factual story; and as I write these lines I taste the blood from a fortuitous cut on my mouth. The blood in Havana and Hungary had the odor of the womb about it: as vital a link in memory between past and present as any.

Not long ago I awoke to report the following half-dream:

Old Havana

. . . *pongee-colored girls in white dresses the sun
shone through in multiple haloes
where they lay alongside streets like sofas
reading José Martí behind potted ferns
in avenue-knolls paved with Key West grass
and long-leaved tobacco shaved and scented like
  bark strips.*

That was half the impossible dream, which must have had its own oneiric reasons: Havana early on, when the *soi-disant* "Spanish Cubans" built, with ex-slaves, a colonial reality, which for all its unreality was more real than the dreamed-up "social realism" of the material-less materialism which has put Cuba's past into the hands of UNESCO planners "at the end of a totalitarian century breeding new slaves / freed into nightmare-bondage to an Ever-Glorious Future," my dream "poem," or prose, went on, when I awoke.

And the latest issue (Summer 1989) of the literary journal *Salmagundi* carries—along with a memoir of my 1986 return to Cuba—translations of mine of three Cuban poems by the hounded, maligned, brutalized-by-"public-confession," and finally exiled Heberto Padilla. It gives a poet's (modern Cuba's best) sensory water-view of Red Cuba seen through its all-encompassing sheath.

A Swim Off Havana

At times I immerse myself in the sea, for a long
    while,
and surface with a sudden gasp,
but I swim from the coast as far as I can
and see the receding indefinite line of the shore,
and the sun boiling in oil-stricken waters.
The shoreline drowns in the haze,
and I close my light-blinded eyes.
There, as if a hand's breadth away from the
    waves
is the country
which so long we thought we bore
on our shoulders: white as a warship
glaring against the sun and against all poets.

Padilla's best-known poem is a quatrain of summation regarding what has happened in what was the Cuba of my youth:

The Old Bards Say

Never forget, poet,
that in any time or place
where you make or suffer History
some dangerous poem always lies in wait.

No sooner had he written this, than Padilla was, of course, detained by the "People's" Red Army. He endured some ten years of house arrest subsequently, before he was brought out of Cuba into exile. (His fate is tendentiously not recalled by people who decry "censorship" or even "censure" in the USA.)

Once my childhood's mock-fatherland, only natural following on a Caribbean boyhood, an adolescent's mock-Eden, Cuba is now a mock-Albania, its rich past traduced, reduced to a mockery of a theoretical mock-Utopia. As a duty to my childhood homeland, as a Hail and Farewell, I have given some special priority to seeing Padilla's poems—and the work of other Cubans—into print: and they have appeared widely, as has a report on my last trip to Cuba ("Literacy Yes! Books No!" was the title in one of three magazines which printed it), while a "pseudo-fiction" of my recent voyage Miami-Managua-La Habana ("In Nicaragua with Nelson Mandala [sic] and My Girlfriend") appears in *Partisan Review*.

The fashionable deconstruction-cultist Julia Kristeva writes: "A person of the twentieth century can exist honestly only as a foreigner . . ." What kind of "person"? Certainly not the rooted, or even unrooted, mass of people. (Certainly not most women. Tutelary goddesses belong to a place, as do earth mothers.) To be a frontiersman (certainly not a "frontiersperson") is the opposite of being a foreigner. The frontiersman bridges two (or more) cultures and stands for one specifically, or for an individualist combination. Unlike Gaugin, me and mine were raised abroad (from USA), with our own frontiers, and are products of two or more cultures, from Catalan to Irish. In the USA the frontiersman stood for the expansion of one culture over and above others, for he held his own to be superior, more hardy and viable in any case—and so it proved. This is another age, but some things are still better than others. A frontiersman is in a good position to know which are better and where. Of course, Kristeva doubtless means a "foreigner" in one's own country. In short, one either lives locked up in "alienation," in a mental institution, in a Bedlam, or is an individualist eclectic; a marginal man, perhaps, but why "alienated"?

And as for the "semiotics" of it all: For me, the public consequences of the spirit of populist semiotics include the way billboards and signs are larded with cute misspellings along the highway. It also accounts for some of the entries in the latest editions of American dictionaries (illustrated "Afro," etc.) and the tit-for-tat omissions consequently of trusted words ("mandorla," say). *Corruptio optimi pessima.*

I have qualified, I believe, to serve as a volunteer *franc-tireur* in what Joseph Epstein (the essayist and editor of the *American Scholar*) calls The Resistance: resistance to a lockstep *Zeitgeist,* and to the entrenched dogmatists, the new Establishment, who run Academia.

One last note on Cuba. Somebody in power in Castro's Cuba is a castrate. Some certain number of Cubans have been *castrado* (I reveal my own subjection to that subject at the end of this memoir). "Thousands," I used to hear in school in Havana, were being *capados.* That was when Machado was president, and we all learned it was his favorite *castigo,* the "chastisement" we would meet if we went to the wrong demonstration or participated in illegal political activity. And then Batista! If Machado was hard on upstart boys' testicles, Batista was not easy, so everyone said. Now there may not have been "thousands," but some . . . some number or other. . . . A lot of smoke for no fire otherwise. Since I am still alive, testicles (chemically compromised by the latest wonder drugs) still intact, waiting brazenly for the miraculous resurrection of the flesh by grace of the newest monocloning, I muse on the fate of my schoolmates, those of my generation and later generations now alive, dozens or hundreds if not "thousands" of the politically punished. In power? Somebody, I repeat, is a *castrado* (not just a *castrato* for musical purposes) and living in Cuba. Quite a few, according to all my youthful gleanings of the terrible truth. Why not now in power? For it was the students, the politically active students, who were the target of this Hispanic custom inherited from the Moors in Spain. The student-radicals came to power under Castro. Some of them must have been docked . . . That condition changes one's point of view, may lead to paranoia, so evident on every hand in the *nomenklatura* on the island. Only consider the anti-Semitic homophobe Red Fascists (Stalinist "conservatives": right-wing left-wingers) presently in command of Cuba!

The exiled Cubans alone refer to all this. Perhaps the subject is too raw for the American media, so loath to mention anything squeamish except mayhem and murder and mugging, a press which dotes on child abuse in detail, and on other sexual frolics, like televised gang-rape trials.

The present regime on the island is shot through with, precisely, eunuchoid paranoia. And with superiority-inferiority complexes. Behold the new Conquistadores, the Castro brothers, aquiline imperialists, the first pure-blooded descendants of Spanish settlers to achieve power, and not by election, in the last half of the twentieth century. I consider them daily, in a picture up on my kitchen wall, just as I did in Dublin in a photo with the then all-white Politburo, all theoreticians of racism, and I noted the fact that this was the first time Cuba has ever been ruled by lily-whites. They have built the largest permanent military force in the world in relation to population, in proportion to the country's size, and Cuba is the only Latin American country with troops overseas ("*con tropas en ultramar,*" to use the historic imperialist terminology).

In Florida, more than 90 percent of Cubans who can vote do so against the inverse racism of the liberals who once ran their area. As regards foreign affairs they are experientially and existentially anti-Communist. I identify with *them.* On *that.* On their home island they never knew of $\frac{1}{32}$-Negro drinking fountains and in their voting now naturally reject the inverse racism of the "anti-racists," the reverse racism of those who cry "racism" at every turn. The party they vote for, within the narrow gamut of choices in the USA, may be the Party of the Rich elsewhere, the Party of the Dumb, and it may sport racists of its own, but there are none at the visible top: at least none the likes of that maximum aberration in American political history, the Reverend Jesse Jackson, ridiculous anti-Semite and Reverse Master-Race-Monger, and his ilk.

On my last trip to Cuba (1986) via Managua, with foundation support, I found a people which had lost its look.

In the days of my growing up in Cuba (fourteen years), and then when I went back to university there, the Cubans were the greatest lookers found in all my travels. The Cuban stare (at women, for example) outdid all other peoples', including those of the Mediterranean world, most notably those of the Italians or Spaniards. It is the stuff of novels, even if unmeasurable. "*Que miras?*" was a warning signal in my youth. "What are you looking at?" meant flight or fight among boys in school or street. Since everyone stared, a longer stare had to *mean* something: a challenge, or *desafío,* defiance or engagement. Of hatred or of love, of engagement in any case. People engaged themselves by looks. In present-day Cuba I found that the Cuban does not engage with his eyes, or make contact as before. He, the *macho* on the street, or even the *dama* (who tended to *avert,* self-consciously, her eyes from the ever-present gaze which tried to engage her), characteristically looked at everything (the trees, the colorful street scene). On this last trip to Cuba I was struck by people *not looking*—at anything in particular. There was none of the brightness of the Cuban look, of the Cuban looking.

People did not seem to look at anything. They walked along unstaring. I was reminded of Bucharest, Romania, my month there one year: another captive people, and other streets full of unseeing people. Will those who pile up hopeful, ever-burgeoning statistics of food production and distribution challenge this psychological (novelistic?) observation? Non-stare replacing stare, non-looking in place of looking. Such evidence, as that of the eyes, has no place on charts, of course. But is it not part of scientific observation? It is true that people in the street in Lisbon do not look at others as people do in Madrid; or that in Paris or Manhattan people seem too busy to look. And in Dublin (or Ireland as a whole) it is not good form to stare or even to look at other people with minuteness in a detailed manner.

But here I am comparing Cubans now with Cubans heretofore. Is it beyond significance, immeasurable altogether? I do not think so.

The critic John Richardson ("Picasso's Apocalyptic Whore-House," *New York Review,* April 23, 1987) tellingly notes the Hispanic *"mirada fuerte."* John Golding (*New York Review,* July 21, 1988) speaks of it, as it occurs in Andalucía, as "the way in which the Andalusian grasps a person or an object with his stare or steady gaze, possesses it, rapes it." Picasso used it, this stare, not from men but from women, five naked women, in his *Demoiselles d'Avignon,* his most famed painting (along with *Guernica*), most certainly his most revolutionary and influential work, and perhaps this century's most iconographic—and heresiarchal—canvas. In Cuba, where this stare, "raping" or not, but certainly intense, on the part of both sexes was classic—this Hispanic look is now reduced to lackluster unlooking. Even the police seemed dispirited and uninquiring in their perambulating scrutiny.

In Octavio Paz's magnificent book *On Poets and Others* (New York, 1986), Paz points up the dangers of *not-looking* when he speaks of Jean-Paul Sartre's reneging on his own senses: "Though Sartre has written subtle pages on the meaning of the look and the act of looking, the effect of his conversation was quite the opposite; he annulled the power of sight" (p. 41). And Paz goes on to say that Sartre, in the course of his own writing, "did not perceive in the freedom movements of the so-called Third World the germs of political corruption which have transformed those revolutions into dictatorships" (p. 44). In regard to Cuba he adds: "In each of the Communist states the Caesar imposes his style on the regime . . . the Caesar of Havana makes use of dialectics much as the old Spanish landowners used the whip" (p. 122).

In *Behind the Wall: A Journey through China* (Atlantic Monthly Press, 1988), the British novelist Colin Thubron writes of the new look in communalized and collectivized China, where people stare "not with the acquisitive glitter of the Arab but with a dull,

hopeless disconnection, as they might stare at fish." Since I had seen a similar look in Bucharest and in Havana I now wonder if there has not appeared in the world a radically new way of looking. Is there not now perhaps a "Collectivist Look"?

Metaphysical Music

As a lad I swooned at the thought of a temple within me, of a sanctuary chamber where God would linger.

And when, at the Colegio de la Salle in the Vedado section of Havana (*vedado* means forbidden, as in China's Forbidden City, ground posted against hunting, off limits to the chase), I was told to prepare my soul to receive the First Visit-in-State from God, I complied with mystic obeisance. And I was told by my French-born confessor that when Napoleon was asked, at the end, which had been the greatest day of his life, he had answered—not Marengo, not Hohenlinden, not Austerlitz, not Friedland, not Wagram, not Borodino—but the day of his First Communion. I believed this tale—it might even be true, for all I know—and that day in Havana was my first epiphany. I walked in a trance of withdrawal. And singed the hair of the boy in front of me in the holy line (he noticed the singeing as little as I did) with my baroque wrapped candle, all enveloped in silver foil like a *banderillero's* gaudy weapon. Thanatos, Eros, and the odor of mother's milk from the Virgin Mary all combined with clouds of incense. And the music of Bach! The "divine plan" and order of things: in the massed banks of flowers, the all-white boys' suits in the tropical shade shot through with bands of sharp sunlight, the incantations in mysterious Latin. Why should that not have been a Great Day for me or Napoleon? Need I bow, now, to the notion that it was a mere simulacrum? That scientifically it was mirror-play?

Saul Bellow writes that he always thought people who never, "never ever" (in their proud boast), showed any otherworldly sentiments were "pathological." It struck me from the first that anyone who could not understand such feelings was possessed of a spirit so wizened he could not respond to any music from "beyond." How could such a one respond, not alone to Bach, or Mozart's *Requiem,* but to anything like Hopkins's "grandeur of God"? Or even to deepthroated Dylan Thomas for that matter?

If the Red spectre of Marx has haunted me since young manhood, the spectre of religion has not: it is no bogeyman for me. The notion of the soul, of the spirit, of immortality, and above all of Bach's divine order in music, his (I could as well write *His*) "divine plan" has always been immanent in my senses once they were awakened, and has imbued me with a wonder which is as simple, and grandiose, as the awe behind the question "Who made the flowers?" Who, indeed, thought up the waterfalls, and the redwoods? Or rather, who was behind the lightning? The ancients thought Jupiter or Jove, though they also thought the lightning had always been there and had never been "thought up," just as Science suggests and as far as technological man is concerned. Or, if not who made anything, simply what does nature's sometime order, the order of a flower in blooming, say, respond to? What is the scheme behind, or in, the harmony of flowers—or music? Now that we know so many answers we know there is no answer. Then why are we driven to ask the question? These rhetorical questions are not, of course, real questions at all, not for scientists or the reasonably well informed, not for the median modern man. They are only the questions of legend, of the savage, of wild men, evocative only to the ears of the unreasonable and people of poetic

"My da, Thomas Aloysius Kerrigan, on horseback in the Philippines," 1910

nature, a few painters or musicians perhaps. Or simply to simpletons. Divine fools.

Consider the zebra, a giant half-dead sycamore, a bed of yellow pansies. Or lilacs last by the dooryard. Hydrangeas! *Mandelbaum, Mandelstamm!* They are the prototypes of art, of a perfection beyond telling, a model of ideation, the pattern of thought, the nub of existence. Do they respond to the Scientific Spirit alone? They entail a longing in men's minds which does not yield to botanical or zoological analysis. Man's constructivist equivalent is the keystone arch of Gothic building, the stained glass at the Sainte Chapelle in Paris, even Gaudí's trees in stone which are columns holding up parks. Only consider the still fruit of Zurbarán: can one regard his pewter plate of lemons and not be God-smitten? Or, if that is too definite, simply awe-stricken.

Or the note of erotic death, the note beyond the tomb, even or especially in *The Magic Flute.* Or in Telemann and Bach cantatas. Veritable Appeals beyond—not to—Reason! Bach believed. Why shouldn't I, who can batten on his echo or stand in his shadow only if the auspices and haruspices are favorable.

A Catholic, Roman, by birth and Irish history, I am not about to renounce my birthright because the Church of Rome was emasculated, lost its testicular privileges in procreative history at Vatican II. It was docked of its universalism when it suffered the cut to the groin from the "with-it" communalist anti-magic anti-Latinists. *Corruptio optimi pessima.* It lost the ritual sense I had first found as a boy in Havana. When later I became a Communist, I called myself a "Catholic atheist"—and God remained for me in the word "a-theist." I never childishly celebrated the death of God. Instead I childishly went on wanting to believe. My own religiosity was my own contribution to my own history's myth. (History: the lack of irony in the collective unconscious—or, as I put it a little differently in an epigram I wrote in Spanish, *"La Historia es la falta de ironía en la memoria colectiva."*) When, as a lad, on a fruit boat bound for Honduras on a cruise (courtesy of my father, the imperialist), I was asked my name, I gave it and, in the same breath, announced that I was "an Irish-American Catholic." If I had known more, perhaps I could have said I was a Puseyite, or "Ritualist," like T. S. Eliot . . .

Unable to believe in any mass-doctrine, and certainly not in the new shake-hands-all-around church in which the celebrant priest faces the congregants in massed confrontation, as lovingly aggressive as a Puritan preacher, I do not attend these or other rallies. Ethical discussions, especially on such private matters as abortion—I proffer the names of my six children as my end of the argument and as exorcism against the subject—strike me, from either side, as a new public barbarity, a disorder proper to the streets, a violation of decent discourse.

And as for the Church's all-too-this-worldly Liberation Theology: it appears to be a poor caricature of Marxist populism, a plan to win over the mob with the most banal form of "Love," Beatle-love, like rancid treacle. "'Social Christianity' has as much to do with religion as 'blue chemistry' has to do with chemistry," Unamuno wrote. Moreover, the history of Catholicism is the history of Europe—and none other. Preaching Catholicism in China—or in Africa—is exactly as unhistoric, and pointless, as preaching Judaism there.

And in general I prefer among people those who have an aptitude for worship, even believing believers, those believing with a belief in which I can only "believe" (believers in almost any imaginary higher order of things), to soul-shrunk believing unbelievers, especially to those who *believe* in their unbeliefs. (Reds of course are believers, not my kind, but deeply religious in a pagan sense, as Noam Chomsky made clear when he announced, in public, in Managua, when asked why he had not mentioned Marxism there, that he had not come down to the tropical heat of Nicaragua "to discuss religion.")

In short, "I would as lief pray with Kit Smart," who was mad, as Dr. Johnson well knew when he lauded the poet, or any other madman, and go down on my knees to the sweet mystery of banked flowers or the trees and mountains and sea and Niagaras beyond.

At Niagara Falls one summer while teaching at SUNY in Buffalo I was carried away, quietly burning in my spirit as with spirits in the belly of a pub-frequenting Dubliner, overwhelmed by the wonder that had inspired the Iroquois there when they intuited a tutelary presence in the immanence behind the veil of mist rising from the crashing waters, an emergent spirit in the falls at the thundering site. *O fons Bandusiae splendidior vitro.* I edged toward the abyss, ever more ready for sacrifice to whatever lay behind the misty veil of thunder. I was surely, or only perhaps, preserved by the Irish poet John Montague, who had apprehended my Celtic purpose and who had followed at a discreet distance. "The madness of the Cross" became the madness of a Celtic wood, or waterfall, in this case one haunted by the Iroquois.

In formal terms I would proffer to myth my offsprings' geo-religious history: my Antonia baptized at the font in Notre Dame de Paris, Camilo in the Seu

de Mallorca, the cathedral at Palma, Patrick and Malachy by the holy water in the same "fortress-cathedral" (Havelock Ellis), and Elie at the font in the church of the "Green Nuns" in Dublin.

Music

Music! I have read only a very few lines of verse in English, say (or in Spanish, for that matter), earthshaking as English is from Shakespeare to Gerard Manley Hopkins, to equal some of the phrases which animate the great German music from Bach to Beethoven, and in Telemann, Schubert, Mozart, and Haydn, and many lesser composers, including two kings, Leopold and Frederick the Great, music from a culture with a "destined singularity" (Heidegger's *geschick*). Music remains for me the perfect mystery, in a religious sense. A *mysterium* (q.v.: *quod vide*): and one that can scarcely be explained, a holy rite and the purest of the arts, to which all other arts aspire. Of course a train whistling on a winter night also suggests a deeper meaning or mystery, but there is no willful cohesion in it, only romance and nostalgia.

The will and its workings, the mystery of any possible meaning, the very notion of order in thought and the world, a glimpse into eternal beauty ("beauty is truth, truth beauty"), is latent in Beethoven's sonatas and trios and quartets, crystalized in the chamber works of Schubert and Haydn and Vivaldi and Mozart (though somehow not in Brahms, whose music is an echo chamber with a dead end, despite the haunting melodies. Brahms, moreover, somehow seems all gesso. Enamel. Grisaille. At best nacre, mother-of-pearl).

I am not of course speaking for musicians here, not from a musician's point of view, for some of them are simply functioning athletes, some prestidigitators, who may entertain no notions of grandeur at all. Very many musicians, in fact, as opposed to composers, have no more idea of the grandness of the music than translators have of the moral and aesthetic authority of their texts. I have watched with astonished disbelief a slew (Irish *sluagh*) of Borges translators who have gotten nothing, nothing of significance, beyond facets of technique, have not been influenced in their lives in the slightest by association with Borges or his texts. *Corruptio optimi pessima.*

Instrumentalists are, by and large, as translators are, by and large, mediums. Everything depends on the text in front of them—not *their* text, after all. They are interpreters. Akin to interpreters in a court of law, except that they do their work, ideally, before a Grand Court, a court of grandeur.

To the scandal of musicians, it may be (I don't know any musicologists at this time), and of many cerebral *aficionados,* I listen to music *all the time,* and well into the night, or all night if possible, especially when alone. "Scandal," I say, because they would be scandalized, with some good reason, at the notion of "background music," music as background to quotidian activities. True-blue listeners want to *listen* when they listen—and there should be no extraneous distractions of any kind, they would maintain (in truth, I know only a few such purists, and they are all of them people of dramatic and mathematical intensity). People committed to true music on the highest intellectual level may also require the most finished of performances. And they will not be content with fragments, as often I am. No Sappho in music for them!

If I were not, for several reasons, already pro-Israel, I would have to become so if only because in Israel—surrounded by twenty-two Arab states, some far richer monetarily—Mozart and Beethoven (German music!) are part of life. This fact alone would necessarily make me a partisan of this outpost of the West.

My office (granted to me "in perpetuity" by the Kellogg Institute for International Studies, University of Notre Dame, Indiana, at a moment when I was expected to attain room temperature), where for some years my door has read, "Senior Guest Scholar," and my pied-à-terre in South Bend are situated on the steppes of Siberia USA, and there(!) I can hear good music all day, and most of the night, without any palaver, some twenty hours without chatter or commercials (O rue *that,* New York!). It emanates miraculously, quite unbelievably at least, from a tiny fundamentalist college, Andrews University, in Berrien Springs, Michigan, a station which, as a subscriber to the "Beethoven Satellite," boundlessly emits the true music (the fundamentalists are surely not Platonists, but they too seem to believe in the "true," and the "good" as well: and they apparently consider music to be sacred by nature).

Alternatively, as well as to records and tapes, I can listen—on the fundamentalist's Sabbath—to the Notre Dame station, committed in theory at least to good music, sacred and profane, but which, run by students, will wander off at any excuse into Irish folk songs at best and into popular nonsense at worst, and which suffers from gauche pronunciations of the composers and their works at all times.

The University of Notre Dame, Notre-Dame-du-Lac, which should perform L van B's *Missa Solemnis* once a week or a month, doesn't celebrate it once a year—at least not in the decade that I have been in and out of Siberia USA, back and forth from my exile's *dacha. Corruptio optimi pessima.*

For me, music is as food, as vital as bread used to be, when it *was* bread.

Though the voice is surely the most wondrous of all musical instruments, especially in cantatas by Bach and Telemann, in duets and solos by Monteverdi, in masses by Mozart and Haydn, I am not an opera fanatic (except for Mozart, or for *Fidelio*) in the usual sense (the most popular, Italian, or French, is not—not precisely—my cup of tea), though I celebrate its existence. And there is much drama in it.

Now, any Haydn symphony lasts invariably the exact time I take to exercise under the shower. A *bêtise?* I listen intently enough. Sometimes I listen with utter concentration, struck dumb, but musically. Impressions and thoughts about thoughts sunder my total attention, ancillary reflections on words and world matter pullulate in my mind, but the underlining sense animates me and my mind's mindfulness. Sweet bastardization! (The narrator in Saul Bellow's *The Bellarosa Connection,* 1989, speaks of his own "two-in-one habit, like using music as a background for reflection.")

But much the same takes place in the concert hall. Music is the continuation of philosophy by other means.

I listen to music, or live it, outside a designated and confined space, the music of composers from Monteverdi to Bartók—and not much beyond. (There must be sensibilities as fine tuned as Mozart's wandering the world of music today but . . . *nada!* Another kind of mystery! Answered by Spengler and Heidegger to their own satisfaction—and mine.) Except, of course, for the unison medieval—who could help it?—the plainness of plainsong and the like: and how now can then anyone find a moment for the noise of "Rock," when there are endless hours of plainsong chant, so much more deeply tense than the latest racket? The Beatles? I never understood how this soft exudation, this loose fungus, this ooze, could have spread beyond the pools of suds in Liverpool saloons, beyond the pubs of the Mersey. What a pop counterpart to Nazi hysteria were the squirming masses of pubescent and pimply adolescents, mostly not-yet-ripe girls, who squealed the hours away while the Beatles and their ilk opened their mouths and—were not even heard above the savage beat! Such music was pabulum for a mass hypnotist and hysteric like the psycho-political sect-murderer Charles Manson, who doted on this dope and followed the instructions he deduced from the Beatles' *White*

Album and its song "Helter Skelter." (And who was hailed by the Weather Underground as a "Revolutionary Hero.") And was there ever a more wan parody of romance than the love-as-a-public-spectacle put on all over the "in" parts of the globe by the Brit High-Mannequin Lennon and the Japanese Businessman Ono for the benefit of the world's pandering press and the masses at their worst? It struck me as contra-natura. Vaguely anti-sex. Publicity in place of erotic privacy.

Jazz? Nothing in contra (though I have no trouble turning off Thelonius Monk, say—grand name: God in it, Theo, I take it, and the service of God—whenever such sounds as his take over the airwaves in my car, while I find it impossible to interrupt a Beethoven quartet). There is only so much time and space. I'd rather fill them with the most substantial fare, the best food for the brain, the richest music, what sticks to the imagination's bones with the longest-lasting effect.

There's an undertone of baseness about most jazz and it takes over and becomes dominant, inexorably, in the long run (after a remarkably limited number of bars). The best of jazz composers ("songwriters" is what they, mostly, have the grace to call themselves) are, like Scott Joplin, say, "stand-ins" for composers of the real music.

Rock? Beneath the dignity of any person with a minimal ear, or a mature mind, to mention.

Music and Women

The sensual choice of serious music has determined my own choosing among women. The three women who have been wived to me or borne children to or with me are more basically musical than I am, two of them being active musicians. It seems to be the *sine qua non* in life for me, even marital life, the without-which there is no marriage of true minds, bodies for that matter.

When they want to be sexually mocking, ironically anti-*femme*, American men may cynically say as regards their feminine prey: "I'm only interested in her *mind*." (Spanish men would not understand such irony or conceive such a conceit.) I, without being in any part "feminist," nor even, like Robert Graves, masochistically subject to theoretical notions of White Goddesses, have never been interested in any woman without a mind, an important mind. Not only not interested for procreative reasons, but also not even for pleasure.

Unlike D. H. Lawrence playing the sodomite through the medium of the two smitten characters in his *Lady Chatterley's Lover*—or unlike the tongue-tied Marlon Brando playing the rhythmic-catatonic deaf-mute Method-ravisher in *Last Tango in Paris*—I never found any deep eroticism in someone with whom it would be impossible to converse or exchange a thought, so much as an erotic thought, even in the course of sensual play, in so-called "lovemaking." If true love cannot always express itself in song or poetry, as ideally it will, it surely requires converse among equals-in-love, at least among those who are not given over to contra-natura sport.

As for true love, in the beginning is the Word, and the Word is with true lovers. And the Word is poetical, musical.

True music: the majestic, the incomprehensible, the godly. Much like love.

In my years I met three women concerned with the great music as the sensual and rational axis of life—and married them. The senses of these three, and their sensual expression, were, are, of a higher level in all other aspects of life as well. They not only understood great art and literature along with music, they were far closer to being centripetal Messalinas (especially if all-encompassingly monogamous) than the most brazen hussies and everyday sexpots. They were even more imaginatively built, more artistically modeled, whether or not they were archetypes of the Earth Mother. They were—and are—the most interesting women I've ever met; also rampant tigresses, painterly Eves, meaningful Cleopatras, houris, concubines, geishas, comrades. Even *without* their minds they would be most attractive—but not to me.

It goes without saying, and given all due reservations as to intelligence-measuring tests, that each one possessed a higher IQ, on the face of it, than I boast, for whatever it's worth (and it's most convenient, at the very least, to have a high IQ, for carrying on in life and letters): sharper, quicker, adept at mathematical matter and musical instruments, and with better memories in all areas.

My first wife, Marjorie Burke from La Jolla, California, mother of one son (who was born when she was nineteen and I was twenty), I met and married at seventeen, when we were both Communists (the Party paid for our underage marriage in Yuma, Arizona, and we spent our honeymoon on the floor of Party HQ in San Diego). She was soon back to being the aristocratic opposite of our mock "proletarian" affectation, and taught herself ancient Greek before going on to Berkeley, where the great Professor Friedlander declared there was little the school could offer her besides practice. She also taught herself calculus and read widely in philosophy, in

With sons Camilo (already a painter), Elie, and Patrick, and wife Elaine, at their home in Palma de Mallorca (formerly Gertrude Stein's), 1965

which subject she published a book dedicated to Mnemosyne. She particularly read Kant, Nietzsche, the classics in Greek—and, always, there was German music. But she did not want to go to Europe, especially careful to avoid a Greece so degenerated from her cherished classical time, and I *did* want to go (and before the cutoff date for GI Bill benefits for study abroad) and so ran off to Paris with Elaine Gurevich, and there we had a daughter, bigamously, so to say. *Mea culpa.* (All pictures—drawings, paintings, contemporary photographs—of the Burke-Kerrigan family, after our son Michael, a satellite engineer in the USA and Italy these many years since, was born in 1938 into the dishevelment of revolutionary doctrine, were lost in a trunk for want of some two hundred dollars to pay the railroad shipment between St. Augustine, Florida, and New York City. Trunk and contents were returned to "Unclaimed" and auctioned off in a railroad sale of lost-forever goods.) Marjorie Burke has a taste for pure form. She finally began going to Europe, and in her latest communiqué, after a visit to Rome, she wrote (in 1989!): "It's too Baroque." She deserved a Greek tycoon for a

shipmate rather than a Red "Fellow-Traveler." *Mea culpa.* However, all was not lost, for, once liberated from my poverty, she presently married a refugee banker (from a Middle European country in the hands of state banking); soon widowed, she married a Jewish refugee professor of French literature at Columbia University and Yale, also born in Europe.

Elaine Gurevich studied music at Champaign-Urbana and under Carl Friedberg (a pupil of Clara Schumann) in New York, and is now translating and teaching music in Spain in our jointly owned home, Gertrude Stein's former house (of which she writes in the *Autobiography of Alice B. Toklas*). But Gertrude Stein in Spain, in her day, was one thing. The Kerrigans' Spain is another. Stein had written Robert Graves in England, luring him to Mallorca: "Mallorca is Paradise. If you can stand Paradise." Today it is Paradise as terminus of a jet stream called Mass Transit Tourism. Elaine Kerrigan translated many books from Spanish while bearing and raising our five children born and reared in three countries (France, Spain, and Ireland), and is active in the world of bilingual publishing with our daughter Antonia, owner of the Kerrigan-Miró Literary Agency in Barcelona (founded and funded by and from the estate of the painter Joan Miró). She continues to play the piano beautifully, having added Bartók and some French music to her Scarlatti and the basic and "historically inevitable" German repertory. She also oversees the (tenuous) fortunes of our son Camilo, the possessed painter, in New York and Palma. She put up with a great deal of roughhouse. And penury. My role became increasingly unclear under guerrilla attack, in the way of American marriages (even abroad); it was not in the cards that I should play the part of a paterfamilias in the age-old tradition, backed up with family funds, preferably, Tolstoy-like, inherited. (But then, could I have ever played that role, or was I the eternal bohemian? A bohemian paterfamilias? There's the conflict. An authoritarian anarchist? I couldn't carry it off.) *Tant pis!*—for all, I ingenuously believe. With her beauty and high spirits she should have been an ambassador's wife and not a bohemian vagabond's. I have never been able to repeat the American refrain, "Another day, another dollar," because I have not been year-round on a regular salary or payroll—all these years. *Mea culpa.*

Moreover, I did not have "the moral heroism . . . to win family happiness . . . and hold on to it" (Valiunas on Tolstoy's "ideals," *Commentary*, June 1989). And then, the drink in Mallorca (and in Ireland, too) breached our defenses. She was a Good Drinker, but . . . I should have . . . ?

Mea Maxima culpa.

My first wife wouldn't go to Europe—out of too much love for its ruined past. The second won't come away from it. The third, though also American, was born there.

Judith Barnes-Weinstein (her mother's surname last, in the non-feministoid Hispanic fashion, two patronymics, two patrilineal surnames) was born in London in 1958. I slept in her bed as a guest of her parents before she was delivered at home on the Chelsea Embankment onto the same bed; and I knew her Russian-Jewish grandfather, whom she never saw, before she was born. Brought up bilingually in Rome, then active as a sculptor in New York, she is a mezzo-soprano at the School of Music at Indiana University in Bloomington; she is also a translator from Hungarian and Spanish. At our first supper with Cynthia Ozick in 1987, that prescient writer said we two were Yiddish *Bascherte* (fated for each other), most precisely and especially because of the age difference (twenty-nine and sixty-nine). My old friend and true (mythical) scholar Mark Mirsky, who believes in fiction and is editor of *Fiction* and perhaps believed

we were fictitious, did not concur; but then, he is strictly Orthodox. We celebrated our first true anniversary in my son Camilo's studio over the East River in New York at the turn of the year 87/88 and our second in London close by the British Museum.

An aside: on Judith's mind: as shown by her arrangement and presence in our bedroom on this day of writing.

Item: an opened book on the bed by a proclaimed "atheist" Hungarian bishop (Janus Pannonius's *Epigrammata*) with pornographic maunderings, asides, in Latin. Item: two paperback "volumes" of a little girl's *The Adventures of Tintin*. Plus: a black-stone lingam from India; a page from a current issue of the Spanish daily *El País* lengthily captioned with a photo of my *compadre* Camilo José Cela, seventy-three, and his new "*mujer*," thirty-three—the same forty years difference between them as between us. *Overhead:* some poems of mine she has pinned up, centered by a photo of Queen Victoria above our un-Victorian, unpuritan bed. Pinned to the door: a flyer announcing her public talk (in Italian) in Milan: SCULTURA E SESSUALITA 10 Ottobre 1987 Movimiento Freudiano Via Torino 2 (overlooking the Duomo). *En face* the bed: an ancient uncloven-footed satyr figure engaged in fellatio with a nymph: a baked-clay sculpture by herself; also a "Portrait of glasses with water in them," she titles it, and two dead-tree drawings, ditto and signed by her. In the background, she is singing: "Der Engel," an adulterous love song by Wagner. (She is not in "good voice" today and asked me to close the door to her piano, adding that I was "slightly dishonest," in asking her to sing something so I could write it into the "background.")

All in all, as regards the three: there are not many of their ilk. And, *nota bene:* I've never *believed* in divorce. Not then or now. But . . . it seems impossible to live life without a certain amount of criminality. Into every life a little crime must fall.

An attempt at justice, or at least factual fair play, having been attempted above as regards the three women, and never having been uxorious, I would like to bring the ideological contention between the sexes (an *à la mode* compulsion these days) into a more general focus, by most conveniently citing a question, perforce almost a remark, made just now by my nonacademic university-student wife when I read to her from the obituary page (of the *New York Times*), a habit as quotidian with me as with Proust and Joyce:

"Don't women ever die?" she asked. "Why so few women's obituaries?"

Needless to give my unnecessarily virile ("*macho*"), man's answer, here. But it made clear that

I was not only not uxorious, but scarcely *encoñado*, as the Spanish say, not to any great extent befuddled as to the bio-historical role of the sexes, not mesmerized in any case out of all sense of proportion, of *"historical"* (to throw feminist cant in the teeth of the modish) reality. No *her*story, as some feminists claim, about it.

"Well, if women had AIDS there'd be more of them on the obituary page of the *New York Times*."

To this, I had no rebuttal.

After a pair of heart attacks and a subsequent diagnosis of cancer had inconvenienced my small ritual life in the USA, in my exile from my chosen exile abroad, in Europe, where I belonged, it was Judith, born and partly raised at the Front Door of the Atlantic (a title I gave a collection of poems published in Ireland to express my own orientation), who took me up after a lifetime (*her* entire lifetime) of seeing me intermittently, in a fatefully routine manner, in Ireland, Spain, and Italy. We near-missed seeing each other in Hungary, a country of great importance to her. We learned our true and further fate, and accepted it in New York on New Year's Day, 1987. We at last knew each other. She knew a Lazarus. And willed resurrection.

El'āzār: A Post Epitaph

After I knew her my recent death
became posthumous, future doom
entombed. And life-after-death
an iridescent present, a breathing of her breath.

More than two years later, while beginning this sketch, I added the following:

Composed on the Heels of Love Cries

When I was rent, death-cleft,
she appeared in the fissure.
I'd lived by night's-gait best:
now dawn's a headlong shout.

And days are days are days
brazen even at sunset:
they lope like deer, imagine chase.
I follow the hunt in graced amaze.

(Love cries: a leitmotif insufficiently accounted for in literature; without any entry in Grove's great *Dictionary of Music*.)

"Le Nozze, September 4, 1987, after a wedding banquet for two in a Brooklyn café": Anthony and Judith Kerrigan

Music and Politics

The reason I became a Communist in adolescence is directly traceable to music. I had come north from boyhood and early high school in Cuba already disposed toward the Red Star of . . . the Future.

In Massachusetts I first discovered Stravinsky in my grandmother's house when I heard his work on the radio. I learned there were concerts by the Boston Philharmonic (under Koussevitzky), and took the train from Winchester one Saturday afternoon on my own. I was fourteen and in my junior year at Boston College High. No one I knew had any idea of music; my mother had, but she was in Cuba, and she had taught me only a very little piano, though she had been a piano teacher before her marriage, and was now utterly distracted and out of mind following the untimely death of her man, my father, at forty. She soon followed him, in any case. The concert included Schubert and Schoenberg—and the first act of *Die Walküre* in concert dress. My fate was sealed in the spiritual realm. After the concert I wandered over to Boston Commons. Some youthful Reds were making propaganda in the park: Yiddish accents were notable. I listened briefly and fell into converse: I told them the thoughts I had brought from Cuba. In a nearby delicatessen I told them about the concert, too. They had ideas on that as well: Red politics out of Russia and German music. The two became instantly fused in my mind.

The year after my first concert, now fifteen and about to graduate from Winchester High School (the eighth school in four years in two countries and on both the Atlantic and Pacific coasts, reflecting the chaos of our deracination from Cuba), I announced in the senior-class yearbook, under "Ambitions, Future Plans," my megalomanic plans succinctly: "President of the USSA." (I meant: the Union of Soviet Socialist America!) In print, it appeared as "President of the USSR." Either way, it was not the "Ambition" my imperialist father had in mind when he "designed" to have me born in the States so that I would be eligible to run for President of the USA rather than of the "USSA." Absolutely no one at all asked me what I meant.

The reason I was a senior at fifteen in a very good American high school was that a cousin of mine who was a schoolteacher brought me to the new school's principal and told him what she, to her surprise, had found me reading.

"He should be in the top class here, never mind his age," she urged.

The principal, a dry Yankee, asked me: "What are your favorite books nowadays?" I summoned up a list on the spot. I remember it clearly: *The Brothers Karamazov* (my first choice, I said), Hawthorne's *The Blithedale Romance* (I can still sense my child's guile in avoiding any mention of *The Scarlet Letter,* which I assumed would be taken for granted), Balzac's *Seraphita* (same reasoning and assumption), a volume of Emerson's *Essays,* Whitman's *Leaves of Grass,* and H. L. Mencken's book on Nietzsche. (No one of the books had been recommended to me by anyone I'd met so far.)

He wasted no time on forms. He arbitrarily assigned me to the top class, only noting, as a kind of regretful aside, that I had not mentioned the most important of all books: "The Book," he said almost wistfully, "you didn't mention the Bible . . ."

That year of silent and personal discoveries was to be the high point of my private intellectual trek through the world: from that height of clarity, up there on that peak, the gravity of chance precipitated recurring, ineluctable landslides. Avalanches! In ef-

fect. A trajectory of avalanches! From that point on it has been a forward thrust intellectually, but in the social arena, in relation to propitious social circumstance, all down-the-hill, officially, in the world thereafter.

When I crossed the country to California, I quickly became part of the YCL, the Young Communist League, and then because of music, I became a friend of a violinist in the San Diego Symphony. He was a Trotskyite, and I had already been warned that they were all "class enemies" and "police agents, provocateurs." It was startling, but the violinst was physiologically a dead ringer for Trotsky, down to the beard. One day we went to a movie house. At the end of the film the violinst advised me to sit quietly with him until the entire audience was gone: the two main leaders of the CP were in the house, had been in the audience. We waited, but when we finally left, the two were waiting in the lobby: "You'll be brought up on charges!" Etc. I knew the violinst was no police agent. I faced my comrades on the charge of "association with a provocateur." Before the vote to expel me was taken, I handed over my Party card and walked out of the secret meeting. I had enrolled in the fight for "freedom"—so I promptly became an active member of the Fourth International. An adolescent, I went from folly to folly. Now revolutionary duty called for me and my new comrades to infiltrate the Socialist Party of California and take it over so that it would speak with our voice.

There was some built-in Marxist "economic determinism" in my fealty to the Party at first. Apart from their sponsorship of our underage marriage in Yuma, they also provided me with a lovely job: they controlled, totally, the WPA Writers Project in San Diego. The top comrade was called the comrade-Project-Director, appointed by and paid for by the government of the USA (which we were all committed to "overthrowing"—what dreamers!), and I was soon the youngest paid-in-advance writer in southern California outside the movie industry. When I moved to Los Angeles the situation was, with ideological modifications, roughly the same, though they ignored or didn't care that I was now calling myself a Trotskyite: it turned out that the commissar-bosses (on USA government salaries) were by way of becoming Trotskyists themselves. Everyone on the project was some variant of Red—except for one anarchist and two token unemployed Hollywood writers hired as cover. I never told the FBI or anyone else any of this. I was never an informer (like so many of my former comrades who fingered me). But now . . . ? The news is scarcely of any use to anyone, except to historians of anecdote. Some of my fellow-writer comrades went on to a certain fame: Harvey Breit became editor of the *New York Times Book Review;* Kenneth Patchen became a cult poet, which he still is, posthumously; Irving Foreman wrote the film script for *High Noon,* and emigrated to England after being blackballed as one of the "Hollywood Ten." And, just as I did, they all evolved—simply grew up; Patchen and Breit soon died.

My first substantial assignment was a pamphlet for the Los Angeles school system on the history of the avocado from its primitive origins in Guatemala to its West Coast development. I next contributed to the *California State Guide,* writing on the architecture of Hollywood mansions and, at the opposite end of the spectrum, on the Digger Indians (what oma-dhauns!). This pleasant routine began my life of dedication to non-"useful"-work. All in all it was certainly rewarding. Every morning in Los Angeles we began the day's theoretical discussions at a cool saloon next door to our office with ice-cold beer and good talk from the novelist Ward Moore (who had

Seventeen, just married, living in La Jolla, and a Bolshevik on the WPA Writers Project, 1935

been expelled from the Communist Party because he was an avowed Orthodox Jew, and was ousted subsequently from his synagogue because he was an avowed Communist, and of whom the poet and critic Max Eastman, become an anti-Communist after learning Russian in order to translate Trotsky's *History of the Russian Revolution,* wrote that Moore "has inherited the mantle of Upton Sinclair with honor"). Beside Moore, our morning table invariably included the poet Rabinowich—a disciple of Laura Riding, who was also mentor to Robert Graves—as well as two lesbian bluestockings, and an anarchist. Moore and Rabinowich were among the greatest of influences on my taste and love for the Great Music, being total devotees in a religious sense themselves. Once again: music and Red politics.

My FBI file kept building, especially after I was discharged from Douglas Aircraft Company after a year as an aircraft worker, following the Writers Project idyll. I had been assigned to Department 20, Experimental, the exact spot that any spy would most naturally have chosen for his work. My FBI record reports that I was sent into the aircraft factory to take it over:

"As a result of the success of the Vultee Aircraft Co. strike, a truce and agreement has been reached between the Socialist (Trotskyites) and the Communist Parties locally. The two activities [sic] have agreed to work together to obtain further control of the aircraft industry. Their particular aim is Douglas." [From my FBI file, secured under the Freedom of Information Act.]

Two men had been assigned to carry out this feat, two men had been sent in to do the job, but I was the only one whose name was known. "KERRIGAN was described to me as a Left Wing Communist . . . now editing the paper, 'Clarity.' " I had never heard of such a journal, of which I was certainly not the "editor." It seems sad that grown men earning a salary for counterespionage should be so incompetent, paid for their ignorance, so utterly misinformed, especially about the two "activities" uniting for any purpose whatsoever: I had just been expelled from one of them for going to a film with a member of the other "activity."

Needless to say, in all my time at the factory I did not convert any fellow worker to anything, not even to good music. In fact, my zeal for the working class as the "Hope of Humanity" was waning. They struck me as, less and less, the possible saviors of mankind, even though there is a folk wisdom that leads them more soundly than most of their theoretical representatives do (if not in Poland, in the USA).

The most amusing lines in my file are those devoted to my "aliases" (my baptismal name is Thomas Anthony Kerrigan): "ANTHONY KERRIGAN, TONY KERRIGAN, THOMAS A. KERRIGAN, THOMAS KERRIGAN, TOM KERRIGAN, T. A. KERRIGAN" [capital letters for all "aliases" in original of my FBI file].

I had never used an alias, as was common in the "Movement," such was my faith in the impending absurd "Revolution" about to sweep the world, including California.

Eventually, after having been led out of the aircraft factory by plant security (their biggest job ever?), an order for "custodial detention in the event of a national emergency" was approved by the attorney general of the United States and the War Policies Unit, and by the chief of the FBI, J. Edgar Hoover.

Meanwhile, I had volunteered for service in Military Intelligence, US Army, in the war against Hitler (which was not meant to save the Jews, as I had thought, and never did so) and been inducted directly into that branch, another very natural place for a spy to choose. (I studied Japanese because I appreciated that culture; German might have been more rewarding, but there was a plethora of savants in that area.) After graduating from the lengthiest OCS (Officer Candidate School) in the army, the MISLS (Military Intelligence Service Language School, Japanese Section, assigned to Combat Infantry), specifically after six months at Camp Savage, Minnesota, following six months at the University of Michigan's Ann Arbor campus, which was taken over by the army, all of this instead of the usual three months OCS course for other services, my commission as a second lieutenant was held up—forever, awaiting the signature of the president, Franklin Delano Roosevelt. My commission was held in abeyance for months along with that of five others (out of thirty-five graduates). We were the first class to graduate into the Combat Infantry of the Japanese Section, and investigations of our past had been stringent, meticulous; so much so that one of the five dis- or un-commissioned men, Jim Lucas, was held up because not only he himself but his father had been born in India, though he and his family were West Coast Anglo-Saxon. I fell on the sword of the by-now dreary FBI record, although I was confronted with the information that there was also a file on me at the Office of Naval Intelligence and another at Army Intelligence as well. McCarthy me no "McCarthyism"!: I was the victim of quotidian institutionalized ignorance. "McCarthyism" is the shibboleth catchword used against all anti-Communists,

even those who *están de vuelta,* who have been there and back—by the disingenuous media clones of anti-anti-Communism. (And, note: the US Army worked with the Russian Army, Stalin's army, for the duration of the war.) Why was I allowed to complete the training? Instead of a commission in Army Intelligence, the *raison d'être* of all the training, I was made first sergeant of the next OCS, and drilled the new officer candidates, marching the men around the snows of Minnesota. On my first day as drill master, issuing a wrong command, I marched the entire group, a platoon, into a snowbank. Obediently they walked into the wall of snow until they could go no further. Abhorrent at first, in fact inconceivable to me as a human activity, brainless, I thought, drilling soon proved to be no more farfetched than surrealism's "automatic writing," or than choreography's routine.

While the men went to class to study the language and geography of Japan and Japanese order of battle, I was assigned the translation of captured Japanese naval manuals on submarine operation: I became an expert on torpedoes, as seen from the Japanese point of view, even on their construction and maintenance.

In the end, assigned to Combat Infantry at Camp Lee, Virginia, I volunteered for the Battle of the Bulge, and found myself nonplussed as to further study. I gave up the Japanese language for good. My name appears as cotranslator of the classic *Hōjōki* by Kamo no Chōmei (composed in the year 1212), fully titled *Notebook of a Ten Square Rush-Mat Sized World: A Fugitive Essay,* published in Canada and then as an art book in Ireland. But I only helped, perhaps, in the English, the difficult text being done by my *compadre* (both of us padrinos, godfathers, to each other's child in a joint baptism at Notre Dame de Paris after the war), Colonel Tom Rowe, now living and writing in Greece and France. By the time I was paying the price for having been a boy-Communist, I had developed on my own into a knowledgeable anti-Communist.

I had had time, however, to volunteer to fight in Spain, in the ranks of the POUM, incorrectly called "Trotskyist," though we in the Fourth International supported it. The great actor Edward G. Robinson—a secret sympathizer of the Old Man, of Trotsky himself, who was then exiled to Mexico, where he would be murdered by the KGB—was to cover the costs of our trip to Spain (no actionable secrets are revealed by my telling all this now). But, a mysterious "comrade from New York" with a German accent came to address us and convey the latest development in person before we could pack our bags and embark:

"They're murdering our comrades as soon as we get to Barcelona! Killing our comrades before we get to the front! Not the Fascists, but the Stalinists who command all the armies!" This generally unknown piece of news was a sad blow! It was a greater shock to my Faith than any known world event in the news. I truly began to see the light, once again, and with ever clearing vision. We did not pack our bags.

My absence from the Spanish Civil War is embodied in an echo years later (v. below) in the collection of verse *At the Front Door of the Atlantic*, from the Dolmen Press, Dublin (distributed by Oxford University Press), with a frontispiece made for the book by Picasso as a return gesture for a poem I had written (in English and Spanish) paraphrasing his iconoclasm. The poem, *"El atentado contra la virgen del piropo,"* and my English adaptation, "The Terrorist Attempt against the Virgin of the Flirtatious Remark," concerning a bomb thrown at a procession bearing this mythical Virgin, was considered blasphemous by the censorship office of the Spanish government at the time, although that was very far indeed from my intention. The editor of the monograph devoted to Picasso, Camilo José Cela (another *compadre:* he was godfather for my son Camilo at baptism in the Palma de Mallorca cathedral, and the boy's name was given him by the godfather, in Spanish fashion), was an elected member of the Royal Spanish Academy, and had fought in the Spanish Foreign Legion against the "Red Army of the Republic," and he was therefore endowed with much might vis à vis the censorship. He was able to force through a revocation of the ban at a private banquet for the censor when the moment came for brandy and Havana cigars (these *puros* never stopped flowing into Spain under Franco though the profits went to Castro's Communist Cuba) and Cela pointed out, tongue-in-cheek, that "Modern poetry is dedicated to the proposition that poetry means nothing," a thesis with which the censor readily concurred, in accordance with his lights. A convenient Mediterranean solution was thus found, and so the monograph appeared in print, including my bi-lingual text, with illustrations by Picasso.

A subsequent visit by Cela and myself to Picasso's longtime exile in France, to one of his castles, this time to his villa "La Californie," in Cannes, resulted in a farmhouse and surrounding land for our family in Mallorca: for he made me a gift of several drawings, mere *garabatos,* playful crayons. After they had hung for years, unmounted and unframed, on our walls in Dublin and Palma, they were deposited, after Picasso's death (it never occurred to us in all

that time to sell them, certainly not while he was alive, though he could not possibly have cared a fig about what we did with them), as collateral in a Swiss bank. The cash loan which accrued allowed the purchase of some terraced farmland (the terraces dated back to the Arab occupation of Spain) on a hilltop facing the Mediterranean at Bañalbufar, the next town down the coast from Robert Graves's Deyá. Every window gave on the sea and the day's sunset over some orange groves below. We planted many trees, I concentrating on easy eucalyptus.

Picasso had proven procreative (for us, fructiferous), the quintessential Spanish *macho.* In one ten-hour day he had also managed to show us his *cojones* twice, perhaps to prove he had two. We spoke only in Spanish; Picasso had a slight Catalan accent (from his years in Barcelona) and seemed to want to talk in French—but Cela knew none. (Picasso and Cela, two Iberian toughs, fretted about death like Gypsies: they ruled out, *forbade,* their own birthdays or any mention of them in their presence, and on their day were black-humored all that day long. I endured more than one of these enforced non-celebrations with Cela, *mi compadre.*)

A book of mine appeared with one of Picasso's drawings (a "portrait," he called it, of me), and it included a poem which pertains to absence—a Doppelganger's going "missing"—on and from the battlefields of the Spanish Civil War. It concerned the front I had volunteered to fight on, where I would have been sent, if the Stalinists were not "killing our comrades before we get to the front," as the Trotskyite delegate from New York had put it to us.

The Ebro Front—An Offering:
Twenty Years Later

I found the cave where we crouched that
night: O'Bannion had never come out.
No one had ever had time to look for him.
I had not gone back there before.
Inside, in a niche
        in a side wall far back
there was one shoe
        with a hole through the bottom.
A plate filled with mud, shining
        in the yellow glare of my lamp.
And six spent shells
        in the wet.
Six 45-caliber shells in the mud of the plate.

Item: Concerning the O'Bannion in the above poem, I can here bring him up to date, to 1988.

There's a character who bears this name, my pseudonym, in the latest book by the true writer and novelist William O'Rourke.

O'Rourke and I are true friends, all the more so in that we disagree on every political issue. First of all, he declares himself a Populist (though on television lately he called himself "an authorized solipsist"). He refuses to read the past's great writers: no Czechs, Russians—"foreigners," he says frankly, speaking clearly (and so he disdains Kundera, *en passant*), neglecting even to read Babel, whose masterpiece of a story "My First Fee" I've tried to foist on him, as a minimal bow to all Russia, for years. Instead he reviews the latest Books, and most lately has shown a great interest in Black Woman Books, for the media. A man can't do two things at once: in the time of one's life there is only Either/Or. But then O'Rourke is in no part a cad or a miser, the least of either of any man I've known. O'Rourke is a defector from the Roman Church and from his Irish heritage (he is of minimal blood from Monte Negro, a kingdom abutting Albania and now part of Yugoslavia, and a lover of things Negro, especially basketball). Our discrep-

ancy of disposition and views makes us complementary: we attack reality or irreality, from opposite directions. As regards the spurious: it is difficult to fool both of us simultaneously.

My pseudonym in Spain under Franco, e.g., when I wrote a piece on Job (the biblical Job) for *Iberica*, the New York journal espousing the cause of the Spanish-Republic-in-defeat (and funded by the Crane toilet-plumbing-family-fortune), was Timothy O'Bannion, and thus I signed my name, to avoid any possible trouble with the Spanish authorities at that time.

Now, this is the very name for a character in O'Rourke's latest novel: O'Bannion is described with precision, a look-alike for O'Rourke's friend, the original behind the pseudonym, me. The word portrait includes the salient details, from long white hair, "a kind of ivory color . . . the tint of old piano keys" (Oh?!) to "unlit but half-smoked cigar in his mouth" (a habit of O'Bannion's, of mine, a mode I affected at the time the novel was written). O'Bannion is bilingual! There are not so many such people, and no others within O'Rourke's acquain-

Kerrigan (left) at a waterfront restaurant in Cannes with
1989 Nobel Prize–winner Camilo José Cela and Pablo Picasso, 1960

tance. O'Bannion speaks, in the book, to his "nephew" in Spanish. I often spoke to my son Elie (part Jewish, he is sometimes taken for a Sabra), "a cedar-colored fellow," writes O'Rourke, during his first two years at university, preferably in Spanish, for a variety of reasons: it was his best language, and we could talk in public in our own privacy, and we did so in O'Rourke's company while he was writing his novel. O'Bannion inveighs against Fidel—"Fifo," he calls him, using the Cuban exile's term. He employs the exact words and arguments I employ daily, unvarying as they are. Only: O'Bannion seems to work for the CIA! At something never explained but dimly ominous. This is a twist that's stylish, the kind of thing an *à la mode* reader expects to hear when things point in the Wrong Direction.

If the reader has read this far, he will know that the CIA and FBI investigated me and that I did not, could not, investigate anything for them. And that's what O'Bannion is doing in the book, some investigative scouting, presumably, for the CIA. Conspiracy-theory anti-Establishmentarianism!

But we are dealing with a novel and the author invoked O'Bannion as a character and thus he is O'Rourke's. It's fiction, for heaven's sake! There are few rules, and I only use the incident here for my own purposes: to continue my existential act. O'Rourke makes O'Bannion live, for this author of men has earned the right to give his characters whatever fate he wants. But wait . . . this pseudonymous O'Bannion has a fictional fate of his own to think about. And by Fiction's laws of history, by the internal logic of myth and story, it has already been proven that he is pursued by the likes of the CIA and cannot, in accord with his fictional past, pursue any objective designated by the CIA. That would be violation of Fiction.

O'Rourke does not traduce me, for I am not a character in *his* novel, where the author is master, but only in my own novel of myself. But O'Bannion?

O'Bannion, as evidenced in "The Ebro Front," went into a cave in Spain—and never came out. Was he working for the CIA on the Republican front in the Spanish Civil War? Scarcely.

There were "six spent shells / in the wet / in the mud of the plate": some CIA setup? Or rather, *some* CIA setup!

O'Bannion had and has a fictional past, a history of his own in fiction. Has a novelist the right to tergiversate it? To apostatize O'Bannion, to equivocate with his history?

But nevertheless and moreover: here is good writing, and a closely researched study of Florida exotica, and a colorful narrative of an actual crime, the theft of Audubon bird prints from a Key West museum. I urge, then, ambivalently (politically speaking), any reader of these pages to read—with the necessary caveat—William O'Rourke's *Criminal Tendencies* (Dutton, 1987), to find out more, in Chapter 22, about O'Bannion and his putative dealings with the very CIA which had denounced him (and some incisive pages on dog-track racing in Florida as well). O'Rourke, by the by, is also author of *Idle Hands,* a masterwork of the picaresque, decried, nevertheless, by several of our mutual, feminist, friends.

Before I was O'Bannion in Spain, before I went to Spain to live, after my War and three years in the army and a year in the merchant marine, in my last year in the USA before expatriation, I decided to acquire an aircraft pilot's license, which any fool—or most fools—can acquire. The truth is that it should be harder to acquire an automobile license—for a far more lethal instrument. I think the idea was to be able to speak of aesthetic matters with more realistic authority.

When one is called an aesthete often enough, an "elitist," by middling Americans, one may well decide to try out one of *their* activities. Once I began to fly, most notably down and over the sea and Inland Waterway of Florida (I liked seaplanes by far the most, though I soloed in a land plane), I could sound off on Beauty with a firmer note. It was even more true after I crashed into Miami Bay (I was planning to fly the length of pre-Castro Cuba and over to the Dominican Republic on some aircraft business having to do with the Florida Air National Guard, of which I was a member until my commission in that service was withheld after some months for the oft-repeated and increasingly dreary reason of my *having been* a Communist in my youth).

I was caught in a crosswind coming into Biscayne Bay. I said "crashed," but actually, after a score of buffeting smacks against the high-running tidal currents and after one wing dragged along the water, I taxied the craft to a stop at a seaplane pier. The plane had already been condemned as UNSAFE by the FAA (Federal Aviation Authority), which was why I was free to use it any time, the owner caring little what I did with his be-damned plane. It had been anchored off his house on Davis Shores, St. Augustine, gathering salt rust. It was not exactly a reliable plane. Manipulating the controls like a wrestler doing his best with some Proteus-like opponent I had not a second to ponder the possibilities, to think of disaster, or to entertain Fear as a guest in any guise—or in fact to "think" at all. Ex post facto, it merely made for an interesting paragraph of personal history. I never regretted a moment of it. It was a rare exhilaration to dock that day. When I called the owner to speak of possible structural weaknesses as a result of the buffeting, especially to the wing, which in dragging had guillotined a field, an acre of whitecaps, he told me to offer it for sale, "for the parts." I had been able to use it whenever I wanted for a couple of months. I never managed to count on a plane more or less my own again. It was a glorious end to my flying career, such as it was, a mere excuse, a touchstone of experience of living in the air, a point of experiential reference.

I am buffaloed by the media's morbid obsession with fail-proof safety aloft. Is no one supposed to take risks, not even those born to dare? Columbus would not have been funded by the USA today—"no way." That so few aircraft fall, that there has only been one shuttle failure (though even the Challenger failure served a purpose), shows that flying is far safer than sailing in 1492. (But why should safety have anything much to do with it? It didn't in the days that America was discovered, I take it.) Today's flyers obviously are as brave and venturesome as ever, but in a consumerist society stampeded by a poisoned grape early in 1989 . . . ?

Reporting on the Visual Arts

Once, when I was "on the beach" (as sailors say when they do not have a berth on a ship), I opened an art gallery on fashionable Oak Street, No. 106, almost at the edge of Lake Michigan in Chicago. (This was while waiting for the mother of our Paris-born daughter to marry the child's father, me, and return to Europe.) I was working as Fine Arts Editor of an encyclopaedia by day and as an art *marchand* and gallery owner by night. The offices of *Poetry,* the magazine, were a couple of blocks away in a Maecenas's building owned and larded (with patronage) by Mrs. Adlai Stevenson, who was manic and insane, busy attacking her husband, noisily proclaiming that he was a homosexual. There was much contact with bohemia and I published prose and poetry in *Poetry* and met celebrated poets, from Robert Lowell to Roy Campbell. (We waited in vain for Dylan Thomas, who drank away his scheduled appearance in Chicago and chose to die instead). (And Death had no Dominion over his verses, which we chose to go on reciting, to this day.) Leon Golub was the *vedette* of the gallery, coming by to call daily, and he went on to fame and great fortune—and social silence; he stays away now from the masses he eulogized. Allan Frumkin, the

dealer, traded some Skira art books, a new departure then, and a Nolde print taken from a rare early German magazine in exchange for a pair of Max Beckman originals (small) from me. I was quite a trader when I came up against the professionals!

We left the gallery to go directly back to Europe (landing in Lisbon on 16 August 1956 to stay "forever"), and there I continued as North American editor of the leading Spanish art journal, *Goya,* for a couple of years. They sent payment by hand, and we were delighted to see, every month, an officious special money-messenger come to our door with a packet of cash in *pesetas.* Some months it was our only income, two thousand *pesetas* per chronicle; other months it was art entries for the encyclopaedia which I had assigned to myself before leaving the USA. There were cheques from *Arts,* in New York. Did anyone ever live solely from pieces on art from exile? The Bollingen Foundation saved us from this fate.

My only contribution to art history, to art journalism that is, was that I apparently managed to be the first person to write, in Spanish, on Francis Bacon, the untaught English paint-genius (another

Oil painting of the author by son Camilo José Kerrigan

man of the drink: born in Ireland after all); and the first, as far as I know, to write, in English, on Gutierrez Solana, the eccentric Spanish mock genre painter (in *Arts*).

While I am about it, making claims, I might as well mention that I have not been challenged when I assert that I was the first in the history of the *New Yorker* to publish translations (of Borges) in their pages—not counting Vladimir Nabokov's son's translations, with his father's help, of early work by that great Russian exile and except, perhaps, Singer translating his own Yiddish into English for the magazine (the first book of his translated by someone else was done by Saul Bellow).

I gave up writing on art when I found most of the paintings from "North America," mainly New York, rather beyond my words, which the paintings scarcely required; the latest dynamic art, or that of the "let it all hang out" order—or disorder—struck me as beyond language altogether, certainly beyond my language.

The galleries and museums were supplying me with an endless flow of photographs, but it seemed inauthentic to be commenting, in Mallorca, about the latest developments in USA sight unseen *in situ, in situ* USA. My very last report covered a tour of Spain, a personal inspection in the studios of the leading avant-garde artists there, from Miró and Saura to Millares and Tapiès, all of them delightful people as well as painters, a holiday trip paid for by *Holiday* magazine.

My most notable conversations on art in these years were with the anarchist painter Emilio Vedova in Madrid and Venice; and with Sir Herbert Read, a *soi-disant* anarchist Lord and fellow editor of the seven-volume Unamuno series for Bollingen/ Princeton, at his rectory-house, "Stonegrave," near York in England; and in Ireland on a lovely estate with a waterfall; in Spain, in Madrid and Palencia; and in Portugal, for the last time, as we sat in the luxury around him on splendid grounds at Azeitao, he unable to eat because of tongue cancer, from which he was painfully dying, quite bitterly complaining over the difficulty of chewing a piece of decrusted bread, he who had endured trench warfare and been decorated with the Victoria Cross for bravery.

There is probably no connection, but I never wrote about art again.

Apart from the gifts of work from Picasso, Miró, and the other artists mentioned above, my collecting included a bronze head of Unamuno by the powerful sculptor Pablo Serrano, and paintings from the madhouse for drinkers (St. Patrick's athwart or abaft

the gates of the Guinness Brewery in Dublin, I don't remember their relative position exactly), and the unique selection of the primitive work of the veteran of the Spanish Blue Division on the Russian Front, the ex-soldier Rivera Bagur. As a writer, art criticism is the only field from which I gladly retired.

Borges and I

One of the high points of my years in Europe (though I was no longer spending most of my time there, but rather working out of my pied-à-terre *dacha* in Siberia USA) was the month I spent in the company of Borges, first in Milan and then in Rome, in the last December of his life (1985).

I had translated and/or edited six titles of Borges's work. On this meeting he insistently called me *Sean Bhean Bocht*, which he said was the designation of a secret Irish society, and repeated the phrase vaguely from time to time through the weeks, even though I told him the words stood for Ireland, "The Poor Old Woman." Perhaps he thought the literal description befitted me, suited me after all.

We worked on some pages of his (offhand pages on Virgil and on the Tower of Babel), but mostly we chatted away in daily meetings and lunches and dinners—he ate only *risotto* by that time, though I ordered grand suppers on my own, for the restaurants were luxurious and *il conto* was always paid by the Freudian organization which funded our voyage to Europe and all our expenses there. Neither he nor I was in any part of us a Freudian, and the irony was delightful . . .

When begged to speak of Freud by the audiences of the converted and the faithful, Borges could not, did not try to, conceal his utmost scorn. The beauty of the situation—and a tribute to the Freudians—was that our hosts never batted an eye, never failed to pick up each and every check for whatever extravagance. Seats costing hundreds of dollars were put at our disposal for the Opening Night of La Scala in Milan. I got stranded in the Freudian foundation's headquarters far outside Milan, Villa Borromeo in Senago, but he was in Milan and went. And was applauded by the audience when they caught sight of him before the performance, an applause which doubled when the former president of the Italian Republic embraced him, and tripled when the incumbent president did the same. Only in Italy! But then . . . disaster. The performance was of the gaudy *Aida*, a showy display opera indeed—but scarcely for a blind man! "I was bored stiff!" he repeated over and over to me through the following days. "What nonsense!" He spoke in English. Nineteenth-century boredom was the same enemy for him as it had been for Oscar Wilde or Baudelaire; he spoke the phrase like an Englishman. But Verdi's music? "I know only tangos, milongas . . ." We did not talk Bach or his kind . . . and again I was disappointed on this head.

Of all the great figures—men of name fame—in arts or letters with whom I have consorted, perhaps only Saul Bellow proved to be a man of high culture. Picasso, or Miró (a neighbor in Mallorca), did not know so much as the names of the great composers, or the great writers for that matter. My *compadre* Cela's idea of music seemed to be limited to Negro spirituals and tangos. *"El bel canto yace putrefacto en la tumba,"* he wrote: bel canto is putrefying in the tomb. It was easy for him to believe this *oltraggio*, for he is tone-deaf. Robert Graves's idea of music (another neighbor on Mallorca, who often used "we Irish," when speaking to me) was the bongo drum—and he put his money where his words were, for he backed, paid for out of royalties, an unspeakably noisy nightclub in Mallorca, called, I believe, "El Mood Indigo," or some such thing, and there his Catalan son-in-law banged the drums dementedly loud for hours: glasses arrived at one's mouth trembling from the sound waves.

On the other hand, Gabriel Marcel wrote—and told me in Paris: "It was no book or work of theology which brought me to a belief in God, but Bach."

Still, the dull catalogue is tedious. The fulminating and irascible stylist Edward Dahlberg hated music—except for Al Jolson, whose records he played surreptitiously after midnight, as I learned on visits to him in his Dublin quarters across the street from "Hartigan's Pub," the sound of the incongruous Jew-playing-the-Darky on old records filling the night air one summer.

Leslie Fiedler, however, said one night in our Dublin place on Fitzwilliam Square (after blasting one and all as overt anti-Semites from a banqueting table where, at a James Joyce conference, my wife and I sat alone with him in apparent *gemütlichkeit*), while he sipped Paddy and listened to Mozart, "Who could think of greater bliss!" He loved Mozart above all composers, he said. A distinguished minority of men-of-letters who care for the music of Music.

But, Borges . . . Every word he spoke in public—and sometimes at the dining table—was transcribed, a microphone thrust into his face by Italian cousins of the *paparazzi*. He did not seem to mind in the least. The Freudians also videotaped his every gesture in Milan against a backdrop of the Duomo

Elaine Kerrigan with Robert Graves, in the Palma café where he contributed an epigraph to Irish Strategies *(Borges-Kerrigan): "God does not love Ulster as he did in the time of Cuchulain," 1974*

standing as a lace lyric in stone outside the wide windows. Subsequently a book was issued with his every word put into Italian, *Borges: Una vita di poesia*, with a *Prefazione* by me: I had contributed a memoir of his Italian days to the journal *Spirali* and was surprised to see the piece turn up as the preface to Borges's torrent of words: I had not been consulted on this transposition nor paid for either work. Only in Italy!

In his flow of words Borges had spoken in public of him and me being "exiled Europeans living in the Americas." And at table in his last days he had said that he would not go back to his "exile" in Argentina. Some have expressed surprise at my report of this statement, but his soon-to-be-deathbed-wife, Maria Kodama (Maria Dryad or Echo, to translate her Japanese name), said the same thing as regards going back to South America.

On the "question" of non-being: Borges was enamored of annihilation. He was obsessed with oblivion, just as Unamuno, his immediate predecessor in these matters, had been obsessed with everlast-ingness. In the same Hispanic way, Borges longed for the obverse of eternity, nothingness. He was cancer-ridden in that last December and would soon die (on 14 June 1986) and said not a word to me or anyone by way of celebrating his good fortune but was as quiet as an ideal Greek about his proximate relief. He did intone variations of "Farewell," principally by reiterating lines from Rossetti, randomly reciting,

Look in my face.
My name is Might-Have-Been.
I am also called No-More, Too-Late, Farewell.

There were other surprises, scandalous some of them. After adolescence, Borges had always called himself a conservative. But no one seems to have noticed—or asked him further—about his mature politics. He spoke about "the superstition of democ-racy" and said that America "can't make up its mind to become an empire" (I quote now from his early story "The Other," which first appeared in English in *Playboy,* but he repeated it all to me again). When I asked him if he had, as reported to me by my friend and his guide in Austin, Texas, Professor Angel Delgado, whether he had really said, on reading the epical words of a defeated Confederate general carved on a monument, really uttered and iterated the lapidary word *"Perdimos!"* "*We* lost!" he repeated the exclamation again and added: "Of course, we all lost, we Europeans. And the businessmen won, Marx's bourgeois. And with that we've gone on to the next step of 'historical determinism,' the brutality of Communism, which is as bad, or more complete, more lasting, than Fascism." And we spoke of the deteriorating state of Academia (again I quote here from "The Other" because it is printed and is at hand at this moment). In our conversation I alluded to his published statement "It wouldn't surprise me if the teaching of Latin . . . were replaced by that of Guaraní." I told him the University of Chicago was now offering "Cuzco-dialect Quechua" in place of . . . "What atrocious deterioration!" he inter-rupted with Latinate grandiloquence.

And there was more, much more. He denounced Neruda's *two* odes to Stalin. "He wasn't asked to write *two,* was he?" Castro in Cuba was "a gangster." Academics dealing with Borges like to claim that "he had no politics." But what could one call what I heard? He was so unfashionable, so unstylish. He affirmed his loyalty to Israel. "I'd go there if I were a Jew, and live and teach. But then, perhaps I am a Jew, Portuguese Sephardic, you know . . . My surnames

could be Sephardic . . ." I told him that my own personal theory was that the Nobel Prize had been denied him most likely because of his very numerous poems and eulogies of Israel . . . "Yes, the Swedes see through me . . . And, then, there are many more Arab states than the one Israel . . ."

There is such a deal of rubbish written in Academia about Borges! The latest news on this front is summarized in a flyer which has just reached my hands, sent to me by Jean O'Bryan, a clear-headed graduate student in Ann Arbor:

The Department of Romance Languages and Literature

of the University of Michigan

announces a lecture

Z/Z

Borges' Emma Zunz, midrash and *écriture féminine*

by Professor B. McGuirk of the University of Nottingham

"The fiction of Borges has been notorious [sic], according to mainstream criticism, as much for the exclusion of woman [sic] as of the ideological," says the flyer. This first sentence is a nonsequitur: Borges wrote not only the story the lecturer will discuss, but such poems as "Whorehouses like Angels" written in a lupanar in Mallorca, where he speaks of "trembling like flame" in the "sheer arms" of a "sheer girl." Borges was no Don Juan, whom he detested, in the manner of his sometime master Unamuno, but he doted on women, even if more or less "Platonically." Besides, who is to say what sexual orientation a man of letters must take? "Mainstream criticism": i.e., the lecturer's position is no doubt that of "Everybody" and thus "mainstream"—some waterway! There is no "ideology" in Borges: that is, there is no "main-stream" or standard "progressivist" Left ideology in him: none of the right kind, in any case. O the quirks of McGuirk are a-plenty! He, or his publicist, con-tinues:

"The feminine has had to be deciphered be-tween the signs, between the lines . . . :" Borges's text "operates within the generally more subversive layers of the political *unconscious.*" (In New England all this could be called "swill.") A non-serviam as to whatever is "mainstream" is a continuing part of my Autobiography-to-come in life.

How this "mainstream" operates is well illus-trated by the history of my own work on Borges. I translated and edited and introduced the first two *books* by Borges in English. (Another work appeared between the two, but it was a made-up collection and not one of Borges's choice, not Borges's idea, but one based on publisher's views in New York.)

Living abroad I have never been a member of the New York "mainstream" cabal. I did all the work on a total of six Borges titles, including his first book—and his last. Borges's goodwill and enthusiasm were conveyed to me repeatedly. In between the first and last book, the "mainstream" held sway: its self-serving contractual arrangements enforced a "closed shop." The fact that in the end I was called back is an indication of the disconformity with what was done after my initial departure from the field. The malaise was detailed to me; it included the dissatisfaction of Borges—and even, finally, of his American publisher.

Borges had grown increasingly alienated from the "mainstream" as his work appeared in English. And so he told me at our first meeting, in Madrid in 1963, and repeated the *histoire* at our last meetings in Rome (like almost all of the great writers I have known, he repeated himself endlessly, fortunately). My most successful piece about Borges was titled "Borges: A Non-Meeting": it concerned his first visit to Spain since his youth in that country. I had *not* gone to Madrid to meet him. The piece was first published in French, then in Hungarian, Hebrew, and then, finally, in English, in a book we put

With Jorge Luis Borges after supper in the Albergo degli Ambasciatori, the Ambassador Hotel, on the Via Veneto, Rome, 1985

together with his permission in Dublin: it included two stories by the Argentinian rendered into Irish—from my English—by a Provo (Catholic IRA) school-teacher who worked on them in prison.

To give a source other than myself to describe the mysteries of the "mainstream," I turn to Mark Mirsky, editor of *Fiction,* a faculty member at CCNY and a notable author himself, who wrote a memoir in which he tells of a supper with Borges "at an expensive New York restaurant." Mirsky had gone there with Max Frisch, the Swiss novelist, and his wife, a translator ("who left the room upset . . . at what she perceived as condescension towards Borges"). Mirsky writes: "There at the other side of the table were several of the literary brokers of New York . . . I turned to this half of the table first and thinking to ingratiate myself, mentioned that I had met Anthony Kerrigan, one of Borges' translators, before. The tablecloth curled and stormed with wrath, condescending adjectives, disparagement . . ."

So, there, in absentia, through the persona of Mark Mirsky, I encountered the "mainstream" in full virulence:

"At the end of the evening as we rose to go, my other tablemates' remarks about Anthony Kerrigan—whose generous letters had been an education, under whose roof I had slept, whose wife and daughter were close friends as well [Mirsky was scarcely neutral]—were rankling. Tony had still not met the writer he had translated and admired. I could not resist a sudden lunge at Borges, with whom I felt I had made no contact at all. 'I want to extend,' I called as loud as I could through the tinkling of silverware and scraping of chairs, as if the Argentine were half deaf not blind, 'Greetings from Tony Kerrigan.'

"'Tony?' whispered Borges incredulous.

"'Tony Kerrigan,' I shouted.

"'Tony Kerrigan,' cried Jorge Luis Borges across from me and fell halfway over the table to grasp me in his arms, throw them around my neck, kiss my cheeks. 'Tony! My benefactor. Tony, my benefactor.'

"It was a minute or so before I was able to explain that I was only bringing him greetings from Tony Kerrigan instead of standing there as Anthony in the flesh. The faces at the end of the table were redder than the wine."

Jascha Kessler, the writer, translator, and poet, reported almost exactly the same experience from UCLA. Thinking that Kessler had said he was Kerrigan, the blind bard had embraced him effusively before Kessler could explain that he, too, was not Kerrigan, but merely conveying regards.

In the early days, while Borges was still a prisoner of the publishing moguls, the reports to me in Spain echoed the Argentinian's great goodwill toward his out-of-the-mainstream translator.

In Milan in his last year he said in public, as recorded and printed in Italian, though he said it in French: *"Kerrigan! mio inventore, mio benefattore . . . Noi siamo due esiliati in America . . ."*

I hold the "mainstream" publishing cabals responsible for having truncated my destiny with Borges.

Awards

John Cheever wrote a most comical letter on how to win a National Book Award (in *The Letters of John Cheever*) which begins: "First you have to have at least three good friends among the judges and then you have to have . . . a commodious bladder and a good supply of Bourbon." And the letter ends, after describing the award festivities: "All the publishers got drunk and sang Down by the Old Millstream."

Of course my NBA was merely for translation (of one of the seven volumes—any one, it turned out—of the *Selected Works of Unamuno*: Princeton/ Bollingen) and I had none of the necessary qualifications as listed by Cheever. And still: it was given to me twice! And retracted once. And finally given to me to keep. Cheever recounts how, on the night of the awards, the plaque of commendation was given him once, taken away, and them given him for a second time: a parallel to my experience. The Indian-giving with me, however, was stretched over two years . . . I was awarded the first NBA in 1974 for my edition of Unamuno's *The Tragic Sense of Life*. I read about my prize, in Mallorca, in the Paris edition of the *International Herald Tribune*. Before I received any word from the officials, I instead received telegrams of congratulations, among them one from Hungarian PEN, and from other far-flung entities; a *Life* photographer was dispatched from Madrid; long distance calls and letters began arriving. But by then I had read in the same Paris-based newspaper that the jury's decision had been revoked, and the award re-given to a most worthy writer/translator, Jackson Mathews, for his work on Valéry, a splendid labor. How was it done, I wondered? Princeton University Press, for whom both Mathews and I did our volumes under the auspices of the Bollingen Foundation, which paid all the bills from travel to publishing, had wanted, the press had wanted, the prize to go to Mathews, for he

was dying. It couldn't have gone to a better man, but . . . to substitute a man because he was comatose? The mystery grew thicker when the next year's totally different jury gave me a second (unrevoked) NBA for a lesser book of Unamuno's, *The Agony of Christianity* . . . How did this second jury, made up of different people, decide I was the best translator in USA, for the second year in a row? and what were the pressures, the committee contrivances, what were the five-year plans? Who leaned on whom? I was never invited to partake in the bibulous ceremonies, because the bosses at Princeton, with whom I was totally at odds, decided that the other editor of our series, also en route to room temperature, rushing toward rigor mortis, would give the speech of acceptance. The next year I was made one of the three judges for the 1977 NBA (now become, temporarily, the ABA), and I held out for the award to the translators of Osip Mandelstam, and won my case on the basis that he, Osip, had written more importantly than the author of a certain Chinese "proletarian" novel, no matter how well the latter was translated. A good original is worth more than a mediocre text, however brilliant the translation.

The award for my work in translation hangs along with the previous (substituted) award in the Princeton Press office to this day, as far as I know, the only NBAs any of their authors had ever won. So much for my experience with these publishers' saturnalias.

My row with Princeton continued until I threatened suit and they modified their plans for shuffling editors about—but that was after grievous damage had already been done: the second volume in the series carries a fraudulent memoir by a hack Red completely traducing the spirit of Unamuno: it was inserted behind my back, and I, in Spain, one of the two editors of the entire series, was never consulted. It was a surprise, though not the first one in dealing with USA publishers, to open the book and see unauthorized matter violating all contractual arrangements. It's difficult to sue after publication of a "creatively-edited" book.

There was one other academic contretemps: it involved the publication of Ortega y Gasset's classic (the adjective is used advisedly) *The Revolt of the Masses,* issued by the University of Notre Dame Press. An "Editor" of the book appeared on the title page, with a Library of Congress listing for library indexing citing only him. Thus this "Editor" is cross-referenced to Ortega, while neither Saul Bellow, who had contributed a foreword, nor myself, who actually edited the book, translated it, and added a lengthy introduction, are to be found in the card catalogue. I had gone over the official "Editor's" suggestions and rejected them practically in toto in my final version. The wages of Academia!

I would hope that key phrases from the twentieth century would include The Tragic Sense of Life, and The Revolt (or more correctly, Rebellion) of the Masses. Though they are the titles of two books, by Unamuno, and Ortega y Gasset, the concepts summarized in these two phrases surely help to explain modern man and his "circumstance." The fact that I resurrected the two books, incarnated them into the best English, represents my most important contribution to life and letters.

My latest NEA award was, in its immaculacy, a cosmic delight. My daughter, Antonia, the literary agent, was visiting from Barcelona and was in the next room with my son Elie, who had just been named a letterman on the varsity fencing team at Notre Dame—what auguries!—when I opened a routine government unstamped envelope. A two-paragraph note informed me that I had been given forty thousand dollars—which I had not solicited: not a sheet of paper asked for or sent. There were to be no restrictions on my spending the sum, which had been assigned to me for reasons approaching the historic. It was disclosed that the "award was intended to support and honor writers who have made an extraordinary contribution to American letters over a lifetime of creative work . . ." I had entered the fiction of American letters on my own terms: I hadn't asked for anything and was asked for nothing in return. It was the cleanest bit of non-business business I had ever done in the arts: I had dealt with no committee and made no pitch. My anti-State soul was unscathed, and I had made no compromise. I should not have accepted the money, of course.

The Drink

In Ireland I doted on a tot of Bushmill's with a jar of Guinness to set me on the road, particularly driving across the country from Dublin to our place in Donegal, most specifically to the fisherman's house we bought on Gola Island off Bunbeg. What clarity of mind and spirit! What drunken driving! What aggression! And in Palma, among the international lushes, how impressively chaotic, insulting, what wild lashing out! Great meals all over Spain with a bottle of robust wine, which became bottles, until the after-dinner cognacs, which also became many. I was not bad to chance women, whom I mooned over, but I was certainly rude, and worse, to all manner of men,

especially Americans abroad. A veritable rooster! I was not a good drinker.

The last time I drank, I spoiled (for my young wife) a wedding dinner for her brother at the commandeered French restaurant "Le Zinc" in Manhattan. And that was my last escapade forever. My first, at seventeen, had been when I stormed a YWCA in San Diego (blinded by raw Stalinist gin: a Stalinist comrade of ours owned a liquor store) demanding to be bedded down in the room with my Communist Party wife-to-be; I ended up in a jail cell, and next morning evaded my uncle, an attorney, who was in the courtroom defending some other prisoner; I scorned his help, and in any event, was not sentenced.

As with any tippler, my stories are repetitive and only infamously legendary, as the occasion when I broke a bottle over the head of the burly just-elected sheriff of St. John's County, Florida; he was blinded by a sheet of blood from his head, so that he could not see to react, and next day decided not to begin his career as sheriff by arresting and charging a mad newspaperman (I was both: sometimes violent when drunk and editor-publisher of the weekly *St. Augustine Observer*). As irregularly as squalls, in spells, I was quite a berserker!

I would like *not* to have to banish from memory certain Irish hoolies, certainly not the night-long party at Lady Oronmore and Browne's estate, Luggula, in County Kildare, where I sat all aglow at a Georgian table next to John Huston, listening to his outrageously ribald stories until he quit the table himself, insulted by *another* drunken Irishman (who accused Huston of being a capitalist *gombeen-man*, a usurer!), the gifted composer and Communist Sean O'Riadah, as gentle a man as breathed when sober, but dead of the drink at forty. Or, warmed by Paddy, swimming naked off the icy coast of Donegal, whose luxuriant northern sands make those of California pale, if not gray-green, in comparison. Or drinking poteen with the poet Tom Kinsella, poteen distilled by his father, "the last Stalinist in Dublin," said Tom of his Da. ("Stalinist" hooch again!) Or the day in Palma Bay, with the Irish novelist Aidan Higgins, when we were carried away by enemy beer served us in the bowels, the galley, of a British submarine tied up in bright sunlight flooding the Spanish port, and, courtesy of Her Majesty's drink, we laced into the Empire's presence in Ireland, and had the sailors roaring while a pair of Irish tars kept serving us ever more beer. But I must remember that Patrick Hooligan, in London in 1898, gave his name forever to Irish bad conduct. There's a bit of the hooligan in a respectable few of the Irish, and none at all in the soft-spoken gentle majority. Still, in many an Irish pub I've heard much bloody talk on the wonders of dynamite and the IRA. And many a chancer claimed he was a member, though the internal laws of that organization (both branches, Catholic Provisional and Marxist Official) are puritanical on the matter of drink and the like, as are all conspiratorial cabals.

Still, through the years there was glorious seaside and portside wassail at Amsterdam, Le Havre, Dublin, Lisbon, Barcelona, Marseille, Naples, the Piraeus, and Tangiers, and even on the Thames. I was very lucky to survive each one, and all. Now I am a *bornemissza* (wine-not-drink), as they say in Hungary for a teetotaler. A sober clown. A drinkless fool forever.

I haven't drunk now in . . . years it's getting to be. I believe in the Marsala wine in Zabaglione, but then I can't be trusted with the plethora of egg yolks; and in wine sauces, say, or in a splash of sherry in consommé. But, in Siberia, I don't get to it. Not even nostalgia remains of all that divine wine. In Italian they say, "Wine works more miracles than a church full of saints." But they also say, more frequently, *"Non frutta niente"*: it yields no fruit, no benefit. There are proverbs to prove that milk should be drunk before wine. I did that, like many in Ireland, and got to ordering varieties of syllabubs, always calling for milk with my whiskey, which helped my belly but didn't always appreciably curb my wildness.

The only "vice" left intact, for over a dozen years now, is snuff. A continuity of snorts a day, an hour. Of course I do not speak here of the American misnomer—"snuff" as chewing tobacco. Snuff is for sniffing, by that most refined sense organ, the nose, and always was until the etymologically-rootless arbiters of words in the media chose to circulate some variant dialectical misuse of the word. Snuff (apart from use with candles) is a variant of *sniff,* "to draw in air violently through the nose," not the mouth: it all has to do with the nose (cf. Skeat, who gives it as Old Dutch, and Swedish, going back to Icelandic).

I picked up the (snuff) habit in Europe, out of the Zurich airport, and it was either a Lancashire man now living in Canada or an Argentinian yachtsman now living on his boat in Mallorca who brought me the first tins, but both supplied me with English snuff—the only kind worth the bother—for the first years. By now I must have gone through a few thousand tins. And never the slightest known harm, apparently. And cheap, too, manifestly. The *Lancet,* of England, the UK medical journal, has consistently *lauded* the habit—especially as an antidote to the rightly dreaded cigarette habit. If any harm should

come to me "eventually," it will be within the confines of a mausoleum, and I will report on it, from *ultratumba.*

The "conservative mind," Russell Kirk, and I used to smoke cigars *mano a mano,* one on one, all the way from Rome to the cigar shop in Remus, Michigan. But I gave up cigars about the time Fidel Castro did. Russell is now rationed to one a day.

Castro, by the by, never learned to smoke a cigar. He is the only man I've ever seen who could let a *habano* go out in his mouth, and he repeatedly had to relight, a desecration of a Cuban tobacco artifact or art object in the eyes of connoisseurs. I had learned, after much musing, how to turn a *puro* into a long-drawn-out sensual delight . . . especially in the morning. Castro used his priceless—even in (rationed) Cuba—"Cohibas" not for his senses but as a political baton. Or perhaps it was simply a phallic device stuck in the mouth of a castrato, of a *Castro castrado,* as the exiles chant, though this colorful juxtapositon is probably more applicable to the other Castro, his *barbilampiño* brother, who grew up beardless, from having been . . . ? "Castroed?" Still, he has three children! His own? And Fidel has none. And is surely paranoid, as both brothers are . . .

In any case I'm a type of drunk, even drinkless. I moon around vaguely, like a romantic in his cups, or rave like a lunatic, whether I've had anything to drink or not. When I talk on and on about the contradictory—antinomical—nature of life, the unknowing would be hard put to say whether I was entirely sober.

Now: this morning there was no citrus juice to mix into my daily pre-breakfast concoction (without coffee) in the blender: a whole banana (as *pocho,* half gone into ultra-matured sweetness, as possible), "orange-pineapple-guava" juice, fresh apple cider in season, always prune juice, and—always—milk, skimmed. Since neither number one or number two of the above ingredients were at hand, I used iced white Chilean wine. A fine tingle for this rainy morning, sharp, and a mellow dilation of the capillaries. Wine as food, then, not as liquor; though, as soon as I added cocoa powder for the second round, the mixture became comparable to the kind of liqueur-filled chocolates I was served every morning on a silver salver in a cafe in the shadow of Giotto's Tower in front of the Duomo in Florence one year while working with the filmmaker John Barnes (father of the diva Judith who was to become my wife so many years later) on a script for his "The Italian Renaissance," in the course of which I ransacked Vasari and André Malraux for filmable notions.

Chilean wine in my fruit juice and liquor-filled chocolates! And liquor in the kitchen: the grandiose as cookery. That's what's left.

And cautionary memories. I watched John Berryman throughout his year in Ireland drink himself (as he knew he would, and so planned, going to check out the available drying-out facilities in his first week) into St. Patrick's Hospital (for drinkers), established cheek by jowl, within sight and smell, next to the Guinness Brewery gates by the wisely magnanimous Dean Swift as his gift to the Irish caught up in their national vice. ("Guinness: the only brew black enough to toast Death!") The roster of its temporary residents has included practically every man of letters (and numberless whiskey priests) in the country in this century (with the disdainful, lordly exception of W. B. Yeats). Berryman wasn't a good drinker either (though many patients in the hospital were "good drinkers," or at least better drinkers than Berryman or me), even his frame was against him, and he seemed to drink every day all day, something I had no gift or stomach for at all.

Like Berryman I courted death more than once. I wasn't looking for it in New York but may have come closest to it there, on the glorious day when, in my role as purser in the late wartime merchant marine (after discharge from the army under a cloud as a Red), I picked up a payroll for a ship's crew anchored off Red Hook. Early that morning I collected thousands of dollars in currency from a bank on Wall Street (the men wanted cash for immediate shore leave) and then traveled from bar to bar around lower Manhattan, increasingly loud and boisterous, my pockets reassuringly stuffed with enough for a hundred Celtic celebrations. I finally lurched aboard a launch at the bottom of the East River just before dawn with a boatload of cutthroats, the makings of pirates, the sight of whom mercifully caused me to clam up. The launch made the rounds of the ships at anchor, so the pirates went on decreasing, but there were still a few left when we reached my "Liberty" ship. There I had to clamber up the Jacob's ladder let down over the side; I secured a hold after a few wild swings around the rope ladder, missing a few times. The only casualties were the men's thirsts, and the captain laced me up and down, for the men had "missed a whole day ashore of whoring and frolic," said the German master. (I was stupidly surprised to learn this.) The captain had been the youngest U-boat commander, "U-boot Führer," I think he had told me, in the German navy in World War I, and hadn't changed all that much since his underwater teens. He had taken me to Yorkville one night and I had

learned about German-American Nazi sympathizers among the lumpen proletariat for the first and only time. He, of course, boasted no FBI record to mar his captaincy of a large US-flagged freighter carrying goods for the front in the dire war against his former comrades. He drank fiercely but, though a small, lean, wizened ancient by then, held his liquor like a brave man. He was a "good drinker."

Under-accounted-for, or in effect, undetected in literature or even documentation, are women "alcoholics" (I here use the term I reject in connection with a person of markedly individual characteristics, that is, those who are not subject to generalization). I've known a good dozen such women, highly original each one, in Ireland and Spain and USA. All "good drinkers." All thin thin thin. Skinny witches. All above average intelligence. All from the northern races (in Spain, all of them foreigners who battened on the low prices and, because no one drinks much except visiting Swedes or Irish or North Americans, were enchanted with the availability of liquor at all hours, even in soda fountains and ice-cream parlours). They all drank night and day—and it was scarcely remarked, even by their mates. (Edward Dahlberg never seemed to have noticed that *both* his wives were in effect simultaneously smashed all day long: each hid a bottle of the strong stuff around the house and each finished her allotment daily. It was a defense against the thundering prophet, no doubt, but they continued the habit after his death.) I don't much fancy women in pubs, except young unattached ones—not wives, surely—but my hat's off to the thin and wily hags who drank, in their time, instead of wasting money on analysts and "counsellors."

Of all that raging and wildness and the flood of interior clarity and clairvoyance (black crows flying through the endlessly diffuse sunsets of northern summer lights in Ireland), I regret too little. Blinding days and rampaging black nights I regret insufficiently; not to say, *"Je ne regrette rien . . . Rien de rien . . ."* The damage done by my indulgence in farfetchedness was done to others, however, and unfortunately. I was not a good drinker—*tant pis!*—but I was in my own irreducible mind a glorious drunk. My apologies to all, or none. Long live the grape now for others, no longer for me: in my desuetude is whoever I have insulted avenged! Long live the memory of that drinking man, Max Hayward, who did the greatest translations of meaningful Russian into English in this century with the lucidity of the drink upon him. Up the drunken bards! Long live the company of Dylan Thomas—and his manner of dying too: fine early on, though pathetic later. The greater enemy is ennui by rote; for some, it is "adjustment" to unworthy least-common-denominator values.

And how condemn that "herculean boozer" William Faulkner? His dense writing is laced with booze, and all the better for it apparently, or all the richer. Not to mention Hemingway, who in Spain was considered a troublesome drunk even as bullfight critics hailed him as the best taurine critic of all time and one of the finest writers on Spain. And not to mention (as we reiteratively mention them both) Kerouac, the *reactionary* Beat (!) (v. contemporary issues of *National Review*), as delirious with the drink as half the true bards of the world. Whenever I talked or supped with the poet Roy Campbell, in Spain or in the USA, drink was present. *Pourquoi pas?* And only consider the schools of drunken poets of China: they made verse flower in Cathay. Even the banal poetry of Mao ("Wonderful. So much better than Hitler's painting," said Arthur Waley) somehow echoed them, perforce. In the case of such writers as Faulkner or Dylan Thomas, some connection is apparent between the scope (grandeur?) of their writing and the scope (grandeur?) of their drinking. *E vero o no?* Though perhaps there is no "(grandeur)" about it . . . Still, Wilde asked: "What difference is there between a glass of absynthe and a sunset?"

The final truth about The Drink: it all depends on who is doing the drinking. But given some love attendant to life, the world seems more resplendent without any distilled drink at all, without "the convivial glass," even for Romantics or for a goodly number of excruciatingly-nerved people who need buffering against the raw world. Doubtless, too, the spirit is more intense, not only without spirits, but with the barest of cupboards: the least of grains, good bread and good water. And an occasional fish from the water. The least amount of food, even more than the least amount of liquor, especially in the USA, is doubtless the *summa*, the sum of husbandry-wisdom. *Food is the enemy,* most particularly mob food in the USA, and in some of the burgeoning nations: a greater enemy than drink.

"Summer at 144 Columbia Heights, over the East River, the Kerrigans at the Barnes' place, next door to Norman Mailer's": (clockwise from left) Elie, Elaine, Maria Del Mar, Camilo, Malachy, Judith, and Anthony Kerrigan, 1987

Of course, hunger may also lead to hallucination, as I found once in Paris after a suicidal, spirit-less fast following my daughter's transatlantic abduction.

As regards the thinking behind such as AA, Alcoholics Anonymous: I always despised it and despise it now. I mean the "thinking," the theory, not the effective work. "Alcoholic"? The human race is too variegated—each individual unique—to be categorized according to a generalization based on median biology. AA-ism is a black sheep's antidote, gelding's vaccine, brain-numbing quarantine for little minds, for communalists, docked analysands, for those who frequent "marriage counsellors," for pacifist Unitarians, and fit for SPCAers who wear the button which proclaims (or claims) that "Dogs Are People Too."

Exultation or entropy. (I do not speak of mass-man, for whom there is no advice from the likes of me.) It is as it is for raging aberrant souls: acceptance of life—and defiance of dying.

But behold another form of inebriation. August 16, 1989, was a day of full lunar eclipse. Judith proved a lunatic, in her charm disaffected, quite out of sorts to find I was not as entranced a moon-gazer as herself: four solid hours of watching. She was the microcosmic equivalent of one of those moon-gazing parties they organize in Japan. As I composed these lines that night I heard her thinking: "Why don't you live life and look at the moon, and never mind writing about your life before *this* night." The charge seemed to be: a lackluster love for the moon. Eventually she announced peremptorily: "It's over. No more eclipse." She spoke almost sullenly. We went to bed unsatisfactorily. It was our most meaningless disagreement over a meaningful matter.

Cancer—and Eros

When I was a young man . . .
I'll tell you, now that
I'm an old woman . . .

About my twin ills: it has never occurred to me to ask the maudlin question "Why me?" I'm content with the grace of the gambler's "Why *not* me?" Is my physique of any possible interest to anyone else, or even to me? Except for the eroticism, which, for its unexpectedness, might interest. An hour or more of nymph's [sic] play, say, so very often, hours of venery, abstract and concrete, globes and forms and substances making up a private history of art, and one's own Venusberg . . . And yes, venery, too, and when one has been rendered a woman . . . For the

routine results of the trimonthly laboratory tests are now to be read, by me and the witch doctors, from the female side of the figures, the feminine column: my gamut is measured according to the woman's scale, the acceptable limits for women: a "feline" gamut of grace. The result, perforce, of the prescribed chemicals; for me or anyone else, perforce; I am, perforce, a woman on the charts, I say, am saying. (Elaine Gurevich Kerrigan, mother of five children of ours, writes: "Well, perhaps that was the trouble . . . All this time you've been over-maled.")

Yet now, as chemically woman, I ritualize all the same procreative acts, my part of them, as before. And ritual makes for reality. With all the same results physiologically, even if not in accord with the rules of biology, and except for population increase. The roles are not reversed: they are the same and the delayed surcease is the same, the spasm and release ("the spasms of bright surcease," I wrote in one poem). That I can't describe it with any scientific measure, by any male measure, doesn't mean its lineaments are not the contours of Elysium. Chemically testesless, I penetrate to the interstices of origin, by the grace of Judith, not a Holofernes-cutting-decapitating-Judith, but the Judith of whom I had written in a poem, all full well unknowing, in a collection of verse, *Espousal in August* (Dublin, 1968), in the last two lines of the volume's "Envoi," the final two lines of the foreordaining book,

your armpits Judith's
being awaited: your waiting being awaited.

Those lines had come to me from nowhere, out of the blue, in relation to no known conscious thought of mine, years before we . . . not met, for we always knew each other, but understood.

Is all this of any possible general interest? There is the one feature, death, common to mortal man, and some urgent advice from Dylan Thomas:

Do not go gentle into that good night,
Old age should burn and rave at close of day;
Rage, rage against the dying of the light.

The other feature perhaps is the fact that this kind of phenomenon seems unknown to American writers from Hemingway to Mailer when they act out of the sexual turmoil between the sexes in their writing . . . or in their lives, apparently. They seem to have no idea, so often, of the far-ranging possibilities between a man and a woman. So many sensual men seem driven to distraction when they can't . . . or

"Bloomsday with Bellow, June 16, 1989": Judith and Anthony Kerrigan (right) at Saul Bellow's summer house in Brattleboro, Vermont

even at the thought of . . . And they commit suicide of a sort long before their time, or before this stage of what median men consider to be The End, anticipating the presumed incapacity to act on an Empty Stage, to fight in a vacated bullring. They are stopped, like charging bulls who have been confounded. They seem baffled in their intuitions. They seem, in American, to have been buffaloed. In the last stage they seem to have been gelded—by themselves, and never mind the women, the American women they think did it. *Basta!*

Perhaps though, I should add, perhaps all this alternative drive I speak of is simply a product of the young Judith's imagination. "The imagination," she wrote me once while we were still forcibly apart, "is the finest sexual instrument." And so we cross the frontiers of femininity into virility, and back again. And, another time she wrote me: "We are limited only by the scope of that most crucial of sex organs, the mind."

The medical tycoons amass their wealth—of knowledge and fees—and look askance at my news: always the same smile and the look to one side. Are

they amused? Do they muse? Have they a muse? Perhaps they disbelieve. It's all nigh impossible, according to the data from the laboratory. Do they perhaps think I'm dreaming? Perhaps. Perhaps so. Perhaps it *is* oneiric, dream arousal, like an erotic drawing for an eccentric collector. Perhaps it is as poignant as a nocturnal emission recalled. Perhaps so . . . so what?

I think: no need for a Hemingway to have blown his brains out like Juan Belmonte the bullfighter because he couldn't . . . No need for a Mailer to disremember all pleasure, as he says he does, and take none now. What is involved? Will? The will to hallucinate? A febrile brain? Redolent memory? Rampant imagination? A heterosexual Sappho or a monogamous Messalina for a mate . . . ? Or simply love . . . sensual, psychical, spiritual, in the end imaginative . . . ?

And then and after all: the Irish god of love, the Celtic Cupid—or Eros—was not only fat in the belly, but Old!

Pourquoi pas?

Sketch of Anthony Kerrigan by Judith Barnes

Last Words

I have already written (and published: as "Druidi-cal") my last words, and hope to rehearse and recite them again in due course. If I cannot, because of a definitive pistol shot to the brain or a lucky thrust to the heart—in a duel, let's say—then let them now stand in, here, in place of a schematic, Socratic Apology, merely as skeleton for a prayer:

> Fell death
> deliver me
> from the verses in your eyes
>
> Old oblivion
> succor me
> from any more surprise
>
> Obvious tomb
> cover me
> from insidious clothes
>
> With a blank inscription
> hide me
> from the closest prose

> From pedestrian prayer
> spare me
> or un-Latin mass
>
> Immured in rue
> buttress me
> with windblown grass

(Borges's oblivion and Unamuno's foreverness as one and the same.)

And then up and away to the stage-right side and top of the under-ceiling mural in the Sistine Chapel! Or will it be the opposite: the stage-left and bottom just above the sacrificial altar at the Vatican in Rome?

In the end, My Religion is the history of art writ small, an archaeological dig's fragment. And so, erotomachia writ small, are my Confessions, my Sentimental Life and Loves. And so, writ infinitely small, in some small sum a burlesque, is the Novel of Myself.

BIBLIOGRAPHY

Poetry:

Lear in the Tropic of Paris, Tobella, 1952.

Espousal in August, Dolmen Press [Dublin], 1968.

At the Front Door of the Atlantic, frontispiece by Pablo Picasso, Dolmen Press (Oxford University Press), 1969.

Nonfiction:

Gaudí restaurador, o la historia de Cabrit y Bassa, Papeles de Son Armadans [Madrid], 1959.

Gaudí en la catedral de Mallorca, Mossèn Alcover [Palma de Mallorca], 1960.

El "Maestro de Santa Úrsula" y su mundo, Papeles de Son Armadans, 1960.

Editor:

Hiro Ishibashi, *Yeats and the Noh: Types of Japanese Beauty and Their Reflection in Yeats's Plays,* Dolmen Press, 1966.

Translator:

(And editor and author of introduction) Andrés Barcia, *Chronological History of the Continent of Florida, until the Year 1722,* two limited editions, University of Florida Press, 1951, Greenberg, 1972.

(And editor) Pedro Menéndez, *Pedro Menéndez, Captain-General of the Ocean-Sea* (autobiography), University of Florida Press, 1953.

José Suarez Carreño, *Final Hours,* Knopf, 1954.

Vicente Marrero Suarez, *Picasso and the Bull,* Regnery, 1956.

Rodrigo Royo, *Sun and the Snow,* Regnery, 1956.

(And author of introduction) Miguel de Unamuno, *Abel Sanchez and Other Stories,* Regnery, 1956.

José Maria Gironella, *Where the Soil Was Shallow,* Regnery, 1957.

(And author of introductory essay: "The World of Pío Baroja") Pío Baroja, *Restlessness of Shanti Andia and Other Writings,* University of Michigan Press, 1959.

(And editor and author of introduction) Jorge Luis Borges, *Ficciones,* Grove, 1962, published as *Fictions,* Weidenfeld & Nicolson, 1962.

(And author of introduction) Camilo José Cela, *The Family of Pascual Duarte,* Atlantic-Little, Brown, 1964, Weidenfeld & Nicolson, 1965, Avon, 1966–71.

(And editor and author of foreword) Borges, *A Personal Anthology,* Grove, 1967.

(And editor and annotator with Sir Herbert Read and, later, others) Unamuno, *Selected Works of Miguel de Unamuno,* Princeton University Press, Bollingen Foundation, Volume I: *Peace in War,* 1980, Volume II: *The Private World,* 1980, Volume III: *Our Lord Don Quixote: The Life of Don Quixote and Sancho, with Related Essays,* 1967, Volume IV: *The Tragic Sense of Life in Men and Nations,* 1972, Volume V: *The Agony of Christianity and Essays on Faith,* 1974, Volume VI: *Novela/Nivola,* 1975, Volume VII: *Ficciones: Four Stories and a Play,* 1975.

(With Alastair Reid) *Mother Goose in Spanish,* Crowell, 1968.

Con Cuba (bilingual Cuban verse), edited by Nathaniel Tarn, Cape Goliard Press [London], 1969.

(And editor and author of foreword) Borges, *Poems,* New Writers' Press [Dublin], 1969.

(With W. S. Merwin, Reid, and Nathaniel Tarn) Pablo Neruda, *Selected Poems* (bilingual edition), edited by Tarn, J. Cape, 1970, Delacorte, 1972, Penguin Books, 1975.

Rafael Alberti, *A Year of Picasso Paintings: 1969,* Abrams, 1972.

(And editor and author of introduction) Borges and Adolfo Bioy Casares, compilers, *Extraordinary Tales,* Herder & Herder, Seabury, 1971, Souvenir Press [London], 1973.

(Adaptor into English and editor and author of foreword and afterword) Borges, *Irish Strategies* (trilingual edition in Irish, English, and Spanish), Dolmen Press, 1975.

(With Thomas Rowe) Kamo no Chōmei, *Notebook of a Ten Square Rush-Mat Sized World: A Fugitive Essay* . . . (adapted from the Japanese Hōjōki), Dolmen Press, 1979.

L. M. Vilallonga, *The Angel of the Guitar,* Ambito Literario [Barcelona], 1979.

Reinaldo Arenas, *El Central,* Bard/Avon, 1984.

(And annotator) Borges, *Atlas,* Dutton, 1985.

(And editor and author of introduction) José Ortega y Gasset, *The Revolt of the Masses,* foreword by Saul Bellow, University of Notre Dame Press, 1985.

(And author of foreword) Fernando Arrabal, *The Tower Struck by Lightning,* Viking, 1988.

Other:

Regular contributor to *Encyclopaedia Britannica* and *Britannica Book of the Year.* Contributor of short stories, essays, poems, art criticism, and translations to periodicals in the United States, Canada, Ireland, and Spain.

Samuel Menashe

1925-

"You should have been a dancer," 1954

Descent

My father drummed darkness
Through the underbrush
Until lightning struck

I take after him

I am a bachelor older now than my parents were when they died. Since I have never been a father, I am still only a son. My father was born in the Carpathian Mountains of the Ukraine in 1899. My mother was born in a large market town of Bessarabia in 1901. Bessarabia was once part of the Ottoman Empire. After a war, it was ceded by the Sultan to the Czar in the nineteenth century. My grandmother came from New Constantine. I was born in New York City in 1925.

My father and his bourgeois family fled the Ukraine in 1921. As Jews, caught in the crossfire of the civil war, they were accused by the communists of

223

being capitalists and by the Ukrainian nationalists of being communists. When they looked back through the trees as they fled, they saw their house burning. They escaped across the river into Bessarabia, which was now occupied by the Rumanians. My parents met when my father was a refugee in my mother's town.

> When my mother
> Was a young girl
> Before the War
> Reading sad books
> By the river
> Sometimes, she
> Looked up, wisely
> But did not dream
> The day I would
> Be born to her

After their marriage in 1922 they went west, first to France, where they remained for almost two years, and then to America. In part their stay in France was imposed upon them by the American

immigration quota, but they also thought of living there because it, too, was a free country—a republic. Cousins of my mother had studied in Paris before the war and were now French citizens. One of them had even been an officer during the war.

My parents were graduates of the *gymnasium,* the classical high school on the German model which prevailed in czarist Russia. Its diploma, like the *bachot* of a French *lycée,* was the equivalent of a bachelor's degree from an American college. Had the war and the revolution not intervened, they would have gone on to the university to complete their studies for a profession. There was not the poverty in their childhood or youth which gave other immigrants the drive to success in America, nor was there anyone to help them here so that they could continue their education without great hardship. They both worked in factories and for a while my father attended law school at night. He became a small-business man. My mother was a housewife. She scoffed at the literary tag *lost generation.* "We are the lost generation," she said in the exact self-appraisal which characterized her. She used to help me with my algebra and geometry homework. Sometimes, when I am coming to the end of a poem, I feel that I am doing a kind of algebra where each word or syllable is a counter, like x and y or a and b, whose value depends on its exact placement. Some of those who approve of what I do have called my poems economical or concise, terms which are used to praise the solution of a problem in mathematics. One day, many years after the homework was done, my father said to me, "You're a poet. You know what I mean—the fleeting moment."

Nightfall, Morning

> Eye this sky
> With the mind's eye
> Where no light fades
> Between the lines
> You read at night
> Binding that text
> Which days divide
>
> I wake and the sky
> Is there intact
> The paper is white
> The ink is black
> My charmed life
> Harms no one—
> No wife, no son

"Wedding picture of my mother and father,"
1922

Since my parents were literate in at least three languages before coming to America, they learned

"My mother (center), aunt, and cousin," 1923

English well and they were well read in it. When this fact came up in a conversation with an acquaintance who, with her brother and sister-in-law, considers herself the founder of a literary dynasty, she refused to believe me. Her parents had been in this country for forty years, but they spoke only a broken English. Her achievement was her own. She was self-made, an American concept. In my life I sense a continuity with my parents and grandparents, who read Tolstoy and Turgenev in Russian. However, because some distant family connections derided Russian as a language for me, I was taught Yiddish, which—although I spoke English by the time I was three—is my mother tongue, by a hair. We were to visit my maternal grandparents in Bessarabia, and my mother wanted me to be able to speak to them in one language or another. As it turned out, Yiddish—without my knowing it for a long time—gave me a vital connection to the German root of English. Paul Bowles, to whom a mutual friend gave my book, *To Open,* wrote to me praising my Anglo-Saxon diction!

In one of those moments of mindless mirth *en famille*—he liked to use a French phrase occasional-ly—my father would say to me, "I knew French before you were born." When he asked me how my students were doing, I replied, "It will take a lifetime for them to learn French." Now I know how brief a lifetime is, flying—indeed—faster and faster as you near the end, like the acceleration of an object falling from a tower. Its speed increases as it approaches the earth. My father also liked to use the legal term *issue*. I was his issue, and as he knew himself—the severed self of the immigrant—he insisted that I, his son, issued from him, must be a misfit. When he said that I was "a square peg in a round hole," he did not want to change me. I cannot make the cliché complaint of the sensitive son misunderstood by his philistine parents who try to make him conform. However, my mother, who called me Oblomov, did want me to work. When I said that I could not work indoors on a beautiful day, she asked why I could not be a bricklayer. "The buildings in New York are too high," I countered. If I whirled around the room to some classical music, she laughed, "You should have been a dancer, but it's too much work."

My mother was brought up on traditional poetry. Most of the poems she still knew by heart were much longer than mine. If I told her that I had revised a poem since my last visit, she would ask, "How much shorter is it?" One evening as we went into the living room after dinner, I handed her a poem called *Dusk.* She stopped near a lamp to read it. As she looked up from the paper in her hand she said, "When one sees the tree in leaf one thinks the beauty of the tree is in its leaves, and then one sees the bare tree."

Dusk

Voices
rise
from
earth
into
night

When I was being battered by rejects, she cited a Ukrainian proverb, "One day there will be a feast on our street." In my first book there is a poem which begins with the line "Are dreams crimes?" On July 24, 1961, the day my book was published in London, the following telegram reached me there: "Dreams are not crimes. Yours brought the feast to our street. Love, Mother and Dad." On July 22, 1962, my mother died in Jerusalem. She had brought the book to the hospital. One afternoon, two or three days after the operation for inoperable cancer, when I came into her room, I found her nurse, a young woman, reading my poems. To divert my mother I started to tell anecdotes of my recent success in London. The nurse turned to my mother. "You must feel great pride," she said. "Not pride, joy," my mother whispered. Joy, the capacity for joy—well named *joie de vivre*—is what she gave me. It comes to me from her as definite as any genetic inheritance, as the shape of my nose or the color of my eyes or the timbre of my voice. With joy comes the festive spirit. She taught me that it is a sin to stint the feast, not to celebrate when one has reason to celebrate. God knows there are enough times for grief and mourning. After she died I wrote a sequence of poems for her which I called "The Bare Tree."

> The silence is vast
> I am still and wander
> Keeping you in mind
> There is never enough
> Time to know another

One weekend, walking with my father in Central Park, I said to him, "Your life seems like the expiation of a crime you do not even know you committed." At once he replied, "For the crime of having been born." My Catholic friends were pleased by this response. It proved—to them—the truth of the doctrine of original sin. On another day, when I was home for dinner after an absence of several weeks, in his blunt, abrupt way—no preamble—he said, "Your mother tells me you're not happy these days. You have to be happy. If you are not happy, you are not a poet." I know that this astonishing assertion contradicts the image of the suffering poet, the *poète maudit.* Yet, I know that it is true at a depth of experience deeper than that romantic cliché which, nevertheless, is also true.

For himself he boasted, "I have the unhealthiest mind in the healthiest body." He was sick for a month before he died, but without pain. His eyes were lucid, but he did not speak. One evening when I asked him how he felt he said, "I feel receded into the distance." Another night he said, "All of my life my spirit has been in a race with my body, and now my spirit has overtaken my body."

In Memoriam

1

> You had your say
> Said what you saw
> That day I stood by
> Your bed to draw you

> Out of your silence
> Your head in profile
> Pillowed, your brow
> Your unfailing eye

2

> Now he lies dead
> In a white shroud
> Eons behind
> His closed eyes
> Bear him out

Years before, he had written a note to introduce me to a friend in Israel. "The Hebrew is Bible pure, but somewhat stilted," his friend told me. It is from him that I learned that my father, as a youth, wrote poetry in Hebrew. As for myself, although I was brought up in a house where there was a reverence for literature, I never expected to meet a poet—let alone become one. Poets were dead immortals. I was twenty-three years old when my first poem happened one winter night. It was in Paris where I was a student under the GI Bill, after having been an infantryman during the war. Had anyone told me when I went to bed that night that I would wake up in the middle of the night to write a poem, I would have thought that person demented. A sudden awakening under a bare window thrust me among the stars—no need of rockets or spaceships:

> All my life when I woke up at night
> There was darkness in a room
> Here the bed is near the window—
> No purpose in this place, and yet
> By an unpatterned hazard of neglect
> In its crossing of my mediocre fate
> It is among stars that I wake

I enclosed these lines in a letter to my parents. My mother replied that she liked the poem, but she did not want me to call my fate mediocre. I changed the word to "ordinary." I had been writing autobiographical short stories—prose poetry, no dialogue. These stories were evocations of my childhood and my experience during the war. From the particulars of my own life, I felt enlightened about Life. I had also matriculated at the Sorbonne. Since no attendance was taken in the airless lecture halls, where one could not open a window because of the French dread of drafts—*courants d'air*—I often skipped lectures to walk along the Seine or on the Isle Saint-Louis or in the Marais. I read avidly from Rousseau to Stendhal to Gide and Camus. It was something to be in Paris and to be possessed by *L'Etranger* or by the poems of

Baudelaire, some of which I learned by heart. There was the Comédie Française for Molière and Racine, and the contemporary theater and movies for the great actors like Gérard Philippe and Louis Jouvet. Certainly, this self-education could not be faulted, but then I went to see Etienne Souriau, a professor of aesthetics at the Sorbonne, who had just supervised a doctoral thesis on the creative experience of a professional instrumentalist—a violinist, not famous but known in musical circles.

I began to write a thesis called "Essai sur l'expérience poétique (étude introspective)." With the phrase "introspective study" I tried to give this personal essay the guise of research in a psychology laboratory. By "the poetic experience" I meant that awareness—call it mystical or religious—which is the source of poetry. Baudelaire says, *"Dans certains états surnaturels de l'âme la scène la plus banale devient son propre symbole:"* In certain supernatural states of the soul the most ordinary scene becomes its own symbol. My total assent to these words—this revelation—was instantaneous. I did not have to test it to prove it to myself. Nevertheless, I quickly jotted down: a symbol

is a sign. The most ordinary scene becomes *sign*ificant, matters. I also read Simone Weil, who said that the duty of the writer is like that of the translator. The writer must stick to the text of reality without adding or subtracting a syllable. I had no doubt about my experiences, my enlightenment without drugs or a guru, but I was uneasy about presenting myself as a poet with scarcely a poem to show for it. My professor said that those who read the essay would know if I was a poet. Its major premise is that Jerusalem and Rome—to use Blake's terms—or Imagination and Empire, are eternal adversaries. The imperial imposition of power destroys the imagination. I claimed that it was a complete misunderstanding of both culture and civilization to use these terms interchangeably when they are in fact in mortal opposition. Civilization always uproots the culture which is the specific, local plant created by the soil, air, water of a particular place. In its stead Rome—pagan or Christian—paves the earth where it grew with stone. Thus, uprooted from the original creation, civilized man is given over to destruction. In both the individual and mass psyche the uprooted roots writhe like snakes in a rampage of murder and war. It is only in a few poets or artists that this civilizing process does not prevail. A few children survive their schooling—the extirpation of the imagination.

> Strange are those fortunes of war which make a few the survivors of many. Having accepted the certainty of death for such a long time, one is suddenly released into life and its normal expectancy. It is as if one should have died but finds himself alive. Maybe there is a feeble attempt to invest what has been called chance with purpose: This is my fate for reasons still unknown to me—the worn ego relining itself with hope, but daydreams are full of the faces of the dead.

"Myself and a cousin," 1927

I wrote this paragraph when I was twenty-four years old. When I was about thirty I read Thomas Mann's novel *Doctor Faustus*. His young protagonist discontinues the treatment for syphilis when his doctor dies, suddenly. The visible symptoms of the disease have disappeared, but it is eating into him like the acid which eats into a copper plate so that the lines which it does not cover emerge in relief to be printed. Elements in him that might have remained under the surface, submerged, now delineate him—give him his definition. At once this analogy applied to my experience as an infantryman. The one who emerged from the war was not the one who enlisted. I am sure that I would have had a more normal life and occupation had I not been in the war, although I know that it could only bring out what was in me. It is not that I was placid before, but the war intensified, defined me.

On the second night of combat I went out with a message and came back to the remnant of my platoon in the cellar of an old farmhouse. The incessant barrage of the artillery was more violent than any storm. I sat down on the earth floor with my back against the wall. My eyes met the eyes of the sergeant sitting opposite me. At once we looked away from each other and I knew why. I saw someone who might die very soon and he could not bear to look at me for the same reason. Years later I wrote "Warrior Wisdom":

> Do not scrutinize
> A secret wound—
> Avert your eyes—
> Nothing's to be done
> Where darkness lies
> No light can come

A long time after the poem was published I saw the verb *secrete* in "secret." The wound secretes darkness. To survive a month in the infantry was to be a veteran. I remember trying to give a few pointers to some replacements—the sound of an eighty-eight shell, for example—so that they would not die on the first day or night before a face could be seen or a name was known. After five months of combat, six of the original company of some one hundred and ninety were left. These figures were not unusual for the infantry.

When I was in Paris for the first time on a three-day pass from the front, I went to look for those cousins of my mother. The concierge told me how she tried to save the piano when they were deported. One peaceful morning, only five years after the war, I was sitting below three judges, with a portrait of the cardinal behind them, in the *Salle Richelieu* at the Sorbonne. I was defending my thesis at the *soutenance*, the oral examination. One of the professors, an Englishman called Farmer, was furious because I had dared to present myself for the doctorate with a personal essay. As he turned its pages, ripping sentences out of context, he would not allow me to answer his questions. *"Passons"* (let us go on), *"passons,"* he said. At last, when I was able to get in one telling response, he slammed his copy of the thesis

down in front of him: *"Moi, je n'y comprends rien"* (As for me, I don't understand anything there). Jean Wahl, the president of the jury, a little birdlike old man—about my present age—turned to him quietly saying, *"Moi, j'y comprends quelque chose"* (As for me, I understand something there). Wahl allowed me to answer his questions, which gave me the opportunity to extend what I had written in the essay. Since he was a well-known existentialist philosopher—he had taught at the University of Chicago during the war—his counsel prevailed. It amazes me now that I was declared "worthy of the title of Doctor of the University of Paris" when I was not quite twenty-five years old. Professor Wahl said that my essay was "heretical and without precedent as a thesis for the doctorate, but perhaps it has created a precedent." He also commented about my style, wondering whether it was original or due to the fact that I was a foreigner writing in French.

When I went to say good-bye to Professor Wahl after almost four years in France, he told me to take my thesis to Meyer Schapiro at Columbia University. I did not know about Schapiro's renown when I left the essay with him. A month later he telephoned to *ask* my permission to show it to a publisher. I thought that I was living a scene in a movie. The heavy door was opening for me. Schapiro was told that it would be feasible to publish the essay if it were written by Stephen Spender. Therein lies the story of my life, almost: I have not made a name for myself. However, Professor Schapiro circulated my thesis among his colleagues at Columbia and through them I got my first job at Bard College, formerly an extension of Columbia. The late Henry De Cicco, a friend studying philosophy under William Barrett, said that my essay out-Heideggered Heidegger, whose very name I did not know—I was a biochemistry major before the war. Henry also said—knowing how ignorant I was—that I would teach *Inspiration 1* and *Inspiration 2*. In the essay I affirmed a timeless presence in the physical world: "the spirit illustrating itself in a path, a pebble."

Enlightenment

> He walked in awe
> In awe of light
> At nightfall, not at dawn
> What ever he saw
> Receding from sight
> In the sky's afterglow
> Was what he wanted
> To see, to know

The night before I was to start teaching I was awake. It was a vigil night for me. I knew that I would be accused of being an anti-intellectual. Indeed, I did have an aversion to the autonomous intellect given to abstract thought, turned in upon itself, prizing itself for its own sake: "Gray grinding I know the mind / That makes the great gray mill grind." Yet, I was not against intelligence. I remembered a phrase which sounded like the English of the eighteenth century, *intelligence of*. Washington might have written, "What is your intelligence of the enemy positions in Saratoga?" Intelligence of, the intelligence which is perception, which has as its object a face, a place. The intelligence of which the eye is the epitome. We say, "I see what you mean."

My students were troubled by the French word for now: *maintenant*. I wrote it on the blackboard and told them not to worry about its length, to pronounce it a syllable at a time. I drew a line after the first syllable and, suddenly, I saw *main/tenant*. *Main* means hand, and *tenant* is the present participle of the verb *tenir*, which means "to hold." Now is what the hand is holding, what you have in your hand. Reality is not ephemeral, a fugitive mist forever escaping us. It is palpable, concrete. We are alive at this very instant, in the flesh, in three dimensions. We are here now. "If not now, when? If not here, where?" The Jew in the ecstasy of presence proclaims: "And David danced before the Lord with all his might."

A few years later when I was in France again, I told some intellectual friends there about my "discovery" of *maintenant*. They consulted a huge dictionary. *"Tu as raison."* I was right. I had chanced upon the original, literal meaning of the word. At the outset language is alive, close to reality which is physical, can be grasped. Later it becomes more and more abstract. It dies.

I was a good teacher. The students were awake in my classes, but since I had not come up through the ranks as an English or literature major—even in getting my doctorate I had evaded the system—I did not have the conviction necessary to impose term papers and to give marks. I did not believe in what I was doing. I quit. Ten years later I made a second attempt at a teaching career—to no avail. The first book that I read after leaving Bard was *Pride and Prejudice*. How happy I was knowing that I did not have to teach it! I read it for my own pleasure. I was liberated. I was a private citizen again.

The Spright of Delight

The spright of delight
Springs, summersaults
Vaults out of sight
Rising, self-spun
Weight overcome

Fort Benning, Georgia, 1943

Like most children of my generation I went to the movies on Saturday afternoon. There were the Hollywood films which I saw on my own, locally, and the Russian and French films which I saw with my parents when we went into town, Manhattan. In May 1945, a week or two after the war ended in Europe, I was in London on a pass. No monument there meant more to me than Olivier's *Henry V*. Later, there were the Italian films, *Open City* and *Bicycle Thief*. I was transported by these European works, but I was back in America now. When I left Bard I drove out to Hollywood where I hoped to apprentice myself to Fred Zinneman, the director of *High Noon*. I did not even know that there were schools where one studied cinematography. I don't think that they were as widespread as they are now. Excerpts of my thesis and a short story had been published in the *Quarterly Review of Literature*, whose editor rejected my poems saying that they were "too pure for the contemporary taste." If Zinneman read my published and unpublished work he would see these pure images. He would know how visual, rather than literary, my imagination was. The movies were the frescos of our age and I would learn how to make them! The face of Anna Magnani was in a pietà by Giotto. As I neared Los Angeles in my little open car, after a journey of thousands of miles, I was exalted as if I were about to see the towers and domes of Florence or Siena in the fifteenth century.

Paradise—after Giovanni di Paolo

> Paradise is a grove
> Where flower and fruit tree
> Form oval petals and pears
> And apples only fair . . .
> Among these saunter saints
> Who uphold one another
> In sacred conversations
> Shaping hands that come close
> As the lilies at their knees
> While Seraphim[1] burn
> With the moment's breeze

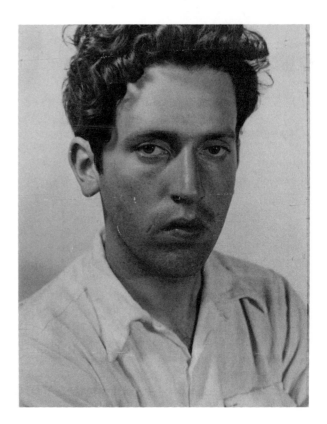

Paris, 1948

Of course, I had no introductions. In the Infantry Manual we were told that the scout must be "bold and aggressive." I made some astonishing penetrations of the hostile fortress of the studios, but I had no artillery to back me up, no big guns, no important people. After almost a year, I did track down Irwin Shaw, who was in Hollywood for the filming of *Young Lions*. We had drinks together at the side of a swimming pool in Bel Air. I must have impressed him in some way—at least in part because I had discovered where he was staying. He made an appointment for me at the studio. I was to be a production assistant for the filming of his novel. On a Monday morning, well tanned and with the collar of my white shirt open over my charcoal jacket, I came through a tunnel of wild geraniums down the ramshackle wooden staircase from my hideout, a shack high up in Laurel Canyon. I picked a bud for my lapel, a touch of red. As I drove to the studio in my little English convertible I was singing, "Lift up your heads, O ye everlasting gates and be ye lifted up, O ye doors, that the King of glory may come in. Who then is this King

of glory? . . . The Lord is the King of glory" (Psalms 24:7-10).

After so many improbable escapades I was finally coming to this appointed meeting at ten o'clock in a studio which I would enter—not by stealth—through the front gate, my arrival announced. I was waltzing my open car in and out of lanes as I chanted. A large, heavy American car swerved in front of me. My head shattered the windshield. When I left the hospital the blood was thick as glue sticking as I unfolded my jacket. The surgeon who sewed me up told me that the same blow an inch lower on my forehead—where two bones of the skull meet—would have done me in. I did not think of calling the studio the next day to explain why I had not kept my appointment. I was stunned, benumbed. My idealized image of Hollywood as a Renaissance city was gone. I had been punished for hubris and for worshipping the golden calf.

Yet, during the months that I spent reading Thomas Mann's Joseph novels and working on poems, when I looked across the canyon to the mountains on the other side it seemed that the last

---

[1] The Hebrew word *seraphim* means "the burning ones." They are archangels, the angels nearest to God, the divine fire. *Hallelujah* and *hosannah* are also Hebrew words which could be translated literally (Praise ye the Lord, etc.), but they would lose their evocative power, music.

veil was about to be lifted. One morning I woke up with the words "I can even forgive myself." This self-absolution was not for any particular sins or failings. It just welled out of me in a simple state of well-being. It might be called an experience of grace.

> All things that heal
> Salve, herb, balm
> Goodness I feel
> Established calm
>
> What form is as fair
> As sunlight in air
> As poultice to skin
> Thorns instantly tear

There had been a productive balance between my hermit's retreat, where I read and made my poems, and the warrior's forays into Hollywood, miles below the magic mountain. Several years before, when I tried to read *Joseph and His Brothers,* I was indignant, angry at the author whose heavy volumes destroyed the poetry of that biblical tale which had been read to me by my grandfather. Now, as I read, the essence of the story ramified like a tree of light. I knew that Mann's knowledge of the blessing—and most specifically the Jewish, patriarchal blessing—was foreign to the secular, literary world which had—nevertheless—bestowed its laurel on him.

Fastness

> I shoulder the slope
> Which holds me
> Up to the sun
> With my heels
> Dug into dust
> Older than hills

Recently, I read that the San Gabriel Mountains, where I dug in, are crumbling as they rise. A few months after the accident, there was a notice in the *New York Times* that the federal government was looking for Americans with a French background to be liaison officers in Indochina (later called Vietnam). I went down to Washington to be tested and interviewed for the job. I even got the FBI clearance, but at the last minute when the job was offered to me I came to my senses—what a wonderful expression—I turned it down, in part because the man on the other side of the desk called me Sam. Even Samuel would have seemed too familiar, since I could not reply in kind calling him John, let alone Jack. I never nick

names. I had been going through the motions of a self-inflicted penance for my departure from the norm—quitting the job at Bard, for example—but now I was myself again.

At thirty I reached Ibiza—then a pastoral island, now noisier than an aircraft carrier—where I lived for a year. The first of my poems to be published (the *Yale Review,* Autumn 1956) was written there. It was there, too, that I wrote a war story which, with a group of poems published in the *Berkeley Review,* was given an award by the Longview Foundation. It was the only grant or award I have ever received. One did not apply for it. The judges were Louise Bogan, Saul Bellow, and Alfred Kazin. When I was to leave Ibiza, a friend—to whom I had shown my poems—suggested that I stop in Majorca to see Robert Graves. I had read, with great pleasure, *I, Claudius* and *Claudius the God,* but I did not know that Graves was a poet. My friend assumed that I did—that's why she sent me to him. It was only when I sat in his study, rapt in his oracular presence, that I learned this fact. He seemed to incorporate the mythology of the Mediterranean on that island in the midst of that sea. Only his poetry mattered to him, he said. All the other books were "potboilers to put bread in the mouths of my children." I was so grateful that I had not betrayed my ignorance of his poetry that as soon as I was back in New York I read *The White Goddess* as well as his poems. He told me that as a young man he had gone to see Thomas Hardy in the same way that I now came to him, and he had received from Hardy the same confirmation that he now gave me: I was a true poet. After two meetings in the village of Deyá, I spent my last evening in Majorca with him and his wife in their apartment in Palma, the capital of the island. They drove me to the boat. He asked me to write to him. He told me that he had a son called Samuel. I was aware then, but it seems even greater to me now as I look back at that meeting, how extraordinary Graves's hospitality was to me, a stranger who came to him unannounced as I did. Later, I learned that he sometimes employed a poet as the tutor of his many children. The career of one of them had been launched by this connection.

After that first publication in the *Yale Review,* other poems were accepted now and then by *Commonweal, Harper's Magazine,* and the *Antioch Review,* but none was ever published by *Poetry,* where acceptance meant that you were in. When I looked at the literary or little magazines, I could see no correspondence between what was in them and what I was doing. If I ever got to see a book editor by eluding the receptionist at the door, he would boast that he did not

"Old Flame," 1957

read the poetry manuscripts despite the fact that he had been an English or literature major at a good college. Poetry was sent to the house poet who, inevitably, published work that buttressed his own position in the world of poetry politics. Like the editors, most literate people in this country do not read poetry. They have been estranged from it by its obscurity or difficulty. My father would say, "This can't be a poem, I understand it." Above all, no poem should express well-being. It should be plaintive, morose, soulful.

> Using the window ledge
> As a shelf for books
> Does them good—
> Bindings are belts
> To be undone,
> Let the wind come—
> Hard covers melt,
> Welcome the sun—
> An airing is enough
> To spring the lines
> Which type confines,
> But for pages uncut
> Rain is a must.

In June of 1960, armed with an introduction from a friend in Paris to his patron in London, I went to look for a publisher there. The morning after my arrival I was received by that important person—the second son of a Scottish lord—who told me at once, "You'll never find a publisher in London." This dire

prediction struck me like a curse coming from the very man who was supposed to open doors for me. Certainly, it was issued with more malevolence than wisdom. Anyone who has lived long enough knows that anything may or may not happen. I knew that the odds were against me now that I was not going to get any help from my friend's patron. However, I did find a literary agent in less than two weeks, and in itself this was a success, especially because my agent in New York had given up in his attempt to get a publisher for me. With my manuscript in the new agent's hands, I had no reason now to stay on in London, where I had been living in a dingy hostel. On the eve of my departure I was strolling in Leicester Square. Suddenly, I saw the great actress Dame Flora Robson, whom I had seen a few nights before in a play, *The Aspern Papers*, based on the novel by Henry James. She was parking her car. She smiled to see the expression on my face as I recognized her. When she got out of the car I told her how moved I was by her in the play. She was on the way to the theater for that night's performance. She suggested that I walk there with her. She hoped that I was enjoying my stay in England. When I told her why I was in London, she asked me to come to her dressing room the following night. I did not let her know that I had intended to leave London the next morning. I just stayed on. In her dressing room that night I met an impresario of poetry readings whom she had summoned to meet me. Later I learned that she had also telephoned a publisher friend in my behalf. Through the impresario I found a quiet room overlooking a small park in Fulham, which was then an unfashionable part of town. I remained there through a cool summer, working on some poems and checking in with my agent occasionally. Rejects, all too familiar to me, were reaching him: my poems were too "short, slight," etc. Although he was confident that in time he could find a publisher for me, I was not.

I was in Foyles bookstore one rainy afternoon when Kathleen Raine, the poet and Blake scholar, came to mind. We had never met, but I had heard her read her poems in New York a few years before. I found her name in an authors' directory. She was teaching in Girton College, Cambridge University. I sent ten or twelve poems to her. In the attached note I asked if I could come to see her. She replied praising the poems, but she said that she was unable to give me a definite appointment because she was taking care of her sick daughter's children in a house without a telephone. Her letter reached me in the morning about ten o'clock. As the hours passed I endured a dilemma of indecision which became unbearable and made me bolt out of the house. Although I am known for being on time, I missed the train to Cambridge because I stopped at the American Express on my way to the station. I hoped to find a letter from my parents which might encourage me in this new attempt. I did find a letter but it was a pessimistic one. My mother, who as I later knew was succumbing to cancer, wrote that she could only root for me from the sidelines, she did not have the strength to do more. I knew that my misadventure in Hollywood had depleted her. Of course, for my parents, the job I left at Bard was the one they dreamed of for me. There, they thought, I would have the dignity of an intellectual life which they never had in America. I had survived the war and come to that safe port, but now I was at sea again in an uncertain voyage whose goals eluded me, or so it seemed. Yet that year I wrote the following poem:

Cargo

Old wounds leave good hollows
Where one who goes can hold
Himself in ghostly embraces
Of former powers and graces
Whose domain no strife mars—
I am made whole by my scars
For whatever now displaces
Follows all that once was
And without loss stows
Me into my own spaces

Made grim by her letter and by missing the train, I rushed to the station on the other side of London to get the next train to Cambridge. My tourist visa was about to expire and I did not know if it would be renewed, but it was a few days before my birthday and one wants to believe in one's luck at that time of year. When Kathleen Raine opened the door of that house in Cambridge, she did not know who I was. When I told her my name she said, "Oh, you've come just on time." It was about four o'clock in the afternoon. It was time for tea. She put the kettle on.

A pot poured out
Fulfills its spout

Had I caught the earlier train, I would have reached that door too soon. I would have interrupted her at her work. Now, as she turned the pages of the manuscript I brought with me, I heard more and more of the praise I had read in her letter that morning. At the same time she said that the London

literati would not understand my poems. I sensed that I was being given a spiritual accolade: I had a beautiful soul. I could sleep out in the open under the stars in unobstructed communion with them, but I knew that I needed a roof over my head, a house for my poems, a book. Five years before, Robert Graves's confirmation of me as a poet had been enough for me, but now I needed more than that. I gripped the arms of the chair on which I sat. "Miss Raine, I've come to ask for your help," I said. She turned red, "I have no power in London." However, after turning a few more pages, she looked up from one poem. I could tell which one by its shape—upside down on the page—as I sat opposite her. She thought that Victor Gollancz might respond to my work. He was a famous publisher in London, to which I returned that night with a note she wrote to him. Two months later he telephoned to tell me that he was going to publish the book with a foreword by Kathleen Raine and a jacket endorsement by Sylvia Townsend Warner. When I went to see Gollancz for the first time after he accepted the poems, I told him that I had no name for the book. He started to turn the pages of the manuscript and he stopped at this poem:

O Many Named Beloved
Listen to my praise
Various as the seasons
Different as the days
All my treasons cease
When I see your face

He crossed out the *O* which begins the poem and wrote *The* above it, *The Many Named Beloved.* My mother said that the book was her first grandchild. It is dedicated to my parents.

In her foreword Kathleen Raine wanted to call me a young poet. I pleaded with her to drop the adjective. It would be assumed that I was a young man of twenty-three, publishing that first slender volume which is both blamed and praised for its requisite literary derivation. I was thirty-five years old. She did drop *young.* Raine, now in her eighties, is a Neoplatonist. Her foes, as she sees them, are those secular intellectuals who deny the "perennial wisdom" of which all ancient cultures and religions are an expression in their own way, and of which William Blake is the great English exponent.

A week or two after the book was published, Dr. Raine telephoned to tell me that she had just heard from Donald Davie, who knew from her foreword that she was responsible for its publication. He wanted to meet me—to know more about me before writing his review of my book. Raine was exultant. She had gone out alone on a limb for me, expecting to be cut down. Now she was joined there by a captain of the "enemy camp." Davie, like Raine, was a professor as well as a poet at Cambridge University. I was to have lunch with both of them. This time when I got on the train to Cambridge I was no longer an anonymous petitioner.

Never before and not since have I basked in more worldly glory than I did during that interview under the high ceiling of a refectory of a college in Cambridge University. Professor Davie asked me about any literary influences of which I was aware. He also wanted to know if I had always written short poems. I told him about an experience I had when I was fourteen years old. Posted in front of the old Quaker meetinghouse in Flushing, New York, was the following passage: "And, behold, the Lord passed by, and a great and strong wind rent the mountains, and brake in pieces the rocks before the Lord; but the Lord was not in the wind: and after the wind an earthquake; but the Lord was not in the earthquake: and after the earthquake a fire; but the Lord was not in the fire: and after the fire a still small voice" (1 Kings 19:11-12). In a split second Elijah became my prophet, and not long after him William Blake—in his short poems—who depicted Elijah on his chariot of fire:

> Bring me my Bow of burning gold:
> Bring me my Arrows of desire:
> Bring me my Spear: O clouds unfold!
> Bring me my Chariot of fire.

Perhaps the piercing economy of the poetry and narratives of the Bible—the Book of Jonah, for example—did stir up my own tendencies in that direction. However, I never thought of anything I read—either on my own or in school—as a literary model. Except for the assigned homework of book reports and compositions, I was a reader, not a writer. Davie sees poets—in part—as exponents of their ethnic backgrounds, whatever these may be. I was doubly foreign to him as a Jew and as an American. Yet I knew the Bible in English, not in Hebrew, and the rivers of Babylon never seemed more pleasant than they did that afternoon on the banks of the Cam.

Donald Davie gave me the lead review in the *New Statesman*, which was read like holy writ by the New York intelligentsia—the *New York Review of Books* was yet to appear. He reminded his readers that Robert Frost, too, had come to England for the publication of his first book. He called my work "a testcase for readers and a challenge to writers." He was joined by Austin Clarke, the foremost Irish poet of his day, with the lead review in the *Irish Times* and by P. N. Furbank in the *Listener*. Neville Braybrooke in *John O'London's Weekly* urged the literary magazines to take up Davie's challenge. Few did. However, the book was reviewed in provincial newspapers like the *Newcastle Journal* and the *Oxford Mail*, whose critic called the poems "a saltspoonful of words." So many years later I hope that salt has not lost its savor.

> *Salt and Pepper*
>
> Here and there
> White hairs appear
> On my chest—
> Age seasons me
> Gives me zest—
> I am a sage
> In the making
> Sprinkled, shaking

In a campaign of less than six months in London, I had bypassed, gotten around, the siege of years in

Central Park, 1961

my native city. The luster of this victory was in contrast to the total debacle in New York. I was a foreigner in England. I was the first one in my family to speak English as a child, but now I was given the imprimatur in the "mother country" by the English themselves. I began a letter with a fanfare from the Apocrypha, "Let us now praise famous men and the fathers that begat us." In his reply my father wrote, "I don't see my part in your success, but if you choose to credit me with it, I am immensely happy. For us the center of the world is London."

With the publication of *The Many Named Beloved* and the reviews that called it to his attention, Stephen Spender started to accept my poems for *Encounter,* an English magazine, which was then at the peak of its transatlantic circulation. In his last month as its poetry editor he published "The Niche":

> The niche narrows
> Hones one thin
> Until his bones
> Disclose him

It was an unlucky day for me when Spender left *Encounter* because he learned that it was funded—in part—by the CIA, an organization that has not given me any trouble. I am no revolutionary. I was never an angry young man. I did not revolt. I seceded. This is still a free country. One can still do so. As my father put it, "It is a good thing you are a poet in this country. In Russia they take their poets seriously. They send them to Siberia. In this country they know they are harmless." In my "hovel," as he aptly called it, I live outside the walls—the stronghold—of poet-professors who, like the abbots of medieval monasteries, exchange visits, reading at each other's colleges, where they mould students in their own image.

When I came back to New York some friends said, "We always knew that you would have a book." It was their way of expressing their loyalty to me, but I knew that I never would have had a book had I not been lucky once, by chance. The French word for luck is *chance.* They also expected an American publisher to be waiting at the pier for me. It took ten more years before a small, unknown publisher brought out my first American book. Those poets, readers for publishers, who had dismissed me in New York, were not glad to see me turn up in London with a publisher and reviews any one of them would have welcomed for himself. I had stepped out of line by going to England. Not only did my success there not open the door for me here, but it was

slammed even harder in my face. It was as if I had a British passport professionally and I could not get an American visa for it. They would not let me in. When a book was finally published here, *No Jerusalem but This* (October House, 1971), Stephen Spender reviewed it and Ted Hughes's *Crow* in the same essay (the *New York Review of Books,* July 22, 1971). Although he was respectful in his treatment of Hughes, now the poet laureate of England, Spender expressed a fundamental reservation about the unmitigated blackness of his poetry: "By an extraordinary coincidence (because he cannot have read *Crow* when he wrote this) Samuel Menashe even has his answer to *Crow* prophetically flickering across his pages, and making the poem he calls *Sudden Shadow.*"

> Crow I scorn you
> Caw everywhere
> You'll not subdue
> This blue air

Spender continues, "He also sees, like Hughes, the necessity of investing one's spirit in something that will not vanish":

> The shrine whose shape I am
> Has a fringe of fire
> Flames skirt my skin
>
> There is no Jerusalem but this
> Breathed in flesh by shameless love
> Built high upon the tides of blood
> I believe the Prophets and Blake
> And like David I bless myself
> With all my might
>
> I know many hills were holy once
> But now in the level lands to live
> Zion ground down must become marrow
> Thus in my bones I'm the King's son
> And through death's domain I go
> Making my own procession

Again Spender: "His poetry reminds me of some kind of biblical instrument—tabor or jubal—and the note he strikes is always positive and even joyous. Here is a poet who compresses thoughts into language intense and clear as diamonds . . . Before leaving Samuel Menashe I will say that nothing seems more remarkable about him than that his poetry goes so little remarked. The best of writing a review is that sometimes one can persuade someone to read something. I hope, as a result of this, a lot of people will read Menashe."

If, using Spender's word, my work was not so little "remarked," I would not have to fall back on what critics have said about it. In the *New York Times Book Review* (February 18, 1973) Calvin Bedient wrote, "Menashe's hard clarity and brevity may be his protection money for being a high romantic in the contemporary world. Perhaps he speaks in a small voice because a loud one would be less persuasive, less audible." *No Jerusalem but This* is dedicated to John Thornton. By the chance of enlisting on the same day in 1943, we met. Our old school tie is of the infantry school in Fort Benning, Georgia, and the campaigns in eastern France, the Ardennes (the Battle of the Bulge), and the Siegfried Line. Thornton is my first reader and an astute critic. One day, when I showed him still another version of a poem I had been struggling with for months, he said, "You do not merely thread the needle, you try to go through the needle yourself."

John's telling image is about the process which may produce a poem. My own image of myself in the world where poetry is published, reviewed, and rewarded with grants and prizes—I do not get—is

"My mother and grandmother," 1906

that of a cliff-hanger whose wrists are sometimes strengthened from unexpected quarters. One afternoon when I walked into the Gotham Book Mart, I was greeted with some excitement by a young man who works there. He asked if I knew that there was an essay about me in a new book by Donald Davie, *The Poet in the Imaginary Museum: Essays of Two Decades.* I had read that essay in the *Iowa Review* years before, but I did not know about the book. Almost a year later someone congratulated me on the Hugh Kenner review of Davie's book. Of course, it was assumed that I had seen the review. I did not even know the name of the magazine in which it appeared (*Inquiry*, May 29, 1978). In his essay Kenner writes, "But no other critic could have written—I'll open this collection almost at random—'The Poetry of Samuel Menashe,' which begins from the rare ability to believe there could be an interesting poet of whom one hadn't been told . . ." Kenner's review of the book, in which there are forty-six essays, concentrates on Davie's essay about my work as an example of his expertise as a critic. Until he read that essay Kenner did not know of my existence. A few years later, when he was lecturing in New York, we met for the first time. I introduced myself to him and he introduced me to his charming wife: "This is the man Donald Davie discovered in London." I said, "Yes, but I am all covered up again." I had been trying for years to get a publisher for my next book here, and in London Victor Gollancz Ltd. was no longer publishing poetry. The poet who has the security of one publisher, to whom he goes when he has enough poems for another book, lives a different life. Hugh Kenner is connected to the National Poetry Foundation of the University of Maine at Orono—a small press with a big name. He telephoned the editor there. Thus, I continue to live a domestic exile in my native city: with all the publishers in New York, I had to go elsewhere again for my most recent book. I dedicated it to Kathleen Raine and to Donald Davie, my English "godparents." "There is a world elsewhere," Coriolanus says.

It is a winter morning. My desk is at a window that faces east. This room is a bower of sunlight in the apartment, which was called a cold-water flat when I moved into it thirty-three years ago. For many years there have been radiators and hot water here, but the bathtub is still in the kitchen and the hall toilets are still in use, although mine is inside the apartment. It may be part of one's bohemian youth to live in a place like this, but in my seventh decade I am still here.

At a Standstill

That statue, that cast
Of my solitude
Has found its niche
In this kitchen
Where I do not eat
Where the bathtub stands
Upon cat feet—
I did not advance
I cannot retreat

Almost every afternoon as I get out of the subway as fast as I can, looking over my shoulder if I hear a footfall, I imagine the bliss of living near Central Park—of walking into the park which a friend calls my living room, rather than commuting to it. I cannot afford the rent of an apartment uptown, not even one smaller than mine. Another friend dubbed me the weatherman when those who gave themselves that name were making bombs in the basement of the paternal townhouse. For me the event of the day, barring catastrophes, is its weather. John Thornton once said about me, "The climate is good, but the weather can be bad." For no more than a day or two, I must add, although I hate to be put to the test of a heat wave. At an exhibit in the Jewish Museum I was glad to learn that the early gods of the Near East—little stone statues—were called the weather gods by those who made them and worshipped them. I am a sun worshipper myself, but not in the summer. "Send my roots rain," Gerard Manley Hopkins cried to the one god, "the Lord of life." *Right as rain* is a rural expression inspired by the rain that comes when the farmer needs it. "Too late and in the wrong rain," has been a refrain for me for years—is it from a poem by Auden? I would sing it in my shower, if I had one. It brings to mind, "The man life passed by," a line from the first stanza of a poem I called *Curriculum Vitae*. I wrote it after a fallow period.

Scribe out of work
At a loss for words
Not his to begin with,
The man life passed by
Stands at the window
Biding his time

Although a word or a phrase never comes into a poem unless it is part of my ordinary speech, sometimes I look it up after I've used it. Everyone knows that biding one's time means to wait, but when I read in the dictionary, "To wait for a favorable opportunity," it seemed that this definition was made to order for my poem, converting pathos to the pleasure of irony: a man who has waited a lifetime for a favorable opportunity. Yes, here I am biding my time in my adobe abode, my own name for this flat where the plaster always cracks.

Last summer I was very sick for the first time since I was five years old, when I almost died of peritonitis. What was supposed to be a simple procedure of preventive medicine led to blood poisoning and an emergency operation. During two weeks in the hospital I was often in pain. My body was a wounded animal that could kill me. I despaired, "If it is my time to die, let it be now rather than a month from now." One day the sentence came to me quietly, "I've lived my life."

Self Employed

Piling up the years
I awake in one place
And find the same face
Or counting the time
Since my parents died—
Certain less is left
Than was spent—
I am employed
Every morning
Whose ore I coin
Without knowing
How to join
Lid to coffer
Pillar to groin—
Each day hinges
On the same offer

A few months after the war I came back from Europe on a sunny afternoon in October. I put on one of my father's suits. It was gray. The shirt was blue. I had not worn civilian clothes for a long time. I felt well dressed, elegant. "I want to live a glamorous life," I said to my parents as we walked around the curve of Flushing Bay.

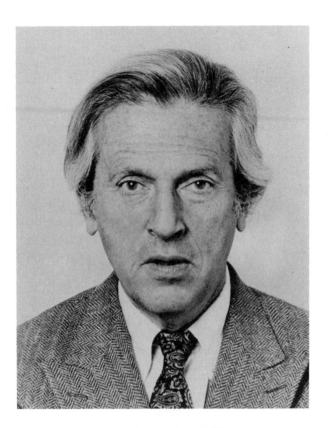

Samuel Menashe, 1987

Awakening

Like one born again
To the same mother
I wake each morning
The same, another
Who takes my name
But cannot place me
In dreams, nightmares
Where I became
The one she bears

Transplant

I would give
My liver, kidneys
Heart itself
For you to live
In perfect health
With me, your clone
Whose grafted cells
Grow marrow, bone

If all else fails

Do not reject
My skin or nails
Whatever's left
Of me for you
By a hair's breadth
Will see us through

Forever and a Day

No more than that
Dead cat shall I
Escape the corpse
I kept in shape
For the day off
Immortals take

Stone

Stone would be water
But it cannot undo
Its own hardness
Rocks might run
Wild as torrents
Plunged upon sky
By cliffs none climb

Who makes fountains
Spring from flint
Who dares tell
One thirsting
There's a well

Sheep Meadow

French spoken
Across the snow
On Sheep Meadow
Evokes a very rich hour
Of the Duke of Berry . . .
Three men traversing
A field of snow—
One of them alone—
Hedged by trees
On the south side
Where the towers
Of the city rise . . .
One of those hours
In early afternoon
When nothing happens
But time makes room

A-
round
my neck
an amu-
let
Be-
tween
my eyes
a star
A
ring
in my
nose
and a
gold
chain
to
Keep me
where
You
are
*

The Dead of Winter

In my coat I sit
At the window sill
Wintering with snow
Which did not melt
It fell long ago
At night, by stealth
I was where I am
When the snow began

Paschal Wilderness

Blue funnels the sun
Each unhewn stone
Every derelict stem
Engenders Jerusalem

Tangiers, 1950

As the tall, turbaned
Black, incense man
Passed the house
I called after him
And ran out to the street
Where at once we smiled
Seeing one another
And without a word
Like a sword that leaps from its lustrous sheath
He was swinging his lamp with abundant grace
To my head and to my heart and to my
  feet . . .
Self-imparted we swayed
Possessed by that One
Only the living praise

> "The dead do not praise Thee"
> —Psalm of David

BIBLIOGRAPHY

Poetry:

The Many Named Beloved, Gollancz, 1961.

No Jerusalem but This, October House, 1971.

Fringe of Fire, Gollancz, 1973.

To Open, Viking, 1974.

Collected Poems, National Poetry Foundation, University of Maine at Orono, 1986.

Contributor to anthologies, including *My Kind of Verse* (Macmillan, 1968), *The Best of Modern Poetry* (Pocket Books, 1975), *A Green Place: Modern Poems* (Delacorte, 1982), *Messages* (Faber & Faber, 1985), *A Feast of Poetry* (Burke, 1988), and *Wedding Readings* (Viking Press, 1989), as well as to textbooks and numerous periodicals.

Toby Olson

1937-

Toby Olson with one of his bird feeders, Truro House, 1988

Last summer my wife and I bought our graves. They're in Pine Grove Cemetery, Truro, Massachusetts, and there seems nothing morbid about the place. Most of the stones are old and dated from other centuries, familiar Cape Cod names—Rich, Cobb, Ryder, and Mayo—and the only literary person I could find was Waldo Frank.

Pine Grove is small, just over two hundred plots in all, and tucked well back in the woods, a metal and stone fence, gnarled trees, plenty of air and light. We've thought to take some lawn chairs out there and cool drinks. We've thought to put our stone up with our names and birthdates on it. Certainly, we'll set in corner markers; that way we can find our places easily when we need them, whatever the changes.

It's May of 1989. I sit at my Truro window, the place where I have written virtually everything for twenty years. It's 6:00 A.M. and foggy and I can't see the bay, but I begin as usual with permanence and death . . .

> Always
> it seems better in the past;
> it's very hard to live
> where body is
>   & I get startled when I think
> I didn't know you well at all
> & that some details of this yard
> will inevitably escape me
> leaving only
> partial understandings.

This place where I sit, this table, window, and chair and this house and the land that surrounds

Toby Olson, one year old, 1938

I begin with one of my real names, Merle Theodore Olson, Jr. I lost the tail when I was seventeen and my father died. It was August of 1954, shortly before my birthday. He was forty-two years old, and it was only when I was thirty-three and wrote a novel called *The Life of Jesus* in 1971 that I was able to place him in my past in any appropriate way.

I was ready to begin my senior year at Hinsdale High School, in a town beyond the west side of Chicago, living again with my mother, sister, and brother, when he died, and I remember the day of his death and something of my behavior when I learned of it. I was working at Fairyland Park in Lyons, had finished my shift on the children's miniature merry-go-round, and had driven back home to Marion Hills in my first car, a 1937 Ford coupe that I'd badgered my father to sign for a few months earlier. He'd been very ill and bedridden at the time, and my mother, sister, and brother were still in Arizona. He may have been slightly delirious, but I fought him and his profound illness, got him to rise up feebly in his bed and sign the paper. When I got home no one was there, and I think I knew something was up. Then the phone rang and my sister said I should come back to Lyons, to my grandmother's house, where my father was then living.

They had taken him away already when I got there, and what I remember is that I left my family in their grief and went out to my old Ford and sat in it, in a dull rage, dry eyed and alone. I think I must have come to a self-destructive resolve there, but I knew nothing of that understanding until much later. Before the end of my senior year, I was in jail. I wrote my first poem there, something about facts and sand, details of the present world and the more real one, fallen down through the hourglass.

I was born on August 17, 1937, in Berwyn, Illinois, just one town over from Oak Park, Hemingway's home. And Frank Lloyd Wright was a presence there as well, though I knew more of his houses in the nearby town of Riverside, across the Des Plaines River from Lyons, when I was fifteen and drove a grocery delivery truck for Mahler's market.

The time was 4:36 P.M., and in a letter my mother writes, "On his way home Dr. Chaisson stopped for a drink in one of the Lyons bars—Henry Frank (Grandma's & Grandpa's friend) was there—. The Dr. said he had just delivered the fairest child he had ever seen. Then he told them whose baby it was & so Grandma heard it from Ida Frank just before your father came to her house with the news."

them, has been the only constant physical permanence in my life, and though the Cape too is changing (tasteless development and awkward wealth), unlike those other places I have lived, the past has a way of remaining here: Corn Hill and Pilgrim Pond, High Head, the beach Thoreau walked upon, the Atlantic no more than a mile away. I'm trusting I can count on Pine Grove too, and on my wife, Miriam, who will rest there with me. Now the fog is lifting, and I can make out scrub oak and my old juniper.

As I look back I see that death has been at center in my writing, and emanating from that focus, issues of nostalgia, memory, and the past. I've thought of poetry as truth-telling and salvaging, of fiction as an invention of what might have been, its buried purpose to redeem personal waste. All this has made the present hard to live in, to settle in, and so another preoccupation has been a concern for luminous details, not as signs or touchstones, but as elements in the sanctity of textures of the immediate, both in the physical world and human commerce. Therefore, the sensuous, the erotic, an aversion to the symbolic, to systematic explanation.

That was the Lyons I remember as a child, one of a cluster of small towns along the railroad and river. (I lived in a few of them until I was nine years old, and then returned again for my last two years of high school.) People knew each other. The towns' communities were church based. Small parades on the Fourth of July, walking to the corner for hand-packed ice cream, talk on open porches in the evenings: all of this before television. I remember neighbors standing in backyards, watching a plane fly over. I remember, though vaguely, beating on metal pots out in the park on V-E Day.

My mother's grandparents, Niels Skowbo and Marie Madsen Skowbo, came to this country from Denmark with four children in 1877. They came directly to Illinois. Both Niels and his son Christopher where skilled cabinetmakers, and they both found work in that trade at the Western Electric Company in Chicago. Niels died in 1923, thirteen years after his wife passed away, but not before he'd acquired a few houses, one of which went to Christopher, who had married an Irish girl, Frances Bastick, my grandmother. The house was in a town called Congress Park, and when Christopher followed his father into death in 1925, he left the house with Frances, who was then fifty-one and had five children, the oldest of which, Ella, was only twenty-two years old.

But they got along, and the house became a family house, and as the children married and left, they didn't go far, and from time to time they moved back in, to care for my grandmother and be with her. My mother, Elizabeth, was the youngest child, and there came a time, a few years after my birth, when she and my father moved into the house. My sister, Jill, had been born by then, and the house in Congress Park became *our* family home, at least for a few years. It's still there, and though there are two other houses that remain constant in the past for me, the one in Congress Park is strongest in my mind these days. A good portion of a novel I've just finished is set in a town of the same name, next door to a house very much like that one. In the novel, called *Dorit in Lesbos*, the house remains familiar from the outside, but the inside is mysterious, filled possibly with details of the narrator's past. Yet he fears that it has all changed and that the past is gone.

My mother is not a sentimental person as far as I can tell, surely not like me in that regard. But changes

With sister, Jill, in Congress Park, 1945

Father, Merle Theodore Olson, early 1930s

and smiling. My mother is seventy-six years old at this writing. I admired her pleasure at the rock's recovery and hope the past turns up such easy joy for me someday. But then I'll find a way to write about it, and that will never do.

In 1912, when my father was only eleven weeks old (and I have my niece Sue, family chronicler and oral historian, to thank for this information), my grandmother, Alvina Carolina Gerny Olson, set out on a train for New Mexico to join her husband, Ted (Theodore Olson), who had gone there with tuberculosis for "the cure." He was twenty-two, she twenty-three, and "on Sunday the lady who had rented Ted a tent to sleep in before I came, would let us use her buggy to take a ride in. When we had to see the doctor, about once a month, she would also lend it to us because the doctor's office was about four miles off." They spent less than a year in the West, and "when we arrived home we stayed at Grandma Olson's and Ted slept out on the screened in porch. He died a couple of months later, in March."

I knew Grandma Olson (Hannah Magnuson) and Grandpa Olson (Tobias) as well. They had come from Sweden and Norway respectively, and story has it that the second *o* in Olson is not a Norwegian *e* at her insistence. I know now that even Olson was only taken on in America, and that my great-grandfather came to this country as Tobias Gusevik. He was born in 1864, died only after I was old enough to know him (rich, Swedish coffee at their house in the nearby town of La Grange when I was seven years old). Great-Grandma Olson, his wife, finished her years living in the house in Lyons with her daughter-in-law, my grandmother. She was in her mid-nineties when she gave it up.

My father's mother (Alvina) was known to me as Grandma Reuss, for she was married again (to John Reuss) while my father was still a child. Grandma Reuss's father, Charlie Gerny, was a teamster and road and house builder. He rented teams of horses out and hauled construction materials. He built the house in Lyons in 1903, and when he died (early in the century) my Grandma Reuss and her youngest sister, Edna, inherited it and moved in. Charlie Gerny's name is on the cornerstone of the Lyons Village Hall: he helped build that as well. My Grandma Reuss died in 1977, but the house in Lyons remains in the family. My aunt Edna (great-aunt really) still lives there, up in the attic apartment she has always occupied in my memory. She's eighty-seven years old now, the last sister from a group of six, and still going strong, comic and ribald as she's

in that house bother her. The porch has been altered over the years, dormers added or removed. She doesn't like to drive past the place or talk about it. And yet last Christmas we did make a visit, parked in front of Aunt Marge's old house next door, and looked it over.

What bothers me is the park itself, that oval that extends for a block, separating the rows of houses facing into it. It used to be a community endeavor. There were flower plots, huge Dutch elms, a plaque commemorating the dead from World War I. But that's all gone now. The park seems barren, uncongenial to ghosts.

We stood on the sidewalk for a while, each in our own evocative memories, and then my mother spotted her rock, a low, broad boulder set in the grass verge between the sidewalk and the curb. Her face lit up. "Why, I used to play on this rock! When I was *very* young." Something like that at least. Then she was jumping in little steps, on and off the rock, laughing always been. She could talk your ear off, and still does mine from time to time. But her stories of the past are rich and labyrinthine, peppered with jokes and lurid reference. Her Lyons might well have been in Chaucer.

The constancy of the house in Lyons has been important to me. It seems to have always been there, and I can see its alterations and my own in photographs and memory. I returned there at various ages, never really lived there, but always felt it as a permanence, an unchanging home. That was surely because of my Grandma and Grandpa Reuss, the rich world of their small-town life, church, community, friends, and family associations that never really seemed to change much at all. My grandmother liked natural light, would wait until it was almost dark in the kitchen before flicking the switch. My grandfather liked to sit by the window in his chair, positioned like a train engineer as I remember it, arm on the sill. I still go back to that house when I visit my mother and my sister and her family for holidays. I like to go there as dusk is coming on, stand in the darkening kitchen, in the presence of still-familiar scents, dusty objects, and remembrance. The rooms are very much the way they always were. Upstairs, my aunt Edna talks on the phone endlessly. She's chosen not to rent out the downstairs. The basement has been emptied and cleaned, but there's still a remnant of the old cistern, broken cinder block and dank smell, my personal archeological site.

As with many relatives on both sides of my family, my father was working at the Western Electric Company in Chicago when he came down with back trouble and lost his job in 1938, the year after my birth. My mother thinks that was the beginning of his arthritis, the chronic illness that would finally end his life, but he'd had rheumatic fever as a child, and that could have been a cause as well. It was all mysterious and it remains so.

At any rate, my mother and father moved to various places, even back to my Grandmother Reuss's in Lyons for a time, before they finally settled into the house in Congress Park. My father managed a few jobs in those years, everything from insurance sales to metallurgy at Electro Motive. My mother had started work upon leaving high school, a clerical job at the Chicago Insurance Exchange, where my father also worked (though for a different company), but I don't believe she worked outside the house in the early years of her marriage. Her real and constant work life would begin later.

I was out and around a lot, even as a little boy, and my first clear memory (I must have been three or

Mother, Elizabeth Skowbo Olson, early 1930s

four) is getting caught sneaking through the Petrones' downstairs apartment, a quicker way to the backyard. I remember Mr. Petrone chasing me around his dining-room table, grinning and laughing, and that it wasn't so funny for me. I went to kindergarten, where I slept on my little rug on the floor and remember scooting around on it for better positions, then entered Saint Barbara's Catholic school in Brookfield, the next town over. I broke my clavicle on the playground, and I remember my horror (slightly erotic?) as a nun held my sweaty face against her starched, white dickie to cool me down. I went fishing in a deep and dangerous quarry, bringing home three-inch bluegills in the bottom of a huge gunnysack. I remember my mother cooking them for me, in a big black skillet, managing to remain serious about the whole thing. I had a dog named Lady. I had a sister, only two years younger than I, but I think, even in these early years, we went our own ways, spending time together only at home. Jill remembers more than I do, more variety and richness, very different things. I remember almost nothing negative or fearful, only the death of a young child, a son of my mother's friend, and that he had blue paint under his nails as he lay in the casket.

I was a very poor speller, and I was ruler rapped many times across the knuckles for that by the nuns at Saint Barbara's. But the nuns also told us Bible stories (as would the ones who taught me later in California). It was they who conveyed the mysteries of the Church, gave us both our guilty consciences and our obsessions. The priests were dark images, intruders in the classroom, only to be met in silence or avoided. This is not my sister's experience. She's kept in touch even with nuns who taught her in grade school, and she now has friends among the clergy. I meet them at her house at times when I go home for Christmas, but I still feel in their presence that I'd better watch my step.

Most of the family socializing in those years was with relatives, and I have good memories of uncles and aunts, cousins, picnics and family parties. Uncle Ray would tell us his own versions of fairy tales, tickling us at appropriate moments. He'd work in the park across from our houses—he and my aunt Marge and their three daughters lived next door from us—keeping the plaque, flowerbeds and flagpole in good order. And we spent time in the house in Lyons as well, my mother and father, Grandpa and Grandma Reuss, sunny Aunt Edna, relatives and neighbors, all sitting and talking on the porch or in the bright yellow kitchen, while Jill and I explored the basement.

Then in 1945 my brother, Jack, was born, eight years younger than I. Things had gotten worse with my father. He hadn't taken up his cane yet, but photos show his loss of weight, the slump of his body. There was no cure for his condition, not even good medicine, but there was the hope of dry weather, a common hope in those days. And so plans were made to move to California, to sell the house in Congress Park and take my Grandmother Skowbo along with us. My father had traveled west alone to set things up, and there was an insurance-company job waiting for him there and a house deal in the works. But the house arrangement collapsed, and when we arrived we stayed with family friends, the Stewarts, in a town called El Monte, near Los Angeles, until we could get properly located. We drove there, in a tough old Oldsmobile, stopping to sightsee and visit Aunt Pearl (my Grandma Reuss's sister) and Uncle Joe in Coffeeville, Kansas. I remember Uncle Joe showing me his gun, a bright revolver in a dresser drawer. My Grandmother Skowbo made the only flight of her life, joining us when we'd found a place to live, our

only house in those California years, a small stucco affair in El Monte's outskirts, near the wash.

The drier California climate provided no cure. My father kept his hand in as long as he could, various part-time jobs. He even tried a tavern for a short while, the Shamrock Inn. That lasted for a year and is memorable only for the Chicano man who brought his banty hens in to walk on the bar—my sister's memory—and for the first television in our family, something for the customers, one channel. My father would hit the vertical hold, getting the people on screen to do the "hula."

A year after we arrived, my Grandmother Skowbo died, and then my mother entered the beginning of her working life. She began at Ball Brothers, inserting cardboard fillers in boxes. My father was mostly at home in those years, and once, in 1950, he traveled back to Illinois for treatments (a new drug, called Cortisone), taking my brother, who was five then, with him. My mother couldn't work and care for Jack at the same time. They were gone for six months.

Toby with his father, Grandma Reuss, mother, and little brother, Jackie, in El Monte, California, 1948

I've spoken to my brother about that time, the way it cemented for him a private and separate relationship with my father. I think it's true that he was raised in a different family than the one I know. At least his memories are distinctly his and not mine. But this is true of my sister, Jill, as well. Only two years between us, yet hers was a different world. Such is the tangibility of time, I guess.

In the fiction I've written, travel plays a central part, not just movement from place to place, but lingering stops in various places, each with its own circumscribed qualities, each set off from the other, so that the pasts of places seem separate and distinct. From the time I arrived in California as a nine-year-old, my life began to feel like a series of episodes, an accumulation of little pasts (very rich ones), and though I was too young to long for them, I couldn't fix myself too well in the present either.

I attended five grammar schools in our first two years or so in El Monte, and then I settled in for fifth through eighth at Nativity. There were sports, and when I reached the seventh grade, dances in garages, girls I was in love with awkwardly.

There was little learning at school, for me at least. I was a poor student, but once I was Monarch of the Gypsy band, in an operetta called *Zurika*, and I had a solo I still remember. It's in *The Life of Jesus*, as are transformations of other things from that time: Father Ghinty, the feared priest who heard my first confession; grace, less than amazing; that sense of the failed son, who could not be Jesus and cure his weak father.

But my father *wasn't* weak. I remember him on crutches, coaching our grade-school football team, being careful not to favor me, but kind in the circumstance and in control. That lasted only for a few games, then he was too ill again to continue.

When I was eleven and ready for the seventh grade, my sister and I traveled back on the train to Illinois, to spend the summer with Grandma and Grandpa Reuss in Lyons. Grandpa Reuss was a serious fisherman, and sometime in that summer we drove to Crivitz, Wisconsin, and spent some time at the lakes. There was plenty of fishing and eating, the novelty of wrestling on television, visits with other relatives. When Jill and I returned to California at summer's end we had both gotten very fat, and my mother put us on serious diets.

I'm moved by that summer in Illinois, something about its pure wholesomeness. Everyone is young and vibrant in my memory, yet old enough to be settled in their lives and in the larger life of community. All of it seems permanent, a place we could always return to. I remember my grandfather's fishing gear in the basement, the smell of it. Aunt Edna had a chart listing the weight of each of her nightgowns, and I would go down into the basement with her and watch her climb carefully on the scale. My grandmother made her coffee cakes, huge and numerous, and Jill and I would eat them up while they were still hot.

The water-drainage system in Southern California was an interlocking series of underground tunnels, large enough to stand in, all emptying into broad open washes, and it was the practice of some of us to explore these winding depths. We'd travel for miles underground, coming up at times under grates at busy intersections where we had never been before. Later, in Arizona, I made similar excursions, working my way through tighter tunnels. I still dream about such passages, and they appear as caves and other below-ground systems in places in my novels. We found nothing tangible on these trips, but there were times we frightened each other, holding a flashlight under our chins.

My sister and I had a babysitter once who wore a truss to make her stand up straight. She took her shirt off to show us, revealing at the same time the white cups of her breasts: frightening. But later she invited me and friends to see her skin, in a wood of twisted, smelly eucalyptus where we would go to smoke slim tubes cut from berry vines. The poem is called "Smoke."

I remember your body it was dancing timber
smell of eucalyptus burning
the endangered house

      and stood apart in the woods together
in smoke, and revealed your breast to me
I was 9 years old.

Each
experiment with love starts
with a body on fire at a distance
      a woman always
standing in full length across the room

Timber: the aureoles of your nipples
I could not touch

your skirt was moving in smoke
your ankles, covered with leaves.

El Monte was a working-class town, a mix of Chicano natives and new arrivals like us, and many of the kids at Nativity had to find jobs to earn spending money. I started out as a shoe-shine boy, but that lasted only a few weeks. Then it was a paper route, the *Los Angeles Times.* I had to rise daily at four, then ride my bike a good five miles to pick up the papers. I'd have them delivered by seven or so, then it would be off to school. At times I missed the alarm, and before she would go to work my mother would have to get up and drive me and my bike to the pickup station. She was always very good to me at these times, bright and cheerful as we drove the empty streets in the morning dark, my bike held outside the car, its tires on the running board. She knew what work was like, for she had become the breadwinner in our family and would remain so. I think she must have known even then that my father would not come back to health. But this was something never mentioned. Not that we had much hope really, but it was impossible to be biding time.

I spent a year working at a riding stable, weekends during the school year, full-time all summer long. I'd act as a guide, taking groups of inexperienced riders out. Mostly, the job was feeding the horses, currying them, and shoveling up their droppings.

The last job I had in California was at a collie kennel, working for a young, but crippled woman who had submitted herself to experimental surgery. She'd had hip replacements, and they had failed. She walked on crutches, her legs stiff from the hips and slightly spread. Her husband traveled and was seldom there. The kennel was a strip of yard behind their house, a common kind of thing in our neighborhood. People raised rabbits, mink, and chinchilla. We had no sidewalks and some of the streets were still dirt, our houses on the edge of town, not yet drawn fully into its refinements.

The woman loved the dogs. There were a dozen of them, and they were very high strung and smart. One of them would hold wet clothing on its back, and as I shoveled and cleaned the kennels I would watch it move beside the woman as she hobbled along her clothesline, hanging things, her bag of pins strapped to her waist.

The woman wept at times, unaccountably to me, and at times she would lie on her bed, her stiff legs spread, dogs on the floor around her, and ask me to bring her things. We ate what the dogs ate, horse meat, from cans. She called me up once so I could come and watch a dog give birth; she took me to a dog show, a marvelous thing. She provided collies, females (because they were smarter), to work in the Lassie movies. She may have wanted a child. I don't know. It was all sexually charged, but I remember no hint of an overture. I was thirteen years old then. Did

I leave the job because we were moving to Arizona? I hope so, that I didn't quit on her, or she on me. She would be close to seventy now, limber and without her crutches: at least in my romantic mind that way.

We left for Bisbee, Arizona, shortly after I had enrolled in Mission High School and even "gone out" for the football team. My father's health had failed dramatically. Bisbee was high in the dry mountains, close to the Mexican border, but my mother tells me that the real reason for the move was so that my father could get easily to Tombstone, only twenty-five miles from Bisbee, where there was an old woman who was known for her "treatments."

We arrived in Bisbee in 1951, and I entered high school there and stayed for a year and a half before leaving, on my own, to head back to California. Though brief, it was a rich and eventful time. I played football, made my first close friend in Paul Justice, together with whom I was suspended for coming to school barefoot and other offenses. I fell in love with Mary Lou, who let me hold her hand at times, but treated me badly, which I probably welcomed. I lost my virginity (strange to think of it that way) in Naco, across the border, and later transformed that event and other flavors from Bisbee in *The Woman Who Escaped from Shame.* I learned to drive, and would take my father to Tombstone for his treatments and wait in the pool hall until he was finished. My mother started work at the telephone company, something she would stay with until retirement. My father was operated on, exploratory laparotomy, in Tucson, but nothing significant was found. My mother and I slept in our car in the hospital parking lot.

I remember coming home once at midnight from the bowling alley in Warren, where I was a pinsetter. I was sweaty and tired, it had been hard to hitch a ride back to Bisbee, and I leaned on the bathroom sink and the pipes broke. Hot water was flooding out. My mother was working the graveyard shift at the phone company, but my father, bedridden again at the time, was there. I remember calling out to him; he awoke and spoke with quiet reason to me: "It's okay. Go out to the side of the house. There's a faucet there. Just turn it off." How he knew about that faucet, I'll never know.

And there were other jobs in Bisbee, too. I worked as a stock boy at Woolworth's, was a salad man at a restaurant twenty miles out in the desert, packed groceries at a store in the nearby town of Lowell. My friend Paul Justice had a better job, as night man at the YMCA. The Y was kept open so that soldiers in town from the nearby fort could spend the night, in cots on the running track above the basketball court. At times, there were no soldiers, and Paul and I had the run of the building. We'd bowl, play pool, swim, use the court and track and the various board games that the Y provided. Those could be long nights, kids in the cookie jar, a perfect pleasure.

In school I was in the senior play, though a freshman. I read few books and didn't study my lessons. I did well in English, but failed other subjects. I was out most of the time, in mountains and desert, in deserted mines, hitchhiking to other towns, underground in the drainage system. Both my sister and brother were searching for community too then, but I was at my own loose ends, and when in '53 my father returned to Illinois and my grandmother's house in Lyons, returned for further treatment, at Illinois Research Hospital and the Ball Clinic in Ohio, I too left, quitting school, and headed back to California. I moved into a trailer with Jimmy Blankenship (a grade-school friend), got a job as a dishwasher, midnight shift, took a few courses at a high school in El Monte, where I learned typing.

The trailer was behind Jimmy's house. We listened to popular music late at night on the radio, and once we drove some sailors back to their base in San Diego and were accused by his parents of going down to Tijuana. My mother was called, and I returned again to Bisbee.

But I didn't stay there. I was restless and too much trouble I think, and it was decided that I would go back to Illinois, stay with my aunt Marie and uncle Eddie, in a town close to my father in Lyons, to enter high school again, and to wait for my mother, sister, and brother to join us, which happened a year later.

In my year at Riverside-Brookfield High School, I slept on a chair folded out into a bed in my aunt and uncle's living room, heard Elvis Presley for the first time, and had my hair cut in a flattop with ducktail. I made friends with Bob Baldachi (went to Chicago and got drunk on wine with him), got involved with a teenage gang called "The Big Ten," fell in love with Marie Buban ("braces of high-school sweetheart / cutting the lips / not the time or place / inappropriate"), and visited my father, who stayed in bed most of the time, at my grandparents' house in Lyons.

I remember a late afternoon. My father was up, sitting in a chair in the kitchen, feeling better. It was summer, and I was taking geometry in order to catch up because of my missed semester in Bisbee. My father had not gotten beyond high school, but he remembered things, and to my surprise had solved a particularly complex problem, then explained it to me clearly. I must have laughed or in some way showed my amazement. We were sitting across from each other, and he took the pencil he'd been working with and wrote, in quick and careful block letters, upside down and backward so I could read it: *What did you expect? 183 IQ!*

In my junior year at RB, I earned money by cleaning hallways in an apartment building and driving a grocery truck for Mahler's market, delivering to the rich folks in Riverside (maids and cooks in uniforms, in large back kitchens), and at the end of that first year, I went to work running rides at Fairyland Park.

As with my time in all other schools so far, I had no thought for education, study, or reading. It was something to do with a complete lack of community or school spirit. Everyone seemed to have been there in their lives for a long time; all had a history in the place but me. I didn't know the school song, knew nothing of important events from previous times. Still, it was at RB that I was first moved by literature, by a young teacher, Mr. Lumbson, who for some reason one day read to us from Kafka's "Metamorphosis." Everyone thought it weird, thought *him* weird, as did I, but for me that weirdness was concrete, the projection of a mind in language, which *is* a reality (though I would never have put it that way). I wrote a story, a man sitting by a fire, alone in the woods. Plenty of nuance and texture. I confused the word "sensation" with "emotion." I presented it to him, trying to get into his story-writing class. But I couldn't spell.

In the beginning of the summer of 1954, my mother, sister, and brother arrived from Arizona, and we moved into our small house in Marion Hills, in the Hinsdale school district. This would mean I'd be leaving RB after only one year, and though I might have been used to moves by then, I balked at that by keeping in close touch with those I was leaving behind, especially "The Big Ten." It was summer, and I was working full-time at Fairyland Park, had graduated to the larger rides, and then in August my father died.

I fought for some involvement at Hinsdale High, but my friends were on the fringe. I saw myself as a cool (though reluctant) hood, but unlike those at RB, the toughs at Hinsdale were separated off by class, and it was the poorer kids, who lived as I did beyond the rich town's limits, that I ran with, keeping in touch with my friends at RB. But I did begin to write, short stories then, pieces with simple plots that counted almost totally on language, articulations of troubled minds. And I began reading too, taking refuge in long, historical romances: Sigrid Undset, Marguerite Steen. I might have turned to other authors, but I was totally untutored in any canon. I found *The Amboy Dukes*, but my mother replaced that with the Bible when I was in jail for fighting.

It happened near the end of the school year, a senior picnic at RB, which I went to though I was attending another school. There was a fight, some of us against a group from another town who shared the forest preserve with us. People were badly injured. I think I remember throwing only one punch, with a force I might have used to strike my father for his dying.

Jail put an end to those involvements, but I remained at loose ends after graduation. My sister had gotten married, at sixteen, to Otie Bates, and they'd begun their family, which now numbers six grown children. The pipes and radiators in Marion Hills had frozen and burst, and we'd had to sell the house and move again. The uncle and aunt I'd lived with kindly offered to pay my way to college in Minnesota, but I would have none of that.

I went to work for the Chicago, Burlington, and Quincy Railroad, first loading boxcars, then delivering company mail in and around Chicago, and at that time I fell in love with Geraldine McLynn, gave her a ring, and had her name tattooed on my shoulder. Then I quit both Geraldine and the CB&Q, and took a job with Reynolds Aluminum, in the physical-testing department. That lasted a year, and then I became a gas-station attendant, and it was at one of the stations where I worked that an odd young fellow lent me two books, *The Trial* and Ray Bradbury's *Dark Carnival*. I read them both, then dumped the latter, and went to the library seriously for the first time in my life, devouring everything that I could find of Kafka. Still, I had no thought of college or the future, except that I wished to return to California, which I finally did, traveling with a friend named John Culpepper, when I was twenty.

On our trip west we stopped in Fort Worth to see my Arizona sweetheart, Mary Lou. She would have kissed me then I think, but I refused her. Then, in California we looked up Joanne Headley, a girl I'd gone to grade school with, and loved secretly. Her brother helped us get set up at his girlfriend's house, a good woman who suffered our presence while we tried to find work. But there wasn't any. Our hair got longer. My car quit, and I decided I'd better join the navy. John had been hanging in with me all the while, but the navy wasn't for him, and he headed back home.

In the navy I found a certain order that I needed, and from the beginning I succeeded within the regulations. Though I'd left some girls I loved behind, the sadness at their loss, and even the loss of my father, didn't keep me down, and after boot camp I entered Hospital Corps School in San Diego.

We had to wait for our full class to gather, were told to volunteer for temporary jobs—mostly cleaning and such—and when morgue duty was called out, my hand shot up, and I found myself in the presence of eviscerated bodies, an intense interest keeping me focused and away from shock. Later, I would work a month of night duty in the morgue, sleep there, be awakened often by the dead. It would be my job to tag them, list marks and scars. In the beginning I'd confuse postmortem lividity with bruises in the crook of the elbow. It would be a month of vivid learning, seeing, and touching those pathologies that I had read about. The young doctors were kind and instructive. I remember my finger in the calcified valve of a diseased heart.

Corps School lasted four months, eight hours of classes each day, and we had very good teachers: nurses, petty officers who had been corpsmen for many years. I remember a moment in Mr. Manetti's class in diagnostic procedure. We were struggling with symptoms of appendicitis and had missed one. Manetti went to the blackboard's side and drew a small face with an open mouth. Then he took his chalk at his shoulder and slowly walked the length of the board, scribing a line from the mouth to the far edge. When he got there he raised the window and threw the chalk out, then turned to us. "Projected vomitus!" he said, knowing that none of us would ever forget it.

After Corps School, I worked the wards: retired enlisted men mostly, cancer of the neck and throat. They'd had tracheotomies, and we taught them to speak again. When they learned, they'd tell jokes to each other in the solarium, belching up air, would speak of family and past experiences; then they would die. One had a wooden leg, a fine and natural-looking one. He'd hand it to new corpsmen on the ward, saying, "Would you stow this?" We'd all get a good laugh out of that.

I started night school at a junior college in the evenings, a psychology class, in which I brought in and presented the bones of the middle ear: show and tell. In my second year in the navy I entered Surgical Technician School, gaining a skill that would support me when I entered college full-time, a few years later. Balboa Naval Hospital had twelve operating rooms, a large variety of cases daily, and I was in on open-heart surgery (a novelty then), complex brain surgery, everything from orthopedics to OBGYN.

I spent two years in San Diego, and it was in that time that I met Morris Smith and Dennis Richardson, two fellow corpsmen who became lifelong friends, though Dennis's life may well be ended now; I saw him over the years, as he drifted down into heroin and crime. Morris went through some troubles too, but he seems to have his life together now.

We listened to jazz, had very profound and naive discussions, thought we knew things far deeper than others did. I followed Dennis to Corpus Christi, Texas, for my final two years in the service, but I kept in touch with Morris, who remained in California, married and with a child.

The surgery in Corpus was very small, and the doctors gave corpsmen room for participation that may not have been legal. I assisted at many operations, even got the chance to do some while the doctors assisted. I learned suturing, a little X-ray and pharmacy work, but the best duty was washing the newborns. We had a rubber trough, a fat rubber hose, out of which warm water fell in a soft flood.

They looked like small mummies, wrapped in their linen. But they were vibrant. I'd unpeel them. There was a soft brush, soap with a texture like cream.

Dennis was there in Corpus, but he was traveling with another crowd, and when Julian Olivares arrived from San Antonio, he became my closer friend. We drank in bottle bars near the base, made quarts of suntan lotion in the pharmacy and took them with us to Padre Island, then a stretch of empty beach running along the coast for eighty miles or more. We found jazz clubs and girlfriends, played basketball together on the base team, sat on the barrack's porch, eating grapefruit and listening to Radio Moscow, well into the night. Now Julian's teaching Spanish literature in Houston and editing for *Arte Publico Press*.

I started writing poems in Corpus, long things with a Beat flavor that I had picked up somewhere, and I spent some time in the two junior colleges there, Spanish and history as I recall. I also got very religious for a time, trying hard to enter back again into Catholicism. Lent became forty days of self-imposed restriction to the base. I ate no meat, went to mass and communion every morning, lost twenty-five

Olson (top left) in the 1959 graduating class of Surgical Technician School, Naval Hospital, San Diego, California

pounds. It all ended, rather abruptly, with Mary Grace, "sweet bucktoothed Mexican girl / hugged in the arc of parking lights / lit up the beach and the Gulf of Mexico / foolishly."

It was 1961. Both Dennis and Julian had finished their tour of duty and left me alone in Corpus to contemplate my future. There'd been a tentative plan for us to meet again in California, join up with Morris, and go to school there. I was twenty-three years old and had no real prospects, though college now seemed a reasonable thing to me.

I left Corpus in the car of another ex-sailor, and we drove the route I'd hitchhiked many times, making our way the thirteen hundred and fifty miles to Hinsdale, where my mother was living with my brother, who was now in high school. My sister and her growing family were settled in that community as well.

I went to work in what I thought of as a "civilian" hospital, and that *did* make some sense. I was the first navy-trained corpsman they'd ever hired to work in surgery, and for a while I had a tough time with the nurses. The doctors had a way of treating me as one of their own, and I remember a breast biopsy on the first day I scrubbed for surgery. The doctor finished removing the sample, then pulled off his gloves and said, "Why don't *you* close?" So I was playing surgeon on my first day, and the nurses saw me, quite rightly, as another male interloper. But I won them over in a while. I was a sweet and naive fellow still then, and they couldn't keep a cold shoulder for long.

But I only stayed in Illinois for a short time. Morris and Dennis were waiting for me in California, or at least I thought of them that way. Actually they were both knotted up in their lives. An entrance into drugs and the dark life for Dennis, marriage problems for Morris. I hadn't heard from Julian and suspected he wouldn't get there. It was summer, and the school year would start soon, so I gave notice at the hospital and got ready to go. I was seeing a young woman named Helene, who I think now would have liked some deepening of our somewhat platonic relationship, but I was still tortured over Marie, my old high-school sweetheart. She'd gotten married, but was separated, and we had gone out and talked, kept at arms' distance, which made me love her all the more.

I remember the day before my leaving. It contained a kind of touchstone of my state then as I see it now. I'd said my good-byes at the hospital, and the nurse they'd hired as my replacement, a woman who had just arrived in the States with her husband

from England, asked me if I would drive her home. We got to her house in the early evening. Her husband wouldn't be home for a long while, she said, and she invited me in.

Then she told me a story of infertility, how fortunate it might be that I was here now, but would soon be leaving. They'd wanted a child for a long time, but couldn't have one. It was her husband. "And I was very close / to being convinced, could see / the bedroom thru the door." The poem is called "A Moral Proposition," a title that comes through Creeley, then Blackburn . . .

> potency, I thought
> this is the perfect gift,
> transcendent; she was a nurse
>   I was her patient
>
> —she turned to me
> a little flushed,
>
> and when I saw her lust
> I left.

And kept going. And when I got to California, I moved in with Morris, who was separated, into a small apartment costing thirty-five dollars a month, which we split. It was walking distance from the speed-file manufacturing business where Morris worked. He was back with Lois, his wife, before too long, and I was alone there until Julian showed up (and Bob Page, too, yet another lost sailor from Corpus). Julian and I took another apartment in the same building,

With Morris Smith, San Gabriel, California, 1962

ten bucks more. Dennis was there, but in another world by then. Still, all of us entered school at Pasadena City College.

Work was various for the next year and a half. I cleaned yards and cut hedges, drove an ambulance for Lamb, did a stint at a gas station (where I was accused of stealing money), cleaned a few laundro-mats—traveling between them on my motorcycle (a Triumph TR-6)—did a brief, depressing stint on a drill press at a small but very loud machine shop, even worked with Morris in the speed-file business.

In a while both Julian and I found our way to Northside Medical Clinic, near the city jail, and it was that job that carried me through my full three and a half years of undergraduate study. The shift at Northside was from five in the afternoon until eight in the morning. But I could sleep there, awakened only occasionally for emergencies. And it was a place to live, too, rent-free.

The doctor who owned and ran Northside didn't like to come in at night, and I was left with most everything: X-ray, casting, suturing, even some diag-nosis and some free (though uninformed) medicine for the local community, hardworking Mexican Americans mostly, but victims of teenage gang war-fare too, winos who had overloaded, the sweet and sexy young Chicana who lived above the place. Still, I had plenty of time to study there, to listen to jazz and poetry programs on KPFK.

I believe it must have been at Pasadena City College where I first read a book with great attention and care. It was a text in symbolic logic, and I had a fine teacher, Mr. Leavis, a math professor who was teaching the course for the first time. Though I was writing some poetry and had found teachers who were friends and remain so—Bob Trevor, Roberta (and Peter) Markman, Woody (and Marie) Ohlsen—for some reason it was philosophy that interested me, and I took other courses in the subject, loving it.

When I entered PCC I'd been placed in remedial English, tested into it, and I was there for a few weeks before the teacher read my first paper and got me into a regular course. What I remember about the paper is that the first word was "Irregardless," but that was the *only* error. I remember the teacher's look, but not his name, a big and serious man, whom I thank now for getting me into Bob Trevor's English class, a poetry course. I showed him my poetry, and it was he who suggested I apply to the Aspen School of Art for their summer program, which I did, receiving a scholarship.

That first summer in Aspen, I turned twenty-five, older that most of the other students in the workshop. A large surprise party was planned, and I was moved by it. I met people from New York for the first time, and was taken with their sureness about things. Robert Vas Dias, who ran the workshop, was the first poet I had ever met. We became friends, and it was near the end of my second summer in Aspen that the two of us decided to separate from the art school and form our own summer program. We would arrange things over the school year, and Morris, who had always painted and been good at graphics, would be our art director.

I graduated from Pasadena City College with all intentions of going to LA State, but my wiser teachers suggested I apply to Occidental College, which I did and was accepted. So were Julian and Dennis, but both of them dropped out in a while, Julian because of illness, Dennis because he thought of education as a scam. Morris, in the meantime, had started the *add gallery* and was beginning to make his way both as a painter and entrepreneur.

In my two years at Occidental I studied English and Philosophy, finding most of my interest in Kant, Wittgenstein, Moore, Russell, and the British mo-derns. The late Donald Loftsgordon was my teacher, a dynamo in the analytic tradition at the college. He managed to get large numbers of his students quite passionate about philosophy, ready to argue against those sloppy aestheticians and religionists at every turn. We were surely bores, but we were at least engaged in what we saw as the life of the mind. Exhilarating.

My studies in English at Occidental were piece-meal; I read what I wished, but deeply, counting on that to carry me through the comprehensive exam I had to take before graduating. I was also editor of the *Occidental Review* and, together with Joe Fitschen and others, publishing writers like Diane Wakoski, Theo-dore Enslin, and Denise Levertov, for which the college took away the magazine's title, not wishing the school to be associated with such authors. As with the Aspen Writers' Workshop later, I found a way to bring Morris into the project, and he did one of the magazine's covers. Another was done by Ansel Adams, uncle of a staff member.

In that time I won the school's poetry contest (with a somewhat graceful imitation of D. H. Law-rence), was harassed at Northside by drug dealers who were after Dennis (the figure of Richard in *Seaview* is not unlike what Dennis might have be-come), and worried about my brother, who had come out to California and gotten involved with Dennis and his crew. My mother had moved to California too. She was involved with a man then, and I think her moving had something to do with that. Later they were married, and shortly after that, he, like my father, left her for death.

And I got married to Anne Yeomans as well. I was twenty-seven years old and it seemed the right thing to do. Annie went to school at Oxy too, we had classes together, and a couple of friends in the Fitschens, Joe and Linnea. Years later I dedicated *Utah* to them, only to find out shortly after that they too had divorced. Mine was an awkward marriage at best, exacerbated by night work at Northside, little money, and no prospects. We gave each other pain and a little pleasure. We both knew we were mistaken from the first, I think, but held out for a while, secretive about that, and ashamed.

Then there was graduation and Aspen, getting free of things, and new beginnings. I had a job waiting for me in Portland, Oregon, as a book salesman. My car was packed with all my belongings. We would spend the summer in Aspen, then head north. But on the day of our leaving, Annie decided not to go, and I set out on my own.

Those rich summers in Aspen tend to merge in my mind, and I can't be perfectly accurate about them. Yet, they were a watershed for me. I moved through them and into the East, into graduate school. They took me from one marriage into another. And it was in and through Aspen that I put a way of writing behind me and took up the direction I am still following.

At Occidental, in 1965, our course in modern and contemporary poetry included fifteen minutes of demeaning talk about the Beats. We had considered two poems by Ezra Pound, none by William Carlos Williams. It was a very good course, in the way it went: what was seen as the Eliot strain pushed into the present, and it was my model. I was writing poems that married D. H. Lawrence and Robinson Jeffers (who was our famed Oxy alumnus), and though my work on the *Occidental Review* opened some doors a little, I was bent on a kind of received artifice that had nothing to do at all with how I felt. I'd seen Williams's poetry in the magazine *Contact;* I was curious, but that was all.

The "Sixties" were never the sixties; they began really to get under way around '63, extended almost

Teaching a poetry-workshop class with Robert Creeley (left), Aspen, 1966

to '75, and for a few years Aspen was a place through which a variety of writers moved. Poetry was growing in favor on college campuses, and celebrity (though never noted as such) was coming the poet's way.

In one of my first summers in Aspen, I met Jonathan Williams and Ron Johnson. Nathaniel Tarn was over from England, and we all had lunch together and talked about W. C. Williams, whom I had begun to read. There was an evening at a bar with Paul Goodman (a long poem of whose Jonathan had just issued from his *Jargon Press*), Roy Innes, Robert Vas Dias, and others. Poet friends closer to my own position were Bobby Byrd, John Taggart, and Carl Thayler.

Once we had our own version of the Aspen Writers' Workshop under way (thanks almost totally to Robert's efforts), we were able to hire faculty, and Edward Pomerantz came out to teach fiction, Paul Blackburn for poetry. In our first (or was it our second?) year, we had writers-in-residence for two weeks each, Robert Creeley and Donald Barthelme. Morris was hanging in as our art director, doing poetry broadsides and such. Tim Reynolds was there, and in future years Edward Hoagland, Gilbert Sorrentino, and others.

And there were various artists and musicians there too. They came to spend time at the Aspen Institute and Music School. We once had a softball game—artists against poets. Claes Oldenburg made a soft bat for the occasion, and Allan D'Arcangelo was their best hitter as I remember. The poets won of course. There were volleyball games with violinists, rock climbing at the edge of town. And we hiked in the mountains as well, two- and three-day trips, up above timberline, to a place called Pierre Lakes, where we would fish for trout, sleep in high meadows under the stars and often a huge moon.

But it was Paul Blackburn who made the largest difference for me, not as mentor so much (though there was that), but as someone whose interest in the details of the world seemed the same as mine. His poetry seemed to be what I later came to call "good talk about important things," and that brought me to feel that I too could do that, could say that the textures of the world were enough, and I need not *give* them a dignity through that artifice that had never been mine. Whatever else, there was a seamlessness between Blackburn's writing and his daily rounds, and I knew immediately that I wanted that for myself. I never got it, but I did come to that sense that what I wrote must be measured against

some concrete authenticity in myself, and that the measure of that was at its base the speaking voice.

There was more, I'm sure, for although Paul was not much older than I was, I took him on as a second father. He too was to die on me, but that came a little later. Fathers can be distant, of course, either in the privacy of their illness or their art, and Paul had a mask as well, one I'm sure I've in part constructed. It was a difficult thing, since I wanted more from him than a friend should be asked to give and had no idea at all of what that was. But I did read a perfect father's understanding in his enigmatic smile, and then there was his poetry: "The Art" . . .

> to write poems, say
> is not a personal achievement
> that bewilderment
>
> On the way to work
> two white butterflies
> & clover along the walks
>
> to ask .
> to want that much of it .

That summer when I arrived in Aspen with my car packed and a job in Portland, both Eddie and Robert said, "Well why not come to New York? We can get you a fellowship." They both taught at Long Island University in Brooklyn at the time, and I quit the job in Portland before I'd started it, and headed east. The fellowship didn't come through at first, and I pawned the fine watch that Annie had given me and found a job at a tissue bank at Saint Vincent's Hospital. I quit that before starting too, aid came through, and I moved in with Larry Smith (an Aspen painter friend) on East Eighty-fifth Street, and started the M.A. program at LIU. I also bought a thrift-shop suit, figuring I ought to wear something like that since I would be teaching. It was the big city, after all.

In my first year in New York, Paul showed me around, introducing me to other poets, calling me on the phone when there were readings he thought I ought to attend. It was through him that I met Jerome Rothenberg, David Antin, and in a while Robert Kelly, George Economou, and Rochelle Owens: those involved in the seminal press Trobar. He also introduced me to Armand Schwerner, Jackson Mac Low, Joel Oppenheimer, Theodore Enslin, Diane Wakoski, and younger poets, such as Harry Lewis and Paul Pines. I met Phillip Lopate at that time as well, and I was drawn to him and his work. His poetry had that casual edge that I, too, was after, and though we traveled with different groups, he seemed to be on the fringe of his as much as I was with mine.

I read for the first time in New York at one of the open readings at Saint Marks Church. Paul ran them then, taping everything, and I remember there was a poet/heckler in the audience, ragging many of the readers. Paul went and talked to him just before I read, and he kept his mouth shut as I delivered a few poems.

In the summers we all went back to Aspen. Ed and Sandy Pomerantz had introduced me to Miriam Meltzer, an old friend of theirs, who was to become my wife, and she came with us, to make the summer richer. Gil Sorrentino, his wife Vickie, and his son Chris were there that summer, and I remember another hike in the mountains, to a hot springs in a high open meadow this time, poets all naked under a jet of water, Jonathan Williams taking photos that I have never seen.

Annie and I got divorced, and a few days later Miriam and I were married by a friend of hers, the rabbi who had done the same for Marilyn Monroe and Arthur Miller. The ceremony was outside New Haven, and a week later there was a big reception in New York City. I'd moved into Miriam's apartment, on Fifty-sixth Street and Seventh Avenue, to the rear of Carnegie Hall, and while I finished graduate school at LIU (and for a long while after), Miriam supported us. She'd been in the social work profession for a while, and it was from her in those years that I began to understand the ways on the insides of human beings, including myself.

As I finished my degree, learning powerful things about literature from my teachers—George Economou, Seymour Kleinberg, and Robert Spector—all of whom became friends, a position at LIU was in the offing, and I took it. At the same time I was teaching a poetry workshop at the New School for Social Research, where I met the poet Tenney Nathanson.

The Vietnam War had begun to heat up, and with it those various activities on college campuses. I remember reading trips to Kenyon, five hundred or more students in attendance, to Franconia, where drugs were undermining a good experiment, to Duke, where nothing seemed affected. And I remember Paul Blackburn saying we were going to sneak into a student-occupied building at Columbia to give a reading, but that we had to pick someone up first. That someone was Allen Ginsberg, and we spent a half hour in his apartment before heading uptown on the subway.

"Colorado hike": Olson, Paul Blackburn, and Bobby Byrd, Aspen, 1965

I was writing a lot in those years in New York and Aspen, and there came a time when a book seemed reasonable. *Maps* was printed by a student press at Kenyon, but the job was so poor that I had to ask them to destroy the edition. It was Paul, once again, who came to my aid. He showed the book to Walter Hamady in Wisconsin, and Walter agreed to publish it as a Perishable Press title. It was my first book, a physically beautiful thing. Walter quickly became a friend, and he has published numerous things of mine in the years since 1968.

In the late sixties in New York, at least among the poets I was traveling with, print publication was not much of an issue. There were many readings, much talk about only knowing that a piece was finished after it was read aloud in front of an audience. I bought into this fully (still do, in fact), and I count it as a measure of a certain relaxed attitude in me when it comes to having my work published. Then, too, the kind of poetry I was interested in was mostly disenfranchised. Certainly university presses weren't interested, and the few more maverick places, like Grove, couldn't handle the amount of material that was being produced. There were magazines of course, Clayton Eshleman's *Caterpillar* among them, but there weren't really that many yet. It was a time of community, though I'm sure I romanticize that a little, and it was enough to have one's work heard, or published in very "little" magazines, one-man or -woman operations.

Community was fine, but it meant, among other things, at least some little history among its members. Most of the poets I was interested in had been at it for a while, and I as a late starter (thirty-one in 1968) hadn't been together in the coming-up times with those whose work I valued. Also, there was a New York thing. Coming from the Midwest and Southern California, more inarticulate places, I always felt outside the almost European sophistication of the City. I was to the side of things, but then I think I'd always felt that way.

The Aspen Writers' Workshop ended in 1968. It had burgeoned in its years and had run its course. We'd come into financial difficulties, something to do with a laundry bill, but I think in the end it was time anyway. The next summer Miriam and I went to Cape Cod, and in the following summer we bought our little house in North Truro. It's almost twenty years since then, but I'm looking out at some of the same trees, the constant bay.

Paul and Sara Blackburn had broken up their marriage in our last summer in Aspen, and maybe Paul was already growing the cancer that would finally bring him down. He took a trip though, to Spain and other places, and he met Joan, who became his third wife, on that trip. And he would finally, before his death in Cortland, New York, have his only child, Carlos.

I'd written a few short stories in these years. I don't know why. Really, it was poetry I was centered in. But I'd been reading Sorrentino, Hawkes, and Coover. I'd come back again to Faulkner and Lawrence with a new eye. Then I wrote a very odd piece, called "Walking," something set in Bisbee, a story about the desert, rabbits, and friendship. It had Jesus in it too, and I didn't know quite what to make of that.

Then two poems got written, and I remember showing them to Paul when he visited us on the Cape. He looked at me strangely, a "*you* wrote this?" look in his eyes. Disapproval? I'm not sure. Then a fairy tale–like piece called "The Early Years" got written. Russell Banks took it for his magazine *Lillabulero*. Finally, I saw that these various pieces might add up to something, and I began work on *The Life of Jesus,* my first novel, only after I was halfway through it. I remember the summer of 1971, when I finished it. I was driven to it.

Paul was living in Cortland, New York, then, and was dying, and for some reason—I know now what it

was—I felt I had to complete the book, to somehow give it to him, before he left. I kept hard at it, obsessed with finishing, putting in a good twelve hours a day. Miriam and I were traveling back and forth, from the Cape to Cortland, helping Joan as we could, and near the end of the summer, when the book was finished, I sat with a group of local poets and artists at the foot of Paul's bed and read some of it to him. He listened carefully and smiled at me when I was done. "That's *good,*" he said, or at least I hope he said that.

It was after we left the Cape and returned to New York that Joan called and said that Paul had had enough, and could I come there. I drove to Cortland and sat beside him with the artist Steve Barbash and watched him give it up. Paul had been writing up to the last few days of his life, taking even the details of his dying into his poems, and I remember his manuscript on the coverlet beside him as he finished living. He was something very special, as is his poetry and translation, which we still have.

I sent *The Life of Jesus,* together with a series of poems called "Home," to James Laughlin at New Directions. Laughlin had published a few pieces from the series in his annual, "New Directions in Prose and Poetry." I remember he'd called me on the phone in New York to apologize for keeping the poems for so long before contacting me. I was moved, and still am, by that call. ND had been a model of almost sacred significance to me, and to have poetry published in his annual was beyond what I'd expected.

Laughlin was taken with *The Life of Jesus,* but wrote that he couldn't publish it, not right then (though maybe in the future) and suggested that I try it elsewhere. So I found my way to Ellen Levine, my very good agent, who tried for two years to place the book. I was now in the fiction world, and it was *not* like the poetry one. I was asked by Grossman to "run it through the typewriter one more time." I got a call from Bobbs-Merrill: would I come over, they'd like to talk with me. When I got there they greeted me warmly, said they just *had* to meet the guy who had written this book, but, oh, no, they surely couldn't publish it. Harper's Magazine Press said it was wonderful, but economic matters, etc. I was exchanging letters with Laughlin all the while, and finally, after the book had been to twenty publishers, he agreed to do it, said he thought of it as having the kind of underground audience that had kept Patchen's *Journal of Albion Moonlight* in print. It *has* stayed in print (a major value in publishing with New Directions) since 1974, but the sales haven't come close to that other, very special, book of Patchen's. It would be six years before I would write another novel.

In the years after the sixties drifted into the early seventies, I became a victim of the tenure crunch. Miriam was teaching at Fordham, at Lincoln Center, and I was still at the New School and LIU. But then at the end of '73 I found myself without work and took a position as writer-in-residence at Friends Seminary in Manhattan. Miriam, too, was ready for change, and after she'd had some interviews, she decided on Philadelphia and Temple University. I was quite ready to leave New York, but I know now that a large reason for my urge was that I'd lived there for a period longer than I'd spent anywhere since I was in grade school. I was restless for change again.

Philadelphia began in difficulty for me. Miriam had a job at Temple, and I had none. And I regretted leaving New York immediately, suffering I suppose from loss of place again, but also from loss of position. I'd worked all my life, and the end of that special community and order of the workplace was something that touched me at the core.

But I was writing, poetry exclusively, taking stock of the past as usual, and also facing recent leavings. I was at an age when relatives were beginning to die and enter the past, aunts and uncles, finally my dear Grandmother Reuss in 1977.

I was offered some part-time teaching at Temple, and as the years moved on I managed to get a permanent job there. I remember sitting in my office waiting for the word. I was forty-two years old, and felt that if the decision didn't go my way I'd have to think about medicine again, some work of that kind. But then George Deaux, my champion at Temple, came in with a smile. I was back in the community of work again; I could relax a little now, get on with things.

We've been in Philadelphia for close to fourteen years, and it amazes me to think that's over a quarter of my life. Variety has now taken on different colorations, no longer that uprootedness, movements to other self-contained places, that increasing gathering of them behind me.

There's been some travel, reconnections with Morris and Julian in California and Texas, a powerful few weeks in Norway, where I found a valley of

With wife Miriam, Truro, Massachusetts, about 1975

relatives and learned that I had that other name, Gusevik, that my great-grandfather Tobias had changed to Olson when he'd arrived in America. Reading trips, and recent times in northern Italy, Switzerland, Paris, and Ireland.

I began *Seaview* in the summer of 1980. Cancer had become a reality in my family. Many relatives had died from it, and there was something about the changes in relationships engendered by the knowledge of that condition that seemed more expansive and complex to me than any poem could handle. Once again it was not statements about significance that interested me, but the various flavors of experience, how feelings intertwined and were figured in talk and behavior, how they took their place in, and were part of, the physical world. Not the real world of course, but the one I would set out to make.

When the novel was finished, James Laughlin accepted it for New Directions, and in 1983 it received the PEN/Faulkner Award, something that came to me with the purity of a gift. I'd been going the poet's route for so many years—that world in which there were no gifts, and the only award was the writing—that my feelings about the PEN/Faulkner were unencumbered, and I received it with the greatest of pleasure. It's made a difference, practically, in that it has given me more time in which to write. And I suspect that it's given me some heart too, for in the seven years following it I've managed to write a good deal of poetry and three novels, all of which has been a rich adventure for me.

What can the past mean for us, these Midwest Catholic boys who are finally inarticulate and without sophistication? In the time of my life, the Midwest has always been a place to leave, heading for either of those frontiers, California or New York. I made my way to the former without intention or choice, and in the way the pioneers lightened their wagons as the journey became more arduous—leaving a trail of valuables behind them—I left pieces of my father's health and the textures of growing up along the road. It has never been writing itself that has moved me, beyond that egocentric power that doing it always seems to contain, but a need to validate that waste that I see behind me, to find a way to speak of it with some dignity, hoping that others will hear that and find some value in it, but not caring much at the same time.

Living with Miriam all these summers on Cape Cod, I've learned to think of the future, to draw myself even into the present from time to time. I

Toby Olson and Robert Vas Dias, near London, 1984

write of the present, wanting its luminosity, but its presence always seems to be in the past.

I remember Paul Blackburn telling us a joke once in Aspen. It was a Spanish joke, he said, and the punch line was imbedded in the colloquial and was untranslatable. Miriam and I were there, as were Donald Barthelme and his wife and some others as I recall. Paul told the joke in English. It was long and complex, and he told it in a slow and leisurely manner, savoring its twists and turns. That was his way. When he reached the punch line, he spoke it in Spanish. "But what does that *mean*?" we said. He smiled and shook his head.

Perhaps the past, too, is untranslatable, its textures lost to us from the times of its occurrences, and only the fake past of nostalgia as possible entrance into it. I've started a new novel, in my head at least. It will take me to Corpus Christi again and will deal with the filter of memory, its faults and its accuracies. I really do want to live in the present, to look ahead from here, but the past keeps waiting for its redemption.

BIBLIOGRAPHY

Poetry:

Maps, Perishable Press Limited, 1969.

Worms into Nails, Perishable Press Limited, 1969.

The Hawk-Foot Poems, Abraxas Press, 1969.

The Brand, Perishable Press Limited, 1970.

Pig/s Book, Doctor Generosity Press, 1970.

Cold House (broadside), Perishable Press Limited, 1970.

Tools (broadside), Doctor Generosity Press, 1971.

Shooting Pigeons (broadside), Perishable Press Limited, 1971.

Vectors, Ziggurat/Membrane Press, 1972.

Home (broadside), Wine Press, 1972.

Fishing, Perishable Press Limited, 1973.

The Wrestlers and Other Poems, Barlenmir House, 1974.

City, Membrane Press, 1974.

Changing Appearance: Poems 1965–70, Membrane Press, 1975.

A Moral Proposition (broadside), Aviator Press, 1975.

Standard-4 (broadside), Aviator Press, 1975.

Home, Membrane Press, 1976.

Three and One, Perishable Press Limited, 1976.

Doctor Miriam, Perishable Press Limited, 1976.

Aesthetics, Membrane Press, 1978.

The Florence Poems, Permanent Press (London), 1978.

Birdsongs, Perishable Press Limited, 1980.

Two Standards, Salient Seedling Press, 1982.

Still/Quiet, Landlocked Press, 1982.

Sitting in Gusevik, Black Mesa Press, 1983.

We Are the Fire, New Directions, 1984.

Fiction:

The Life of Jesus, New Directions, 1976.

Seaview, New Directions, 1982.

The Woman Who Escaped from Shame, Random House, 1986.

Utah, Linden Press/Simon & Schuster, 1987.

Dorit in Lesbos, Linden Press/Simon & Schuster, 1990.

Editor:

"A Symposium on Diane Wakoski," in *Margins,* 1976.

(With Muffy E. A. Siegel) *Writing Talks: Views on Teaching Writing from across the Profession,* Boynton/Cook, 1983.

Collaborations:

Chamber Music: Three Songs from Home, music by Paul Epstein, poems by Toby Olson, premiere performance Philadelphia, 1987.

BirdSongs, music by Paul Epstein, poems by Toby Olson, premiere performance Philadelphia, 1989.

Other:

Contributor of stories, poems, and articles to more than two hundred magazines, journals, and anthologies, including the *New York Times,* the *Washington Post,* the *Nation, Philadelphia Magazine, American Book Review,* the *New York Quarterly, American Poetry Review, New Directions in Prose and Poetry, Boundary 2, Caterpillar, Contemporary American Fiction* (Sun & Moon), *Inside Outer Space* (Doubleday), *The American Experience: A Radical Reader* (Harper & Row), *Loves, etc.* (Doubleday), *Choice, Conjunctions,* the *Gettysburg Review, Temblor,* and *Boulevard.*

Angelo Pellegrini

1904-

Since this is a personal story let me begin with a few blunt facts about myself. Swarthy of complexion and of fairly good disposition, I am of middle height, middle weight, middle class.

I am a college man and a Ph.D.—a *Western* college man and a *Western* Ph.D. I have seen America from coast to coast. I have contributed my bit, as a section hand, to the construction of our railroads. I have worked on the waterfront, in the lumber camp, and in the sewer ditch. I have played baseball, basketball, football; and I have been knocked cold in a boxing match. I think I have now reached the top in the American social hierarchy, for I am classified in the census as a schoolteacher; that is, "a man employed to tell lies to little boys."

I have a wife, the former Virginia Thompson of Salt Lake City. We have three children: Angela, fifty-four years of age, Toni, forty-five, and Brent, forty-three.

The mortgage on our home was liquidated years ago. Among our modest possessions are the usual gadgets which make the expatriates and the esthetes despair of our material civilization. These include a bathtub, a porcelain toilet bowl, a telephone, an electric stove and Frigidaire, hot and cold running water, a vacuum cleaner, a waffle iron, an automatic washer, an electric iron, a radio, television, and phonograph, recorded Bach, Beethoven, and the rest, an electric coffee percolator, and thermostatically controlled central heating. We prize these ugly symbols of American culture because they contribute to our cleanliness, to our well-being, and to our freedom. To date they have not in any way interfered with our esthetic development. Should we ever discover that they are messing up our spiritual life, we will burn the place down and move across the street into a wilderness of maples and alders where we will construct an outdoor privy and read Thoreau.

This is not likely to happen soon; for we are very happy in our home on View Ridge. Our lives now center pretty much around a well-equipped kitchen; a study (that was *designed* to be primarily my own); a wine cellar whose warmth is being enjoyed by an increasing number of friends; a garden, our source of flowers, fruit, and vegetables.

Angelo Pellegrini, age twelve, in America

These are the blunt facts: husband, father, teacher, middle-class American, resident of Seattle in the far Northwest. And behind these facts is a story which, in the context of our times, may be worth telling.

The tracing of events to their causes frequently involves oversimplification. I recognize and accept this risk when I say it is not likely that I would be here now, writing this story in my study on View Ridge, if my father had not met Swan Sistrom, a burly, amiable Scandinavian, somewhere in the state of Washington early in 1913. How they met, I have never known; but that Sistrom persuaded Father to send to Italy for his wife and children is an established fact.

In 1912 we were a family of seven in Casabianca, a small community a few miles west of Florence, where we worked a bit of land as sharecroppers. The children, of whom I was the third, ranged in age from two to fourteen years. The central, dominating fact of our existence was continuous, inadequately rewarded labor. It was not possible then, and is much less now, for a peasant to make an adequate living in Italy without owning his home and a few acres of land.

Education beyond the third grade was out of the question. The overwhelming majority of literate Italian immigrants in America would tell you, should you ask them, that they quit school after the third grade. It is not a matter of a magic number. At eight or nine years of age, if not sooner, the peasant child is old enough to bend his neck to the yoke and to fix his eyes upon the soil in which he must grub for bread. I did not know it then, but I know it now, that it is a cruel, man-made destiny from which there is yet no immediate hope of escape.

Father and Mother were an excellent team. Without subservience on either side, with initiative pretty well distributed between them, they were always in agreement on all matters which touched the welfare of the family. They were meticulous conservationists without being in the slightest degree parsimonious. Each felt free to suggest, to propose, to initiate such humble enterprises as investing the meager savings in a half-dozen hens. They shared a persistent, haunting anxiety about providing for their children the best within their means. That was the secret both of their harmonious relationship and of their ultimate, modest success.

Like all peasants, they worked hard; but unlike all peasants, they brought a certain degree of imagination to their labors. They were not ambitious. They were not "go-getters." They had no grand design in life. They were perfectly willing to remain peasants, to operate within the little world in which they were born. But within that little world they were constantly scheming and plotting to defeat the resistance to their modest desires: adequate food, clean, warm clothing for the children, perhaps a penny or two salted away against emergencies. Nothing more than that. Each day they went about their work, sustained by an active hope that the morrow could be made just a little bit better. Had they lacked these qualities—particularly the sustaining faith, the hope that, with their own efforts, they could eventually provide what they thought their children should have—Father would never have left Italy. And had I survived the Fascist bludgeon, the Ethiopian crusade, the Spanish campaign, and all the madness which followed

1939 . . . But these are gross improbabilities. There would have been no sequel to contemplate.

I think it was compassion that finally provoked them to think seriously of America. They had tried their best in Casabianca. They had even ventured so far as France and Algiers. But when they had looked soberly into the future, and taken careful stock of the possibilities available to them, they had seen it only in terms of continued misery, of annoying, marginal existence. Of course we were not starving. There was always an abundance of weeds and vegetables, of beans and corn, of dry cod and stinking pilchards. Furthermore, an Italian never starves! His techniques for survival are miraculous! Those who have had occasion to observe the Neapolitan street urchins, the notorious *scugnitz,* will understand what I mean.

But misery to Father and Mother meant quite something else. I do not mean to imply that they saw—as I can see it now in retrospect—the real tragedy of our existence; nor that they had fancy notions about how the Pellegrinis should live. They were acutely aware of their responsibilities as parents; and they had some idea of the meaning of dignity in human life. For example, there was a certain menace in their reproach when my brother and I were caught in the neighbor's chicken coop sucking eggs like two little demons; but they were also disturbed because they realized that a real necessity had driven their sons to petty robbery, a necessity they had been unable to satisfy. They were anxious that we should wear shoes; and yet when they bought us footwear (not really shoes as we know them in America) they were driven to enjoin its use except in school and in church. So we lugged the wooden sandals under our arm, or strung over the shoulder, until we reached the church or the schoolhouse door. They were outwardly stern when they refused the coin we needed to buy an ice-cream cone, and they tried to put the refusal in terms of some vague discipline; but they knew that they had refused because they did not have the coin. And that hurt them.

They saw our future in terms of repeated frustrations. They perceived, also, what the toll would be on us and on themselves. The kind of gradual starvation which ultimately reduces man, in behavior and in appearance, to the level of the beast, they dreaded most of all. Beyond bread and wine for the stomach, they saw the need of so many little things that children must have to grow in health, in joy, and in decency; and they felt that, if they failed to provide them for their own children, they would live in anxiety and die miserable failures. So to do their duty as they saw it, but more out of a profound

"On my father's left knee," 1905

compassion for us, they agreed that Father should take a neighbor's advice and go to America.

The neighbor was *l'Americano,* so called because he had been in America and had returned with enough money to realize every peasant's dream: his own home and a bit of land. He told Father fabulous stories about America and urged him to emigrate. "In three years," he said, "you can save enough money to do what I have done. Steerage passage across the Atlantic costs very little. When you arrive in New York the employment agents of the railroad companies will take you to the job at your own expense. If you need money for the steamship ticket, I will be glad to lend it to you." And he did.

So Father left for America late in 1912. It was a desperate adventure. He knew no one who would meet him in New York. He had no assurance of a job. He knew nothing of the procedure in looking for one. Crossing the Atlantic was a terrifying prospect to an Italian peasant. It had about it the same smell of doom that the sailors whom Columbus cajoled into accompanying him in 1492 must have experienced. Leaving a wife and five children for three years, or

more if luck failed him, must have scarred his heart irreparably.

I have tried without much success to recapture the exact mood of that departure. All I can remember is confusion, tears, a savage kiss; a feeling that separation was final—that Father was going to a far-off place beyond the ocean, and that we should never see him again. And a dim vision of Mother, for weeks thereafter, trying bravely to conceal the tears she could not withhold.

Upon his arrival in New York, Father was immediately employed by the agents of the Northern Pacific Railway and assigned to an "extra gang" which was eventually dispatched to the state of Washington. And it was there that he met Sistrom, who was section foreman for a pioneer firm, the Henry McCleary Timber Company.

Henry McCleary and his two brothers had established the company at the turn of the century, and by the end of the first decade they were ready to operate on a large scale. They owned extensive timber land, had established a shingle mill and a sawmill, and by the time Father appeared on the scene they were ready to undertake the manufacture of fir doors. They operated their own logging camp and hauled the logs on their own equipment over their own railroad. Father went to work for them and later became Sistrom's assistant. With a gang of about thirty men, all of them Greeks and Italians, the two men constructed and maintained twenty miles of railroad.

Father and Sistrom became close friends. I have frequently wondered about the basis of that friendship. Each spoke a bizarre version of the English language which I could seldom understand. How did they communicate when they first met? They were a strange pair, complete opposites, with apparently nothing in common but their work.

Sistrom was a man of extraordinary strength. His Scandinavian pallor and his unathletic bearing were deceptive. The large, somewhat elliptical head, the heavy neck, and the sloping shoulders formed a single block. His arms hung loosely from his shoulders and paralleled his torso, which was unusually long and tended to a rather deep rotundity. He walked with a lead of the right shoulder and a slight stoop which had nothing to do with age.

He lacked the attributes which ordinarily suggest strength: the square shoulders, the broad chest, the pinched buttocks and narrow waist, the chiseled bulge of the biceps. And he was about as agile and graceful as a bear. He was all of a piece, a roughly molded mass. But he had plenty of primitive, brute power. How much, no one ever knew. Its source was hidden; it just simply met the challenge, whatever it happened to be. I saw him once, observing quietly, as four men struggled to lift a railroad rail with iron tongs. He finally motioned them aside, picked up the rail with his bare hands, and set it neatly in place.

He was quiet and good in a negative rather than a positive way. He minded his own business and was never known to be harsh or cruel. His smile was little else than a slight twitch of the mouth. When he spoke, it was rarely more than a half-dozen words at a time. His diet consisted chiefly of whisky and pancakes, both of which he consumed in large quantities. But I never saw him drunk, although on occasion he dozed in his chair after having leisurely dispatched the better part of a bottle of rye.

Father was in every way a contrast. He was of medium height, somewhat stocky though well-proportioned, and very dark. The high forehead, with the black, curly hair receding beyond the temples, the sparkling, brown, deep-socketed eyes, suggested a man of quality. He had a conservatively elaborate mustache which I believe he cultivated so that he might suck it twice after each glass of wine: a short and a long suck in quick succession. It was a gesture which translated relish into sound.

Although he had no more than the usual three years of elementary education, he was a cultivated peasant with all the instincts of a gentleman. His calligraphy was both legible and distinguished—an attribute which gave him considerable, unsolicited status among his Italian friends. The more so, since he also had a talent for precise, laconic expression, and a knack for untangling issues and keeping the discussion grooved. He did not himself talk excessively. He sat among his friends, listened to their heated arguments, and often dismissed with a nod of the head requests for his opinion. But when he felt inclined to make an observation, and asked for their attention, they listened with respect; for they knew from experience that when Father spoke he usually had something to say.

And he had a taste for good food and good wine. Like so many men who are genuinely interested in food and discriminating in their tastes, he had learned to cook, and he enjoyed cooking whenever he had the opportunity. The cultivated peasant, with the instincts of a gentleman, could be seen regularly at the kitchen range on Sunday: smooth-shaven, black hair parted on the side, the sleeves of the white shirt rolled above the elbows, Mother's embroidered apron tied around his waist, whistling merrily among his pots and pans, in the hot glow of the stove, preparing for

his family and friends the chicken or the rabbit he had dressed the day before.

No man was happier than Father when the food pleased him; and no man more unpleasant when it did not. When the day's work was done he gravitated tremulously toward the dinner table, as if each dinner were the first or the last, or some rare, novel experience. He was not a heavy eater; he ate moderately, but with great care and great relish—almost with deliberation, certainly with absorbed attention. Unlike his friend Sistrom, he seldom drank whisky; but wine was another matter. He approached it as he would approach a friend: with a benediction on his lips. He held the glass of the ruby liquid to the light; he talked to it; he consulted with it; he praised it; he reproached it when its transparence was defective; and he drank it with audible gusto. A quart a day was his measure: a pint in the lunch bucket, a congenial and bracing companion on the job; and a pint at dinner to celebrate the end of another day of honest labor.

Father was excessively cautious in his total behavior, something of a perfectionist in all his undertakings. So much so that, in consequence, he undertook little. Only in his work, in the home and on the job, was he reckless and unsparing of himself. In all else he was somewhat like Hamlet: too much given to weighing consequences. He was particularly diffident in making generalizations. However, when prohibition came upon him like a curse, he threw caution to the winds and quickly branded the noble experiment as the Unforgivable Heresy.

Such were Father and Sistrom. Superficially they were poles apart; but there was something below the surface in each which brought them together in a genuine friendship. I was never quite certain that I knew what it was. When they talked about their common work they understood each other fairly well; but when they talked of other matters—Or did they ever talk about other matters? I did not know; for when Sistrom came into our home—which he did frequently—and sat with us at dinner he did little else than twitch his face into a smile and pinch gently the cheeks of my little sisters. I was curious about that friendship because I attributed to it the most important event in my life: a thirty days' journey into a New World and to good fortune.

When we left Italy, in the fall of 1913, I separated myself forever from a world to which I have frequently returned in memory. Many years later I was to realize that, to a child of nine years, immigration to America meant a new birth, to which a certain inevitable continuity with the past had given an added significance. The seven thousand miles which separate the state of Washington from Casabianca is the distance between two worlds fundamentally different. At this distance, and after having revisited my native land, I can state confidently that, for me, the distance was the interval between two births. It is no exaggeration to say that, in my childhood, I twice discovered life and the world; that, in fact, I have lived through two childhoods. The experience of an American child born, let us say, in Maine and transferred to California at the age of nine is in no way analogous.

May I allude briefly to the world I left behind, the world of a nine-year-old child, so many aspects of which I have never forgotten? What I shall have to say about that first world will be helpful toward an understanding of my reactions to the second. I had been many years in America before I could see that world in perspective; before I could evaluate those early experiences, some of which I remembered so well. To be sure, it was the landscape of a poor child; but, even so, there was much in it which was utterly delightful. For I was born in the incomparable Tuscan countryside, in the vicinity of Florence, in the shadow of the Leaning Tower of Pisa, outside the

"Mother and the children a few weeks before we came to America. I am on her right with watch chain and bow tie, nine years of age."

medieval walls of Lucca, amid olive groves and vineyards. I remember particularly the early autumns, when the leaves were beginning to fall and the earth to harden with the early frosts. I remember walking barefooted to school, under the bright skies of Indian summer, quickening the pace to traverse more rapidly the shaded portions of the path, looking intently at the wayside vines for that last, possible cluster of grapes which had escaped the sharp eye of the gleaners. How precious, when found, that last sweet cluster! the final taste of the grape until the next season should come!

And I remember the winters! The long winter evenings I remember, with the family and the neighbors huddled at the hearth, with only the illusion of a fire to keep us warm; and how we took turns blowing on the coals to start a flame which soon thereafter subsided into thin ringlets of smoke. How the peasants unleashed their morbid imaginations and summoned forth horrible stories about the spirits of evil. The singing I remember; the passing of the wine jug; the final retreat into dark, cold, damp rooms, to sleep several in a bed, between sheets of homespun, rough, almost thorny, linen.

And the spring and early summer I remember! Like the hibernating animal, the peasant subsists during the barren winter months on his own substance. When spring comes he returns again to the soil to gather the mushrooms, the tender shoots of the turnip, the succulent core of the chicory; then to spade and to rake and to sow, that later he may reap the fruit, the vegetables, the grain. I remember the anxiety with which we, sugar-hungry peasants, awaited the first melons, the first fruit on the tree, the first grape on the vine. Who, more acutely than the peasant, is aware of the intimate, personal significance of the miracle of life? Rich, proud, centrally heated America, mark well my word: you know not the agony of winter and the bliss of spring! Some day, perhaps, when you may be old and shriveled and exhausted, you will know their meaning. But today, you know it not.

All these things I remember. They were the excitement and the drama of my early years. But the experiences I remember most vividly were even more intimately related to my life as a peasant boy. I remember labor, unremitting toil, exalted in the home, in the church, in the school, and its necessity quickly realized by the growing child. I remember the stonecutters crushing rock by hand for the roadbed; the women in the fields hoeing, weeding, harvesting, and then rushing to the kitchen to prepare dinner for the family; the men setting out with their tools before the break of day; the bent grandmothers spinning, weaving, and tending the children for their daughters; the draymen hauling rock, hay, and sand from sunrise to sunset; and the vendors, the beggars, the peddlers plying their trade in sun and rain.

It is not an accident that after these many years I remember a certain picture in my second reader. It shows a group of children seated around a table studying in the lamplight. The caption reads: "Dopo il lavoro lo studio." (Study after the work is done.) Nor is it any more strange that the only story I remember in the same book had to do with Cecco, a lazy boy who was taken to an island by a strange little man on the assurance that there he would find a world of delicacies. When he arrived at the enchanted island, where fruit was growing in profusion, Cecco reached for an orange; but the orange burned his fingers and then lectured him in these words:

> Alto la! Cecco sfacciato,
> A rubar chi t'ha insegnato?
> Se mangiarmi tu vorrai,
> Lavorar prima dovrai.

(Hold on there, my brazen Cecco! Who taught you to steal? If you want to eat me, you must first *earn* the right to do so.)

Nor was I by any means a disinterested spectator of the laborious routine. I learned to work as I learned to walk. In bright-eyed, well-fed America, engrossed in devising community projects to keep the young out of mischief, where the strapping lad of sixteen must be bribed to mow the lawn, in America the vast playground, where everyone is either a playboy or an athlete, such things may seem incredible: but at the age of seven I worked for wages. I hired out as a human disc harrow, an adolescent clodbuster. Barefooted and in abbreviated breeches, I went to a neighbor's field to pulverize the clods of earth with a wooden mallet. All for a nickel a day! And when I wasn't working as a hired hand, I went forth in the summer sun as a rugged enterpriser to retrieve sand from the river. At convenient intervals on the steep bank, I carved out ledges. Then I shoveled the sand from the riverbed onto the first ledge, from which I relayed it to the next, and on up to the top, where the drayman, to whom I sold it, could load it on his wagon and haul it away to the mason to whom he, in turn, sold it.

For a child under ten years of age, that kind of work was more than could be justified as wholesome discipline. It was discipline, I now realize; but in Casabianca the child worked as a matter of grim necessity. Among less arduous tasks, I remember particularly stripping leaves from the mulberry tree to feed the silkworms, and cutting grass, especially clover, to sell in small neat bundles to draymen along the highway. I went frequently to the main thoroughfare early in the morning with two or three dozen bundles of grass, to await the prospective buyers. During the autumn months I gathered fuel for the winter—any combustible remnants that could be found on a landscape where everyone was a gleaner and a scavenger. I also helped with the spading, the hoeing, the weeding, and—most pleasant of occupations—the harvest. On market days I followed the cattle and horses along the highway. For amusement? For diversion? Of course! A child must have his fun—even in Casabianca. But I pulled behind me a two-wheeled cart on which was strapped a huge basket—in case! Why? Because we needed the manure to fertilize our small plot of land. And I kept my eyes fixed expectantly on the animals. When one of them hesitated in his jaunty strides, then humped his back and arched his tail, quick as a flash I was right there,

"My mother's brother, Narciso Palidoni, and his family," 1900

shovel in hand. When the basket was full I retraced my steps to the stone cottage, as rugged and as proud and as confident as the president of the National Association of Manufacturers—though much less certain about the future.

Notwithstanding the constant labor, in which every member of the family participated, each according to his ability, I remember want—modest desires, humble yearnings, frequently immediate and vital needs, unfulfilled. There was always an abundance of such foods as I have already described; but our desire for meat, cheese, eggs, coffee, sweets, citrus fruit, and white bread was *never* satisfied. Except on rare occasions, and in microscopic quantities, we simply did not have them. Luxuries I am leaving out of account, because we never pretended to have, nor even desired, what we knew a kind Providence had reserved for another class of people.

And I remember the awful distance that lay between us and what Silone has called the "citizens." In our village they were the doctor, the priest, the schoolmaster, the mayor, and their various brethren of the bourgeoisie. They expected and received from us obsequious acknowledgment of their superiority. They entered our world for favors; we entered theirs in service. One was expected to stand bareheaded in their presence and to address them only in the most formal terms. The relationship was accepted as a matter of course; it was only in retrospect, after I had been several years in America, that I realized there was something cruel and disgraceful about it.

Very early in life I learned that, except as masters, the chosen people were inaccessible to the poor. The haughty schoolmaster had a beautiful daughter—the only blonde in the community—with whom I had the misfortune to fall passionately in love at the ripe old age of eight. Her name, of course, was Beatrice. Because she was of the elite, she had a special seat in the schoolroom, by the side of her father's desk and facing the commoners.

Every day I found more and more irresistible the desire to be close to my Love. With an instinct which only young lovers can understand, I found a way—a thorny, painful path, but a path which led to the feet of my Beloved. The standard punishment for behavior unbecoming a scholar, conceived with a certain diabolical finesse, was to make the villain kneel with bare knees on grains of corn scattered on the floor by the teacher's desk. One happy day, as I writhed and wriggled in the agony of unrequited love, I had an inspiration. I took my pen and jabbed it fiercely into the neck of the scholar who sat in front of me. The shrill, pitiful scream which followed, and which I had

anticipated, brought me instantly to my feet. With more of pride than of sorrow I confessed my guilt—and, presto! I was kneeling at the feet of my Beloved. Thereafter, I became the most incorrigible brat in the schoolroom; but the schoolmaster's daughter, happily, was later wooed and won by someone else.

And I remember fear. Horrible memories of fear! At different times, in different places, different people fear different things; for certain species of fear are endemic to time, to place, and to culture.

Some of my fears as a child were of real, others of illusory, objects. But at the time they were all real to me; and the expression "We have nothing to fear but fear itself" would have left me simply bewildered in fear. I now realize that those fears were rooted in the culture. Among the real objects of my fear were the priest and the schoolmaster. I feared them because they were authoritarians who called the tunes, to which I could not always dance. They were the giants in a world of order and absolutes, with the privilege and the power to enforce their wills; while I was the dwarf whose inner necessities required a little anarchy and much flexibility in the precepts I was expected to follow. The schoolmaster operated with the rod, and invoked the law where he felt inadequate; the priest imposed the repetition of catechisms, and invoked the demons of hell and the wrath of God to allay recalcitrance.

I think I was a good rather than a bad boy. To be really bad requires time; and in the first world I discovered I lacked the leisure indispensable to villainy. I don't remember ever having been severely punished; yet both my lay and my spiritual guides succeeded in making my life miserable. They were not exceptional in any way; they were simply the agents of time, place, and culture. I cringed under the threat they held over me. I remember the times, after having committed some horrible crime such as devouring a neighbor's apple, that I got to my knees and implored the Lord to forgive me, while I insisted that I had intended no harm. Perhaps it was my misfortune to have been born a rather decent creature. At any rate I lived in horror most of the time. I feared the two people whom in any decent society a child should love.

I know now that the most terrifying objects of my fear were illusory, although the culture insisted that they be accepted as real: witches, the devil with his three-pronged fork, serpents spawned in hellfire, and the whole evil hierarchy of a cruel religious mythology. The atmosphere of the whole community was charged with real fear of the invisible world. It was sustained by gossip, by spectacle, by rites, and by myth. Shrines were set up in the fields and along the highways. Priests blessed vineyard and olive grove against the invisible enemy. Death was shrouded in a slimy mess of superstition. If the American funeral is too much a business transaction conducted in an atmosphere of piety and soft organ music, the Italian funeral was a transaction in piety conducted in an atmosphere of horror and garish symbolism. Its effect, whether intended or not, was to make the survivors strengthen their ties with the parish church.

The imagination of the community was morbidly preoccupied with witchery and the demons of darkness. There was a babe in the neighborhood who had been seriously ill for a long time. He was not more than two or three years of age. No one seemed to know what was wrong. I remember him in his crib, set near the threshold in the sun. He lay there, pale and motionless, day after day. I remember that his mouth was always open, that the flies buzzed over his face, entered into the mouth, the nostrils, and darted at his eyes. He never moved to protect himself.

When the peasants gathered at the hearth during the evening, they frequently speculated about the causes of the little tragedy. Of all the theories advanced, this has stuck in my mind: the child was bewitched. That had been "proved" by ripping open the mattress of his little crib, with the discovery that the feathers in it had been woven into intricate designs. It was, so the peasants concluded, the work of a witch who had entered the mattress and idled away the hours weaving feathers into patterns while she held the babe in her evil spell. That led to further speculation about the identity of the witch. Innuendoes were made about several people in the neighborhood, among them an old woman whom I loved, and a vicious crookback whom I feared and hated. I have forgotten what finally happened to the child.

But I remember tales about the crookback. He was a bad man and a tyrant, twisted into a knot perhaps by paralysis. He frequently passed the day in the local pub to which, since he could not walk, he was wheeled in a barrow by his wife, who was a fine woman, or by his daughter, who was a cruel wench and a match for an All-American fullback in strength. I remember him crouched in the barrow, growling and striking at his wife with a club, as she patiently wheeled him to his cronies at the pub. And I saw him one day giving the same treatment to his daughter—inadvisedly. For when she had had enough abuse, she picked up the barrow and pitched father and all into the ditch.

It was the opinion of the community that the crookback was a devil, in disguise. Which, of course,

Father, Piacentino Pellegrini, 1922

he was; but not in disguise. He was frequently held responsible and abused for community misfortunes. He was thought by some to be implicated in the babe's tragedy. Even my mother on one occasion accused him to his face of being the agent of evil. For some reason that I have forgotten—probably for plucking a cluster of grapes in the crookback's vineyard—the savage daughter beat me severely, and I ran home in tears. Mother usually took the view that if someone flailed me I must have had it coming; but on that occasion both the extent of the beating and the administrator thereof enraged her. She took me by the hand and went to the crookback's house, where something awful which I have forgotten must have happened. But I remember Mother's parting thrust, delivered through clenched teeth and accompanied by a brandishing of the fist: "The good Lord has marked the agents of evil."

On another occasion—again as we were seated around the hearth in the evening—I listened to a strange tale told by a man who had some education and presumably should have known better. He told us that one night, a little past the midnight hour, as he was walking home along the top of the high riverbank he was attracted by a noise in the riverbed. Although he was terribly frightened he stopped to observe, and he saw three old hags splashing in the water. He yelled to them to get to their homes and to leave honest men like himself to walk the night in peace. When they did not move, but continued splashing, he fired several shots into their midst, and they disappeared.

After such tales as these, I was expected to go upstairs to my bed and to sleep in blissful innocence. On the wall in my bedroom hung an ugly picture of hell with the devil presiding over the damned, and huge serpents gliding over the flames of burning brimstone. Is it any wonder that even as a grown child I had to be taken to bed by my mother, who stayed with me until I fell asleep?

I would not deal at such length with this experience of fear if it merely reflected a personal obsession. What I feared was what the community feared. Peasants regarded their superiors with awe and fear. The man who dared walk by the wall of a cemetery in the dark was a community hero. Fear is a way of life, rooted both in ignorance and in a keen sense of reality, and sustained in many parts of southern Europe by a clerical medievalism which time has not yet conquered. My children and the children of my neighbors, living in a different time, a different place, a different culture, know none of these fears.

Such was the world I left behind when I came to America in 1913—the world of a nine-year-old boy. The experiences I have related are not recalled out of the past in the ordinary sense; they were woven into the texture of my being, and are as much a part of me as what happened five minutes ago. They are also the irreducible bond between myself and the landscape of my early youth.

Nor do I want to give the impression that it was an unhappy world to the young boy then engaged in its discovery. If it was not always pleasant, it was at least usually exciting. The participation in the struggle for the day's bread, when the bread is actually achieved and the hunger satisfied, yields certain memorable moments unknown to the boy who is born in luxury. Father's infrequent moments of "good fortune," which he frequently converted into the little things he knew would make us happy—trifles such as a whistle, a striped cotton sweater for summer wear, or a ball of twine with which to fly our

homemade kite—brought the unexpected joys which gave to life some of its most dramatic moments.

The butchering of the hog, for example, when we could afford to buy and to feed one, supplied enough sheer delight to keep us in a glow for months. There were first the elaborate preparations: the selection of the day, the solicitation of aid from certain men in the neighborhood, the sharpening of knives, including a long stiletto used to pierce the heart, the preparation of straw torches used in singeing the bristle, and the boiling of water for the final cleansing and scraping of the hide.

It required five men to slaughter a good-sized hog. The animal was led from the sty to the spot where he was to be killed. Suddenly, and with the skill of primitive men in handling animals, they tripped him onto his back. Then each of four men gripped a leg and held it fast, while the fifth grasped one of the ears, located the heart, and with unerring accuracy plunged in the stiletto. He twisted it round and round in the deep wound while the pig pierced our ears and the countryside with its screams. Gradually the screams subsided into spasmodic grunts, the muscles

"With my girlfriend," 1922

relaxed, and the pig lay motionless on his side. But the men held tight until the heart was still, for they knew from experience that in a last desperate effort to remain alive a pig will instinctively play dead.

When the stiletto was removed, the wound was plugged so that no blood would be lost. Then the bristles were singed, the hide scraped and cleaned with the razor-sharp knives, the carcass hoisted on pulleys, the hind quarters spread for disemboweling. The blood was drained into a tub for blood sausage, a then delectable fusion of blood, raisins, pine nuts, and chopped meat. The caul fat was carefully removed from the viscera and set aside for later use. The heart, lungs, liver, and kidneys were placed in containers. Except for the liver, they would be eaten during the first week. The children eagerly awaited the bladder which, when cleaned, dried, and blown up, became a precious balloon. The intestines were cleaned and then submerged in the riverbed overnight for a thorough washing.

All of this, of course, was a preliminary to the great event: the cutting of the carcass after it had hung in the cold for two or three days. It was

Pellegrini, 1948

customarily cut in the evening after all other work was done. The hams, shoulders, and flanks were trimmed and salted. The meat was scraped off the bones and ground for sausage. (Father would occasionally toss us children little dabs which we broiled on coals, sprinkled with salt and devoured with incredible relish. We looked forward to those gifts from season to season.) The bones were salted down in crocks for use later in seasoning our soups and greens.

When all else was done, we rendered the lard and made the *fegatelli.* It was the grand climax of hog butchering and provided the one exquisite feast of the season. Those delicate morsels, so far as I know, are genuinely Tuscan and have never found their way into the cookbooks. There is no place for them in an urban economy. They are the one luxury which Providence reserved for the peasants. Knowing full well that no reader of this book will ever attempt to make them—he was born at the wrong time and in the wrong place—I must nevertheless record how they were made, in memory of the joy they brought to my childhood. The liver and the tenderloin were cut into small pieces and flavored with salt, pepper, nutmeg, allspice, and cloves. Then a piece of liver and a somewhat smaller piece of the tenderloin were wrapped with enough of the caul fat to go around once. (The caul fat, technically called the omentum, is a transparent, fatty lacelike veil which connects the viscera and supports blood vessels.) The two were speared together with a sprig of dry fennel, an herb that looks much like dill. The bundles were arranged snugly in shallow pans, covered with freshly rendered lard, and cooked slowly for an hour in the boiling fat. What was not immediately consumed was left to congeal in the lard and in that way conserved for as long as one could resist the temptation. *Fegatelli!* One of the infrequent blessings of the Tuscan peasant.

I have tried to re-create the atmosphere of hog-butchering time because it dramatizes the little things that were big things in the world of a peasant boy. But there were also other, if lesser, excitements in a life so completely preoccupied with the struggle for existence; and if butchering a hog was the major event, this was because it provided at least the momentary illusion of well-being. When I sold grass or sand, or manure gathered on the highway, or earned an odd penny in some other way and brought the gain home to Father, I experienced one of the greatest and most enduring satisfactions known to man: the satisfaction of having done something urgent and vital, something intimately related to life. Such activities as I have described provided the drama and the excite-

Autographing Wine and the Good Life *for actress Anne Bancroft, 1965*

ment which the American boy finds in comic books, in movies, and in games.

Looking back upon those early years from the sobering distance of several decades, what should I say? Should I now be better than I am had I lived the first ten years of my life in the environment enjoyed by the average American boy? The question cannot be answered. I can say, however, that those early experiences provide a yardstick with which I have been able to take the dimensions of the New World, and a point of reference from which I have been able to evaluate and appreciate its grandeur. Nor is there any doubt that, in my attempt to utilize the resources which America has placed at my disposal, the lesson which I drew from those early years has been decisive. Had I remained in Italy, my childhood experiences would have prepared me to

accept frustration with patience and humility; in America, they have matured into such habits of work, thrift, and self-reliance as are necessary in the achievement of a certain measure of self-realization.

The Tuscan vernacular is rich in proverbial statements such as: "Questa vigna non fa uva." "Scoppiar di salute." "Tagliar la fame col coltello." (This vineyard yields no grapes. To burst with health. To cut hunger with a knife.) Yet, so far as I am aware, it lacks an equivalent for our insouciant "No news is good news." The reason, very likely, is that such a statement reflects a degree of sophistication, and an ability to abstract oneself from the immediate facts of experience, which the peasant has never achieved. His mentality, so drenched in superstition and preoccupied with fear, slips easily into thoughts of disaster and misfortune. To such a mind, no news is bad news.

"Between two waiters in Pensione Rigatti,"
Florence, Italy, 1979

For several months preceding the summons to join him in America, we had had no news from Father. We were terribly worried. I remember that Mother, notwithstanding her effort to keep the family cheerful, was gradually breaking under the burden of fear. From day to day we expected a black-bordered letter which would bring us news of Father's death. We had resigned ourselves to the worst. But when our friend the postman, who knew well Father's handwriting, came whistling merrily to the door, and holding something behind his back, we knew that all was well. All was well indeed!

Father was very much alive! The letter contained an eloquent description of the new home he had found for us in the state of Washington. "Sell immediately everything we own and leave on the first available ship out of Genoa. Money for the passage will be sent within a week."

Within twenty-four hours the Casabianca neighbors had heard that the Pellegrini family was going to America. And what did it mean to them or to us? They had learned to accommodate themselves to the departure of a man who left his family and went to far-off places in search of work; but the departure of an entire family for America was unprecedented, and the peasant imagination could not encompass the event. Their world, and ours, was coextensive with

the area they covered on foot when they went to work for prosperous landowners in adjacent communities, or when they went to market, perhaps once a year, in one of the larger towns not more than ten miles away. Generations of them had lived and died without having gone even so far as Florence, about twenty miles away. During the days preceding our departure they clustered about us, incredulous, dazed, eager to help with the preparations, and repeated over and over, *So you are going to America!* Yes, we are going to America to join our father. Beyond the simple fact that America was a sort of fairyland and that we were going to Father, we had no idea of what was in store for us. We were loaded on a neighbor's mule cart and taken to the train. In Genoa we went aboard the ancient *Taormina* and descended into her stinking bowels. And that is all I remember about our departure.

But I remember that it was a rough passage made the more terrifying by ugly rumors. Peasants who did not understand why some objects sink and others float, and who lacked antecedent experience in such matters, had to accept on faith the phenomenon of a floating ship. Their faith, of course, was severely taxed. Every time the ship rolled, or dropped groaning into the trough of a wave, accompanied by the clatter of falling tin dishes with which each steerage passenger had been provided, she was presumed to go down.

I remember, with lingering traces of horror, one particularly terrifying moment. For several hours the ship had been lunging uncertainly, the heavy water splitting against the bow, sweeping over it, and reuniting in a mass of foam and spray on the foredeck. With every thrust forward she seemed to be driven back by the watery walls which the wind raised across her path. Then she apparently got astride a mountainous wave which lifted her higher and higher, as if a reversed gravity were hoisting her into the sky. She paused for what seemed an interminable instant upon the crest. Then, bow foremost, she plunged down, down, down, propellers screaming in the air, the water rising on both sides, the crash of dishes and baggage mingling with the shrieks of the steerage passengers. What had happened? No one knew. There were rumors that the propellers had broken; that the engine had exploded; that we were drifting in the Atlantic with death our destination. Fortunately, all such reports had little else to them than a certain metaphorical truth.

Of the "huddled masses" who poured into America at the turn of the century, the passengers aboard the *Taormina* were fairly representative. Most of them were southern Italians who had come aboard at Naples. Apparently out of habit, the men carried their jackets in the crook of the arm—as if they were about to go somewhere. The women were hooded in black shawls. Some of them stood or knelt in the posture of prayer. Frequently someone screamed an invocation to San Gennaro, their patron saint. Day after day, for three long weeks, the scene never changed: the same faces, pale with sickness and with fear, stared vacantly, or cast furtive glances at one another, as if each sought reassurance in the presence of his doomed companions. An elderly woman expressed the common plight. She complained of her misery to a member of the crew. When he assured her that she would not die she shot back at him, with unintended humor, that he had taken from her her last hope.

We had left the Old Country. We were moving slowly toward a mysterious New World, where we had reason to believe life would be better. But, of the blessings which attended us beyond the new frontier, there was no intimation aboard ship. Passage across the Atlantic seemed to have been so calculated as to inflict upon us the last, full measure of suffering and indignity, and to impress upon us for the last time that we were the "wretched refuse" of the earth; to exact from us a final price for the privileges we hoped to enjoy in America. We were packed in filthy bunks like herring in a barrel. All our belongings were crowded there with us—even the tin dishes in which we ate the awful food we were served. In the vomit which, in various stages of desiccation, littered the floor, one might have easily identified the constant ingredients in our diet: macaroni, lentils, beans, salt cod. Honest enough food—until it had undergone the evil alchemy in the ship's galley.

Nor could we escape the sickening stench—something very palpable and substantial. We felt as if we could touch it, lean against it, move it from place to place; but we could not escape it. It originated in the galley: a heavy, warm, humid, sour odor of desecrated food. It fused with the smell of acid vomit. It gathered overtones from the exhalations of sour stomachs and of dirty, sweat-drenched, peasant flesh. Then, whichever way we turned, it blew into our nostrils in thick, pulsating blasts.

We had longed for debarkation in New York. It should have been as a release from a dungeon; and in reality it was. But there were several layers of reality. The first one was a nightmare.

At long last we had arrived in America! We had thought that Father would be somewhere near by,

Pellegrini on his eighty-fifth birthday

and that in a few hours, at most in a day, we should be in our new home. That was the hope that had sustained us through the discouraging days aboard ship. We were like a lost child who controls his sobbing long enough to repeat intermittently, "I want my daddy." Nothing else mattered. We did not see the Statue of Liberty, which every immigrant is presumed to behold in tears and in silent adoration. In fact, we had never heard of that colossal symbol of America. We had never heard of America as an "asylum for the oppressed." I was to discover all that much later. What had excited all the passengers was the first sign of land; and what had brought joy to *our* hearts was the assurance that Father was on the far shore. Seductive illusion!

We debarked, of course, at Ellis Island, though we then knew nothing about it, nor about its purpose, nor about the annoying routine to which all aliens who entered America had to submit. Had we known, the experiences would certainly have been less terrifying. I remember only interminable, uncertain waiting, complete bewilderment. And the horrible rumors! How prone to woe and to despair is the peasant mind! Why were we herded into those barren rooms? Why were we not taken to the trains so that we might proceed to our several destinations? There was a variety of answers. Someone said that a terrible disease had been discovered among the passengers, and that no one would be permitted to land. Someone else suggested that America was filled up, and that there was no room for anyone who sought employment. An interpreter finally told us that everyone would have to submit to a rigorous eye examination; to which information some starry-eyed optimist added a footnote to the effect that in a large family someone was certain to be rejected.

Well! The Pellegrinis were not rejected. The long journey from Casabianca to America, thirty wretched days, had brought us to a land that Charles Beard, writing at about the same time as our arrival, said was blessed with the greatest natural endowment of any nation in the world: the broad plains, the mountains rich in minerals and fossil fuel, the navigable and fish-rich rivers, the forests which in 1913 were still primeval, trees that ranged from seven to fourteen feet in diameter. The resources of the New Land, both physical and spiritual, were best described by its greatest poet, Walt Whitman:

Fecund America!
Thou envy of the globe! Thou miracle!
Thou, bathed, choked, swimming in plenty,
Thou lucky Mistress of the tranquil barns,
Thou mental, moral orb.

When our family settled in the Northwest corner of that land, Grays Harbor County, in the state of Washington, I was ten years of age. That area I have called the opulent Pacific Northwest. Having engrossed my share of its vast cornucopia, I have lived a long, happy, productive life. I am now eighty-six, and have formulated a credo that accounts for that tranquility. I shall state it here as the appropriate conclusion to my miniautobiography.

Michel E. Montaigne, noted French essayist, stated that our "Great and glorious masterpiece is to live appropriately." And what does this mean? I suggest that the very essence of living appropriately, especially in an age of scarcity, is living in harmony with Nature. Use its bounty with prudence. Renew what is renewable. The soil is a community of organisms. Respect them. When you take down a tree, plant another in its place. Respect the integrity of lakes and rivers. By virtue of their metabolic processes, plants respire oxygen in our atmosphere. Add to the process by planting where you have space. Return all organic waste matter to the soil. In these creative ways, none of which imposes what could be called a burden, we shall contribute significantly toward maintaining what ecologists call the balance of Nature.

This credo, which has given my life a meaningful direction, is also in accord with what I learned from my immigrant father: "It is the duty of every member of the human family to leave that section of land whence he draws his sustenance in better condition than it was when he acquired it."

This I have done by cultivating a kitchen garden, fifteen hundred square feet. The dollar value of its produce, vegetables, culinary herbs, a peach and a fig tree, is about enough to pay for the real estate tax on the property. May I suggest that you do what I have done? And bless you for the effort. It will make you a more worthy member of the human family. The human family! As Bertrand Russell said: "Remember the human family and forget everything else!"

BIBLIOGRAPHY

Nonfiction:

The Unprejudiced Palate, Macmillan, 1948.

Immigrant's Return, Macmillan, 1951.

Americans by Choice, Macmillan, 1956.

Wine and the Good Life, Knopf, 1965.

Washington, Coward-McCann, 1967.

The Food-Lover's Garden, Knopf, 1970.

Lean Years, Happy Years, Madrona Pubs., 1983.

American Dream: An Immigrant's Quest, North Point Press, 1986.

Charles Plymell

1935-

From Kansa, Land of the Wind People

I was told that my great-grandmother walked on the Trail of Tears. My grandmother moved on westward to the Cherokee Strip. As a young girl, my mother lived a somewhat cruel, austere life with little but the buffalo grass and sunflowers to give her joy that a stepparent thwarted.

The earliest account of my father's ancestors was that they sailed from Ploërmel, France, in the early 1700s. My grandfather was deeded 160 acres by President Cleveland in the Oklahoma Territory called "No Man's Land." My father was a wanderlust, a cowboy; he left his cup of coffee on the table in the sod house he built before going on a cattle drive to Galveston, Texas, where he signed on a ship to sail the world for the next two years. When he returned to No Man's Land, his coffee cup was in the spot where he had left it.

Still, nothing much happened there, nor the places he and my mother moved to raise my four sisters and me. Yes, I'm the only boy and the youngest, which always seems to evoke a recondite nod by all who are told. I have never understood why, but include it for the record. My family moved to the land of the wind people, which the Indians called "Kansa," where my grandfather had begun a stage line that ran from the Territory to nearby Dodge City, Kansas. A few miles to the southwest remains a settlement called Plymell where the stage headquarters were. It consists of the Plymell school and the Plymell Union Church. Later we lived on a farm near Ulysses, Kansas. Not much happened there either, except for what I felt as a raw and forceful cosmic energy that seemed to gather in space and etch itself on the landscape and everything in it.

The Plymell family had established itself in the community, and there were many published accounts of my grandfather's worthwhile deeds and attendance at social functions. One newspaper's account heralded him as one of the best ranchers in the Territory because of his quick actions to protect the herd from a great blizzard. Another account was in a book about the Dalton Gang where he helped back down a gang of marauders. He died young, and a respectable

Charles Plymell (front) with his father and three of his sisters, Norma, Sue, and Dorothy, on their farm in Kansas

dynasty of gas, oil, and cattle that would have rooted itself in that time and place was pulled up to drift like tumbleweed across the blowing topsoil, and never again to find conditions favorable for growth.

By 1935, my father had sold his part of the ranch and took his family to Holcomb, Kansas, where I was born in a converted chicken shed built to protect us from the black dust storms that had long covered the once-thriving stage line a few miles away. My mother had to put wet rags over our faces so we could breathe. When she wasn't busy with us, she was gathering cactus and shooting jackrabbits ("Hoover steaks") to feed us. In my poetry, I speak of the madness that this desperation could in frailer women evoke, and of seeing in a Washington, D.C., gourmet market a half-century later the kind of cactus she had gathered.

As a baby, I was placed in a wooden box on the floor of the tractor my mother drove around the field. When I grew older, I sometimes sat in the cab of the truck, and waited while the tractor and plow went around the section (640 acres) in a square. I listened to the wind's pitch that blew through the doors of the truck and watched and heard the two-cylinder John Deere tractor ping into what seemed to be infinity and then come back around as its two cylinders popped louder. The lines the plow made around the field and the sound of the tractor left in me impressions of space, metaphysics, and physics.

Some of my early nightmares were of similar graphic dimensions with seemingly unending lines and planes converging until fear awoke me. This abstraction, with its diminished volume, would later feed my interest in such matters as Pythagorean versus Aristotelian geometry, and provide some allusions for my poetry as well a basis for reading Robert Lawlor's essays concerning sacred geometry.

My family was part of the migrations from the dust bowl that went from Kansas and Oklahoma to Southern California. Some of my earliest memories are of riding and living in the back of the International farm truck. My sisters made up crazy jingles to help me with my preschool activities. One that I remember is "Votcha peacha; Votcha peacha; Votcha peacha-voo. Hip, hip, hooray, the dogs are coming!" I can't, however, get my sisters to acknowledge the invention of these lines that made a lasting impression on me. None of my sisters, except perhaps the oldest, would ever appreciate the songs of Annie Ross or King Pleasure. My love for scat, bebop, and later rap, may have had its roots here. The more formal rhyme schemes of the Burma Shave road signs that were placed in verse distances along the seemingly endless miles helped to educate a generation of migrant children. "Solomon Grundy . . . born on Monday . . . fell in love on Tuesday . . . married on Wednesday . . . took ill on Thursday . . . saw the doctor on Friday . . . died on Saturday . . . was buried on Sunday . . . that was the end of Solomon Grundy. BURMA SHAVE."

We moved to Yucaipa (Indian for "green valley"), California, where my father rented a house, and my sisters set up my "official" preschool and named it "Yucaipa Valley Basement School." My memories of this place range from far-fetched tales of what might be hanging in those huge sacks in our

Father, Fred Plymell, Oklahoma Territory, 1916

landlord's basement window to the authenticity of whether or not it was indeed Bing Crosby's brother, Bob, who stopped his car and visited. This argument was resolved by the fact that his brother would not have worn a particular color of socks. Having tired of such intellectual problems, I would run and play in the washes. To this day, I feel slightly faint when I try to recall the still enthrallment and scent of the brush and the orange groves where the clear water trickled magically over the smooth, colorful rocks. Later we would be taken to the San Bernardino County Orange Festival, where I remember a world made from oranges. This would be as close to paradise as anything I have experienced since. That valley is now immersed in a deadly black smog while the Kansas sky is clear.

My father was trying to make a living "trucking" during the Depression and had left his family in California. He told of having hauled a truckload of apples to Chicago and having to dump them as worthless. Then, some men held a gun to him until he voted for their candidate. These stories probably had something to do with my regarding any political system as eventual folly. I never was a flag waver and thought jingoism reprehensible, though the thought of doing anything against my country was equally reprehensible. A line I later worked into one of my political poems that first appeared in *Evergreen Review* about "Woodstock" recalled the words I had heard my father say when talking politics on the high seas, "The likes of you and me, sailor, are just ballast."

I am a drifter, a transient, the very thought of setting out for somewhere has always stirred me. My politics lean toward anarchism, and in general I am wary of government and authority. I do not vote, but I consider myself more politically informed than the average person. Philosophically, as well as politically, my thoughts eventually had to rest, albeit paradoxically, in an open-ended rather than a closed system. My wilder side could be attributed to family traits and a constantly changing environment; nevertheless, I liked having a little bit of the "outlaw" in me, tempered by the realism of a timeless lyric.

By 1940, we had returned from California to Kansas, and my first years of schooling were in a one-room schoolhouse where I was frequently stood in the corner and made to memorize poetry. I was in the

Mother, Audrey Plymell, Grand Valley, Oklahoma, 1924

same room with my sisters; my teacher taught all grade levels and also cooked the school hot lunch, baked beans. She was also a woman from the temperance movement, so our music class consisted of singing, "What's the matter with wine, sir? ALCOHOL. Alcohol is a drug you see, leaving a trail of misery." (Over and over we sang it.) My parents were busy working the farm, but not too busy to take the farm truck to gather scrap metal for the war effort. Their lunch, eaten on the tractor, was pork and beans, Vienna sausage or potted meat from the can, along with some white bread.

Woody Guthrie's ballads of hope had been tempered by the cry of other country-music singers who sang the songs of despair and aloneness, of death itself. Even the good gospel intentions of the Carter Family's "Everybody's got to walk that lonesome valley" left in me a spine-tingling portent, and in the old farmhouse, I remember the song "Twas on the Isle of Capri where I found her," and a full-color picture that my father brought from Italy that hung on the wall as the only decor. Real places far away sounded better than the abstract far-away one, and that might have had something to do with my own restlessness and unwillingness to concede to time.

We frequently took shelter in the cellar from the rolling cyclones. Someone would invariably make a last-ditch effort to retrieve my toys. My selfish thoughts of existence and childhood frights over the "big question" were interrupted by the newspaper headlines and radio which roared Pearl Harbor news of billowing smoke like the black tornados—then Roosevelt's voice. I remember the words and symbols when my mother, while talking to a friend, picked up a souvenir ashtray that had a picture of the Statue of Liberty in the bottom of it, and said, "And he'll be the right age for the next one." Something new to think about. I began to be puzzled about wars and more immediate fates.

When we moved into the small town of Ulysses, Kansas, World War II was at its peak. Added to the pathetic songs of the cowboy and the lonely prairie were the songs like "The Soldier's Last Letter" that played over and over on the jukebox at the Bon Ton Cafe, where my mother and sister "slung hash." A B17 from the base at Liberal, Kansas, crash-landed near our house and the crew had to stay on site. Since my sisters were of dating age, I was immediately filled with a cultural influx of talk from newly enlisted Yanks from the big cities; some had seen combat. My head was filled with stories, and my continuous errand was to go buy saltines and Velveeta cheese to serve with their beer. I immediately converted combines and other farm machinery in the yard into combat vehicles from which I gunned down the "enemy." My collection of insignias sewn to my jacket was unchallenged.

My oldest sister was the wildest in our family. She left the farm as soon as she learned to hitchhike, and never slowed down. She died on the streets of San Francisco in 1969 after having been evicted from Kaiser Hospital with casts still on both legs. She swore that the government agencies used experimental drugs on the bums they pulled in off the street. She always wanted to write. I still have her old Royal typewriter, on which I wrote my first prose book, *The Last of the Moccasins,* for which she was the inspiration. I am a romantic. My other sisters became Christians, conservative, conventional, and, as the expression goes, kept close to the willows.

Farming was a "sure thing" in hobo lore and song. Expansion and growth, most of it subsidized, would make instant millionaires of those who stuck to the land, but my father was too restless to accumulate such a respectable fortune. By the late forties we had moved to Wichita. My father had sold the farm in western Kansas and soon thereafter had made trips to South America and Australia looking for that perfect cattle ranch and great space. My mother remained working in the aircraft plants. My father left my second-to-the-oldest sister in charge of the house in Wichita. I had been put in a private military school in San Antonio, Texas, for my first and only year of high school. By the time that year was over, my father had returned with his new South American wife. He bought me a new '51 Chevrolet in which I followed him to Yuma, Arizona, and Blythe, California, where he had bought some cotton land as well as some wild land on the Colorado River at Cibola, Arizona: population two, a brother and sister who lived in the same house, which had a dirt floor. There was a sod post office with a yellowed Wanted poster, one or two inoperable Model T Fords, and a pile of burro hooves from their usual meal of wild burro.

It was around 1948 when I was in junior high that I spent summers helping drive tractors and trucks, though my first experience at driving was in Kansas when I was six years old. My mother was on a tractor and plow, and my father was on a tractor and plow. This left me and the International truck, which had to be moved a few miles to a different field. My father put the truck in gear for me and jumped from the cab. I drove it in low gear, which was about the speed of the tractors, to the other field, where I brought it to a stop. There was nothing I could run into except the dirt of flat land, so it really wasn't that big a feat. My father later bought a big Reo truck and a smaller truck called a Reo "Speedwagon." He liked that name, which was chromed in script on both sides of the hood and recalled that when Reo first made vehicles, they were called "Speed Wagons." The name was used again by a rock group who apparently liked its double meaning. I am sentimental about trucks, and even have dreams about those we owned.

Into the pathos of my environmental energies came historical words, symbols, and the logos of my deeds, which would mark the crude beginning of my creative expressions. It was no longer the childhood singing of a cowboy-song metaphor about herding the dark clouds out of the sky when I would stand in the middle of a field with no one or nothing as far as the eye could see and sing louder and louder . . . thinking that my voice was in the wind . . . could stay in time . . . or through time . . . a plaint of someone, like an imaginary Greek Islander who had sung to himself thousands of years ago to establish his own ethos, to say, in effect, I am here—but now, of the street in this life, the poetry became the idiom, the tempo, the time.

After following the rodeos for a while, and writing a poem about riding the bulls and broncs, I hot-rodded my new car and concerned myself with drag racing around Southern California. I wore my hair in a "ducktail" and adopted the L.A. look, which was a flower-patterned shirt with the collar turned up and new Levis that were never washed until they turned stiff and shiny black. I went cruising the streets of Los Angeles, Americana in the making. Central Avenue for the old bebop and tenor sax, Hollywood and Van Nuys Boulevards for the great drive-ins with would-be movie stars on roller skates serving the cars. My father watched both me and my car become more and more worthless. To his dismay, I traded it in on a new Buick Roadmaster and began working on the pipeline in Arizona.

Having grown up in the Bible Belt and seen an appreciable amount of powerful bible-thumping hypocrisies, I grew disdainful of dogmatism, but not entirely disrespectful of canon. My mother was always "prayerful," but my father, usually while figuring out his land or cattle deals on his marathon car trips over the western half of the continent, would offer a philosophical aside that: "Whoever or whatever is behind this whole thing ain't gonna let a little thing like man figure it out, and you'll just go crazy if you try to." Instead of hearing declarations of Truth in church, I was rather struck with Truth itself and developed a strong dislike for what I perceived as dishonesty or phoniness in established culture. I eventually had to resolve whatever belief I held into a simple statement that I believe in Belief. In that respect I was a hippy. I saw them arrive and shared. But I was never a joiner or belonger.

My music appreciation was eclectic, and at the infamous and rowdy Cowboy Inn, a holdover from early Wichita when it was called "Cowtown," there were always barroom brawls to add to the excitement. But where else and when else could I have parked my Buick at the door of a honky-tonk and paid a dollar cover charge to drink and dance until daylight to Hank Williams' singing? All the greats played this famous dive, most of them now in "Cowboy Heaven." And of course there were the other "greats" in their own right who played the honky-tonk scene, did radio shows broadcasting over the endless waves to small lonely towns. Many performers had jars full of Benzedrine tablets in their guitar cases, like in the poem from the battlefield of World War II (a .45 in one holster and bennies in the other). Their audience was made up of truckers, housewives who needed to lose weight, veterans, all who added to the frenzy of postwar growth . . . and overdose, an amplified frenzy in the soul of country, Hank Williams, dying in the backseat being driven to the gig he never made in Canton, Ohio.

Crude or cool, my feelings were expressed in music. Near the converted chicken house where I was born was one of the biggest dance halls between Denver and Kansas City. Whole families would go there to dance. Kids would run around the floor, drunks would stagger outside to throw up; my sisters would jitterbug to the big-band sound that broke the silence of the vast plains. My eclecticism grew naturally, from the honky-tonks to the back-alley clubs with combo musicians who like split from Kansas City after the Norman Granz jazz scene dissipated, like its music emanated from the doorways of little clubs on the Kansas City streets, like bebop, blues, progressive— the soul of Bird. A great war spawned a great romantic period in America. Society was busy stabilizing itself, but the music kept on rocking.

I drifted around and lived with a sister in Santa Paula and then Ojai, California. At that time, these Gardens of Eden were inhabited by working-class generations from the Okie population of Bakersfield who mainly followed the oil fields. Later this "world desirable" real estate was to be devoured by the

Oldest sister, Betty

wealthy. I worked on the pipeline, rode in rodeos, moved northward to Oregon, and then returned to Wichita. My father had lost most of his dreams and money while looking for a "spread" of a bygone era and rented some land in the Flint Hills, near Wichita, to run some cattle. I quoted him in a poem as saying, "The best cattle country since Uruguay." He would leave no will, probably because of an aversion to such documentation.

The Fabulous Fifties from Ducktails to Eggheads

I recall my one year of high school as being not terribly interesting compared to the excitement of being wild and free while my biological and intellectual demands were radically out of sync. In those days there were drug problems too, but nothing like today. The drugs then, as now, were an integral part of the music, except for classical and opera, which demanded the performers' absolute control. But those were simpler times; although there were losses, there were fewer problems because the drugs belonged in the subculture. There seemed to be more fun to life, less hype. Even if one did not belong to the life-style of the rich and famous, one could rebel against the shallowness and conformity of creeping oppression, and have fun doing so, "without a cause." There seemed to be more hope and a great deal more to look forward to than just upward mobility. Instead of programs, we had friends, and one, Robert Branaman, would later encourage some of us to go to college, which seemed a very square thing to do. But slowly we integrated with some of the squares on the quads, though unlike the future generations, we were not eager to share our trappings from the subculture. Movies and popular songs helped provide the common appreciation and intercourse with the squares. Even the most eggheaded couldn't resist the voices from that generation which spoke to everyone . . . James Dean, Brando, Elvis, Johnny Ray . . . who came out of Ohio, Nebraska, Mississippi . . .

In the fifties, before the "secular-humanism scare," most universities retained strong philosophy departments that served not only as a foundation for the humanities, but also as an academic framework for those who were going into the ministry. These studies at Wichita University naturally appealed to me because they seemed to be an extension of the all-night-talkative Benzedrine discussions that took place in the nightclubs of Wichita and Kansas City when I was a hepcat turning hip, in that particular age that changed the terminology. I continued my nonacademic life with friends in nightclubs listening to small combos during my "lounge-lizard period," and we always managed to find professional mentors who graciously shared their time; one such was the actor Mickey Shaughnessy, who was particularly good at the stimulating conversations that took place after his "gigs" and ran to brunch the following day. That was the advantage of nightlife in Wichita, Kansas. In Hollywood or New York, time would be in demand. Here it was spent for the good of it, not for the duty of it.

I look back on it profoundly, as if I were a good citizen of an ancient culture; my sensibilities were being heightened by the work of the great hipster Lord Buckley as well as by Aristotle, in a blend that kept me from being too pretentious and pedantic—undesirable traits I made a conscious effort to avoid. I studied semantics with Professor Walpole, who with heavy British accent and dry humor complained that the academic life was deteriorating with too much Aristotle and marijuana. Later, Patti McLauglin, who saved me at a point of self-destruction and gave me a twelve-string guitar, was to help defray a mad argument between Professor Walpole and a banjo picker-fundamentalist barkeep who had violently different views on the use of the first obscene word learned by all cultures, according to the authority, Walpole, who had written a book on semantics. Such was the mixing of cultures that seemed to join the lay with the professional during my new experience of college. I became keen enough in metaphysics that, in my freshman year, I was asked by the department chair to tutor the class.

I would experience the secular side of this impressionistic-linguistic fervor again when I would share a flat in San Francisco with Neal Cassady, the protagonist in Kerouac's novels. And I would be ashamed years later to tell Patti, at her Gate Five, Sausalito, California, houseboat party, that I had hocked the twelve-string she had given me to accompany her beautiful folk songs on. Such were the reoccurring influences that were a constant weave in my life, which were to be learned as "Karma" in the language that Ginsberg was to bring from his stay in India when he shared the Gough Street flat in San Francisco with me and Neal. But the street-culture wisdom of the fifties included feelings, close friendships, a versatility of word usage, and mental associations—the altruistic inquiries were not mere Benzedrine-stimulated loquacities or hemp euphorias; they became a part of traditional cultural, or subcultural, mores.

Charles Plymell, Wichita, Kansas, 1954

I was fairly naive as to what people thought about me. I always made friends, though I did not mix easily in polite company. I could not master small talk and hated introductions. I would never be a candidate for a fraternity, nor, as I was later to learn, a candidate for much else that was offered in a competitive, materialistic, success-oriented culture. A strange feeling of alienation from my time was within me. I would even go so far as to make up the story that introductions were not used in my culture (whatever that was) and that those who needed to know each other always found each other. Neal Cassady, the subject of many well-known seers who made tapes of his past lives, was himself sometimes the savant, and would say on occasions, in his multilevel talk, that I had a problem with time.

Long before I knew about academic degrees, I knew the longitudes and latitudes and had dragged the main streets in almost every town immortalized in song along the famous old Route 66. From Flagstaff, Arizona, I headed north to Oregon to live with my oldest sister, who had quit the wild life long enough to marry a lumberman from New Jersey who owned a mill in Prineville. He was an epicure of the finest houses of ill repute and gambling, and was prodigal when introducing his new brother-in-law to that historical remnant of the wide-open West. I worked construction during 1954 and lived on a small houseboat on the Columbia River while helping to build the Dalles Dam. Afterward, I bummed around with my sister and her new friend, Frank Lockhart, the son of a Black madam and an Irish sheriff from an area around Deadwood, South Dakota, and picked up some jargon from the rounders before heading back to Wichita.

Race music began to surface in Wichita in the early fifties. A phone call from one of my cronies alerted me to the songs of a "cat" whose early work sounded like zydeco. He was a rhythm-and-blues artist that we HAD to check out. He and his combo were playing at one of our hangouts in "Colored Town" known as the Mambo Club. We knew the bartenders and musicians and there was no problem in our being the only whites in the clubs. We parked my Buick Roadmaster next to a '49 Caddy that still had the red dirt of Louisiana on its dented fenders, paid a dollar cover charge for the live music, and the bartender introduced us to Fats Domino, who joined us at intermission and between the sets. There weren't more than a dozen people in the club, and we danced and raved all night in Wichita of the fifties, across the tracks in the right place at the right time to dig the great artists and then go to Mrs. Dunbar's for the kind of barbecued ribs that I have never since found . . . even in New York.

But into this cool subculture rhapsody came a change. Bob Branaman had been working as a "bellhop" at a large downtown hotel. He had previously painted pictures and drawn cartoons during his stay in reform school, and, like the rest of us, had not finished high school; but by expounding on the virtues of a formal education, he persuaded—either because of his altruistic feelings or because he didn't want to make a new scene by himself—some of the more sensitive and reflective of us to enroll in the university. It was while goofing at one of our all-night, lounge lizard, pink and black plastic dives, that he read to us some lines from the collected poems of the radical scholar himself, Ezra Pound.

I studied philosophy and art and gravitated toward English. There was at that time a strong contingent of women folk singers and professors, around whom I had spun Sapphic fantasies. This was fertile ground for sensitivity to happen. There were many very good professors who seemed genuinely interested in their own subject area, and one got the impression they liked to teach it. There were plenty of characters to add to the fun of those years. The folk singer Joanie O. Bryant taught English. After I had taken all her courses, she (undoubtedly with a great sigh of relief) hinted gently that she had nothing more to offer me. There was the semanticist Hugh Walpole, whose behavior finally made him a recluse. There was Professor Nelson, who lectured brilliantly on Hart Crane and the American expatriates of the Lost Generation and tolerated the campus "aesthetes." There was Professor LePell, the artist, who got everyone excited about painting as well as the other fine arts. It was at his parties that I began to acquire taste, if not a hunger for all the arts, for the plains were artistically austere compared to the coasts and one had to make an effort to generate art. He had what seemed to me every classical album available, and I listened to everything from the madrigals to the atonal moderns—intensely, and for hours. I was so enthralled that I spent all my time involved with the arts and ignored my classes except for metaphysics and, subsequently, flunked most of them one by one.

The students who wrote poetry and made art formed a special coterie; I can see how fortunate I was to be in such an environment. Like the eighties, society in the fifties was determined by a strong sense of conformity that implied its own sense of success and virtues. We were probably made fun of by the fraternity/sorority crowd, but for the most part, we were oblivious to it. Besides, there were allies forming among the more serious Phi Beta types, who were called "eggheads." Robert Branaman had been elected to an honors arts society, and due to his high grades in art, he was asked to pledge a Greek fraternity, but he stated in his reform-school idiom that . . . "Hey, man, them people have some very funny rules." We had our own crowd for whom the doors were open when we wanted to "cool it" in the clubs across the tracks, inaccessible and unknown to the college crowd, where Bo Diddley, Chuck Berry, or some great seminal tenor saxophonist "wailed" all night long.

As I broadened my music appreciation to include classical music, I became friends with Crandal Waid and his wife, Mary Joan, who gave me much support and welcomed me to stay with them when Crandal was with the Santa Fe Opera, and later when they lived in a loft in the section of New York City that was to be known as SoHo. I had gotten a job operating an offset press on which I learned printing skills. At Wichita University Professor LePell conceived the university's literary magazine, to which I contributed. One semester I collected the money for the printing of an issue and used the printing press on my job to print it, but there was no binding equipment, so I perfect-bound it myself. I found some glue used for cloth binding and heated it in my cooking pot, but it didn't hold and the magazine came apart after a reading or two. It was a good issue, one professor said, "but it came apart after the first reading." "Haven't you ever heard of Dadaism," I rejoined. It wasn't funny to Mary Joan, who was on the magazine's board of directors.

Those of us who wrote poetry influenced each other, and we were irresponsible. We seldom went to classes, "partied" continuously, stayed out all night in the clubs across town, and took drugs. We had sent to Texas for a carton of peyote and had purchased a blender to help get the stuff ingested. We became mystic visionaries as we lay awake in profound madness for what seemed to be whole semesters, missing our courses. A brilliant poet, Alan Russo, with whom I was later to live in San Francisco, ventured outside one day and said he "heard it crack." He announced that it was spring and that he had heard the equinox.

We began having "creative energy" parties sitting around a fire on the riverbank, or dancing naked in the moonlight in the fields. There was usually music from flute or strings. Our parties took on a profound reverence, and we were not far from the Potawatomi, who still used peyote in their religion. I saw a shift in drugs and culture. Gone were the days of cutting up the amphetamine cotton strips from nose inhalers. I saw less of my friend who played bass and ingested so much cotton from nose inhalers that he began to smell like one. Peyote didn't seem to be the drug of jazz. While in my new life-style as a student, I invited an old saxophonist over from one of the clubs to show him a peyote cactus. He jumped back and grabbed a handkerchief from his vest pocket to touch it with.

I began to write more poetry and give artsy intellectual parties at my house located near the university. I probably had a poster of a bullfighter on the wall. Professor LePell lent me a copy of *Howl*. Alan Russo, whose father was a professor, translated from the Latin some poetry for Dr. Nelson and wrote a small sheaf of poetry that I published. Russo then left for San Francisco to join the artist Bruce Conner, the poet Michael McClure, and the publisher of Auerhahn Press, Dave Haselwood, who had left Wichita a decade earlier. I would be going to San Francisco to stay with Russo, who would introduce me to Philip Whalen and other Auerhahn Press poets who would witness the "Now" generation. Bruce Conner would paint "LOVE" on the pavement outside our Oak Street flat in the same block letters as Right or Left Turn.

I was told by my father to enlist in the air force when I was eighteen so I could retire at full pension after I became thirty-seven years old. That was good advice, but then thirty-seven years old seemed like a long time in the future; now of course it seems eons in the past. I was, though, able to keep out of the draft by attending college and joining the air force ROTC. I kind of liked it because it reminded me of military school. I didn't believe I would have been a good candidate for the service, and just to be sure, I told the draft board that I didn't believe in killing. Just then a couple of friends, one carrying a white jacket, and the other a philosophy student who preached part time, ran up to me waving the Bible acting as if they were trying to restrain me. They shouted to the clerk that I was a dangerous poet in trouble with the State, and then they pushed me out the door and "forced" me into a car. I don't know if that was effective, but with my school deferment added as good measure, my draft-card classification kept falling below conscription.

My creative work at that time was deplorable, barely as good as what I see nowadays proliferating from local arts councils throughout the country. Then, there was no financial support to speak of, and probably just as well. I was, though, developing, or perhaps dulling, my sensitivities, together with my capacity for a daily bottle of codeine cough syrup, while all the things I was expected to do to be a successful college graduate never seemed to transpire. I blamed a "genetic disposition" for my tendency for opiates, and modeled a destructive creative kinship with Coleridge. While the danger and potential for self-destruction from the use of drugs and alcohol increased in our society, the greater problems became the profit and criminality in them, rather than the chemistry. I simply outgrew them, but not without close calls. I have no way of knowing how drugs affected my creative work, but I reached the point where drugs did not interest me. It may have been that I became tired of hearing, for a half-century, about the drug problem. I remain an advocate for the decriminalization of drugs.

Having proved the future my mother saw in the ashtray wrong by not being the right age, or by obtaining deferments, I had missed the benefits of the G.I. Bill, but managed to put myself through college by working nights. I never had a goal and never really thought about what I wanted to do or to major in. It all sounded good to me, except for sports. Other than having a little fun playing football, basketball, and track, I never cared for sports. I never liked baseball, and the idea that a ball was being hurled at me made me nervous. Besides, I was never a team player. I don't know if my life has been filled with too many ironies, karmas, and anachronisms, but I now live near the Baseball Hall of Fame and witness a cross section of America in the ungainly form of a tourist, which invades this location every summer and stirs in me a pleasing feeling of justified nonconformity and mild unorthodoxy—a poem in making.

I followed politics and became more cynical while some of my friends in college became scholars; there was an interest in politics then on campuses that may have helped usher in the turmoil of the sixties. I got to see JFK when he came to speak in Nixon's conservative stronghold. I thought he was somewhat of an upper-class brat, but I became hooked on his mystique. Tears came to my eyes when I saw him and Jackie visit the poor Mexican households which exhibited his picture beside the crucifix and a saint or two on their mantels. Besides, the country was finally being led by a swinger.

I was busy dulling my senses and having an orgy of whatever I wanted. I found a book by Kenneth Patchen in the university library that contained the axiom: "Hurrah for Anything!" I would stay in my room all day listening to classical albums and rarely attending classes. When I did attend a geology class one day, I happened to be seated alphabetically next to Roxie Powell, who was to become a lifelong friend. It was one of the rare times he attended class, too. His father had been a Methodist minister in Ulysses, Kansas, and had known my father. Roxie was distinguished at that time for having more hours of "F" than anyone who had ever attended the university. He was able to confound the administration just enough to keep himself enrolled, and though he carried a heavy course load every semester, his immediate interests prevented him from attending classes. He could usually be found on one of the library floors going through all the books on whatever subject he was into that day. When he wasn't on that floor he could probably be seen helping Professor Walpole off of the floor at a local bar. His manic activities and verbal hyperboles gave him a life-style that could hardly be matched by the movies. He wrote some of the most original poetry I had ever read, and I used it as a milestone to my own efforts. Roxie Powell was writing the poems for *Dreams of Straw*, which Dave Haselwood and I later published in San Francisco.

The Sixties and Psychic Cataclysms

I made many more trips back and forth from Kansas to California in the late fifties and by the early sixties had begun to acquaint myself with artists from Wichita who had gone to San Francisco: Bruce Conner, Michael McClure, and Dave Haselwood, who would later publish a fine edition of my first book of poems, *Apocalypse Rose*.

I had friends in Southern California as well, and liked Venice, where I stayed with the artist Larry Albright, who introduced me to the Beat aficionado Eric Nord and the infamous degenerate poet Taylor Mead. I thought Taylor was one of the best poets of that generation, and I would see him again in the eighties when we read at a new bar in Baltimore. Larry was then working on some of his fantasy metal sculptures that incorporated electronics. He was later to be credited for the special effects in the movie *Close Encounters of the Third Kind*. I felt at home in the Los Angeles area, having lived in Southern California as a

child and later in my teens. I had cruised Central Avenue in the early fifties, picking up vibes from the great jazz spots. I had also cruised Van Nuys and Hollywood Boulevards during the "drive-in carhop era" when I owned a classic hot rod, a chopped and channeled '34 Ford coupe which would be priced at over twenty thousand dollars today. During the fifties there was always work if one wanted it, and things didn't cost much, so there was usually enough money with gas at fifteen cents a gallon to go anywhere.

Before one of my many departures from Wichita, I hung around with a couple of friends who were in theater at the university. Brad Hammond's aunt was one of the English teachers I was in love with. I would go over to Brad's apartment to drink and talk. The decor was different. No bullfighting posters or art nouveau. It was all fishnets and Hollywood. His roommate, Dean Hargrove, who would become the writer and producer of television fame, was also getting ready to leave for Hollywood after graduation. Brad Hammond, his girlfriend and later his wife, Celeste (a folk singer), and I were to drive out later. I settled in San Francisco about the time my oldest sister arrived to get off the road for a while. I found, through friends, a little room (pad) in a very nice and quaint Russian neighborhood on Ashbury Street off Haight Street; the neighborhood was later to be trashed. This was in the early sixties, and there seemed to be something stirring, but no one knew to what proportions it would grow. Sausalito intellectuals like Alan Watts and Hayakawa, who had tempered the earlier "San Francisco Renaissance" poetry scene, would be caught by surprise. By the time they awakened, the sixties were in turmoil. I was at San Francisco State College during its unrest, when Hayakawa behaved irrationally, grabbed the microphone, and "fired" Kay Boyle. Reagan was watching Hayakawa's debut into the conservative party.

By early 1963 we began to remark how there seemed to be more "heads" on the street, and each day they seemed to be a little more outrageous. We were dancing wildly to Ray Charles while those heads were blooming into "hippies." Good Mexican marijuana was as plentiful as beer and a lot more fun and less expensive. It seemed that I and my friends at various times lived in pads all over the city, but at this time we had concentrated on the "Haight." Alan Russo had kept in touch with Glen Todd, whom I had last seen in Wichita when I went next door to his house as he was getting ready to go see an Elvis performance. Glen Todd became the master party-goer and chronicler of the scene.

At his pad (which was later to be called "end pad") everyone was holding hands and beaming smiles, or looking at their faces in the mirror. I was asked if I wanted to take a trip. There were two kinds of lysergic acid available: one was the Owsley acid on a bluish vitamin pill, and the other was in a glass vial and could be ordered from Sandoz Laboratories for experimental purposes. As my consciousness was being expanded beyond anything I had read about hallucinogens, I put on Haydn's "Ode to Saint Cecilia" and began making up words to it. I entered those worlds that had been described by researchers I had read. Fortunately, I was with people who saw these experiences as discoveries that would enhance our knowledge of reality; they didn't treat the experience lightly. Soon we added to our chemical cabinet pure mescaline from Light Laboratories in England. Some prominent doctors became interested in the creative and experimental atmosphere.

A psychiatrist had bought a famous avant-garde gallery on Fillmore Street named "Batman Gallery" by its founder, Billy Jharmark. It became a space for artists such as Bruce Conner, who had come from Mexico with a suitcase full of marbles to exhibit; poets Michael McClure, Philip Lamantia, Robert Duncan, and their publisher, Auerhahn Press's Dave Haselwood. Glen Todd was the seminal historian and later became a printer for Andrew Hoyem, who had disbanded Auerhahn, which specialized in fine editions of living poets, and founded Grabhorn-Hoyem, which published expensive fine editions of dead poets.

I was working on collages and experimenting with images on emulsion screens that when laid over a photo created an hallucinogenic effect. I put together a show of my collages for the Batman Gallery. Most of them were sold, and the show was reviewed favorably in *Art in America*. Bruce Conner was working in film, and my friend from the early jazz-club days in Wichita, Bob Branaman, was also working in film and had discovered another filmmaker from Kansas, Stan Brakhage. I had been inspired by their films and made two films of my own, which were shown at the Ann Arbor Film Festival. They were later archived at the New York Filmmaker's Co-op.

The San Francisco scene kept growing, and I kept trying to move away from it, but it was everywhere. I blended in sometimes, but being from an earlier generation, I was content to remain invisible. Though I attended concerts and parties that identified the hippies, I didn't take on the trappings. The earlier Bohemians and artists who had migrated to San Francisco were mostly educated, or at least had

some basis of reference for history and culture. These newcomers seemed uneducated, innocent of worldly experience, and not aggressive enough for a competitive society ". . . whose action was no stronger than a flower," so they quickly became both prey and predator of the street. When their numbers increased rapidly, they created culture as instant as a chemical sprayed on a pill.

The *Oracle* was their newspaper. Having little culture of their own like many who embark anew, they sought religious orientation, especially Eastern mysticism, and were ripe for new cults and the many budding self-awareness organizations. Others were victimized, put in institutions, or disconnected entirely from the mainstream or even a subculture society. In front of City Lights Bookstore in North Beach, an established artist who had spent his years in the coffeehouses playing chess and listening to the folk singers asked me, "Hey Man, which way is the Haight Ashbury?" I made use of some of the anachronisms and the new mysticism in my writing at the time.

There were a lot of things coming together by 1963. It was like some great cosmic charge opened and sent ripples through every level of changes; as if the *I Ching* had been shuffled. I rented a house with Glen Todd and Justin Hein, a painter from Kansas. The house had been used as a meth factory, and before we had moved in, it was rented to a new wave of youths from Wichita who had by then immersed themselves somewhere in the Haight. I didn't know it at the time, but Ginsberg had lived at this address with the painter Robert LaVigne. Diane DiPrima had been there years before to gather material for her magazine *The Floating Bear*. She will visit the Gough Street flat again in the city of floating scenes.

During the summer of 1963, at the infamous 1403 Gough Street residence, a blast was in the works. It was an address well known to the Auerhahn regulars: Dave Haselwood, who would move his Auerhahn Press soirees to that address and entertain a steady stream of poets; Jonathan Williams and others from the Black Mountain school; McClure and the San Francisco Renaissance; Ed Sanders, another Kansan, who migrated to New York's Lower East Side and started the Fugs. He performed across the street at the Avalon Ballroom.

The Hollywood "alchemists," whose strong image collages and film montages mixed the word medium, also came to Gough Street and contributed to the scene: the publisher Wallace Berman and the actor Dean Stockwell. Dennis Hopper and Dean Stockwell sent collages and drawings to be included in an underground magazine I was printing at that time called *Now*. Later, when I lived in Hollywood with Brad and Celeste Hammond and had no money, Dean's hospitality allowed me to explore the scene. There was some common ground in Hollywood, Barney's Beanery, where I wrote some "pop" poetry.

History in the making was the feeling at the Gough Street party in San Francisco that night. Parties were open affairs and strange people always showed up. It was like a cosmic gene pool, a *Star Wars* rehearsal, an archetypal convention with hidden messages and timeless meanings that manifested themselves with a look, a dance, a conversation; where everyone communicated on multiple levels, as if Carl Jung had met pop culture, where group consciousness was saturated with lysergic acid. It was as if enormous cosmic forces were coming together and the weave and warp of time was overlaying itself in a history that I suspect a keen Herodotus meditating on Mount Tamalpais (Marin County) might have enjoyed. Even the tile inlay on the stoop resembled a superimposed swastika over a Star of David. Or were things really that significant? When I answered the doorbell, a group was on the stairs. Allen Ginsberg, who had just returned from India, entered. Behind him: Lawrence Ferlinghetti, Michael McClure, Philip Whalen, Lew Welch, and a host of other luminaries. The songs and dancing grew wilder, and a crazed poet, Dave Moe, started flipping out, dancing wildly, in a tantrum, for the famous guests.

After a while Ginsberg introduced himself and said to me something that sounded rather cryptic, like, "I guess you're the one I'm supposed to meet." And I said, "I guess you're the saint," and he said, "No, I don't want to be," or something to that effect. I tried to make small talk with Ferlinghetti and told him he reminded me of someone a master painted. He looked puzzled and never said much. Within a few days, Ginsberg took me to Ferlinghetti's house on Portero Hill. Ginsberg said he had come to San Francisco to help his old lover, Neal Cassady, write his novel and was looking for a place to stay. I said I had this seven-room flat for a hundred bucks a month that we could share.

I had met Neal once when he had dropped by Maureen Kegwin's flat in North Beach where I'd been staying. Allen said Neal would be bringing his things to move in. A '39 Pontiac pulled into the driveway and jerked to a halt. I learned later that a brake line was damaged and Neal drove it that way, gearing it down as far as possible, then pulling on the emergency brake. It was in that car we went on a white-knuckled ride down the coastal mountain road to Bolinas with Neal driving and pulling the emergen-

Philip Whalen, Charles Plymell, Allen Ginsberg, and Lawrence Ferlinghetti, San Francisco, 1963

cy brake to slow down while physically fighting with his girlfriend, Ann. Allen and I were being tossed around in a backseat like a couple of Marx Brothers' extras.

At Gough Street, Neal unpacked three or four cardboard boxes with his belongings spilling out of them. He moved much faster than a normal person and left his girlfriend, Ann, standing in a daze. His last parcels were a grocery sack and a shoe box full of marijuana which he tucked under one arm while putting his other arm around Ann to carry her up the stairs. I later characterized them in a poem as Popeye and Olive Oyl and began making collages-notes of scenes that would go into my book *The Last of the Moccasins*.

From then on there was a steady stream of writers, artists, and media people coming to Gough Street. I got caught up in the excitement of history as the moment which seemed to follow Ginsberg. I saw how busy he kept himself and to what ends he would go to be as much a part of it as possible. He told me he had once worked as a market analyst, and I saw how those skills paid off. I tried to become as analytical and sensible about poetry and its audience as he was. He was not only a tireless promoter, he worked generously as an agent for those poets he liked. He showed Ferlinghetti a draft of my poem "Apocalypse Rose," which he published in the next issue of *City Lights Journal*. I began to publish poems in *Poetry* and *Evergreen Review*; the latter illustrated two of my longer poems and paid me over three hundred dollars each for them. The publishing of poetry was changing too. With the growth and funding becoming available for small publications, the event of being published was no longer as important, but payment for poetry was to become almost nonexistent.

Underground publications were becoming more concerned with political movements and new-age thought, even the poetry had common themes. The psychedelic generation in San Francisco was at full tilt by the time Timothy Leary showed up at Gough Street. For the first time I saw what too much acid could do to a person. People were flocking to hear him speak. I thought he was superficial and academic but quickly able to capitalize on slogans and strategies of the happenings. I began to see signs that consciousness expansion could also shrink people into their own idiocies and immobility, especially in the face of ordinary courtesies and civilities. I took more mescaline and LSD no matter how much it felt like I was being pulled through myself, and, like the flower children, used weed as the daily mental food. The Grateful Dead were acting childish, walking down Ashbury Street scaring the aged Ukrainian immigrants. A couple of young entrepreneurs from Reno set up the first head shop on Haight Street. Things would never be the same. The rallying cry became "revolushun" and the hype was "underground" but the reality was more like a rash, an inflammation on the societal body, and the co-optive power of capitalistic enterprise would absorb it all. But these were heightened times. Oracular. A myth wafted again through the orbs of history to defray the mechanization of the soul. Where was Joseph Campbell? I saw it as:

The Great Goddess Moon, inviolate and pure, reflecting the untouched love for millenniums shown through the cold November sky. The King of the most powerful land was preparing his reign of peace, justice, freedom and equality, but there were problems. His armies were engaged in conflict they could not get out of and he was enamored by the spell of the sex goddess. In order to give the people something to get

their minds off the conflict, like the ancient Lydians who invented dice and ball games to alleviate the misery of a national famine, playing and eating on alternate days (or to perhaps impress the sex goddess); the young King had a plan. He promised her the Moon. There was a tremor through space and the Great Moon Goddess put a curse on the sex goddess that she take her own life and that the King be assassinated and the event so obscured that the truth can never be known by the sorrowful queen and her people.

I was sitting in the front room at Gough Street when Neal Cassady burst through the front door followed by John Bryan from the *Los Angeles Free Press*. "Turn on the TV, Charley, Kennedy's been shot!" As we watched the story unfold, Neal and I looked at each other and said that Oswald was a patsy. Ginsberg wrote a poem about the assassination in his typical style of recording insignificant details that detailed a larger historical moment. He mentioned in that poem, "Charley's underwear strewn bedroom." Underwear could be an important detail in the lives of poets in that it might reflect the poet's rearing. His mother had probably trained him to pick up his clothes off the floor, but I had little training in such matters, so I reasoned that since I didn't have housekeeping utensils, I could use my soiled laundry to keep the floor dusted. I never liked the idea of my mattress on the floor anyway, and was concerned about dirt being tracked in. Ginsberg was the traditional and better housekeeper, though most of those chores were Peter Orlovsky's obsessions. If fifties swaggered, the sixties asked: "What is this, anyway?"

Frank Lockhart had been attending Alcoholics Anonymous meetings in some of the old buildings that were relics from the Barbary Coast. He was on the seniority list at the union and came to Gough Street until he got on his feet. Everybody loved and respected old Frank, who helped prepare the Thanksgiving dinner that November in 1963, which fed some of us mentioned in the poem Allen Ginsberg was writing about Kennedy: Glen Todd, Justin Hein, Maggie Harms, Robert LaVigne, Neal Cassady, Anne Murphy, and many more at Gough Street that Thanksgiving Day. And there was always an invitation to a stranger from off the street. I include them in my book *The Last of the Moccasins*.

Neal took me to his godfather's place in the Japanese section of town. Gavin Arthur was a "seer" who was Neal's mentor, guide, and the closest thing to a father Neal had known. The nation was recovering from that November; and Gavin, the grandnephew of President Chester Arthur, mentioned that Herb Caen had quoted him that morning in the *Chronicle* as saying, ". . . My friends were appalled when I had told them I had voted for Nixon, but I knew whoever was in office during this term was to be assassinated." The country was still shaky and President Johnson was keeping its attention on the Vietnam War. Neal was wanting to travel and said we should go to Wichita or somewhere, but Kesey suggested the famous Hell's Angel party in Palo Alto that resulted in a bust.

My collage exhibit at the Batman Gallery was on a night of the Goldwater convention. Neal had gone to the convention and showed up later at the gallery wearing a Goldwater (whom I thought he resembled) button, a little straw hat, and sporting a red, white, and blue cane. There was still plenty of excitement brewing. So much, I felt like Neal did about his writing duties. Who wanted to spend time on it? The more dutiful poets like Phil Whalen and Michael McClure would be gentle guides. I was reminded that if I wanted to be a poet, I had to write. Ginsberg was even more dutiful, while grabbing the moment. He recorded what I thought was the most insignificant detail. As we rode down to the Monterey Jazz Festival on my motorcycle, he chanted all the way (probably out of fear). We began making verse out of the signs in shops, what we saw people doing, painting with the spontaneity of life as Kerouac had taught him. It was indeed a splendid trip, which I thought had roots in progressive jazz scat. Ginsberg talked about *Howl* and drugs with Thelonious Monk, who seemed to regard conversation as an anchor to his mind, the occasional word grounding the vast cosmic charge his mind seemed to produce. On the way back to San Francisco, Allen and I stopped by Kenneth Patchen's house, but he was too ill to see us.

Karen Wright, a friend from Wichita who was later to return to Lawrence when I moved there, came by Gough Street with a new album she said I must hear. I liked it. It reminded me of Woody Guthrie. It was Bob Dylan's first album, and I asked her if I could borrow it to play for Ginsberg when he came home; he didn't have anything to say about it. We never talked music, except for a reference or two about Bessie Smith and Lester Young. Later, when all I heard was slightly nostalgic adolescent whine turned cynical, Allen was raving nothing but Dylan. Poets of the fifties began to realize how much music was going to influence pop culture. The Beatles arrived and

reacquainted a new generation of Americans with its music roots.

Peter Orlovsky had an old chartreuse Ford convertible, which we all packed in to go to an organized peace gathering at Joan Baez's ranch. I wrote a poem that included in it the actions of Peter's brother, Julius. We were introduced politely by Ginsberg, and Joan Baez was quick to label us as his "entourage," which annoyed me, but was a useful cliche to precede "groupies." My father was a fan of hers, so I wanted a closer look. From then on, the meeting became a comedy of errors. Julius accidentally broke one of Baez's windows, for which Allen dutifully paid. I was drinking too much and had to vomit, but when I went to her sink of hammered copper, I felt ashamed and ran outdoors regurgitating. She had organized a walk, but I didn't go, saying I would get my shiny black boots dusty. She served sandwiches (at a charge of sixty-five cents), and then decreed that we all had to sit for thirty minutes without speaking. I asked her to move her Jaguar, which was blocking Orlovsky's Ford, so I could hop a bus to the Tenderloin. Peter drove me to the Greyhound station, where I began a poem. I learned a new phrase from her, "that's my bag"; I later wrote "my bag" all over a collage I made using a picture of a model with two hand grenades and a bayonet. It later appeared in some underground magazines in England and France. When I arrived at the Tenderloin, I sat with the crazies in the lobby waiting for Frank and Betty and wrote some poetry, "above the ghettoes of clamoring style."

At Lawrence Ferlinghetti's suggestion Mary Beach and Claude Pelieu, with Mary's daughter, Pamela, came to San Francisco. Mary was the distant cousin of Sylvia Beach, who had helped foster the American expatriates and writers of the Lost Generation. Mary and Claude had come to visit Allen Ginsberg at the Gough Street address, where I was introduced to them. Mary's daughter, Pamela, was underage at the time, but I took her to Mike's Pool Hall in North Beach, where Ferlinghetti and other Beats hung out and wrote poetry. At that time, it had not gone chichi, as everything thereafter was quick to do; it still had the best salami sandwich and minestrone available, served on tables covered with slightly soiled red and white checkered tablecloths. A dime in the jukebox would turn a 45 RPM record of Caruso singing arias while old Italian men would sit and study the billiard games.

After a time, the pictures on the television returned to the Vietnam carnage, and I wrote poetry and made collages that reflected the sadistic actions of forcing a will upon a people. I saw LBJ at a North Beach rally and believed he might have had more immediate reasons to keep the war going. It helped draw the people's attention away from the possible chaos that might result from the question of who killed Kennedy. The antiwar movement was growing. I would sometimes drop by the Peace and Freedom party and the Black Panther party headquarters to test my skills in rhetoric by picking out which leaflets were actually authored by CIA or FBI operatives.

I admired the Black Panthers, who were ready to lay down their lives at the State House in Sacramento. Watts was burning. I could no longer walk safely to the Batman Gallery on Fillmore Street. I was attacked while going to the Fillmore Ballroom to see Lenny Bruce. Not because of fear, but a general malaise, and so many things to attend, I did not make the effort to hear Janis Joplin and the Grateful Dead though I had complimentary tickets. On another night, at Dave Haselwood's suggestion, I didn't walk to a nearby club to hear a new group called the Jefferson Airplane. Such was the malaise of EVERYTHING.

The art of this generation was psychedelic posters, and the music was psychedelic rock, which was beginning to use the mixed media to simulate a psychedelic world, and amplification to convey its vibratory message. I attended some of the multimedia concerts, but there were two performances I attended that were anachronistic. One was a Chuck Berry concert in the auditorium at Berkeley, which drew only a handful of people, the other was at the Avalon Ballroom, which usually had a full house. About thirty kids turned out to hear an "unknown" Bo Diddley, who began by saying something like, "Mercy . . . here I am now playing for you." He sounded as if he were slighted, and I felt too old for the crowd. I turned toward the avant of Burroughs and Pelieu.

By 1964 a new generation had arrived in San Francisco and made City Lights their rendezvous. Claude Pelieu, a young Frenchman with a thorough understanding of surrealism, had arrived with Mary Beach, the distant cousin of Joyce's publisher . . . and Charles Plymell, a jazzy poet from Kansas, onetime editor of *Now*, who did sadistic collages. The two *Bulletins from Nothing* and *Grist* from Wichita give the prevailing mood. . . . Funk in San Francisco, rather different from Ed Sanders's blithe scatology and the total sexual gluttony of Tangier, has at least something to do with the tough spirit that Kansas gave to the West Coast. (Jeff Nuttall, *Bomb Culture* [New York: Delacorte Press, 1968], 194.)

Dave Haselwood published my first book of poems, *Apocalypse Rose*. I was publishing magazines such as *Now* and a newspaper tabloid called *The Last Times*, which, like the *Oracle,* was meant to make money by being hawked on the street. There were only two issues, and one contained some drawings of a new cartoonist, Robert Crumb. I remember Ginsberg's quip upon hearing for the first time about the "Haight-Ashbury" while recording his impressions on his new tape recorder that Dylan had given him. He said it might get back to John Ashbery in New York that a hate movement about him was starting on the West Coast.

The influential literary work of enough magnitude to penetrate the expanded mind of the intellectual or the fool, the doctor or the paranoid, as well as be able to reveal national and international madness and a cosmic warp, was *Naked Lunch*. If this cosmic trip was too heavy, there were softer works that seemed to catch the cosmetic. I sat with Richard Brautigan in some of the new head shops and discussed the scene. He had a sense of what the new generation liked to hear. I took some of his poems to publish in an issue of *Now* magazine. Burroughs had sent me a cutup of an article I had sent him which he used to illustrate his method.

Bored with the scene, I asked Ferlinghetti if he wanted to go see Neal on his bus, but he was content to stay at Mike's Pool Hall and write another poem about the Vietnam War. I was happy to visit Neal, who was driving his expressed bus, "Further," to keep the scene new. He introduced me to Tom Wolfe, who with Kesey and the Merry Pranksters was to set out on new adventures. That was the last time I saw Neal. I recall the lines from Burroughs: "The Frisco Kid, he never returned."

Ginsberg had purchased a van with a grant that would enable him to ride across America while Peter Orlovsky drove. We were leaving from City Lights Bookstore in North Beach when I saw Pamela and asked her to go with us. The Haight-Ashbury scene was growing larger in numbers, which, to me, was about the only thing left of interest about it. I had published three issues of *Now* magazine that included drawings by Branaman, some cut-up prose by Burroughs, poetry by Ginsberg, McClure, Whalen, Russo, Richard White, et al. Richard White had been a pianist/poet in Wichita who came to San Francisco with yet another new wave of people who were

With Neal Cassady, Gough Street, San Francisco, 1963

making films, writing poetry, making the scene. In this contingent were friends of the Tulsa group who had migrated to the Lower East Side to start the poetry scene at Saint Mark's Church. Maureen Owen, who published two of my chapbooks, *Over the Stage of Kansas* and *Blue Orchid Numero Uno*, while at Saint Mark's-in-the-Bouwerie, was part of this group that spent time in the Haight before going to the Lower East Side.

Pam and I travelled to Wichita. I broke my ankle on a skateboard and she continued on to New York. Ginsberg and Orlovsky wanted to visit the "vortex," and while in Wichita gave a reading that brought out the Wichita police. They had been called (of course) because of the obscene poetry. The reading was interrupted and turned into a grass-roots happening. Some John Birch members were in the audience and, though disgusted with the filthy language, supported the poetry as the right of free speech. The cops didn't know quite what to do, so they "got on the two-way radio" to the chief of police. Allen asked to talk to him and began a rather involved dialogue as only Allen can—over the police radio. He mentioned that Barry Farrell from *Life* magazine was coming to do a

story about him. Over the radio, the chief instructed the cops not to interfere, saying, "Well, they're doing this all over the country."

I took Allen Ginsberg to meet my mother; we picked her up after work at the factory. We ate at a Chinese restaurant where the waitress asked him for his autograph, having seen his picture in the paper. He asked if there were any poets at the university, so we went to Bruce Cutler's house for a visit. He shut the door in our faces and said we'd have to make an appointment to see him during his office hours. The people in charge at the English department were reluctant to sponsor Ginsberg, even for free. The friend who had visited the draft board with me was now teaching philosophy, so he arranged a place for poetry to be read. We also read at Moody's Skid Row Beanery, a flophouse and beanery which was a personal Goodwill Industries complete with ice-cream wagons if you wanted to earn your beans. The proprietor, whom I suspect was an old Wobbly, became notorious in showing underground films that the police couldn't figure out. The only "art" movies they knew about were the porno flicks down the block. I showed Ginsberg and Orlovsky some of the seedy hotels and bars in the old part of Wichita. The photographer and filmmaker Robert Frank had flown out from New York to visit. By dawn we were ready for great breakfasts at the ancient Hotel Eaton, where Robert filmed the giant portrait of Carry Nation. Wichita's skid row had a long history on the frontier, but compared to larger cities wasn't that bad. I've written many poems around it; one of my latest is a recollection of "Sam Shusterman, the shoe store man."

I went with Ginsberg and Orlovsky to Nebraska, where they read at the university and later visited Karl Shapiro, who remarked that he couldn't understand why Bruce Cutler (his student) had treated us so oddly. It was my first encounter with an academic poet. During the trip, Allen recorded on his tape machine the Kansas landscape of his "Vortex Sutra" poem. He had asked me earlier to edit his long "TV Baby" manuscript, from which I had thrown out whole pages. I wanted to know how his current impressions-turned-expressions could become important poetry. He sometimes asked me for localisms of the Kansas landscape. We then travelled to Kansas City, where Barry Farrell joined us to work on his Ginsberg article for *Life* magazine. I watched the power of publicity.

After Pam returned to Wichita, we went to Lawrence, Kansas, where we met the curator of the special-collections archives at the University of Kansas, Terence Williams. I got a job at the Van Camp Pork and Bean factory in Lawrence, and later wrote about the experience in my book *The Last of the Moccasins.* I hung out at the Rockchalk Cafe and, in the company of Ken Irby, edited and printed another issue of Gene Fowler's *Grist* magazine. Through Gary Brown, a friend of LePell's from his university days, I met S. Clay Wilson, the cartoonist, with whom he was sharing a house surrounded by ''hogs'' and various Harley-Davidson parts. S. Clay gave me some drawings for *Grist* as well as his earliest portfolios of the ''Checkered Demon.'' While in Gene Fowler's bookstore, I saw a lad browsing through the underground publications and asked him if he had read any of Burroughs' work. I gave him some publications I had printed, which contained some work Burroughs had sent, and said he might like them. He introduced himself as James Grauerholz, and, when he became old enough to leave home, he set out for New York and a new life-style which was highlighted in Burroughs' biography *The Literary Outlaw.* Many years later, he returned to Lawrence with Burroughs, where they currently reside.

I had bought a '50 Plymouth in Hollywood and drove to Big Sur to stay at Branaman's place for a while before returning to San Francisco. While Pamela and I were baby-sitting Richard White's puppy, we decided to get married. We packed the car complete with the puppy and went to Reno, Nevada, and, leaving the roulette wheel for a few moments, stood in line to get married. When we returned to San Francisco, the flower children were doing their pseudopastoral, the beginnings of be-ins in Golden Gate Park. There was a party at Bolinas welcoming Gary Snyder's return from Japan. I felt put off by his piety and the tainted abalone that had been picked, and in the bathroom wrote a ''serious parody'' of an Oriental soul poem:

> An ant climbing up
> the toilet bowl
> slipping all the way
>
> I will give him a raft
> An ant floating
> on the tissue paper

Charles Plymell, James Grauerholz, William Burroughs, and John Giorno,
Cherry Valley, New York, 1975

The Bolinas party was to produce a haunting image for me. I saw for the first time a beautiful child, a girl with innocent blue eyes, who was reportedly mine. She lived with her mother, Maureen Kegwin, and was generously taken care of by Bobbie Creeley, Joanne Kyger, and other kind folk at Bolinas. Due to personal problems that evolved, I was to see her but one other time.

There was a strong international little-magazine scene going on then which had a boost from Claude Pelieu. Doug Blazek had moved to San Francisco, and through him I met Brown Miller and Seaborn Jones. Blazek was publishing poets Charles Bukowski, Harold Norse, Marcus J. Grapes, Opal L. Nations, and other names in the underground magazine scene. Carl Weissner was the German correspondent who was the force behind the magazine *Klacto* and translator of my work as well as Charles Bukowski's. This scene was to continue into the eighties when Jorg Fauser would write articles on us for *Tip* magazine in Berlin, which did two articles on me. Carl Weissner translated my poetry into German for Pociao of Expanded Media Editions, publisher of one of my books, *Panik in Dodge City,* that appeared in Germany. The issues of *Grist* magazine I edited included many of the international figures in the underground movement.

In the People's Park March, I sensed that the leadership of the intellectual left not only lacked humor and wisdom, but their strategy was obviously naive. The route to the park had been approved and mapped out by the authorities; I took no chances, my country or not, and ran my own test just to see to what extent authority could go. At Berkeley, certain streets were lined with barbed wire, tanks, and armed personnel. Governor Reagan was taking no chances. When I saw the cross streets blocked off at the intersection, I knew that this was not a revolt because it was being played according to the other's rules, but it could very well be lambs to the slaughter.

When I told one of the guardsmen that my wife and I wanted to leave the march, he said we couldn't leave the designated route. I said that my wife was pregnant and we did not want to continue. He said we'd have to go all the way to the end of the route. I glared into his eyes and said the hell we would, and walked past him. That may or may not have been the best thing to do, but on more than one occasion, there were incidents where students were shot for no reason but power. As I write this, I think of the Chinese students. The books of William Reich that Patti had lent me years earlier when I first entered college were not entirely a study in paranoia, but had confirmed my unarticulated childhood observations of growing up in a violent land. Kent State was no surprise to me.

I felt like an outsider when I said what I thought of the organizer's strategy. Again, I felt alienated, too old, neither Left nor Right. I was fond of saying that, at my age, I had learned a couple of things. Neal and I liked to be didactic in a frontiersman kind of way, so I made a mental note that the next time I saw him I would discuss the virtues of knowing when to call someone's bluff, or when to play the fool. I wrote a poem treating these didactics which was published by a rare and beautiful press, Loujon Press, in Arizona, in its magazine, the *Outsider.* Hugh Fox, at the Department of American Language and Thought at the University of Michigan, was to write a critical analysis of my poetry and coin the words "Invisible Generation." It never became famous, and its name implied it should not have.

When we returned to San Francisco, Pam and I rented a flat near the Fillmore Ballroom. It was the time of nude parties and free love, when women's bodies were painted on. The last time I saw Richard

Elliott Coleman and Pamela Plymell, Baltimore, 1970

Brautigan was at such a party. There was a public nude beach south of San Francisco where many of us partied. I would write anecdotes of the time I watched a Mexican, who had walked up the coast from the border, awaken from his sleep of muscatel to rub his eyes in disbelief under the day's sun, which produced a game of volleyball above him, played by naked women.

Robert Crumb, whose comics I had printed in one of the underground publications, had arrived in San Francisco. His apartment was furnished from the street and contained some nice vintage radios. Don Donahue, who was about to become an underground-comic entrepreneur, came by our apartment one day with a sheaf of Crumb's drawings. We had an old Multilith in our bedroom, and we went over some of the technicalities for printing colors that were explained to Crumb. I decided on a format that would fit the Multi, which later became the standard for many comics to follow. With much love and effort we printed the first *Zap* comics of Robert Crumb, which sold for twenty-five cents. I put my name on the back cover as printer. I forget how many copies we managed to get through the machine intact, but there was a gathering party at Crumb's afterwards. I don't think we delivered as many copies as we were supposed to, which made that first adventure in printing become all the more rare. Recently, S. Clay informed me that the "Plymell *Zap*" was listed by collectors in San Francisco at four hundred dollars a copy.

In 1968 Pam and I drove a new Mustang convertible from San Francisco to New York City for a fellow who wanted it put on the boat to Paris. Otis Redding on the radio. I began writing my *Neon Poems* as we left Frisco Bay. Past the wild rose of Utah. The Lower East Side and a flight to Paris which had to land in Belgium because France was under civil law. After a bootleg bus trip from Brussels we arrived in Paris, and I began writing poems about the revolts which seemed to be popping out in every major city in the world. We visited Burroughs in London and of course I wrote a poem about it. Contrary to reports that his line was "don't drop in," he was very nice and cordial. He took us for a drink at a pub on Duke Street.

We returned to New York, where I got a job as a guard on the graveyard shift at MOMA. I guarded all the floors of the museum and a fellow from Jamaica covered the Rockefeller mansion. Actually, neither of us knew much about the job so we drank and played with the electronic surveillance machine. He didn't cover the mansion because he said there was a headless ghost in it. I took strange forays among the objets d'art, alone with them until Gotham's daybreak. I was later to write some "spoof" poetry designed to make the curators gasp about what I did with the paintings and sculptures. After a while, the long journey back to Wichita and San Francisco.

Frank, from Deadwood, South Dakota, had been living with my sister in various skid-row hotels and had begun working on the docks in San Francisco. He got me into the union, and I thought I pretty well had it made. I could earn in a few nights what the average worker earned in a week. I could call in when I didn't want to go to work, and then call in when I did. I thought it was the best job a poet could have, and with my recent publications, I began to consider myself a writer. I carried a longshoreman's hook in my back pocket and was able to live out the Brando movie *On the Waterfront,* where there were Ph.D.'s who hated the academe, ex-cons and druggies, alcoholics, and even a philosopher, Eric Hoffer. Learning psychology, sociology, and politics on the job helped lend insights and emotions to my writing, which would eventually be labeled proletariat.

It was at that time an opportunity from the academe called again. Marc Mendel, a poet from Baltimore, came to visit us and mentioned his mentor, Elliott Coleman. He made Baltimore sound like a place we should live. Afterwards, Nidra Poller, another student of Coleman's, came from Baltimore to help convince us to go there. She later wrote the introduction to my City Lights book.

We packed up cats and belongings and drove across country to Baltimore just in time for me to enroll in Mr. Coleman's class at the prestigious writing seminars. Mr. Coleman had awarded me a fellowship with a stipend. We lived on about two hundred dollars a month and rented an apartment that was home to our newborn daughter, Elizabeth. It proved to be a very exciting year at the seminars, so much so that, at times, Mr. Coleman seemed to pull out all stops to survive the rowdy class that fate had dealt him that year. He was from "the old school," but could rise to any occasion in such a way that no one doubted his credibility. He was always generous to the students and at Thanksgiving brought us a turkey, which we shared with Warren Fine and his family. P. J. O'Rourke added to the rowdiness of the classes, which tried to be as out of control as the parties that ensued. He lived down the block with his beer cans and motorcycle parts spread all over the sidewalk, no doubt gathering humor for his next adventure, *The Harvard Lampoon.*

Josh Norton, who was at the seminars that year, later became one of our publishing family and an inspiration for me to continue writing. We formed a special bond that we needed to help turn the tide of what we saw as an encroaching mediocrity in poetry and art. Though he was crippled since birth and had a tiny body, he had a great strength. When I thought something needed challenging, I would but hint to him, and he would bang his cane on the table until the points would be resolved. The seminars became so animated that we could sense when Mr. Coleman was in need of his evening cocktail and meal at the faculty club or a nearby restaurant, to which he would often invite students. At one seminar meeting, a student jumped on the table and began to dance wildly. Even such professional pranksters as P. J. O'Rourke became meek and docile under Mr. Coleman's mastery. In short, no one could get one up on him. He was a special person who enriched the lives of many of his students. I was especially pleased to have been able to introduce him to my lifelong friend Roxie Powell, who was able to help Mr. Coleman live out his greatness and rage against mediocrity, even meet death with repartee.

My father died in 1969, just before Christmas. We had planned to visit him with our new family. From his shrunken estate, the amount of $5,000 was finally filtered down to me, and by that time I wanted to settle down with my family. Again, my wife, a new daughter, and a cat or two, with our belongings and the cat box, were packed into an old Ford. We lived on the Lower East Side for a while. I remembered the countryside around Cherry Valley, New York, where we had stayed at Allen Ginsberg's place in the nearby hills after having attended Buckley's "Firing Line" television show in the city with him, Sanders, and Kerouac. There were two old stores for sale next to the post office in Cherry Valley that were used by the inventor Samuel Morse to develop his coding machines. I wrote a check for $3,500 and unloaded our belongings. We later sold the buildings to the jazz keyboard artist Paul Bley.

Josh Norton came to stay with us while we pursued Pam's vocation as a publisher. We began to publish many books and magazines under the Cherry Valley Editions imprint. We rented a Xerox machine and in two months produced four issues of the *Coldspring Journal* and seven chapbooks. The seventies were spent publishing, living a back-to-earth lifestyle, and squabbling for grant monies to publish literature. There seemed to be a general decline of exciting literature and a proliferation of what we thought of as unimportant art and poetry. Our

Charles Plymell, Wichita, 1965

publications reflected our thinking and consequently we were not popular among those who were connected with arts monies on the state and federal level. We finally quit applying for funding entirely, which curtailed our literary productions; we later sold the printing equipment and continued publishing on a small scale.

Writers who sold, like William Burroughs, helped the press. He came to Cherry Valley with John Giorno and James Grauerholz to stay a few days. Pam fixed Texas barbecued ribs for them. Giorno assembled my poems for Kulchur Foundation's publication of *Trashing of America*. He got the artist Les Levine to do the cover. I had a publication party at the Gotham Book Mart, and upon seeing the portraits of writers who had formerly occupied that space, felt honored.

Our son, Billy, was born in 1978 on my father's birthday. Financially, things had gotten worse during the recession, and Pam and I couldn't find jobs in what was essentially a rural area. I had parlayed the Samuel Morse building into a nice house and carriage barn on three acres of good land, but the mortgage was due. I had hopes of getting a writing fellowship to keep the house together, but, as always, my application was turned down. I was particularly bitter about it, because it seemed all my friends as well as the combined household of Orlovsky and Ginsberg had gotten one. To me, $12,500 was a staggering sum. More than I could have saved in a lifetime. Just a fraction of it would have saved the day for us, but we had to sell and relocated in Washington, D.C., where we had heard jobs were available. I thought that I at least should sell to an artist who would appreciate the place, and my friend in the city, Crandal Waid, had a painter friend who wanted to get out of the city. We sold him our place for a nominal amount and used the money to pay the astronomical rent in Washington until we could get on our feet.

Before we left Cherry Valley, a representative from Europa Verlag who had just been to California, where he had signed up Christopher Isherwood, visited us, and I signed a contract for the Austrian publication of *The Last of the Moccasins.* He paid City Lights $1,000, which they split with me. I received two copies of a very attractive book, and that was it.

Washington worked out fairly well. My wife began working at *The Wall Street Journal,* and I began teaching part-time. We met many interesting people who could help me find a job. Through them I found all the work I wanted as a part-time English composition instructor, but I soon learned that I was in the wrong profession at the wrong time, at least for the tenure track. The old-boy network of aged Caucasian males in English departments was being purged. I was able to teach in prisons and at some of the many campuses in the area. I had gone to a party at Michael Mooney's house, who had just quit his editorial job at *Harper's* and was writing a book about arts funding in which he quoted me on funding experiences. At his party was the enfant terrible poet of Washington, Eric Baizer, who had skills in writing about the unfairness of literary funding. The Washington papers did an article about it, and I was mentioned in the "Notes on People" section in the *New York Times.* Michael's friend had read that I was in Washington and told another friend, Reed Whittemore, that I was in town. Reed invited me to the University of Maryland president's house for the posthumous birthday party of Katherine Anne Porter. It turned out that I had met Katherine Anne Porter and was able to contribute an anecdote. Reed was on the committee to grant tenure to a program director who hired me to teach part-time upper-level composition courses, though my teaching poetry was out of the question.

Other poets didn't care for our public statements, nor did they like it when Joshua Norton and I staged a reading at a university at which Rod McKuen read my poem "In Memory of My Father." I learned how serious, political, and fragile poets are (especially those in the academe) when it comes to what might be considered a threat to their rank. I used the analogy of a type of rats in the city that squeal, shriek, and attack when a different clan invades their territory. Philosophically, I took the point of view that if my work can survive after I make an effort to offend the establishment and political sycophants, then it might have some substance.

Washington, D.C., became too expensive when the economy was getting better and we decided to return to Cherry Valley. Once again I was with family and cats in a U-Haul truck camped temporarily at Allen Ginsberg's farm. By this time our old solidarities were frayed, and he was concerned that I might not be the best guest for his "Committee on Poetry" farm. I was convinced that since he had supposedly landed $100,000 for his book which mentioned me against my wishes, and since he has more than one domicile, he could have been more helpful. With the payout from Pam's retirement fund from her job in Washington we scratched together enough money to pay down on a house in Cherry Valley and were thus spared the realities of the homeless.

My demeanor, I sense, is as raw as a wind-whipped fence post. As a person from the plains, I have etched into my features what some mild Easterner might construe as violence. I am comfortable with "Zane Grey" talk and have not tried to affect a more sophisticated speech. I spent much time in my youth in a landscape with nothing but wind and space as far as I could see. I lived in extremes, felt the violent power of cyclones' charges next to the quiet of whisper. I became part of the natural etching, uprooted as the tumbleweed. Three of my favorite contemporary writers and mentors also came from the plains states: William Burroughs, Robert Peters, and Loren Eiseley.

Though I had little regard for the time that was ticking away on the white man's analog, I was naive, or not caring, about many other things and was late to learn that there were many people throughout my life who apparently had an aversion to me and my art. Aloof, cool, and mystic, I took on the persona of a gunslinger, riding in and out of towns. I found comfort in the words of Alan Lomax, who sang about the dark night, himself, and his pony . . . a long way from home: ". . . If them people, they don't like me, they can leave me alone." I never learned how to be a good sycophant, which, towards my eventual career, seemed an essential skill for obtaining rewards, or even a good job. I learned that there was no certainty in distinguishing what the serious writer should become, inside or outside the system, and poetry was surely not something in demand.

Out of step with the literati, uneasy with the regional parlor humor of the *New Yorker*'s sophisticates, and at the age of fifty-five, I am a white-bearded old man reading the want ads, seeking jobs, usually part-time, to help support my family, and still finding very little time to write in not a very well-planned career. Even with the earnings of my wife contributing to the income, I still had a lifelong conflict with what I did, opposed to what I should do to earn a good living. This lack of middle-class progress was many times problematical and difficult for me to explain to my children. My life's work was the unemployment line, unskilled labor, or part-time teaching. I would be thankful to my mentor for higher education even if I were unable to parlay that into the security of position and title. I was, however, fortunate enough to meet people who influenced my life and my writing. Tomorrow I have to go to the unemployment office.

BIBLIOGRAPHY

Poetry, except as noted:

(Editor) Roxie Powell, *Dreams of Straw*, privately printed, 1963.

Apocalypse Rose (introduction by Allen Ginsberg), Dave Haselwood Books, 1966.

Neon Poems, Atom Mind Publications, 1970.

The Last of the Moccasins (prose), City Lights, 1971, published in Austria as *Moccasins Ein Beat-Kaleidoskop*, Europaverlag, 1980.

(Contributor) *Mark in Time: Poets and Poetry*, New Glide Publications, 1971.

Over the Stage of Kansas, Telephone Books, 1973.

(Contributor) *And the Roses Race around Her Name*, Stonehill, 1975.

The Trashing of America, Kulchur Foundation, 1975.

Are You a Kid? Cherry Valley Editions, 1977.

Blue Orchid Numero Uno, Telephone Books, 1977.

In Memory of My Father, Cherry Valley Editions, 1977.

(Contributor) *Turpentin on the Rocks*, Maro Verlag (Augsburg, West Germany), 1978.

(Contributor) *A Quois Bon*, Le Soleil Noir (Paris), 1978.

Panik in Dodge City, Expanded Media (Bonn, West Germany), 1981.

(Contributor) *On Turtle's Back: A Biogeographic Anthology of New York*, White Pine, 1983.

(Contributor) *Planet Detroit: Anthology of Urban Poetry*, Planet News, 1983.

(Contributor) *Second Coming Anthology*, Second Coming Press, 1984.

Forever Wider: Poems New and Selected, 1954–1984, Scarecrow, 1985.

(Contributor) *Ebenezer Cooke Poetry Anthology*, St. Mary's College of Maryland, 1987.

Was Poe Afraid? Bogg Publications, 1989.

(Contributor) *World*, Crown Books, 1989.

Contributor to numerous magazines and journals, including publications in Canada, France, Germany, Holland, Mexico, and Switzerland. Guest editor, *Grist* magazine, 1967; contributing editor, *Nola Express*, 1969; editor, *Coldspring Journal*, 1974–78, and *Northeast Rising Sun*, 1976–80.

Tom Raworth

1938-

Tom Raworth at his
Sutter Street, San Francisco, home, 1976

Avondale Road, Welling.

I was born on July 19, 1938, at Bexleyheath on the southeast border of London. My mother, Mary Moore, came from Dublin; my father, Thomas Alfred Raworth, was a Londoner from Hammersmith. Our home was a semidetached redbrick house built in the early 1930s, during a speculative building boom, on what had been apple orchards and fields of raspberries. Two rooms, a kitchen, and a bathroom downstairs; upstairs, two bedrooms, another smaller, and a boxroom. A tiny front garden with a longer one at the back. Lilac and laburnum trees near the dining-

room windows. Honeysuckle and lavender. A patch of grass through which a line of square white paving stones led to five apple-trees (three eaters, two cookers) and a clump of raspberry, loganberry, and gooseberry bushes. Slightly to their left (looking away from the house) was the air-raid shelter. A corrugated-iron Anderson that smelled of wet earth and contained two oblong wooden bunks with flat metal-weave springs, a torch, and a shovel. My first memory, from between eighteen months and two years old, is of sitting on the sloping piece of concrete behind the house, a hot sun, a new wooden horse with red wheels, and me trying to pull off its tail to put onto my old broken one. Feelings of being smaller than the table and how rough khaki cloth was. Of my father going around the corner of the street. I had a toy rifle he'd carved from a plank and painted with chocolate-brown gloss. A summer hot enough to melt the paint into soft bubbles. I pushed them in with my finger sitting on the lump of tree-trunk that kept the kitchen door open. Noises of planes, guns, and bombs. My mother wouldn't have me evacuated to the country-side so, with most children gone, classes at my first school (Saint Stephen's Catholic Primary) were small. I went there when I was four-and-a-half to sit at a long table with Roger Markey. On the alphabet board "b" and "d" were confusing. My sixth birthday was spent in the school shelter (a brick building next to the fuel store) moulding a small mouse from a piece of white candlewax softened in the heat.

My mother was from a large family of Republicans living in a tenement on the North Circular Road. Sean O'Casey rented the room underneath them, and it was from his autobiography I learned part of her history and read the description of my grandmother's funeral. My uncle Liam was arrested trying to tunnel into Mountjoy Jail and imprisoned. My mother was in there too. I discovered only this year, reading O'Connor's biography of O'Casey, that the characters in *Juno and the Paycock* were based on my mother's family. In the mid-1930s she went to London and, through her friend Bridie McGrath, met my father. He had been working since the age of fourteen to support his mother and sister after his father had been crushed to death on the wharf at

Hammersmith. This grandfather, another Thomas, had run away to sea one day when he was thirteen, after throwing an ink-pot at the head of a teacher who had insisted that as our name is pronounced RAY-WORTH he must put a "y" in it. His older brother Will went with him. One went to sail, the other to steam. It was two years before my grandfather got home, and by then he had been around the globe twice. Once swept off the deck by a giant wave while rounding Cape Horn and washed back on board by another. When courting my grandmother in her Suffolk village of Lavenham he had thrown a stone over the church tower, one of the tallest in England. So his Protestant son met a Catholic Irishwoman, converted to Catholicism, married her, and moved to a new working-class suburb. And I could sit in the fork of an apple-tree to watch for Spitfires, Hurricanes, and Doodlebugs.

Sometimes during the bombing we slept under the table near the bookshelves and I would idly scan titles: *Kim* and *Three Lives* and *The Road to En-dor* and the *Seven Pillars of Wisdom* and *Lives of the Pirates* and

"My paternal grandparents around the turn of the century"

wonder about them. Later, after the war, I'd lie awake listening to the trains shunting at the end of the street. Or in autumn and winter to ships' fog-horns from the Thames.

When I was seven my father came home, after India, Burma, and Ceylon, and I enjoyed the hard chocolate and oatcakes from the iron rations in his kit-bag. In 1949 I won a scholarship to grammar school (Saint Joseph's Academy—run by the de la Salle Brothers) and took the 89 bus over Shooter's Hill each day wearing my green blazer, green and gold striped cap, and green, gold, and scarlet tie. My first day there I had a fight with Georgie Grist. Prior to the Education Act the school had been Public (i.e., private), and a boy named Manchester, in one of the upper forms, still rode in on horseback. The only universities that counted were Oxford and Cambridge.

In 1952 I made my first trip to France. A school exchange, with a boy named Emmanuel from Lille. The ferry to Boulogne. A week in Wimereux, on the northern coast. Sand, sun, beach tennis. A girl singing "La Paloma" at night. Then a drive to Paris in his father's black "traction avant" Citroen, a car I've loved ever since. At the Chatelet Theatre we saw *Le Chanteur de Mexique* and the lead singer came onstage riding a white horse. Then up to Lille for some drab days steering mopeds between tram-tracks in the rain. Home a few weeks, my parents sent me over to Ireland for a month to stay with my aunt Annie. She had thirteen children (luckily only eight remained at home) and they lived in a three-roomed thatched cottage some miles north of Dublin. I helped my cousins pick potatoes, fingers worn raw in the sandy earth. Tasted banana ice-cream for the first time. Walked the lanes to Lusk to play handball in the shadow of the round tower. Fought with my cousin Jim by the low stone wall that separated the cottage from the schoolhouse where Thomas Ashe had taught. My cousin Johnny let me hold the steering-wheel of his van as we drove on his milk-round. Then back to school.

I'd started there with enthusiasm and finished, at sixteen, bored. The outside world interested me much more. One morning during my first term in the sixth form I took a train to central London and got a job as a claims clerk in an insurance company. From there to a company booking films, to construction work on a power station, to packing costume jewellery, to a small canned-food importers, to any next thing that came up when I was bored. In late 1955 I was called for my army medical and a hole was found in my heart. This was sewn up the next year and I went to work in the transport department of a drug company. Interspersed in those years were the Festival of Britain, dance-halls, commercial television, modern jazz, Edwardian then Italian suits, long then short haircuts, and a lot of books. For a while I worked nights on the door at Cy Laurie's Jazz Club opposite the Windmill Theatre in Soho and got a taste for salt-beef sandwiches and chopped-liver rolls. One lunchtime at work I met Val in an elevator; we went out a few times, I borrowed eleven shillings and sixpence and a tie from her uncle Morton and we got married. She had been brought up in South Wales by her grandparents, had won a prize by answering every question on radio's "Top of the Form," had been offered a scholarship to the Royal Academy of Dramatic Art that she didn't bother to take up, and you didn't have to slow down to talk to her.

Eton Road, Haverstock Hill, London NW1.

A large ground-floor room with a broken pull-out bed, a table, a couple of chairs. A complaining landlady who forbade children. Val and I were both working. Lloyd was looked after by her aunt in Islington during the week. At weekends we had to smuggle him in and hope he'd be quiet. Long walks up the hill to Hampstead. Running down the spiral staircase at Chalk Farm Underground Station each morning to save waiting for the lift. A separate small kitchen with torn linoleum. A shared bathroom upstairs. Not many memories.

Amhurst Road, Hackney, London E8.

Two basement rooms, a kitchen with a lavatory half-outside. A shared bathroom upstairs. The back room dripping with damp, the wallpaper peeling. We shared the flat first with Val's cousin Carolyn and her husband Nigel. The landlord was a rabbi: Mr. Kon. I began to think of doing a magazine after finding a few writers who interested me: Christopher Logue, Alan Sillitoe here; Ginsberg, Corso, and O'Hara in the U.S. Nigel's father died and his mother moved down from Yorkshire and bought a house in Stoke Newington. We all moved to

Fountayne Road, London N16,

but not for too long. The only advantage was that the house was near the terminal for the 73 bus so we were always sure of a seat to work. After a few weeks little notes began to appear everywhere: "PLEASE DO NOT USE POWDER IN THE BATHROOM," that sort of thing. Val was pregnant, and when one night going downstairs she almost fell over a vacuum cleaner strategically placed on a small landing, it was time to move again. Rabbi Kon, with great kindness, let us move back to

Amhurst Road.

I began to comb the bookstores in Charing Cross Road for magazines, and in a copy of *Between Worlds* I read some poems I liked by an Edward Dorn. His address was in the contributors' notes, I wrote to him, he replied at the end of 1960, and for some years we corresponded two or three times a week. In a small magazine from the midlands, *Satis*, I found poems I liked by Anselm Hollo. I wrote to him care of the editor and we met outside his flat near Regent's Park one evening in January 1961. Val was in hospital having Lisa. Through Dorn I was soon in touch with Creeley, Dawson, Snyder, LeRoi Jones, Olson, and other Americans, and through Anselm I met Piero Heliczer and David Ball. Plans for a magazine rumbled on. I had to do it as cheaply as possible, so when Val's stepfather gave us a belated wedding-present of one hundred pounds I bought a small treadle letter-

With parents, Thomas Alfred and Mary Moore Raworth, 1938

"Edward Dorn, around the time we started to correspond"

press machine, some type, borrowed some books on printing from the library and taught myself how to set type and print. Christopher Logue had introduced the idea of poetry and jazz in England on his recording "Red Bird Dancing on Ivory" with the Tony Kinsey Trio. Michael Horovitz, Pete Brown, Spike Hawkins, Bob Cobbing, Libby Houston, and others were giving readings, sometimes with musicians like Dick Heckstall-Smith and Graham Bond. There was Michael's magazine *New Departures* (the first issue of which I'd bought in the French Café in Old Compton Street some months before, on the way to work at Cy Laurie's). Another called *Sidewalk* from Edinburgh. Steve Fletcher, a photographer friend, had a brother Sid, an engraver who shared a loft in Soho with a letterpress printer, Richard Moore. He let me move my press there and in exchange for his using it for small jobs, I was able to print the magazine and store paper. I made two wooden frames, each the size of a page of type, with loose tops and bottoms of hardboard. Each night I'd set two pages (after distributing the type from the day before) into these boxes, tie them with string, take them into work with me, walk down Tottenham Court road in the evening to the loft, and print. To save time I'd use whatever colour ink was still on the press. We were always poor, and for a time Val's brother John

moved in with us to share the rent, sleeping in the back room with Lloyd and Lisa. There were the usual events. Mr. Goldman in the flat above left the bath running and flooded us out. One evening when our friend Ken Lansdowne was over John got into an argument with another neighbour and Ken and I had to dance around the street at midnight trying to hold John back and avoid the neighbour's breadknife. People slept on the floor in sleeping bags. Sid was a black-powder fan, and through him I got interested in guns for a while. We went down to Bisley to shoot. All this time I was working in the drug company in Euston Road, down in the basement. Ken worked with me for a while. He'd been in the navy at Suez, overseeing the troop landing. The cocky army major he'd bawled out on the dockside turned out to be our boss. For some months we were completely forgotten. No work to do, our pay envelopes delivered every Friday. We'd draw, type stories, make paper aeroplanes. One Friday two workmen appeared and began to brick up the doorway of our room. We were rediscovered and, typically, promoted. When the Fascists started meetings again in Ridley Road, John and I were there throwing oranges. Eventually 750 copies of the magazine were printed, collated, and stapled. Val took them around to bookshops in a carrier bag and, although some complained "we only stock REAL poetry," they all went. As did we to

Temple Fortune, Finchley.

The first floor, over a pub. Four rooms, a kitchen and bathroom, but in bad repair. Still, it was near the Panzer Delicatessen and not far from Hampstead Heath.

David Ball had stayed with us briefly in Amhurst Road on his way up to the Edinburgh Festival. He was taking his doctorate at the Sorbonne, and in August 1963 I visited him in Paris for a few days. A minute garret room on the sixth floor with a sloping roof that made it impossible to stand upright. A cold-water tap on the landing. Piero was living in equally bad conditions: a room in a hotel on the Place de la Contrescarpe one wall of which had almost completely fallen into the street. But he had a tiny printshop on the Rue Descartes where he had handset his *Pulp Magazine for the Dead Generation*. Out at the University City I met a friend of David's, Joseph "Pepo" Angel. A Jew from Cairo, he had no papers, only a Nansen Passport. He was married to Anya, one of three Finnish sisters. Another later lived for a while with Piero. The third with the Finnish writer Pentii Saarikoski. Pepo had a doctorate in chemistry, and was going to Cambodia for two years to teach. Back in Paris later he became a photographer and filmmaker, doing construction work in between jobs.

We managed to paint two rooms and the kitchen. In the smaller painted room I delivered Ben one icy February night in 1964. The midwife wasn't able to get there in time through the snow. To keep him warm the two-bar electric fire was on twenty-four hours a day. Just after we'd moved in, Jonathan Williams and Ronald Johnson arrived in the country. For four weeks, with great good humour, they slept on the floor, a cold wind cutting through the rusted metal windowframes. Then they moved on to luxury in Well Walk, Hampstead. I remember a party there for Burroughs when he would only talk to John, to the chagrin of a university type in full evening dress. Irritated, Burroughs spilled a drink on him then slowly and considerately wiped down his lapels with the snottiest handkerchief I'd ever seen. It was at a reading Jonathan and Ronald gave that Val and I were introduced to Barry and Jackie Hall. They'd been to California on some sort of painters' grant for a year and Barry was back working as a process

engraver. We got on instantly, and in 1965 started the Goliard Press together in a stable behind Finchley Road. By this time I was working as a French-speaking telephonist at the Continental Telephone Exchange near Saint Paul's. Evenings, nights, and Sundays, the rota constantly changing. I'd started to write things that interested me to read. The first sense I had that anyone outside my family found them interesting too was in a pub called "The Orange Tree" off Euston Road. I met Anselm and Gael Turnbull one lunchtime to give Anselm the first copies of his book *History*, and showed him the poem "You Were Wearing Blue." He was enthusiastic and we had another drink.

Gene Mahon, who worked in the International Telephone Exchange, lodged with us. He was very handy and built himself a fitted bed and cupboards. Occasionally we'd go round to another friend, Mikes Zambakides, a librarian who'd grown up in Larnaca, Cyprus, where his mother ran the cinema, to watch his television and eat baklava. One evening at the Halls' we met Asa and Pip Benveniste. Asa, an American, who after the war lived for a while in

David Ball, Nicole Ball, Tom Raworth, and Lotte Harding, London, late 1960s

Tangier where he edited the magazine *Zero*, had tired of his job in publishing and had started Trigram Press. It was on his machine that Barry and I printed Basil Bunting's *Briggflatts* for Fulcrum Press.

In the late summer of 1965 the Dorns arrived in England. Ed was to teach at the new University of Essex. Val and I, along with Race Newton, went to Waterloo Station to meet the boat train. With them was Jeremy Prynne, whom I'd never met, but who had sent me a congratulatory postcard four years previously when the first issue of *outburst* appeared. A few weeks after their arrival, after a long dispute with the brewery who were our landlords, we were evicted, losing clothing and furniture in the process. The Hollos generously took us in, and for a while four adults and six small children shared their apartment. A couple of weeks before Christmas we moved to

Manor Road, High Barnet,

the last stop on the Northern Line. A large house recently "converted" into flats. Two rooms, a kitchen, and a bathroom on the ground floor. But enormous rooms, the front one over thirty-five feet long. Bruno was born in one corner of it four days after Christmas. Shortly afterwards large white mushrooms appeared along the skirting-board under the window. There was a musty smell, and Val's foot went through a floorboard. Dry rot. The landlord sent in two builders who were there for such a long time they almost became part of the family. One of them, George, a Glaswegian, started each day with whiskey and tea, and would even baby-sit while Val went shopping. Jeff Nuttall lived a few streets away and would drop in on his way home to see how things were going.

The press was doing well. Along with publishing under our own imprint, we printed books, posters, and various ephemera for others. Barry and I were still working, so when Nathaniel Tarn and Tom Maschler from Jonathan Cape wanted to take us over, put money into the press and work it full-time, Barry decided to go with them. I felt uneasy about perhaps having to print books I wasn't too interested in, and having to plan months in advance. It was the autonomy and immediacy of the press that I liked. The last book we printed and published together, at Barry's suggestion, was my first: *The Relation Ship*. In 1967, through Dorn, and Donald Davie (who was head of the literature department at Essex), I was offered a place there as an undergraduate. So for the first time we moved outside London.

Ted Greenwald, with Valarie Raworth and Joan Simon, Bleecker Street, New York City, 1972

Victoria Road, Colchester.

A five-roomed flat on the first floor where we lived for five years. The university had only been open three. Built in a hollow on parkland Constable had painted. I was to study Latin-American literature, so the first year was a Spanish language course. At a party at Gordon Brotherston's we met John Barrell. Herbie Butterfield was teaching in the department and several Latin-American writers spent time there. José-Emilio and Cristina Pacheco. Marco-Antonio and Ana-Luisa Montes de Oca. My Spanish teacher, Carlos Lazzaro, was from Argentina. I have an image of him dancing a spectacular tango with his wife Lucy in their room at the top of one of the bleak grey concrete dormitory towers.

In the spring of 1968 Val and I went to Paris, and drove from there down to Provence with David and Nicole Ball in their old 2cv. We stopped overnight at a small hotel in Chalon-sur-Saône and at breakfast the next morning heard the news of the assassination of Martin Luther King (or "Lew Turpin," as I thought the French radio announcer said). After some days in the sun Val went north, and I started from Nice with another student, Roy Wallis, for Spain. The train was almost empty and we were able to spread out and sleep on the seats. I woke somewhere around Valencia to see my first oranges on trees. A quick walk through Barcelona between trains, then on to Granada. We were lodged with Spanish families and my room overlooked the railway station forecourt: handy for the parades of Franco's troops. Nobody wanted to talk about Lorca. Roy and I spent a lot of time in the Alhambra. There were visits to Malaga and to an avocado pear plantation. Once we took a bus along the coast to Estepona where Race Newton was playing piano. Steep cobbled streets and retired English. From Paris David was sending thick envelopes of newspaper clippings about the May events. The University of Granada was quite staid, so we made posters inviting students to meet and discuss what was going on elsewhere. Immediately the police descended and Chris Allen was thrown into prison. Full, of course, mostly of gipsies. We had to take him food and drink every day until, after much work by Carlos and the British Consul, he was released. Then we got word that deportation was in the air. We burned our University Identity Cards in protest, and left from Malaga.

Back at Essex there were meetings, marches, occupations, television cameras thrown in the fountains (which were rarely playing: the wind, funneled by the tower blocks, soaked everyone in the square if the water jetted up more than six inches), and boycotting of lectures. There was a new friend, Peter Gilpin, a Scot from Dumfries. Another "mature student." By this time Asa had published two books of mine, and I'd given my first public reading. For Tom Pickard at the Mordern Tower in Newcastle. A friend of Anselm's, the Swedish poet and translator Gunnar Harding, came to visit. Lee Harwood called to meet him, and he translated several of our poems into Swedish.

By the end of my second year I was bored and thought to leave. It was suggested I do a master's instead of finishing my B.A. This seemed more interesting, and, as my grant wouldn't cover postgraduate study, the literature department found a small amount of money and appointed me their "Poet in Residence." As part of my work I translated a prose book by the Chilean Vicente Huidobro, and four sections for *The Penguin Book of Latin-American Verse*.

I'd met the American painter Jim Dine in London, and one evening we had dinner with him, his wife Nancy, and the poet Kenneth Koch. Koch asked me if I'd ever been to the United States. I told him no, and he said when he went back he'd invite me to read in New York. I discounted this, but a few months later he wrote, giving a date for me to read at the Loeb Student Center with Dick Gallup and Aaron Vogel. When I wrote to Anselm, who by now was teaching at the University of Iowa, he asked me to do something there. As did Ray DiPalma at Bowling Green.

I arrived in New York early in the evening. The Dines had had to go upstate, so Koch told me Anne Waldman had said I could stay at her place. John Godfrey was also staying there and thus he was the first American writer I met in America. We talked for a while, Koch came by with Red Grooms, and we all drove uptown to see the first showing of Grooms's and Edwin Denby's film *Tappy Toes*. For a few days I stayed in Newark with an old friend, Rosalyn Williams, did the reading (where I saw Piero again and met Fielding Dawson), then took the Greyhound west. I did another tour in 1971, and again in early 1972.

In the spring of that year I was staying with the Greenwalds on Bleecker Street when I had trouble with my heart. A couple of years previously I'd collapsed in Colchester. Scar tissue from the openheart surgery in 1956 was interfering with the electrical conductivity of the muscle. Ted Greenwald's parents sent me to their doctor, a Morris Perlmutter, who slid me into Bellevue one night where I was shocked back to normal rhythm and shot onto the street early the next morning sloppy with Valium. He charged me nothing. Reeling, I went with Ted to the airport to meet Val and Aram (who'd been born in January 1970). People drift through this period. Bob Grenier, Barrett Watten, and Darrell Gray in Iowa City. Coming back on the bus from there to New York with George Kimball. Andrew Carrigan, and Ken and Ann Mikolowski in Michigan. A coked-out drive from Boston to Franconia, New Hampshire, with Harvey Brown, Ted Greenwald, and David Ball, after an evening with Aram Saroyan at Ken Irby's listening to Tibetan music. For some days I stayed in Bowling Green with DiPalma and Betsi Brandfass. He introduced me to Howard McCord and Philip O'Connor who ran the writing program there, and when I got back to England I heard from them inviting me to teach as a "Fiction Instructor." In the early autumn I returned to Ohio, found a house, went to Detroit Airport, and, after a long argument with Immigration (resolved when Val said to the officer, "Well, fuck this: I'm going home") we were all driven down to Bowling Green by Andrew Carrigan.

Barry Hall and Kathy Ainsworth,
New Mexico, early 1970s

Liberty High Road, Bowling Green.

The frame house was some miles out of town, in the middle of corn fields. A completely flat landscape: the drained "black swamp." Our water was dark and sulphurous. Bleach and salt had to be added to it in the usually flooded cellar. And people did stop their cars to stare curiously at us when we went for a walk. I learned to drive, getting my licence after a test in Defiance which consisted of driving around the block and parking, and we bought a secondhand station wagon. On one corner of the campus was an artificial hill, a few feet high. People would come from miles away to walk up it and change their perspective. I taught some freshman English courses and some literature and writing classes for the M.F.A. program. A few of the graduate students became friends. Bill Welbourn from Chicago. Evelyn and Sam Koperwas from New York. Then the accidents began. First I skidded on ice into a tree. Then we set out to drive to visit the Balls in Massachusetts. All went well, we even picked up a hitchhiker, Terry Pfaltz. Then, outside Herkimer, New York, one of the rear wheels broke on a curve over an icy bridge. The wagon somersaulted twice, crossed the barrier, and stopped upside down in the opposite lane. A quick-thinking truck driver swung his rig across the road to stop traffic and miraculously I was the only one hurt. My head was cut by the crushed roof. We spent the night in a motel where the owner's husband had just died of cancer. The next day David came and picked us up. From his house I talked to Harvey Brown. "Hmm . . . " he said. "Herkimer. I was driving past that town last year and the engine dropped out of my car." Back in Bowling Green Val decided to take me, in a borrowed Pinto, to the hospital. Turning the corner at one mile an hour, nervous of the deep ditch, she drove straight into a parked Cadillac hearse. Several other smaller accidents followed, the sequence only stopping after one morning, sitting on the porch, I noticed a giant semi coming down the absolutely flat and straight road in front of the house. No truck had ever used this road before. I watched it approach, and when it was directly in front of me it stopped and the engine burst into flames. That was it. We took what money we had, drove down to Texas, and caught the train to Mexico.

Calle 57. Mexico City.

The train had been standing in the station at Nuevo Laredo in full sunshine for several hours before we boarded. The few Americans immediately began to complain about the lack of air-conditioning and stared blankly when told to open a window. The carrriage was an old Pullman with seats that made up at night into curtained beds. Stretches of arid landscape with occasionally, miles from anywhere, a figure riding a donkey. Towards the evening of the second day a conductor ran down the cars crying happily, "Only eight hours late!" At the station we were met by the Pachecos, who took us to the Hotel Gillow, where Zapata had stayed on entering the city. After a few days, with the help of Ana-Luisa Montes de Oca, we found a house to rent. Reputed to be haunted, and empty for some time, it was owned by a parapsychologist and was in a working-class area inhabited mainly by small craftsmen, carpenters, electricians and such. There were rumours it had once been a brothel, connected by tunnels to the nearby monastery. We found no tunnels, but there were certainly plenty of mirrors, and a tiny windowless oratory where Lloyd chose to sleep. I was working on a sequence of poems called *The Mask* and remember with pleasure writing by a first-floor window at a carved wooden desk, lit at night by a lamp in the shape of a polar-bear. Everything was going well, the children had friends and were out every day exploring the city. The neighbours' initial distance had disappeared when they discovered that (a) we were not Americans and (b) we were not much better off than they were (they noticed Bruno standing in the queue at the corner shop with his bucket for beans). Bruno, having red hair, was particularly at ease. He went shoe-shining each morning with Chucho and explained one evening that even that wasn't necessary. "You just sit down," he said, "and people come and give you money." To touch the lucky red hair. Then, one morning while I was working, there was the thump of an explosion. Val had, classically, gone looking for a gas-leak with a lighted match. She had Aram in her arms, and to shield him had taken the full heat with her left hand and face. I flooded her with cold water. Neighbours, hearing what had happened, brought the complete stock of ice-lollies from a passing vendor. A doctor arrived, gave her some morphine, and said we had three choices. She could go to the American hospital (impossibly expensive); to the Mexican hospital; or I could treat her at home. Money was low, so we decided on the latter. Val's face was painted with something called Verde Brillante, a tincture of aloe vera that set like dark green shellac. I had to repaint her face and hand every few hours, give her injections and plenty of vitamin E. She looked like the jade Palenque mask in the museum. Neighbours brought us food, and eventually she was able to go out again, fearful of what was happening beneath the mask. In fact, being poor and having to use the traditional remedy proved better than if she'd been burned in "civilisation." After some weeks the surface began to peel away and the skin underneath was perfectly healed. The only scars were a tiny one on her chin, where she'd anxiously picked away a little to see what was happening, and a thin white band on one finger where the flesh had been burned to the bone.

At this particularly low point, our money almost gone, a telegram arrived from Ted Berrigan saying he had been offered a job in England for a year, and would I be interested in taking his place in Chicago. We borrowed enough money to fly to Texas, then drove north, getting lost in Gary, Indiana.

West Waveland, Chicago.

A first-floor railroad flat. Above us lived Alan Bates, a playwright who also taught at Northeastern. This had been a community college, recently accredited as a university. I was to teach similar things as in Ohio. The writing program had its own building, a converted storefront a little way off campus. We were two blocks from Wrigley Field, and four from the lake. Of all the places we lived in the United States we have the warmest memories of Chicago. Even though hairs broke off my frozen moustache one January day walking to the lake. Lloyd by this time was in high school, which was dominated by two gangs, the Royals and the Latin Eagles. On his second day there he was surrounded by Latin Eagles, backed nervously

to the fence, then relaxed as they asked him to tell them what things were like in England. Lisa was taken over by her Puerto Rican friend Vicky and went off to mass every Sunday. I rode the El to work and back, and one day in the middle of writing a postcard to Merrill Gilfillan, began a long poem called *ACE*. Bill Welbourn, a student from Ohio, was back in town, working putting in windows in Lakeshore high-rises. We spent time with him and his wife Marilyn. With the poet Bill Knott, who lived in the Bates's flat for a while. With a few of the Northeastern students, some current, some who'd studied with Berrigan, or with Dorn before that. Terry Jacobus, Al Simmons, Henry Kanabus, John Paul, Steve Pantos.

In May 1974 I went to Budapest at the invitation of the Hungarian PEN Club to work on some translations with Gyula Kodolanyi. Stopping off on the way in London I stayed with Barry, who read *ACE*, liked it, and wanted to publish it under our old imprint. I left him the manuscript, he did some illustrations, had the book printed and bound, then lacked the last payment. Before he could raise the money, a flash flood during a freak rainstorm flooded the printers' basement and destroyed all but thirty-five copies. It had to wait another three years before Geoff Young republished it in California.

Back in Chicago there were a few more incidents. Aram, then four, was knocked down by a car and rolled between its front wheels and out between the side ones. Our usual mixture of bad and good luck. Lisa had appendicitis a week after my health insurance expired, but the hospital took the number and never sent a bill. And I was offered a job at the University of Texas at Austin, thanks to David Wevill and Christopher Middleton.

East Oltorf, Austin, Texas.

The only place we could find to live was a new tract house to the south of the city. The sort of place with imitation coach lamps outside the door. But there was a swimming pool that no-one except us bothered to use. When we first arrived a woman named Karen Kuykendal was extremely kind, inviting us to stay in her house for several days while we looked around. We never took to Austin, despite the generosity of many people there. It was a combination of things. A climate so hot and humid it was almost impossible to move. A university so rich as to be depressing. I remember once being invited to eat with an expert on some English poet. Not at his town house, but his country place, where we ate barbeque and listened to him moan about his lot while through the window three mechanical excavators ceaselessly dug out his lake-to-be. We couldn't afford a car, and as the bus into town was only a quarter, I decided that was the way to go. It was only after a friendly black woman gave Aram a dime one day, and a black man came over to me at the stop and said, "I'd like to shake your hand. . . . You're the first white man I've ever seen waiting for a bus here," that we realised the transport system was purely to get the servants in and out. I do remember a few pleasant days out at the (real) lake with the Wevills. Some evenings with Raja Rao, an Indian novelist and philosopher I'd met once in Saratoga Springs. And a delightful Thanksgiving with Lorenzo Thomas and Dee Lang in a beautiful colonial house lent to us for the weekend by a painter from Birmingham. But the last straw was being told to mark creative-writing assignments on a bell-curve. We had neither the money nor the inclination to return to England, so early in 1975 we packed up and drove across country to California.

Geary Boulevard, San Francisco.

As the Dorns were in England we stayed in their place on Geary at Masonic for the first few months. A typical Victorian frame house. Next door was the press run by Holbrook Teter and Michael Myers. Sometimes I worked there with them, usually on fast runs of ephemera. It was very like working with Barry; we'd think of something, do it, change it on the press. The children went to school. Aram started, and for a while was bussed to Chinatown where he could understand nothing that was going on. The period, 1975–77, was about the last time it was possible to live reasonably cheaply in San Francisco. We enjoyed it, but overall it felt like village life. A few friends came through. I remember Hugo Williams over from England. We took him out to Bolinas to meet Aram Saroyan and they instantly got on: talking about the problems of having famous fathers. Peter Gilpin and Gayle Foster stayed for a while. We drove down to Pescadero to eat artichoke omelettes. Then the Dorns came back, and Holbrook offered us a wooden cabin up in Sonoma for a while.

Camp Meeker, Sonoma County.

A large L-shaped room with a wood-stove. Two tiny rooms off it, and a gallery where bats flew across. An open porch. Redwoods all around. A couple of miles to Occidental, the nearest town, which was famous for three large Italian Family Restaurants where people from San Francisco brought their parents to eat on holidays. On the following days the town's

"Val and Edward Dorn," San Francisco, 1975

sewage system always backed up. Mostly hippies who'd moved not quite back to the land. Long-hairs who made jewellery but were "getting a gun now" as "kids break in and steal your stash." If they stopped to give you a lift to town, "Rhinestone Cowboy" would be playing on the cassette. Aram, Bruno, and Ben went to school, but there was nowhere for Lloyd and Lisa. They had six months to roam about and throw stones at loggers' trucks. We got a taste for the local towns; Santa Rosa, Petaluma. Friends would drive out and we'd sit on the deck deciphering the rebuses inside the Lucky beer-caps. Once I bought a Danish pastry from the supermarket, about eight inches in diameter, one half red (strawberry), the other half yellow (custard), and nailed it to a redwood. It was still there when we left, neither decayed nor eaten by anything. A German shepherd scratched at the door at the beginning of the rainy season, came in, lay by the stove, and stayed a month. "Wolf" was on his collar. Our black cat disappeared into the woods. On Halloween there was a scratching in the roof and it dropped onto our bed. At midnight. An Alastair Johnston (originally from Newcastle) and a

Frances Butler turned up one day and asked if I had a book they could publish. They ended up doing three. David and Nicole Ball arrived with their son Sam, this time in an old Volkswagen they'd driven across country. In Occidental one day, broke, I was walking along the boardwalk and saw with joy a sign saying "FRUIT PICKERS WANTED." But the town had been taken over by television, and I'd walked onto the set of an episode of "Streets of San Francisco."

Richard Gates had a bookshop down the coast at Half-Moon Bay. It was there we met Dale Herd. They'd been surfers, along with the painter Michael Balog, and now Dale was writing sharp short prose pieces. He came up to Camp Meeker to visit, driving a red Karmann Ghia he'd bought for around eighty dollars. One side had been smashed in, and was held in place by a mass of yellowing sticky-tape. "Watch this," he told Val as they stood in the library doorway in Occidental, "people can't stand it." Sure enough a crowd began to gather. The leather-workers, the quilt-sewers, the candle-makers: all the liberal right-thinking folk of the town. They started to mutter angrily. "Piece of shit," one said. "Who'd drive a thing like that? . . . No self-respect." Dale grinned and drove back down to L.A. A couple of years afterwards his path crossed Barry Hall's. After some time in New Mexico (he had stayed with Cape Goliard for a few years printing a series of excellent books including Olson's *Maximus Poems* until one day he got bored, left the rollers halfway across a page of type, locked the door, and disappeared) Barry had married Kathy Ainsworth and they'd gone to Africa. He'd worked on several films, and in Los Angeles made one of Dale's book *Dreamland Court*.

For some months we shared the cabin with a photographer, Rob Rusk, his friend Betsy, and her daughter Rachel. The ten of us survived. Betsy had a car, and was manager of the local Round Table Pizza, so we got to see the coast around Bodega Bay, to go to the cinema in Monte Rio, and to eat regularly. Eventually Holbrook and Joan sold the place to Michael's mother, and we moved back reluctantly to the city.

Sutter Street, San Francisco.

A flat on the top-floor of an all-black apartment building. Two rooms, a kitchen and bathroom, and a small hall. At the top of Sutter, near the trolley-car terminus. It was staring downhill from the front-room window early one morning that I began *Writing*. We weren't there long. Already San Francis-

co was changing, and realtors in trendy suits arrived to measure the rooms and stare through us. Holbrook and Michael were off to a mountaintop near Healdsburg. There were a few months to go before their house was demolished, so we carried our stuff a few blocks to

Anza Street, San Francisco.

Another old frame house. Three rooms and a kitchen, with a garage downstairs where Michael had had his studio. I took the train across country from Oakland to do some readings, and at the bus-station in Buffalo was seized by two Immigration officers in maroon jackets. I'd left my passport in California, and of course the visa had just expired. We had to wait for a deportation hearing. In the meantime, without papers, it was impossible to find work. Holbrook's wife Joan worked for the Social Services and suggested Val try there. The wages were below scale, and they were so glad to get anyone that they checked nothing. She went to work for the city looking after aged alcoholics in the tower block they lived in since the city had destroyed all the small hotels for redevelopment. Her charges were fascinating. One, Mrs. Philips, had worked in vaudeville having cigarettes flicked from between her lips by a partner with a bullwhip. From that she went on to be the first woman photographer for Associated Press. Another, Mr. Toma, had been chauffeur to King Carol of Romania before taking up boxing and becoming, by beating Benny Lynch, then on the way down, European Bantamweight Champion. Once he managed to cash a Xerox of his social security check in a local bar. I found work first stacking underground comics in a basement in the Mission, and then for a few hours a day as a guinea-pig for research into "Visually Evoked Potential" at the Eye Hospital. Barrett Watten turned up one day. Realising we had no car, he asked us to call if there was anywhere we needed to be taken: a generous gesture we've not forgotten.

Old houses were going down and tidy condominiums were going up, each with an iron grille behind which Chinese could be seen polishing their cars. Our house had been bought, with a couple of others, by an Irish builder named Linehan. He took a fancy to us, and when our time came to be demolished, he moved us into another house, with a few months left, around the corner on Masonic. The Greenwalds were staying with us. We took our belongings to the new house, went back, and watched the bulldozer drive straight into the room we'd slept in the night before.

John Barrell, Helpston, Northampton, England, early 1980s

Masonic Avenue, San Francisco.

A stucco house, one floor above the garage. A sage green carpet and a brown swivel chair left by the last occupants. Opposite the side entrance to Sears.

Geary, Anza, and Masonic were three sides of a block. At the junction of Geary and Masonic, in the shadow of Bekins Storage, was a bar called The Pub. In there one evening I got talking to an Andy Berlin. He was riding a Harley, living in Bolinas, working as a short-order cook in Point Reyes, and writing prose. We saw him often after that. And his friend Steve Emerson, another prose-writer.

In the spring of 1977 I was invited to the Cambridge Poetry Festival and, with a special permit from Immigration, went back to England. I visited my parents; stayed with Gilpin and Gayle in London, with John Barrell in Cambridge. A few weeks after I got back to California there was a letter asking me to be Poet in Residence at King's College. We'd been out of England for over five years. Lloyd and Lisa were leaving high school. There was no way we could

ever afford for them to be educated further in the United States. In the early autumn Val flew to London, the children giggling as they arrived because everybody they saw sounded like someone from Monty Python. I went across country first, giving a reading at Duke for Andy Berlin, who was back living in Durham, North Carolina. There, in their house in the woods, I met David and Susan Southern. He was to design *Writing*, and to publish another book of mine. Together we drove to Carolina Beach and swam in the warm sea under a full moon, luminous insects flickering in the sand we scuffed walking back up the slope.

14 Cosin Court, Cambridge.

A college flat, down an alley opposite the Fitzwilliam Museum. My duties at King's were not exactly heavy. I had to give two readings, at either end of my stay, and be available for anyone who wanted to talk to me about their writing. John Wilkinson and Geoffrey Ward came by. We had friends in the town. John Barrell and Harriet Guest. Jeremy Prynne was librarian at Caius. John James and Wendy Mulford lived near. At the university we met Colin MacCabe and John Higgins. I spent a lot of time in the Botanical Gardens, finished *Writing*, and began another long poem, *Catacoustics*.

During early 1978 I was invited to festivals in Rotterdam (where I met Harry Hoogstraten and saw Piero Heliczer for the first time in many years) and Amsterdam (with Tom Pickard). I found the Italian writers—Franco Beltrametti, John Gian, Rita degli Esposti, and Corrado Costa—good company. These were really my first trips to Continental Europe since 1968, apart from the time in Budapest.

At the end of 1978 we had to leave Cosin Court, and after a few weeks' hospitality at John Barrell's, Val found a furnished house for a year.

Cavendish Avenue, Cambridge.

A large semidetached house with a garden. Enough shelves for books and a room to work in. Lloyd went off to Camberwell School of Art. Lisa and Ben were punks for a while. Lorenzo Thomas and Barrett Watten passed through. Aram learned to ride a bicycle. Bruno had girlfriends. Lisa moved in for a while with a Graham who supplemented his dole with the occasional roast duck trapped by the river. My heart began to play up again and one evening I collapsed. A slightly surreal event, as a Richard Tabor who'd dropped in continued to explain to me, flat on my back, how nobody paid any attention to his writing and he was sure it was because he'd never been to university. While Val and Gayle rushed about calling for an ambulance. After a few days in intensive care my heart was shocked back to normal for a while, our lease ran out, and we moved to a council house.

Ditton Fields, Cambridge.

Here we stayed for eight years. On an estate where the "problem families" were put. No furniture, bare boards, broken windows. In London, Lloyd had found a squat in Brixton, and Lisa moved down there. We got the house into shape, and even grew vegetables in the garden with the advice of the old man next door. Bands of stray dogs roamed the streets. Front gardens were filled with bits of cars. An enormously fat woman who walked past every day had a watch tattooed on her wrist. I never found out what time it said. But it was possible to escape from this. Behind the football stadium was Coldham's Common, one of the few remaining pieces of true common ground in Cambridge. Had we owned a cow or a pony we could have grazed it there. Wildflowers

Gunnar Harding and Anselm Hollo, Stockholm, 1987

and thistles sprouted everywhere, and except for a few mown football pitches no attempt had been made to pretty it up. Cattle wandered freely, as did several retired horses. In hot weather they'd gather in the shade under the railway bridge and terrify cyclists.

Early in the 1980s I began to hear from two writers in Paris: Claude Royet-Journoud and Dominique Fourcade. Claude had lived in England for a while (when we were in the United States) with the poet Anne-Marie Albiach. Their letters were interesting and they seemed much more aware of what was happening in poetry than their contemporaries in the London literary world. I was invited to give some readings in North Italy, so went by train, stopping off in Paris. There I stayed with Pepo in his new place, a loft in a courtyard near the Bastille. And there I was fortunate enough to meet and become friends with Clive Unger-Hamilton and Cordelia Chitty, who were busily turning three tiny maids' rooms on the sixth floor into one large flat. Claude, Anne-Marie, Dominique and his family became close friends too, and shortly afterwards Claude and I were awarded an exchange bursary by the British Council in Paris to spend a month in each other's countries. In the meantime I went on to Italy, reading with Beltrametti in Venice and Udine. In Venice I felt at home more than in any other place but Chicago. I stayed first with the poet and painter Francesco Giusti. Met Armando Pajalich, who invited me to talk to his students at the university. Looked at the house Gian and Rita were working on. Learned how to marble paper from Daria. Delivered armchairs on Piccio's tiny blue boat that he'd rebuilt from fragments of one once owned by Hemingway. Many times during the 1980s I was invited back to Italy, France, and Switzerland. And several times I toured the United States, with occasional ventures into Canada. Winnipeg at thirty below zero.

Ben, after a bad time early in the decade (he and some friends had been attacked by a gang of bikers at a seaside resort in 1981. His friend Richard Ellis was killed, and Ben was badly stabbed in the back and legs), moved to London. Bruno, as bored with school as I had been, left as soon as he could, decided one day he wanted to be a sign-writer, walked into the oldest company in town and was given an apprenticeship. Val, nervous about working after so many years at home, found a job with a computer-software company that had never previously hired anyone over the age of twenty-five.

My mother grew frailer, and died in the spring of 1983 shortly after her sister Annie, whom she'd not

Tom Raworth (center), with Franco Beltrametti and Giovanni d'Agostino, Milan, 1986

seen for thirty years, visited. My father had cared for her by himself, refusing all offers of help, for two years. Now, exhausted, he began to weaken. Every two or three weekends Val and I would go down by train to cook and clean. Lloyd, his friend Hannah, and Lisa took turns too. My father would sit in my grandfather's wooden armchair and talk about his life; something he'd never done when I was a child. He'd wanted to be a printer—in the seventeenth century one of our family, a Ruth Raworth, had printed Milton's first collection of poems—but there was no possibility. Most of his life he had worked as a lawyer's clerk, until the late 1940s when he'd become assistant to the editor of the Jesuit journal *The Month.* He'd written reviews, and the occasional article. One I remember was an account of how he'd tracked down the clock in the background of the Holbein picture of Saint Thomas More and his family. The only person able to decipher the handwriting of Gerard Manley Hopkins, he had prepared the typescript for an edition of *Sermons and Devotional Writings.* By early 1986 he was unable to leave the house, but refused to go into hospital. In the autumn I had to move in to care for him. Strange to be back in the

house where I was born, looking at the same books on the shelves. He held out until October, then died a few hours after entering hospital. John James drove us to Lavenham to scatter his ashes in the shadow of the church tower.

My parents' house translated almost exactly into a small terraced one in Cambridge. The woman who was selling was ninety-three and had lived there all her life, for the last decade or more in one room. The rest of the building was unchanged from when it had been built in 1887. There was no bathroom, an outside lavatory, and no kitchen—just a small scullery. While the builders were in I went to an arts festival in Gothenberg, Sweden. Anselm had been invited too, and Gunnar came over from Stockholm to read his translations. We took the train back with him and spent a pleasant week together.

St. Philip's Road, Cambridge.

After months of work we moved in during October 1988. The following month my *Selected Poems* were published. And the month after that Lisa gave birth to our first grandchild, Cato. This spring I was fortunate enough to spend two days with Anselm and Jane in southern Utah, to see Ed and Jenny Dorn in Boulder and Ted Greenwald and Lorenzo Thomas in New York, and to take the train down to North Carolina to visit the Southerns. John Barrell and David Ball were here recently. Jeremy cycled over for tea and a digestive biscuit last week. Franco called from Switzerland. There was a postcard from Rosalyn in Barbados and a letter from Piero, now married and living in Amsterdam. This weekend Val and I leave for Scotland with Gilpin and Gayle. On the way up we'll see Asa. And Race and Lizzie Newton on the way back. Last night I watched Tom Pickard's TV programme on the Sutherland shipyards and talked to him afterwards on the phone. Cato has a temperature and Lisa has taken him to the doctor. Val's bringing hamburger home, Aram's out on the town, and it's been windy all day. Photographs from thirty years are spread out on the bed. Dark grey clouds scud from the west across a nearly white sky and the bathroom door slams in the wind. To my left are the bookshelves I stared at from under the table (now downstairs in the kitchen) nearly fifty years ago. I can see *The Road to En-Dor* on the top shelf.

BIBLIOGRAPHY

Poetry:

Weapon Man, Goliard Press, 1965.

Continuation, Goliard Press, 1966.

The Relation Ship, Goliard Press, 1967, Grossman, 1969.

The Big Green Day, Trigram, 1968.

(With John Esam and Anselm Hollo) *Haiku,* Trigram, 1968.

Lion Lion, Trigram, 1970.

Moving, Cape Goliard, 1971.

(With John Ashbery and Lee Harwood) *Penguin Modern Poets 19,* Penguin, 1971.

Pleasant Butter, Sand Project Press, 1972.

(With Asa Benveniste and Ray DiPalma) *Time Being,* Trigram, 1972.

Tracking, Doones Press, 1972.

Here, privately printed, 1973.

An Interesting Picture of Ohio, privately printed, 1973.

Act, Trigram, 1973.

Back to Nature, Joe DiMaggio Press, 1973.

Ace, Cape Goliard, 1974, The Figures, 1977.

Bolivia: Another End of Ace, Secret, 1974.

Cloister, Sand Project Press, 1975.

That More Simple Natural Time Tone Distortion, University of Connecticut Library, 1975.

Common Sense, Zephyrus Image, 1976.

The Mask, Poltroon Press, 1976.

Four Door Guide, Street Editions, 1978.

Sky Tails, Lobby Press, 1978.

Nicht Wahr, Rosie?: Miscellaneous Poems 1964–1969, Poltroon Press, 1979.

Writing, The Figures, 1982.

Lèvre de Poche, Bull City Press, 1983.

Heavy Light, Actual Size, 1984.

Tottering State: New and Selected Poems 1963–1983, The Figures, 1984, expanded edition published as *Tottering State: Selected Poems 1963–1988,* Paladin, 1988.

Tractor Parts, Spectacular Diseases, 1984.

Lazy Left Hand: Notes from 1970–1975, Actual Size, 1986.

Visible Shivers, O Books, 1987.

Other:

(With Anselm Hollo and Gregory Corso) *The Minicab War* (parodies), Matrix Press, 1961.

A Plague on Both Your Houses (screenplay), 1966.

Betrayal, Trigram, 1967.

A Serial Biography, Fulcrum Press, 1969, Turtle Island, 1977.

Little Trace Remains of Emmett Miller (recording), Stream Records, 1969.

Sic Him Oltorf! (broadside), Zephyrus Image, 1974.

Logbook, Poltroon Press, 1977.

Translator:

(With others) *Con Cuba: An Anthology of Contemporary Cuban Poetry,* Cape Goliard, 1969.

(With others) *The Penguin Book of Latin-American Verse,* Penguin, 1971.

(With others) John Gerassi, editor, *Third World Political Documents,* Wiedenfeld & Nicholson, 1971.

(With Valarie Raworth) *From the Hungarian,* privately printed, 1973.

William Pitt Root

1941-

William Pitt Root under an umbrella of sea-grape leaves, Fort Myers, Florida, 1988

Birth

The first human voices I ever heard, or over-heard, were discussing the pros and cons of my decapitation and dismemberment. This was during a blizzard in Austin, Minnesota, in 1941, on December 28, a day officially described as the unluckiest day of the year. For me it could have been worse.

But to begin an autobiography at the beginning is a risky business. When *is* the actual beginning anyway? Who but Athena, leaping whole from her father's head, has arrived in any condition to be taking notes? And some cultures date life from conception rather than birth, while Carl Sagan is famously fond of stating we are all children of the stars. . . . You'd be a fool to argue against such a distinguished origin, a blind fool not to note that any power conferred by this star-stuff shooting atomic through our veins and wildly arcing across our delicate synapses is the same power that fuels the two-toed sloth, the sea slug, and those polyester suits that make Johnny Carson shine.

However, I'm told, by the one who would know best, that my birth was hard. My shoulders caught in the birth canal so for some time my head dangled in this new world while my body was locked in the old. While I did manage to slip free before the debate concluded, I still do gaze with more than the usual interest at images of those shrill brilliant faces protruding from the vaginas of ancient Mother goddesses.

313

First Memories

My earliest memory is of being carried on my mother's shoulder through a railroad yard where, as she walked, the ceramic crunching of cinders underfoot made the first sound I recall. Wrapped in a shawl, I could scarcely get my face clear of its blue nimbus to look down through that soft wool of the ethereal to the grit of the earth below.

My next memory is more complex. I am with my mother, walking in a strange city with hills. Alongside the sidewalk runs a little low wall. I want to walk on it and mother helps me up. I'm thrilled. I run. But the sidewalk goes downhill as the wall rises higher, higher. I am exhilarated by my daring as I balance there. Then a dog from nowhere charges out barking fiercely. It crouches between me and mother. She cannot reach me. If I run from it, I get farther and farther above my mother, who is holding up her arms and calling for me to jump. I am terrified. It is too far to jump but clearly the dog is going to do something dreadful if I don't. The next thing I know, I am looking down on this scene from above: I see the boy, myself; I see the woman, my mother; I see the dog, snarling—but I am like a balloon that has slipped from a hand and serenely floats unnoticed safely above.

My Parents' Courtship

My father, William Pitt Root, was thirty when he met Bonita, then sweet sixteen, in Austin. He was directing a minstrel show for John B. Rogers Production Company in the late thirties. He cast my mother-to-be in both a trio and the minstrel chorus, but she, having a clearer sense of destiny, cast herself, more ambitiously, at him, first pursuing him with glances and then with letters when he returned to the road. Flattered, he considered her a sweet schoolgirl with a crush until a couple of years later, when he came through Austin again. She was no longer a girl but a woman, sights set and heart cocked. She got him, too, hard-bitten bachelor that he was.

He had travelled in those days with only one companion, an unaltered Gila monster he kept in a shoebox. It escaped one afternoon while he napped in a hotel room. He woke to find it nestled under his chin, breathing foul breath in his face. He lay deathly still until it stirred and moved off, then he clapped it back into its box for good.

Bonita Joy Hilbert was a real beauty, with dark hair, dark sparkling eyes, and lively spirits as innocent as an active imagination permits. Her high-school drama teacher told her there would be no difficulty in getting her a drama scholarship to Case Western Reserve University but her stepfather disapproved.

Later, when she posed for some publicity photos for Cypress Gardens in Florida in 1940, she was offered a tryout in Hollywood which my father, then her fiancé, discouraged. She was utterly taken with this worldly fellow, who, from photos of that time, bore a passing resemblance to the young Frank Sinatra. He had a lovely tenor voice and would sing "O Danny Boy" or "When Irish Eyes Are Smiling" anywhere, anytime. Mother, too, had a rich, lovely voice. Her "Mares-eat-oats" was my favorite. It fascinated me how the words blurred through pure music into new meanings.

Early Years: Florida 1941–1953

On my folks' honeymoon trip West, they drove one of the first two-tone Pontiacs to come off the line, tan with maroon fenders, a convertible to boot. A dashing pair. In California they ran into trouble finding accommodations because Mother, of German-Danish descent, looked Mexican, and her name,

"My father, William Pitt Root," 1938

"My mother, Bonita Joy Hilbert Root, in a publicity shot for Cypress Gardens, Florida," 1940

Bonita, clinched it. No room at the inn, again and again. Which infuriated my father, a proud man. I wrote my first "serious" poem, "Equality," at 16, after I saw on TV the old movie *Ramona*, in which the hero and heroine suffered from similar discrimination but with tragic effect.

They spent their first two years on the road, settling briefly in Orlando, Florida, where my father was a trouble-shooter for the newly formed National Airlines, then moved to Jacksonville, Mobile, and New Orleans, where he got an offer of a partnership truck-farming in Florida. In those days choosing the crops to plant was a kind of gambling, and that appealed greatly to my father (a non-smoking teetotaler), who believed good luck and hard work were twins. This was in Fort Myers, Florida, then a town of about ten thousand, a dozen miles from the Gulf and even closer to the verge of the Everglades. [See "The Storm," *The Storm and Other Poems*.]

He was a devout Christian Scientist. As a teenager in New York State, he contracted polio before it had the name. He was bedridden for a year and the doctors said he was dying. His mother, Charlotte

(known to me as Toadie), a woman of astonishing strength of purpose, was not about to let her only son die. She brought in every kind of specialist imaginable, resorting to the borderline occult—a Christian Science practitioner, a sort of neo-Christian shaman. He insisted on seeing my father alone. Toadie relented, waiting outside for hours. When the door opened, her son was infused with a faith from which he never wavered, a faith partially the cause of his death later.

The doctors, who abhorred Christian Scientists then as now, conceded he might live, but warned he would never walk again. Then they conceded he was, indeed, walking, so they assured him his lurch would never improve. Two years later, he auditioned with Rogers Brothers as a choreographer. Fifty years later I would correspond with poet Fred Lape, of Esperance, New York, who had been the auditioner. He said when Bill came on stage he was painful to watch but he insisted on trying to dance. His body ran with the sweat of his agony, his movements were hopeless, and, Fred added, his courage was impressive. A year later, at a second audition, he did get a job, though the dancing would come later. Meanwhile he and Fred travelled doing gigs, Fred playing dance music on his cornet, my father singing. "We were," Fred wrote, "what you might call adequate to our audiences." [See "The House You Looked For," *Striking the Dark Air for Music*.]

III.

Father, you could dance
and you learned to dance
with pain. They told you
you couldn't walk again.

Young and sure to die,
you lay and wept, wasting
in the bed of a closed room.
Then changed.
        Changed
with such fierce strength
that curse became command.
You lived despite them all,
You rose, you walked, by god
you danced back into life.
. . . pale and agonized,
you made them watch you dance.
They did not understand.
You called it dance
and dancing it became.

(from "The House You Looked For,"
Striking the Dark Air for Music)

"Street angel, House devil" his mother called him, and his wife knew why. When I knew him, my father was still extremely charismatic. Men clearly respected and enjoyed him, women seemed to enjoy him even more. Each year he would direct and choreograph the Pageant of Light memorial for Thomas Alva Edison (who'd lived many years in Fort Myers), a kind of minstrel show quite popular then. He would drag one leg, almost imperceptibly, when very tired, and he would surreptitiously cough blood in handkerchiefs he always carried with him. He had TB but would be treated only by his practitioner. He was active in the church, taught Sunday school, visited the sick and elderly every Sunday, often insisting I go along. The experience of regularly seeing so many people afflicted by so much tragedy, dire poverty, loneliness, and despair, inevitably set me apart from the kids for whom such suffering remained unknown. I stood in awe of my father, whose spirit remained steadfast through these visits that sometimes left me trembling. [See "If a Fish Ignores the River," an unpublished story.]

When I began going weekends to my father's farms, to hunt pests and varmints and to work alongside the field hands a few hours each day as my father made his supervisory rounds, I began meeting for the first time Puerto Ricans and Cubans. Few spoke English. They worked hard, fast, and after work they set campfires near the quarters provided (my father flew them up from the Caribbean for the harvests, paying more, I was proud to learn, than most employers but still very little), then they'd drink and start to sing and dance. I was astonished to see grown-ups behave as they did, with a pitch of gaiety unimaginable among my parents' friends, the only other grown-ups I knew. I loved it and I wanted more than anything to be Puerto Rican or Cuban. When my father noticed and forbade me to spend any more time with them, it nearly broke my heart.

For years I idolized Gilbert Roland, star of such movies as *Beneath the Twelve-Mile Reef,* a Hispanic who seemed to me to be everything a man should be, and his laughter intimated an attitude toward the world I longed to share. I still think he was terrific.

In many ways, my childhood so near the Everglades was idyllic:

I went to the farms every Saturday, and to church every Sunday of my childhood, but where I got my sense of reverence was knee-deep in swamp-water looking at alligators and flamingoes, hearing the owls at night, seeing the way a doe bent her neck to drink from a pond, watching utterly awe-struck as a cottonmouth swam by or a rattler buzzed in the saw-grass, seeing the brown pelicans fly in formation overhead along the Gulf shore, studying the horizon at the beach before I ever set foot in the water to be sure there were some porpoises out there to fend off the sharks. . . . Childhood experiences are probably the strongest, most formative, and if the child is fortunate enough to be around wilderness of any kind, he will develop a sense of proportion about existence and significance which man is not at the center of. There are grander things out there, and to know that as a child is to know it always. My sense of creatures wasn't that they were friendly but that they were just, gave fair warning, defended their own, and that there was in wild creatures a magical quality I respected beyond anything else I might imagine. Without them what was stirred in me might never have been touched. Without the external wilderness to stir and order the interior wilderness of the heart, a human being cannot be fully human.

Creatures had, for me, a vitality and perfected grace I seldom saw in humans, with important exceptions. The Seminoles who came to town in their native dress, to shop, awed me. The Cubans and Puerto Ricans, who carried on physically with such eloquence—such people seemed to me, as a boy, infinitely more alive and enviable, more serious and joyful, than most people I knew. This yearning for basic connections is probably strong among all people, but certainly it distinguishes those I am most drawn by: one sees it in Rilke's fascination with caged animals, Levine's interest in the old working class of his Detroit childhood, Roethke's love first of the greenhouse and then of the Pacific Northwest, Garcia Lorca's love of Gypsies, in Neruda, in imprisoned Hikmet—the list of writers who have hungered for such connections is endless.

(from *CutBank* 22, interview
by Randy Watson and Jim Gurley)

I was pretty solitary, and happily so, though I did have friends. Tommy and Skippy Phillips, Jules and Reiner Haneburger, Michael Perry, Billy Weber. And girls—Susan Shelby Shanklin, in particular. I intended to marry her, whatever that meant, and even offered, as an inducement, to take her name so she wouldn't have to lose the lovely sound of hers, which, just then, was her main objection. We'd ride our horses, arm wrestle, go to matinees, play spin-the-bottle, and run before anyone got kissed.

I loved certain trees and took my favorite people up into them. SSS (above) had a wonderful Australian pine in her backyard. We would climb to the top, peer down, trading wishes and dreams, listening to the world in a different key. We had a sea-grape tree in our backyard at home which I climbed and clung to through many an afternoon and listened to before sleeping:

At night, late, when I was supposed to sleep,
I lay in bed, my chameleon
nestled along my nose,
his belly a horizon rising and falling
by one eye; sometimes
I lay there hearing you like a ghost at sea
                              creaking and rustling
by the sleeping porch,
giving the winds
a body to whisper through; sometimes
when the house was still
I lay for hours, radio
held to my ear and tuned to Havana,
dim red tubes miraculously
wiring my skull with a language that sang
even without the music
songs so quick my heart skipped beats to hear.

(from "Sea-Grape Tree and the Miraculous")

The Caloosahatchee River, over a mile wide, flowed by the foot of Coconut Drive. It was splendid to have one's own river. From the seawall I hooked catfish, crabs, sheepsheads, sand sharks, rays. I would venture out onto the forbidden sewerage pipe twenty-five yards or so into the river and test my skills at balancing as the tidal waters rose and wetted the moss on the pipe, making it slick. Once I looked down and saw an enormous sawfish beside me. I'd never heard of such a creature, thought it was a monster, promptly set off running for shore and just as promptly slipped into the water. I thought it would cut me to ribbons and I'd vanish without a trace. When I got home, smelling of sewerage and ranting about a monster, Mother explained for the first time what "sewerage" meant, and the experience completely lost its horrific dignity. [See "Tree of Water," a story, *Nimrod* 30, no. 2.]

Much of childhood's charm consists in misunderstandings. One day I was looking through a stack of black-and-white snapshots of the Fort Myers beach area and came across a picture that made my blood freeze. It was a road I knew, but crossing it was a dinosaur, hissing, with fins on its back and gatorish jowls at its throat. I'd thought they were extinct! I showed it to Mother. Instead of asking what it was, I asked if it was real. She assured me it was real, that it probably had swum in from much farther south. So for years I thought dinosaurs were at large in the sea. Had she mentioned the term "iguana," those magic years of believing I knew something few people knew would never have occurred.

How I Began Writing

I began drawing stories before I could write. When words eventually crowded out illustrations, I was a writer. My stories mostly concerned a boy with

"Here Billy (a.k.a. William Pitt Root, fils) gets the drop on the world, by the Coconut Drive house in Fort Myers, Florida," 1947

wild beasts for companions—a wolf-dog, a cougar, an eagle; basically these creatures took turns saving his life. My actual companion was a cocker spaniel, Honeyboy, who saved my life more than once when I ventured too near the Caloosahatchee. After Honeyboy died of heartworms one Christmas Eve, eventually I got my "wolf-dog," a solid black German shepherd named Dinah von Babenberg. When I saw her (she was two years old, nervous and exhausted from her car trip), my first gesture was to grab her throat to hug her; her response was to bite me about the head and shoulders. For her fierce spirit, I loved her all the more, and we grew inseparable.

My fifth-grade teacher, Mrs. Foster, encouraged me to read my stories aloud to the class during recess. My friend Jules offered five dollars cash for one story. I declined, but it seemed clear writing could be a lucrative profession. Mrs. Foster, a painter, lived with a writer of "paperback books." Romances or thrillers, most likely. She invited Mother to bring me over to meet him one Saturday afternoon. I was excited, not knowing what to expect. Mother read paperbacks, which my father sternly discouraged as a waste of time. She had books stashed all over the house. When we arrived at the Fosters' trailer-house, Mrs. Foster met us at the door and suggested we sit outside to have tea while Mr. Foster "got ready." Minutes passed, an hour—no Mr. Foster, and no further mention of him either. Finally we left. The episode left me with a powerful curiosity about writers. Strange, perhaps unfriendly, perhaps just a little wicked in some undefined way. In retrospect, I sympathize with the man, who doubtless preferred getting soused to the prospect of entertaining a fifth grader with literary ambitions.

Going North

My parents would take their summer vacation among the northern Minnesota lakes. We would stay at fishing camps, hire motorboats or canoes to troll for pike or walleyes, and fish at dusk for red-eyed bass from the docks. It was glorious. The fish were delicious and the lakes had rubbery leeches that stretched out to unbelievable lengths and could suck your body dry of blood in minutes if you fell in and couldn't get out in time. Or so we kids agreed, by campfires at night.

In 1953, Mother and I drove North alone. I thought my father was coming later. Then, at her parents' house, Mother announced she and my father were "separated." She explained it but life without my father and mother together was unthinkable. The

next day he called, asking forgiveness, and she happily told me he was driving up to join us immediately. A day later, another long distance phone call. There had been a car accident. I remember seeing her crouched over the phone as over a fire, a last hope that was going out, crying "No, no" over and over. No one had to tell me he had been killed. I went outside and hid in bushes, exactly as I had once seen a puppy of mine do after it was crushed by a car tire, and I made the same noises that puppy made as it died. But I didn't die. I lay face down and smelled the grass and realized my father would never see grass again, or see me again, and I tried to stop breathing, as he had stopped breathing. But at last I took that searing breath he could never take.

He had pulled off the road to avoid an oncoming driver passing on a curve. Pulling back onto the road the car flipped, and in those days before seatbelts his chest was crushed against the steering wheel. He lay by the road for an hour, several ribs broken, two through his lungs, drowning in his own blood. When an ambulance arrived, with rescue equipment, he refused oxygen because it would be a betrayal of his faith, like taking medicine. His religion taught whatever happened was God's will: you perfected your own vision of His will through your acceptance of it. This he did. Unknown to my father, just the day before his longtime "practitioner" also had died. My father died August 1, 1953.

In the days following, the radical integrity of that act thrilled me with pride in my father and utterly horrified me as well. I was bound to admire him because I understood why he did it and how anything else would have made a different man of him, a diminished man. Yet I knew, too, that I had taken that breath myself, in the grass, that I had not been able to do as he had done. I imagined no one else had such terrible knowledge of righteousness or its cost to those who, loving him, would have held him back. [See "If a Fish Ignores the River," a story.]

Leaving Home for Good, Heading North

We lost the house, the farms, our way of life along with our means of livelihood. We moved to my mother's hometown in Minnesota. My one companion from childhood was Dinah, the "wolf-dog." We would protect each other. The theme of my early stories was coming true, and I quit writing.

I came down with a mysterious fever about this time and its intensity enhanced my reading of *The Old Man and the Sea*. I embraced that book, that author, and some vague sense of the calling of such art, with the fervor of a convert. Here was someone else, I thought, who had known something great and had it taken from him and was made different than those around him by that experience. I wept the tears I had not wept at the funeral—for my father, whose death had been courageous in a way few understood, for the old man whose great fish became a curiosity for fools and who tasted the taste of pennies as he dreamed of lions, and for myself, the life I had lost forever.

But a new life was beginning. I saw snow that winter. And each morning I delivered newspapers, sometimes in a twenty-five-below-zero degree world as dreamlike and unreal as anything I'd ever read of in books.

> There I learned the seasons
> in a long strange year.
> I saw the crippled trees
> crumple into colors, shedding
> their brilliant disease of leaves
> that left the branches dead
> and trembling in the snow-white wind,
> magical and stark
> between streetlamps and starlight.
>
> . . . .
>
> And each dawn of the long first winter
> silent in the moonlight, I hiked
> through the frostbright
> dreamlike sleeping trees
> that jutted like black bone
> from wounded snow.

> (from "Circle of Struggle,"
> *Striking the Dark Air for Music)*

In the seventh grade, Miss Daniels, a bleached blonde English teacher, assigned our class to write an ad. I wrote in couplets, scarcely knowing what couplets were:

> Use Ma Fletcher's girdle grease
> And your snap will never cease.

It went on for thirty or forty more lines. Read in class, it was a great success. When another teacher asked everyone in his class to tell what he or she wanted to be, I mumbled my ambition and was asked to repeat it.

"An arthur," I declared.

Heading West

After two years, in 1955, we moved to Washington State. My father's life insurance had made the down payment on a house in Austin we sold just before it was foreclosed on. Mother bought a trailer-house and a new Studebaker. We drove across the Badlands (where Mother nearly fell into a ravine when she lost her footing sightseeing in high heels), through Montana (where we got lost on a mountain road and I had to take over the wheel and back us down because Mother had a phobia of heights; when we drove by Missoula, I vowed to return there to live one day, and I did, over twenty years later) and on through Idaho, toward Seattle.

But Seattle had become a city since she'd last seen it. We ended up in Redmond, twenty-five miles east. It was wilder there and I liked it. A movie, *Blackboard Jungle*, with Bill Hailey and the Comets' "Rock around the Clock," had just been released. It gave kids my age—we'd never before thought in terms of "generation"—an identity that romanticized the rebel. Soon, James Dean would even more deeply instill that ideal in us. In Junior High School, I liked some of the wilder kids but I was tolerated rather than accepted into their ranks. I was "a good kid," returning home immediately after school to clean the trailer and care for my young sister, Wendy. Having little chance for after-school socializing, I drew into myself, reading, fantasizing.

Love, Despair, Philosophy

Shortly after arriving in Washington, I fell hopelessly in love with a girl I met at a family picnic (Mother had shirttail relatives there) and scarcely saw again until high school. By then, Diana was the most popular girl in school. It was an odd relationship, for I was as darkly shy and reclusive as she was radiant and effervescent, and she always went steady with older guys. But we would take long walks and swims together, talking and talking, with an undercurrent of passions approaching delirium.

As a high-school senior, when I read *Hamlet* I became suicidal. He knew my every thought and impulse, though my grasp of his character was a bit feeble. I wrote a free-verse poem about my particular agonies—nine parts glands gone mad, one part philosophy—which seemed to provoke a mixture of admiration and alarm among the teachers who shared it with each other. At the time, I despaired of ever living long enough to own my own car. I had begun to write again because it was the only way I knew to express my bewilderment, my sense of the impossible possibilities without which life was not worthwhile.

My classmates were preparing for college or careers at Boeing Aircraft, where my mother, having gotten one of the highest scores ever recorded on Boeing's standard IQ test, was given an entry-level job as a secretary. I'd worked at part-time jobs since I was eleven, supplementing her income, which seemed calculated to fall about 20 percent short of what we needed. On one job at a local Rod and Gun Club, I lost part of my hearing because the manager neglected to mention I should use earplugs. We lost one, maybe two trailers to foreclosure, and I noticed that, ever after, when bills began to mount we would move. We moved a lot.

I, meanwhile, began reading Sir James Jeans's *The Universe around Us,* pondering such questions as "How do we know when others say 'red' or 'middle C' that they really mean the same things we mean by those words?" and "If any one thing is eternal or infinite, how can anything else in the same universe be finite and defined in time?" I also began memorizing the atomic weights and numbers of various elements and the speeds of various atomic particles and the density of outer space (three atoms per cubic yard) and the names and numbers of the moons of the various planets, information I could scarcely believe actually existed. I collected such statistics as others might collect gemstones or butterflies.

When I discovered Will Durant's *The Story of Philosophy,* I had my introduction to the wide world of ideas: Aristotle, Socrates, Plato, Spinoza, Hume, Nietzsche. I was hooked. Here were guides who asked hard questions, rejected easy answers. Not only were they undaunted by anxieties that reduced most people to despair, but the style of their phrases and the audacity of their insights made them loom as heroes of the intellect, knights of the crucial nuance, victors over the philistine assumptions fueling most lives I saw around me. Here was a pursuit worth exploring, in company I truly enjoyed.

College seemed out of the question for several reasons—I didn't think I was smart enough, we had no money for it, and it had long been understood that upon graduation I would take a job and help support my mother and sister. Hoping to win money for college, I entered a United Nations essay on peace contest with a paper suggesting that since enemies only united in the face of a greater challenge from without, perhaps we could resolve the current tensions between the Free World and the Communist states by releasing the real information we had on UFO's so that we earthlings could unite to form a common defense. It didn't win. For my senior honors English paper, I wrote a fifty-page essay on "Ideal Government," arranging to have myself locked into the school library two nights in a row so I could have full, uninterrupted access to the classics I was gorging

"Billy with the reins; my father with Wendy, my sister; my mother; and the real, unidentified driver of the surrey with the fringe on top," Saint Augustine, Florida, 1953

on with an inexplicable ecstasy. I began to harbor more seriously the notion that I might indeed be a writer myself someday. In fact, it was the only thing I could imagine wanting to be.

Undergraduate Years

From high school I went immediately to work in Todds Shipyard, Seattle. The pipefitter to whom I was assistant, an old union pro, constantly told me to slow down and get lost on my way to and from the supply yard with the materials for our jobs. He mostly napped or smoked. So did almost everyone else. [See "Old Timers," *Invisible Guests*.] There was no Caribbean after-work high-spiritedness to relieve the exhausting tedium, just heavy-handed, locker-room obscenities which smelt to me of brutalized sensibilities. I longed for escape.

When there was a general strike at Todds, I used my meager savings for tuition at University of Washington. I rented a basement room for twenty dollars a month in the university district, signed up for courses. Having no money left over, I stole paperback texts about philosophy and history and art to read and bacon to eat. In fact, until I was able to get a job that paid minimum wage, I possessed few things not the shape of a pocket. But I was on my own, in very heaven, an outlaw-scholar-poet-philosopher, or so I fancied myself. And foolish as those fancies may have been, never before in my life had I felt so innocent, so free.

About this time, I met Tim Riley, who would soon become my closest friend. His ability to describe the most ghastly catastrophes of life in such a way as to unearth all their mercilessly comic possibilities has left me breathless from the giddy mix of tears and laughter countless times over the years.

In my freshman year I took Leonie Adams's poetry workshop. She was replacing Roethke, on leave. At the time I hadn't heard of Roethke or anyone else since Lord Byron, except for Sandburg and Frost. Adams was a grey lady, very quiet, private even in the classroom. She perpetually wore a wool coat, scarf, and cap, often sat at the desk, slumped over the work for the day, without speaking. Except for her occasional excitement over a line or image, I recall little of the workshop because I understood almost none of it. My poems, with titles like "Do the Bells Bemoan Rebirth," were stuffed with lit'ry diction, and she was reading verses to us from Thomas, Stevens, Eliot, Hopkins, all of whom rang in my ears like foreign tongues set to beautiful rhythms and relieved with occasional moments of English

lucidity. But I was in over my head, bewildered. I also had to take a job that conflicted with the class, so we met weekly in her office. The sessions were seances in which she conjured the dead with quotations I didn't understand but admired not least for their grip on her imagination. She was charged by a life of memories and knowledge that had galvanized her with an unflagging intellectual vitality. She encouraged me kindly, but I didn't take another poetry-writing class until I graduated and came back for night courses before going on to graduate school, so intimidated had I been by her erudition, my ignorance.

I pursued Hemingway, Twain, Emerson, Nietzsche, Schopenhauer, Freud, Jung, Blake, and Diana, with about equal ardor, through class after class. I also took courses from David Wagoner, William Dunlap, Nelson Bentley, Grant Redford, George Bluestone, all writers teaching writing. I even met Theodore Roethke, briefly, when he kicked me out of his last class because I was not yet a senior. "Come back next fall, old shoe," he said, arm around my shoulder.

Much later I did occasionally visit one of John Logan's workshops conducted on a houseboat in Elliot Bay. I remember bringing him a poem in a particularly demanding form I'd just discovered. He asked me to read it. "Totems poke from Rana Raraku on Aku Aku," I began. He stared, aghast. "What," he finally said, when I had finished only a couple of stanzas, "is that?" "A pantoum," I answered, shaken by his tone. "But is it a *poem?*" he moaned, shaking his head.

Later he approved a few of my poems and suggested I try them with his friend Robert Bly. Knowing nothing of Bly, I sent sonnets, roundels, rhymed quatrains. He replied, in spidery handwriting, "These poems are knock-kneed with objects." [See "Stockroom," "Grandfather at a Picnic," in *The Storm and Other Poems*.] I was chagrined. A year later I sent more work. He replied simply, "Empty." This time he was wrong but that judgement rang in my ears for years until I purged it by beginning a poem "I am empty" and exploring the worst fears I knew. [See title sequence in *Striking the Dark Air for Music*.]

I had had, at best, a checkered undergraduate career. By the time I approached graduation, I had refused to attend mandatory ROTC classes, nearly flunked statistics, did flunk prescriptive grammar, and waged a pitched battle in one philosophy class against the alleged inevitability of Socrates's suicide. The teaching assistant, rumored to be the philosophy department's brightest grad student ever, insisted that Socrates lived and died by rules as clear as those governing baseball. I knew nothing of game theory but I loved Socrates and wasn't convinced he merely struck out.

I achieved little intellectual or aesthetic distance in those years. It seemed to me there was already too much of that around.

Marriage

In one short-story writing class, I met Judith Bechtold. Her stories were much better than mine. And she was beautiful. She deigned to have coffee with me one day, and another, and to go to a movie, and another. A year later, after she returned from a summer in Europe during which we wrote back and forth almost daily, we married and moved to Bolinas, California. Our daughter, Jennifer Lorca, was born later that year.

My writing had become real almost overnight once it dawned on me that anything I wrote would one day be read by my own flesh and blood, the child Judy was carrying. This was in the late spring of 1965. What had been, I realized in retrospect, apprentice exercises in craft and technique, became work in earnest, my legacy to my child; perhaps the legacy I had never received from my own father. [See *The Storm and Other Poems*.]

Judy already had an M.A. in creative writing. I applied to various master of fine arts programs and was accepted by University of Iowa and by University of North Carolina at Greensboro, which offered a teaching assistantship and had Randall Jarrell on its faculty. I wanted to return to the South.

Graduate School

I also wanted to study with Randall Jarrell. But Randall wasn't teaching the M.F.A. people. He wasn't well. Soon after we arrived, in ambiguous circumstances many people felt had been suicidal, he was killed. It was a blow to everyone, but the aftermath somehow solidified us. Maybe part of that came from realizing that, even with such clear accomplishments, something in a writer could still feel *that* empty—*The Lost World*, his last poetry collection, was heartbreakingly sad—so we were all jolted by the realization of how deadly serious the task of a writer might be, after all: he must first save himself, clearly a matter more complex than achieving success among peers, even among friends, of whom he had so many.

It was the first term UNC-G, "the women's college," had gone coed, and it was coed only at the grad level. There were about half a dozen male students on campus, all in the M.F.A. program. As we all stood in the hall awaiting the first workshop—uneasily eyeing each other, wondering how it was going to be, what our teacher, someone named Fred Chappell, would be like, whether it might not all be a terrible mistake—down the hall came someone whose general appearance made us feel relatively suave and debonair. He gave the impression he'd just dropped off his bedroll somewhere. His hair was slung carelessly over his forehead, rumpled shirt unbuttoned half down his chest, gait a shuffle, and a cigarette hung smoldering from his lips. He turned into our classroom.

Once we were all seated, he looked up, a bit pained despite the grin, and said, "Name's Fred Chappell," the Tarheel accent thicker than cigarette smoke. "This is the creative writing workshop." Pause. "If things go as they should, inside two weeks we'll hate each other's guts."

But he was wrong, as we were wrong. Within two weeks, we knew we had a teacher as good as they get, and we were vying to write something, anything, that might earn an approving nod or remark. There must be some things about writing Fred didn't know, but we never found out what they might be. Intuitive, intelligent, he was as learned in the classics and French surrealists as in the best of the "new" writers (he put me onto Kinnell and Merwin and tried unsuccessfully to interest me in Ashberry, with whom Fred would share the Bollingen Prize in Poetry two decades later).

Fred was often to be found at the Pickwick Bar a mile off campus in those days, surrounded by books and, once we discovered his hangout, by us. He was generous with his time and tactful enough to be supportive without compromising his critical sense. Our flawed drafts would glow in the borrowed light of Fred's intelligence.

Fiction workshops were the province of Peter Taylor, immediately recognizable as a Southern gentleman of the old school—his kindly smile was just slightly askew, his eyes bright blue and friendly, his accented speech soft and genteel. He raised courtesy to a high art in his workshops, encouraging critical readings of each other's work but, by temperament and example, making tact an indispensable aspect of any comment. One learned to listen very closely to Peter's remarks, to decode their kindliness for whatever hints of shortcoming they might reveal.

In this M.F.A. program we learned that the business of teaching and learning about writing could be conducted quite effectively without the cutthroat atmosphere rumored to prevail at many other programs.

Into this time and place came Allen Tate, well into his sixties by then, with his relatively new, relatively young wife, Helen. We knew by rumor that she had been in a convent when she took a literature class from Allen at the University of Minnesota and fell in love with him, leaving "all that" behind. Certainly we were impressed.

Mr. Tate was delightful, loved to amuse and be amused, told anecdotes about old Possum and Red and Cal, even told once, over lunch, in grave tones, about packing his daddy's dueling pistols and boarding a train for Palo Alto, where he intended to challenge Yvor Winters to a duel for his remarks alleging Tate's culpability in Hart Crane's death. "But I had a change of heart when I hit the Mississippi," he concluded, "and I came home." His eyes twinkled. "Just as well for Yvor, too!"

As a teacher, he simply led us to the materials and watched with interest as we tried to respond, whether to the theories of Aristotle or Charles Olson, whom he regarded as a Pound franchise. The old war-horse no longer needed to prove a thing, and was thoroughly enjoying his glory years. He and Peter together passed some of my work on to Robert Lowell, by whom I was later recommended, I'm told, for a Rockefeller grant. They also helped me get a publisher for *The Storm and Other Poems*, basically my thesis.

Several years later, after *Striking the Dark Air for Music* came out, I visited Mr. Tate at his home in Tennessee. He was bedridden with emphysema (he had chain-smoked True Blues in Greensboro) and was hooked to an oxygen tank. I was appalled by his condition, he by my beard. His greeting was, "Why, Allen, my boy, you've come to pay homage at last!" He meant Allen Ginsberg, his way of chiding me for my beard. At the time I mistook wit for confusion, but frailty hadn't diminished his appetite for amusement.

First Teaching Job

Having graduated midyear 1966–67, I sought work immediately at the Modern Language Association of America meeting in New York. Arriving on a Sunday evening, we parked our car, got out to look around, returned to find everything had been stolen. Over a greasy-spoon hamburger, a fair omen of things to come, I did get a job—teaching five basic courses spring semester 1967 at Slippery Rock State College. We lived ten miles from town: The Yellow

House, Volant, Pennsylvania. It was so cold I had a 6:30 A.M. appointment with the local tow truck to start the car for my 7:30 A.M. class, this despite having bought the biggest battery in the county—so large I had to strap the hood down to keep it from flying open. I wrote not one poem, despaired ever of being able to teach and write.

The next year I taught a much lighter load at Michigan State University, began to write again. I didn't yet know that the periodic dry spells I would experience would tend to be followed by changes in style, and the new poems seemed dreadfully flat, dismal in mood. ["Year of the Monkey," "Burning," "Curse of a Quiet Citizen," *Invisible Guests*.] My prospects appalled me. A. J. M. Smith, the distinguished Canadian poet and anthologist then at MSU, asked me one night at a party how many poems I had published. I said around 150. He sighed. "I haven't published that many poems in my lifetime." Tenure, promotions, dwindling energies siphoned off into extrania—I felt like a bowling ball working its way in

*Assistant professor at
Michigan State University, 1968*

slow motion toward the pins, and, win or lose, that would be that.

I was fortunate. By the end of that first year I had been awarded both a Wallace Stegner Fellowship to study creative writing at Stanford and a Rockefeller grant. I accepted the Stegner, postponed the Rockefeller, and we headed west. We could never have made it that year at Stanford had Judy not diligently saved from the MSU wages. We summered, as we had the previous year, on the Oregon coast. The previous summer had been a relatively lovely and cheerful time of walking the coast, picking the ubiquitous blackberries for pies and preserves, and caring for my lovely seven-year-old sister, Jan (the older of two daughters my mother bore from her second marriage). That next summer, however, was foggy and dreary, and during that time it was becoming more difficult to ignore that our marriage was in trouble. Our daughter, Jennifer, whom we both loved wholeheartedly, had become more and more our best reason for staying together.

Stanford Years

At Stanford, Wendell Berry, as visiting writer, taught both the fiction and the poetry-writing workshops the first term. His first novel and collection of poems had just appeared. Few of us knew his work. But everyone admired Wendell from the first word. Even Ken Kesey has remarked on Wendell's resemblance to Gary Cooper, as much in manner as in appearance. Tall, lanky, clear-eyed, high-minded, kindly, accustomed to demanding a great deal of himself, his standards were high, his judgements fair.

I recall one particular session of Wendell's workshop. A young Kentuckian—very young, wispily bearded, and hell-bent on cracking the workshop's civilized veneer, even if it took Raw Sex and Drugs to do it!—came in with a new story he asked to read while it was fresh. The young man read clearly intending to blow our minds and fully expecting to be martyred for his trouble. He read without once looking up. Long on psychedelics and sex, short on everything else, the tale involved a demented San Francisco orchestra director who somehow had contrived to wave his baton over a stoned couple making endlessly permutative love in the orchestra pit—with detailed, magnified, quadraphonic, Fujicolor attention to the vast, throbbing, foaming, empurpled genitalia prominently featured.

At story's end, he sighed, raised his head with the slow, sad, triumphant smile of one about to be crowned with thorns, and found, instead, a dozen averted faces, two dozen shuffling feet, and total silence. We all liked him. We were embarrassed not by the story but by his intentions. Not even Wendell spoke. The silence lengthened. Finally Ian, a hard-boiled Aussie with Sunny Jim looks, broke the spell. "I say there," he began, "that 'great, throbbing, luminescent prick' you kept mentioning, was it *attached* to anything?"

The author's next story improved by a quantum leap.

Divorce

Judy and I were living in La Honda, twenty miles or so from Stanford. It was a small town near the coast, and we had a ramshackle house on a hillside sloping to grape arbors and fronted by Recreation Drive, a name whose optimism we tried to take to heart. But things between us were not working.

As the publication date for *The Storm and Other Poems* approached, I noticed how many of the poems in it derived from the past. I determined I would write new work in the first person present tense. The resulting Reckoning poems of *Striking the Dark Air for Music* probed areas which, once opened, were hard to ignore. Years later, in selecting and arranging that work for a book, I tried to depict something other than the sadly familiar struggles of husband and wife growing away from each other—which I realized, gradually, was not the true center of the poems—but rather the underlying dramatic tensions of the naturally bipolar psyche in which the primal elements, a male "I" and female "you," out of synch, fiercely contended among new balances of a shifting interior power, often via interior dialogue. This hadn't quite been done before and it seemed to confuse most reviewers, though at least one, the poet T. R. Hummer, read it very well.

Song of a Blind Traveller

As a blind man negotiates
rutted backroads, marvelling,
if he maintains his balance,
at his grace, so some men
leaning upon fences on the way
will amuse themselves
with the clumsiness they see,
while others, witnessing
his grace,
will share grace with him.

(from *Striking the Dark Air for Music*)

Marriages all around us were shattering. Max and Sue were in trouble, Ed and Kitty. My friend Tim's wife, Karen, had died following childbirth. Peter and Mary up in Portland. Judy and I tried counselling, in vain. We split up, then decided to give it one last try, on a trip into Mexico. [See "The Anonymous Welcome," *Faultdancing.*] After that, Judy eventually took Jennifer and returned to Oregon, to her parents. I took off alone in an old Volvo and drove the perimeter of the country, ten thousand miles in a month, visiting everyone I knew along the way. Then I returned to Palo Alto for a while, and moved in the fall of 1970 to a commune in Albion, near Mendocino, living part of the time in a teepee on an open meadow surrounded by huge trees, enjoying it all at first, then feeling increasingly alienated by certain aspects of that Eden.

East

When Amherst College offered me a job as visiting writer spring term, 1971, I took it. The Rockefeller money was long gone and a subsequent Guggenheim grant was going fast. So I taught at Amherst, wrote, took my last few hundred dollars and flew to Europe for the summer. My mother had previously vowed that if Nixon was elected she would take her younger girls, Jan and Heidi, and leave the country until Nixon was gone. She'd spent the first year in a village near Salzburg and wanted to move either to Crete or Majorca. I would help with the driving. Over several weeks, we drove down through Yugoslavia to Athens, from Athens to Rome, on to Barcelona, and finally out to Palma on Majorca. I took occasional sidetrips, hitchhiking and meeting up with the family down the road.

I returned to live on another commune, in southwestern Vermont, near Packers Corners. When I'd first visited, it had been half men, half women. When I returned, the men had left. I was uneasy because this is basically what had happened earlier in Albion. I asked if I was welcome or if they'd rather remain an all-women group. *No problem,* they said. *You're our friend. If things change you'll know.*

So we all lived in the old farmhouse insulated with cornhusks long since rotted to meal and fallen to the base of the walls. It had a wood stove for heat. Before I left we'd planted the nearby field with vegetables, but everyone else also left for the summer, and by September weeds were more plentiful than tomatoes. Farmers we were not, although we had enough zucchinis to reach to the moon and back. Nonetheless, we were contacted by *Ramparts* maga-

zine to write a series called "Rainbow Farm: Notes from the Counter Culture." It was an interesting period of which I may write more another time.

PITS[1]

My life changed somewhat when I accepted an invitation for a poetry-reading tour in Arizona, winter of 1971–72. I expected college readings but as I stepped off the plane, the organizer, Neil Claremon, said, "Just think—this time tomorrow you'll be standing in front of a classroom full of Navajo kids!" "Why?" I gasped. "Because this is a poet-in-the-schools program you're on. You have done it before, haven't you?" I had indeed read in the *New York Times Book Review* about Kenneth Koch's innovations in teaching poetry writing to children, and I had admired him for it, but I had also thanked my lucky stars I would never find myself in that circumstance. I had not, it seems, knocked on wood.

So we drove north into higher, colder country (in Tucson, it had been hot and sunny) to arrive at a place so old as to be timeless, unspoiled by the native generations there for hundreds of years. Perhaps because I have so little admiration for "dark satanic mills" or "the great white way," I have always been happiest where natural landscapes provide an alternative scale of values whose humbling grandeur and ferocity I instinctively trust. This was such a place.

Approaching that first classroom, we overheard the teacher, an ancient Bureau of Indian Affairs crone, instruct her class in how to regard us. "You mustn't take these people seriously—they're only poets." We rounded the corner, and the whole class turned to stare. They were fourth or fifth graders, little kids with wide brown faces and bright eyes, black hair hanging loose over their foreheads or in neat braids. She then called us aside to say, so everyone in the room heard, "Now listen, these are Indian children. They don't know anything and they're slow to learn, so don't expect much."

By now the kids were looking down at their desks in that attitude I had been warned to expect: "Indian kids tend to be impassive. Don't expect them to pay much attention to you." And no wonder! Turning from the teacher, laden with turquoise jewelry and girded by a Navajo belt worth a fortune, I said, "Well, hello. It seems like we have some things in common—you aren't supposed to pay any attention

---

[1] Poets-in-the-Schools

"My daughter, Jennifer Lorca Root, just after we finished painting our first car together," 1971

schools in Arizona, New Mexico, Vermont, Mississippi, Idaho, Wyoming, Montana, Oregon, Washington, Texas. Along the way, I would work with Black students in the delta country around Greenwood, Mississippi; in Natchez I would teach mornings in a white high school, afternoons in a Black high school, carrying their poems back and forth to each other, a kind of cultural smuggler. I worked on the Navajo and Hopi reservations, on the Crow, Northern Cheyenne, and Wind River reservations. I worked with kids in remote logging communities, in coal country. In Alaska, I worked with kids from villages made of ice and hides. Other than my immediate living expenses, generally very low, all I needed was enough to maintain child support, which, though modest, proved difficult to manage through these years.

> . . . Here
> most faces are flat as the earth
> and colors of the earth, and when their speech
> erupts with Crow, earth fills the air
> as words the stomach somehow hears.
>
> Speak, and you will be heard.
> But question these faces
> expecting what you would expect
> of stone, or an old stump,
> the wide blank gaze, neither
> friendly nor hostile,
> of a flat rock, or bark
> with eyes. It is not
> a gaze that isolates
> a tree from its forest
> or mistakes
> words from the tongue
> for the heart's talk.

(from "Teaching among the Children of Chief Plenty Coups," *Reasons for Going It on Foot*)

Jennifer and Me

Jennifer often spent her summers or parts of them with me in Oracle, Mendocino, Portland. We lived part of a year in London and Cornwall. And we would visit other times as well. But there was never really enough time for us, and parting was traumatic.

In 1972, after a visit in Greensboro (Judy returned there for her M.F.A.), when it came time to leave, I decided on the spur of the moment to spend our last day together painting my car, an old gray Saab named Sebastian. We bought can after can of Rustoleum, two brushes, spray cans of gold paint. First we repainted the whole thing white, then added

because we're only poets, and we aren't supposed to expect much because you're only Indians, right?" I winked. Soon the kids were smiling, glancing back and forth at each other, then looking straight at us. And they listened.

My doubts and fears had fallen away like shadows when I'd heard that teacher. This was not a place I could waste time indulging my insecurities. I'd glimpsed how it was for these kids, and how it would be. Maybe it was a rerun, in a way, of my father versus his field hands, of certain values he stood for versus values I was slowly discovering were my own. It didn't matter. Imagination, once you have the feel of it in your heart, your mouth, your hand, is something no one and nothing can take away. It is "red veins full of money." At the time I knew little of *their* traditions, but I soon began learning about the Blessingways and Songways, the ceremonial poetry and ritual dances that have histories old as the heart of the bristlecone pine.

So, for the next ten years, off and on, I would partially support myself working as a poet-in-the-a wide gold stripe over hood, roof, and trunk. It was nearly Valentine's Day, so on one fender went a red heart. On another, a picture of my shaggy dog, Sam. On another, a flower. On the last, a horse. The car glowed like a magnificent Russian Easter egg on wheels. When we stood back to look at it, Jennifer's face fell and she began to cry. "We ruined it," she wept. I assured her it was fine, that it would run better than ever now, and our day together would always be with me anywhere I went. But as fate would have it, the car blew its engine two hundred miles north. Then blew it again in Vermont.

So the next year, I made a point of painting my next car, a '61 Valiant, with Jennifer—this time over turquoise Rustoleum we put a dragon on the passenger's door and planets on the driver's door. It ran like a top for years. A sailor in Galveston, Texas, once staggered out of a bar and flagged me down in the street to ask where I had gotten the dragon design. I told him we'd made it up. He asked if I would tattoo him with that design if he got me tattooing equipment. Reluctantly, I declined, but when I passed the word on to Jennifer, she was delighted. [See "A Natural History of Unicorns and Dragons My Daughter and I Have Known," *In the World's Common Grasses.*]

Rancho Linda Vista

Another benefit of that fortunate trip to Arizona was my discovery of Rancho Linda Vista, an eighty-acre former dude ranch (Andy Warhol's *Lonesome Cowboys* was filmed there shortly before I arrived). Tom Mix, Lana Turner, the guy who wrote Arthur Godfrey's "I Wanna Go Back to My Little Grass Shack" and Arthur Godfrey all had visited there in its heydays of the thirties and forties. But when I saw it, it had been recently purchased by ten couples wishing to create a place where they could live cheaply and support themselves by means of their artwork in a community supportive of such pursuits. It still thrives, a sprawling assembly of adobe houses and dry washes and a huge barn converted into studios, which is where I am writing now. [See "Writing in the Studio of a Friend," unpublished ms.] Its population ranging in age from toddlers to sexagenarians includes painters, sculptors, ceramic artists, weavers, woodworkers, an anthropologist, a psychiatrist, an acupuncturist, a sandal-maker, dancers, musicians, a mine foreman, teachers, and so on. Nearby is Sun Space, where the first large-scale artificial environment is near completion. Since that first visit nearly twenty years ago, I've considered this place my home away from home, and

I've seldom let a year pass without living some part of it here.

Other Places, Other Jobs through the Seventies

Eventually I did less and less PITS work (I was burning out), more and more visiting writer-in-residencies: Wichita State University, University of Southwest Louisiana in ragin' cajun country, and University of Montana, where I was hired five times between 1976–1985, usually to replace Dick Hugo when he was on leave, then again, sadly, when he died.

Besides the Rockefeller, Stegner, and Guggenheim, mentioned earlier, there's been a National Endowment for the Arts grant, a United States/United Kingdom Fellowship, and so on, several (unsuccessful) nominations for the Pulitzer, National Book Award, and American Book Award, various

"At the base of a crater behind Little River Cemetery, Mendocino Coast, California," 1980

prizes and awards including three Pushcarts, hundreds of readings at colleges and universities, bars, bookstores, and coffee shops across the country, numerous symposia and writers workshops, all pretty much the standard fare for a working writer. Individual poems have been included in over sixty anthologies and have been translated into Japanese, Croatian, Macedonian, Russian, Yiddish, Hebrew, and Swedish. But such stuff, so exciting as it happens, incrementally, tends to be deadly boring in summary.

In 1979, I was visiting writer at Interlochen Arts Academy in northern Michigan, an idyllic spot in woods among lakes. When I left Interlochen—perhaps the first school where I never heard a teacher complain about the students—I drove with my dog, Grizzly, in "Casa Blanca," an aging white station wagon (the rear axle was forever coming loose on this car so I learned to replace it myself and carried a junkyard spare always), heading for Oklahoma City,

where my good friend Bill Gammill lived. Interlochen hadn't paid much and I was dead broke. Gammill had a friend in construction who needed an extra hand, finishing drywall.

For me the slide from glory to grits had long since grown familiar. Over the years, I've worked a number of odd jobs to stitch together my sporadic income from PITS work, poetry readings, and visiting writer jobs: I've worked twenty-four hundred feet underground in a copper mine near Oracle, Arizona; in a book factory in Brattleboro, Vermont; as a dishwasher in Fort Bragg, California; as a bouncer at the Sweet Chariot in the pre-restoration Pioneer Square of Seattle, as a Teamster in North Carolina and California, as a factory hand in Stockton, and so on. Most often I was glad for the work, some interesting in its way just so long as I could always see the other end of the tunnel.

The Russian Connection

At Interlochen Arts Academy, I had a fateful call from a Pamela Uschuk, a poet arranging poetry readings for the local arts council. Advised by a friend that "Pamela is a good poet—and gorgeous," I returned the call suggesting we see the movie *A Little Romance*. Except for the adjective, the choice of movies proved prophetic. I wasn't long in Oklahoma City before I found myself missing Pamela and told her so. We soon hooked up, spent a few months in OKC, a few more in Oracle, part of a year in Port Townsend, Washington, part of another in Missoula, then back to Oracle for two years, then back to Missoula long enough for Pamela to earn her M.F.A. (years before, she'd quit her graduate studies in Russian literature, just shy of her degree, to retreat from academia to the northern woods of Michigan, where I found her).

During the years since, constantly writing and publishing poems and stories, gathering prizes and awards, working with PITS programs on reservations in Montana and in prisons in New York, eventually she found time to make as honest a man of me as the law allows.

"My youngest sister, Heidi Sena Petersen (far left); my mother, Bonita Joy Maria Petersen (seated); my eldest sister, Wendy (Gwendolyn Frances) Clisham; my middle sister, Jan Kristen Goldthorpe," 1985

Leaving Missoula

Summer of 1983 we bought an old rustbucket in London and drove across Europe to Athens, sleeping on its reclining seats every other night. In Greece, after exploring the islands of Patmos and Paros, we visited Yannis Ritsos, the Greek poet, at his home on

*"My wife Pam with Mu on a water tower
at Rancho Linda Vista in Oracle, Arizona," 1982*

Samos, before circling round to Thira. Back in England we visited Laurens van der Post and his wife, Ingaret, at their summer place. These writers, still hard at it in their seventies and eighties, respectively, were enormously inspiring to us. Politically at opposite ends of the spectrum, at heart both men are warm, astonishingly courageous. Each having spent years imprisoned—van der Post in a concentration camp during World War II, Ritsos during various Greek regimes—they've both remained steadfastly passionate in the constant and unsentimental dedication of their art to the service of humanity in ways that far exceed the simply literary function. And each, in fact as well as in figure of speech, has been declared a hero many times over in the course of their extraordinary lives. It was my only meeting with Ritsos. I'd met and corresponded previously with Laurens, at whose invitation I addressed the World Wilderness Congress in Findhorn.

At the end of our third year in Missoula, my job ran out and I took a position at Hunter College in Manhattan where I direct the Creative Writing program. Faculty and students alike are generally excellent and serious. Two-thirds of the students from working class or immigrant nonwhite backgrounds are Blacks drawn variously from the city, the Caribbean, or Africa; Hispanics from the U.S., Mexi-

co, the Caribbean, Spain, South and Central America; others come from the Middle East, India, Pakistan, China, Japan. Just last term, I worked with students from Poland, Turkey, Spain, Harlem, Italy, Little Italy, Chile, Queens, Brooklyn, Scarsdale, Puerto Rico, Ceylon, Costa Rica, China, Detroit, and so on, a full spectrum of Christians, Jews, Hindus, Muslims, Communists, a Hungarian who spent a year in prison at hard labor for participating in Free Speech demonstrations. A course I offer in Twentieth Century Native American Literature always draws students with Native American heritages. One could scarcely imagine a richer mix of students.

The glimpses I get through these various eyes of what America still means to the rest of the world are invaluable and challenging. And often humbling. Since being in New York, I've also taught in the graduate writing program at New York University and in the Westside Y's "Writers Voice" series, each of special interest in its own way. Pamela also teaches writing, through Marist College, at Greenhaven Maximum Security Prison, and through Poets-in-Public-Service up and down the Hudson Valley.

We had to search long and hard for a place in New York we might find tolerable for us and our three large dogs—Mu, Drambuie, and Oscar Wild (no e)—each, by the way, part wolf. We've now rented a house in the Shawangunk Mountains, bordering the Catskills, five miles from New Paltz and nearly a hundred from Manhattan. It has a creek running by one of the decks, a lake a hundred yards below the other. Across the dirt road is a waterfall we hear as we write, I in my first-floor study with Oscar wrapped around my feet, Pam in the study above with Mu wrapped around hers. The Jotul wood stove is highly efficient, and having found this place makes living in New York unusually pleasant, though we both yearn, incurably I suspect, for the open faces, rugged regions, and wild creatures under the big skies of the West. Coyotes have just been reported in New York City's northern boroughs, but as Gary Snyder has said, no woods without grizzlies can quite be true wilderness. (In Missoula, the campus police sometimes had to roust the occasional feeding bears before students started arriving for morning classes.)

Usually we summer in or near Oracle, with frequent trips down to the coast of the Baja Peninsula. Last summer I came close to being food for a pair of ten-foot hammerhead sharks, but that's a story for another time. Come spring term, l990, we will share a writer-in-residency at Pacific Lutheran University in Tacoma, Washington, which will put us in a part of the country we both love, for a change, nearer my

"With my daughter, Jennifer Lorca, and my wife Pamela Uschuk," 1981

family, who are spread out from Los Angeles (where my daughter, Jennifer, is completing graduate studies at USC's Annenberg School) and Fort Bragg (where my oldest sister, Wendy, is a weaver) to Everett (where my middle sister, Jan, is a nurse and my mother lives, retired) and Bellingham (where Heidi, my youngest sister, works as a fitness trainer).

Current Projects

My first project is to find publishers for a number of manuscripts recently finished or nearing completion: *Under the Umbrella of Blood*, poems concerned with current issues and events "an informed consciousness incurs like debt"; *The Collected Poems of Heinrich Boll*, cotranslated with Hannelore Quander-Rattee; and a story collection, *Who's to Say This Isn't*

Love? And Other Stories. I'm at work on new collections of poetry and short fiction, a miscellany of translations, imitations, and adaptations of poems from around the world called *After Others*, miscellaneous essays, reviews, and interviews tentatively entitled *Where Heart Is the Horse and Head the Rider, Poets Must Be Centaurs.* And I hope one day to publish a collection of my photographs, accruing since I got my first 35-mm SLR, a Canon Pelix, in 1966.

My recent poems tend to reflect wider concerns I found hard to incorporate into the earlier, more often personally oriented poetry. How successful those efforts are, time will tell, but as years pass I feel—and who doesn't?—more and more powerfully the urge to broaden beyond what I've done, and it has seemed to make publishers, who'd been happy with my more pastoral work, a bit nervous. Here is one such poem:

Under the Umbrella of Blood

In the shower not ten minutes ago and blind from the vinegar rinse
I was thinking 40, I'm 40
when the stinging reminded me how Turks used to bet on
just how far a headless man could run—
                                        It was orderly, in its way
with bands of selected prisoners, troops in attendance, distance markers
a hammered copper plate glowing solar at the end of a pole;
as the prisoners one at a time ran past the sword took off their heads
and the plate scorched the neck-stumps shut to keep blood pressure up
so the runners ran farther, each stumbling on under an umbrella of blood
until the disfigured collapse, all legs and loose elbows.

Do you suppose that as each head fell staring and revolving
it could hear the tossed coins clink on the outspread blanket?
Could it see the body running off without it?
As it lay speechless, facing dirt or the sky, as chance would have it,
would it know whether it won or lost for its learned critics?

I wonder, and I rush off to the typewriter wiping my eyes clear,
knowing if I am to get it right
the images under the final downpour must be running
faster than the applauding coins of the world can ever fall.

BIBLIOGRAPHY

Poetry:

The Storm and Other Poems, Atheneum, 1969.

Seven for a Magician, Freestone Press (Limited Edition), 1973.

Striking the Dark Air for Music, Atheneum, 1973.

The Port of Galveston (photographs by Jean-Claude Marchant, Richard and Betty Tichich), Galveston Arts Center, 1974.

Coot and Other Characters: Poems New and Familiar, Confluence, 1977.

A Journey South, Graywolf Press (Limited Edition), 1977.

Seven Mendocino Songs, Mississippi Mud Press (Limited Edition), 1977.

Fireclock, Four Zoas Press (Limited Edition), 1981.

In the World's Common Grasses, Moving Parts Press, 1981.

Reasons for Going It on Foot, Atheneum, 1981.

The Unbroken Diamond: Nightletter to the Mujahideen, Pipedream Press (Limited Edition), 1983.

Invisible Guests, Confluence Press, 1984.

Faultdancing, University of Pittsburgh, 1986.

Other:

(Editor) *What a World, What a World! Poetry by Young People in Galveston Schools,* Galveston School District, 1973.

(With Ray Rice) *Song of the Woman and the Butterflyman* (film), 1975.

(With Ray Rice) *Seven for a Magician* (film), 1976.

(Editor with Diana Katsiaficas) *Timesoup: Poems, Stories, and Graphics by Young Alaskans,* Southeast Alaska Arts Council, 1980.

(Translator) *Selected Odes of Pablo Neruda,* Four Zoas Press, 1989.

(With Ray Rice) *Faces from the Poems of William Pitt Root* (film), in progress.

Martin Jack Rosenblum

1946-

BECAUSE I HAVE BEEN ASKED TO DO SO

I rely upon experience that has a mystical quality to provide depth beyond surface detail, but stick to that detail in my poetry. My poems are at the root of existence, but through a harvesting of life-style. I work with language as a trusted companion who shares my sense of wonder about how internal reality shapes external events.

My aesthetic is derived from uncommon material achieving common expression. Transcendent ventures are incomplete until spoken and heard—maybe not immediately understood, but voiced to the extent that comprehension will occur once tribal members have really listened.

The improvisation of living produces knowledge of a classical organization that always stays just beyond language, and while poetry never gets far enough it moves closest when objects are put into action. I would not consider placing my old Colt Peacemaker in a nylon camouflage holster; leather is the best fit, and then we must have it in a floral pattern to suit the pistol's historic domain. The context will make that which occurs in it either awkward or suitable. Poetry has to be made from specifics in motion, and it must be placed on the page in such a way as to create authentic forms.

In 1989, I created the proper context for an expression of my life-style. And therefore it is predictable, yet tremendously humbling, that this text sells in greater numbers than expected of real poetry books; it is unpredictable, maybe, but just as humbling, that my image and poetry appear on a line of Harley-Davidson T-shirts, also selling in record numbers. My new book is called *The Holy Ranger: Harley-Davidson Poems*. It is a Cabala for poetic awareness of self and culture, written not philosophically but in aesthetic terms, that, by virtue of rendering complexities in simple imagery, defines reality for those who are of the same tribe. The Holy Ranger is a buckskin shaman, and his story is one I want to tell now because I have been asked to do so.

I was born in Appleton, educated in Madison, and now work in Milwaukee: these Wisconsin cities map the autobiographical explorations.

Martin Jack Rosenblum, "The Holy Ranger"

Exploration One: Appleton

Sander Rosenblum lied about his age so he could leave Sweden for America before he would be permitted by emigration law to do so, and this resulted in two birthdays. Our family eventually lost track of which one was real and which one was imagined, so we would celebrate our choice according to its convenience in a given year. On my father's marble tombstone in Appleton there is one of the dates, and the other one is there as well on the bronze marker erected at the grave site by the Veterans of Foreign Wars in honor of his World War II military service. He had served as a palace guard in the Swedish army, and was selected to be a member of the elite guard corps known as Lightning Troopers; in the American army, he was a sharpshooter but wound up as a typist because he was the only one in his unit who could handle office duties. He stayed in this country as a technical corporal when the 127th Engineers went to Europe, coordinating communications by phone to typewriter using a typing system that he developed and that I now use after years of watching him.

By the time he went to war as an American citizen, he had already married my mother, Esther Ressman, who was born in Appleton of Sarah and Harry Ressman. Sarah was from Poland and Harry from Russia, and they met in a Chicago tailorshop but soon moved to Appleton, where Ressman Clothiers was established and still stands, now owned by my cousin. My father also opened a clothing store in Appleton, called the Rose Shop. Father's store sold women's apparel and Ressman's sold men's. Grandma and Grandpa did the tailoring for both, and then for another store my father briefly had after trying premature retirement from the Rose Shop due to a heart ailment. He finally went to work as a salesman in a men's suit department of a store run by a friend until retirement by choice. He made it well into his eighties with the heart problem that killed him in 1988 after raking October leaves then settling into his chair to catch his last breath.

The day Sander Rosenblum died I woke up earlier than I normally do, because I had dreamed something that shook me awake, and I in turn woke my wife, Maureen, to tell her of the dream I had that Father would die this day. It was a Sunday. He called that late October morning and we had our usual weekly phone conversation. But I did not recall the dream until I got an afternoon call from my parents' neighbor, informing me that Dad had just died. Father went for a longer walk than was customary, raked the leaves, then sat in the den after telling Mother he felt he was more out of breath than he should be. She heard the gasp and called in their neighbor, who could not wake him up. There was blood on the rug after the paramedics tried to make sure there would be no liability involved with their ambulance call, and Father died on his own, refusing to respond to the injections and thumping, having gone alone but first making certain I knew it would be the right time for him.

In violation of Jewish tradition, I opened his casket right before he was buried. I was going to deliver the eulogy because I could not trust a rabbi to say anything concrete, and as I finished what I was to say there in his presence, I came to terms with my own mortality. The eulogy in that little Jewish cemetery was an inspired one, then, as I had just resolved my own sense of destiny, projected by the dream in which my father's death was indicated through details that related to my circumstances as well. I shoveled the dirt onto his casket, took off my obligatory yarmelke, and walked away.

Father was always inappropriately hard on me, but soft when it counted. He never seemed to know me at all, and his temper would often flare when I had done the least offensive thing—such as when I put my license plate in the spokes of my new Schwinn American, instead of behind the seat where it usually went. Dad flew into the most peculiar rage and nearly hit me. Perhaps I remember this event the most because I fought back.

My father was very strong. He once got tired of Aunt Diana's complaints that her grand piano was not in the right spot in her living room, and got even more fed up with Uncle Ben's inability to move it as

Martin with his parents, Sander and Esther Rosenblum, April 1947

he was having one of his hypochondriacal ailments, so Father just picked the piano up by himself and dispatched it to where it was supposed to be.

So when he grabbed me in the garage, where I went that night when he discovered my break with license-plate-placement tradition, and I held him off with preteen strength and fury until he gave up, there was a standoff not unlike the one, years later, when I finally was able to beat him in a game of chess. My father's temper was a dark secret few outside of the immediate family ever knew, and it would flash out of apparent calm over issues seemingly inappropriate to such rage. He quickly gained his composure and went into the house. I sat for hours admiring my new Appleton bicycle plate with its magical low number set neatly into the rear-wheel spokes. I have stayed in that garage until quite recently, having finally realized I could put my damn license plate anywhere I pleased without having to worry about where it should go by rule or opinion.

My father was a man who would not permit any kind of disagreement with even the most irrational house law, and for many years I lived in contempt of all that would govern me, sorting out what I really did not want to obey from what I could without attendant emotional discomfort. Obedience has never been easy, but now I have an understanding of it, sometimes fastening those plates behind the seat, sometimes crimping them in the spokes, and more often than not I build custom fender brackets for them like the one on my Harley-Davidson Sportster that is painted to match the original bike colors.

Dad never approved of motorcycles, having ridden on the buddy seat of one driven by an inebriated Swede on what must have been an impressionable journey, so a continuous disagreement between us was my need for one and his need to be relieved of fear if I had one. Though he led an adventurous life before marriage, he showed little of this once he settled into family ways and instead demonstrated hysteria regarding anything that might not suit his concept of safety. I decided that a 1939 Ford Sedan with a 1948 Mercury flathead engine would do as well as a motorcycle, but lived in passionate fantasy of owning this primer grey hot rod instead because Dad immediately shouted that the machine was as dangerous and equally uncomely to the middle-class driveway.

So without these items of rebellion, I got into the real object and rebelled with the vengeance of a demigod ripping through Appleton's quiet streets. I traveled with rotten eggs in hand when younger, rocks when a little older, and finally a pearl-handled

Mexican switchblade when old enough. I went into fistfights with willpower and strength, and learned my fighting technique while trying to survive against overpowering odds; that gorgeous knife reminded me of my Stallion .38 cap gun with its bright silver finish and mysterious mechanical action, so I rarely had it out of my pants pocket like I seldom loaded caps into the toy pistol: the purity of the thing was more essential than its function. I would make gunshot noises with my breath. I would slice my opponents once the fight was over in the air with my knife. I became a decent fistfighter, but I was suffering too many permanent mouth injuries.

When I carried the Stallion .38, I would prefer to play alone at being a cowboy in the ravines that led to the Fox River near my house, always on the verge of lawlessness but ultimately saving the day by heroic deed in support of the law, deputized right before nightfall and the ride home. While I had friends with whom I roamed as if in a posse looking for the next street fight years after those days of solitude in the ravines on horseback, I was relieved once I got back to my yard after a night of chasing and fighting so I could sit alone listening to the tree frogs and tending to the slight facial wounds suffered by boys in the fifties. By the time I walked inside to the kitchen and pressed a cold, white milk bottle to my forehead just that way James Dean did it in the movie, I was already dreaming of ways to recreate the epic qualities of these evening crusades.

I started to write about the same year I quit wanting to fight. Fighting was exciting, but I was losing as much as winning, and writing seemed to be the place where objects got used instead of just preserved. The cap gun could get dirtied, wonderfully soiled with the residue of explosive materials, and that knife could click into use with such marvelous, abrasive force, so one always had to maintain them, tempering practicality with preservation. But through the act of writing caution was unnecessary and one could push guns and knives to maximum potential, being rid of oil and cleaning brush in favor of ink and fountain pen.

I listened to early rock and roll before most kids my age did, as my cousin, older than I was, brought it into my house along with an early sex education. My love for the music of Gene Vincent, Eddie Cochran, Ricky Nelson, Little Richard, and all those wild men of portable-radio rock music, tuned in from Southern stations late at night then ordered from local record shops, changed my sense of language forever. I wrote those kinds of songs and sang the lyrics as I rode my bike in the wind with my head tilted just so to keep the bird's nest hairstyle curled in place. I switched to writing tales of the Old West, and, when in the seventh grade, upon completion of a story about the U.S. Cavalry that I turned in to my English teacher, I was falsely accused of copying it and gave up writing for girls. My teacher said my story was too good for a kid my age and therefore I must have plagiarized it. I went into LeeAnn's blouse with a passion as a result. I discovered something better than writing, I figured, and its pursuit was even more genuinely of the senses.

Most tend to have their early sexual experiences in college, but I got mine in before then, and when I got to college I had already settled down to a studious, timid approach worthy of most high schoolers wanting to make class rank. By high school, in the backseat of my Corvair Monza that my father bought for my mother but that I took over with chrome tail pipe and skull gearshift knob, I enjoyed the abandon most middle-aged men destroy their marriages to recover. I missed the sexual revolution in the sixties because I already invaded, conquered, and saved the world for democratic sex. I fell in love constantly and wanted to live forever with lots of beautiful girls at various times, and sometimes variously. I was honest about all this with each one, professing exactly what I felt, which was loyalty, adoration, and extreme togetherness upon the neat Chevrolet backseat that could fold down to make this quasi-sports car into a two-seater with a flat rear compartment.

My rebellion worked well on the outside but on the inside took a toll. I began to experience psychosomatic illnesses very early in life and nearly died from the complications of one in the early eighties. Migraine headaches started first, usually coming on Friday nights to ruin weekends; these were apparently capillary letdowns from tense weeks spent acting more casual about it all than I felt. Colitis kicked in later, then ulcerative colitis much later. Every doctor I went to came up with the same result, which was that there was nothing physically wrong with me that could be absolutely traced to a functional problem; the medicines prescribed by physicians made matters worse, so I decided to control these illnesses through my own resources. Solitude seemed to act as a healing process, as did simply behaving exactly as I needed in any given situation; nobody thought of psychotherapy until years later, and even then I really cannot say there were benefits galore. Most of the time I did things my own way, which was the best total cure, or I separated myself from all interactions and in silence healed from a psychosomatic episode.

Every summer Father would rent a cottage in Waupaca, which was near Appleton, and we would move to the lake for awhile. My grandmother and grandfather lived just across the Pacific Street Bridge from our house on Pacific Street, and my aunt, uncle, and cousin just another block or so further down, and this proximity in Appleton narrowed when we all moved in together at the lake. It was a tiny place built above a boathouse, and I enjoyed swimming across our lake to an island where I could watch muskrats and turtles. It was at the boathouse that I finally lost my patience with my cousin Alan, who was four years older and who usually spent more time with my family than I liked because, it seemed, his mother, Aunt Diana, and father, Uncle Ben, enjoyed being without him.

My mother, never one to speak her mind on anything, except on the rare occasions when she would have a couple highballs or pink ladies, gave in to her sister, the selfish aunt, or her brother-in-law, the henpecked uncle, while her mother and father, Sarah and Harry Ressman, continued their emotional shunning of Mother that apparently began when she was born. My mother, Esther Pearl, always talked about how my dad even paid for her wedding as her own parents had spent what money they had saved at the time on some whim of her sister's. Esther was pressured to take care of Alan by her family, so Dad and I went along with it; though neither of us especially cared for the continual presence of this ungrateful bunch, my father and I cooperated to the detriment of our own relationship at times.

Understandably, my cousin was nasty to all living things. The day I lost all ability to tolerate him was when he trapped a turtle and kept it in a bucket. When he was in the hammock reading a comic book, I let the turtle go. He heard the turtle plop into the water and started pushing me around, and I beat the living hell out of him. Grandma, Aunt Diana, and Mother were all there and they proceeded to swat me until I let his head drop, which I had been holding steady with my left while I banged it with my strong right. Then they all chased me into the lake.

I went underwater as far as I could go until I was sure I had lost these strange people, and surfaced right next to Uncle Ben in his inner tube. He could not swim, and enjoyed bobbing around in the water; once, the Waupaca police boat had to rescue him as he fell asleep and wound up in the middle of a channel between lakes. He looked at me sympathetically, but it was obvious there was nothing he could do without endangering his own tranquility. I was a strong swimmer even at this time, which was when I

Sander Rosenblum, "pointing to the train coming to take him into World War II"

was in the fourth grade, and easily made it to the island after surfacing near the inner tube to look back at those harpies on the shore. I felt very strong all afternoon as I walked around on the sandbars, pretending I was a lost explorer having arrived at the West Coast after adventures out West, having lost my horse in an ambush and my gun, too, so I just had my briefs and a wooden pole taken from a tree. A worse ambush took place when my father and grandfather came to the boathouse that night for supper from their stores: before they drove back, each got mad at me, and my father's harsh words constituted a serious betrayal, so as I walked out on the dock and got into the rowboat I decided upon a life of integrity and justice. As the oars dipped into the night waters, I heard the distant sound of a houseboat party and could see the running lights moving further away from me.

It was in the fourth grade that my entire world became extremely unreliable. My truancy up to this point was under control somewhat, but now it became a real problem to my parents as I developed a phobia

about leaving home, though, of course, getting out of there was what I needed. This unresolved conflict started a succession of terrifying nightmares. Sitting in school would bring them back, as my consciousness had to be directed so far from their resolution. I had long ago created a mythical beast, a werewolf, to guard me from the other monsters I had seen in the hall since kindergarten, but while in third grade I came up with a powerful entity who waged war better than another, though companionable, monster. This figure was initially either a U.S. Cavalry officer or a Royal Canadian Mounted Police adventurer, and I did a lot of library and movie-theater research to determine exactly how he should look; he eventually left the mounted service to ride independently against bad guys and injustice in America. I rode with him, and these rides are my fondest memories of childhood.

I would leave Edison Elementary School and get on my horse, and trot along in conversation with him. I called him The Holy Ranger. I would wear a cowboy hat to school, and cowboy boots, but Mother would not let me take my cap guns; so, instead, I took a pocketful of toy soldiers that I collected and still to this day collect, and they would shoot up the inside of my desk during class and then be put into the posse that rode home with me to give us official command of the territory. (I had hundreds of realistic little soldiers then, and now have a couple dozen or so that I paint myself based on research conducted in my library of militaria. The toy armies I marched then went the way of my electric trains, which were discarded when I went to college, and I have spent years building new ones, based on historical settings such as the one on my office shelf of the battle of Little Round Top at Gettysburg in 54-mm scale.) In third grade, I actually organized a cavalry troop, handing out ID cards to my playmates; I put this Holy Ranger in the lead and myself second in command, and all of us, in formation, rode the ice rink in a blazing hail of lead as we captured renegades, making all sorts of neat horse and gun noises, sending those not fortunate enough to be in the troop running away from our charge. But I soon lost interest in this organization, and continued to ride alone with him.

I remember one ride home from school in particular. I stopped at Zussman's Grocery to buy penny candy and suddenly realized that maybe I should play a musical instrument like the bugle I heard when in a cavalry charge. I got home and talked my parents into letting me play a horn. For the first time, as I practiced my trumpet (which was substituted for the bugle by my music teacher because

Martin Rosenblum, "getting ready to hit the trail"

band solos were more appropriate than military ones, apparently), I got an idea as to how I might release my feelings into productive, recognizable forms. But I soon tired of playing scales. My teacher, a foreigner, had his office at the end of the local music store, and I had to walk the basement steps and then across the entire length of the dark building to get to him. He sent me a postcard once while he was back in his homeland, and I thought it was a good idea to quit, as he would not be back for a long time and I stopped practicing the trumpet when he left anyway. I could not understand his dialect and usually made up my own lessons, so easily decided I could do without him if I ever wanted to play again. My father got furious that he had wasted money on lessons. He took his anger out on me until he realized that the music-store owner owed him money for unused lessons, and grabbed me as we went to collect the twenty-five dollars and fifty cents.

Father took an old Stella guitar from the rack in the store when the owner refused to reimburse him, telling the man that he was a crook for hanging onto the money. That guitar changed my whole life. It sat in the closet until I was a junior in high school. Then a houseguest happened to pull it out and play an E-major chord. When she left, I played that chord over and over and bought a book of chords and made folk

music, especially the blues, the center of my life for years to come.

I became a respectable blues guitarist, harmonica player, and singer in the sixties. I played at many local hootenannies and was written about in the local papers often. My vocal style was rough and I played a mean harmonica. I blew mouth harp, in fact, with every name rock-and-roll band that came through the Fox River Valley. They would ask for me. I would get drunk and blow my heart out. I joined some other musicians once I got to the Fox Valley Center of the University of Wisconsin, where I went to college for my first two years before transferring to UW–Madison, and we had ourselves a real hot jug band. (The musicians with whom I played have gone on to become known nationally as a down-home music act.) I played solo blues and we all worked on traditional American music. I studied ethnic American folk-music styles, moving on to Autoharp and five-string banjo, and soon we were actually making money at it. We were recognized on the street and respected by other "folkies," and I eventually became friends with John Hammond, Jr., whose guitar method I learned from records, and with Dave "Snaker" Ray, "Spider" John Koerner, and Tony "Little Sun" Glover, whose styles of guitar, song, and harmonica I also learned from my old hi-fi speaker. (In recent years, I have met with Hammond to discuss a proposed book I have in mind on the urban, white bluesmen of that time. Their influence on music and culture is untold.) I had been a beatnik toward the end of high school, publishing my first book of poems when I was a senior (which was a shock to all, as I appeared to be little more than a long-haired greaser, but one with an excellent social rating, as I combined low and high culture easily even then; I was the only student-council member photographed for the yearbook with a collar turned up and hair in a wondrous bird's nest with ducktail), and moved right into the urban folk scene. The transition from Jack Kerouac to Blind Lemon Jefferson was in the same mythology of daily experience as guided by mysterious forces beyond but still within the beat and blues soul.

I became enamored of Gibson guitars and played only these, having traded the Stella, which I had painted jet black with flame decals around the sound hole, for my first Gibson. I was working in a shoe store and had spending money, which went for music supplies, beer, and cigarettes. I really just smoked because I liked the smell, and soon switched to the pipe which I still enjoy, but the beer was consumed to get as drunk as possible as often as necessary. To get that first Gibson guitar, I went on the only trip I ever went on alone with my father.

Father always worked. Even on weekends, he would be in his pressed suits with the handkerchief in the pocket; he might take the suit coat off if it got too hot in summer, but he would always be in his dress shirt with suspenders which matched his tie. He smoked Chesterfield straights and did so European style, either with a holder sometimes or usually with his first finger wrapped around the cigarette, until he had to give these up. He kept the smokes in a silver case, with a place for the holder and a built-in lighter. He could perform a trick with a cigarette underwater. He would somehow keep the cigarette lit while he went under. We would all gather at the boathouse dock as he took a drag, smiled, then went way under with the butt in his mouth and came back up still smoking a dry cigarette. Nobody could figure this out. I went under once next to him to take a look through my goggles, but he just winked at me there under the dock and stopped the show. Such class, I thought, and my love for him was felt. My love for him was really experienced on this journey to get my Gibson. We went to Milwaukee for it. I had located a prized J-50 which could not be found in Appleton stores, so at the spur of the moment he left work early, which was never done before or after, and, leaving closing that night to Mother, we drove in the Buick Special with its smart vent holes on each side of the hood right into downtown Milwaukee to pick up my Gibson Dreadnaught in its plush hard-shell case. Then we stopped for dinner on the way back.

It was at the dinner table at some roadside cafe outside of Oshkosh that he told me the story. I knew my Gibson with its fresh spruce top was safe in the Buick's trunk. Dad adored this Buick coupe, which he got after having a sleek Oldsmobile Rocket two-door that cracked an engine block. He eventually bought a succession of Pontiac Catalina coupes, all in gold with full wheel covers and chrome exhaust tips that I would add, but this two-tone blue Buick with its Dyna-flow transmission was his favorite; and as he talked, he kept looking at it under the lights in the parking lot as though he could see more than I saw there. He told me about a night spent on the road with his father in their peddler's horsecart.

He worked with his father, as did his three brothers, while his two sisters stayed at home with his mother in the city, selling various wares from village to village in rural Sweden where the family had moved from Norway. Dad was traveling alone that night with his father and wanted to go into a nearby town to a dance. He had met a girl earlier in the day when they stopped at her parents' farm to sell their goods, and knew she would be there. His father gave him permission and so he went to this girl's farm, and when she left he walked up to her and they went together. It was raining but they kept dry beneath the tree line near the path.

They danced until after midnight, then he accompanied her home. He talked with her and they kissed. He knew he would never see her again, so he headed back to the campsite slowly with much on his mind. He saw an old woman coming toward him.

There was just enough room for her to pass by him if he helped her by holding onto her elbows, and she onto his, so that they could balance on the path that on one side had a thick forest and on the other a deep puddle from the night's rain. He thought that her clothing was unusually rough to the touch, and to himself said that homespun fabric was not as smooth as the materials he had seen in city stores. As she went by with his help, he looked aside for a moment at the water to make certain he would not step in it, and in doing so felt he could let go of her as she was safely behind him now. He looked right back to watch her walk further on, having just taken his eyes off her for less than a second, and she was gone.

There was nobody there. He said that he froze. He told me about this as he put down his coffee cup with a clunk into its saucer on the cafe table. I looked out at the Buick to make sure it was safely parked under the late fall moonlight. He said that he saw her coming toward him under a full moon. He poured cream into his cup, and repeated that the moonlight was so bright he could still see her face clearly some forty years later now, and he would still dream about her and be unable to sleep. He said that after he recovered from her absence on the path, he ran back to camp and sat at the fire until morning. It was soon after this that he decided to go to America. He told his father he wanted to go, and they forged a birth certificate to make him old enough to be granted official permission; and after he said good-bye to his family he never saw his parents again, for they died while he was making a new life for himself and sending home more money than the remaining family in Sweden earned altogether. I asked him if he figured that old lady on the path to be a harbinger of good fortune. He replied that I should finish my steak and french fries, because my new Gibson was heavier than the Stella and onstage now I would need more strength to hold it up.

I was into weight lifting and bodybuilding in high school, and was a record holder for the military press in my weight classification; I enjoyed flexing my biceps and breaking things with my bare hands that one normally could not break. I was powerful, but never an athlete. I tried to throw the shot put and run the 440, but hurt my knee so badly that I required surgery. At that time, I just was not ready for the success at long-distance running and the prowess in martial arts that would come years later; I was not able to do much beyond work with free weights, which I did with a passion. There were no bodybuilding organizations and magazines on the subject, so getting into this, and so-called health food, was quite a radical move to make in the early sixties. I alternated between this life and the life of drinking and debauchery, balancing for months until a migraine put me under and I would surface with solemn dignity and a desire for real friendship, even though I needed solitude more.

I had close friends. I always was surrounded by boys who were quick to help and laugh, drink and play cards, and girls who wore bright clothing and would undress now and then with lust in movie-theater balconies and upon the soft, cold grass alongside the Fox River. Lots of times I would just want the reassuring company of these girls, and would walk with them by the river or under the Pacific Street Bridge, telling them secrets I never intended to keep. I loved all of them. They each had their special smells, and favorite songs.

My boyfriends were crazy. We loved each other and fought like enemies, making up as though lost family members reunited; once, in City Park, my pal Tim and I were challenged to a fistfight by some older hoods. They rode around in their own cars and wore their blue jeans nearly below the bottom of where a studded belt can no longer hang onto the lost waistline. Louie fought with me and Don fought with Tim. Tim and Don went at it the hardest. Louie and I just shoved each other a lot. I was scared and he knew me to be a fighter so was timid. He could have killed me. Tim nearly got killed. It was all very frightening, and Tim and I went to the Pizza Palace afterwards, which was filled from the Methodist dance that night, and acted like tough heroes. But both of us kept looking at each other, knowing we were definitely through with heroism. We embraced as we walked down Wisconsin Avenue, and he turned his way under the viaduct to the less amiable part of town and I went my way over the Chicago and Northwestern tracks to a little finer neighborhood.

I saw Tim at my twenty-fifth high-school reunion. I had not attended any before this one in 1989, and came to it as a celebrity because of the success of my present book (noted in the preamble), and actually just a few weeks after our reunion the hometown newspaper put it at front-page status with a color photo of me on my motorcycle wearing full cowboy gear, and the local bookstore sponsored a book-signing soon after as well. Tim was at the reunion and I sat with him for dinner and we talked about that night and, as I was leaving, he cried. I would have but I already did after I left him that night to cross the railroad tracks and saw the headlamp of a 400 Streamliner on its run to Green Bay. I watched the people on the cars go by and took a shortcut then through the ravine, coming up near Nawada Court nearly blinded by tears. Tim looked terrible the next day; and as we played poker, then rode around in a friend's Ford pickup on country roads, sitting in back drinking Adler Brau beer brewed in Appleton, I knew changes were coming. Our wounds would heal, even his which required stitches, but I felt there was something that would not get any better.

Being a musician made high school tolerable, for I could express myself, finally, with life-style and originality. I got kicked out of Appleton Senior High School for having my hair too long, my sideburns untrimmed, and I loved it. There finally was some substance to my rebellion. I played the blues with hellhounds on my trail. I learned bottleneck guitar

At sixteen

from the Mississippi Delta, I could wail those Texas blues, and from Louisiana came finger-picking that would rattle windows on Pacific Street when I cranked up an old amplifier to which my first electric guitar was hitched. I learned it all from records and by playing it with others. I took a lesson once, but the guy had never heard of Robert Johnson, only those superficial British rockers, so I just learned the scale I could not figure out myself and split halfway through the session. I listened and watched, then did it by myself. I got real good at this.

Exploration Two: Madison

After two years of living at home while attending the Fox Valley Center, I moved living and schooling to Madison and immediately went into culture shock. I walked into an English class in Bascom Hall and saw dozens of guys who looked like I did. In Appleton, the males were blond and could not grow beards; in Madison, I suddenly appeared normal. The Jewish community in my hometown was not large and they just wanted to blend in as most were immigrants. My heritage was Orthodox, but still there was no insistence upon the Talmud as a way of life as it would conflict with being Americanized; I happily ate bacon, lettuce, and tomato sandwiches at home while my parents somehow insisted they were keeping kosher. My grandparents also insisted upon a kosher house, but with one set of dishes; the duplicity was confusing to me, but I soon decided that being Jewish meant just enjoying my grandmother's fresh challah every Sunday along with greasy varnishkas steeped in chicken fat on the holidays. God? I never met Him in any synagogue. I heard him, though, in the fall leaves crackling underfoot on the way to chader class every day after school from the fourth grade on until my Bar Mitzvah; but to the manhood celebration He was apparently not invited, for I was unaware of His approval until I walked along the Fox River bank in my white sport coat and white bucks, black pants and white belt. I was hip. I pulled the Bar Mitzvah off without a hitch, singing those ancient melodies with the punch I heard in Buddy Holly songs, and then quickly dropped any pretense of being Jewish except when I ate Grandma's fresh bread.

In Madison I applied all my energies to studying literature in English. I had to make up for lost time, as in high school I did nothing academically and when I decided to excel in my senior year I was shut out of all the interesting honor classes because I had a bad reputation as a student. At the Fox Valley Center,

after a rocky start because I was still playing music more than studying, I did extremely well; in Madison, too, I did very well and graduated with distinction, going on there after being admitted easily into a doctoral program in American literature. I learned how to learn in Madison. I gradually stopped playing music because I had to stay out too late at night and get too drunk. This interfered with the act of writing poetry, which I preferred to do early in the morning. So I began to turn to poetry writing and scholarship with intensity, and let the blues go. As I opened myself up to the poetic ability I had starved for so many years, just having fed it now and then in moments of reverie, I had a mysterious experience that has forever altered my perception of reality.

I had something like it happen once when I refused to go to elementary school and was sitting in my room. Mother came in after Father lost his temper with me and left early to open his store, and sat down next to me on my bedroom rug. It was late autumn, and the streets were wet and the early morning light was unable to break through that northern Wisconsin cloud cover settling in just before winter. She asked me why I would not go to school, and preferred to sit in silence looking out the window. It was a decent question and one I answered internally with an implosion of sights, sounds, smells, and tactile sensations: the vision was of a garden in which there was a stone fountain, and I sensed a light rain on the flowers, which gave off sweet odors. A red brick wall encompassed the scene, and a black wrought-iron gate let me in and out. I chose to stay in for the rest of the day, answering her question amidst this place with its birds chirping and cool marble rooms off the garden entrance. It was years later, in the writings of Hermann Hesse and Carl Gustav Jung, that I had an intellectual network from which to ponder what I saw as a child and witnessed again in my Madison room.

It was June in the later sixties. I had gone to part-time status in my undergraduate work because of what we will call a nervous breakdown: one night I just let go and could not grab on again. So I reduced my course load and read further in Hesse and Jung, and studied Zazen with the Buddhist scholar Richard Robinson, whose class I took along with one in literature to keep my writing going. I read Rilke, continued my serious investigation of William Butler Yeats, absorbed Blake, and went back to Theodore Roethke; but I also began my lifelong study of Ezra Pound and William Carlos Williams, and read nearly every important poet with the exception of the Projectivists and Objectivists, the most important ones to my development as a writer, which I got to a couple of years later once I was in graduate school. I completed the education I was not getting in college and which I needed to handle the imagery I experienced: this time I spent much longer in the garden, having burst into it with bright speed on a hot night after coming back from a walk along Lake Mendota then ceremoniously pouring myself and a close friend some tea. Visions convince me that I have something to say, and I have had many since these, but the one in Madison was an electrifying vector, for it left me knowing I was a poet; I was back in school full-time in fall, and I wrote a paper that year on the difference between a saint and a poet, as seen in the lives and works of A. E. and W. B. Yeats. A. E., the saint, preferred his experiences untouched and wrote less-concrete poetry; Yeats, the poet, particularly in "Vacillation," worked toward a poetry of specifics in order to bring his psychic life into action. I understood A. E. but relied upon Yeats. William Carlos Williams says it best, and I used this quote in my first quality book of poetry because it takes care of all the questions regarding the solipsism of pure numinous experience versus the rugged force that poetic composition can be: "The poem / is complex and the place made / in our lives / for the poem. / Silence can be complex too, / but you do not get far / with silence." One must move out of vision into communication based upon it, or one will not move at all in this lifetime toward anything but a misunderstanding of God's unconscious whisper, heard in the magnificent rustle of fallen leaves blown there to fertilize conscious recognition of the human struggle.

I had tried painting in my Appleton basement, shoving the Lionel New York Central Freight train aside that ran on schedule every Saturday, pumping fake smoke into the damp air, but my canvases were always unsatisfactory. On one trip to the artist-supply store, the lady who owned it asked me what I thought of her painting. "Tundra," I said, as I looked at this abstract entity done in swirling but stable earth colors; she looked at me mysteriously and reported that I titled her painting, and so it was called in an exhibit catalog I saw at Lawrence University about a month later at an opening. I should have stuck with titles, words, for my paintings done in a year's flirtation with an M.F.A. in painting were inspired but technically deficient. My major professor was a student of Zen, and he knew I knew so let me go until I knew enough to stop. I learned much from Klee and Kandinsky that I later applied to poetry, and dropped the whole painting idea, because what I understood as visionary had to be reported verbally. I kept a daily journal, and had for some time, so I turned to it for imagery and listened to classical music, in which I had become quite a self-educated expert, as I wrote my poems, my first real poems.

I worked all that summer on my poetry. I had always written in a stilted free-verse style, and I continued that way until, by summer's end, I realized there had to be more control. I reverted to a classical methodology, perhaps influenced more by the Schubert, Barber, and Bartók I heard each day than by the poets I read every evening; these composers were classicists who still could allow for the fiery center to heat the surface just enough. I discovered Schoenberg and really concentrated on a more rigid definition of what my poetry must become. I felt like I had made a deal with the devil, and while reading Thomas Mann's *Doctor Faustus* pronounced myself a member of the dark world where style had to be maintained in order to make the awesome sights verbal. *Magister Ludi* convinced me that there was a secret organization to which I belonged.

I worked very hard, did little else but study and write. Years before, the first year in Madison, actually, I had met Maureen Rice. She was a close friend for awhile and somehow always seemed to show up at my apartment to talk, or in an Italian restaurant where I was sitting alone in a booth, and I gradually got to know the woman to whom I've been married now for nineteen years. I initially met her in an English class, which was the first Madison campus class I walked into: Maureen wore tight jeans and high leather boots, and had the longest hair I ever saw on a woman. She came right over to my desk and sat down and talked to me as though I knew her already. I liked that, and watched her hair move with her intense conversation. We did not become lovers until four years later. During those years of friendship, we conferred almost nightly on the telephone about shared tales of broken engagements, and, at one point, she was dating my roommate to whom I had introduced her. My roommate was a dear friend, but he possessed an immature soul; I spent many hours over countless days with him in discussions having philosophical and spiritual content, and was as close to him as a man is to another man, but when I saw how foolishly he behaved when infatuated with a woman, as he was with Maureen, I got real sick of him real fast. He lived in an ideal world, not an active one.

One night after I had a lovely dinner of shrimp with lobster sauce prepared for me by a married woman while her husband was out of town on business—I met her in a Chaucer class and was her backdoor man for a year—and after we spent our

Maureen and Martin Rosenblum, 1989

postmeal time together, I called Maureen. The sweet cook had sent me hitchhiking back to town with a rucksack full of leftover food—for how could she tell her husband that she prepared that kind of meal for herself?—and I arrived at my lonely room around daybreak and woke Maureen up with a call. She had just broken up with my roommate for good this time, and was in the mood for company. I suggested we finish this oriental delight for breakfast, so after shaving and showering I hitchhiked further. I never left. We walked and talked and over her home movies I fell hopelessly in love with this gorgeous, brilliant lady.

But she was expecting some guy from Canada whom she had been dating as well, and apparently he had intentions of marriage. He called the next night and they talked while I walked around Middleton, which is just outside of Madison and is as rural and sweet as was Appleton, reflecting upon my entire life up to this juncture. I had gone abruptly, leaving my shoes behind, so came back with sore feet and a certain heart and asked Maureen to marry me. On this walk I saw it was going to be Maureen or nobody. I could live by myself, it seemed, or if I wanted to

share my life with another it had to be her. The next morning I overheard Maureen on the phone telling her mother that she needed a wedding dress because she was marrying Marty. "Marty Rosenblum, you know, my friend," she said. We have stayed friends and are the best of lovers.

That guy came in from Canada and Maureen had her hands full with his petulance as well as my roommate's hysteria, so I left town after a phone conversation with Maureen with her talking calmly to me and my roommate wailing in the background. She had accidentally met him while on a walk with the Canadian, and he started crying so much that to escape it she called me. I decided then to get rid of my roommate as a friend. I am very loyal and expect loyalty from my friends. But I am also intolerant of behavior that demonstrates failure to act courageously, especially when it violates the friendship creed. He and I had talked matters over, and he needed to be a man about it all; he was not, and I still cannot return to our friendship. I told Maureen that I had some writing to do, and went to Appleton while she dealt neatly with the two wimps; I was about to do an important poetry reading, and wanted to finish a poem, called "The Assumption," that gathered together all the years of experience I brought to my love for her. I read it to her on the telephone while she was in Chicago, visiting her mother after having resolved things in Madison, and I was still in Appleton; we met back in Middleton, I did the reading, and we set the marriage date for the following September 6, 1970, the same date as my parents' wedding. We were married in the Chicago synagogue her mother and father used for their wedding. We shared ourselves that summer as though we had just met and knew nothing about one another. I still have this feeling at the end of a day, when I come home and we begin to talk: she is the most refreshing, beautiful woman I will ever know. Her talk is brilliant and beauty impossible to get enough of in one lifetime.

Before I applied myself to the task of becoming a poet, I was a scholar. I was walking with my briefcase in hand and my cuffed and pressed trousers, my wing tips, coat, and tie (a complete reversal from the leather jacket in high school, and the tight, pegged pants and pointed shoes) neatly coordinated, and as I came to the building right behind Bascom Hall on the UW–Madison campus I saw Maureen in a picket line protesting the Dow Chemical Company's recruitment activities that day in 1967. Dow made napalm. Maureen was a member of Students for a Democratic Society. I was reading Hawthorne under Harry Hayden Clark and did not know much about her political sentiments, but her legs looked good as usual so I stopped to chat. Suddenly, all hell broke loose and the entire world changed forever.

In the movie *The War at Home,* you can see me knock out the University Police chief. The view is from the back, so I am unrecognizable except to those who were there. I caught him with a sucker punch because he told me I was a "little bastard" for asking him to call off the Dane County Police, who were seriously injuring people I knew. I simply put my briefcase into my left hand and caught the arrogant jerk with my right. I calmly walked away as he rolled over and down a little grassy knoll. I went over to my journalism professor, who had not seen my punch as the situation was complete chaos, and he looked at me in horror, saying he had never witnessed anything like this police riot, and that he had seen disturbances all over the world when he was a reporter. At that precise moment, a cop shot a tear-gas cannister at us, and as we stepped aside it ripped into the door of a white car parked behind us. Having just escaped what could have been severe injury, he asked me if I wanted to go to the Rathskeller for coffee, and by this time Maureen had joined us, so we all left as the skies turned as threatening as the mood on Bascom Hill. The three of us just sat there, looking out over Lake Mendota as it churned, drinking coffee; I kept seeing the blood splashed on the cement, and the head of a coed smashed by a nightstick, and wondered where this would take us all.

I was attacked on Langdon Street by Madison policemen in plainclothes the following spring, and when they could not pin me down to trounce upon me, for I was much too fast and strong for these three overweight slobs, they tossed a tear-gas grenade right at me, which I promptly tossed back into their car as it sped away. It was war between cops and students, and though I had no political disagreement over which to fight, I fought for survival. I gave up my student military deferment, feeling that if I wanted to go to Sweden I could, or if I wanted to serve I could handle the adventure involved; I just no longer wanted that student privilege, even though I was a serious scholar and writer. I received a medical deferment in the mail. My knee injury was the disqualifier. It was that simple for the Appleton draft board. My father telegrammed that I was freed from having to make a decision; by this time, he was against the war in Vietnam, although he was very much in support of it at first. I remember that he watched the McCarthy hearings when I was a child, and he believed in a Communist threat then; I would be amazed later on, though, when he decided that fighting communism was not worth the Vietnam War because our government was in a losing battle there and at home. I do not know what I would have done had I not received my medical deferment. Now, many of my buddies are Vietnam veterans and I have great empathy for their courage, waging war to survive when even their own country had not adequately backed them up in the field. I would have fit in well with my fellow warriors and am certain I would have been swept up in the mania of combat to protect myself and my friends. I doubt if I could have lived in Sweden. I tried that years later for different reasons of escape and it did not succeed. So I wound up fighting on the streets of Madison against fat cops for no other reason than to survive, and studying the poets who brought me into my own style of writing. In order to keep my attention, these poets had to offer a world as specific and unavoidable as the one that had taken over the city of Madison by force.

As a doctoral candidate, I discovered the Objectivist poets and then the Projectivists, working from one into the next with a scholar's mind and a poet's heart. I was in a class on Ezra Pound taught by a maverick who would turn the session over to this poet

Carl Thayler, who would drop in from time to time and since then has been one of my closest friends. That spring in 1969 the University of Wisconsin was shut down by protest and martial law, so we met at one another's apartments, which made the study of Pound and his disciples even more homemade and hermetic.

I also edited an anthology of Madison poetry published by a small press I founded there with some other poets. One of the contributors was Carl Rakosi, who was poet-in-residence at the time, and who later became like one of the family to Maureen and me. His poem, one of the Americana series that was to be the subject of my doctoral thesis, totally turned me into a believer by virtue of its commonality and lack of metaphorical process.

I began studying the Objectivists and publishing my poetry books and making appearances in the little magazines of the sixties and early seventies. I did many poetry readings, and Professor John Shawcross, who came to readings I would do in Madison as I was studying with him in the Ph.D. program, was supportive of my oral style, finding in it the voicings that John Berryman used so beautifully. My investigation of Berryman, hardly an Objectivist, led me straight into an understanding of the poem as notation for oral interpretation that I finished with Charles Olson's Projectivist verse. All this furious activity took place before and immediately after I asked Maureen to be my wife.

The poems I wrote for her, edited from many into my book *Home*, which has just come out in a second edition and which stands as one of the strongest collections I have published, got rid of the archaic methods I had been using to tame the poetic growling. In the midst of this style passage, Carl Thayler introduced me to Toby Olson, and conversations between the three of us, in person and through the mail and by phone, brought me to the brink of the proper poetic method. I studied William Carlos Williams to push nearer the edge, but when I found one of Paul Blackburn's little arcane books in a used bookstore on a trip to Milwaukee for a job interview, I absolutely went over to the other side.

Exploration Three: Milwaukee

I left the Ph.D. program at Madison for the job. I was appointed project assistant in the English department while enrolling as a student in creative writing at the University of Wisconsin–Milwaukee. I went to Milwaukee because all my major professors at the Madison campus resigned due to what they perceived as political repression on campus during the previous years of violence and protest. So I got married and found myself living in Shorewood near the university in Milwaukee. I was the first graduate of the fledgling creative writing master's degree program, and then moved into a spot on the English department faculty as a lecturer. During these opening years in 1970, Maureen and I got to know one another as married lovers and my writing came out as the books *Home* and *The Werewolf Sequence*, published by Karl Young at Membrane Press.

I met Karl immediately upon coming to Milwaukee, and to this day nearly twenty years later he is still the only poet here with whom I can discuss the poetry that matters. We met at the soda fountain in a drugstore near campus, introduced by a poetess who soon left our conversation because Zukofsky, Reznikoff, and Oppen were quite unknown to her, and decided to copublish Toby Olson's book manuscript I accepted with my small press in Madison. That was the first act of companionship as close friends and fellow poet/publishers, followed by many right through to the present; for a time, Karl and I even shared the same shrink, and I would arrive for my appointment as he was leaving, coming in my rattling Volkswagen as he left in his.

Maureen encouraged me to see a psychiatrist, as I had unresolvable psychological problems. Those sessions produced friendships with that one, another after him, and then with a third, the latter being a social worker whose ability to write poetry blossomed during our professional relationship. The second psychiatrist died of a heart attack, and I miss his Existentialist attitudes; the first still communicates with me through Karl, still seeing him, and the social worker and I see one another regularly to gossip. I am not existential in any way, and the psychiatrists seemed to prefer that approach; but the social worker, the most competent of the group, was close to my understanding of life processes, yet I cannot report anything curative there either that would not come from the right kind of friendship. My wife is a very successful psychotherapist, and we will often disagree about the whole impact of the profession, but our marriage is based on communion of spirit and flesh, and intellectual disagreement on most issues. I resolved my psychological dilemmas by virtue of action, not contemplation of them, and enjoyed the friendships, not the input, of those designated by contemporary society to replace the wise person in the village or the best friend in the neighborhood.

Maureen is not fond of my extreme position in support of the Second Amendment to the Constitution, but she purchased a magnificent Colt revolver for my arsenal as a wedding-anniversary gift. I cherish Colt pistols, especially the Single-Action Armys, and absolutely believe that every person in this country should own a home-defense weapon, whether it be of historical value, as mine are, or simply a modern firearm with all the technological advances. I own a couple of Colt Government Models and enjoy the autoloading features for target shooting, understanding that these make better defensive weapons than my old-fashioned Peacemakers; but I prefer guns with an Old West feel to them, and would be pleased to blast an intruder with a .45 Long Colt round shot from one, kept by the bed in a fast-draw rig, should my dog not get the sucker first.

During my first year of teaching at the University of Wisconsin–Milwaukee, I was asked by a promi-

nent East Coast publisher to edit an anthology of Milwaukee poetry as part of its City Anthology Series. This led to a conflict within the English department for me, as I was new there and another person felt more qualified to do the editing who had been around longer; I believe that I lost my job as a result, as I was not rehired and this person was clearly in charge of my lectureship. I also ran into political problems with the publisher, who proved himself to be an unethical sot, reneging on commitments once the book was out and doing well by virtue of my editing abilities and organizational methods. With distaste for both department and publisher, I left Milwaukee with Maureen to live in Sweden.

I had gotten ill before I left, and was being poisoned by the malpractice of a physician who was treating the flare-up of my intestinal disease with

Maureen and Martin Rosenblum with their daughters, Molly Dvora (left) and Sarah Terez Rosenblum, 1989

needlessly high-powered drugs. The side effects of cortisone were devastating. When we got to Sweden, I was coming off these drugs and healing. (I did not get better from them, but from deciding to leave teaching and editing in a hostile environment.) I had been in Sweden with my father and mother while in the first years of college, and saw my father with his relatives and friends as he met them for the first time since he left when in his teens, but this time without him I had little in common with them. My cousin, whom I had met when he was a graduate student in Madison (and who wound up living, by chance, across the street from my rooming house, so we had become good friends), even seemed distant and unfriendly. We stayed with him and his Indonesian wife, whom I also knew from Madison. He was nearly banished from the family for this marriage, but my father stuck up for him by mail, so I found their cold reception to be most disorienting. We soon moved to a little apartment in downtown Stockholm just as winter struck. Previously, I had been in Sweden during the long summer days, enjoying a slow ship voyage there and back, but this time, having sped in by plane, I found us very suddenly in a dark world with few people we enjoyed. Maureen and I walked around during the few hours of daylight, feeling quite lonely, and I got sick again. I was working on an important poem that later would be an impactful book called *The Werewolf Sequence,* and decided to return to Milwaukee to live with friends in a huge, rambling old house near Lake Michigan. I fell back into the improper care of the same physician giving me more of those drugs, and the psychotic episodes along with horrid physical problems as well nearly brought total ruin.

With Adelle Davis's help and Linus Pauling's, Maureen educated herself and brought me back to health through food and vitamin supplements which detoxified my body and mind chemistry. Davis and Pauling wrote in answer to many questions which the medical profession did not even know how to ask. I sued the doctor, but he luckily died from a heart attack and so my desire for moral justice was satisfied out of court. I started seeing doctors at the University of Chicago, where all the basic research is done on my disorder, inflammatory bowel disease, and have relied upon them since the early seventies. I had another brush with disaster in the early eighties that nearly killed me based on this disease, but for the time, with proper dietary precautions and lots of tension-relieving exercise, I was keeping it in remission.

So we were back in Milwaukee, after a camping trip to California in the spring once I had recovered

sufficiently; we tried to recreate the summer we spent the year before in our car on the road, camping and traveling where we felt like going, but we both wanted to settle into Milwaukee again for comfort's sake, so I accepted another position at UW–M in the English department as a lecturer, offered to me by the lady of the house in which we all lived, as she was the chairperson. It was easy to come back in that I worked for her, and so I picked the right mood and went to visit my former associate who had banished me from the English department as a result of the great anthology wars and wound up being a witness on his behalf in a custody suit for his children, which he won. I was an ideal witness for him, as I was not exactly his best friend during the time I knew him and his ex-wife, and so could testify with credibility beyond reproach against her for him; I was asked by his attorney to characterize my relationship with him and said, sonorously from the witness stand, that it ''was one of professional animosity'' during the period about which I was going to speak. I could barely keep from laughing, and he and I looked at one another, as we still do today, with respect and affection.

I have respect for ex-colleagues in the English department, for I was treated fairly there for nearly ten years; now, I have tenure at the University of Wisconsin–Milwaukee in an academic-staff position which I have occupied for almost another ten years since leaving the teaching profession. In the Department of Learning Skills and Educational Opportunity, I work as an academic advisor and admissions specialist on behalf of educationally disadvantaged students, helping them emotionally and academically after admitting them.

My publishing and poetry-reading record brought a permanent collection of my manuscripts and related material to be established at the Center for Contemporary Poetry, Wisconsin State University–LaCrosse, beginning in 1971, and as a graduate student I won an Academy of American Poets award; during my early years of teaching literature and writing, Yale University selected me as one of the promising younger poets for whom Sterling Memorial Library established an ongoing collection of published works. I was a guest lecturer and poet at the University of East Anglia, Norwich, England, in the American Studies Program, because of my seminal work as a scholar and poet of Objectivist technique, and I received two fellowships that allowed me to travel there and elsewhere for research and presentation of Objectivist long-poem method, which is the subject of my doctoral thesis that is still regarded as the original document on it. The dissertation investigation led to a book-contract proposal that was accepted for a critical biography of Carl Rakosi, but Twayne, the publisher, had a trivial pursuit of the subject and switched me from one uneducated editor to another until the National Poetry Foundation at the University of Maine–Orono approached me to do the book there; so even though I agreed informally with the latter institution to complete the book, I am still working on it. My devoted friend Norman Holmes Pearson, just before he died, told me that some projects involve one's total personality and therefore must be completed by some internal schedule, and this book seems to be calendared as such. *Still / Life*, a collection of my poems from the sixties into the nineties, is another book in progress I intend to complete once the significant end of it, too, has been reached. I am very much at work as a scholar and poet, though I do not talk about my investigations into poetic technique nor the poetry that results with anybody now except those with whom I correspond.

My relationship with Karl Young is really one of correspondence, for he now lives in Kenosha, and I also regularly write to Cid Corman, Theodore Enslin, Howard McCord, and Carl Thayler. These dear friends sustain me with letters every week or so, and my relationships with them bring me personal and literary, emotional and aesthetic meaning. I write to many poets, but this blessed bunch are my constant companions and I love each one.

I respect my associates in the area literary community, too, for they are all serious and hard-working writers; Milwaukee has an inspired collection of wordsmiths, and their styles have little in common but the geographical location. I identified this in my introduction to *Brewing: Twenty Milwaukee Poets* in 1972, and it still accurately stands today. While there is this large and productive group of writers here, I am so unlike them in life-style, and am such a loner, that I do not have real close relationships in it. As a poet, not as a guitar player, I have worked with jazz musicians around Milwaukee, and one, Jack Grassel, collaborated with me on an album called *Music Lingo* that has had quite an impact for its original duet of word and music. Jack rides a Harley and shares other life definitions with me, and it is with him that I talk about poetry outside of my correspondence. Steve Nelson-Raney, a jazz and horn player with whom I also record and perform word and music combinations, is the only other nearby person for me relative to poetry discussions of value. It is not odd, though, that I am understood by musicians here more than by

"Equipped for danger," Martin Rosenblum with Howard McCord, 1988

poets, for overall composers work with materials that are closest to mine.

I have a rigid schedule that involves exercise at sunrise, then typewriter time with either correspondence or my journal, or with poetry, though I write poems whenever biologically necessary, until it is time to take my older daughter to school and go to the post office, then walk the few blocks past Downer's Woods to my UW–M office in Mitchell Hall. I studied martial arts in the seventies with a master and have taught the Chinese systems of kung fu and Kenpo karate, in which I have professional ranks, for a number of years; so my morning workout consists of kata to loosen up, and then I move to distance running and working out with free weights. For nearly ten years, I ran eight miles each morning, getting 6-minute miles per run; just before I radically cut back my running, I did a 5:11 mile at age thirty-eight. Now, at forty-three, I run only to get ready for lifting weights after my martial-art wake-up. I enjoy leaving the house with my Bernese mountain dog, "Harley," gotten about the time I got my motorcycle, who goes along for my mile or so at full gallop. The day has to start this way to provide balance for the night's dreams that I consider as I work out and plan what comes next, fully realizing that my morning alone will be the only part of the day that follows my sense of order. But I enjoy the improvisation we call living, so welcome what appears first as chaos and later as hermetic order.

In 1982, I had to cut back on my running, and then again in 1984, just as I was working myself back to those longer runs, I had to back off for the same reason: I got seriously ill. The first time no diagnosis could be made, and the opinion was that I had a flare-up of my bowel disorder. I did not believe this and argued with the doctor and eventually left him; even though he was Milwaukee's expert on the subject, I trusted my own awareness of the illness and was right. I returned to the University of Chicago, but by then I was recovering and we just rode it out, with an agreement that this was not the usual disorder. In 1984, I started the same symptoms and this time a diagnosis was made: in both instances, I had come in contact with a virulent form of dysentery. My guess is that it came from South American or drug-addict students, as both groups can be carriers and I work with both at UW–M. This disease is hand-communicated to the recipient. The second time I came in contact with it, I was given an antibiotic but had an allergic reaction so was struck with the disorder as well as the side effects from the cure. I nearly died.

I was barely functioning, lying in my University of Chicago Hospital bed, when Carl Rakosi came to see me. I was supposed to introduce him at a reading I had arranged in Milwaukee, and he was doing another in Chicago, so came into my room as he was in town and on the way to the one in Wisconsin. We talked and he said something, quite casually, that really caught me. For its full impact, let us go back to 1979 and work up to this awful spring of 1984.

I had stopped publishing in 1979 with the birth of my first daughter, Sarah Terez, because the publishing aspect of being a writer did not appeal to me any longer; after doing at least a book or two each year from the 1960s into 1979, and many magazine publications, I had had enough of the politics of publishing. I knew I would continue to write, always, but maybe I should keep it to myself for awhile and really turn all energies to family life, I decided. Maureen was changing careers. She had been a successful, nationally acclaimed batik artist (while working as a zookeeper on the side), and now was preparing for her life's work as a psychotherapist. I

had plans to leave the teaching profession for a different kind of academic work that I now do with pleasure. Sarah's birth was very traumatic, and brought everything to a focal point. She was to be a home-born baby, but complications set in and we raced for the hospital with our doctor to have Sarah come into my arms by cesarean section. Sarah smiled at me and I fell in love with her there on my bare chest as Maureen recovered. Maureen said to Sarah, "Hello Sweetie, welcome to us," and I cried, making the decision to just be at home with my wife and daughter, supporting them with full attention and with a secure financial program. Our dear friend Barry Bursak came in from Chicago and stayed with me while I talked late into the night about giving up publishing. I meant it. When Maureen and Sarah came home, I stopped sending out manuscripts.

I sold the house we lived in then in a very seedy part of the city. Originally, we lived near the university on the East Side near Lake Michigan, but when we came back from Sweden we eventually purchased an old house for eight thousand dollars and refurbished it with cedar walls and bi-level ceilings. But Michigan Street was turning violent even then, and when someone was shot in my front yard and came to the door for help, I decided to get my wife and newborn the hell out of there. I sold the house the same day, then also sold my Ford truck used to pack Maureen's wares off to craft fairs. I also sold my Volkswagen, which we had for city commuting. All that money, less what I needed to buy a used Saab, was put down on the house in which we now live on Stratford Court in Shorewood. I moved us here and took a job commuting to Chicago, as I had finished my Ph.D. and thought that I should advance financially, which would not happen in academia. I became executive director of Lawyers for the Creative Arts, with an office on Wabash, and hated it. The lawyers were unfriendly and some less than sincere, and when I discovered that the books were not kept properly by the previous administration, I was given severance pay to quietly leave without any publicity. I was proud of myself for holding out for what was honest in the deal, but quite depressed about the quality of human nature on Wabash in Chicago. I immediately was able to move into an academic-staff position at UW–M that I still occupy, without missing a fringe-benefit payment; I went from teaching to administration with a short time off, as it were, to experience the sleaze of the private sector. Now, we were situated on the East Side once more and I had a marvelous job that was very meaningful to me. I did not want to wander the country as a poet-in-residence, and took myself out of the running for a position like that in New York State to take the Chicago job, then returned to academia with a new attitude that I still have. Maureen was getting situated in her new profession. Sarah was starting to teach me how to be a good daddy. Then I got real sick.

That was the first time. The second time, now, I was near death. Carl Rakosi said that, perhaps, I left something unresolved in my life by not continuing to publish. It was just a passing remark. But it came from him and it caught me. After he left, the machine to which I was attached started to take blood out of me instead of putting nutrients into my veins as it was supposed to: I rang for the nurse for three hours and nobody came. I had not been able to eat, as nothing would stay put, but rushed out in a bloody mess. I had fevers every day of over 104 degrees for many weeks. I suddenly got more angry than I ever had.

I have a ferocious temper; one that, once un-leashed, attacks to kill. I got up and pulled the machine from its lag-bolted position on the wall. I carried it into the nurses' station and demanded that the line from it be removed, shouting that I bought two or three transfusions and now the hospital was apparently trying to take back the blood my insurance company paid for: the line was removed and the doctor called. I told him I was leaving. He said I should not, as I might really die. I said, please do not ruin me financially; sign me out. I was going home. I called Maureen, telling her to drive in early the next morning for me. I ordered solid food, ate it, got sicker than hell, and tried to sleep but wound up in the waiting room near the bathroom writing in my journal. The doctor came in the next morning to tell me I was crazy, and that I should accept psychiatric help to make my hospital stay tolerable. I said I would rather be crazy than accepting of the poor treatment there, and that I would die at home in comfortable surroundings if necessary to get out. He has remained my friend and physician for many years since, and I respect Dr. Hanauer a lot; what he did that morning for me was courageous and quality medical attention. He signed me out and told me to call him each day, and to stay alive. I did call him, and I barely stayed alive.

Each morning I would get up from my bed I had made on my third-floor office floor at home, away from Maureen and Sarah as I would be sick during the night and delirious with fever, and try to eat and then go for a sunrise walk by the lake. I began to plan some books of poetry. This plan to publish kept me alive. I did therapeutic things such as build an H-O model-railroad diorama in a bookshelf that was an exact replica of the Chicago and North Western yards near my Appleton house, collect 54-mm military figures and paint them after studying their uniforms from books I also collected, making American Civil War dioramas with these figures once they were researched and painted, and begin a collection of firearms. I initially got Civil War pieces, such as a Springfield Trapdoor and Sharps Carbine, Colt Navy and Pocket Navy pistols, but moved into Colt Single-Actions and unique Colt pistols that I could use for target and combat shooting. This was the therapy that allowed me to heal: working with precise objects as I wrote my new poetry for publication.

The aspect more terrible than my suffering, however, was that I missed much of Sarah's childhood because I was either finishing the Ph.D. and moving us while changing careers, or being very ill and going through my recovery processes. I have many sleepless nights where I try to find her back then and cannot. While I make some things better for myself now with our second little girl, our baby Molly Dvora, I cannot make better for Sarah what I messed up. But I healed myself, and that sure needed to be done, and the sicknesses were unavoidable, and all that I went through to complete my degree work and situate us more securely had to take place, so my regret is not guilt. It is just that, regret, and I feel it often.

After 1984 I published a series of poetry books and worked myself up to the Harley-Davidson materi-al. While I was recovering from the second illness, I decided that I would finally own a Harley Sportster. I had always wanted one, and when I was in elementary school I imagined myself on one or on a horse. I would see riders dressed in cowboy clothing on Harleys and Indians on horseback ride up Leminwah Hill Road near my house as I was pretending I was out on the plains chasing bad guys and renegades on the bluffs that the road passed between. They would roar up this hill with fringe floating in my imagina-tion. So when I finally bought my Harley-Davidson in 1987, it was delivered to our dining room, where it stood next to the supper table all winter. On week-ends, I would wax it and add lustrous chrome parts in the comfort of my home. One Friday night when all in the house had fallen asleep, I got on my Sportster and turned on the headlamp, which shot a beam right out the window into the falling snow through to my lost childhood, illuminating the trail ahead.

We already had our baby Molly, and her birth and life so far is exactly the opposite of Sarah Terez's: it was a peaceful, natural birth process, and Molly is now about two years old and calm as can be from proper full attention from me and much love from

"The Thirtieth Anniversary Model XLH Harley-Davidson Sportster"

her older sister, now going on eleven. Maureen is an ideal mother, and has brought both of our little girls through all sorts of situations that I, having not gotten the right nurturing myself, could never have gotten through with them. We parent well together most of the time, but I try to take my cues from Maureen. I have this terrible temper and try not to let it discipline, but rather utilize patience and caution instead. I once pushed through a closed car window with a Kenpo hand movement to get at a punk who had cut me off as I was driving with my family. Sarah thought this was great stuff, but Maureen was furious and rightfully so; she understands how to control anger, though she would never stop me in a proper situation, and always insists upon understanding in the home instead of fury like my father's.

Buying the Harley changed my life, because my Harley poetry suddenly became in demand by a huge audience, and this, in turn, altered the way I live. My life-style has always been that of a "biker" but had to be kept somewhat secretive. Now, it is front-page *Chicago Tribune* material and syndicated for national television current-event spots: my first little book of Harley poetry was out of print in a month, and only had trademark approval from the company; but the second book, in an edition that goes well beyond any amount for a book of real poetry, is an Official Licensed Product from Harley-Davidson, Incorporated. It has been assigned a part number, making it a Part and Accessory Catalog feature, and is available not only in bookstores but from any Harley dealer's parts counter. My image is on a line of T-shirts and on a jacket patch and Holy Ranger badge. *The Holy Ranger: Harley-Davidson Poems* is a serious literary endeavor with the commercial success expected of writing that is less so. While it is backed by a Fortune

500 corporation, I organized its funding, design, typesetting, and distribution. The little press I started in Madison and brought to Milwaukee is still small, but it is doing large things in the world of book production, combining what is ideal about underground publishing with what is necessary about commercial printing. It was financed by a municipal judge in Butler, designed on Brady Street in Milwaukee, and typeset in Kenosha, so every word is exactly where I intend it; distribution is primarily through Harley-Davidson, but there are other sources as well as direct sales, and the book was printed and bound down the street from the typesetter's house. When we went to pick up the first copies for its Fourth of July, 1989, release, we gave the very first copy to a biker who just happened to ride past on his custom Sportster chopper. He took the book with casual glory, turned right around in the middle of the street, and headed back to his yard, where he parked the bike and sat reading it on his front porch as I left for the T-shirt company in Waukesha to give final approval of those designs. *The Holy Ranger* comes from a Milwaukee environment to meet American standards of rugged possibility that only poetry like it can handle.

The British Broadcasting Corporation did a television documentary on the spirit of Harley-Davidson that focuses on my book, and Warner Brothers

"The official trademark"

consulted with me for a proposed television-series pilot after the producer read my poetry. I am getting letters from all over the world, written by readers who have established me as a shaman of the biker tribes; and fellow writers, timid at first about all the success factors because failure has been a sign of success for those of us who write the legitimate poetry, are starting to understand the strength of my aesthetic, which marries art and finance, hermetic and common experience. I am the only poet whose book has a part number and who has a Dun and Bradstreet rating, sure, but what makes this all so interesting is that Neo-Objectivist poetry with Projectivist attributes is being purchased and seriously considered by thousands of readers in the form of the book itself and upon three different T-shirts.

I own the registered trademarks associated with my book, and one of them is "EvoPoetics." This refers to the Harley Evolution engine combining with the art of poetry, and also to the aspect of my poetry that makes it so archetypal: it evolves as it discusses itself in relation to that which it is about. There is a great deal of subtext in my work, but I maintain a surface simplicity that I learned when I met Paul Blackburn right before his untimely death in the early seventies. He was in Milwaukee for a poetry reading, ponytail bobbing as he matter-of-factly chanted his odes to everyday reality. In his voice there was deep philosophical resonance, which brought me back to his texts after talking with him briefly about one in particular. My poetry, I like to think, takes his further down the road on a Harley, well away from the cities, toward more rural objects as expressive ends in themselves and as images of complex subjects. As an old blues line I used to sing goes, "I live the life I love and love the life I live"; so do I head toward poetry and life-style as being indistinguishable: The Holy Ranger is a mythopoetic entity just like me.

I believe in what my friend and correspondent Colonel Jeff Cooper means when he insists that we must ride, shoot straight, and tell the truth. Being in a life-and-death situation constantly while on a motorcycle, knowing how to effectively handle a six-shooter to the extent that you are prepared for and cognizant of all that taking aim must be, and always speaking the truth in words and deeds is a creed that works in letters and life. I am writing as I live, living as I write, to take the blues line into another key, and the T-shirts created from my image underline the marriage of work and life I have achieved, as they are life-style garments that others wear in celebration of who The Holy Ranger is and what he says.

My constant buddy is Howard McCord, the Old Iguana, as we call him, and it is with him that I share binding elements of life and writing; it is important to have that one friend beyond one's lover with whom all details of the adventure can be processed for further courage and valid narrative. My politics have been inappropriately assailed as being unkind to the left-wing folk associated with the fine art of social justice for all as long as it is the downtrodden with whom we must be equal. While it is true that I disapprove of government money for the arts and insist upon fair wages for those who work and nothing for those who do not, I also demand that the environment be protected at all costs to the economy and women be allowed the freedom to choose abortion as birth control. I alienate left and right, but in that I am a field editor for the *Shootist* magazine and have such strong convictions regarding the impossibility of peace without first being able to be safe enough to afford that luxury, I tend to disenchant the wimps on the left before the arrogates on the right. Iguana and I write and call each other on these topics, and know we are righteous men.

I am dissatisfied with America in this decade, as she is in the hands of cowards and suffers from a misguided judicial system. Politicians lie a lot and fear action that might accomplish something definitive. Lawyers defend even the most worthless people to win for a cause. We lack the right morality and have no common sense of wrong. While I am not a man who believes that external reality is where we must start, as we enter the nineties there are serious revisions of social and political order that have to be undertaken in this country if we are to experience less mistrust and violence. We must look back to traditional values, restore family and neighborhood love and familiarity, be unafraid to protect ourselves with righteous indignation, and have regular mystical experiences to keep our reverence for the unknown that is our heritage and future.

Because I have been asked, I have done so: I have explored my youth, maturation, and present condition. *The Werewolf Sequence* achieved critical acclaim for its ability to engender a mythopoetic reality founded upon psychic magnificence nearly bursting from everyday commonality, and *The Holy Ranger* has taken this transformational secrecy away from its academic restriction.

As a poet, I work against those who have done nothing more than replace the silk smoking jacket with designer jeans, the cigarette holder with dope pipes made from exotic wood, and the subject matter set in rhyme with the incomprehensible fake verisimilitude of writing that cannot be tough enough to accept daily routine.

As a husband and father, I oppose a world that is unkind to honest effort and unprotective of the tender ability to be strong enough to survive with integrity.

As an educator, I disqualify obstacles to learning set by prejudice and fear.

As an autobiographer, I have mapped the poet, husband and father, and educator, and then discovered entirely different places to explore in search of what I work for, agree with, and qualify as being: so this has been a very practical yet evocative enterprise relative to understanding more about the story I have told.

SELECTED BIBLIOGRAPHY

Poetry:

Halloween Evening, Albatross Press, 1969.

Bright Blue Coats, Art Department, University of Wisconsin, 1970.

First Words the Moon Sings Near Drowning (broadside), Albatross Press, 1970.

Home, Membrane Press, 1970, second edition, 1989.

Settling Attention and Other Poems, Albatross Press, 1970.

Father for My Prayer (broadside), Monday Morning Press, 1971.

On:, Harpoon Press, 1972.

Sequence Fifty from the Werewolf Sequence (broadside), Membrane Press, 1972.

The Werewolf Sequence, Membrane Press, 1974.

as i magic, Morgan Press, 1976.

Scattered On: Omens and Curses, Pentagram Press, 1976, second edition, 1987.

from as i magic / system four (broadside), Pentagram Press, 1977.

Divisions / One, Great Raven Press, 1978.

Holy Screams, Pentagram Press, 1979.

Borne Out, Sutra, 1983.

(With Steve Nelson-Raney) *Brite Shade,* Cody Books, 1984.

(With Judith Marks) *Burning Oak,* Lionhead, 1986.

(With Steve Lewis) *Geographics,* Lionhead, 1986.

Three Poems (broadside), Morgan Press, 1986.

Conjunction, Pentagram Press, 1987.

(With Nelson-Raney) *Hocket Stutter* (broadside), Morgan Press, 1987.

(With Laura Winter) *Stone Fog,* Membrane Press, 1987.

Harley-Davidson Poems, Lionhead, 1988.

(With Cid Corman and John Perlman) *Six Concentrations,* Tel-Let Press, 1988.

The Holy Ranger: Harley-Davidson Poems, Ranger International Productions, 1989.

American Outlaw Visionary, Morgan Press, 1990.

Audiotapes:

Membrane Tapebook Number One, Membrane Press, 1972.

Language Compositions: A Live Performance of Poetry and Blues Improvisations, Roar Recording, 1977.

Other Symptoms, Roar Recording, 1984.

(With Jesse Glass) *Backlit Frontier,* Roar Recording, 1987.

(With Jack Grassel) *Music Lingo,* Roar Recording, 1987, second edition, Frozen Sky Records, 1989.

Critical studies:

Protractive Verse: Movement for Free Verse Parody, Dry Run Press, 1976.

Free Verse Self, Lionhead, 1979.

Editor:

(With others) *Albatross One: An Anthology of Poetry from Madison,* Albatross Press, 1970.

Brewing: Twenty Milwaukee Poets, Giligia Press, 1972.

Postpoems: A Poetry Postcard Anthology, Lionhead, 1975.

Work in progress:

Carl Rakosi: A Critical Biography.

Divisions: Epic EvoPoetic Text.

(Editor, with Karl Young) *An Objectivist Casebook.*

Still / Life: Collected and Revised Poems from 1969–.

Carl Thayler

1933-

During my birth year, and for six years after, we lived in a second-floor front apartment in a fine facsimile of a Moorish fortress, with pairs of black balconies on the top two of its three white stories. There was a strip of grass in front as brief as a pair of shears, but it sloped just right for sitting under the electric wires and enjoying the sun. The balcony, of course, was closer to the sun, and when she sat there, Mother smeared a white line across her nose. From her lap, the horizon was fairly clear for the several miles between us and the beach. When it rained, as frequently it did, Mother said that the rain was unseasonable. In a good wind like a Santa Ana, the wires swayed, and Mother said it was unseasonably hot. Fronds from the scruffy dismantled palms littered the street. Palms in brownish cracked groups commanded most of the city's height. They parted in tossed clumps for the tracks for the swank Los Angeles Limited, thirsted by the washes of the Los Angeles River, and almost clandestinely linked fronds to the north where they climbed the dun-colored hills. Hollywood was north, out there, between the hills and the schoolyard we directly overlooked.

Or anyway Hollywood was out there as Mother talked about it with the girl from next door, was out there like a lost ring. Mother had witnessed Tom Mix climb the steps of the Hollywood Hotel on his horse Tony. I was in her stomach then, a most unprofitable place from which to see film stars, albeit we were only a trolley ride from Hollywood. When Mother and the girl from next door walked my carriage, they headed north.

The neighbor girl was always singing. She sang behind my carriage; she sang on the balcony, her back to the pigeons; she sang on our strip of grass when mother sunned me. She could sing real songs, but she rarely did. Rather, she made them up, although not well. I could tell. Quarantined in my carriage, I distinguished good songs from bad, the real from her half-hummed, stumbling anecdotes of love betrayed and resentments fostered. In my newborn's head, I revised her moons that fell always into the sea, and her maidens, likewise.

Carl Thayler, 1989

I navigated by language through the seclusion that silence imposed upon me. It lessened the gloom of nap time. I listened to older children on the stairs, and still older ones in the schoolyard across the street, and to Mother and the neighbor girl discussing whether or not to sin and eat chocolate. I understood the arrangements each made, and why. I understood firm decisions and feeble songs. I felt like a spy and liked the feeling. Language was a big deal, and mine. For awhile anyway, it remained beyond my parents' watchful eyes and sharp ears. Like Mother's chocolates, it was a bit sinful.

When finally I officially talked, it was anticlimactic. Mother used to say that, as a girl, she had preferred to dance alone, in her room, with her private thoughts of the great Isadora. Talking to myself was like that, a dance, too, and done best among the pitfalls of self-absorption.

When Father and I first spoke, white gauze covered his mouth. He was in a sanatorium with TB, and we drove with family friends across the desert to visit with him. I believed, somehow, that good manners occasioned these visits, and that illness and the possibility of death favored family ties, and love, and even speech. But Father and I rarely got beyond a warm wave of greeting, and the premature coolness that often follows upon condolences. Mother would notice then that his shirt lacked a button, or his shoe a lace, and they'd arrange to administer to those needs. He seemed grateful, and the desert cooled and darkened, and he'd cough and complain of weakness, and in his customary slump he'd say good-bye. Mother left with his shirt, or sock, a promise for a Sunday visit next month, and a pain in her back. "That's life," she'd say. And if I complained of anything on the ride back, she raised the specter of an enema. I'd put my hand across my mouth like a white flag of surrender, like the gauze over my father's mouth. I never doubted that Mother's enemas could raise the dead, but I had merely swallowed dust in the still sweltering car.

When I was three, a phantom appeared in the apartment. It took advantage of Mother's stomach. She visited the doctor often. I accompanied her, and we'd share a malt afterwards in the pharmacy. Father was home now, and a lot of bustling about turned an improbable corner of their room into a nursery. The neighbor girl was there, pale, like her tunes. She wore Mexican peasant blouses, which Mother favored on her, with an eye-bludgeoning number of flowers stitched wherever the cloth rode against her frail body. Her teenage face already sagged at the mouth, and her songs seemed resigned now to betrayal.

The phantom kicked at Mother's stomach, which mysteriously pleased her, and she waited impatiently for the next one. When it kicked, I was invited to touch her stomach, which I did quickly, knowing a pat was a sign of encouragement. And that was the last thing I wished to offer.

Later, Mrs. Gilbert from upstairs visited. She rarely came downstairs. Rather she listened all day to the radio. Her balcony was above ours, and I'd heard hundreds of thundering choruses of "The Donkey Serenade." Her son was off fighting in Spain with the Loyalists, and between spins of the interminable serenade, she got bits of news, almost always bad. Stranded and mournful in the midday heat, she said, "You birth them and raise them. Why?" Then she

went upstairs, and Mother sat with her hands laced tight enough across her middle to compress the baby. I knew Mother would protect us, would, if it came to that, raise us from the dead with a sympathetic, if bowel-clutching, enema.

When he arrived, my brother already had about him the sour smell of old age. But the neighbor girl sang that he was a pure white dove. He wiggled and squirmed as if to extract himself from his wrinkled red skin. While I played around the shrubbery row dividing our building from its neighbor, Mother and the girl took the baby for a stroll in the carriage. Mrs. Gilbert's radio said the Fascists had bombed a village in Spain. I recall a picture in the paper of a bomb-blast by a carriage. Some people would have considered that a matter of civic pride.

He'd arrived in October, Christmas followed almost immediately, reviving my flagging eagerness for surprises. My parents discussed money, trancelike and daily. Father's business wasn't doing well. While he was in the sanatorium, his partner had robbed him. It was now a prodigious feat for Father to cart sample cases of embroidery up flights of stairs. With equal frequency he talked of money, of his partner and his partner's suits which should have been a warning, he coughed, and he napped.

In spite of prohibitions and warnings, I was up early on Christmas morning, standing on a chair before the stockings on the mantel. Mine encased a blockish, remotely cylindrical object. A roundish one filled my brother's. Both were dismayingly lumpy. In deference to my curiosity, my heart raced. I removed the socks and looked into them. From mine I withdrew a headless chocolate bunny. My brother's sock contained the head. He was, of course, too young for chocolate. But Father believed we should learn early to share. The misshapen head rather resembled a sticky brown rose with an extravagant pair of petals insolently cocked forward at the top. Neither half was a confectioner's dream, nor mine. I flung them onto the floor, the head following the somersaulting body. They stuck to the rug, and I tried to rub clean my hands against the mantel, leaving traces of the mutilated bunny where Father had hung the socks. I spent most of Christmas morning standing in a corner, face to the wall, with a sore butt.

Before I entered kindergarten, Mother and I walked the several blocks to the grade school I would attend. We stood before the fence surrounding the remnants of her girlhood memories. "Look," she said, "a sandbox." She spoke as though it were a sanctuary. I pulled at the straps of my leather aviator's helmet, and watched other little aviators exchanging joyous fistfuls of damp sand. At last, a war! Recriminations and evasions stopped. The sandbox was Europe, and death to Fascists!

The kindergarten teachers ranked George Washington high on the list of presidents of the United States. Apparently he, unlike Mr. Roosevelt, told the truth, and that was the cardinal virtue. For no transgression in kindergarten was too banal to fess-up. George Washington's portrait hung at the end of the perfumy hallway—lavender and resin, the odor of consolation after a mishap. Mrs. Thompson, my teacher, naturally encouraged us to emulate the illustrious George whose little axe launched a God-fearing nation, one whose capital virtue, so to speak, was telling the truth. What burden on the heart did teachers have to know that so galled them?

"Young George, one knew early, was destined for great service to his country," and Mrs. Thompson, for the umpteenth time, recounted, ". . . there was in his father's yard, a cherry tree . . ."

What would she cajole from us: a twist of a kid's arm in a shady deal for marbles, a father's sacrifice ignored, a protesting turn of the lock on the bathroom door? The neighborhood cat I'd invited in to suck the baby's air? Did my silence condemn me to spiritual exile from my native land—drifting like *The Man without a Country?*

George dared confession and won control of his country's destiny. At best, I could be only a marginal president like FDR. But that was OK because he'd get us a crack at the Fascists, no matter what lies the nation endured. Mrs. Gilbert's boy was dead, and I had plans. To the other kids I bequeathed the dubious honor of coming clean. I continued to die in the sandbox during recess with my lips sealed.

When war came, I was in Whittier, California. The radio told of the American dead, many of whom were very young. "Theirs," said FDR, "was the final sacrifice." Pearl Harbor must have been named for the eyes of the dead underwater. And from their sockets what could bloom like in the poppy fields mother talked of in France? For young men to drown with their teeth still in braces seemed wrong, yet worldly and noble. The family friend whose house we were visiting said he'd worked hard every day of his life.

"Of course the Japs hadn't considered that. The public be damned," he said.

Father always told the truth, and he had prospered. At least we had a house to ourselves now. Never a town for idleness, Whittier, California, had

orange groves and pickers. The pickers reached furtively through the leaves for the fruit, the dusty hard dry oranges that apparently bore, in California, the shiny seeds of happiness.

"Water," said the family friend, "that's the whole goddamn problem. You've got to bomb Colorado to separate it from its water."

The groves would prosper, Father said, in the hands of honorable men. Meanwhile, there were the Japs to lick; America's Pacific pathways would lead to victory; the coppery sun sinking behind the friend's flagstones would arise on buzzards over the Jap homeland. Father and the Whittier businessman enjoyed the security of fine principles. Before we returned home, the man gave me a gift of long trousers. But when we got home, Father took them and put them on a closet shelf.

"Where they'll remain," he said, "until you behave honorably."

A new home, a new school. This one was much like the old one, except it was further east. In the secular lingo of the day that gave the balance of power to the chokes (Mexicans) and the jigs (Blacks). As if by civil decree, at the three grade schools I attended, fights were settled at three o'clock by the bike rack. The chokes fought the jigs and, by a predictable providence, both fought the anglos. For their part, the anglos also fought each other when a space became available by the bike rack. Needless to add, short pants hindered my incursions into peer groups.

"Thayler as grist for Fox's nickelodeon," about 1955

Carl and Marcia Katz Thayler, about 1968

My knees were continually puckered raw from scraps in the gravel by the bike racks. But having in mind a moral lesson, Father didn't relent. And for her part, Mother knew when to keep her counsel to herself. Over the year, I grew to believe myself predestined, and not for happy circumstances.

When I was eight, Father mysteriously relented and allowed me to wear long pants, my antics apparently now honorable. Certainly my desperation turned into fear and cruelty. Father tended to find moral resonances in congenital misfortunes. Meanwhile, the trousers were now tight in the butt, and too short. With other fashionable Californians, I learned that fear, redolent with mothballs, could fell one. With that oddly suitable odor, I waited for the three o'clock bell to ring, the eyes of the Mexicans as unblinking as those of sunning alligators.

Afterwards, I carried a knife to school and tried one afternoon to erase the past by cutting a boy's palm. The Vice Principal called my father and, in his funereal style, said that I'd crossed the line, had gone from a fallible lad within the guidance counselor's domain to an object of growing interest downtown, to the district's psychiatrist. Father took the news som-

berly. Jesus, I thought, a trickle of blood on a palm. Come on. After all, close by at Belmont High, a choke shotgunned another gang member from the auditorium balcony. Killed the kid. I'd only brought to grief a hand raised to do me mean-spirited harm.

Back then, when school psychiatrists were itinerant characters, and few in number, they were considered only a cautious defense against antisocial behavior. The district psychiatrist had several meetings with my family, in various groupings and singly. He permitted me to hear him confide to Mother that "Your husband needs help fast."

Father entered the office when we left. Mother was still distracted and didn't reply either to the psychiatrist or to Father, who liked to pacify her with a word about the help I was getting. Father's displeasure with the psychiatrist sounded in the crack of the door against the wall as he stormed out of the office. He marched out of the waiting room, motioning for us to follow. He removed his eyeglasses by the elevators and dried the bridge of his nose. He demanded disjointedly to know what malicious lie I'd told to turn the psychiatrist against him. Needless to add, as a precaution against my untruthfulness, we stopped seeing the psychiatrist. And over the next year, daily, Father had two questions for me at the dinner table: "Did you turn out the bathroom light?" and "What did you tell the psychiatrist to poison his mind?"

I ran away from home, and the police brought me back a couple of days later. I continued to run away, sleeping on the roofs of friends' garages, at the beach, in movie theaters. I wasn't terribly nostalgic about home. But then I didn't manage to stay gone for long.

At home and away, I continued visiting the library on Friday evenings, a ritual for which I thank Mother. She loved to tell me about Jack London, and I believe that if Father hadn't had other ideas, she'd have named me for him. Her great figures were Isadora and London, and when she told the story of his house burning in the Valley of the Moon, her sense of loss was unendurable. She knew scores of details of his life in which to embody her infectious enthusiasm, and once when I ran away, I headed for Oakland to become an oyster pirate. I read all of his books, and liked the dog stories best. For a year I identified with heroes who answered to names like "Buck," and "Fang," and "Jerry of the Islands." Barking in vacant lots provided me with the masculine virtues founded on healthy teeth and body hair. And being outdoors a lot, I adopted the moon as the lonely hero's companion.

After my first year of high school, I was hustled off to Brown Military Academy: a clean slate, according to Father, who knew it was a national theater for God's bullies. Dr. John Brown, an Ozark evangelist, opened the academy in San Diego, and questions of home turf aside, he had no difficulty understanding Californians. San Diego was a retirement center for the military. The Pacific War had recently ended. And if the military officers discarded their uniforms, they retained the prejudices of their caste. For theirs was an early and impressively affective brand of self-realization. In his welcoming sermon, Dr. Brown put it well: "Eagles and Dodos divide the lot of Mankind. And contrary to the Hit Parade, there ain't no Mr. Inbetween." To that, Jack London would have given a rousing *Amen.*

I loved BMA: the barrack's polished hall reflecting sea light; the football team, undermanned and underweight, that charged and sometimes beat the Sunset League's best; the battles on the beach with kids from La Jolla and Pacific Beach. Unlike the crude brutality of home and public school, at Brown's

it offered clarity, and afforded a measure as accurate and as chilling as the eye of an expert marksman.

I did however succumb to temptations, although the Spanish fly I slipped into Dr. Brown's Kool-aid was only a Tijuana aspirin. But what a Sunday dinner for an overambitious cadet! Dr. Brown's guests included a general from Washington, and a score of elderly women, his financial backers. The suspense was unbearable as they passed the pitcher I had set before them on the head table, light entering through the wire-meshed windows of the converted gymnasium. Only *Paradise Lost* could make a nonevent so vivid, so staggering. The cold beads on the pitcher winked with frenzied calamity. Possibly George Washington was behind my itch to discover the real inclinations of those ineffable dowdy cousins of pornography. Cadets' doors at Brown's had been removed to curb the bad habits of boys who'd take advantage of hands empty for the moment of swords and rifles. The guests drained glasses of Kool-aid, but no orgy ensued. The Eagles remained somewhat present, shadows on the covers of hymnals on a dozen covetous laps.

When my year at Brown's concluded, I refused to return home. Instead I got a job on Hollywood Boulevard, cleaning a gymnasium after-hours. During the day, I attended Hollywood High, and continued to evade an education while playing football and messing around. What books I read were stolen from shops along the Boulevard: Henry Miller, Kenneth Rexroth, and Kenneth Patchen. Then, William Carlos Williams.

While reading of WCW's "stark leaves," I decided I'd been a poet all along. On the evidence of letters I'd written to Mother from camp years earlier, she'd praised my way with words. On that, my scruples comfortably allowed me to proclaim myself a poet. But my immediate desire was to race cars.

For years I'd desperately attempted to look old enough to convince the United Racing Association I was eighteen. According to rumor, the great Troy Ruttman was only fifteen and, while he was tall, height didn't seem necessary to drive midgets. But I failed to convince the midget racing association. I even had a respected driver, at whose garage I hung out, to lie for me. But the association that controlled the tracks in California said I wasn't old enough to enter the pits before a race, and that I only looked silly wearing dark glasses at night. So I looked for better opportunities to lie; it was as good a way as any to nurture a young poet. I convinced a mechanic to entrust me with the 1200-cc Harley-Davidson, an old cop bike, he had for sale. I assured him I'd ridden hundreds of them. Of course, I'd never been on a motorcycle. I did know, however, that Mulholland Drive offered the steepest turns to take at speed. The canyon road snaked along the terraced divide between the Los Angeles basin and the San Fernando Valley. Easy, I thought, the shift positions were marked. I didn't reach Mulholland for a couple of years. I dropped the bike after a skid through an oil patch about a mile from the garage. I took the bike into a parked car and lay under it, the pipe burning my leg. Eventually a kind soul assisted me upright. I waited until early morning to return the dented bike to the garage. A police call might have been out for it. I never returned to find out.

Mulholland Drive was a homegrown race track that nightly howled with the exuberance of engines, on a trail of lights. After running up there first with an MG, then with a TR-3, I felt ready for the Riverside Speedway. A month before a race there, I continued to rely on Mulholland for experience, and the car with a shudder gave it to me. One night the road was damp and I missed a shift and plummeted down the canyon wall. My destiny to drive race cars

appeared at the moment short-lived, and oblivion on the rocks below, and coming up fast, seemed a dismaying prospect. Then—as if partially reverberating with the handsome destiny I'd imagined for myself—the car stopped tumbling, stopped cold, as if it had been suddenly fixed in the misty air. The front end nested neatly in the crotch of a tree, the car hanging, unhurried now, the engine still running under the trashed bonnet. The rocks below resembled weird lunar graves. The tree recoiled, but held. It was the only tree in sight. My dreams of racing glory ended where some might unkindly say they began, on a warped frame.

My first excursions into poetry were less dramatic, although with their share of wrecks behind them. Language was as obstinate as a cowlick, as unmanageable as a libido—a poet, appointed but unlettered, threatened to become an untenable role. But I relied upon the authority of calculated rudeness. It worked as well as my imitations of WCW and Thomas Campion, about whom I'd learned from Pound. It kept me from worse trouble as I drifted in unsavory directions—no laurel wreaths, but no arrests for major felonies either.

I discovered, circuitously, the "Evenings on the Roof" concerts and Stravinsky, the Ferus Gallery painters and Barney's Beanery where they hung out, a few typewritten poems by two writers in San Francisco, Jack Spicer and Robert Duncan. And the Coronet Theater. In Los Angeles in the early fifties the Coronet showed films by René Clair, Buster Keaton, Stan Brakhage, Man Ray, Jean Vigo, Cocteau. The Coronet helped to open my eyes, albeit for the dark glasses. Bertolt Brecht directed Charles Laughton there in "Galileo." After discovering the theater, I lost patience with those who bitched about LA, claiming it was a wasteland of used-car lots and pink homes for movie stars.

The city herself began to interest me. Vigo was wonderful, but so too was Captain Horace Bell, leader of the constabulary of ex–Texas Rangers who brought the law to Bellflower and then to LA proper. When he retired, the Captain built the Southwest Museum by himself. And it's still there, with as fine a collection of relics of the early tribes as one could hope for. That's why I must gently demur when friends compare my stories (unpublished) with Nathanael West's. He was a tourist in Los Angeles, and a nervous one to boot, rather like a shaken guest at a funeral. If I hold a mirror to the face of the Lady in the box, it's to collect her breath on the glass to show that she's fine. A quick head trip through the fumatorium and she'll do her encore.

Daughter, Emily Thayler, age three

Over the years, the work of three artists has settled as naturally in my affections as the scent of oranges blossoms did when I ditched school to drink beer in the groves and inhabit a few images of Rimbaud's from the *Illuminations* that I carried with me for a long time. The poems were luminous and totally bewildering; the scent of the blossoms was hot, and the light through them after I had a few beers was astonishing—the same light, I was certain, had shined off the patio tiles of a rancho in early California. It was a maddening light, one in which God might have been present. I have since seen hints of that light in the labels placed by some packers on orange crates, and in the poetry of George Oppen, the photographs of Edward Weston, and the paintings and drawings of Richard Diebenkorn. Between them, these three artists, as the saying goes, bring it all home. Kenneth Rexroth, I recall during the beat/academic hoopla, distinguished more accurately between geographical sides of the Great Divide. And as Mother used to say, in California it was always unseasonably hot, or unseasonably wet, or unseasonably windy. It's there, a signature on the coastline, and on the heart.

When fighting began in Korea, I'd been in high school, and it continued when I was out. I was in the Naval Reserve and for reasons mysterious to all, including my chief, I got excited about submarines and applied for active duty.

"Think the air's bad in LA?" he said. "Try it when you're under the ocean for days and the guy beside you has gas."

As a child of chilli peppers and seismic tremors, I was not deterred. My boot-camp company consisted of three Mexicans from LA, a doleful black from Mississippi, and a pizzle of rednecks. The worst of it: we were expected to share one radio. "I didn't know God made honky-tonk angels," whined Hawk Williams. And the rancor of his fellow rednecks, I suppose, needed no more issue than that. One afternoon, Caldrone, a Mexican kid in Little Fence, a choke gang whose customs were felt throughout the Southwest, commandeered the radio, and we listened for the first time in weeks to the blessed Dominoes sing: "Rock 'em, roll 'em, all night long, I'm a sixty-minute man."

As the case has been with good art throughout history, controversy ensued. Given the impertinence of the critics, Caldrone's exposure to sophisticated hardware hadn't, fortunately, convinced him to abandon the simple flip-knife. The music scene improved.

Emily Thayler, age eighteen

I qualified for sub school and joined my training class at New London, Connecticut. Among our many tests was a day of psychological tests. After they were assessed, I was invited back for more, and then more, and then more.

"Ah . . . ," said the psychiatrist, "we don't all function equally well in group efforts. Obeying orders is, ah, a social skill. A sub's like a galleon, sort of. We all pull our oar. You don't belong on the boats, on any naval vessel either. Can't discharge you, your lack of, ah, facility isn't a dischargeable category. But let's keep you out of trouble. Suggest a duty."

"Diving."

"Sorry, they're lined up a thousand deep for that."

"The Hollywood recruiting office."

"Got to maintain an Atlantic Fleet setting."

"I'd like to play football."

My accomplice signed the papers and Bayonne Naval Depot gained a linebacker.

The season ended and I laced on boxing gloves, and got laced by Jumping Joey Trippy of Boston, and that was very discouraging. Without burdening the chain of command, I dropped in on the base commander to discuss my disenchantment with the military. He asked a few sly questions and phoned for the military police. I was, forthwith, reengaged in exhaustive discussions with shrinks. Their decision was unanimous: abort.

Days later I was delivered by ambulance to the mental ward of Saint Albans Military Hospital. For the next four months the shrinks offered me the opportunity for martial redemption: "Confess, come clean, you can obey orders," they said during midnight sessions, a lamp shining into my face.

"Admit, come clean, obey," sayeth my confessor. It seemed Mrs. Thompson was right. I didn't fess-up, and received a "general discharge" with the news that I'd blown my chance at the presidency.

I enrolled at Los Angeles City College to recapture the comparatively happy days of high school. Looking for Mickey Mouse courses, I became a theater major, not without qualifications: at Brown's I'd similarly enrolled in Speech to avoid homework, and Major Collins volunteered me for the debate team. I placed first in a dramatic declaration run-off with contestants from throughout the Southwest. Acting was fun, and the earnest actresses were, occasionally in intimate performances, incandescent.

Fall came 'round, and football season. I was kept so far down on the bench, for so long, that I waited not to play, but to be repatriated. I only got the coach's attention when, during a game, I smoked a cigarette on the bench. In fairness, his nostrils emitted twice the smoke mine did when he bellowed me off the field, and off the team. School was no longer fun, so I quit, and got a job instructing in a gym, and caring for the gym's alcoholic owner. After a year, simultaneously, his liver and my patience gave out. He returned to careening his Jaguar across Ventura Boulevard, and I hitched to New York.

I figured on a job with Will Geer's Folksay Theater, a company with whom I'd performed in Topanga Canyon. They'd only recently left for New York City and had invited me along. They were currently touring high schools in New York State, in spite of the composition of the group which included a score of blacklisted performers—both Woody Guthrie and Pete Seeger were associates of Geer, along with other House Committee on Un-American Activities favorites. I left California with five dollars and the trip took eight days. When I arrived in NYC, the company was on tour and I had three dollars. It hardly degraded Father's judgement of me when I collected sheets and a towel at a Bowery flophouse: "You'll end up a skid-row bum." Always a sucker for a *fait accompli,* I was depressed.

It was the mid-1950s. At the Museum of Modern Art I saw my first Jackson Pollock, *Autumn Rhythm.* I remained in front of it for the afternoon; everything responsible for bringing me to that canvass was a fair reckoning. In a few days Geer returned to NYC, and I joined the company both on stage and on the floor of an apartment in the Albert Hotel where most of

them bunked. Although not resolutely, I managed to make financial ends meet by playing young men provoked by their resentment of the social system to commend themselves to justice, justice, justice; by selling Scrabble at Macy's the year of its introduction and subsequent rage; and by sparring for dollars with the welterweights at Stillman's Gym.

While listening to Seeger was pleasant enough, I preferred Miles Davis and Bud Powell, and so spent my free evenings at Bird Land and the Royal Roost. Within two years I returned to California to test for a role in a movie starring an actor I'd met in New York, James Dean. The movie was *Rebel without a Cause.* I didn't get the part, but got one instead in a Tony Quinn western. Nick Ray, *Rebel's* director, saw it and brought me to Twentieth Century Fox. My horizons widened: I shoot Robert Wagner in the back in *The True Story of Jesse James.* I admit, the movie offered the kind of tarnished truth I could understand, and yet I wasn't happy. At a studio conference, Nick had a good word for me. The studio boss asked "Do we own him?" Nick said no, and the studio boss said, "Get him."

Carew Hartwig

For what was an indecent salary at the time, I was gotten. The contract was for seven years with six-month options. Suffice it to say, things quickly became a tangle. I now had the opportunity to race, but Nick, of whom I'd become quite fond, was hurting over Jimmy's death in a race car. So, contrary to Mrs. Thompson's lessons, I kept secret the Lotus Spyder I'd ordered. The situation worsened when Tom Pittman, an actor in *Jesse James,* crashed and died racing on Mulholland. In deference to greed and ego, I stayed at the studio, while sputtering about the phony this and the phony that. Writing seemed to be an unsalvageable dream; I hadn't even completed reading Pound's list in the ABC's.

And yet the freshness of those plums in that poem WCW wrote to his wife remained long after the charms of studio starlets, and many of them were unbearably nubile. The control of the studio changed hands, and I was ordered to make an ass out of myself in a part that later went to Pat Boone (ho-ho). I refused, I shot too much dope, I learned from my shrink during the day of urgent calls I'd made during the night.

When I'd first spoken with him, he'd laughed. "You've got a hard life, boy. I should kick you out of here," he said. "But I'll take your money instead. I've got no more integrity than you."

For the remaining months of my option, I collected a weekly pay check while my conduct militated against a permanent union. At the end, we parted without a word. In fact I learned from Mark Robson, who'd tested Diane Varsi and me for *Peyton Place,* that the studio officials walked out of a screening, refusing to look at film on Diane until Robson found another partner for her. My death, apparently, was as close as they were willing to broach a *modus vivendi.* From then on, as Gilbert and Sullivan might say: "His career was a bit austere." I did occasional supporting bits on TV, a cheapo movie, a snarl in a film Nick did at MGM. I floated, directionless. Although I read most of Pound's suggestions, which allowed me a few pretensions.

From Gene Frumkin, the editor of the literary journal *Coastlines,* I learned of Black Mountain College. The college had drawn almost all of the handful of poets I'd taken the effort to copy by hand from Gene's magazines: Olson, Creeley, Dorn, and Duncan. Plus, Paul Blackburn was associated with them. In the end, it was Blackburn to whom I'd give the most care, trying to preserve the look of his page—for more fully than I'd found elsewhere, his poems reconciled a warm nature with an intransigent world, a harsh contemporary music with an old world sense of charm, grace, and honor. Finding the well of Blackburn's poetry, I could only say: "Horseman, dismount."

I wrote to Cid Corman and he graciously responded with *Origin.* I started for North Carolina a few times, but my life was too unsettled for me to attend school. Instead, I wrote a play. It was a fetid bit of romanticism, but it had a virtue. I learned I could pass off my nonsense on a persona. Of course, I fooled no one who knew me.

By a circuitous route, the play reached NYC. S. had been looking for a play to produce, and he and his wife surprised me by flying to California and offering me an option. The fairly regular income almost convinced me I was trafficking in literature. I returned to drugging a bit too much. The role of a generously talented but self-destructive youth delighted me. Not everyone is afforded the pyrotechnics of destruction: Dean's red jacket, Chet Baker's golden horn. In east LA, they shot you down, and afterwards bitched about their privations.

A year later, S. was back in LA, in my doorway, in response to a mutual friend's overheated account of my health. As the tendency goes among the wealthy, he figured the impetus of a really good vacation would move me back on track. We enjoyed drinks served in frosted glasses, served on marble tabletops, in the mountains. Before he left, he offered me his summer home in Connecticut, and I snapped up the offer. He gave me a check with the understanding I'd write a new play, since the early one, like too much that's hallowed in theater circles, was disarmingly sincere trash.

Since the house was isolated in the woods, and the store was several miles along a narrow, rutted road, S. provided a car for shopping, and for compromising his trust. However, the isolation was a sanctuary and I remained in it through snow, rain, sun, and drizzle, living on staples and minimizing trips to town. Familiarity with drugs, alcohol, and fellow humans dissolved in the long nights and the disclosures of such simple endearments as deer at the salt lick. There was little to worry about save the wild dogs the pig farmer up the roads allowed to run free. While my writing was hardly irresistible, it lightened up by struggling free of an expectation of justice—I quit retaining past misfortunes for future profit. And unforeseen humor entered the writing.

The best laugh came when S.'s wife demanded confirmation that she too was a person, and her husband, in complicity with her lugubrious demands, gave her the new play to produce. She was bored with

Carl Thayler, Howard McCord, and Ted Enslin

her affairs, dance classes, shrink, and chatty afternoons with girl friends at the Russian Tea Room. Producing a play must have seemed a fine way for her to formalize her independence. So much for Broadway. The last I heard of the couple, they were divorced and she was conducting self-esteem workshops for Feminists.

After a year in the woods, I returned with the play to California, where it received two short runs, and received a prestigious little award that came without cash. My suitcase contained scores of exercises written at Pound's suggestion. I'd experienced reserves of affection for the unredeemable world as it might be articulated. A formal education seemed a good idea, and I enrolled at Kenyon College.

Before leaving California for the class of '68, I married Marcia Katz, as she completed the University of California, Los Angeles, class of '64. A juggling act, indeed. But she was good-natured and hardworking, and I was the author of a play her mother hadn't found at all funny. At the close of summer, we skipped town.

The choice had been between Kenyon, and joining Cid Corman in Kyoto. Corman's response to

my decision was ". . . hereafter our friendship shall thrive on silence." And while I, too, disliked Kenyon's English Department and the *Review,* that clique accounted for only a small public sampling of the college. The philosophy classes were first-rate, the equal of graduate seminars at the University of Wisconsin–Madison. First-rate, also, were history, classics, math, and religion. And to my benefit, few people there were interested in my writing. In retrospect, Black Mountain would not have worked out half so well for me. I say this after speaking with ex-students, reading accounts of the college, and having lived for a year among unrelentingly self-proclaimed humanists in a "free-wheeling" co-op. So, from '64 to '71, when I left graduate school at Madison to return to writing, I mired myself in the obsessions from which Wittgenstein claimed his thinking would free me.

Thanks to meeting Blackburn in '67, I severed the dumber relationships I had to my writing, and booted the poems out into the world: let them stand on their own, kid stuff or no. With Paul's death in the early seventies, which I witnessed, I finally accepted his poet's kiss, full on the mouth, and determined to write full out. I left the Philosophy Department, and the end of my marriage could be traced there, to that costly decision. Preparation for the divorce meant saying good-bye to my daughter Emily, then a very young child, several times a day. Another *fait accompli,* but one hardly to be relished.

Almost twenty years have passed. Emily begins college this month. It's fitting for me to be writing in a rented room with my belongings, mostly manuscripts and books, in boxes. In two days I'll move across the hall. It will be cooler there. I like those manuscripts, the stories and the poetry, they read OK to me. Publishers don't care for them, although they claim to admire the writing. They claim also to be puzzled, and they ask why I'm "perverse." They talk about an admixture of "realism" and "surrealism." Whatever they mean, there's no room in their theology for my brand of hermeticism. Well, far be it for me to discourage perversity.

In '85, I passed fifty and got scared about living hand-to-mouth, and enrolled at Bowling Green State University for one of those tickets writers get for jobs, a master of fine arts. Well, there're no fixed rules, so perhaps one will still come through.

I did, however, meet splendid friends at BG; delight in teaching elementary-school kids for an Arts Council; learn from the old Iguana to admire fire-arms; rid myself of bad habits after a heart attack and today have the stamina of a slightly over-the-hill woodwind band; continue an animated, if redundant,

series of breakups and reconciliations with Carew Hartwig, my lady fair for the past dozen years; and admit that no time was, or will be, favorable for literature, or for love, or for the presidency.

My mother, who I once believed could raise the dead with an enema bag in one hand and a cup of chamomile tea in the other, is herself dead, as of the fourth of this month. If requests are answered in such matters, then, by that, she was kindly treated.

For reasons that should now be clear, I consider the manuscripts beside me as spoils of war—love is ephemeral, but war is solid and bitter. Mother knew that in marriage and alone in old age. I guess that is what is meant by "perverse."

August 14, 1989

BIBLIOGRAPHY

Poetry:

The Drivers, Perishable Press, 1969.

Some Ground, Modine Gunch Press, 1970.

The Mariposa Suite, Tetrad, 1971.

The Providings: Poems, 1963–1971, Sumac Press, 1971.

Goodrich and the Haggard Ode and the Disfiguration, Capricorn Press, 1972.

The Drivers, Second Series, Bloody Twin Press, 1988.

D. M. Thomas

1935-

A WRITER'S ALPHABET

D. M. Thomas, *"standing against a mine-ruin, with Carnkie behind,"* about 1970

Prologue

A half-serious game I sometimes play, over a drink with some new acquaintance, is to invite him or her to run through the alphabet, specifying things he or she likes. And after that, the dislikes. It's a quick way of finding out if there are any shared enthusiasms or antipathies. It has its limitations, of course—it is hard to believe that he or she really cares strongly about xylophones, Xenophon, or Xerxes; but by the time *x* is reached I've usually discovered whether we're going to have much in common.

Since the intention of this present piece is to allow the reader—who has probably read only one or two of my books—to gain some impression of my life and personality, I thought I could do worse than play the alphabet game for him, in a slightly more sophisticated form. Each entry represents something that is or has been important to me, has influenced me for better or worse.

As a consequence of this approach, chronology is overturned, with a risk of confusion. Therefore at the beginning a chronological summary may be helpful:

1935: I was born in a tin-mining village of west Cornwall, in the southwest of England.

1937–49: Lived in a bungalow that my father, a plasterer, built.

1949: Immigrated to Melbourne, Australia, in the wake of my sister, who had married an Australian airman she had met in the war.

1951: Returned to share the family-house in Cornwall.

1953: Began my compulsory military service, during which I learnt Russian.

1955–59: New College, Oxford, reading English. B.A. degree, first-class honours.

1960: Death of my father.

1959–63: English teacher at Teignmouth Grammar School, Devon. I also began to write poetry.

1963–78: Lecturer in English at Hereford College of Education. Head of department for the last two years.

1975: Death of my mother.

1976: I began writing my first novel.

1979: Became a full-time writer.

1981: My third novel, *The White Hotel,* became an international best-seller.

1987: Moved back to Cornwall.

1989: Concluded *Russian Nights,* a quintet of novels, with *Lying Together.*

Aunts

Carnkie, the Cornish tin-mining village where I was born, was rich with aunts. Shrunken, white-haired, often arthritic from the drizzle that swept in off the Atlantic, they coiled up small in deep arm-chairs, surrounded by stuffy plants and furniture and photos of dead husbands. They would smile at me, say to my mother how much I'd grown, and press sixpence into my hand. They were honorific aunts, though I guess I was distantly linked to them all, through the inbreeding of a tight community.

Auntie Perry, moon-faced, surprised to learn there was the same moon shining on America, lived away from the village in the tiny white-washed cottage where she and my mother had been born. Perry was a genuine aunt. When her husband died she refused to budge from her cottage except once a week to pick up shopping: committing a slow, deliberate suttee. Auntie Susan-Jane was more sociable after her husband—my mother's brother—died of miners' silicosis; yet maybe Auntie Perry's way was better, because one night Auntie Susan-Jane stripped off her clothes in front of the Methodist chapel and started singing hymns.

I suppose she was taken "up Bodmin." Bodmin housed the mental hospital. Quite a few people from the village had at least a spell "up Bodmin": perhaps it was a genetic effect of a century's radiation from the tin-mines, long since derelict, that ringed the village. If you were not taken "up Bodmin" you might be sent "down Tehidy," where there was a sanatorium for TB sufferers; though TB was in decline, fortunately.

I had little contact with the aunts on my mother's side; but the paternal aunts were part of the intimate family-circle, and are woven deep into my life. Auntie Nellie, her fiancé killed in the First World War, ran a sweet-shop and retired early into severe arthritis. She was genteel and gracious; recited with impeccable elocution "Our England Is a Garden" at concerts; dressed up as a gypsy-woman, with loose false teeth, every Christmas, and came calling at our door; invited in, spun us yarns which didn't vary from year to year but still had us laughing. She also scared me a bit, till I was old enough to be sure the crazy, yabbering crone was actually my gentle aunt.

Auntie Ethel didn't laugh much; she could not have been expected to, having lost her husband, her two beautiful daughters, and a grandchild from TB. She was accepted back into the family-house at Carnkie in the spirit of Frost's words: ". . . when you have to go there, / They have to take you in." But she was too long-faced, and too slow-moving for my favourite aunt, Cecie, who scurried from morning to night, bearing chamber-pots or pasties, blackberries from the lanes or cups of tea (maddeningly never quite full), her stockings flapping at half-mast, her face and hands grubby as an urchin's. A couple of hairs jutted from her chin; you couldn't see her for steam as she churned the mangle for the washing; the lawnmower she propelled frenziedly was taller than she. She never stopped. I've never stopped loving her.

Beverly

Two years after my birth in 1935, my father built a bungalow, at weekends and after work, with his own hands. It was on the outskirts of Redruth, a working-class mining town two miles from the village of aunts: far enough for independence, near enough to stay in close touch. In the twelve years we lived there, I don't think we ever failed to walk to Carnkie on Sunday afternoon.

The small, neat bungalow was called *Beverly* after Beverly Hills. I was never allowed to forget that my parents had spent years in Los Angeles. My sister, Lois, was born there. ("It's not tomatoes, it's tomay-

"Mother, Father, Uncle Percy and his wife, and Uncle Leslie," about 1925

toes!" she said to the waiter on the ship bringing them home.) California loomed as vast as its redwoods in my parents' imagination—and even, through photo-albums, in mine. My father, especially, loved America's prosperity, big heart, classlessness. "What college did you attend, Mr. Thomas?" the Reverend Hunter, their minister, had asked him. Thinking quickly—in his mind's eye the humble village-school—my father replied: "I was educated in England."

And so—*Beverly*. Its kitchen held a "breakfast-nook" and a "cooler." Far across green fields, from the breakfast-nook window, one could glimpse Carn Brea, the ancient stony hill under which nestled the village of aunts, that other, deeper home. We lived in two places; or in three, if one included the white, Spanishy Californian bungalow of the photo-albums.

Beverly was a house of hospitality. Although my father would say it was better to own a spare umbrella than a spare bedroom, because you could lend a guest the umbrella and he could get home before dark, he and my mother loved it when friends called unexpectedly. Sometimes Lois would play the piano and my parents would sing duets. They had strong, sweet voices, soprano and baritone. They built a paradise for two, would gather lilacs in the spring again, confessed they were longing to hold each other to their fevered breasts.

Winter night falling, a drizzle blowing across the fields, my father, home from work, would clench a plate of stew on his lap, eating and warming at the same time. Then listen to a comedy-show on the wireless—which they almost alone called the radio—and my recovered father would thunder a rich, inimitable laugh.

I often slept with my father, pleading fear of ghosts. He was warm and tangy, as I slid off to sleep. His breast, I think, was often fevered, whereas my mother's was cool.

Cornwall

England's first colony, conquered a thousand years ago. An all-but-island, it has never been insular; Roman and Phoenician vessels landed here, to trade for tin; saints from Ireland and Wales sailed in, and unsaintly Yseult to the court of King Mark. Wherever in the world there are, or were, hard-rock mines, you will find a hidden diaspora of the Cornish. It was much more natural for my father, at twenty, to sail to America to find work than to go, like Dick Whittington, to London.

Cornwall's spine is granite, and around it cluster the poor, bleak, worked-out mining villages. The rugged, dramatic coast is home to tens of thousands of drowned voyagers. Soft, lush river-valleys cleave the coast and snake towards the granite moors. The shifting sky holds a pure, mystical light, summoning artists. The Cornish, like other Celts, are simultaneously down-to-earth and imaginative.

I lived away from it for thirty years, but never lost touch. Night after night, latterly, my dreams insisted I should go back to live. Two years ago I did so. As my car, in advance of the removal-van, nudged into the narrow, high-walled drive of the property I had bought, my heart sank. It was a grey, bleak day; I felt drawn back into the womb, from which it had taken such energy to escape. I rushed to the phone and called my lawyer.

"Has the sale of my house in Hereford gone through?"

"Yes. This morning."

"Damn!"

Otherwise I would have stopped it, and sent the removal-van back to the Midlands without unloading. It would have been a big mistake: the claustrophobia lasted a few months then vanished. If this is the womb, it's very pleasant. I live just eight miles from *Beverly*, and ten from Carnkie, but in a very different environment: softer, more middle-class. It is a small but necessary distance: as my father may have felt when he built *Beverly*. For me, though, the distance is necessary because the people I loved are dead.

Cornwall means a lot to me. It's become mother, father.

Dad (Harold Redvers Thomas, 1900–1960)

I know almost nothing about him and almost everything. My relationship with him was almost

D. M. Thomas playing rugby with his father behind Beverly, *with Carn Brea on the horizon, about 1941*

inarticulate. I was too young to question his periods of broodiness and melancholy. I knew that Mum would soon shake him out of it, and he would come to life with some droll tale of one of his workmates. "What do you think Freddy said today? He was up the ladder, and he overheard a nurse say to a patient, 'You're very low.' She obviously meant he needed another pillow. But Freddy came scrambling down the ladder. 'What'ee think, Harold?' he said. 'Bleddy nurse, tellin' the bleddy man he's dyin'!'" Dad's laughter would cascade, his head thrown back, auburn hair gleaming. The story would be retold to others, for months, never staling because his laugh never failed to make it new.

To say I admired his gentleness, kindness, courtesy, would be wrong, because it lapped too closely around me. It was an ocean I was borne up by. A fine, proud plasterer, he talked to his bosses as an equal. Addressed curtly by a boss as "Thomas," soon after his return from California, he said to him, "I've got a handle to my name." He was far more intelligent and sensitive than his bosses—and one or two of them had the grace to sense it; he was an ardent Union and Labour supporter, yet completely without class rancour. Our home was curiously classless.

As I approach the age at which, with brutal unexpectedness, he died, I catch myself coughing his smoker's cough, hunching into my overcoat in the same way, throwing back my head with the same movement. But that is no compensation for his absence, these past thirty years. His death, coinciding with my moving away to take up a teaching-post, severed me from my roots. I needed him to earth me. His death shattered our family-house; Auntie Cecie lay in bed, too grief-stricken to move. The chapel-choir was never the same again, since his fellow-baritones, disheartened, gave up coming.

I suspect frustrated sexual passions, a frustrated creativity. A certain timidity (I have it too) kept him often in the background. With his voice and personality he should have been a leading light in the local amateur operatic society; instead of which his only role, ever, was as a sentry who had to say, "You can't come in, Emile; you're drunk!" He rehearsed it endlessly with us. I have lived my adult life under the shadow of his loss. Psychoanalysts talk of the "family romance," but I do not think I romanticise him. In his gentleness and reserve, in his earthiness and mystery, he was the most remarkable human being I have known.

Early Religion

By the time I was sixteen, in 1951, I had fared far, had voyaged. Few youths in England had sailed to Australia, stayed for two years, and returned—though many had emigrated for good. We had followed in the wake of my war-bride sister, intending to stay; but by about the third day afloat, to my infinite homesick relief, my father had decided it would be a temporary sojourn. Now I was back, with infinite reluctance: living in the village of aunts, since of course *Beverly* had been sold.

Explosively I had discovered poetry, in my antipodean years, and the popular musical classics; most explosively of all, sex, though it was still entirely in my head. I strangled if a girl approached; but few did.

It was back to chapel-going on Sunday evening, sitting in the pews my grandfather, a mining carpenter, had made. At least the hymn-singing, with my parents dominant in the choir, was sweetly harmonious; and the sermons, from pious but uneducated local preachers, occasionally allowed a moment of entertainment to interrupt the boredom. "As Charles Lamb said, the other day . . ."

Deep into Swinburne and Hardy, I decided I was an atheist. At school I would only read the lesson if I could choose it from the Apocrypha. My passionate arguments made Auntie Ethel cry—she lived to die, to see her daughters and granddaughter again, I guess—but no one else took much notice. The family didn't wear religion on its sleeve.

But their lives were pure. There was no drink in the house, and sex didn't exist. I knew it existed, as huge and hot as Australia; but I couldn't reach it. The closest I came to it was at the social evenings in the Sunday school. Curiously, the prim Methodist elders allowed a mating ritual. It was called Postman's Knock. During the interval between the formal games, when the aunties poured cups of tea and laid out homemade cakes and sausage-rolls, the youngsters were allowed their own informal fun. A youth stood guard at the door leading out to the damp porch. A male or female went out, then requested a partner. He or she was summoned in a loud voice, often giving rise to catcalling hoots as the blushing man or maid responded, vanishing behind the door. It was sometimes a few seconds, sometimes an age, before the door opened, and the one who had been summoned became the summoner. It was impossible to refuse. Easy to imagine the fumblings and probings that went on, in the sacred porch. Anyone who wasn't hopelessly decrepit might be called. What assigna-tions the village rakes must have set up, in those dark, intimate seconds! What tremors they must have set going in virginal breasts! What jealousies burned, over who had asked for whom. I was seldom asked for; and when I was, my kisses were quick and clumsy.

And there was an interesting formal game in which someone in the centre demanded an object, and the members of two teams strove to be the first to bring him it. I remember Tommy Webb, our cleft-palated shopkeeper and church-organist, demanding a lady's stocking, and with shrieks and giggles skirts were hoisted to unclip a nylon. "You only want to see what I got on!" teased Sylvia Combellick, and Tommy laughed soundlessly, his rheumy eyes twinkling. Sylvia was too young and glamorous to be an auntie; she was married to a "quiet" man, "a great reader"—in other words, he was a bore in bed. Having put on her stocking again and smoothed her dress down, Sylvia followed her remark to Tommy by momentarily, gratuitously, in an excess of high spirits, sliding her dress up again, revealing a scarlet suspender-strap cleaving a shapely white thigh. It was rumoured that, at a social at a different Sunday school, the women had been invited to compete over who would lift their skirts highest; and some hussies had raised them to their waists. This was shocking, quite beyond the pale. Since religion was supposed to be joy, I didn't see the sense of that. It sounded wonderful.

Flying

The British Airways Boeing took off from Sydney, heading for a stopover in Adelaide and then the long flight home to England. It had been a sentimental return journey to Australia for me, more than thirty years after my cross-world voyages. But I was glad to be going home. It is always good to go home. In mid-rise into the blue, I heard a descending twang like a harp-note. It bothered me. No one else seemed to notice. But then the pilot came over the intercom, announcing that an engine had failed and we were turning back.

Panic seized me. The old fear of flying. I fought to control my breathing. What saved me was the *sangfroid* of my neighbour, a silver-haired old lady who went calmly on reading her newspaper. I thought, My God, if this little old lady can be so calm, it would be shameful for me to yield to hysteria.

I was relatively calm when we landed. The old lady looked up from her newspaper, blinking in surprise. Turning to me she said, "We're not in Adelaide already, are we?"

Waiting once for a plane to take off in North Carolina, I chatted to my neighbour, a befurred, rather attractive blonde. In no time—I don't know how it happened—we were kissing, passionately, shamelessly. We must have kissed for half-an-hour, until takeoff. The polite stewardesses ignored our frenzy of desire. Once in flight, we buried ourselves in books and magazines, strangers again.

I like these moments of delirium.

Greyfriars

Greyfriars—actually, 10 Greyfriars Avenue— was the house I have lived in longest. Almost a quarter-century. Exchanging a grammar school teaching job for a college post, I moved there with my wife and two small children in 1963—just before Kennedy's murder. It was a modest three-bedroomed semi in a modest, rather elderly avenue near the River Wye. Its garden was overgrown. It had a cherry-tree which blossomed resplendently each May. Strangely we use the past tense for houses we no longer inhabit: the cherry-tree is still there, in a tamed garden.

There was a lot of turbulence and a good deal of unhappiness at Greyfriars, yet my memories of it are almost uniformly happy. My older children, Caitlin and Sean, grew to adulthood there; fragile though it often was, the nest collapsed only after their departure. What I remember about it is that calmness which, as Pushkin said, is essential for creation. Maureen, my wife, had the gift of creating a silence, a tranquillity, for me, within which I could write. I wrote first on a card-table in our bedroom; later we had a study built on. Poems came, then novels.

It may have helped that the site on which our house stood had once, as its name implied, held a Franciscan friary. The monks had built it deliberately on marshy, fetid ground, outside the city wall. Now it was an avenue of three-bedroomed semis, occupied mostly by ageing couples who religiously washed their cars on Sunday morning. We saw no ghosts of cowled monks, but the ground felt serene. I discovered that a Franciscan poet, William Herebert, had lived there in the fourteenth century. I took it as a good omen.

A stray white cat gave birth to four kittens, secretly, in our garage. The kittens were wild when we found them. One of them bit the hand of the Animal Welfare lady who came, and she cursed roundly, saying we'd never tame them. It wasn't long before the wildest was curling up in our arms.

I spent many years there wondering how I could escape it—perhaps to return to Cornwall; yet now it

is forever a part of me. I would love and hate to see it again; I find it hard to imagine my study turned into an ordinary room.

I sit there at my desk, moody, dreaming; a clatter of dishes from the kitchen telling me that supper is being prepared. I await her voice summoning me. We shall catch the start of the TV news at six, as usual. I am a creature of habit.

Hereford

I came to Hereford, to the Greyfriars house, with some guilt, since my schoolteaching post in Devon had kept me relatively close to my widowed mother; but a College of Education was a step up, and I wanted more time in which to write. The holidays were longer, the working-hours shorter and without the strain of imposing discipline on unruly boys and girls. It was, indeed, a delightful job; all the students, in the earlier years, were female; many were attractive; some were intelligent and sensitive. In the English department we could set our own syllabus and concentrate on the *genres* and authors we liked best. I tended to specialise in poetry, with a scattering of Russian novels in translation. It was good to teach more informally, casting off the black gown, leaning back in an easy chair with a cigarette between my fingers, discussing Yeats, Frost, Pasternak.

All the students were training to be teachers, mostly in primary schools—of which I and most of my colleagues had had no experience. Yet we had to supervise their teaching practices. That made me feel like a charlatan. It was quite pleasant, on a sunny day, to drive out into the rich, sleepy Herefordshire countryside, but as some dreary redbrick village-school approached my mood always gloomed. I kept my visits as short as possible. On one memorable occasion I watched for twenty minutes an earnest, bespectacled student moving building-bricks around with some six-year-olds, scribbled some inane comments on a memo-pad, and beat it to my car with a sigh of relief. I wasn't sure where the next school was, only that it was about a mile away through winding lanes. I drove slowly, drawing on a grateful cigarette. At last, turning a corner, I saw the little, lonely school, redbrick, Victorian, nondescript—much like the last school. I entered, and to my utter astonishment was greeted by the same earnest, bespectacled student I had left at the other school, a mile away. She looked almost equally puzzled. "What are you doing here?" I demanded. Her mouth goldfished. I realised I'd made an awful mistake, driving in a circle. I apologised, grinning, beat it again, and decided to give the second school a miss. It was time to head back to the college for a prelunch sherry—like a staff brigadier returning to headquarters from the trenches.

My confusion on that morning was characteristic of my feelings about Herefordshire. I never responded to it enough to get to know it. For me it was too landlocked and stuffy. Perched on the Anglo-Welsh border, it seemed too gloomy to be England, too bland to be Wales. I wrote poetry about Cornwall.

About a year after our arrival in Hereford, a slim pamphlet of my poems was published: *Personal and Possessive*. It wasn't a vanity publication, the publisher took no profit, but I had to pay for it myself by getting subscriptions. Many staff and older pupils at the school in Devon subscribed, as did many lecturers and students at Hereford College. I was summoned before the principal and the director of education. Some of my poems acknowledged sexual desire for my former schoolgirl-pupils. One poem, at least, suggested more than mere desire. I was severely reprimanded. I offered to resign, but my principal, a formidable lady, said I was not to. She offered to buy up all the copies intended for college students, who would be told the publication had fallen through. I accepted the deal, and crawled away. She took possession of twenty or thirty copies of a booklet which is now, absurdly, quite valuable.

Intimations

They are working quietly now,
heads bent, pens scratching away,
their heels lifted abstractedly out of flat shoes,
and I have time to think, and look down.
I look down at myself furtively
and see it was not I that had caused their
     laughter,
the ripples of lewd-eyed mockery that raced
—as if one were suddenly naked—
up the row from swarthy Susan's
dirty chuckle . . . Oh well, whatever the
     cause,
not I, at least . . . I feel the flush dying
and I hate Susan a little less perhaps,
though I still hate her, for that laugh.

Yes, they are quietly at work now,
puzzling over a difficult piece,
and I remember Lawrence and his troubles
and momentary consolations. An October
     sunlight
leans on them through the window, and I
am alone out here, looking at them,

beginning to love them again as a peace
leans on me like sunlight.
My gaze runs up and down the rows
of bent heads and stops
at Penny, in the front seat, her tall
and gawky and graceful frame twisted sideways
out of the desk in concentration,
as at that moment a look of dislike, sheer
dislike of the passage, born of
exasperated incomprehension, baffles her face.
She looks up, and sees my eyes
aware of her, divining my feelings,
and she smiles, shyly and confidingly,
her brooding dark face lighting up
in friendliness. And I'm aware,
sharing, so suddenly with them,
aware of their beauty and their life.

A faint belch disturbs the class into spurting
     giggles;
it is Susan of course, her dumpy face wreathed
     in blushes,
and I love her. None of them suspects
I am so close, concerned and intimate,
or that the warm, quiescent
body of their life is flowing to me
as I stand stiff in my gown.
I have suddenly seen them, not as children,
but as all-but-women; I watch,
not the ties and crumpled childish collars, but
     the laps,
which are womanly-curved and almost
     maternal.
Cross-legged, they might be women beside a
     cradle,
waiting patiently for their baby to sleep,
so warm and womanly the crossed thighs,
     suspender
nuggeted faintly against the navy skirt;
and I feel in sharp intuition
how strange and frightening their new bodies
are to them, how wonderful and exquisite
with sharp sexual feeling.

And then I look at the boys, decently
apart on the other side of the room—
and I don't feel anything of this about *them*.
Guiltily I walk between the rows of boys,
suggesting a word here, hinting, cajoling,
pretending to get annoyed over a smudge.

(1961)

"Ready to fight the Nazis," 1940

Jews

When I published *The White Hotel* many reviewers and readers assumed I must be Jewish. Not only am I not Jewish but I wasn't aware of Jews, as any sort of "problem," when I was growing up in Cornwall—not until I saw the first photographs from Belsen. When I went to Australia I found there were many Jews in my class, though they didn't stand out particularly from the rest of us. The whole class was quite serious-minded and polite, in contrast with the boys I had left behind in my Cornish school. One Jew, Oscar, heavy and blue-stubbled at fourteen, intended to become a brain surgeon; and no doubt he has done. I fell in love with a girl called Sara, but it didn't occur to me until years later that she was a Jewess. She was just a lovely, slender, graceful dark-haired girl. I loved her dumbly, shyly, tenderly, unbearably; I could say to her across the years, in the words of Pushkin: "God grant another love you half so well." Save for an accident of geography, she would have

drifted into the Auschwitz air as a five-year-old Jew-child.

King Solomon's Mines

My father read the *News Chronicle* and, every month, the *National Geographic* magazine, but never a book. I can't recall my mother reading anything except uplifting religious booklets in her later, arthritis-crippled years. Yet they encouraged me in my love of books. With my sister ten years older, out dating almost every night, I was virtually an only child. I escaped into my own romances, as a counterpart to my sister's. I loved a few books very intensely, constantly rereading them. The first I remember was *Robin Hood,* an illustrated version of the Hollywood movie starring Errol Flynn. I loved the movie-stills as much as the words; thrilled at the sight of Robin and Maid Marion embraced at the end. I gulped back my tears over *Black Beauty;* frightened myself with the gloomy old house of *Kidnapped,* which I much preferred to the fresh-air gusto of the same author's *Treasure Island.*

Kingsley's *Water Babies* was eerily haunting. I didn't reread *Alice in Wonderland* because it seemed too real, too scary. *Westward Ho!* was a struggle, but I was moved by the exotic settings of its illustrations. *The Final Reckoning,* a story of Australian bushrangers, drew me to Henty, and I devoured all the books of his I could find: a sweep around the British Empire. Probably because I was well-behaved, I loved the antics of William in Richmal Crompton's series. I loved Captain W. E. Johns's Biggles and, just as much—to show I was no chauvinist—Worrals of the WAAFs. I read and reread *Little Women.* When I woke from a tonsillectomy, my mother comforted me by reading to me from *Gulliver's Travels.*

But the book which stood out above all the rest, and which has haunted me all my life, was *King Solomon's Mines.* I became entranced as soon as I saw an illustration of the desert that had to be crossed, with Sheba's Breasts, shimmering and snow-nippled, beyond it. It was full of wonderful incidents: finding the skeleton of the Portuguese explorer, José Silvestra, in the mountain-cave; the old witch Gagool spinning and spitting as she prepared to dart her spear at the one chosen for sacrifice; the lunar eclipse, just in time to save the intended victim; the descent into the mountain . . . But it was all wonderful and magical. Rider Haggard's story is crammed with erotic symbolism, and I surely responded to it, unconsciously, at eleven or twelve. Above all, it was Sheba's Breasts which haunted me. I had never seen real breasts, having been bottle-fed. The first breasts I saw were created by two artists: a writer and an illustrator. I owe them a debt. Like virtually everything connected with sex, breasts became mythologised, aggrandised, to my imagination.

Lois

I saw my sister's breasts often enough—but in her brassiere—because she had a tendency to dash around the house while changing to go out. For a "forfeit" at one of the village socials I mimed my sister changing to go out, and brought a great laugh. She was bright, and went to the grammar school; but insisted on leaving early so that she could earn some money. A freckled, attractive, exuberant redhead, she had the run of all the servicemen who swarmed into Cornwall during the war. She was a spitfire, a hurricane, a bazooka of a girl; though she was almost never at home, she dominated the house. We lived by the eternal Scheherazade of her romances. And, when the Australian flight-sergeant was victorious over the American major, we followed her south.

Her husband died of a heart-attack in middle-age, after which she resumed her confused but heroic romantic quest. An affair of the heart while she was revisiting her birthplace, California, led her to stay on. The affair fizzled out. One evening her son, a choreographer with the Scottish Ballet, phoned me, and in his still strong Australian accent said, "Uncle Donald, Mum's been caught in an earthquake." I was not surprised. She was at the dead centre of the tremors. Her heart is still molten lava, in her sixties. She has come to live near her son in Glasgow. She and I are closer than we ever were, but as different as chalk and cheese. She believes the universe is taking care of her, and I guess she's right. Her red hair has greyed, though not her temperament, and I see more and more our mother in her.

Mum (Amy Thomas, née Moyle, 1903–1975)

My mother's hair was already grey in my childhood; I have to turn to the photograph-albums to find her black-haired—which I do with pleasure, for she was beautiful, *gamine*, sparkling, mysterious. Or perhaps it is only the effect of the old and hazy snapshots to make her look mysterious. She waited four years for my father when he went to California seeking work; he returned for her faithfully, they married, saw a rugby-match, and sailed for America on the

"*With my father and Lois at* Beverly," *about 1942*

same Easter Day, 1923. In the snaps she huddles among a band of male Cornish migrants, and my father looks very proud of her.

Her mother had died when she was young. She never talked much about her parents, and I never thought to ask her. As in some peasant-culture, she settled almost completely into my father's family. Therefore she seems to me to have no history, to have sprung, already beautiful, into my life—the life of the snapshots—many years before I was born. Born in fact on the first day of spring, she was perfectly named: Amy. She was lovable and loved. Her character, too, seems to have the sweet fragility of spring. Like an April day, she was "all smiles and tears." She would dissolve at someone's sad plight, or some sadness of her own; then instantly brighten, and laugh at her own ready tears. She chattered like spring birds; she did not work too hard. In contrast to my father's well-phrased, expressive letters, hers were slapdash and without full-stops; though, as she liked to boast, she could spell well.

If she were a flower, she would be a daffodil; if a book, *Little Women;* if a bird, a swallow; if a metal, silver; if a tree, aspen; if a piece of music, the Moonlight Sonata. She wasn't passionate; she enjoyed a cuddle, she would say, but could do without anything else. She wasn't an earth-mother, though she looked after us well. Giving birth to me late, she worried that I would get hurt, and wouldn't let me play with rough boys. It is for that reason, perhaps, that I grew terribly shy and reserved; stood separate, observing—and became a writer.

Her two favourite expressions were "What's to be, will be" and "The Lord will provide." He always did, though she was—to my guilt—lonely in her last years. She had a mystical streak; a nun warned her of my father's imminent death, and Jesus knocked on her window one night, checking that she was okay. She had a natural dignity and wisdom; when she decided she had had enough, that life held no more pleasure, that she wanted to be with my father, she made her heart—as strong as a lion's—stop.

Novels

I'm not addicted to reading novels. If my doctor advised me to cut out reading novels for a year, I would not be perturbed. There is a puritanical streak in me which makes me think, even after a novel I've enjoyed, "But it didn't really happen."

I feel this less, and often not at all, with Russian novels; partly perhaps because Russia herself is so fictional and surreal. When I first read *Anna Karenina* and *War and Peace,* my actual existence seemed less real, and infinitely trivial, compared with the events and characters in the novels. I lived like a sleepwalker between the periods of reading. Turgenev's *Nest of Gentlefolk* brought tears to my eyes at the end—not only the first time I read it, but the second, years later. Since we never step into the same river twice, this was a rare experience. Even more extraordinary were my reactions to Turgenev's novella *First Love,* in which a youth finds that his father is his secret rival for the love of a beautiful girl. Reading it at twenty, I identified totally with the youth's emotions. Rereading it in my forties—totally with his father!

Doctor Zhivago overwhelmed me with its poetic beauty and changed my way of viewing the world. Nor was I the same person after reading *Ulysses.* *Madame Bovary* disappointed me when I first read it; but when, inspired by Julian Barnes's *Flaubert's Parrot,* I tried it again last year I felt it was one of the greatest novels I had read.

Hardy's novels became a part of me early on; Lawrence's too, but I don't care to reread him. I can't get beyond a few pages of Proust. I struggle with

"My mother, with Lois," about 1925

Dostoievsky, Dickens, Conrad, Henry James, Jane Austen, George Eliot, the Brontes, Nabokov—though I love his autobiography, *Speak, Memory.*

After twenty years of writing verse, I had an impulse to try a novel. Two Russian novels that I happened to read at that time helped me to overcome my aversion to the laborious build-up of plot and characterisation: *Torrents of Spring* (Turgenev again) and Bulgakov's *Master and Margarita.* The first flowed with a flawless, lyrical simplicity; the second dazzled with its mixture of tragedy and comedy and its apparent indifference to logic.

Oxford

While I was an undergraduate, reading English, at New College, Oxford, Khrushchev paid a visit. He spat at Epstein's statue of Lazarus in the college chapel, muttering curses against decadent modern rubbish. The English and French invaded Suez. I joined in the passionate denunciations of our imperialistic stupidity and double-dealing, which were distracting the world's attention from the tragic events in Hungary. I trembled lest I be called up. Having done my two years' national service, I was on the reserve.

The vacations were longer than the semesters. My life fell into a twofold pattern. At Oxford I worked hard and had little social life. I was conscious of my privilege, a working-class boy at Oxford; I intended to try to deserve it. Also I loved the plunge into literature. In the vacations, at home, I stayed in bed late reading; took quiet walks; played snooker and bridge at the Men's Institute; walked in the evening to the next village to see my fiancée; and walked down the hill, late, to a light supper left on the kitchen-table by my mother.

It seems, looking back, a perfect existence. I had the intellectual adventure of Oxford, but was still a part of the village and my family. It was still whole, and seemed set fair forever; in fact, my father's time was running out.

During my final student year I developed a nervous breathlessness and saw spots before my eyes from overwork. I could only type essays, not write them. For my finals I was allowed to sit alone in a room at college, with an invigilator, typing my answers. I was struggling to identify the location of some Chaucerian passages when the invigilator, who happened that day to be one of my own tutors, leaned over my shoulder and whispered, "No, it's from the Pardoner's Tale, my dear fellow." I still muddled it, for some reason, and typed the wrong answer.

Poetry

While I was at Oxford I wrote two appalling Petrarchan sonnets, and a decent, rather Lawrentian, short story which was published in the university magazine *Isis*. Working, after I had got my degree, for a diploma which would allow me to teach, boredom and a street-accident I observed gave rise to a *frisson* of excitement as I settled to write a poem—an instantaneous conviction that I wanted to be a poet beyond all else. Yet I was soon trying my hand at a novel, intensely autobiographical. Someone offered to show it to the novelist Philip Callow, to get an opinion. His response was that it was not only unpublishable but clearly the author would never publish anything. I have lost the manuscript, which is a pity, because I would like to see the awfulness responsible for such a discouraging comment.

I have roamed the border between prose and poetry, even when—as happened for fifteen years—I was sure I could never write—didn't want to write—prose. My poems were strongly narrative; and the poets I loved best were those who kept to a narrative line, had something positive to write about: Frost, Donne, Yeats, Emily Dickinson, Anne Sexton; and increasingly and almost obsessively the Russians, Akhmatova and Pushkin above all. I translated, and learnt from, both. An inspiration closer to home was Charles Causley, Cornish and of working-class origins like myself, with a pure lyricism I could not begin to match.

When, after I'd published six collections of verse, the novels started coming, I thought them a temporary aberration. I even believed that the Russian term *poema*, meaning a long poem, better suited such a fiction as *The White Hotel* than the word *novel*: it had indeed started from a narrative poem. My wish to incorporate into fiction documentary material, as in the "Babi Yar" section of *The White Hotel*, fitted perfectly into the poetic tradition exemplified by *The Waste Land* and Pound's Cantos; whereas in the novel it was not a tradition.

With the government-decreed closure of Hereford College in 1978 and my casting myself adrift as a full-time writer, I sensed that I would go on writing novels, or *poemas*, rather than short poems, since I would need to feel absorbed. I would find it impossible to write poems for eight hours a day, so I would need the longer, more time-consuming *genre*. Even so, the days seemed terribly silent. Gloom overcame

The author with his wife Maureen, 1959

me. What helped to save me from a deeper depression was reading an anthology of Armenian poetry. The courage and beauty of such poets as Varouzhan and Siamanto, faced with their country's extermination, put my problems into perspective.

Questions

Just and truthful God,
I wish to protest;
there is so much we don't understand,
but you hurry away from our questions
like a politician from the cameras.

Why are the huge eyes of so many children,
too weak even to blink,
opened to your world,
only to become glazed pools
where flies swarm?

Why do you give, to the murderer
of the just ruler, a steady hand,
good luck, fanatical accomplices;
but to the executioner of the tyrant
a clumsy hand, bad luck,
weak and treacherous followers?

Here, an old woman, lonely, wanting death,
pulled alive from the smoking ruins;
there, the young mother of children,
blown to pieces.

Why, out of five of equal aspiration,
do you make one a Mozart, another a Hitler,
another a Campuchean peasant,
another a rich woman's aborted foetus,
another swept away with millions
in the vaginal fluid?

One a man, another a stoat, another a flower,
another a stone, another—not even a stone?
Any fisherman
who used a net with such wide holes
would leave his family starved.

God, do you ever shudder
with the thought of your non-existence,
as we do with the thought of ours?
With the thought of *why?* Why *you?*
I might have been you,
and you might have been here.

Are you a slave to the dice?

I have a humble place at your table,
but how can I eat your bread,
and drink your wine,
when there are the poor, outside your palace,
stretching their skinny arms through the
    railings?

Do you envy us our courage, patient endurance,
passion for the unattainable:
qualities you cannot possess?

You are like a quizmaster,
who hasn't himself been given the answers.
You wrap your cloak about you,
your cloak of night and stars.

(After a medieval Armenian poem by Frik; 1980)

Russian

At eighteen, a horrible shadow hung over me. Instead of going straight to university I had to do two years of military service. Though I had been to Australia and back, I had never spent more than a night away from my parents; I had had a soft life, and dreaded the iron army discipline I was about to experience. The send-off at Redruth station was like a wake; it could not have been gloomier if they had been seeing me off to the trenches.

The reality of 6:00 A.M. reveilles, drill, boot-bulling, and general dehumanisation was even worse than I'd anticipated; and my homesickness was also worse. I'd experienced a lot of painful yearnings during the past four years—for Britain (when in Australia), for Australia (when back in Britain), for a girlfriend. None was more piercing than this: for my parents, and the comforts of home. Through the horrific two months of basic training, I wrote a few lines home almost every day; and almost every day I received a finely written letter from my father, describing in detail the latest rugby-match, etc. Given that he always came home tired-out from work, these letters were a marvellous labour of love—though I simply saw them, and my mother's loving scrawls, as my due.

Then, a huge stroke of luck. The Cold War had led to a demand for Russian-speakers, which had resulted in the setting-up of a Joint Services School for Linguists. I was selected for it. As if that wasn't miracle enough, the school had been deliberately sited in Cornwall so that the students could work hard without the distractions of a nearby big city. I could go home every weekend. And kindly providence soon provided me with an attractive, sexy girlfriend, called Maureen, whom I met at an Old Tyme Dancing class. Our relationship was established by the time I moved on to the second phase of the Russian course, at Cambridge. We wore civilian clothes now. Our tutors were mostly Russian émigrés, messianic about their mission. They exhorted us to "work, work, work! so that you fall in love with yourself!" We spent six hours a day in class, and had massive word-lists to learn.

I found it difficult and tedious. I didn't want to fall in love with myself—I was in love elsewhere, and lived for my home-leaves. Intellectually my mind was looking ahead to Oxford and English. With my fairly generous pay I bought a couple of English-literary books each weekend at the impressive Cambridge bookshops. Yet I came to like the maddeningly complex language, imperceptibly; and these early contacts with Russian literature were to lead, in later years, to an obsessional interest.

When people tell me, now, that the English language is beautiful, I can't believe it. Presumably I'm too close to it, it's a part of me. Whereas I remain dazzled by the beauty and expressive power of Russian—which I see, still, through a glass darkly, having been graded by my teachers "suitable for low-level interrogation after further training."

Sons and Daughters

My daughter, Caitlin (named after Dylan's wife), was conceived a few weeks after my father's death in 1960. She is like her mother in many ways, yet the Thomas inheritance is very clear in her. She is auburn-haired, well-built, and broodily good-looking. Highly intelligent, she has always been uncertain what she wants to do with her life. The question has been answered, for the foreseeable future, by marriage to a young Scot, a wizard in the stock exchange, and the birth of their son Alexander. She is sentimentally attached to "family," and I regret there is only my sister left, on my side, for her to know.

Sean, born in 1963, read philosophy at London University but wishes he had read English. Graduating at a time of high unemployment, he decided to live by his wits for a time, and to write. He has written two novels, both of which have, to date, hovered frustratingly on the verge of acceptance by a publisher. But he has plenty of time and talent. A couple of years ago he was falsely accused of rape by an ex-girlfriend, arrested, and put into prison on remand. He was found not guilty at the Old Bailey. I admire his courage in surviving his ordeal.

Daughter, Caitlin, and second wife, Denise, at Padstow, Cornwall, 1989

Ross, my younger son of a second marriage, is twelve. He is mad about computers, and is very sensitive and thoughtful. He becomes understandably exasperated with me when I can't operate the video-recorder.

Tensions

While the Americans and Vietnamese were killing each other, changes were occurring in my life. Maureen and I were divorced, but discreetly, even secretly, and continued living together as if nothing had happened. I got married, also discreetly, secretly, to a teacher and former student, Denise. Ross was born. Denise and I, who had never lived together, obtained a discreet, secret divorce. These apparently surreal events could only be understood through an awareness of all the circumstances of those years. Though I was the person responsible, I had the feeling of sleepwalking through events I could not control.

In 1985, Maureen left to marry a divorcée whom she had met. Shortly after, I fell ill with kidney-stones, had four major operations, followed by an undiagnosed glandular fever and severe depression. Denise and Ross moved in. Very slowly, over about two years, I recovered. We moved to Cornwall.

Uncles

There weren't so many uncles in the village of my childhood as there were aunts. Those who would have been honorific uncles were mostly dead. Women are everywhere tougher.

I was left with my real uncles, of whom one, Uncle Eddie, lived in the family-house with his three sisters and his son, Gerald, who was four years older than I. Gerald was looked after by Auntie Cecie; his mother had died when he was very young—I think also of TB, the great scourge of the time.

Uncle Eddie lacked the black-haired or auburn-haired good looks of his brothers, and was different in other ways. He wasn't practical. He worked gently at a men's outfitters; and after his retirement he sat gently around, smoking his pipe, reading the *Reader's Digest,* strumming the piano. And in the evenings he walked to the Men's Institute for a game of cards and a chat. He was dignified, kindly, and courteous, with a quiet air of authority. He became president of almost everything in the village, and was a kind of honorary squire. He had never emigrated like his other brothers; but alone had been in the First World War. He would talk about "Mespot," where he had served, but I didn't listen. I liked him very much; he was my favourite uncle.

Uncle Leslie, who had a small farm some miles away, was a different kettle of fish: ambitious, energetic, somewhat aggressive, tight with his money. He once answered my passing father's greeting in the street with, "Hello, Charlie," being absorbed in a business-deal. Yet he and my father were close; they had lived together, couple with couple, in Los Angeles. He was a good bass singer, without my father's expressive, soulful quality. He mourned never having had children, and grabbed my hand when he was dying, as if wanting to claim possession. Just like my father ten years earlier, he died of a stroke following a routine prostate operation. I don't think it's surprising that I fear operations.

Uncle Percy, the eldest, stayed in California; I never met him. Willie, gentle, pacific, a devil for the girls in his youth, went mining in Colombia. He married a demanding neurotic woman and settled with her in London. Whenever he planned a holiday in Cornwall, his wife would fall ill and he would have to send a cancelling telegram. He retired to Cornwall, but too late, after all his brothers and sisters except Leslie had died.

"From left, Uncle Eddie, Mother, Auntie Nellie, Father, Auntie Cecie, Maureen, myself in college blazer, outside the family-house at Carnkie," 1958

Uncle Donald, the youngest, was by all accounts a vivid, redheaded charmer. He joined the flying corps after the First World War, and was killed in a plane-crash on Salisbury Plain. His death shattered my ageing grandmother, and brought my parents and their infant daughter home from America to comfort her.

But for his death I would probably be an American, and with a different Christian name.

There was also Uncle Tommy, an uncle by marriage to my Auntie Lilie. She, with the characteristic red hair but also a kind, gentle personality, was forever being shamed by her husband's crudity. Fat, bald as an egg, he would lift an enormous buttock off his chair and fart, loud and long; then chuckle as Lilie scolded him.

Lilie died in middle-age of stomach cancer. So far as I was concerned, she died discreetly, the family keeping me out of their grief. It was as if she had gone away on holiday. Tommy eventually remarried, and passed from my life. I remember him only by his fatness, baldness, and farting.

On my mother's side there was an uncle, stocky and grey-haired, a Methodist preacher in the States, who came home for a visit and—one evening when my parents crept shamefacedly out of *Beverly*—told me the facts of life. I was utterly incredulous and a little disgusted.

Virginals

Our voyage to Australia, which began on my fourteenth birthday, was psychologically momentous. It would have been enough, emotionally, to be stunned by new physical worlds—the creaking, teeming life of a migrant ship, Maltese and Arab traders, Suez, Ceylon, dolphins, new constellations—and racked by homesickness; it was altogether too much to experience also the onset of puberty in mid–Indian Ocean. Not yet a wet dream—I think—but erections, pulsating and exquisite.

I was ripe for them, of course; and doubtless the changes of diet and climate helped. The immediate provocation was browsing through adult novels—innocuous by today's standards—in the tiny ship's library. But I am grateful the burst-through into sexuality came on that voyage. Every boy or girl's first bodily change at puberty must be profoundly affecting; but in my case it was as if it had been created by the leaping dolphins, the Buddhist temple at Kandy, the Southern Cross, the ocean's phosphorescence. The experience mythologised sex for me, and helped towards the belief that it was wondrous and awesome.

Creative also, for I had decided to keep a journal of the voyage. My sister, who worked as a secretary, typed it up for me after our landfall in Melbourne. It contained no hint of the most important event of my crossing.

Since I had no contact with girls at all in Australia, until the last few weeks before our return voyage when my class at school became mixed, the mythic, creative, imaginative element in my concept of sexuality went on expanding. The young women who occasionally crept into my sweating bed, to embrace me and bring me to orgasm, were figures out of *Photoplay* magazine—Esther Williams, June Allyson, Doris Day, Kathryn Grayson . . . And she *might* turn, as my wet dream awoke me, into a gross black spider hanging on my wall near the window. During the waking hours there was no way that I knew of re-creating the divine but interrupted release that sleep sometimes brought me; so there was intolerable tension. Sex was as tense as the tight-belted waists of the film-star sweater-girls; as the gripped nylon-threads of my curvacious sister's stocking-tops as she exercised on the lounge-floor; as the silences between the sinister and magical crescendo-ing piano-chords of the Rachmaninov concerto that always introduced *Popular Classics* on the radio. It was as stifling as the heat before a breeze from the Antarctic came. There was no lotusland of soft, cool, easy fulfilment. It certainly wasn't a recreational romp. It was awesome, oceanic, magical, tense, fetishistic, creative (it still is)—and I longed to experience it.

War

And from my earliest years I associated love with war. Vera Lynn's was the first siren-voice, woman-call, I listened to: that throbbing, sweet, plangent voice over the radio; not intimate but from the echoing spaces of some hangar, assuring the boys in blue that she would meet them again, though she didn't know where or when, but it would be on some sunny day. And in the second verse their mingled, throaty voices would join hers as a chorus. A discarnate gang-bang.

My sister was meeting them already, on sunny or rainy evenings; a little companionship between missions. I experienced all her romances vicariously.

I suppose I was too young to be conscious of the disasters and deadly perils of the first two years of the war; yet something of the fear of imminent invasion came through to me. Was I more frightened or excited when the siren sounded and we went to

"Sean, Denise, and Ross at my daughter's wedding,"
1989

crouch beneath the stairs in our cellar? I learned to pick out the drone of the Messerschmitt, and fear it. But in the silently wheeling searchlights there was an unreality, a distant beauty. I couldn't imagine a bomb falling on me; and in fact only a handful of people were killed in our town, from a stray bomb.

We had a refugee from London, a pretty teenager called Pam. When eventually she left us I asked her for a kiss, but she said I was too young. My father said, "And I suppose I'm too old," and she replied, "Oh, I wouldn't say that!" I only know of this because my father kept mentioning it to people, in a joky way: but it was clear that it pleased him and that it responded to a secret fantasy.

By the time I was wholly aware of what was happening in the war, at seven or eight, we were winning. From this point, all was excitement as I followed the advances of the Allies and, nearer to home, my sister's campaigns. Sexually, she was as stubborn and intractable as Leningrad; emotionally, frailer than Singapore.

As D day approached, Cornwall was swarming with troops; unknown to us of course, Eisenhower's

headquarters was just a few miles away. I observed the war closely yet was never actually in danger; nor was anyone close to me involved—my father, just too old to be called-up, was in the Home Guard. I was immensely privileged, and the experience has obviously shaped me. In a way, everything later becomes an anticlimax. I still feel the Second World War as a living, contemporary event.

XXX

It was 1984; XXX porno-movie neon signs lit up Collins Street, which in 1951 had been the staidest in Melbourne, a collar-and-tie street of bankers and businessmen.

My publishers put me up in a plush hotel, and I feared no spiders on the seventh floor.

My bedroom was air-conditioned.

A real, live woman climbed into bed with me.

Otherwise nothing had changed.

Yelabuga

Yelabuga is a small Tartar town on the River Kama where, in August 1941, Marina Tsvetaeva, lonely and in despair, hanged herself.

There is a Yelabuga on every artist's map, and increasingly in our century writers have ended up there. Yesenin hanged himself (and perhaps shot himself too, to make sure); Mayakovsky shot himself; Virginia Woolf walked into a river; Dylan Thomas drank himself to death; Berryman threw himself off a bridge; Sylvia Plath put her head in an oven; Anne Sexton sealed her garage and ran the engine.

I have glimpsed the faint lights of Yelabuga, but my train has never stopped there, fortunately. One can only pray it never will.

Zeiss

I own a fine Zeiss camera, but it's wasted on me. I've used it about half-a-dozen times in twenty years. Whereas my father, with a clumsy Kodak bought in California almost seventy years ago (I still have it), took thousands of snapshots, filled album after album. And how I envy those smiling groups, those happy couples and brothers and sisters, cousins and close friends. I curse them, in the most affectionate way, for having been so barren, those six brothers and four sisters; for having stayed abroad, died in plane-crashes, married wives who died young, lost

"With the Armenian poet and translator Diana Der Hovanessian (to my immediate right),
in Boston," 1982

lovers in a war, lived in damp cottages that produced fatal illnesses . . . In a word, left so few of us in their wake. Is there some especially fine Zeiss, I wonder—product of Germanic brilliance—that could make them burst out of the photograph, laughing, singing, joking, and with potent loins?

BIBLIOGRAPHY

Poetry:

Personal and Possessive, Outposts, 1964.

(With D. M. Black and Peter Redgrove) *Modern Poets 11,* Penguin, 1968.

Two Voices, Cape Goliard, 1968.

The Lover's Horoscope: Kinetic Poem, Purple Sage, 1970.

Logan Stone, Cape Goliard, 1971.

The Shaft, Arc, 1973.

Lilith-Prints, Second Aeon (Cardiff, Wales), 1974.

Symphony in Moscow, Keepsake Press, 1974.

Love and Other Deaths, Elek, 1975.

The Rock, Sceptre Press, 1975.

Orpheus in Hell, Sceptre Press, 1977.

In the Fair Field, Five Seasons Press, 1978.

The Honeymoon Voyage, Secker & Warburg, 1978.

Protest: A Poem after a Medieval Armenian Poem by Frik, Five Seasons Press, 1980.

Dreaming in Bronze, Secker & Warburg, 1981.

Selected Poems, Secker & Warburg, 1983.

(With Sylvia Kantaris) *News from the Front,* Arc, 1983.

Prose:

The Devil and the Floral Dance (juvenile), Robson, 1978.

The Flute-Player (novel), Gollancz, 1979.

Birthstone (novel), Gollancz, 1980.

The White Hotel (novel), Gollancz, 1981.

Memories and Hallucinations (memoir), Gollancz, 1988.

"Russian Nights" series:

Ararat (novel), Gollancz, 1983.

Swallow (novel), Gollancz, 1984.

Sphinx (novel), Gollancz, 1986.

Summit (novel), Gollancz, 1987.

Lying Together (novel), forthcoming.

Translator:

Anna Akhmatova, *Requiem, and Poem without a Hero,* Elek, 1976.

Akhmatova, *Way of All the Earth,* Elek, 1979.

Alexander Pushkin, *The Bronze Horseman,* Secker & Warburg, 1982.

Yevgeny Yevtushenko, *A Dove in Santiago,* Secker & Warburg, 1983.

Pushkin, *Boris Godunov,* Sixth Chamber Press, 1985.

Akhmatova, *You Will Hear Thunder,* Secker & Warburg, 1985.

Editor:

The Granite Kingdom: Poems of Cornwall, Barton, 1970.

Poetry in Crosslight (textbook), Longman, 1975.

Songs from the Earth: Selected Poems of John Harris, Cornish Miner 1820–84, Lodenek Press, 1977.

Other:

Translations performed as radio plays, including *You Will Hear Thunder,* 1981, and *Boris Godunov,* 1984; work represented in anthologies, including *Best SF: 1969,* edited by Robert Vas Dias, Anchor Books, 1970, and *Twenty-three Modern British Poets,* edited by John Matthias, Swallow Press, 1971; contributor to literary journals in England and the United States.

Cumulative Index

CUMULATIVE INDEX

For every reference that appears *in more than one essay,*
the name of the essayist is given before the volume and page number(s).

INDEX